AN HISTORICAL GEOGRAPHY OF
WESTERN EUROPE BEFORE 1800

Revised Edition

BY

C. T. SMITH

LONGMAN
London and New York

To the memory of my dear wife, Susan.

Longman Group Limited London

Associated companies, branches and representatives throughout the world

Published in the United States of America by Longman Inc., New York

© C. T. Smith, 1967, 1978

First published 1967; second impression 1969 Revised edition, first paperback edition 1978

British Library Cataloguing in Publication Data

Smith, Clifford Thorpe
    An historical geography of Western Europe
    before 1800.—Revised ed.—(Geographies
    for advanced study).
    1. Europe, Western—Historical geography
    I. Title   II. Series
    911'.4   D967   77-30746

ISBN 0-582-48986-5

Printed in Great Britain by
Whitstable Litho Ltd., Whitstable, Kent

CONTENTS

LIST OF MAPS

LIST OF PLATES

ACKNOWLEDGEMENTS

We are grateful to the following for permission to reproduce photographs:

Aerofilms Library Ltd: Plates 1, 2, 5, 6, 7, 12, 14, 15, 18, 23, 24, 37, 38; Hansa Luftbild G.m.b.H.: Plates 3, 4, 10, 11; The French Government Tourist Office: Plate 39; Foto K.L.M. Aerocarto N.V.: Plates 16, 32, 41, 42; Ed. E. Mignon: Plate 27; Royal Netherlands Embassy: Plates 13, 40; Service Commercial Monuments Historiques, Paris: Plate 17; Swissair: Plate 26. Plates 9, 25 and 28 are from the Collection at Keele University by permission of the French Embassy and the Air Ministry.

PREFACE
TO FIRST EDITION

Any writer on the historical geography of Western Europe faces many problems of organisation, selection and definition, and the decisions that are made about these matters must frequently be arbitrary and sometimes controversial. Western Europe has been broadly defined to include Scandinavia, Germany, Italy and Iberia as well as France and the Low Countries. Inclusion of the British Isles would have changed the scale of the whole work, and no detailed treatment has been accorded to this area. Nevertheless, Britain has by no means been rigorously excluded and reference will be found to it at frequent points in the discussion of particular themes. Similarly, reference to central and eastern Europe or the Mediterranean as a whole has been freely made at points where comprehension of Western European conditions would have been difficult without it. Thus, the peopling of Europe in prehistory is a theme treated largely for the continent as a whole. In some ways, a regional treatment is logical for a geographical study, but to have divided the work into separate sections on Scandinavia, the Mediterranean lands and north-western Europe would have involved much repetition and would undoubtedly have destroyed the unities which have been common to many geographical situations of the past in the area as a whole.

This is not the place for a discourse on the nature of historical geography, but it may be well to record the point of view from which it has been approached in this book. The author takes it as axiomatic that geographers are interested in places: what they are like now, and how they have come to be what they are. Indeed many have thought of historical geography as essentially a study in the changing landscape or as 'man's role in changing the face of the earth'. There is much to be said for this view in that it focuses attention on the analysis of present 'landscapes' in historical terms, on the legacies of particular periods to present conditions, and some emphasis is here given to the patterns of fields, roads, villages and towns and the ways in which they have evolved. It is an approach that invites us to ask questions about why this or that feature of settlement, for example, was laid out in precisely that way at the time of its creation, how it may have changed, or how it may have survived long periods of intervening change to the present.

In some cases, survival of a 'relict' feature may be just that and nothing more. It has become so irrelevant to subsequent change that it has survived more or less intact, like the burial mounds of megalithic invaders or the lynchets which adorn some of the hillsides of Germany, France and England. But the 'inertia' of ancient features may also be expressive of continuing functional value, like the Roman roads of northern Italy, or the drained polders established by the Dutch in the Low Countries. In other cases, original functions have been lost, but subsequent changes have brought new values and new significance. Again and again, the great towns of the Middle Ages, or even modest centres of an ancient industry have been revitalised by a tourist industry, as for example Venice, Bruges or Aigues Mortes. 'Rejuvenated' features are not wholly confined to the world of physical geography! Nor should it be forgotten that the creation of early patterns represented a heavy investment of labour and capital in altering the face of the land, and it has frequently been the case that investment is equally necessary to obliterate them. The small fields of Brittany or Cornwall surrounded by high mounds and hedges or the dispersed strips of open fields in France or Germany are only now being radically altered with a new-found agricultural prosperity and a new technology. But to organise a study of the historical geography of Europe wholly in terms of relict feature from the past or in terms of the evolution of its landscapes would make it much more difficult to view the larger themes of geographical change and to set them into the context of the circumstances which gave rise to them.

The reconstruction of past geographies is frequently regarded as the orthodox task of historical geography, and to some extent this concept has shaped the present study. But a series of static portrayals of geographical conditions in periods of stability is neither possible nor desirable in a work of this scale, even if such periods of stability could be found. It is the periods and processes of geographical change, of active settlement and colonisation, of urban foundation and growth, or of industrial and commercial change, that stimulate most interest and that have been most significant in the formation of the landscape. 'Geographical change' is a loose term, however, and requires explanation. It would certainly comprehend changes in the use of resources and of position as a response to social, economic

and technological conditions, but it should also be concerned with
the processes involved in bringing about new spatial distributions:
colonisation and settlement, migrations, the spread of innovations,
the relationship of towns to the regions they serve and the regional
effects of urban growth; the localisation of agriculture and industry;
and the processes involved in the concentration or dispersal of settlement, commercial activity and industry.

Indeed it may be that historical geography is now on the threshold
of a new major task, though it is one which is only occasionally
hinted at in these pages. A corpus of new ideas, theories and models
relating to spatial patterns and processes is in the making. Haggett's
study of locational analysis, for example, a pioneer work in this
field, classifies the subject matter of locational structures under
headings of movements, networks, nodes, hierarchies and surfaces
in a form which cuts across the traditional distinctions between
economic, social and urban geography. This emerging body of
doctrine is at the centre of geographical study, concerned as it is
with location, and much of it is certainly applicable in principle to
historical situations. Before 1800, statistical data are hard to come
by, and there are as yet few studies in this vein, but it may be that
the approach and the concepts of locational analysis will open up
new lines of research and new methods of integrating the knowledge
about the past as well as the present.

Many of the most exciting trends in recent geographical studies
have been in urban geography and particularly in the analysis of
relationships between towns and their surrounding regions. To
analyse these relationships in the past by the precise quantitative
methods used in urban studies of the present is rarely possible, but
the corpus of theory and the approach of the urban geographer can
be profitably applied to many historical situations, if only in a
qualitative fashion pending detailed study of available data, or of
data yet to be unearthed. There are many points at which further
research from this point of view could illuminate geographical situations of the past.

The origin and early growth of towns in medieval Europe is a field
in which the military, administrative and religious as well as the
economic functions of towns could be integrated in terms of the
flow of income and services, rents, revenues and dues between the
town and the area served. The spacing of medieval towns in relation
to the chronology of new urban foundations of the twelfth and

thirteenth centuries needs much more detailed analysis than it can be given here. Urban spheres of influence need careful reassessment in the light of changing urban functions in marketing, the growth of retailing and distributive trades and the changes in 'service' industries. The growth of capital cities and the great ports in the early modern period has always attracted attention, and their impact on regional growth and agricultural change has received more and more attention since Fisher wrote in the 1930's on the importance of the London food market. But there is still need for more careful study of the changing urban hierarchy between the sixteenth and eighteenth centuries. The spread of rural industry and the fortunes of industries such as textiles and iron have perhaps been over-emphasised in studies orientated, consciously or no, towards the industrial revolution of the nineteenth century, and insufficient attention has been paid to those crafts and service trades which made up a very considerable proportion of much of industrial activity.

Certain themes, however, recur throughout this study of Western Europe, undertaken to a great extent on an empirical rather than a theoretical basis. The patterns of rural settlement in Western Europe are, of course, extremely varied and many classifications of them have been made, but the interpretation of contrasts between villages and scattered farms and hamlets can best be understood, perhaps, as the resultant of forces making for concentration or dispersal. The balance has varied from one period to another according to the dominant needs and aims of rural society.

But a similar alternation between concentration and dispersal is to be discerned operating in other spheres and at different levels. The spread of industry from medieval towns into the countryside from the late thirteenth to the fifteenth centuries, exemplified by the cloth industries of England, the Low Countries and Italy is one such movement; a trend continued on a much larger scale in the early modern period, and affecting a much wider range of industries. It was not until the nineteenth century that this trend was substantially reversed, sometimes because rural industry agglomerated to the rank of urban status, as in the case of many coalfield towns, or because of a general decline of rural industrial occupations.

The pattern of medieval trade, too, shows great variation in relation to urban growth and prosperity. Thus in the great period of the Champagne and Flemish fairs the flow of commerce appears to have been fairly widely spread through the towns of north-western Europe and no one town dominates the pattern. But the trend towards concentration and the commercial dominance of a few centres can be seen to operate in the growth of Bruges, then in the outstanding concentration of trading activity in Antwerp, and the 'reign of Amsterdam' which followed it. The concentration of leadership in Amsterdam must be qualified, for the towns of Holland and Zeeland shared in it to a considerable extent. But in the eighteenth century new conditions intervened to spread leadership in commercial enterprise more widely in a period of expansion and change, particularly in the colonial trade.

One of the products which one may expect to be distilled from studies of successive geographical 'cross-sections' is that elusive quality of place sometimes described as 'personality'. The uses made of the same location by successive generations with different motivations, technologies, political concepts and so on should, in principle, yield conclusions about locational values. Some attempt is made to characterise 'the personality of Europe' in the section in prehistory, following the time-honoured example of Sir Cyril Fox's 'Personality of Britain'. But it could be interesting to pursue the theme further into medieval and early modern history to the point at which the dominance of the nation state begins to obscure regional unities such as those which link the coastlands of the Western Mediterranean or the coastlands of the North Sea basin. One of the concepts which helps to illuminate the interpretation of the economic geography of the Middle Ages is that of a commercial axis of Western Europe extending from the Low Countries to Northern Italy and composed of many strands—from those linking Flanders with Champagne and the Rhône in the west to those which link the Rhine with South Germany and the Brenner Pass to the east. And this is also the industrial axis of the Common Market in the modern world.

There are many people to whom I would like to acknowledge my indebtedness during the time this book has been in preparation: first of all, to Jean Mitchell, who has inspired many student generations of historical geographers as well as my own. From her dedication, knowledge and enthusiasm I have learned much, first as a student and then as a colleague. Her constant advice and encouragement have helped at all stages of the work. My thanks must go also to B. H. Farmer and to J. A. Steers as friends and colleagues who have given advice and help in a more general way. And it is certain that

H.G.W.E.—1*

this book would never have been written, and certainly the indexing would never have been finished, without the help, guidance and support of my wife and family.

C. T. SMITH
St John's College,
Cambridge

ACKNOWLEDGEMENTS

We are grateful to the following for permission to reproduce copyright material:

Edward Arnold (Publishers) Ltd for a slightly modified version of a table from *The Quaternary Era, Vol. II* by J. K. Charlesworth (p. 1032); Methuen & Co. Ltd and Stanford University Press for a table from *Prehistoric Europe* by Graham Clarke, and Roger Mols, S.J. for a table based on material from *Introduction à la démographie historique des villes d'Europe du 14ᵉ au 18ᵉ siècle, Vol. II* (p. 47) by R. Mols, S.J.

PREFACE
TO THE REVISED EDITION

Apart from the few textual corrections, the major change which has been introduced to this revised edition has been the inclusion of a Postscript which attempts to chart the directions of change, not only in knowledge of the topics which are included in the book, but also in the ways in which scholars have brought new attitudes towards the interpretation of evidence about the past. It attempts to review some of these interpretations, and includes a select bibliography drawing attention to some of the recently published works which extend, revise or confirm the content and the conclusions of the original edition.

My thanks are due to Paul Laxton for his helpful comments on the Postscript and the select bibliography.

C. T. SMITH
University of Liverpool,
1977

Part 1
Prehistory and the Classical World

CHAPTER 1

PREHISTORY

EARLIEST BEGINNINGS

There are few places in Europe which have not in some way been altered by the hand of man. A few coastal features, high barren mountain tops, or remote regions in northern Scandinavia may lay claim to such a distinction, but rural landscapes are almost everywhere deeply rooted in a long history of settlement. The patterns of fields, farms and villages, varied as they are from place to place over the face of Europe, may be seen both as the result of and as clues to the arrangements which have been made by many generations, possessing different economic and social structures and equipped with changing technologies, to use their physical environments to best advantage. Many of the lands which are forest, heath, moorland or high Alpine pasture have been modified by the clearing of original forest, by the grazing activities of domestic animals, or by the introduction, wittingly or no, of alien species of plants. An outline of the peopling of Europe is thus an essential prerequisite for the greater understanding of man's rôle in changing the face of the earth, quite apart from its intrinsic interest to the historical geographer and its relevance for the understanding of the fragmented linguistic and political character of Europe.

Change through time lends itself to a neat division no more easily than geographical change in space. The unity and boundaries of periods are subject to exactly the same qualifications as the unity and boundaries of geographical regions. With these provisos, then, the peopling of Europe may be seen in terms of five major divisions, and although there is much overlap, each is characterised in a general way by its contribution to the patterns of modern Europe. In the first long period of prehistory the initial settlement of Europe by hunters, fishers and food-gatherers altered the land but little. But the introduction and expansion of farming by new immigrants in the Neolithic period is of fundamental importance. Although much has been claimed, little is known for certain of the extent to which modern settlements may be traced to Bronze Age or even Neolithic times. But there is some plausibility in the view that many of the physical characteristics found among modern populations were already present and that the Indo-European languages, from which most of the modern European languages derive, were already being spoken over much of Europe by the end of Bronze Age times.

The age of Greece and Rome is one of new achievements in the peopling of Europe. In the west, population increased to an entirely new level, and so also of course does the evidence, both literary and archaeological, by which these achievements are known. The introduction of towns and town life, the great expansion of population and agriculture, the spread of Latin, the construction of roads, the foundation of new villages and the planned settlement of farmers form a part of the classical heritage which is still woven into the fabric of the rural and urban landscapes of Western Europe.

The age of migrations which began with the final irruption of Germanic peoples into the Roman Empire and ended with the incursions of Scandinavians and Magyars into western and central Europe changed yet again the linguistic patterns of Europe, added much to the settlement of the countryside, and saw the beginnings, or the revival, of urban life in many towns which are still of importance. The stage was set for the great economic and demographic expansion of the Middle Ages, to which our landscapes owe a debt second only to that of the period after the industrial revolution.

If the age of migrations had established a new pattern of language in much of western and central Europe, the expansion of the tenth to the fourteenth centuries did much to stabilise the major outlines and to modify the pattern itself in some important ways. Almost all of the villages and hamlets of Western Europe had been founded by 1350 and though some were lost in the great contraction which followed, few new ones have been founded since except in Scandinavia and in politically troubled areas. Expansion took place mainly at the expense of virgin forest, to the extent that it has been called the 'great age of clearing', but men were driven too to the reclamation of marsh and heath, and to the irrigation of semi-arid lands. This was also an age which saw the foundation of most of the towns and cities of western and central Europe, and the frequency with which the survival of medieval town plans hampers the free flow of modern traffic, and presents problems in the planning of industry and urban land use, is comparable with the efforts which must be made in farming to fit a twentieth-century technology into a framework of cramped fields or scattered strips which are a legacy from the same period.

Much of the interest of geographers in prehistory has focused on the relationships of early economies with their physical environments. From the premise that comparative studies of human adaptations to similar environments could yield useful conclusions, it is obvious, for example, that the societies of Western Europe during the last glaciation might be compared with Eskimo cultures of the modern world. Similarly the occupation of Europe by successive peoples equipped with changing technologies provides a series of examples of the ways in which different peoples have used the same environment. Preferences for particular kinds of site for settlement and defence, the repeated use of certain routes of migration and the regional groupings of material cultures are the elements out of which one might build a concept of the 'personality' of Europe along lines analogous to those used by Sir Cyril Fox in his book on the *Personality of Britain*.[1]

The peopling of Europe in prehistoric times took place in a physical environment that was changing, for the earliest cultures of the Palaeolithic, brought by the precursors of *homo sapiens*, probably appeared in Western Europe during an interglacial period. This is not the place to enlarge upon the details of climatic change and the evidence by which it is known,[2] but it is important to recognise that understanding of climatic change has rested partly on the nature of late Pleistocene deposits—moraines, boulder clays, fluvioglacial terraces, solifluction deposits and löss, for example. In some of these distinctive flora and fauna give a clue to prevailing climate. The detailed elaboration of a chronology of climatic change has been heavily dependent on the analysis of fossil pollen grains preserved in such deposits, as well as seeds and other plant remains. Fossil fauna, especially the ubiquitous population of non-marine mollusca, have yielded their quota of information, but the remains of large mammals are not so widely distributed and are therefore not quite so useful. Absolute chronologies have been mainly dependent, however, on historically datable events, the counting of annual layers of silts, as in the varve clays of Scandinavia, and the dates provided by the estimation of the ratio between radioactive and non-radioactive carbon in uncontaminated carbonaceous deposits. But all of these more certain methods of estimating an absolute chronology are applicable only for relatively recent periods, and even the Carbon 14 method is reliable only for dates more recent than about 70,000 years.[3]

The physical environment of Europe was changing in other respects as well, for the patterns of land and sea were altering (see Table I). Sea-levels were at times lowered to the extent of a hundred metres by the locking up of water in the ice sheets of glacial times, to rise again in interglacial and postglacial times. Eustatic changes of this type were complicated, however, by the isostatic movements of land masses in response to the imposition or removal of the weight of overlying ice sheets. Changes in sea-level were therefore complex. Much of the North Sea basin was exposed as a marshy area of lakes and bogs during a period of relatively low sea-level in the Mesolithic, for example.

PALAEOLITHIC AND MESOLITHIC EUROPE

Of the predecessors of *homo sapiens* who occupied Europe in the Lower Palaeolithic to the height of the last glaciation (Würm I) little need be said, for in spite of the long duration of their sojourn in Europe they have left few traces, and have contributed little to our equipment and almost nothing to our hereditary make-up. A mandible from the neighbourhood of Heidelberg suggests the presence of one such group as early as Middle Pleistocene times; the incomplete skull of Swanscombe man, associated with flint axes in interglacial gravels of the lower Thames is another such predecessor, both of them considerably earlier in the scale of time than the fairly widespread but still sparse population of Neanderthal men who occupied much of Europe during the first phase of the last glaciation. With their short, thick limbs, massive brow ridges, chinless but massive jaws and large faces, they were probably less like modern men than some of their own contemporaries in Europe and Africa, and it has been suggested that they may have represented a highly specialised type which developed at the very margins of the habitable world at a time of extreme climatic conditions, but which was replaced by *homo sapiens* at the beginning of the Upper Palaeolithic.

The making of tools is perhaps the most useful of the criteria which have been suggested as the touchstone of humanity in its early evolution, since it is by his tools of durable material, mainly flints, that early man has left most of his traces. The existence of the earliest of these tools, or *eoliths*, roughly worked flints gathered from Pliocene or even earlier deposits, is a matter of some controversy, however, for it has been shown that there is a fairly high chance that many of these so-called tools might well have been the product, not of the directed human intelligence of Palaeolithic man, but of careful selection by modern archaeologists from the products of wave action, freeze-thaw, solifluction or other natural processes.[4]

Among the undoubted products of Palaeolithic flint-working techniques a basic distinction must be made between core and flake tools.[5] Core tools were produced by the chipping away of flakes from a nodule of flint so as to produce a tool such as a hand-axe. Flake tools were made from the flakes which were struck from the original lump of flint. The more skilled Levallois industry prepared the initial flint into a shape roughly that of a tortoise shell before flakes were carefully struck from it. Later still, much more elaborate shapes, including blades, could be produced by skilfully applied pressure as well as carefully controlled blows.

Both core and flake industries existed from an early date in Europe, but the distributions of the earliest industries appear to be significantly different. Few hand-axes, which were the main product of the core industries, have been found east of the Rhine, but they are abundant in western France and they occur in Iberia, southern France and Italy. There are, moreover, close links between the hand-axe tools of Western Europe and those of south and central Africa where a continuous evolution from primitive chopping tools to the hand-axe has been traced. Early flake industries of southern Britain, Belgium and parts of Germany, on the other hand, are to be associated with flake traditions in the Old World, north of the Alpine Caucasus-Himalayan belt. For the most part these early cultures existed in warm interglacial conditions during which a forest vegetation was widespread in Western Europe. In western France a warm fauna included hippopotamus and the straight-tusked elephant. But to the north and east, steppe conditions probably prevailed. The hand-axes of Western Europe, associated with a forest distribution, may have been better suited to deal with trees, wood and roots than the scrapers produced by the flake industry, tools more adapted to such tasks as the skinning of game hunted in the steppes.[6]

With the onset of colder conditions at the beginning of the last glaciation, steppe and park-steppe or park-tundra spread further south into Europe and over wider areas. At approximately the same

TABLE I

	LAND AND SEA		BLYTT-SERNANDER PERIOD	CLIMATE	POLLEN ZONE (Firbas)	VEGETA
	NORTH SEA	BALTIC				NETHERLANDS
0 A.D.	Dunkirkian Transgression .... slight regression		Sub-Atlantic	cooler, wetter	IX	beech, then hornbeam; forest clearance
1000 B.C.		Limnaea Sea	Sub-Boreal	drier, more continental; warm	VIII	oak forest; elm and lime less important; appearance of beech; beginnings of forest clearance
2000 B.C.–	....	....				
3000 B.C.–	Flandrian Transgression	Litorina Sea	Atlantic (climatic optimum)	warm, moist	VII	
4000 B.C.–						Mixed oak forest
5000 B.C.–					VI	
6000 B.C.–	Inundation of the Dogger Bank	Lake Ancylus	Boreal	warm, dry, rising temperature	V	pine and hazel; increase of mixed oak forest
7000 B.C.–		Yoldia Sea	Pre-Boreal	rising temperature	IV	dense birch and pine
8000 B.C.–			Younger Dryas	cool sub-Arctic	III	park landscape, birch and pine
9000 B.C.–	North Sea part land, part ice-covered	Baltic ice-dammed lake	Alleröd oscillation	warmer, cool sub-Arctic	II	first birch, then pine/birch
10,000 B.C.–			Older Dryas	cold sub-Arctic	Ic	park 'tundra'
11,000 B.C.–			Bølling oscillation	cool sub-Arctic	Ib	park landscape, birch
12,000 B.C.–			Oldest Dryas	sub-Arctic to Arctic	Ia	'tundra'

VEGETATION		FAUNA DENMARK		ECONOMY DENMARK
DENMARK	ENGLAND			
pine revertence; beech	birch revertence; beech	sheep more important than swine; tame horse	Iron Age	sedentary farming; herding; herding; and fishing
oak forest	oak forest; alder	red and roe deer, wild pig, beaver, bear, dog	. . . .	. . . .
spread of grasses and ling; weeds of cultivation	spread of grasses and ling; weeds of cultivation		Bronze Age	forest clearance
. . . .	beginnings of forest clearance		Neolithic	shifting cultivation; herding, hunting, fishing
(oak, elm, lime) and alder		aurochs, red and roe deer, wild pig, beaver, bear and dog	Mesolithic	hunting, fishing, fowling, strand-looping gathering
pine and hazel; . . . . beginning of mixed oak forest; pine and birch	pine and hazel; beginning of mixed oak forest	aurochs, elk		
birch forest	pine and birch . . . . birch forest		Mesolithic	
tundra', park 'tundra'	birch, park landscape	reindeer, bison. wild horse	Upper Palaeolithic	hunting, gathering, fowling and fishing
park 'tundra', birch forest	park 'tundra' with birch and pine	reindeer, bison, alpine hare, giant Irish deer, elk, beaver, bear		
'tundra'	'tundra'	reindeer		
park 'tundra'				
'tundra'	'tundra' ·	reindeer		

time the hand-axe culture of the west disappeared and flake industries of Levallois type spread over much of Europe and south-
west Asia. Within the domain of Levallois industry and Mousterian
culture (closely associated throughout northern Europe with
Neanderthal man) it again seems possible to distinguish a regional
contrast.[7] West of the Rhine and the Rhône the use of hand-axes
revived, but they were smaller and the product of a flake industry.
East of the Rhine and in Italy, hand-axes of this type were absent,
but tools were smaller, more varied, and included characteristic
plano-convex flakes. Here, too, then, the tool-kit of the west may
reflect an economy adjusted to milder, wetter conditions and more
abundant vegetation, while that of the eastern zone is again adjusted
to the hunting and preparation of game in dry, continental steppe-
tundra south of the Weichsel ice in the Baltic and north of the Alpine
Würm ice. Nevertheless, Mousterian culture as a whole was widely
spread over northern Eurasia, and its equipment remained very
largely restricted to tools of flint and wood, with probably little use
of bone.

Even though the hunting and food-gathering economy and habitat
of early and middle Palaeolithic Europe can be but dimly discerned
from the archaeological and geological record there is something to
suggest that adaptation to the varied environments of tundra, steppe
and forest had taken place. The possession of fire, and clothing of
skins prepared by specialised flint scrapers, mitigated the rigours of
cold climates, and so also did the choice of shelter. During the milder
conditions of the interglacial periods open sites in close proximity to
water, and frequently on river terraces were preferred by, for example, Chellean and Acheulian man, but with the onset of colder
conditions during the Mousterian phase, sites near the mouths of
natural caves constitute the chief sources of finds. Figures tabulated
below illustrate this change:[8]

		OPEN SITES		ROCK SHELTERS AND CAVES		
		NUMBER	%	NUMBER	%	TOTAL
Upper Palaeolithic	Magdalenian	17	10	148	90	165
	Solutrean	10	14	62	86	72
	Aurignacian	24	18	112	82	136
Middle and Lower Palaeolithic	Mousterian	45	34	88	66	133
	Acheulian	36	78	10	22	46
	Chellean (Abbevillian)	32	94	2	6	34

Some thirty to forty thousand years ago, during the last glaciation, and probably during the less severe conditions of an inter-

stadial phase within it, two great events affected Europe. One was the appearance of *homo sapiens* and the ultimate extinction from Europe of Neanderthal man. Differences among skeletal remains in cranial and other measurements have led anthropologists to suppose that even at this early stage there was perhaps some differentiation into races, but there is so little agreement that it seems wiser to suspend judgment on the issue. Thus 'Grimaldi' man, short and slender, with a long, relatively narrow skull, so known from a site in the Riviera, has been seen as an ancestor of either negroid or Mediterranean man. Cro-Magnon man, tall and heavily built, with broad face and relatively long, narrow skull, and named from the type site in the Dordogne basin, has been seen as an ancestor of the peoples of northern Europe. More doubtful similarities between the Eskimo and the Upper Palaeolithic Chancelade man have been stressed by some and minimised by others.

The second great event was the introduction, quite possibly by these new men, of new and finer flint-working techniques by which more delicate blades, gravers and burins and points of various kinds could be produced. Not only did these methods involve a new economy in the use of raw materials, but they also made possible the working of other materials—bone, antler, wood and horn—and thus an enlargement of the variety and specialisation of tools for the hunting and collection of food, the preparation of clothing and the building of shelters. The invention of bows and arrows, the spear thrower, barbed harpoons and finer spearheads opened up new resources. Fishing became more important, birds became a useful source of food, and the hunting and trapping of larger animals became more efficient.[9] Some suggestion, but no more than this, of an increase of population comes from the much higher frequency of finds in relation to the time scale of various cultures. The population of France might still, however, be numbered in terms of tens of thousands, and that of Britain in hundreds.[10]

The early cultures of the Upper Palaeolithic occupied Europe at a time when cold conditions were slightly less severe than in most of the Mousterian period, or than they were later to become in the last readvance of the ice in the Alps and northern Europe. Harsh frost-tundra conditions still made the margins of the ice uninhabitable, but to the south open vegetation persisted to the Pyrenees, diversi-fied by dwarf birch and arctic willow in the west of France and to the east of the cold, wind-swept corridor between Alpine and Baltic ice.

Although frequently labelled tundra, the composition of this open vegetation included many warmth-loving plants not now found in high-latitude tundra. To the south-east, open vegetation was continued in the steppe lands of the Magyar plains and southern Russia. Coniferous forest extended northwards only to Italy and central Spain, and mixed and deciduous forests were pushed even further south to the very margins of the Mediterranean. Reindeer, wild horse, bison, mammoth, cave bear, ibex and cave lion are chief among the animals depicted in the brilliant cave art of the period.

On the open plains of the east, mammoth were the prey of hunters, who probably banded together for communal hunts like the Plains Indians of North America in later years. It has even been suggested, though with insufficient evidence, that the extinction of the mammoth may have been assisted by the success with which they were hunted. Wild horses were common in eastern France, but with the return of more severe conditions in the last phase of the Upper Palaeolithic it was the reindeer, above all, which provided for the needs of the contemporary Magdalenian culture in the west. Indeed the distribution of the Magdalenian cultures is almost coincident with that of reindeer. Its bones and antlers were major raw materials for harpoons, needles, spearheads, and spearthrowers; reindeer commonly constitute 70 per cent or more of animal remains in excavated sites in Germany and Switzerland. Like Eskimos of more modern times Magdalenian men followed the reindeer herds north in the summer months and set up temporary camps (suggested by the tent-like designs which occur in cave sites further south) at river mouths and near marshes or lakes, which were fished for trout, salmon and the like. In the west the permanent and winter headquarters remained chiefly in the caves of the deeply incised and very sheltered valleys of the Dordogne system, in the Cantabrian mountains and further east in the limestone caves of the Jura and the Swabian and Franconian Jura. It was in south-western France, however, in places like the famous Lascaux, that Palaeolithic art reached its full and magnificent florescence in the Magdalenian period, though caves of this kind had religious and ceremonial rather than domestic functions. To the east cave habitats were rarer on the löss plains, and tents of skins and excavated shelters half underground were the homes of the plain hunters of the mammoth.

A different economy again prevailed in the forested margins of the Mediterranean. Cultures were more localised than in the open lands to the north, where movement of men and animals over long distances encouraged greater uniformity. Bows and arrows were more useful and important weapons for the killing of birds and small game. Fruits and honey played a larger part in diet. And there was an increasing tendency to use tiny and delicately worked flints (microliths) set, perhaps, with pitch or resin from the forest in holders of wood or bone.

The succession, provenance and distribution of the Upper Palaeolithic cultures contribute a little further to the idea of a 'personality' of Europe. The earliest of the Upper Palaeolithic cultures, the Châtelperronian, is found only in south-western France, but the more important Aurignacian culture which followed it extended from south-western France eastwards through the hilly country of Hercynian Europe to the Rumanian area and to the Crimea. There is sufficient resemblance in flint-working techniques to suggest an origin in south-west Asia. In France the Aurignacian is succeeded in roughly the same area by the Gravettian, but further east and north these distributions diverge. The Gravettian is much more closely linked to the löss lands of central Europe and is very well developed in the east on the steppe lands of southern Russia. Whereas the Aurignacian was closely identified with cave dwellings and the beginnings of cave art, the Gravettian is distinguished, chiefly in the east, by its great collective mammoth hunts, its half-buried shelters in open country, its little figurines (the so-called 'Venuses' of, for example, Willendorf and Prědmost) and its apparently ceremonial use of red ochre.

The distributions of the cultures which followed—the Solutrean and the Magdalenian—were, however, quite different, since they recalled earlier distributions in their concentration west of the Rhine and the Alps. The Solutrean, characterised by its highly skilled use of flint, may have been indigenous to the west or it might have spread from Hungary towards the end of Aurignacian times. In the west it gave way to the Magdalenian reindeer culture again limited to the west and to the area north of the Cantabrian mountains. To the south the forest was a barrier to the hunting economies of the open park-steppe or park-tundra of the north, and to the east the re-advance of ice in the Alps and northern Europe may have reduced to a narrow corridor the routes which had been taken across central Europe by the Aurignacian, Gravettian and possibly the early Solutrean cultures.

With the final retreat of northern ice, a whole series of changes were set in train which were of the most profound significance for the development of Europe. In north Germany, Upper Palaeolithic hunters began to colonise new lands abandoned by the ice and Denmark began to be settled. Further south the microlith techniques of the Mediterranean lands spread slowly northwards with the advance of the forest. The desiccation of the Sahara and of south-west Asia and the colonisation of Europe by forest were beginning to threaten the survival of the Upper Palaeolithic cultures and to demand new adaptations to an environment that was once again changing.[11]

By far the most dramatic and momentous changes occurred outside Europe altogether. Increasing aridity in south-west Asia must have created critical conditions which could only be met by migration or an economic revolution, and it is in this area, indeed, that the earliest signs of agriculture and the domestication of animals are found. Change was perhaps least in the Mediterranean lands where forest had persisted through late glacial times, and although the forest changed in character and composition, radical adjustments of economy were less necessary. But in north and north-western Europe the equipment and economy of society had to be adapted to a physical environment which was changing fairly rapidly.

The final retreat of ice from the Baltic, delayed twice by the return of colder conditions in the Older and Younger Dryas periods, began about 8000 B.C. New areas were opened up for settlement in Britain, Scandinavia, North Germany, and also on the floor of the North Sea basin. The isostatic recovery of the land from the overlying weight of ice, and also the release of water formerly locked up in the ice sheets themselves, set in motion complex changes in sea-level, represented first around the coasts of Britain by the 'submerged forest' period when much of the floor of the North Sea basin was exposed. At a later stage raised beaches were formed by the higher sea-level of the Flandrian transgression. But the most important feature for human occupation, however, was undoubtedly the invasion of the forest northwards. The cold Dryas periods had been characterised by the spread of *Dryas octopetala* and by a spread of grasses of alpine rather than arctic character, and therefore with a greater carrying capacity for herbivorous animals. Park-tundra with dwarf birch and arctic willow predominated in the Alps and Pyrenees, to the south of which forest vegetation prevailed.

The analysis of pollen and other plant remains preserved in postglacial deposits has made it possible to record in some detail the changes in vegetation which followed the amelioration of climate, particularly in northern Europe, Britain and the Netherlands. The details are complex, depending on many factors, among which may be stressed the regional variations of climate in Europe, and also the variations in the rate of migration of plants from various source regions. Birch, pine and willow were the first to colonise the more northerly areas, pine then gaining ground to be followed later by the rapid spread of hazel. As climate improved to the warm wet conditions of the Atlantic or climatic optimum, mixed oak forest and alder became dominant in the north, extending further than its present limits in central Sweden. This general pattern of succession has been found elsewhere in Europe, but with a large number of variations. In eastern Europe oak was less well developed than spruce and fir; in south-western France oak appeared before hazel; beech appeared in southern France long before its arrival in Britain; and in northern Italy oak followed a short phase of spruce and fir. As climate and vegetation altered so also did the fauna. Elk, red and roe deer, wild pig, beaver and marmot replaced the reindeer, the wild horse, bison and mammoth of the open plains.

The material equipment and the economy of the Upper Palaeolithic hunters had thus to be adapted to a radically changing environment. Tiny flints or microliths, which were certainly used to tip arrows and which had been characteristic of Upper Palaeolithic industries of North Africa and Spain, were used much more widely in the new Mesolithic age of western and eastern Europe. The bow and arrow, more useful in a forest environment, replaced the harpoon and the spear as the dominant weapon. Fruits, nuts, small game, snails, fish and fowl became more important elements of diet. In the west the Azilian economy of western France may have developed from the modifications which were to some extent forced on Late Magdalenian hunters by the change in environmental conditions. Geometrically shaped microliths were characteristic of the Tardenoisian cultures which followed, though the variety in the assemblages of flints makes it necessary to distinguish different sub-divisions of the industry as a whole in western Britain and France, Iberia and Italy. Communities were small and widely scattered, and it seems possible that the greater resources of the forest, the decline of long-distance seasonal migrations over open country, and the isolation of groups within a forested environment combined to bring to an end the uniformity over wide areas which seems to characterise the Upper Palaeolithic world of open vegetation, wide-ranging game, and communal hunting.

Habitat also changed with the climate. There are sites in France in which the gradual abandonment of cave dwellings for open country can be traced from Magdalenian to Azilian times. The Tardenoisian hunters almost universally chose lightly wooded sandy soils or high upland country as in the Pennines of Britain. In western France the caves in the Eocene limestone on the right bank of the Gironde estuary were abandoned for the sandy soils of the Landes.[12] In the Weald, in the Netherlands and Belgium, and between the Loire and the Seine, the concentration of Tardenoisian sites on sandy soils is striking. It was perhaps partly because of this preference for sandy or upland soils unsuitable for cultivation that Tardenoisian cultures were able to persist side by side with the Neolithic farmers on loam or löss soils, occasionally securing by theft or barter the sheep or other domesticated animals whose remains figure in their middens.

In much of the newly colonised lands of the north, in an area centred on Denmark and southern Sweden and extending from the North German Plain across the exposed floor of the North Sea basin to eastern Britain, a different economy developed, and it was one which was well adapted to the environment of marsh, forest and lake of these northern lands. Aptly named after a Danish locality called *magle møse* or 'big bog', the Maglemose economy was one which rested heavily on fishing and fowling as well as hunting.[13] Specialised blunt-headed arrows were invented to bring down birds and wild fowl; hooks, nets, basket-work traps and seine nets were developed for fishing. Paddles and dug-out canoes represent the first evidence of boats, and it was therefore in these times that the colonisation of islands became possible. Islands off western France were colonised for the first time; western Norway was almost certainly pioneered from the sea as climate ameliorated. Axes and adzes were invented to fell trees and to work timber and great use was made of bone and antler as well as flint to create varied and specialised tools.

Unlike the Tardenoisians, the Maglemose pioneers of northern Europe were not restricted to sandy soils, but showed a very strong preference for lowland sites, frequently near marsh and lake. Their possession of means, however modest, for clearing woodland enabled them to settle within wooded areas. Their settlement sites as

well as material equipment betray their interest in fowling and fishing, for in later Mesolithic times when sea-levels had risen, settlement concentrated on the raised beaches in Scandinavia which mark
the limits of the Flandrian and Litorina transgressions. And by then
sea fish, seals and sea birds were being skilfully sought out.

NEOLITHIC EUROPE

The pioneer farming settlement of Europe

While the societies of Western Europe were adjusting their economies
to the amelioration of their environment and were beginning to
colonise the newly opened northern lands, even greater changes were
occurring elsewhere. The northward spread of forest which followed
the retreat of Baltic ice was accompanied by the onset of drier conditions in south-west Asia and the Sahara. Although a causal connection is difficult to establish, it is against such a background of
deteriorating supplies of food and water that the first steps took place
towards the cultivation of crops and later the domestication of other
animals than the dog. Roughly similar dates are, indeed, suggested
for the flourishing culture of Star Carr in Yorkshire (about 7000
B.C.) which presages the Maglemose culture in many respects, and
the pre-pottery Neolithic horizons of Jericho (about 7500 B.C.) where
crops of wheat and barley were already being grown and harvested
with flint implements.

The controversial issues which surround the origin of agriculture
refer mainly to non-European areas and discussion of them must
therefore be brief. It is likely that the harvesting and storing of wild
grains preceded their cultivation. Grassy uplands of easily cultivable
soils where wild varieties of grains were growing are more likely to
have been the home of cultivation than the marshy and naturally
flooded alluvium of lowland rivers where clearing would have
presented difficult problems. At all events two varieties of cultivated
wheat and barley were already evident in the earliest Neolithic
settlements of Palestine and Egypt.[14] The very hardy *einkorn*
(*Triticum monococcum*) accompanied the first farmers into Europe,
but it yields poorly and its modern representatives have almost
disappeared except in a few mountainous areas. Emmer wheat
(*T. dicoccum*) was widely cultivated in the Middle East and Egypt
and, although less tolerant of cold climates and poor soils, it yields
more highly than *einkorn*. The more modern and complex Bread

Wheat (*T. aestivum*) did not become important until the Iron Age. Among the barleys both the two-rowed variety (*Hordeum distichum*) and the six-rowed varieties, the dense-eared *H. hexadistichum* and the loose-eared *H. tetrastichum* were grown in Neolithic times. Six-rowed barley of the dense-eared type was normally cultivated by the Neolithic pioneers of central and western Europe, though it has been largely replaced by loose-eared varieties which were already to be found in Neolithic Britain and Denmark. In so far as the distribution of wild ancestors of cultivated crops offers a clue to the origin of early cultivation south-west Asia seems the most likely area. The wild ancestors of *einkorn* are to be found in the Balkans and two-rowed barley south of the Caspian, but south-west Asia is the only area in which all are to be found, and within this area it is Palestine which has representatives of all but *einkorn*.

The domestication of goats and sheep probably occurred a little later than the cultivation of crops, and was undoubtedly helped by the attraction of the grazings on stubbles after harvests and perhaps by the increasing need of animals to congregate around scarce water. Domesticated sheep and goats were found at the lowest Neolithic levels in south-west Asia where the wild goat was widespread. Varieties of wild sheep were widely distributed over western and central Asia and Europe. The European mouflon (*Ovis misummon*) survives only in Corsica and Sardinia; the western Asiatic mouflon (*O. orientalis*) in Cyprus and Turkey, and the Soay sheep of the Outer Hebrides are said to be their nearest descendants in western Europe. The larger urial (*O. vignei*) was the source of breeds introduced into Europe in Neolithic times, and both the modern merino sheep and the Norfolk Blackface are believed to be related to it. The third variety of wild sheep, the argali (*O. ammon*), native to central Asia, has made little contribution to domestic varieties outside that area. Meat and hides rather than wool were the earliest products of these domesticated animals, to be followed later by dairy produce, and finally their use as pack animals. The woolly fleece of the sheep was probably a result of domestication rather than a reason for it.

The domestication of cattle and the pig, animals widespread over the Old World in their wild forms, took place rather later. Cattle domesticated from the tall, large-boned aurochs or urus (*Bos primigenius*) were introduced into western Europe by Neolithic farmers, but the smaller short-horned cattle (*B. longifrons* or *brachyceros*) did not appear in Britain until late Bronze Age times. Similarly the pig was domesticated both from *Sus scrofa scrofa*, well suited to grubbing in woodland, and in south-east Asia from *Sus scrofa vittatus*, producing a variety of pig introduced into Europe as late as the eighteenth century from China, since when it has largely replaced the older type.

Cultivation and stock-rearing were the most fundamental of the new techniques which have been normally associated with the Neolithic revolution. Weaving, the making of pottery, and the polishing of flint implements were also new. But not all of these features are necessarily found together; pottery was made in Denmark before cultivation was known; farming was known in Jericho before pottery was made. But in much of Europe the earliest farmers and herders seem to have been immigrant colonists equipped with a material culture very different from that of the surviving hunters and fishers, and one which made possible a vast increase of population. Europe had become a pioneer fringe of new farming settlement.

Variations of climate, soil and vegetation within Europe demanded changes in the balance and repertoire of crops and stock, and also severely limited possible areas of settlement. In the Mediterranean lands changes were few, for here the physical environment is similar to that of south-west Asia. The Mediterranean evergreen forest was relatively thin and easy to clear in many areas. Wheat and barley could continue to be the dominant crops and there was abundant grazing. In northern Europe, at the other extreme, the short, cool summers, the infertile, acid podzols and the absence of undergrowth and therefore of grazing in the coniferous forests effectively prevented farming settlement from passing much beyond the margin of the coniferous forest. It was not until historical times that serious inroads were made into them. In the intermediate zones of western and central Europe, in the zones of brown earths and deciduous and mixed forests, suitable sites for settlement had to be carefully chosen and adjustments to the original economy had to be made. Wheat and barley were supplemented or even replaced by other cereals in some areas. Rye and oats probably first appeared as weeds of cultivation in crops of wheat and barley, gradually proving their worth as useful crops on dry, hungry soils or under cool, damp conditions respectively. Pigs were eminently suited to the grazing of woodlands, but when woodland was cleared the sheep came into its own on open heath and grassland. Game continued to be an important part of diet and the range of wild products gathered even increased with new demands for dyestuffs, for example, or with the introduction of new plants which were the unwitting accompaniment of the alteration by man of natural vegetation.

Soils and vegetation severely limited the possible areas of settlement in much of western and central Europe. Marsh and damp oakwood forest were avoided and light, well-drained soils preferred. Light sandy loams, gravelly loams on river terraces, dry, well-drained soils on chalk or limestone, and above all the löss and limon soils of central Europe, Belgium and northern France were the preferred sites for settlement. The coincidence between löss soils and the settlement of the early Danubian peasants, the pioneer farmers of central Europe, is very striking indeed. It was once thought that these light soils supported a heath and grassland vegetation which made settlement easy for societies equipped with only flint tools, but pollen analysis has made it clear that these light soils carried a mixed oak forest which could, however, be much more easily cleared than the damp oakwood of heavier soils. Practical experience has shown that flint tools can dispose of thin woodland fairly easily, though it seems likely that fire was the chief weapon for the clearing of woodland for farming. Löss, rendzinas and sandy loams were also easy to cultivate with hoe or digging stick, and the open forest gave good undergrowth foliage for the pasturing of cattle and pigs. Heath and grassland on such soils were frequently a *result* of the clearing of forest by prehistoric man.

Shifting cultivation of the 'slash and burn' type was normal in temperate Europe. Trees were probably lopped and ring-barked before burning. Seed would be sown in the ashes, with a minimum of cultivation of the ground, and stumps of trees would be left. Yields would be high at first, followed by a rapid falling off after a few years, so that the Neolithic farmer, like modern peasants of the humid tropics, would move on to another site. As late as the seventeenth century Finnish settlement on morainic soils in Sweden followed a similar pattern.[15] The whole sequence of settlement, clearing and burning, then cultivation followed by abandonment and the regeneration of secondary forest is graphically illustrated by Danish studies in pollen analysis.[16]

In the Neolithic settlement of Europe, four and perhaps five primary groupings of cultures have been recognised which may indicate the major routes by which farmers and herders pioneered a new way of life in Europe (Fig 1·1). Yet there are many difficulties in deducing the direction and nature of such migrations. The evidence is, of course, the wide scatter of material objects which have been left. Similarities between such objects or assemblages of objects may be established in terms of typology, stylistic details, or the use of rare and identifiable raw materials (e.g. distinctive shells or minerals with a limited distribution). Even when such similarities are established,

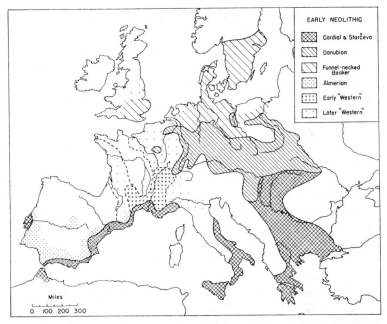

Fig. 1:1   Early Neolithic cultures in Western Europe (after Stier and Kirsten).

it is by no means always certain whether they were produced by wholesale migrations of settlers, by the movement of minorities of traders, craftsmen, warriors, rulers and priests, or even by imitation and cultural spread involving little movement of people. The chronology of movement may be so difficult to establish that quite opposite interpretations of the direction of movement may be possible. Finally the measurements taken from the skeletal remains of prehistoric man have been used to identify types and to suggest population movement, but by no means conclusively.

The only certain representatives of the earliest, pre-pottery Neolithic farmers and herders similar to those of south-west Asia are to be found in the nearby area of Thessaly, but the distribution of blade tools and trapezoid flints have suggested a wider spread of pre-pottery farmers in other areas of the Mediterranean and in France. The second, and much more important group of pioneer farmers in Europe, represented by the round-bottomed pottery of the Starčevo culture, appears to have reached the middle Danube by one of the most important entries into central Europe from the Aegean— the Morava–Vardar gap, from which the culture spread between the Tisza river and the Dniester. Starčevo farmers were shifting culti-vators using *einkorn* and millet and it was not until later in Greece and much later in the Balkans as a whole that they were succeeded by sedentary cultivators living on permanent village sites, now represented by tells (mounds) of debris accumulated over many centuries.[17]

The Danubian culture was the third of the early Neolithic cultures which intruded into Europe from the east and it is a culture remark-ably widespread and uniform over much of central Europe from the Rhineland to western Hungary and Poland. It is characterised par-ticularly by the unity of its pottery and the spiral-meander motif in its decoration. As in the Starčevo culture, a mussel native to the Black Sea (*Spondylus gaederopus*) was used for ornament. Cultivat-ing his *einkorn* and probably emmer wheat, barley, beans, peas, lentils and flax, the Danubian peasant was undoubtedly the pioneer farmer over much of central Europe, herding fewer stock than his successors in this area or than the equivalent pioneers in Western Europe. Large rectangular houses grouped in temporary village settlements were normal, one such settlement near Cologne showing no less than seven occupations. The very uniformity of the culture, and C14 dates which put the Danubian as early as 4000 B.C. at Magdeburg, suggest that it had spread very rapidly across Europe. The remarkable concentration of settlement on easily cleared and worked löss soils together with the reliance on shifting cultivation may help to explain this rapidity. It was not, indeed, until much later that farming spread north from the löss to the less attractive boulder clays of the North German Plain and to the southern margins of the Baltic, and by the time that it did, older Mesolithic traditions of hunting and fishing had been assimilated to the new farming tech-niques in the Funnel-necked Beaker cultures of the area.

Two other primary Neolithic cultures were involved in the transmission of new techniques into Europe, but by way of the Mediterranean. Round the shores of the Mediterranean the earliest Neolithic cultures are characterised by rough pottery coarsely decorated by impressions made in the soft clay before firing, and generally known as 'impressed' ware.[18] Patterns were often made with the edges of shells, particularly the *cardium* shell, so that in the Mediterranean this is sometimes also known as 'cardial' culture.[19] Its strongly coastal distribution suggests a diffusion by sea from the east, from northern Syria and southern Anatolia to the shores of Sicily, the Balkans, Italy, France, Spain and North Africa. It has been suggested, since impressed ware was succeeded by painted pottery in the Near East by 4000 B.C., that its diffusion into the Mediterranean must have begun before then. Moreover, just as the impressed ware of the Neolithic Mediterranean was part of an area of distribution which reaches to the Gulf of Guinea and China, so also was the Mediterranean the western limit for a wider area of the Old World in which painted pottery was made.[20]

Finally, round the shores of the western Mediterranean, and found at their most elaborate in Almeria, are the component cultures of what has been called the 'western' group. Wheat and barley were cultivated but the economy was, in general, more pastoral; swine were more favoured than sheep, and round, bag-shaped pots were made in forms originally inspired by workmanship in leather rather than clay. It has been suggested that the dominance of stockbreeding may have encouraged mobility and the diffusion of a fairly uniform culture from Gibraltar to Liguria. Much of France, Switzerland and even to some extent southern Britain may have received part of their earliest Neolithic cultures from the western Mediterranean by way of the Carcassonne gap and Aquitaine or by way of the Rhône–Saône trough. At all events, the Rhineland, eastern France and Switzerland were at the margin between these 'western' cultures and influences of Danubian inspiration from central Europe, just as Britain was at the margin between western cultures and those which had developed in the North German Plain.

After the period of early Neolithic settlement, Mesolithic traditions sometimes lingered on side by side with an established farming economy nearby. Thus in Belgium, hunters and fishers continued to inhabit the infertile heaths and unattractive uplands while the light but fertile soils of the lowlands were settled by Neolithic farmers. Bones of domesticated stock in the middens of hunting peoples sometimes suggest that either trading or raiding may have taken place between hunters and farmers. More frequently, as in the Funnel-necked Beaker culture of the North German Plain, Mesolithic traditions were assimilated to new farming economies with a resultant fragmentation of culture and sometimes an impoverishment. In later times settlement was pushed on to the poorer soils of what are now often heathlands. Hunting and stock-rearing became more general; hilltop settlements on defensible sites and the appearance of weapons suggest a degree of unrest. It may be that the growth of population had begun to put pressure on the limited resources of the times.

New impulses from the east

Long before the pioneer farmers had begun to make inroads on the woodlands of north-western Europe, urban civilisation had begun to flourish in Crete, a threshold in Europe for the advance of civilisation from the cities of the Fertile Crescent. Varied in relief and soils, Crete was admirably placed to assimilate the richer traditions of Egypt and the metal-working tradition of western Asia to its immigrant Neolithic culture from Anatolia. Material wealth, accumulated from the trade with Egypt, Syria and Asia Minor for which Crete's position was so suited, farming wealth and the newly acquired skills and institutions undoubtedly nourished the Minoan culture, which has been called the first distinctive European civilisation. Knowledge of copper was followed by the technique of working in bronze; the potter's wheel brought new standards of precision; communications were improved with the introduction of wheeled vehicles and roads; and specialised skills and crafts were emerging. A high degree of government and organisation are evident in the existence of central authority and the palace industries of Knossos, and also in the highly developed religion centred on the 'Mother Goddess' and involving elaborate arrangements for the disposal of the dead.

From the third millenium B.C. to its final destruction by the Mycenaean power of mainland Greece about 1400 B.C. Knossos and Crete benefited from the trade of the eastern Mediterranean with Syria and Egypt and also with the small barren Cyclades islands whose wealth must have been derived from trade rather than from their exiguous agricultural resources. Copper from Cyprus and Naxos, emery, obsidian from Melos and Yali, marble idols and vases were shipped from the Aegean islands to Crete, Troy, Lesbos or Egypt.

The lands of the eastern Mediterranean also looked west and north, however, to the barbarian lands. To them they transmitted new impulses in various forms. Objects of copper made from central European ores but with eastern Mediterranean techniques and found in north-east Hungary, Bohemia, and Silesia may represent one such impulse. Elsewhere, copies of copper daggers made in flint may represent another. And maritime traders in their long, narrow ships had pressed westwards to the central Mediterranean by Middle Minoan times, ultimately to reach the Rhône delta and Sardinia.

The megalith builders of Western Europe

There is no doubt of Minoan contact with the western Mediterranean soon after 2000 B.C. and it seems very likely that it was by way of an earlier pioneer movement westwards that some at least of the traits associated with the megalithic cultures of western and central

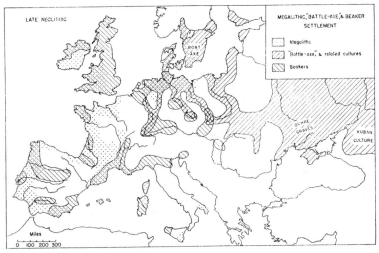

Fig. 1:2   Late Neolithic cultures of Western Europe (after Stier and Kirsten).

Europe were transmitted. The megalith builders are distinguished by the architectural features of stone-built graves of which various forms are to be found over much of western Europe (Fig. 1:2). Some are the graves of single individuals, but the most important and significant are, perhaps, the collective graves, chiefly of the passage grave or gallery grave type. The former is a chamber approached by an access passage, the latter a long, narrow chamber frequently subdivided, but without a separate entrance passage.[21]

The distributions and successions of the megalithic tombs have been variously interpreted. In southern Scandinavia and north-west Germany the sequence was once thought to represent a completely indigenous development, so that passage graves in Britain and western France were viewed as the result of an outward expansion from Scandinavia. But the reverse is much more likely to be the case as soon as it is admitted that the earliest stone-built graves are not necessarily the product of the same culture which was associated with the passage graves. Similarly in Iberia the contrast between the elaborate and complex passage graves, corbelled and rock-cut tombs of southern and eastern Spain on the one hand, and the poorer single chambered graves of the meseta and the north and west, was once thought to be indicative of an inevitable progression of indigenous culture from poor and simple to richer and more elaborate traits. But it is more likely that the more complex structures are earlier and that a cultural impoverishment took place with the penetration of interior Spain.

In France the earliest passage graves probably date from about 2300–2000 B.C. and were constructed in Brittany as a result of maritime settlement from northern Spain, and in southern France as a result of colonisation from the western Mediterranean. The earliest settlements were coastal (Plate 1), but with the expansion of gallery graves in southern France and in the Gironde and later in the Paris basin, megalithic monuments are to be found much further inland (Fig. 1:3). Morbihan and Brittany appear to have been important foci from which colonisation in western Britain and western Denmark took place. Although there are differences of opinion about the chronology, it seems most likely that many of the megalithic tombs of Western Europe derive ultimately from models among the advanced societies of the eastern Mediterranean. Collective tombs in natural or rock-cut caves, or in carefully corbelled and dry-walled structures, very common in the Mediterranean, were modified into the passage grave and then the gallery grave during their movement north and west. In southern France statue menhirs were built to the same deity that was worshipped in the city of Troy I. Incised spirals, 'oculi' and diagrammatic abstractions are all that remain of the more representational art of the eastern Mediterranean. The

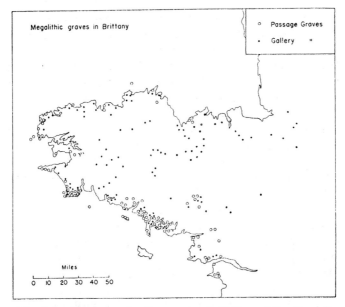

Fig. 1:3   Passage and gallery graves in Brittany (after Daniel).

trephining of skulls was practised in southern France as in the eastern Mediterranean.

There is, then, a striking deterioration in cultural traits from east to west. It seems possible that the builders of the passage graves, frequently seen as colonists, as missionaries of a new religion, less frequently as a 'sort of travelling undertaker persuading the natives to adopt a new style of tomb',[22] were in a sense the explorers of the west, seeking also for sources of precious stones and metals, particularly copper and tin. At all events, as in the early Neolithic, Britain, western France and Iberia are culturally linked with each other and with the Mediterranean, and thence indirectly to the advanced societies of the east. In megalithic times the orbit of these 'western approaches' extended further still, however, to include the shores of the North Sea basin.

'Battle-axe' cultures of central Europe

In central and eastern Europe new developments of the late Neolithic economy accompany the appearance of a series of cultures collectively known by the common features they possess—polished stone battle-axes, quite possibly based on metal prototypes and frequently found deposited with male skeletons, and pottery decorated with cord impressions. From the Vistula and the Dnieper northwards to Sweden and Finland and westwards to the Rhine and to Jutland, 'battle-axe' warriors appear also as pastoral groups frequently settling in areas untouched by existing farming populations.

Even more perhaps than in the case of the megalithic builders of Western Europe there has been scope for difference of opinion about the origins and provenance of these cultural traits.[23] One may discard former chauvinistic views which would make them the Nordic ancestors of the German peoples dominating central Europe from a heartland in Saxony and Thuringia. It has been more cogently argued that most of the basic features could be explained in terms of purely indigenous developments without recourse to the assumption of new cultural migrations. Thus, the increase of late Neolithic population and the acquisition of farming and herding skills by former hunters and fishers would have encouraged, perhaps, the extension of settlement on to poorer soils not formerly cultivated, and thereby, perhaps, a shift to pastoralism. Such a background might also have encouraged the restive conditions in which battle-axes might be a useful innovation and stock a more mobile form of wealth than crops. Hints of a patriarchal society in the archaeological record are also to be explained in terms of the higher status of the male in a pastoral and warrior-ridden society, rather than in terms of cultural influx.

There is, however, greater support for an entirely different view, that patriarchal society and a greater emphasis on pastoralism and other cultural traits were brought by an immigration of newcomers from the east. Links have been sought in the late Neolithic cultures which extended north of the Caucasus and the Black Sea across the steppes of southern Russia to the forest margins. Here too new cultural traits involving different building habits and burial rites, the use of copper and the wheel as well as greater emphasis on stock-breeding and material traces of a patriarchal society, were superimposed on existing communities, but these are also all traits which are closely associated with the 'Kurgan' culture (so known from its large barrows) north of the Caucasus towards the end of the third millenium B.C., and this in turn had contact with the advanced societies of Sumer and Mesopotamia. As in the Mediterranean so in central Europe new impulses from the advanced societies of the

Middle East were slowly carried westwards, becoming barbarised and impoverished on the way.

The routes taken were, indeed, those which were to become the classic entries into Europe from the east; north of the Carpathians to southern Poland and then westwards to Thuringia and Saxony, the North German Plain and Belgium, through the Carpathians to the Hungarian Plain and to the Danube corridor; and by way of northern Asia Minor to the Bosporus and the Aegean.

Beaker peoples

Known by the distinctive shape of the drinking cups by which they have been identified, and from which, possibly, fermented liquor was drunk, the Bell Beaker people were also pastoralists and warriors, armed with bowmen's wrist-guards and flat-tanged knife daggers. They have frequently been regarded as either prospectors for metals or introducers of metal-working into Europe, using copper though very sparingly. The beginnings of mining for copper, tin or gold in the Balkans, Transylvania and Slovakia, south-east Spain, Cornwall and Ireland are commonly attributed to them. They were traders as well, and may have assisted in the pioneering of the routes by which amber from the Baltic shores and west Jutland was taken south by way of the Brenner pass to the Aegean, and by which segmented beads were exported from Egypt and the Aegean to lower Austria and Moravia.

In central Europe the Beaker peoples were widely distributed from the upper Danube to Budapest, across Bohemia to central Germany, and from northern Italy to the lower Rhine. In Western Europe the Bell Beaker peoples seem to have followed, from south-east Spain, the routes previously taken by the builders of the passage-graves; so much so that some of the Beaker people gained admittance to their collective tombs. In the west, at least, there is some suggestion that the Beaker people were a small minority of traders, warriors, and/or smiths, and frequently gained a high social standing. Physical anthropology also suggests an intrusion of a minority of tall, broad-headed and physically distinctive people,[24] though in course of time the alien Beaker people mingled with indigenous populations and adopted many of their cultural traits. The early style of the beakers, remarkably uniform over all those parts of Europe where it is found, changed into very many local varieties as these new and alien traditions were assimilated.

AGRARIAN AND INDUSTRIAL REVOLUTIONS

Bronze in Europe: cities in Greece

The introduction of an urban civilisation to the mainland of Europe based to a large extent on goods, skills and craftsmen imported from Crete took place in Greece in the first half of the second millenium B.C. About 1800 B.C. Greece had been invaded by newcomers bringing grey wheel-made Minyan pottery of a kind which is also to be found in Asia Minor and northern Persia. They were probably also speakers of an early form of Greek, and it was upon their traditions as well as those of Crete that Mycenaean civilisation was built. By the sixteenth century B.C. the royal shaft graves of Mycenae contained a rich equipment of bronze implements and weapons, vessels of gold and silver, ivory-handled mirrors, gems and amber. The power of kingly leaders as well as great technical advance was also symbolised by light war chariots, mounted on spoked wheels and drawn by horses, again comparable to similar vehicles in Palestine and Syria and among the Hittites of Asia Minor. By 1400 B.C., Mycenaean power was able to overthrow the Cretans and to sack Knossos itself. The old, non-Indo-European language of Linear A was supplemented by the kind of Greek inscribed on tablets and was, like Linear B, only deciphered in recent years. Expansion into central Greece, the Peloponnese and Thessaly is indicated by the spread of carefully corbelled, round stone-built graves or *tholoi* which replaced the Mycenaean shaft graves from about 1500 B.C. and which recall in some ways the earlier megalithic tombs of the Mediterranean, and which may, indeed, have been derived from the central Mediterranean. Mycenae itself hardly qualifies as a city, for it consisted essentially of a strongly fortified citadel containing the royal palace and surrounded by a cluster of villages. But true cities certainly existed elsewhere at Argos, Thebes and Tiryns, for example, on sites which still carry buildings of classical or modern age. The urban revolution had reached Europe.[25]

The wealth of Mycenae, like that of Crete before it, was undoubtedly based on trading and possibly raiding in the eastern Mediterranean. Trading posts at Colophon and Ugarit, colonies on Rhodes and Cyprus (worked for its rich copper resources) and Mycenaean pottery testify to the importance of this early trade with Mesopotamia and Egypt. But for Europe as a whole, the trade with the barbarian west and north was much more significant, for the geography of economic development in Europe was to a great extent governed by the demands of eastern Mediterranean markets and the routes of access to them.

The tin necessary for the manufacture of bronze in Mycenaean Greece must have been imported, and there is every likelihood that Cornish tin constituted part of the supply. Links with south-western Britain are indicated by the presence in Mycenaean graves of necklaces of amber beads with curiously perforated spacers of a type fashionable in Britain; segmented beads of faience in Bronze Age burials of southern Britain and a dagger of the thirteenth century B.C. found in Cornwall are from the eastern Mediterranean. British contacts may have been either by western seaways or the transcontinental amber routes. There is, indeed, sufficient evidence of Mycenaean goods in southern France to suggest a transpeninsular route from the Mediterranean by way of the Gironde to Brittany. Mycenaean pottery in eastern and southern Sicily suggests a trading sphere in the Mediterranean not very different from that of the later world of the Greeks.

A network of trade routes linked Britain and the western Baltic with central Europe and Italy, and it is in these latter areas that economic advance and the adoption of bronze were most precocious. Amber, valued for its appearance and its magical, electrical properties, is a commodity at once durable and of identifiable provenance, and it can be traced along the trade routes from its source in Jutland and the Baltic to its ultimate markets in the Mediterranean. No doubt with other commodities, it was exported by way of the Elbe to Bohemia and thence by way of the Danube to the Inn valley, the Brenner Pass and so to the Adriatic. Another route went by way of the river Saale to the river Main and thence to the Danube, while a still more westerly branch was added later by way of the Rhineland and the river Neckar. Cornish tin may have joined these routes in north-western Germany; they were certainly travelled by itinerant merchant craftsmen carrying stocks of manufactured and semi-finished goods, together with raw materials in the form of neck-rings or ingot torques. From about 1500 B.C. and especially from 1250 B.C. the copper resources of the Tyrol near Salzburg were intensively worked; the ores of Slovakia and the tin of Bohemia were being exploited, yet in spite of the unities which are implicit in this long distance trade in a few important commodities, material cultures were different enough, even over small areas, to warrant the idea that traders probably operated within tribal territories, rarely penetrating beyond.[26]

From about 1200 B.C. new burial habits began to be adopted in many parts of central Europe. In place of earlier tumulus burials cremation was practised and the ashes were deposited in urns grouped together in the 'urn-fields' which gave the culture its name. Similar customs had been adopted in Troy about 1400 B.C. and were known soon after in Hungary, from which they spread to much of central Europe. But what is more important is the extent of new changes of technology and economy, revolutionising the use of the environment, both in farming and in the use of metal.

The collapse of Mycenaean power about 1400 B.C. made available a surplus of copper for consumption within Europe itself. Quite highly organised mining and a new abundance of metal served to stimulate other advances. In earlier times metal had been scarce and restricted to ornaments, weapons and axes for the most part; flint, bone and wood continued to be the raw materials for most tools. Now hammered bronze vessels were being made; socketed axes were more abundant and cheaper metal made possible its use for chisels, gouges, saws and the like, which in turn made the working of wood easier and more accurate. Horse-drawn vehicles became more efficient and more widely used, though solid-wheeled waggons had been introduced in earlier times.

The most important changes concerned the expansion of sedentary agriculture. A light wooden plough or *ard* drawn by oxen had been known in early Bronze Age times in the Mediterranean, and permanent village settlement reflected in the accumulation of tells had been evident in the middle Danube from the same period, but it seems likely that the spread of the plough and of fixed fields, small and irregular though they were, came mainly in the late Bronze Age. There can be no doubt that the introduction of animal power for the preparation of the soil for cultivation, and the mixed farming which the keeping of stock entails, must have vastly increased the capacity of the land to support population. The final clearing of the woodland from many areas of light soil which had previously been worked over by shifting cultivators also took place. There is indeed occasional evidence of an acceleration of sedimentation as a result of soil erosion following upon deforestation in some areas during the Bronze Age, and there is also fairly general evidence that sheep became more

important than swine as the proportion of open lands increased and
woodland declined.[27]

Whatever the relationship between technical advance, the growth
of population, the development of the Urnfield culture and ultimately
the collapse of Mycenaean power, it is certain that Urnfield cultural
traits and probably Urnfield migrants pushed west, south, and south-
east from central Europe (Fig. 1:4). In the eastern Mediterranean

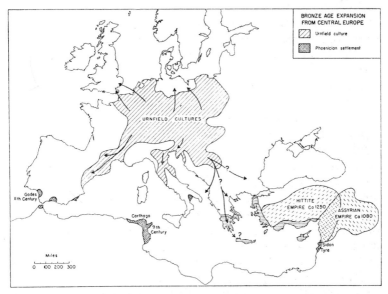

Fig. 1:4   Expansion of Bronze Age 'urnfield' and related cultures from
Central Europe (after Stier and Kirsten).

new invasions occurred, accompanied by the devastation and burning of cities; the Hittite confederacy was broken by invasions from
the west; Philistines settled the coast of Palestine and many of the
most famous of earlier sites were abandoned and destroyed about
this time. Troy was destroyed between 1209 and 1183 B.C. and the
Dorian invaders were ravaging the Peloponnese about 1100 B.C.
Distinctive articles such as safety pins and fibulae common to the
Balkans and also found in the eastern Mediterranean suggest that
all this, too, was related to an outward expansion from central
Europe at about this time.

In the west, the bearers of this Bronze Age culture, identified as
Celts, moved west by way of the Belfort Gap to southern Alsace and

the Saône basin, and thence by way of southern France to Catalonia. Another westward movement pushed emigrants from the Loire region to Iberia, where a bronze industry was set up on the basis of Cantabrian copper and Galician tin resources. A north-west movement reached southern England about 1000–900 B.C. by way of northern France. To the south of the Alps new invaders about 1000 B.C. brought cremation and advanced Bronze Age metallurgy to Italy between the Po and the Tiber and laid part of the foundations on which Etruscan civilisation was later built.

In many ways the geography of Urnfield expansion diverges from the repeated patterns of earlier times. In its lateral east–west movement across France and in its inclusion of much of France, Germany and northern Italy within its sphere as well as the heartland of the middle Danube, it recalls in some ways distributions like that of the Carolingian Empire or the spread of the Teutonic peoples at the time of the barbarian invasions. The fact that all of these movements have in common, is, perhaps, that they were essentially continental in character and owed little or nothing to maritime expansion. Mediterranean trade was in eclipse with the decline of Mycenae, Egypt and the Hittites, and this was, then, one of the few occasions on which the mainsprings of expansion were to be found in central Europe rather than in the cultures with easy access to the seaways of the Mediterranean.

Iron Age expansion

Iron working, which formally distinguishes a new age, and which represents a further extension of man's ability to use his physical environment, is thought to have originated on the southern shores of the Black Sea. Several reasons account for its relatively late discovery compared with copper, notably the need to achieve higher temperatures in smelting, the greater difficulties of manipulating iron, and the rarity of native iron. For long, iron smelting was probably a closely guarded secret of the Hittite Empire, but with the disturbances of the twelfth century B.C. iron working began to spread—to Palestine, where it was fairly rapidly adopted for the making of sickles and ploughshares, and then to Greece. But it was not until the seventh century B.C. in central Europe, and the late sixth or fifth century B.C. in western Europe that the use of iron spread at all widely. The Early Iron Age Hallstatt cultures, like the Urnfield cultures on whose solid foundations they were built,

spread over much of central and western Europe, drawing inspiration
from two new sources as well as the source from which they acquired
their iron-working techniques (Fig. 1:5). From the Mediterranean
the Greek and Etruscan traditions helped to mould the Iron Age
economy of Western Europe, but so also did the customs of pastoral
nomads from the south Russian steppes.

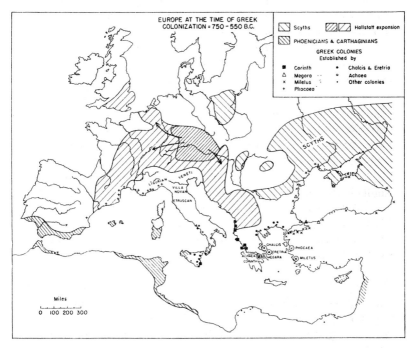

Fig. 1:5   Iron Age Europe at the time of Greek colonisation (after Stier,
Kirsten, Bengston and Milojčič).

The Greek colonial cities, established from about 750 to 550 B.C.
on the shores of the Mediterranean and the Black Sea from the Sea
of Azov to the Costa Brava in Spain, were centres from which Greek
exports and cultural influences spread into the barbarian world. In
the east trade contacts were through the pastoral nomads of the
steppes and the steppe margins; in the west Massilia was the chief
centre to which the tin trade flowed and from which wine, a commodity to acquire great prestige among Celtic chieftains, was exported northwards by way of the Rhône–Saône route. The Greeks

represented the most important, perhaps, of the civilising influences among the barbarian peoples of the north, providing another instance of the use of the well-trodden paths to the west by way of Sicily, southern Italy, the western Mediterranean and the Rhône–Saône and Carcassonne gaps.

In the east, other and quite different neighbours were forcing change on the societies of the late Bronze Age. In the eighth and ninth centuries B.C. Cimmerian nomads, established in the steppes of southern Russia north of the Black Sea, appear to have been responsible for disturbances affecting Asia Minor on the one hand and central and south-east Europe on the other. The Cimmerian push into Europe, however, left little trace and was but an overture to the much more impressive thrust of the Scyths which followed. Known partly from the history of Herodotus and partly from the elaborately furnished graves of their chieftains, marked by great burial mounds up to forty feet high, the Scythians were highly organised and war-like pastoral nomads who had achieved mastery of horse-riding and of the specialised skills needed for their essentially mobile existence in the steppe lands from southern Russia to the very frontiers of China.[28] Indeed, the Scyths had learnt techniques in art and decoration from the Chinese as well as the Greeks. In the west the Scyths moved into central Europe by routes which were later to be used again and again by mobile warrior pastoral groups from the Russian steppes: north of the Carpathians to the upper Dniester, southern Poland and thence to east Germany; across the Carpathians to the upper Tisza, Transylvania and the Banat north of the Danube; and by way of the Black Sea coast to the lower Danube below the Iron Gates and to Thrace. In the Balkans at least, the Scyths came as a minority settling among a larger population and mixture took place to the extent that it is difficult to decide whether individual graves are of Scyth or of indigenous origin.

The Hallstatt culture of the early Iron Age, best developed in its core area north of the Alps in Austria, Bavaria, and Bohemia, owed its character, then, partly to the traditions of the Urnfield culture that preceded it, but the practice of burying chieftains with their waggons, harness, and other equipment in timbered chambers over which great tumuli were built derives from the east and from Scythian influence. The long Hallstatt swords and many forms of ornaments show similar origins, particularly the imaginative use of animal and bird motifs.[29] It does, indeed, seem possible that a minority of horse-riding warriors had established an aristocratic rule over a large indigenous population.

To the east Hallstatt cultural elements are to be found in southern Poland, the middle Danube and Bosnia; to the west similarly, hill forts, weapons and armour, ceremonial burial in place of cremation, horse-riding and four-wheeled chariots characteristic of the south German Hallstatt culture spread to the Low Countries, France and Iberia, and from the Rhineland to south-eastern Britain. There is thus a general resemblance to the distribution of the Urnfield culture. Southern Scandinavia, the North German Plain, western Britain and western France were slow to receive knowledge of iron working and other changes, and the continuity with earlier periods was here more marked.

As in Urnfield times so in the early Iron Age, expansion from central Europe is a dominant theme in the distribution patterns of prehistoric cultures,[30] but it is one which has tended to be obscured by the greater knowledge and, indeed, the very great importance of Greek colonisation of the west and the Mediterranean colonisation implicit in Phoenician settlement. Both of these brought a new, fundamentally important introduction into Western Europe—the city and urban life. The subsequent period, marked in the Mediterranean by the decline of classical Greece and the beginnings of Roman expansion, is much more markedly one of 'continental' and particularly central European dominance, for the period 450–250 B.C. is known among continental authors as the great age of Celtic migrations. Based on Hallstatt cultural traditions, into which stimuli from the classical world and from the Scyths of the steppes were fused, a new artistic form was born in the culture of La Tène, closely associated with the Celtic peoples in Switzerland and south-west Germany (Fig. 1:6). Fortified townships with towers and high walls of clay bricks along the Danube reflect the classical influence which was expressed farther north in the fortified Gallic *oppida*, so well known to students of Caesar's Gaul. It has been observed that some at least of these townships were religious centres as well as fortified camps and palaces, and the presence of traders and artisans adds to their qualifications as towns in the modern sense. Coinage made its appearance, and Greek models from Macedonia and Massilia later inspired a true Celtic coinage. Production of tools, implements and ornaments by specialised artisans on a larger scale than ever before implied a spread of material wealth to peasants and

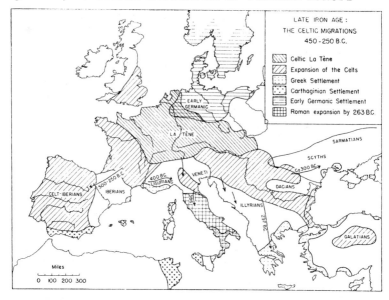

Fig. 1:6   Late Iron Age cultures and the Celts (after Stier and Kirsten).

traders as well as nobility. Iron implements and ploughshares, the widespread use of oats and rye on marginal agricultural land widened the possible areas for settlement in much of Europe. Heavier soils and thicker woodland began to be tackled.

The expansion of the Celts in the west took them to south-eastern Britain from northern France, and from north-eastern France across the central massif to the Aquitaine basin. In Spain they partially displaced the non-Celtic Iberians and came into direct contact with the Phoenicians. They settled in the Po basin, raided Etruscan cities, and sacked Rome itself in 386 B.C. Other Celtic tribes pressed eastwards into the Pannonian basin in the fifth century B.C. and from there they spread into the Balkans by way of the Danube and the Morava–Vardar gap, sending settlers even further afield to the interior of Asia Minor. In southern Russia they came into contact with Greek colonies on the Black Sea coast and were sending a deputation to Alexander the Great in 335 B.C.

From the Black Sea to the Atlantic, Celtic peoples dominated the settlement of non-Mediterranean Europe until their eclipse by the advance of the Roman Empire. The early Germanic peoples of southern Scandinavia and the North German Plain, who had acquired the use of iron as late as 400 B.C. were beginning even by the second century B.C. to reach as far south as Aix-en-Provence on raiding expeditions. They were stimulated perhaps by that deterioration of climate during the sub-Atlantic period which brought about a contraction of farming settlement in Sweden. But the importance which attaches to the Germanic peoples belongs to a later age, on the other side of that watershed, less definitive, perhaps, than it was once thought to be, which is identified by the fall of the Roman Empire.

RACE, LANGUAGE AND PERSONALITY OF EUROPE

The contributions of prehistory to the modern geography of Europe are very difficult to assess. In some ways the land had already been greatly altered. Substantial inroads into the forest had been made in some parts of Europe on areas of light, easily worked loams and in the Mediterranean, but the damp, oakwood forests of the heavy clays in temperate Europe had hardly begun to yield. Moor and heath, grassland, maquis and garrigue may already have been the result of deforestation due to temporary shifting cultivation or the desire to extend pastures. In addition, fixed fields, farms and villages, occasionally on sites which have persisted in use to this day, were coming into being. Mining had made a few light scars here and there, and trade and movement were leaving their mark in trackways (such as the Pilgrims' Way and Icknield Way) all over Europe, though wherever possible rivers were used for transport. These can be but tentative suggestions; in two respects, however, the contribution of prehistory to the peopling of Europe must receive further attention. In terms of both race and language the basic lineaments had already been drawn, though the interpretation of both is a matter of great difficulty and controversy.

Race and the peopling of Europe

Most attempts to distinguish races in Europe have been based on the physical characteristics of modern populations, formerly on the basis of hair and eye colour, stature, pigmentation and measurements of head and face, and more recently on the basis of blood groups. There have been relatively few large-scale studies of skeletal materials from the distant past which might throw direct light on early migrations and the genesis of modern patterns, and by far the most systematic and complete of such attempts has been that of C. S. Coon, published in 1939.[31]

A number of difficulties arise, however, in the evaluation of racial differences, not least the cloud of chauvinistic and social prejudice which often surrounds the subject. Confusion of the physical differences which constitute race with language, nationality, culture, class, and with such indefinable qualities as intellectual and physical prowess, leadership and courage, have endowed the whole topic with emotional overtones very difficult to discount. For example, Ripley's division of European types into Nordic, Alpine and Mediterranean, insecurely based by modern standards, has achieved notoriety through the racialism which has been engendered round it, not least by Nazi encomiums of Nordic man.

Classifications of race have been most frequently based on measurable differences such as skin, hair and eye colour, hair form (whether curly, lank or woolly), the shape of the head, stature and body build. There have been tendencies to measure only those characteristics which differ in a way which is 'meaningful' in terms of ideas about the historical evolution and migration of races, that is, which fit preconceived notions about historical evolution. Or attention has been necessarily concentrated on, and importance unwarrantably attached to, the measurement of those features which have survived from the past, for example, skeletal remains and particularly crania, at the expense of soft and perishable parts of the body. Careful objective measurements have been made of essentially subjectively chosen criteria.

Perhaps the major aims of racial classification have been on the one hand to establish the existence and nature of anatomical differences between populations and on the other to throw light on the ways in which man has moved to and mingled in his present locations. It is in this latter sense, of course, that the historical geographer is interested. It is reasonable to assume, therefore, that those characteristics which are not adaptive to the environment will be those which are most important in throwing light on origins and movements of populations. Features such as skin, hair and eye colour appear to be adaptive to some extent and can therefore be discounted. Stature varies a great deal with nutrition. The shape of the head (e.g. length in relation to width; height of the vault) has been frequently used as a characteristic, perhaps because of the ease with which it can be measured, but it has been shown to alter in some cases over relatively short periods of time from one generation to another. It has, indeed, been said that the maintenance of constant characteristics in skeletal features over a long period of time is more a matter of pious hope than of established fact. Clearly, therefore, a non-adaptive character should be the major criterion in distinguishing human groups from the point of view of their evolution.

Since heredity functions by way of genes which control human make-up in a very complex way, it is desirable, too, that the genetic inheritance of those features which are chosen for racial criteria should be simple or well understood. Few criteria fulfil all the necessary requirements, but blood groups approach most closely to them; their genetic inheritance is fairly well understood; they are not appreciably adaptive to environment; and abundant and accurate modern data concerning blood groups are available because of the needs of transfusion services.[32] There is, however, the very serious disadvantage that no completely satisfactory means have been found of discovering blood groups from the dry bones which constitute the evidence from the past.

The best way of outlining views on the peopling of Europe by groups of differing physical stock must be, therefore, to compare the conclusions drawn from modern blood group data with those which have been drawn from the statistical analysis of skeletal material associated with archaeological horizons. The study of modern blood groups gives no indication of chronology or of the processes involved, but it is methodologically unimpeachable; the analysis of skeletal material is more doubtful, but its conclusions can be referred to a surer chronology. Skeletal material from much of prehistory is rare, however, especially in such periods as the Late Bronze Age when cremation was normal. Interpretation of skeletal material has thus been associated necessarily with accompanying cultural material, and conclusions about movements of population have been based on both types of evidence. Yet there is no fallacy which has been more strongly attacked in modern times than that which associated race and culture too closely. In modern societies race, language and culture frequently do not coincide; and the same may well be true of prehistory.

It may, nevertheless, be useful to present Coon's summary of the conclusions reached by such methods. In west central France and in central Wales small groups of bulky, large-headed people may represent survivals of an Upper Palaeolithic type,[33] but over much of northern and central Europe there are many more modern representatives fairly close to the Mesolithic population of the area, which tended to be characterised by a large broad-headed and broad-faced type. Early Neolithic farmers, however, introduced a new and contrasting element in the predominance of a short, slender, and small-headed type found among Danubian peasants, Mediterranean farmers and herders, and among the Neolithic pioneers of Western Europe. Late Neolithic colonisation by megalith builders in the west and by 'corded' and 'Battle-axe' people in central Europe was represented, on the other hand, by tall, long-headed and long-faced types. Coon sums up: 'The racial history of Europe in the Neolithic, therefore, is a problem in the balance between new racial streams of relatively uniform type which poured in from the south and east, and older residual elements which survived or suffered amalgamation in the west and north.'[34] Only one other major new element appeared in prehistory, according to this view, and this was the immigration of a tall, broad-headed minority very closely associated with the dissemination of the Beaker and of bronze working, and sufficiently important to be interred in collective tombs in Western Europe. Very late in prehistory and in historical times, of course, new elements appeared from the east in Russia and particularly in the south Russian steppes.

The divisions that can be made, then, stress the survival of very early types in central west France and in central Wales; the existence in Western Europe and particularly in highland Britain and western France of a population which has a great deal in common with that of the Mediterranean and North Africa. Another feature would be, also, the contrast between the western populations and those of central and northern Europe (with which, perhaps, eastern Britain may be included). These latter may owe more to a combination of types deriving from the east and the Mediterranean with the autochthonous population of Mesolithic times.

The differentiation of European populations according to the relative frequencies of A, B and O blood groups is shown in Fig. 1:7. In terms of world distributions as a whole, A frequencies are high and B frequencies are low, except in eastern Europe. Within Europe the clearest division is between east and west. To the east of a rough line from the Gulf of Bothnia to the Adriatic the frequency of A genes decreases slightly but it everywhere remains higher than that of gene B which increases steadily from west to east. Tongues of high B

frequency penetrating into central Europe suggest a history of
immigration from the very high B zone of central and western Asia.[35]

In the Mediterranean and to the west of this dividing line, blood
group frequencies are more complex, though more comprehensively
known. B is uniformly low through the whole area. Much of central

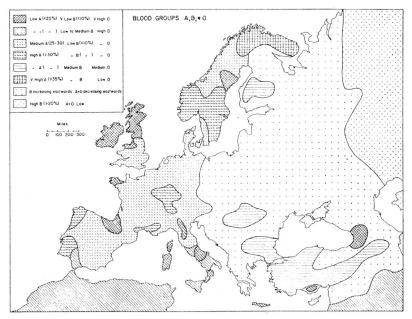

Fig. 1:7   Blood groups and the peopling of Europe (after Mourant).

and western Europe is characterised by high frequencies of A, a feature which has been seen as something essentially European, and
which is to be noted in the Alps, the Pyrenees, the Rhineland, central
Italy, the Balkans and parts of Scandinavia. A general association
between high A frequencies and broad-headedness has been noticed
in central Europe. It has indeed been suggested that this zone of
high A and low B may represent a distinctive element in the population of Europe. Within this larger zone, however, there are several
highly anomalous areas.

The Lapps of northern Scandinavia show very distinctive features.
A frequencies are very high indeed, and both B and O are unusually
low in one part or another of the area. Among other characteristics
there is a tendency to Asiatic values. It would seem that the Lapps

had reached their present genetic constitution through the long isolation of a relatively small population—a conclusion entirely consistent with what is known of their history. The populations of Ireland, Scotland, northern England and North Wales, together with Iceland, present unusual features of quite a different kind. O frequencies are very high indeed, and A correspondingly low. B is low too, but tends slightly to increase to the north and west in the British Isles. There are signs here of an early population pushed to the western and northern margins of Europe. There are, moreover, areas of locally high B frequencies in central Wales which coincide with the area in which Professor Fleure found traces of types which he considered to be 'survivors' of Upper Palaeolithic man. Iceland's population has much more in common with western Britain than with Scandinavia, a strange anomaly in view of the close ties of Iceland with Scandinavia. It may be that Irish settlement of Iceland was more important than that of Vikings of Scandinavian origin; or perhaps the Scandinavian population at the time of the great expansion in the ninth and tenth centuries A.D. was more closely allied to that of western Britain than it now is.

The Basques, culturally and to some extent physically distinctive, and speakers of a non-Indo-European language, share also a combination of low A, very low B and high O frequencies. Here, too, is a population which may, genetically as well as linguistically, be considered as a product of long standing and isolated settlement. But the rhesus factor is entirely different from the north-western European groups, as it is also among the Sardinians, where the characteristics of western British populations find another echo in a blood group composition of very low A, low B and extremely high O.

In general, Italy and Greece resemble western and west central Europe more than east-central Europe, but whereas central and northern Italy, like part of Iberia, seem to have much in common with the Alpine area in its high A frequencies, Greece and to some extent Sicily share once again the combination of high O, low A and low B that is to be met with in north-western Europe.

Analysis of blood group frequencies may, then, yield the following tentative conclusions: populations with similar characteristics of low A and B but high O frequencies exist in western Britain, Iceland, the Basque area, Sardinia, North Africa, Greece and Crete and the western Caucasus. Other blood characteristics, however, show differences between these different areas. It is possible that they may be linked together by a common origin at a remote date if the differences in the other blood characteristics are a result of long settlement in isolation; indeed the location of some of these groups is remote and isolated from the mainstreams of settlement. The second conclusion that seems possible is that the occasional evidence in, for example, central Wales, of an even earlier population with slightly higher B frequencies, is coincident with the area in which physical characteristics attributed to Upper Palaeolithic man also occur. Thirdly, much of western, central and northern Europe is characterised by high A frequencies in a combination which is to be found also in Iberia and northern and central Italy. A rather insecure identification has been suggested with broad-headed Alpine stock, once said to be characteristic of mountain areas of western Eurasia, and there are also similarities in blood group frequencies with Anatolia. Finally, in eastern Europe the groups with lower A and higher B frequencies appear to mark the course of relatively recent and continental migrations across the plains of Russia from western Asia. The picture that emerges is thus one of the peopling of Europe by successive waves emanating from the east and south-east, leaving vestiges of older populations in remote and isolated areas far away from the thresholds by which new populations have entered. It is therefore consistent with the conclusions from archaeology and to some extent with older studies of physical anthropology, though only in a very general sense, for it does not permit of a detailed association with the events of prehistory, nor is it reasonable to ask that it should, since culture and race are not necessarily linked.

European languages and prehistory

Although the distributions of languages in Europe have changed greatly and although languages themselves have altered since prehistoric times, almost all of the fundamental groupings of European languages were present by Iron Age times.[36] With the exception of Basque, and of the Finno-Ugrian languages represented by the Finnish and Magyar languages, the latter introduced into central Europe in the invasions of the ninth and tenth centuries, all modern European languages are grouped, together with some Asian languages, as belonging to, or deriving from, a common language or group of languages called Indo-European. A division among them is frequently made between the *centum* group, mainly western, and a *satem* group, mainly eastern, on the basis of the fact that one group has K where the other group has S. The classification of past and present Indo-European languages is as follows, the extinct or rarely spoken languages being in parentheses:

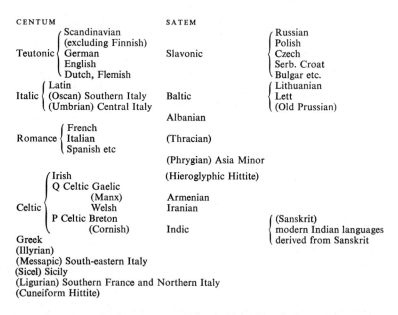

CENTUM

Teutonic { Scandinavian (excluding Finnish) / German / English / Dutch, Flemish

Italic { Latin / (Oscan) Southern Italy / (Umbrian) Central Italy

Romance { French / Italian / Spanish etc

Celtic { Irish / Q Celtic Gaelic / (Manx) / Welsh / P Celtic Breton / (Cornish)
Greek
(Illyrian)
(Messapic) South-eastern Italy
(Sicel) Sicily
(Ligurian) Southern France and Northern Italy
(Cuneiform Hittite)

SATEM

Slavonic

Baltic

Albanian

(Thracian)

(Phrygian) Asia Minor

(Hieroglyphic Hittite)

Armenian
Iranian

Indic

{ Russian / Polish / Czech / Serb. Croat / Bulgar etc.

{ Lithuanian / Lett / (Old Prussian)

{ (Sanskrit) / modern Indian languages derived from Sanskrit

It has been argued that the study of words common to various Indo-European languages may give a clue to the economy and society of the theoretically original language from which various forms have diverged. Words for cattle, sheep, breeding, dairy products, grains and ploughing are similar among early Indo-European languages. The same word for horse occurs in nearly all languages. There are only two sets of words for wheel, one of which may sometimes mean chariot. Axle is a common word, and there are similar words in some though not in all Indo-European languages for axe, bow, arrow, javelin, spear and sword; and also for gold, silver and copper. Such correspondences have been used to suggest that a hypothetically original Indo-European language developed in a society which knew of the plough, agriculture, the wheel, domesticated animals, and the horse, particularly, and for which the sea was of little significance. But the same name is used, of course, both for wild and domesticated animals, and the spread of a technique may be

1 *Carnac, southern Brittany*.
One of the most impressive
Megalithic and Bronze Age
sites in Western Europe. The
proximity of the site to the
coast is evident. Note also
the small hedged fields and
scattered settlement characteristic of the Breton *bocage*.

2 *Arles*. The major Roman port on the Rhône and linked to the sea by the Marius canal, Arles pre-empted the trade and importance of Marseilles after 49 B.C. It controlled the river navigation and possessed the most southerly bridge over the Rhône carrying the road between Italy and Spain. It was a centre of cloth manufacture, had an imperial mint and exported oil and wine. Its arena, built in the first century B.C. with a capacity for 21,000 spectators, and its amphitheatre, for 7,000 people, bear witness to the size and importance of the town. It was still important in the fifth century, and its street pattern still retains traces of its Roman origin. In the Dark Ages, the amphitheatre served as a quarry for the construction of churches and town walls, and the arena served as a fortification for the reduced population which lived in crowded houses within it.

accompanied, after all, by the spread of a common term to describe it. Deductions on this basis about the nature of an 'original' economy may not, perhaps, be so reliable as was once thought.

Written evidence of language is, of course, the only certain source of knowledge about early distributions, though this may take the form of place-names as well as inscriptions and the like. The earliest evidence of this kind is of Hieroglyphic Hittite in about 1500 B.C., probably introduced by invaders of central Asia Minor about 1900–1800 B.C. at about the same time that newcomers brought early Greek to Greece. Place-names and classical writings have yielded much evidence of later Indo-European languages and their distribution over Europe, particularly of Celtic. To trace the movements of language before these indications, however, is a much more hazardous business, depending partly on the identification of pre-Indo-European elements in place-names, and partly on assumptions about the imposition of new languages by immigrant populations whose characteristics and identity must necessarily be deduced (not always with certainty) from cultural equipment. Clearly, however, there is no obvious relationship between the successful imposition of new language and the numbers or even relative proportions of migrants or conquerors; nor can migrations be deduced with confidence from cultural affinities; conclusions based on cultural evidence may therefore be somewhat tentative. Identification of place-names is again tenuous in many cases, though -assos names (e.g. Parnassos) in Greece are thought to be of pre-Indo-European origin and therefore would date back over 4000 years.

The expansion of the Celts in the Iron Age can be traced to some extent in the place-names they have left. P-Celtic was probably taken to Britain in the fifth century B.C. where it was superimposed on, or displaced, existing Q-Celtic speakers. P-Celtic was taken to Italy about 400 B.C. An early expansion appears to be reflected in the survival of -briga (fortress) which occurs in Gaul and Iberia, with one example as far afield as Galatia, which is known to have had a Celtic colony.[37] The names in -dunum, meaning fortified place, occur in place-names such as Lyon, from Latin Lugdunum, or Autun, from Augustodunum, or in Roman names which have not survived to the present—Camulodunum (Colchester). With them may be associated rarer names in -magus (or open settlement). Both of these names are to be found in Britain, Gaul, Catalonia and northern Italy, together with some doubtful representatives in central Europe and the Danube valley which bear witness to the eastward expansion of the Celts from south-west Germany.

It seems possible that there is a fairly strong case for associating Indo-European languages with the expansion of the Urnfield peoples of the late Bronze Age. Thus in Iberia there is a fairly close relationship between the distribution of urnfields and that of early Celtic place-names, except in the north-east, where Ligurian settlement may account for the absence of -*briga* names. But urnfields are not found in those parts of eastern Spain where non-Indo-European speakers (Iberians) survived until classical times. In France and Germany Indo-European languages could have been spread by war-like and agricultural people coming from central Europe who are also identified with the spread of Urnfield culture. But there is little connection between the *satem* languages and the expansion of the Urnfield peoples in eastern Europe.

There are, however, grounds for supposing a much earlier introduction of Indo-European languages in late Neolithic times. It has been suggested that the area north of the Balkans in which permanent agriculture with fixed fields was practised may have been a zone from which Indo-European speakers spread out, for argument on philological grounds has suggested that the earliest Indo-European speakers were essentially settled farmers, organised in an hierarchical and almost feudal system and, possibly, practising a form of open-field farming. And it is from the area just to the north of the Balkans that permanent as opposed to shifting agriculture was passed on from Mediterranean society. Thus, Indo-European languages would have spread from south-eastern Europe and ultimately from the eastern Mediterranean area.

Another and rather more likely hypothesis, however, would link Indo-European languages with the late Neolithic 'corded' and 'Battle-axe' peoples of central Europe.[38] In north Germany, Teutonic languages might have been introduced with cremation in the late Bronze Age, though even here there is little evidence of a large-scale cultural migration. Otherwise, they may have been brought on one of two other major movements: either the Funnel-necked Beaker people responsible for the introduction of farming (see above p. 22); or the bringers of corded ware and battle-axes, who represent the only other major immigration. The latter are the more likely candidates, since the connections of the former are chiefly with the non-Indo-European Danubian peasants. It has been suggested, too, on linguistic grounds that the divergence of P-Celtic from Q-Celtic must have taken up to ten centuries. If so, the introduction of Q-Celtic to Britain may well have been about a thousand years before the introduction of P-Celtic, an order of magnitude which makes it entirely feasible for its introduction to be associated with that of the Food Vessel culture, which had strong links with the corded ware of the North German Plain and Saxo-Thuringia.[39] As has already been noted, corded ware and the battle-axe may be traced back to the steppes of southern Russia (see above p. 28) and thus to those links with the area north of the Caucasus from which Indo-European languages may also have spread eastwards into India. But in the absence of direct linguistic evidence the earliest origins must necessarily be hypothetical and even speculative.

Prehistory and the 'personality' of Europe

In 1932 Sir Cyril Fox recognised a basic division in the human geography of prehistoric Britain between Highland and Lowland provinces,[40] and it was a division which could be seen in the successive distribution patterns of prehistoric settlement, which tended to conform either to a western 'Highland' pattern or to an eastern and southern 'Lowland' pattern, though at certain periods the British Isles as a whole constituted a single unity. The division rested partly on the contrasting nature of the physical environments of the two provinces, and therefore of the possibilities they offered to settlement, but it was also a product of contrasting orientation towards the continental sources of new cultural contacts and trade. Fox noted that the cultures of the lowlands tended to greater wealth and density of settlement because of the greater fertility of soils and suitability of climate. Other contrasts could be found, however, for lowland Britain, most adjacent to and accessible from the continent was easily overrun by invaders, and new cultures tended to be imposed upon it. In the Highland Zone, a region of refuge from the plains of the southeast, new cultural elements tended to be absorbed. Continuity of cultures was thus more characteristic of the Highland Zone and the concept of the western and highland zone as a remote and inaccessible area in which archaic elements were long preserved is only partially modified on those occasions when trade, traffic and migrations along the western sea routes brought western Britain into the van of new cultural changes, for the very distances involved along the maritime routes and the transpeninsular crossings which were commonly used, also tended to mean that newcomers were small minorities among a larger indigenous population able to absorb new traits. Similar cultural provinces may be identified in Europe on the basis of similar and repeated geographical distributions of successive cultural elements. As in Britain, such regions tend to reflect the characteristics of relief, soil, climate and vegetation, but on the larger European canvas one should obviously distinguish not only the mountainous areas from the lowland plains, but also the very different possibilities for farming, herding and hunting which are suggested by the major vegetation belts of Europe: the coniferous forests, the deciduous woodlands, the evergreen forests and the grassy plains of the east and south-east. One must also distinguish within the deciduous forests particularly between those soils which give rise to relatively open and easily cleared woodland, notably on the löss, and the damp oakwoods of the heavy clays. The relationship of these major regions to settlement has already been outlined.

As in Britain so in Europe mountainous areas tended to be settled late, to preserve elements of older and more archaic cultures, and to show greater continuity in traditions and settlement precisely because they are remote, isolated, and less desirable habitats than the fertile acres of the plain. Thus it is in the Massif Central and in Brittany that Celtic place-names survive most frequently in France. It was also in the Massif Central that megalithic culture seems to have survived longest, for graves of a megalithic type continued in use until well into the first millenium B.C. Yet it must not be thought that such areas were necessarily cultural barriers, for it is one of the commonplaces of historical geography that the Alpine passes, for example, conveyed and channelled ideas and trade, as the Brenner did from Bronze Age times. Invaders from the east repeatedly preferred passes through the Carpathians to the circuitous but lowland route *via* the lower Danube.

The differences between Highland and Lowland Britain rest also on differences in orientation to the continent and therefore in the sources of their cultures. Thus the indented coastline of western Britain and the existence of relatively short transpeninsular routes across Brittany, Cornwall, South Wales etc. made possible the rapid spread of sea-borne cultures over the whole area. The close proximity and similar environmental conditions of Brittany are reflected in close cultural similarities with south-western Britain and Ireland in late Neolithic and Early Bronze Age times. Lowland Britain as a whole looks by way of the Channel or North Sea crossing to cultures in the Low Countries, Denmark and northern France. Elements from the North German Plain, the Rhineland and Switzerland are mingled in the early Neolithic cultures of south-eastern Britain. Similar cultural contacts are to be found in the coastal areas of the other marginal seas of Europe: the Black Sea, the Baltic and the Mediterranean.

Moreover, for much of prehistory such areas may be seen in the light of the general tendency for advanced cultures and new migrations to reach Europe by way of the Near East, the Aegean and the steppes of southern Russia. For this period at least, Europe must usually be regarded as a peninsula of Asia, and one composed of four great latitudinal zones differing primarily in respect of accessibility and utility to early man. The northern zone of conifers, mixed woodland and dense deciduous forest on heavy soils was not attractive, but further south the variety of relief, navigable rivers (particularly the Danube) and above all the frequency of either grassland or easily cleared open woodland on löss soils made much of central Europe and the Balkans a corridor for early movement. To the south of this zone, the Pyrenees, the Alps and the Dinaric Alps, with their associated high rainfall, thick forests and steep slopes tended to cut off a central European zone of early movement from the most important corridor of all, that which is represented by the Mediterranean.

A variety of factors combined to make the Mediterranean not only a corridor of early movement but also the largest and most striking of the cultural provinces of Europe. The ease of navigation in a relatively tideless sea blessed with high average visibility and fairly regular winds during the summer sailing season made movement from one part to another fairly easy, most of all in areas like the Aegean where a scatter of islands and a deeply indented coastline made point-to-point navigation possible over large areas, while ships could be beached in many a sheltered bay. Although the earliest Neolithic settlers hugged the coasts and perhaps reached the Tyrrhenian Sea by way of overland crossings rather than by way of the difficult and inhospitable coast of Calabria, the improvements in navigation and shipping, even by the late Neolithic, had made Sardinia accessible and longer coast to coast voyages possible. Similar conditions of climate and vegetation round the shores of the Mediterranean and similar possibilities of rearing stock and growing crops made the transmission of culture, people and ideas a rela-

tively rapid process. The wide dispersal over the shores of the
Mediterranean of the early Neolithic impressed ware and later of
collective forms of burial and the worship of a mother goddess which
characterise the megalithic settlement are examples of such uni-
formities.

But it is also frequently necessary to distinguish other and smaller
unities in the cultural patterns of the Mediterranean. The link between Palestine, Sicily, North Africa and southern Spain which is
evident in the Phoenician settlements of the tenth century B.C. is recalled by the much later, but to some extent similar, patterns of the
Arab Empire in the southern Mediterranean. Unity about the shores
of the western Mediterranean is suggested by the expansion of the
Bell Beaker peoples, to some extent by the distribution of megalithic
culture and much later still, by the sphere of interest of the Catalan
sea-state of the thirteenth century or the Aragonese Empire of the
fifteenth, which included southern Italy and Sicily as well as eastern
Spain, and which was also deeply involved in the trade with North
Africa. The axis of Greek colonisation in the central Mediterranean
from the Aegean to southern Italy and Sicily and beyond to the
Ligurian coast is one along which movement to similar environments
could take place by relatively short sea crossings. It is very similar
indeed to the distribution of early Neolithic settlement and is repeated later by the interest shown by the Byzantine Empire in the
maritime fringes of southern Italy and Sicily.

In the prehistory of Sicily, strategically located at the boundary
between the eastern and western basins of the Mediterranean, two
types of settlement distribution tend to recur.[41] Settlements of maritime origin distributed on the coast have often fallen into two groups:
a north-western one and a south-eastern one. Early Neolithic settlement was mainly concentrated in this latter area; so also are early
Copper Age settlements, evidence of trade with Mycenae and the
cities founded by Greek settlers. North-western Sicily, however,
possessed the distinctive Conca d'Oro culture closely related to western Mediterranean traditions, Bell beakers deriving from Iberia, and
strategically placed Phoenician settlement straddling the Sicilian
straits to the western sea routes and North Africa.

Central Europe constitutes a second unity in much of prehistory
but it is one which is much more varied and less definite. The essential
feature is, perhaps, the relative ease of cultural transmission on the
easily cleared and cultivated löss, together with the frequency of

navigable rivers with terraces of loam soils which attracted early settlement, and the variety of relief over small distances. Three different themes may, perhaps, be stressed. First, migrants and cultural influences from south-west Asia reached the area by several well-defined routes: by way of the Aegean and the Morava–Vardar gap to the Danubian plains; from the Black Sea and Anatolia by way of the Bosporus and the lower Danube; and by way of almost continuous grassland which led north of the Black Sea either to the Carpathian passes and so to the open, fertile plains of the middle Danube, or by way of the löss of southern Poland and Silesia to central Germany. Danubian peasants may have come by the first route; the others transmitted cultural elements like the battle-axe, or corded ware in the late Neolithic, or much later, the long sword and the artistic motifs which originated with the Scyths of the open plains.

The navigable rivers cutting across these east–west routes and flowing to the North Sea and the Baltic, however, carried central European traditions northwards towards Scandinavia and to the heath, marsh and moraine of the North German Plain. Farming and herding were introduced to Mesolithic peoples by these routes; and the brilliance of the Scandinavian early Bronze Age depended on the amber routes pioneered by way of the rivers. Yet if it was the function of central Europe to receive, assimilate and transmit new cultural elements from the east and south to the remoter lands of the west and north in several periods of prehistory, it had also an important rôle to serve on occasion as a cultural hearth from which expansion took place in all directions. All three Mediterranean peninsulas suffered invasions of continental origin in the expansion from central Europe of Urnfield peoples, and similar expansion recurred later in the Iron Age Celtic movements and the Teutonic expansions after the fall of the Roman Empire.

Western Europe is the third major unit discernible in the 'personality' of Europe, deriving much of its character, as does Highland Britain, from its maritime nature and its position at the end of the line for continental migration routes. In the Paleolithic it is, perhaps, the contrast between maritime and continental elements in climate and vegetation that are important in creating contrasts in hunting and food-gathering economies that are briefly discussed above; but from the Neolithic, Western Europe achieves individuality as the area in which elements derived from the Mediterranean met and fused with those from central Europe. West of the Rhine and in Switzerland there was a boundary between Danubian and 'western' cultures of the early Neolithic; the distribution of passage graves, gallery graves and bell beakers conforms to a western, maritime pattern in which there are common elements in western Britain, western France and Iberia.

From the Bronze Age, trade links continued to unify the western sea routes in the trade with Mycenae, the Phoenicians and then the Greeks. The isthmuses of the west by way of the Rhône–Saône or by way of the Garonne basin continued to be important as trade routes, but cultural expansion and settlement seemed increasingly to depend on central European inspiration from the Bronze Age. The expansion of middle and late Bronze Age cultures into France came mainly by way of the Saverne Gap and the Belfort Gap from south-west Germany.[42] Iberia and western France, which had been in the van of cultural advance in the great surge of maritime activity in the age of the megalith builders and the Bell Beaker migrants, became, like Highland Britain, simply the last refuge of peninsular Europe in which ancient cultures survived or which was never reached by new cultural advances in the remainder of the continent. The survival of non-Indo-European speakers in much of Iberia well into the Iron Age, and indeed, the Basques themselves; the racial distinctiveness of western Europe and its common features with Mediterranean areas; and the survival of Celtic languages in the west—all appear as expressions of these characteristics.

Two comments might be made in conclusion. The individuality of central and Mediterranean European provinces, from the point of view taken here, depends essentially on the canalisation of movement and cultural influences from the east into two almost parallel directions, one basically by sea and coast-to-coast settlement; the other by land and river. These two zones are separated to a great extent by the mountain barrier of the Alps, the Pyrenees and the Balkan ranges, broken in four zones by fairly easy passages: the Morava–Vardar gap, the low cols between the Adriatic and the Danube basin, the Rhône–Saône trough and the Carcassonne gap. Assuming still that new cultural advances came essentially from south-west Asia, it is clear that the provenance of cultures reaching Western Europe will depend upon the relative rates of cultural transmission by the sea-route and isthmus crossings in comparison with that of overland movement across the löss belt. With assumptions about such rates and also about the rates of movement in different types of natural environment it is possible to set up a very crude and approximate model of the settlement of Europe. Thus, if sea transport were twice as rapid as overland movement across easily cleared löss, limon and steppe, impulses of common and contemporaneous origin in the eastern Mediterranean would reach Cornwall and Kent or East Anglia at about the same time, but one would have travelled by way of the Garonne basin and Brittany, the other by way of central Germany and the Rhine. Such an advantage to maritime movement may have held good until after the decline of Mycenae, but at later dates continental expansions penetrating into the Mediterranean peninsulas themselves suggest a greater rapidity and effectiveness of overland movement, a change in circumstances which may have been assisted by the development and spread of the horse-drawn vehicle.

REFERENCES

1. SIR CYRIL FOX, *The Personality of Britain*, Cardiff, National Museum of Wales, 1943, pp. 10–14 and 90–4.
2. F. E. ZEUNER, *Dating the Past*, London, 1958.
3. J. G. D. CLARK, *Prehistoric Europe, The Economic Basis*, London, 1952, p. 12.
4. J. K. CHARLESWORTH, *The Quaternary Era*, London, 1957, vol. 2, pp. 837 ff.
5. M. BURKITT, *The Old Stone Age*, Cambridge, 1949.
6. C. B. M. MCBURNEY, 'A geographical study of the Older Palaeolithic stages in Europe', *Proc. Prehistoric Soc.*, N.S. vol. 16, 1950, pp. 163–83.
7. Ibid., p. 175.
8. Charlesworth, *Quaternary Era*, p. 1032.
9. Clark, *Prehistoric Europe*, pp. 62–90.
10. L. R. NOUGIER, *Géographie Humaine Préhistorique*, Paris, 1959, pp. 63 ff.
11. J. G. D. CLARK, *World Prehistory*, Cambridge, 1961, p. 63.
12. Nougier, *Géographie Humaine Préhist.*, p. 140.
13. J. G. D. CLARK, *Mesolithic Settlement of Northern Europe*, Cambridge, 1936.
14. SONIA COLE, *The Neolithic Revolution*, British Museum (Natural History), London, 1961.
15. S. MONTELIUS, 'The burning of forest land for the cultivation of crops', *Geogr. Annaler*, vol. 35, 1953, pp. 47–54.
16. Clark, *Prehistoric Europe*, p. 93; Cole, *Neolithic Revolution*, p. 34.
17. V. G. CHILDE, *The Prehistory of European Society*, London, 1962, pp. 46–7.

18. J. D. EVANS, 'Prehistoric settlement in the Western Mediterranean', *13th Annual Report and Bulletin* of the London Institute of Archaeology, London, 1958, pp. 49–70.
19. Childe, *Prehistory of European Society*, pp. 47–9.
20. L. BERNABÒ BREA, *Sicily before the Greeks*, London, 1957, pp. 38–60.
21. G. E. DANIEL, *The Megalith Builders of Western Europe*, London, 1958, p. 136.
22. Ibid., p. 126.
23. Childe, *Prehistory of European Society*, pp. 134–44; but for earlier views, see his *Dawn of European Civilisation*, London, 1948 (new edition 1950) and *Prehistoric Migrations in Europe*, Oslo, 1950.
24. C. S. COON, *The Races of Europe*, London, 1939, pp. 146 ff.
25. Childe, *Prehistory of European Society*, pp. 78–98.
26. Clark, *World Prehistory*, pp. 150–2.
27. Clark, *Prehistoric Europe*, pp. 97 ff.
28. T. T. RICE, *The Scythians*, London, 1957.
29. T. G. E. POWELL, *The Celts*, London, 1958, pp. 46–51.
30. H. BENGTSON, and V. MILOJČIČ, 'Vorgeschichte und Altertum', *Grosser Historischer Weltatlas, I, Erläuterungen*, Munich, 1954.
31. Coon, *Races of Europe*, pp. 174 ff.
32. W. C. BOYD, *Genetics and the Races of Man*, Oxford, 1950.
33. H. J. FLEURE, *The Races of England and Wales*, London, 1923.
34. Coon, *Races of Europe*, pp. 129–30.
35. A. E. MOURANT, *The Distribution of the Human Blood Groups*, Oxford, 1954; and *The ABO Blood Groups*, Royal Anthrop. Inst. Occas. Publ. no. 13, 1958.
36. H. HENCKEN, 'Indo-European langauges and archaeology', *Mem. Amer. Anthrop. Assoc.*, vol. 57, mem. 84, New York 1955, p. 68.
37. H. RIX, 'Zur Verbreitung und Chronologie einiger keltischer Ortsnamentypen', *Festschrift für P. Gössler*, ed. W. Kimmig, Stuttgart, 1954, pp. 99–107.
38. MARIJA GIMBUTAS, 'Culture change in Europe at the start of the second millenium. A contribution to the Indo-European problem', *Men and Cultures*, ed. A. F. C. Wallace, Chicago, 1960, p. 540.
39. Hencken, *Mem. Amer. Anthrop. Assoc.*, vol. 57, mem. 84, 1955, pp. 45–58.
40. Fox, *Personality of Britain*, pp. 84–90.
41. Brea, *Sicily before the Greeks*, pp. 38–60.
42. N. K. SANDARS, *The Bronze Age Cultures of France*, Cambridge, 1957.

CHAPTER 2

THE CLASSICAL WORLD

GREECE

In a great wave of colonisation between 750 and 550 B.C., in 'a vital step in the development of European civilisation',[1] the Greeks brought a new way of life, new crops, a new culture and new ideals to the western Mediterranean lands, and above all, from the point of view of the geographer, they brought the city to the west in the fluid, adaptable and individualistic form it had taken on European soil in Greece rather than in the more rigid mould into which it had been cast in Asia and Africa.

Roman expansion, nurtured by Greek and Etruscan neighbours, is in itself an excellent illustration of some of the principles of political geography, but in terms of the peopling of Europe it involved a *mission civilisatrice* which recalls in some ways the rôle of the European in tropical Africa almost two thousand years later. Emigration from Rome or Italy was frequently small in relation to the numbers of indigenous peoples but Roman law, language, customs and traditions were to a varying extent assimilated or imposed. Features of Roman age may be relatively infrequent in modern landscapes outside Italy and certain other parts of the Mediterranean but it is to the Roman Empire that one must often look for origins and starting points. Towns, roads and frontier defences were among the chief instruments of imperial control in the barbarian west and they have left their mark on the modern map in many areas. In farming the Romans built on older foundations and their contributions are harder to find, but there was a great expansion of clearing and rural settlement which had permanent effects.

The Greek city-state

When the Hellenic world of the Aegean began to emerge in the eighth century B.C. from the long dark age which followed the Dorian invasions of the twelfth and eleventh centuries and the resultant migrations and disturbances, the Greek city-state had already begun to take shape as a politically independent and self-governing unit, territorially defined, and with its nucleus of settlement grouped below the fortified citadel or *polis* which gave its name later to the city and then the city-state as a whole. The city-states, of which there were about two hundred by 600 B.C., were frequently tiny in size and population. Even Athens had no more than 300,000 people, and Corinth about 90,000. Few others had more than 20,000. Crete, small as it is, had forty-three cities; the state of Corinth was rather smaller than Bedfordshire. It is true that the islands of the Aegean make small natural units and that complex folding, faulting, erosion and subsidence have produced an environment that is greatly varied in relief, with many small valleys isolated from their neighbours and with complementary resources close at hand—the mountain forests for shipbuilding, fuel and charcoal; hill pastures for sheep, cattle and goats; and lowland arable. Yet it would be wrong to attribute the existence of small independent city-states to the fragmented environment of the Greek lands, as some writers have been prone to do.[2] Indeed, the city-states did not even very frequently coincide with natural units of this kind. Federations like that of Arcadia, large territorial states like Sparta and the partition of small islands into several city-states (e.g. Lesbos into six), are examples of this divergence from the 'natural' unit of the valley or the island.

The small independent Greek city-state thrived in a peculiarly favourable political, technological and social context. External threats between the eighth century B.C. and the rise of the Persian power in the sixth were few; self-sufficiency and the predominance of agriculture had not yet been threatened by the specialist interests and pressures which were later fostered by greater emphasis on trade; the specialisation and professionalism of military and naval techniques were not yet far developed. Above all, there had emerged a feeling of community, an insistence that the *polis* was the proper and optimum unit for the conduct of affairs, the administration of justice and the determination of policy. The *polis* was therefore not merely a place and a community, but also the 'state-idea'[3] of the Greeks and the creative force of their political geography. Plato's ideal was a community of 5,000 citizens; Aristotle thought each citizen should be able to recognise all others, so that a city of 100,000 citizens would be absurdly large; Piraeus was planned for a population of 10,000 citizens. Even allowing for the fact that total population may have been five or more times greater than the number of citizens, the ideal is still clearly very small by modern standards. Shortage of arable land and isolation may have restricted the growth of individual settlements, but it has been suggested that a climate which permitted open-air gatherings throughout the whole year may have been a more significant geographical element in the development of the city-state than a physically fragmented environment.

In its early stages at least, the *polis* reflected its primarily agricultural environment and the dwellings grouped around the citadel were more frequently the houses of farmers and artisans than of traders, merchants and shippers. Some of the early cities chose defensible sites close to good agricultural land rather than to the sea. The centre of Corinth was several miles from its harbour; Athens had to build a port at Piraeus. The trading and merchant interests grew up later, and it was thus only at a later stage that Greek cities acquired the emphasis on trade and commerce which qualify them as towns or cities in a modern sense.

The Greek colonial movement

Between 750 B.C. and 550 B.C., as a result of one of the most remarkable colonial ventures the world has seen, the Hellenic world was extended from the Aegean to the furthest shores of the Black Sea, to North Africa and Egypt, and westwards to the coast of Spain and southern France. Such an expansion had been dimly and partially foreshadowed by Mycenaean activity before 1400 B.C, but this new venture from the Aegean has left more abundant and permanent traces, for it meant that the 'urban revolution' was brought to the western Mediterranean. It has frequently been stressed that the Mediterranean, and especially the Aegean, has many qualities which made for a precocious development of seafaring abilities, of which there is abundant evidence in the Odyssey. Population was concentrated near the sea on what level land there was, yet mountain forests for shipbuilding timber were usually not far away; indented coasts provided many sheltered beaches as suitable harbours; good average visibility and high relief together with the wide scatter of islands in the Aegean made point-to-point navigation easy during the summer sailing season between March and November. Moderately regular land and sea breezes and the northern Etesian winds helped, and so too did the relative tidelessness of the Mediterranean and the absence of difficult currents—except, notably, in the Hellespont, the Bosporus and the Straits of Messina.[4] But the Greeks had not been the first to take advantage of these features. The early Greeks had been essentially cultivators and, long before their maritime prowess began, Phoenicians, Mycenaeans, Minoans and even Neolithic societies had used the seaways of the Mediterranean to good effect. The Greek colonial movement occurred at a time when the trade of the Aegean settlements with Syria and Egypt was expanding, when new 'oriental' influences were being felt and new forms in pottery, architecture and literature were being developed. Greek skills in navigation and shipbuilding were developing too. It was also a time of social and economic change when new pressures were bringing about an increase in population, inequalities in landholding, the subdivision of farms, poverty and political discontent. The function of the Greek mercenary in the eastern Mediterranean at this time may be an expression of this surplus population, and so too may the colonial movement itself. Commercial or strategic motives operated in individual cases (in the early settlement of Cumae near Naples, or Almina at the mouth of the Orontes, for example), but for the most part viable and balanced communities were sent out, sponsored by a mother city, to found a new city-state which would be self-sufficient in essentials, autonomous and completely independent from the beginning. A coloniser, or *oikistes*, explored the best location and chose the site, allocating lands and leading the new community to its future home.[5] Certain types of site recurred: islands, high ground near the delta of an important river (Olbia), or the neck of a peninsula easily defended from sea or land and near good arable land (Cumae). Almost everywhere the relative uniformity of climate made it possible to reproduce the crops and farming methods of the home environment, though the deficiency of good wine in some places and of olives in the Black Sea settlements provided reasons for trade with the homeland.

At a later stage when trade had begun to alter the character of the colonial expansion, trading and strategy mattered more in the selection of sites, particularly in the Marmora region and the Black Sea. In some of these cases, too, and among Corinthian colonies, the political independence of new colonial settlements was much less complete than in earlier days. Once colonies were established, however, trade and specialisation followed. Wine, oil, pottery and other manufactured goods went from Athens and Corinth, for example, to the rest of the Hellenic world. Black Sea colonies sent fish, grain, hides, furs, wax and honey drawn from the Scyths of southern

Russia; Phocaean colonies in the West could begin to rival the Phoenicians for the trade in bronze, copper, silver, tin or amber that flowed from the north or from Spain. The distribution of Greek colonies is shown in Fig. 1:5. Three features stand out: the avoidance of Phoenician strongholds in North Africa, Spain and western Sicily; the large part played by a fairly small number of cities in the movement as a whole; and the concentration by some of the colonising cities on certain areas of settlement. Megara and Miletus were active to the east and north-east, Corinth in Sicily and the Adriatic, and Phocaea in the western Mediterranean.

In many respects the Greek colonial enterprise anticipated the problems of overseas settlement that were posed in later days to greater populations and over greater distances. In the selection of a wide range of skills among settlers, in the organisation of settlement and choice of site, and in the effort to attain self-sufficiency and autonomy from the start, Greek aims were admirable, and their success is attested both by the reputation and prowess of *Magna Graecia*, their chief colonial area in southern Italy, and by the enduring quality of some of the sites they chose, such as that of Marseilles. The early maritime colonial movement of the Greeks was not so well recorded or so dramatic as the far-reaching conquests of Alexander the Great in the fourth century B.C., but they left a profound and enduring impression. The barbarian cultures of the Celts and the Scyths had been deeply influenced and so had the advanced Etruscan culture of central Italy. Much of Sicily had been strongly Hellenised, and southern Italy had acquired a coastal scatter of Greek cities.

ROME AND ITS EXPANSION IN THE WEST

Of all the periods into which history can be divided it is the Roman which lends itself most clearly and most temptingly to that task of historical geography which can be labelled briefly as the reconstruction of the geography of past periods. In its political, legal, social and economic organisation, the Roman world of Western Europe was clearly distinct from the Iron Age out of which it emerged and the barbarian world which followed. But it was also a much more articulate and economically productive world, so that its literary output and its material remains provide peculiarly abundant sources for geographical reconstruction. It is indeed a tribute to the modern research of historians and archaeologists that the clarity of these boundaries of the classical period have become increasingly blurred as more comes to be known of Iron Age foundations, internal changes in Roman society and the Dark Age transformations of a fragmented Roman legacy.

It seems necessary to review briefly the historical geography of early Rome and its expansion before proceeding to an outline of the economic and political geography of Rome in its heyday, because it is against this background that one must place the major items in the legacy which Rome has left for posterity in the landscapes of Western Europe: its towns, its roads, its villages and even its field patterns and farming traditions, as well as the peopling and the languages of Western Europe.

The origins of Rome

No variety of determinism is adequate to explain the rise of Rome from its humble beginnings as a collection of Iron Age settlements. Neither can it be interpreted as an isolated and miraculous flowering of civilisation in Italy. It is, however, certain that Rome was sited at a location where the three very different cultural traditions of the Greeks, the Etruscans and the pastoral Iron Age peoples of the hills met and were most profitably mingled. To the south of Rome lay Cumae and Neapolis, northernmost outposts of the Greek colonial world in southern Italy, a world made up of maritime city-states jealous of their independence and thus subsequently vulnerable to piecemeal absorption by Rome itself. They were, above all, the agents by which Greek culture was developed and transmitted to Phoenicians, Etruscans, and, of course, to the Romans. For it has been said that 'the cultural contributions of the western Greeks settled on Italian soil cannot be overemphasised. . . . Techniques, religion and art of the Italian peoples were decidedly and permanently influenced'.[6]

To the north in Tuscany lay the loose urban federation of the Etruscans, responsible for much clearing of the forest and for a great expansion of agriculture in central Italy (Fig. 2:1). They spoke a non-Indo-European language and wrote a script not yet fully deciphered. To the Romans, whose territory they occupied from 616 to 510 B.C. they handed on much of their impressive material culture, including their own variety of urban life and also a 'preoccupation with drains' which extended not only to urban drainage and the building of aqueducts but also to the remarkable *cuniculi*, drainage or water-supply tunnels cut into solid rock and found widespread over central Italy. In southern Etruria, near *Veii* in the Tiber basin *cuniculi* are

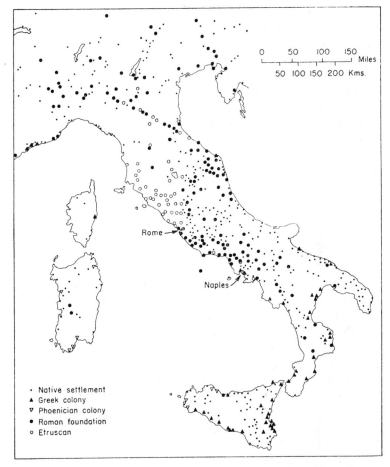

Fig. 2:1 Early settlement in peninsular Italy (after Houston).

found both in upper valleys (for water supply) and in the flood plains of the lower valleys (for drainage), but some also appear to have been designed to reduce soil erosion. Recent volcanic rocks overlying sands, clays and gravels to the east of the Tiber are highly erodible. Flood plains in the area can be shown to have built up by as much as 12 to 15 feet during the period of clearing between the early Iron Age and the end of Etruscan times. By controlling surface run-off, therefore, the *cuniculi* have reduced the rapidity of soil erosion so that the rolling hills and relatively subdued slopes of country drained by these underground tunnels contrasts very markedly with the gullying of land and the sharp breaks of slope where artificial drainage of this type is absent.[7]

Etruscan origins have been sought both in migration from Asia Minor and in development from indigenous Bronze and Iron Age cultures of central Italy. Place-names, blood groups and archaeological evidence show some affinities which argue in favour of such a migration, though not necessarily on the grand scale or at the early date of 1100 B.C. that was formerly suggested.[8] Indeed, migration may have been roughly contemporary with the beginnings of Greek colonisation in the eighth century B.C. and not long before the first flowering of Etruscan culture about 700 B.C. But unlike the maritime Greeks to the south, the Etruscans penetrated deeply inland, founding new towns in the heart of Tuscany and conquering and colonising the Po valley itself in the sixth century B.C., when they also spread southwards across the Tiber to the neighbourhood of the Greek settlements in Campania. Unlike their Greek and Carthaginian contemporaries in the western Mediterranean, with whom they competed for trade and seapower in Sardinia, Corsica and the Tyrrhenian coastlands, the Etruscans qualified their predominantly maritime interests with a concern for overland expansion and conquest which in some ways anticipated the Roman pattern.

Advanced urban cultures occupied only a relatively small part of the peninsula, and much of it was occupied by predominantly agricultural and pastoral Iron Age peoples. South and east of the Etruscans, there were several groups speaking Indo-European languages. They included the Itali and immigrants from the Balkans in south Italy; and in central Italy the Samnites, Sabines, Umbrians, and Latins. In the north, however, non-Indo-European Iron Age peoples such as the Veneti and the Ligures remained undisturbed until the Celtic invasions of 450 and 350 B.C.

Rome was located, therefore, where the civilised cultures of the Greeks and the Etruscans converged on an Iron Age world of the Latins and their neighbours. But the site and situation of Rome also combined a number of qualities which were advantageous at successive stages of her early history and in relation to various functions. In peninsular Italy as a whole the Tiber valley and the plain of Latium has a nodal position near productive agricultural land with which only the middle Arno and the plain of Campania can compete. As Rome expanded, road-building could take advantage of natural routes along the coast and through the gaps in the Apennines; and the navigable Tiber and proximity to the sea facilitated the cheap assembly of foodstuffs and raw materials, particularly building materials, in Rome itself. But it was only as Rome expanded that these regional advantages became apparent, and indeed they were noted by Cicero, Livy and Strabo.

In the early development of settlement, local site factors were more important. Steep-sided hills, capped with volcanic rock, offered easily defensible and habitable sites above the marshy plain. Early Iron Age settlement, traced by post-holes which indicate structures similar to the huts depicted in contemporary pottery of the region, has been located on the Palatine Hill, and there are more or less contemporary cemeteries on the Forum, the Esquiline and Quirinal Hills. Rome began, therefore, as a collection of hilltop villages inhabited by peoples of differing cultural traditions and concerned mainly with pastoral farming. But by the early seventh century B.C. land was being drained in the valley of the Forum; by 650 B.C. it was a small town, still modest by the standards of Etruria but with merchants and artisans as well as farmers. The close approach of firm land to the river, at a point where a midstream island made an early bridging possible, also contributed to Rome's early nodality. Indeed, no other bridge was built across the Tiber below Rome until the nineteenth century. At a very early date then, Rome gained local wealth and importance from its place on both the salt road and the transhumance route from coastal marshes to the summer pastures of the interior hills. Between 550 and 475 B.C. it achieved a truly urban status under the aegis of the Etruscans.[9] Greek pottery reached it in quantity, temples were being erected, a protective wall some six miles long had been built around it, and a major attempt was made to drain the land of the Forum by building the *Cloaca Maxima*—the Great Drain. As a trading centre, a focus of religious observance and as a strategic frontier town *en route* to the Greek cities in the south, Rome already warranted the substantial public investment involved both in its wall and its drains.

The political geography of Roman expansion

The geography of Rome's expansion from its modest beginnings to the Empire of Augustus has long provided a standard topic of historical and political geography. The approach of many geographers has been too much concerned, however, with understanding the directions taken by Roman expansion in the light only of the physical geography of Europe. The motives which led Rome to its policy of expansion for so many years and the basis of Roman military and naval supremacy have either been taken for granted or rightly left for the historian to elucidate. But preoccupation with the strategic geography of 'natural' routes and 'natural' frontiers has led to the neglect by geographers both of the character of the barbarian society which confronted Rome in the west and of the geographical implications of Roman techniques of territorial control.

It is not the aim of this brief survey to analyse in detail the strategy and history of Rome's geographical expansion but the major features must be outlined. Opportunities for early expansion in the peninsula developed in the fifth and fourth centuries B.C. with the decline of Etruria and the Hellenic city-states, and with the new challenge of Celtic invasions. The Etruscan empire had begun a long decline after its loss of mastery at sea at the Battle of Cumae in 474 B.C. and from the time of its defeat in Campania and its ejection from Rome. The city-states of Magna Graecia, like those of the mother country, found it impossible to combine in a strong federation or to defend their land frontiers against the attacks of interior peoples, and ultimately fell piecemeal to Rome. Celtic invasions of northern Italy had culminated in the further reduction of what remained of Etruscan power and then in the sack of Rome about 390 B.C., presenting a new challenge which Rome met by the rebuilding of its walls and by the reorganisation of its army. The cavalry, upon which most reliance had hitherto been placed and which was drawn mainly from the patrician ranks, was now supplemented by heavily armed and armoured infantry drawn from among the *plebs*. Roman concentration of effort on military supremacy and techniques of territorial control extended also to the establishment of roads, fortified military colonies and even purely agricultural colonies of Roman citizens in newly conquered lands. After Latium had been subdued, the interior peoples of central and southern Italy were conquered, and then the Greek cities of the south by 275 B.C. The Romans had thus succeeded in unifying the peninsula south of the Rubicon.

The acquisition of the Greek cities of the mainland inevitably brought Rome into contact with their neighbours in Sicily, still essentially divided between the two dominant seapowers of the Mediterranean, the Greeks in the east and south and the Carthaginians in the west guarding the trade routes between North Africa and the eastern Mediterranean. With the Sicilian Greeks in their pocket, Roman effort was concentrated against the Carthaginian hold in the western Mediterranean, which included colonies in south-eastern Spain, Sardinia and Corsica as well as North Africa and western Sicily. There began the long series of Punic wars by the end of which Carthage was destroyed in 146 B.C. and the coastal fringes of the western Mediterranean had been acquired by Rome. In the process, Rome had become a seapower as well as a landpower and Roman navies were supreme in the Mediterranean (Fig. 2:2). Indeed, by the exercise of its newly won seapower, Rome had everywhere established maritime bridgeheads from which its armies could be deployed in the hinterlands of Africa, Asia and Europe. In western Europe the stage was set for the ultimate extension of Roman power to the Rhine and Danube and beyond, and for the development of that pattern of expansion which has been categorised as a vain search for the illusory *boojum*, the 'natural' frontier.

Even in the third and second centuries B.C. the inadequacy of the Apennine frontier in Italy had been demonstrated by Gallic invasions and the armies of Hannibal. The Bologna gap had proved a particularly vulnerable point. But Gallic settlement superimposed on an Etruscan heritage had made much of the north Italian plain a unity which, as Cisalpine Gaul, was understandably incorporated whole into the Roman territories by 200 B.C., driving the frontier to the crest-line of the Alps. Conquest was followed by the building of roads, the settlement of military colonies, the reorganisation of Etruscan towns and the foundation of many new towns in the north Italian plain including Aquileia (181 B.C.), the Roman port on the Adriatic and the predecessor of Venice.

Southern and eastern Spain had been occupied between 206 and 197 B.C. after the second Punic War in order to preclude the recurrence of tactics such as those of Hannibal in his famous march with elephants across the Alps, and to exploit the mineral resources long known to antiquity in the Sierra Morena. Coastal settlements were linked by military roads from north-east Spain through Cartagena to Malaga and *via* the Guadalquivir basin to Seville and Cadiz. Cartagena and Cordoba, the latter significantly well inland, were made centres of the army and of administration. Nevertheless, the pacification of the interior pastoral peoples, the Celt-Iberians, proved a long and difficult process not complete for the whole peninsula until A.D. 19.

Fig. 2:2   The expansion of the Roman Empire in the West.

The annexation of Gallia Narbonensis in 121 B.C. followed the appeal of Marseilles to Rome for protection against piracy along the Ligurian coast. This action also guarded the all-important trade of the Rhône valley from the attacks and depredations not only of organised Celtic peoples of the Massif Central but also of Germanic newcomers, diverted from the eastern Alps to southern France by Roman arms. What is also evident, however, is the fact that the annexation of southern France also assured overland communications from Italy to Spain by way of the *Via Domitia*. The Romans' pre-occupation with overland movement is perhaps nowhere better expressed than in the subsequent replacement of Marseilles, an excellent natural port, well-sheltered but difficult of access by land, by Narbonne and Arles which had the virtue of being on the system of military roads.

The gaps which pierce the mountain barrier separating Mediterranean Europe from the north—the Gate of Carcassonne, the Rhône–Saône trough, the weakening of the Alpine chain in the east between the Brenner Pass and the passes through the Julian Alps, and finally the Morava–Vardar gap in the Balkans—have already been stressed as important features in the movement of cultures and of trade goods in prehistoric Europe, but their very existence made all of these zones unsatisfactory as frontiers for an empire spreading northward from the Mediterranean, particularly at a time when Celtic tribes beyond the frontiers were gaining in material culture, military prowess and social and political organisation. Fortified hilltop settlements were ceasing to be temporarily occupied refuges and were becoming real urban centres of trades and crafts as well as centres of government and defence. Gergovia, located high above the later Roman foundation of Clermont Ferrand which replaced it, is an excellent example of this type of settlement. New movements of Germanic peoples had also set in train further disturbances at the fringe of Roman control on the flanks of the Rhône trough.

It cannot be suggested that Caesar's campaigns in Gaul were primarily motivated by considerations of political geography and 'natural frontiers'. Internal conditions in Rome and personal aims and ambitions matter most in this connection. But it may perhaps be claimed that the extension of the Roman frontier to the Rhine, covering the Massif Central, the Belfort Gap, the Saverne Gap and the lowland routes north of the Ardennes which were in the hands of the Belgae, represented a remarkable recognition of geographical realities in Western Europe in an age of very ill-developed cartography. In terms of Roman technology the Rhine was an excellent frontier with its wide, marshy tract and confusing distributaries in the lower valley; deeply incised in its gorge section and thus easily defended from either bank; and bordered by a marshy zone even in the densely settled fertile rift valley section.

But the acquisition of the Rhine as a frontier now raised in a more acute form the problems of security and communication resulting from the Roman failure to hold the Alps beyond the crest-line on the Italian side. The existence of a deep re-entrant of independent territory in the western Alps was anomalous. And the Alps as a whole were the source of recurrent threats from mobile pastoral mountain peoples. It was the policy of Augustus to reduce such centres of disaffection not only here but also in the north and west of Iberia from 27 B.C. to A.D. 19. But the incorporation of the whole Alpine massif did not lead to so well-defined and final a boundary as the Atlantic in the west. Conquest of the western Alps gave control over the routes to Gaul; of the eastern Alps, control over the amber and the bronze trade of the Brenner as well as the known and highly valued iron ores and gold of Styria.[10] But no possible frontier could be found among the moraines and the dissected outwash plains north of the Alps until the Danube itself was attained.

The Rhine–Danube frontier was reached and, although it proved in general a satisfactory frontier along which natural features could reinforce normal defences, it was never sacrosanct even after the death of the 'Divine Augustus'. Trajan's expansion into the area known as the *Agri Decumates* in south-west Germany in A.D. 83 (see Fig. 2:3) abandoned the virtues of a river frontier for the advantage of a shorter boundary, using relatively local features such as the crest of the Black Forest and also bringing into the Empire the whole instead of merely a part of the densely populated and fertile land of the Rhine rift valley. The conquest of Britain from A.D. 43 may also be taken to represent a departure from the Augustan policy of maintaining the status quo, but it also emphasises the shortcomings of a frontier along the Channel coast which was even more 'natural' than the Rhine. South-western Britain probably had a closer cultural affinity across the Channel with Brittany than with other parts of England, and the Belgae of south-eastern England had very recently migrated from adjacent parts of the continent. Piracy and raiding from Britain, partly aimed at assisting closely related cultural groups on the other side of the Channel, provided other reasons for the conquest of Britain besides rumours of great mineral wealth.

The Rhine and the Danube seem to have remained the basis of the Roman frontier system, however, not because they were ever regarded as perfect, but perhaps because a zone of equilibrium had been reached against the pressure of Germanic barbarians, who remained very largely outside the Empire except in the neighbourhood

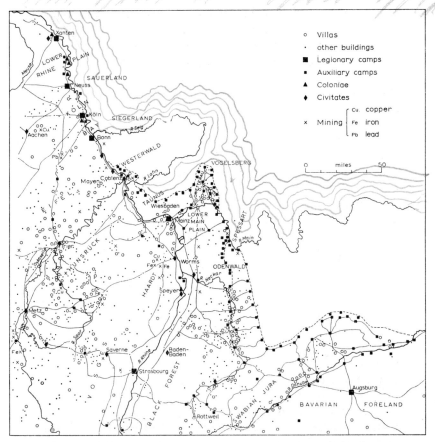

Fig. 2:3 Roman settlement, communications and defence on the Rhine frontier and in the *agri decumates* (after the 1:1,000,000 map of the Roman Empire, *Tabuli imperii Romani Mogontiacum* (Mainz). Note the intensity of settlement in areas of good agricultural land near the frontier, e.g. the Wetterau, the Neckar valley, the Danube valley, the Lower Main and Rhenish Hesse. Note also the concentration of villas and other settlements near important towns, particularly Trier, for a time capital of the Empire, and also near Coblenz, Mainz and Aachen.

of the *Agri Decumates*. Indeed, the attempt by Augustus to reach the shorter land frontier of the Elbe–Bohemia–Danube line suggests that the Rhine frontier was by no means regarded as final. German tribes were to be overwhelmed by penetration from the river Main to the Saale and along the Lippe to the north; and by the conquest of the

Elbe by a fleet from the Rhine.[11] Some of the important towns of the Rhine valley such as Nijmegen, Bonn, Coblenz, Worms, Strasbourg, and Basle owe their initial foundations and choice of site to the establishment of strongpoints from which this conquest of western Germany was to take place. It was, however, the loss of three legions in the abortive campaign of A.D. 9 which brought an end to this further aim, and the attempt was never repeated. The frontier in the west remained stable from A.D. 83 to the loss of the *Agri Decumates* in A.D. 273 and the Rhine frontier stood till its crossing by the Suevi in the winter of A.D. 406.

Several features of the history of expansion outlined above require further comment. Firstly, the main emphasis is put here on expansion in the west, but it must be stressed that the wealth, wisdom and culture of the eastern Mediterranean represented a much more glittering attraction to Rome than the barbarian west. Greek influence remained strong long after the break-up of the Empire of Alexander, and Greek trading cities still handled the richest trade of the Mediterranean, that which came across the Fertile Crescent from Persia, India and the Far East. It was to the eastern Mediterranean that much of Roman effort and interest were directed in the second century B.C., although power was first extended by means of protected states and spheres of influence rather than by direct political control.

Secondly Roman conquests in Europe were, until a relatively late period, almost entirely confined to lands of Mediterranean climate and vegetation. It has been noted that the conquests in southern France were limited at first to what may be very broadly termed Mediterranean France. The boundary of Roman rule in the region of the Pyrenees followed for a very long period a line parallel to the limits of Mediterranean climate and vegetation rather than the more obvious boundary of the watershed or crest-line of the Pyrenees. The uniformity of farming systems established in the Mediterranean long before Roman rule, involving the prevalence of the light, ox-drawn plough and concentration on wheat, the vine and the olive, may have contributed to the ease with which the Romans adjusted themselves to the conditions of the conquered lands and to the possibility of settling them with soldier-farmers. And Romans may have been reluctant to involve themselves too deeply in the alien ways of the mobile semi-pastoral societies of the highlands which flank the Mediterranean. But it seems equally possible, to say the least, that the rough coincidence of the Roman boundaries with Mediterranean climate and vegetation may reflect very little more than a common degree of proximity to the margins of the Mediterranean Sea rather than an effect of climate expressed through the economy and society of the areas concerned.

Thirdly, once predominance at sea had been acquired, Roman expansion followed a familiar pattern for the Mediterranean, consisting of the acquisition of a wide scatter of maritime cities and strongpoints oriented more to the sea than to the development and control of the hinterlands. This maritime orientation had been characteristic of Greek and Carthaginian and probably of Mycenaean colonists, megalith-builders and even the bearers of the Neolithic 'cardial' culture before them. But Roman emphasis on military prowess and techniques of territorial control in addition to naval supremacy brought into being a politico-geographical situation that was entirely new in the Mediterranean, and indeed in north-western Europe. It was, clearly, the Roman need to establish quick and reliable means of communication by road which made it necessary to control the hinterlands of the maritime cities, and it was this need for control which endowed the landward frontiers and their natural qualities for defence with a new and considerable importance.

Finally, a more general and fundamental theme in both the political and economic geography of the Roman Empire arises out of the situation discussed above. The concept of the Roman *limes*, a term as evocative, perhaps, as the term 'frontier' to an historian of the United States, stems from the nature of military strategy and military technology of the period. The Romans realised that the effective strength of their disciplined and highly organised legions was increased enormously if rapid mobility were assured. The need for mobility was satisfied by the excellent road systems in which the Roman genius for engineering was fully employed. Roads parallel to and behind the frontier were, in many places, quite as important as the ramparts and ditches which strengthened or replaced natural defences. Indeed in some cases the *limes* itself had no linear defence works at all and consisted of the open ground of a no-man's-land or a chain of fortresses between garrison towns. Other roads focused on military settlements well in the rear of the frontier, so that reserves could easily be called up to any part of the frontier zone. It was precisely because of the location of much of the military power at the periphery of control in the frontier zones that the natural quality of frontier defences mattered so considerably. In medieval times, when armies were often raised for *ad hoc* purposes, and boundaries simply marked off societies of differing allegiance, the location of frontiers mattered little. Only from the nineteenth century, perhaps, were frontiers again to be so zealously guarded and natural advantages sought. It is against this background, however, that the expansion of Rome can be viewed to some extent as a search for a natural frontier, and although an ideal solution could never be found, it is in some ways surprising how successful the Romans were in their choice of a modified Rhine–Danube line. The frontier was more than a military institution, however. It also constituted a major stimulus to economic development and to the romanisation of barbarian peoples.

THE GEOGRAPHY OF ECONOMIC DEVELOPMENT IN THE ROMAN WEST

General considerations

Annexation of the western provinces meant much more dramatic change than did the acquisition of an empire in the eastern Mediterranean. Imports to Rome from the Middle East and even further afield introduced Roman taste to the more sophisticated products of eastern Mediterranean craftsmanship, and there developed a demand for such products, frequently luxurious and expensive, which stimulated production and trade along existing and established lines in these areas. There followed also an influx of Greek and Syrian slaves and artisans to Rome, which in turn stimulated Roman production. In terms of trade, craftsmanship and even agricultural skills, Rome had much to learn from the eastern provinces, and the geography of settlement, agriculture and trade was therefore much less profoundly affected than it was in the west.

In barbarian Western Europe, already strongly differentiated in terms of its economies, societies, and densities of population, the impact of Rome brought about a geographical revolution. Fresh patterns were superimposed which were the result of the operation of processes that were new and unprecedented in Western Europe. Some of the new conditions—peace, order and efficient administration—prevailed throughout the Empire, and had important effects. Even where production continued to be largely for subsistence among the indigenous population, peace and order sufficed to bring about an increase of population and this alone brought about an expansion of cultivation, clearing and settlement which in some areas has had a profound and enduring effect on the rural landscape of Europe. New opportunities for regional specialisation came with the assurance of security and reasonable economic stability, communications and urban markets. Regional specialisation and the expansion of production were also facilitated by the Roman capacity for organisation and civil engineering, by massive investment in public works, by the spread of new skills and techniques in industry, agriculture and trade, and by new standards of efficiency in the exploitation of mineral resources. In many ways the influence of Rome may be likened to that of Britain, France or Japan in their underdeveloped colonial territories from the late nineteenth century. Rome came to the west as an imperial power imposing a new culture and civilisation, forcing economic development into new forms geared to the needs of the administration, the army and the metropolitan power, Rome itself.

The civil administration, the army and Rome were the three institutions which had the most important consequences for the economic and social geography of the west and their impact varied from place to place in a significant way. Rome and its demands on production were one of the most important influences on the economic development of the west, but the expressions of imperial power which were in many ways dominant and new in bringing about geographical and economic change were the frontier and the army, the towns and the Roman roads, all functionally interdependent and representing the chief of the material achievements which consolidated the conquest and made Roman administration and military control effective and efficient.

Rome itself, city of a million people, was the chief of all urban markets, imposing its demands on all Europe and dominating the economic map of Europe (Fig. 2:4). Financed by tribute and taxation, its industries supported by fresh armies of slaves as long as new conquests were being made, Rome became a great 'parasitical' capital, sending relatively few exports in return for the massive imports it needed of grain and oil, timber and metals as well as more expensive commodities; the sherds of some 40 million jars in which oil and perhaps some wine were imported from southern Spain over a period of a generation or so form a great mound some 140 feet high at Monte Testaccio near Rome. In the first century A.D. the new provinces were all markets for the industrial products of Rome and of Italy: Italian bronze from Rome and Campania, glass from Campania, pottery from Arretium, textiles from southern Italy and from the Po valley were exported northwards and northwestwards to the frontier areas through ports such as Aquileia. But for a variety of

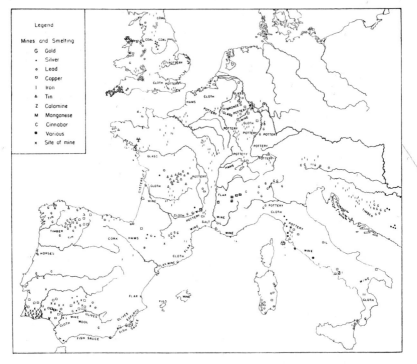

Fig. 2:4   Major products of the Roman Empire in the West (after Davies, Bengston and Milojčič). Note the concentration of mining in Britain, and in north-west and south-west Iberia. Note also the great activity in (a) Mediterranean lands with access to navigable water and (b) the Rhine frontier area.

reasons Roman and Italian industry later declined, though Rome still remained a great centre of consumption, exemplified by the provision of free bread and oil as well as circuses. Although metals, raw materials, and later, manufactured goods such as pottery and cloth were imported to Rome from the west, the main bulk of agricultural imports came from areas which had easy access to water transport. North Africa, south-east Spain, coastal districts of southern Italy and Sicily, and those parts of southern Gaul near to the Rhône were the chief suppliers of grain. Wine came from southern Gaul and oil from the Midi and south-eastern Spain. The urban market of Rome thus revolutionised the farming of the Mediterranean coastlands.

The army in particular was a major instrument of economic development. It was responsible for the massive public investment represented by the engineering and construction of roads; by the building of forts, towns, harbours, aqueducts, canals and drainage works; by the creation of factories and the opening of mines and quarries. Its veteran soldiers supplied the settlers for agricultural colonies which were frequently established behind the frontier. But the army was not only a source of labour and the agent by which much public and social investment was achieved: it was also a market for food, wine, raw materials and manufactured goods and, if some of the specialised tastes of its more affluent officers and administrators continued to require imports from Italy or the eastern Mediterranean, most of the needs of most soldiers could increasingly be supplied from the fields and factories, mines and quarries which were springing up nearby to meet the demands of frontier armies. The attraction of the frontier market in bringing about the shift of the pottery industry from southern Gaul to the frontier[12] or in encouraging the northward shift of viticulture to the Rhine valley are examples of its importance. It is, indeed, abundantly evident that the degree of romanisation and the intensity of economic development in the Empire as a whole increased substantially towards the frontiers of the Rhine and Danube. It was certainly the proximity of the army as much as the very favourable physical environment which assured the intensive economic development of areas such as the Rhine rift valley or the Rhenish Palatinate, or which helped to establish an industrial tradition in the Belgian province.

The introduction of towns and of urban life into much of Western Europe was, perhaps, the greatest achievement of the Romans in the west: and their work was of a singularly enduring quality in spite of all that was lost in the Dark Ages that followed. The characteristics of Roman towns and their relationship to the medieval towns will be discussed below, but it must be stressed at this point that the garrisons and administration of the towns, like the army at the frontier on a larger scale, were also the foci of new and considerable capital investment. The growing populations of servants, merchants, craftsmen and landowners which gathered round the garrison and the officials at once constituted a potential labour supply as well as markets for an unprecedented variety and volume of goods. The concentration of purchasing power in the hands of the soldiers, officials and tax-collectors meant that the towns were becoming significant markets for agricultural surpluses and manufactured goods. In the early Empire at least, growing towns stimulated the expansion of rural settlement in their neighbourhoods (most conspicuously by the establishment of villas), and this was perhaps as much due to the existence of urban markets as to the social needs of romanised landowners for proximity to the culture, amenities, prestige and influence of urban society.

Together with the frontier and the town, the road was the third of the indispensable supports of Roman domination in the west, each dependent on the other, each stimulating economic development and each leaving fundamental traces for later generations to build on. The Roman roads were usually military and strategic in conception but they attracted trade and settlement for many reasons. Proximity to the road meant security and the camps and *civitates* which were linked together by the road system were themselves foci of economic development. The very slowness and difficulty of travel made for greater contact between traveller and local inhabitant. Rest-houses, inns, sanctuaries, markets and market towns grew up along the route. Villas were frequently established near to the roads and their property boundaries were determined by reference to them. Yet in some areas there is a striking contrast between the abundance of archaeological finds near pre-Roman trackways which continued in use through the Roman period and the scarcity of finds on purely military roads of Roman origin. It must also be remembered that water transport continued to be by far the cheapest way of carrying goods. Costs of transport were frequently prohibitive overland; the cost of an oil-crushing machine could be doubled in a hundred miles, for example. By water, the cost of transport amounted to about a third of the price of grain in a journey from Spain to Italy.

Production for the market of all but the most luxurious or expensive foodstuffs and manufactured articles had therefore to take place near the market or near water transport. The Rhône and the Saône carried heavy traffic in spite of the current of the former. Chalons-sur-Saône was an important river port and so was Lyon. Routes from Lyon towards the Atlantic followed the St Etienne trough to Roanne on the Loire, which could then be followed to the

3 *Grossfahner, near Erfurt, Thuringia*. Large irregular nucleated village set in its open fields, much fragmented into small strips.

4 *Breberen, north of Aachen, West Germany*. Regular nucleated village grouped about an open space which includes the church, but is now much divided. Note the clear limit between open fields and enclosed crofts and gardens. In the open fields the orientation of strips gives an indication of the grouping of strips into furlongs.

5 *Open fields north-west of Dijon.* Strips tend to follow the contours, though orchards and woodland can be seen to occupy steeper slopes.

6 *Bocage, south of Paimpol, Brittany.* Characteristic small, hedged fields with much hedgerow timber; scattered settlement.

sea. Towards the Channel, the Saône and the Seine were linked by a relative short portage overland from Chalons; and the Doubs led easily to the navigable Rhine. Strabo's comments on Gaul are worth quoting in this respect:

'Now the whole of this country is watered by rivers which come down from the Alps, the Cevennes and the Pyrenees and discharge into the Ocean and the Mediterranean. Further, the districts through which they flow are plains, for the most part, and hilly lands with navigable watercourses. The river beds are by nature so well situated with reference to one another that there is transportation from either sea into the other; for the cargoes are transported only a short distance by land with an easy transit through the plains.'[13]

Canals such as that of Marius linking Arles to the sea, or Car Dyke linking the waterways of the Fenland, or projects such as that for a canal linking Rhine and Moselle thus had considerable economic importance.

Transport over long distances was possible but expensive. For all but rare and expensive commodities, regions remote from Rome were thus accorded a degree of natural economic protection which encouraged industrial and agricultural development, particularly in the Rhine provinces. The development of regional self-sufficiency in the west in the later Roman Empire was a natural consequence of expansion and of the difficulties of communications, notwithstanding the excellent road system which the Romans created.

Agriculture

In the geography of agriculture, changes were greatest in the Mediterranean area. Techniques of irrigation known to the ancient world of the Middle East were introduced not only into North Africa but also into Spain, where irrigation was important in the south and east. Roman success in conserving moisture for crop production by techniques of dry farming appears to have been very considerable[14] but it was North Africa that benefited rather than Western Europe. There were technical innovations in the introduction of watermills and oil presses, but controversy surrounds the extent to which they were important and it has been suggested that the former were still fairly scarce in classical times.[15] Other technological changes in agriculture were few, but contemporary writers knew of the importance of frequent ploughing and of clean fallowing in conserving moisture. The practice of using a green crop for stock fodder, a practice which dispensed with fallow, increased the number of stock and also the amount of manure available, was also known and practised in the Po basin. Indeed, agricultural knowledge, as in a later 'age of improvement', was codified in the writings of agronomists, such as Varro and Columella. What is known about grain yields suggests that they were as high in Italy in Roman times as at any time until the nineteenth century. In Sicily, on good soils near Etna, classical yields of 8 to 10 fold represent about 20 bushels per acre. On good soils in Etruria grain yielded 10 to 15 fold, but the average was probably no better than 4 fold or about 9 bushels per acre.[16]

As in the Arab world of later years, political unity from the Middle East to the Straits of Gibraltar and the movement of men and ideas over a wide area encouraged the spread of crops and stock. Varieties and breeds were improved and new crops were spread into northwestern Europe. Contacts with China, unified under the Han Empire, also stimulated the exchange of crops, products and techniques. Apricots, lemons, melons, Asiatic cattle, and Egyptian cats, ducks and geese appeared in Rome and Greece from the east. Sesame, clover, alfalfa, cherries, peaches, some varieties of plums and figs, quince, almond, chestnut, walnuts, radishes, flax and beetroot were spread into the west. The cherry, introduced from Asia Minor in 74 B.C. had spread rapidly over the western world even by Pliny's time in the first century A.D. Cultivation of the fig was pushed north to the point at which frost became a major hazard, but the development of viticulture in Gaul presents the best example of the spread of new crops and the selection and introduction of new varieties to withstand marginal climatic conditions.[17]

Introduced into Massilia by the Greeks, viticulture extended into southern Gaul and was widespread by the first century B.C. But Strabo commented that: 'As you proceed northwards to the Cevennes, the olive-planted and fig-planted land ceases, but other things still grow. Also the vine, as you thus proceed, does not easily bring its fruit to maturity.'[18] Indeed, viticulture was unknown in the parts of Gaul conquered by Caesar, though Romans and then Gauls in the area developed a thirst which required the import of wine from southern Gaul and from Italy. But by A.D. 90 Pliny wrote that new stock, resisting cold, had pushed the limit further north. By the end of the third century viticulture was well established in the Rhine rift valley, in the Côte d'Or (near the modern vintages of Beaune and Nuits) and in the Bordeaux area, where a Spanish stock had been acclimatised. By the fourth century the vine was established in the Moselle area, near Paris, in the Loire valley near Tours, Angers and Nantes, and even in Hertfordshire.

The introduction of new crops, notably the vine, was one of the relatively few ways in which Rome affected agricultural practice north of the Alps. The wheeled plough was known among the Belgae and in the Swiss area, but it was probably not a Roman innovation. The Roman influence was in rural settlement and in stimulating output of grain, wool, flax and wine rather than in technological innovation. North of the Alps and the Massif Central, it was the market of the Rhine frontier which stimulated commercial agriculture, not only in the production of wine, but also in the grain exports which found their way to the Rhine frontier from the Meuse, the Scheldt, the Loire and the Seine basins. The wool of England and of northern Gaul was supplying textile industries of more than local importance, but it was, as suggested above, the Mediterranean lands, of climate comparable to that of Italy, with a greater density of population and above all, access to Rome by water, which were most strongly devoted to commercial agriculture. The plain of Campania was renowned for its Falernian wines, its olives, corn and cattle; southern Italy and Sicily were best known for their grain, their wool and their wine, Sicily exporting some 2 million bushels of grain at one time, and well known too for its baggage animals. The Guadalquivir basin was the best developed part of Iberia in Strabo's time, exporting grain, wine and olive oil, not only in large quantities, as he says, but also of the best quality. Wax, honey and pitch were also exported from there, and large quantities of kermes and other dyestuffs. Oysters, fish and fish-sauce, wool and cloth were also produced.[19] Tarragonese and Andalusian wines were known on the Italian market and flax was important in the Ebro valley and in parts of the Costa Brava.[20]

Mining

The intensity with which the Romans exploited the mineral resources of the West stands in marked contrast to their neglect in the period that followed (Fig. 2:4). It is true that many of the major sources of iron, copper, tin and precious metals had been known and worked from Bronze Age times, but the Roman exploration for minerals seems to have been much more systematic and complete. The need for metals was great. A steady supply of precious metals had necessarily to be maintained, not only to satisfy increasing demands for gold and silver plate and ornaments but also to maintain stocks of currency and to maintain the balance of payments with the advanced cultures of southern Asia, then as later, a constant drain on the currency stocks of Europe. Copper and tin resources were well known but the Romans instituted much larger-scale exploitation to supply a vastly greater need for bronze, while copper was also used with calamine in the manufacture of brass. Deposits of lead were ransacked throughout Europe to supply new uses for metal in the construction of buildings and conduits. Iron, too, was more used than formerly, though sources were more widely scattered and trade consequently less well developed than for rarer metals. Nevertheless, the effect of improved bellows in making possible the production of true steel for the first time began to put a premium on the production of iron free from impurities; and Spanish steel was widely known for its quality and was exported over large distances.

In many cases only the richest and most accessible of ores were exploited. In Etruria deposits of ore which would now be counted rich, containing 4 to 5 per cent copper, were neglected; lead ores with less than 10 per cent metal were often neglected, and Roman slag has frequently been worth working over again.[21] The state of mining technology was partly responsible, for only shallow shafts and short adits could be made and simple drainage problems tackled. Lack of skill and power limited the range and quality of ores that could be smelted. But it is also true that the Romans were, in a sense, skimming the cream of Western European mineral resources in the same way that the Western Europeans were to prospect the world in the nineteenth century.

The exploitation of minerals had effects on other aspects of settlement. There is some evidence in the Sierra Morena of an Italian immigration of miners and prospectors in the second century B.C. to work mineral resources which had just been brought within the boundaries of Roman territory. Alluvial gold in the high valley terraces of eastern Styria attracted a gold rush in the second century B.C. But one must distinguish, in ancient mining as in more modern times, between the independent and foot-loose free miner, working for himself and probably by himself on placer deposits of alluvial gold or tin, and mining with shafts or adits which was organised by authority, supported by slave labour and sometimes operated on a large scale. Mining seems also to have attracted urban and rural settlement in its neighbourhood. Towns, villas and sometimes roads were more frequent in the richer mining areas. South western Iberia and, on a smaller scale, the Forest of Dean are examples.

In the Italian peninsula Tuscany continued to be the major source of copper, tin and iron as it had been in Etruscan times (Fig. 2:4); mainland iron ores were supplemented with imports from Elba, from which some 11 million tons of ores were taken in ancient times. Few other parts of Italy had important mining industries and there are signs of decline in Etruria itself in the time of the Empire. Copper, brass, bronze and lead industries of Campania were based on imported metals; Sicily was exploited for its iron, silver and lead; Liguria for silver and the central Alps chiefly for alluvial gold. None of these areas appears to have been as important as Etruria, or even Sardinia, a storehouse of mineral wealth which had been known and worked by the Nuraghi long before the Roman occupation.

The mineral wealth of Gaul was less striking than the industrial skills of its inhabitants. A little gold in the Pyrenees and tin in the west represented the bulk of its valuable minerals, though lead and silver were mined in various places. Iron working, however, was widely scattered, no doubt for local markets, and most of the ores which were being worked in the eighteenth century were already exploited in Roman times. Along the Rhine frontier mineral resources were more fully developed: copper in the Ardennes and the Eifel; calamine, used to make brass, in the Sambre–Meuse depression; silver and lead in the Moselle basin and east of the Rhine at the mouth of the Lahn. North of the Alps, Styrian iron and alluvial gold made the fortunes of Roman Noricum.

But it was Iberia and Britain which supplied, perhaps, the greater part of Roman needs. Strabo among other classical authors was enthusiastic, writing of southern Spain: 'It is rare for a country to have within a small area an abundance of all kinds of metals. . . . Up to the present moment, neither gold nor silver, nor yet copper, nor iron, has been found anywhere in the world in a natural state either in such quantity or of such good quality.'[22] The Algarve and the Sierra Morena represented one great area of mineral wealth in silver, copper, and cinnabar. The tin of Portugal and north-western Spain dominated the Roman market from the time of the pacification (about A.D. 19) to the third century A.D., and in north-western Spain was 'the most important goldfield of the early Roman Empire,[23] chiefly in the basin of the Sil river. The density of mines in south-west and north-west Iberia is one of the most striking features of Fig. 2:4. Copper, calamine, lead, and the iron of Bilbao were worked in the Cantabrian mountains and several places in the Ebro valley and even Toledo itself had a reputation for their steel.

In Britain, too, the pattern of mining heralds later distributions: the Weald and the Forest of Dean were the most important iron producers, though the ores of the Midlands and South Wales were also exploited. Wales yielded gold and copper in Anglesey, Caernarvon and the Dee valley, but it was above all for its lead and tin that Britain was known. Lead from Shropshire, Derbyshire and the Yorkshire dales, and silver-lead from the Mendips indicate how thoroughly the Romans prospected for minerals. And in the third century A.D. it was to the tin of Cornwall that north-western Iberia relinquished its leadership of the tin market.

Industry

The exploitation of mineral wealth at the very fringes of the Empire in remote and inhospitable areas like the Yorkshire dales is explicable in terms of the scarcity of non-ferrous metals and the pressure of needs which made it possible and necessary for very heavy costs of transport to be borne. Yet one of the most striking features of the economic development of the Empire is the tendency for manufacturing industry to spread out from Italy to the frontier regions, frequently at the expense of the metropolitan area. The existence of the frontier markets was certainly important in stimulating industrial production, but so also was the cheap and free labour of the native Gauls, accustomed to a modest standard of living, adaptable to the new Roman methods, and more conscientious and skilful than Italian slave labour. Provincial wares often came to rival and surpass those of Rome and Italy in quality as well as price and the home market itself was invaded by provincial manufactures.

The migration of the pottery industry illustrates this trend. For many years after the conquest of Gaul it was Etrurian pottery, particularly the fine red-ware pottery (*terra sigillata*) made chiefly at Arrezzo (*Arretium*), which was to be found in much of Gaul, but the potteries of the Tarn basin at and near La Graufesenque captured the market of Gaul, the Rhine frontier and even Britain between A.D. 40 and 70; by the turn of the century their products were being imported in bulk to the Italian peninsula.[24] Later still the industry moved even closer to its frontier markets, in factories between Mainz and Strasbourg and then in Bavaria. The cloth industry too seems to show a centrifugal movement to the frontier. Apulia and Calabria, the Po valley and southern Spain were all well known for their woollen or linen goods, but in later years cloaks worth importing into Rome were being produced near the Rhine frontier at Worms, Trier, Namur and Reims. Glass workers migrated to Gaul about A.D. 50, and factories at Arles and Lyon were competing with those of Italy. Fifty years later, glass working was established at Worms, Namur, Trier and Cologne, and it was these which came ultimately to supply almost the whole of the western provinces except Italy.

It forms no part of this study to examine in any detail the processes and trends which changed the economic character of the Empire almost completely in the third and fourth centuries A.D., but it is necessary to mention the main themes in order to understand the changes in urban and rural settlement which were fundamental to subsequent medieval development. The third century was a period of crisis in which the Germanic invasions which resulted in the loss of the *Agri Decumates* were followed by civil wars and inflation. A new world was emerging which was very different from the classical Empire. The tendency towards the development of regionally self-sufficient economies was accelerated, and there are signs of industrial expansion in, for example, the state cloth factories at Reims, Tournai, Trier and Metz, or the arms factories of Autun, Strasbourg, Amiens, Reims and Trier. Towns may have been in decline, but rural industry and rural settlement seem to have thrived in northern Gaul and Britain.

Militarily the empire was on the defensive, needing even vaster armies for its support, so that shortage of recruits and shortage of manpower were pressing problems at a time when taxation necessarily continued to be at a high level. Whether population was declining or not, as some have suggested, it is very difficult to say, for there is little direct evidence. At all events, there is no doubt that the economy was increasingly being regulated by the state, which was beginning to take an even greater part in economic affairs than it had previously done. Policies aimed at maintaining craftsmen in their occupations and farmers on their lands in order to sustain a high level of taxation failed to counter the drift from the towns to the countryside under the protection of powerful families.

THE ROMAN LEGACY IN THE LANDSCAPES
OF WESTERN EUROPE

Towns

The introduction of the town and of urban life into much of Western Europe was certainly one of the greatest achievements of the Romans in the west: and it has been one of the most enduring, for the degree to which medieval and modern towns of Europe are based on Roman sites and Roman foundations is very striking indeed. There are still many towns in which a part of the urban layout or a skeleton of the street plan follows the lines first marked out by a Roman surveyor. But Roman towns had very considerable variety in their origin, functions and geography and the ways in which this varied legacy was handed down to the Middle Ages were also complex. It is necessary to outline, therefore, the characteristics of Roman towns before proceeding to a discussion of the more difficult problem of urban continuity and survival into the Middle Ages.

Many of the Roman towns grew around the military camps which were the headquarters of legions or cohorts. There was indeed a great variety. Some, notably on the Rhine frontier, grew round smaller fortresses or *castellae*. On the other hand an elaborate and formal establishment of urban status and lay-out was involved in the creation of the *coloniae*, where again a distinction must be made between the Roman and Latin (Italian) *coloniae*. Many of the Roman towns were largely indigenous in character from the beginning, for they frequently replaced or grew on the very sites of the Gallic *oppida* which had been primarily fortresses.

The *oppida* of Celtic peoples, frequently mentioned by Caesar, were essentially fortresses, primitive refuges which may once have been no more than temporarily occupied but which were increasingly becoming permanent centres of trade, crafts, administration and religion in the more developed parts of Gaul.[25] They were frequently, but by no means invariably, hilltop settlements like Gergovia, Bibracte or Alesia; they were sometimes defended by marsh or water, like Bourges or Lutèce (Paris): but defensibility was the major characteristic demanded of their chosen sites, even at the expense of accessibility. Many of these *oppida* became the nucleus of a Roman town. Reims, Paris, Bourges or St Albans are examples (see Fig. 2:5). Others proved too inaccessible for the Romans, and new lowland sites were chosen nearby—Clermont Ferrand near Gergovia,

Aix-en-Provence near the fortress of Antremont, Autun near Bibracte. The Roman towns thus took over the regional functions of these Celtic pre-urban centres and superimposed upon them a new pattern of economic development. Thus areas which had been tribal territories of the Celtic peoples became *civitates*, the administrative

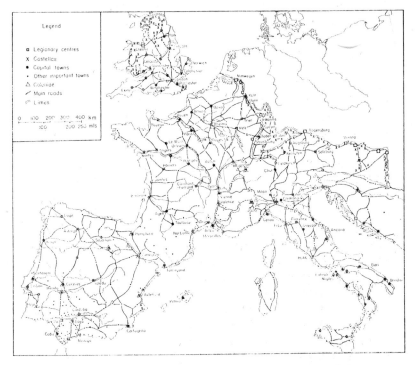

Fig. 2:5 Major towns and roads in the Roman Empire.

areas governed from the Roman towns, and also, very approximately, the market areas of these Roman capitals. The persistence of early Celtic traditions through Roman times and beyond may to some extent be revealed by the way in which it has been the tribal Celtic name rather than its classical Roman designation that has been remembered in place-names. Thus Paris derives from the name of the *Parisii*, not from the classical *Lutetia*, Reims from the *Remi*, not *Durocortorum*, Amiens from the *Ambiani*, Bourges from the *Bituriges*, Limoges from the *Lemovices*, not *Augustoritum*. Bordeaux (*Burdigala*) and Lyon (*Lugdunum*) are examples of Celtic non-tribal names that have persisted.[26] There is, indeed, an interesting contrast between northern Gaul on the one hand and southern Gaul, Iberia and the frontier area on the other, for in the more highly romanised areas of the frontier and the southern Mediterranean areas, the classical name more frequently survives. Narbonne from *Narbo*, Arles from *Arelate*, Cologne from *Colonia Agrippinensis*, Zaragoza from *Caesarea Augusta*, are examples of this latter type.

Many of the Gallo-Roman towns developed gradually and relatively haphazardly, original defences becoming less important in the urban plan than the market or sites near crossroads, quays and harbours. Many remained open towns during much of the Empire. The *coloniae*, on the other hand, were new settlements resulting from an act of state. They had the right to establish defences and they were constructed according to established policy and rules, such as those codified by Vitruvius.[27] Native inhabitants could be dispossessed and ancient property rights disregarded. A founder chose the site, took possession of the ground, traced out the plan of the town and allotted urban tenements. Within the walled area the layout was grouped around the two major streets, the *cardo maximus*, running more or less north to south, and the *decumanus maximus*, running east to west. Minor streets were laid out parallel to them, thus dividing the urban area into blocks of roughly 240 by 260 feet or 260 by 390 feet. A place of significance near the junction of the two main streets was reserved for the forum, the basilica and other public buildings. Among the planned *coloniae* a distinction must be made between the Roman and the so-called Latin *coloniae*. The former had more privileges but were frequently quite small, with a complement of up to 6,000 veterans. Cologne, Béziers, Narbonne or Arles are examples. The Latin *coloniae* had originally been founded as part of a resettlement scheme to relieve poverty and overpopulation among the Roman *plebs* and among rural underemployed in Italy, and they were allowed to have up to 60,000 citizens. Nîmes and Vienne, examples of this latter type, were, in fact, larger than the Roman *coloniae* nearby, Orange and Arles.

Many towns grew on or near the site of the characteristically rectangular Roman military camps. These varied in size and importance from the grand legionary camps, in area some 1000 yards by 670 yards to cohort camps of 220 yards by 170 yards, or to the tiny nuclei of a few acres provided by the *castellae* (Fig. 2:5). Civil settlements of Italian and indigenous traders and craftsmen often grew up nearby to serve the needs of the soldiery, more commonly along the Rhine–Danube frontier than in Gaul or Britain. It was these civil settlements rather than the original camps, which were sometimes most worth defending by wall in the later days of the Empire. Many of the towns strung out near the Rhine from Nijmegen to Zürich had their origin as Roman frontier camps. Regensburg, Passau, Linz and Vienna are examples on the Danube.

The types of site which were favoured for the Roman military camps were very different from those preferred either by Celts or Germans for their strongpoints, or by the medieval nobility for their castles of much later days. The function of the Roman camps was more often offensive than defensive; they were the supply bases and troop headquarters of armies which depended greatly on movement.[28] Easily defended but isolated places on hilltops, in forests or marshes were avoided. Accessibility was important, therefore they were often set up near existing settlements at sites on crossroads, river crossings or near navigable water. Since it was precisely this quality of accessibility which mattered again when the revival of trade in the Middle Ages occurred they were sometimes places which were resuscitated as urban sites at a much later date and under very different conditions.

The qualities demanded of sites and locations for Roman ports and harbours similarly differed in some respects from those which were needed either in earlier or later years. Marseilles presents a fine example. The Vieux-Port, chosen by the Greeks, had been an excellent natural harbour and Massilia had flourished until the first century B.C. It remained an intellectual capital of southern Gaul during the Roman occupation, but its trade declined to little more than coastal traffic. The long hard climb out of the town itself was a serious difficulty for wheeled traffic, and on a larger scale Marseilles lay far to one side of the main currents of land traffic between Italy and southern Gaul and up the Rhône–Saône valley. With the increase in overland movement and commerce, accessibility by land had become at least as important as a deep, sheltered natural harbour. Marseilles was therefore abandoned for the river port of Arles, seriously liable to silting, but the lowest crossing point on firm ground at the head of the delta for east–west routes, and also the point of transhipment from river traffic to the canal cut by Marius to the sea. Arles became the great entrepôt (Plate 2). As late as A.D. 418 Honorius could write: 'It is from Arles that all the products of the entire world are distributed: the oriental luxuries, the perfumes of Arabia, the delicate products of Assyrian art, the grain of Africa, the fruits of Spain and all the wealth of Gaul, are literally unloaded at this point.' Narbonne, too, owed its importance to its position on the *Via Domitia*, linking Italy and Spain, and on the road towards Toulouse and Aquitaine using the Gate of Carcassonne. Although a major port of the Empire, its harbours and beaches were inconveniently scattered over the lagoons which lay between it and the sea.

Towns of very varied origin—administrative centres, *coloniae*, indigenous towns and military camps—were widely spread over the whole Empire (see Fig. 2:5). By A.D. 15 there were some 350 towns in peninsular Italy and as many in Spain. Yet their distribution varied from one place to another. In eastern Spain and southern Gaul the intensity of urbanisation may reflect the greater length of Roman occupation, greater participation in commerce due to the presence of the Mediterranean seaway, or it may reflect the predisposition of indigenous peoples, already indirectly in contact with the classical world, to accept Roman concepts of urban civilisation. It has also been suggested that in Spain the fragmentation of tribes had led to a multiplication of small capitals from which each was separately ruled. Normandy, too, and perhaps for similar reasons, had many small towns; Brittany and northern Belgium relatively few, perhaps because of a greater stress on pastoral farming.

It is paradoxical that Roman towns have left so deep an imprint on the geography of modern Europe in spite of the vulnerability of urban economy and institutions to the insecurity and decline which followed the collapse of the Empire. The pattern of Roman towns may be much more clearly discerned, in fact, than the impact of Roman agriculture on field systems and rural habitat. Many of the major towns and regional capitals of Western Europe have names of classical origin; some can trace the outline of Roman fortifications in the pattern of their modern lay-out, or the major framework of the *cardo maximus* and the *decumanus maximus*;[29] and in the more highly romanised Mediterranean lands, modern street blocks may faithfully reproduce a Roman pattern.

Yet the precise ways in which the connection between ancient and medieval town occurred are frequently a matter of conjecture and controversy. With few written records, conclusions rest heavily on inference from archaeological juxtapositions, and the evidence will frequently bear more than one interpretation. Continuities and relationships have been sought in a variety of fields: in legal and social institutions or in the economic, military and religious functions of the towns in late classical and early medieval times. The geographical interest in the fate of the classical towns concerns all of these, but it is also true that the geographers' interest centres to a considerable extent in the topographical expression of these functions on the ground and the ways in which they are related to subsequent development; and it is in this matter that the evidence is, on the whole, clearest.

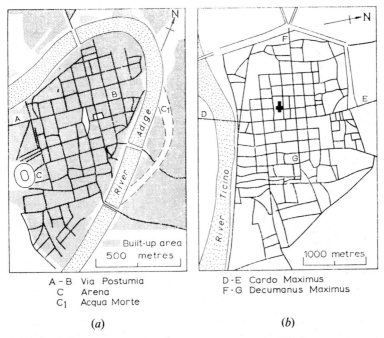

A - B Via Postumia
C   Arena
C₁   Acqua Morte

D - E Cardo Maximus
F - G Decumanus Maximus

(a)   (b)

Fig. 2:6   Urban street plans of Roman origin.
(a) Verona. Classical Verona was rebuilt about 15 B.C. The *Via Postumia* provided the main NE–SW axis for the orientation of the Roman plan, which may be traced by the square blocks averaging 260 feet square, equivalent to plots of 2 *jugera* (240 Roman feet square) and bounded by 20-foot wide streets.
(b) Pavia. The Roman street pattern is strikingly well-preserved, including the main axes of the *cardo maximus* and the *decumanus maximus*, near the crossing of which stands the site of the medieval cathedral.

In some instances the chessboard street plan of the Roman layout has survived more or less intact. It may be clearly seen in the layout of Pavia, a town which commanded an important passage across the Ticino and retained importance in the barbarian world in the seventh and eighth centuries as capital of the Lombards; or in the layout of Verona, which was rebuilt in 15 B.C. in connection with the preparations being made by the Romans to force the Brenner Pass and to conquer Rhaetia.[30] Such survivals are not uncommon in northern and central Italy—in Piacenza, Turin, Como, Brescia, Florence, Lucca, Naples, for example. Zaragoza and Cologne are examples outside Italy. Where the layout of a fairly large section of the Roman town has been preserved in detail, survival must be presumed to be the result of a considerable degree of continuity in urban life, and it is indeed where there is other evidence of continuing currents of trade, notably in northern and central Italy, that this type of topographical continuity is most frequent. But by no means all Roman towns had been laid out by the measuring rod of a surveyor in such a way as to leave us incontrovertible evidence of Roman origins. Many towns had grown haphazardly, notably Rome itself, so that evidence of Roman layout is not apparent from plans alone.

In most cases, however, the relationship between the topography of Roman and medieval towns is much less direct. For the function, importance and layout of Roman towns underwent dramatic changes in the third century as a result of the wave of Germanic invasions, unrest and civil uprisings that took place all over the western world. In A.D. 256 the frontier was pierced and soon afterwards the *Agri Decumates* were lost. Internal security which had depended on the sanctity of the *limes* was now undermined. Layers of charcoal and rubble bear witness still to the burning and destruction of many a Roman town in the west during these uncertain years. There followed a period of urban decline and of a flight to the countryside which was also marked by massive activity in the walling of towns. During the third and fourth centuries masonry walls tended to become higher and thicker and were flanked by numerous towers as greater strength of fortifications was increasingly substituted for scarce and badly needed manpower.[31]

The areas enclosed by the new walls were frequently very small compared with the urban areas of the early empire (Fig. 2:7). Cologne and Mainz were about 240 acres; Trier at 700 acres was very large; but very many were no larger than 5 to 50 acres. Paris and Amiens were 20 acres; Dijon was 28 and Maastricht 5. In Gaul the refortification of much-reduced areas has been traced in some fifty towns. Sometimes the plan was rectangular and based on the outlines of the earlier *castra*, but curved walls were also used. In some cases only the most defensible area was enclosed and fortified

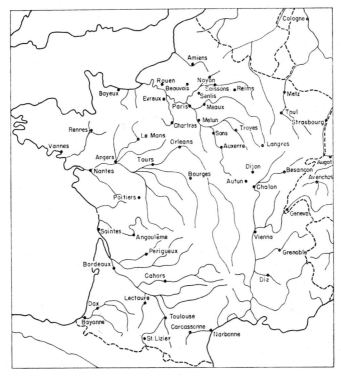

Fig. 2:7 Roman towns of Gaul which show contraction of the walled area during the late Roman Empire (after Hubert).

rather than that which contained the most important buildings and only where it was strategically necessary to enclose a larger area than a citadel was this done, at Bordeaux, for example. The walled area was occasionally constructed outside the old town or at its edge to take advantage of a natural defence: for example, on the Île de la Cité in Paris; on a spur, at Auxerre; or to transform the amphitheatre into a bastion, at Tours or Périgueux.[32] The creation of the reduced walled area would obviously have disrupted the plan of the old open towns and there is evidence that in some cases buildings in the neighbourhood of the new walls were systematically dismantled (Périgueux and Angers) if they obstructed excessively the field of fire or visibility from the new walls. It is also quite possible that urban life continued in the old towns outside the new walled area and outside the cleared area beneath the walls.

It is therefore very clear that the towns of the fourth century A.D. presented a very different appearance from those of the Empire in its heyday, but it was from these that there developed the nuclei for the great expansion of medieval cities.

During the Dark Ages it was, in general, the religious and military function of the town that continued to retain importance. Everywhere the economic function of the town declined. So also did the importance of the market place, though this decline was more marked, perhaps, in Britain and northern Gaul than in Mediterranean lands. Defence obviously increased in importance during these troubled years, but it was primarily through the Christian church that there was the most complete continuity. From the time of Constantine when Christianity became the official religion of the Empire, bishops had their residence in the towns and particularly in the *civitates* which had been Roman administrative centres. It was these which often became the dioceses of medieval Christendom; the *civitas* became the *cité* and thus the city.

In the fourth century, then, it was from the dwindling Roman towns that the countryside was converted. In France more than a hundred *civitates* were recognised in the seventh and eighth centuries; most of them were the centres of bishoprics and were sited on Roman foundations. In the old Roman lands of the Rhineland medieval bishoprics were established without exception on or near the site of Roman settlements. At Xanten, Cologne, Trier and Bonn there are continuous records of bishops from Roman to medieval times. In south-east Gaul Roman towns tended to fade away completely if they retained no ecclesiastical significance.

In these circumstances, the fragment of the ancient Roman town which formed the nucleus for later expansion in the Middle Ages was usually associated with either defence or religion rather than with trade or industry. The walled area itself, massively defended by walls of up to 25 to 30 feet high, sometimes became the residence of royal officials and nobility and the capital of a territorial unit; or it became a citadel for the church, and the cathedrals which replaced classical temples kept alive an urban tradition until merchant colonies began to settle in the protection of their walls.

Trier may serve as an example, though it continued to have a commercial importance which was unusual. It had been a very important Roman centre on the Rhine frontier and was elevated to the rank of *colonia* in the first century.[33] It had a good position, protected by the Eifel and the Hunsrück at the entry to the Lorraine plateau behind the line of the Rhine but at a roughly equal distance from Mainz and Cologne. It was for a time an imperial residence and capital of the Empire. It had important industries connected chiefly with arms and clothing. It had a mint and reputedly 'drained the commerce of the world', possessing a Syrian colony and becoming an exponent of oriental religion and art as well as the new Christianity. Its third-century wall enclosed some 700 acres. From A.D. 314 it had a bishop, acquiring a basilica in the centre and Christian churches in the suburbs. Some trade continued to the seventh and eighth century and merchants from Trier still travelled to Italy from Marseilles, but it was the church which was the greatest element in continuity and the bishops retained a great deal of their power.

In some places, however, new foci developed outside the walls, notably where holy sanctuaries, centres of pilgrimages and then abbeys had developed on the sites of early Christian cemeteries. Since these were outside the walls of the ancient town there was a corresponding shift in the development of the town plan.

In attempting to understand the continuities of site between the Roman and medieval town another possibility cannot be excluded. It may be that some sites especially, perhaps, in Britain had been completely abandoned and that they were occupied afresh by barbarian peoples. Roman sites had been well chosen and the emphasis on defence in the late Roman empire put a premium on qualities which were demanded by the barbarian leaders themselves. Walls were still valuable fortifications and both they and ruined buildings were useful quarries for a fresh start. Thus, for example, materials for a new church built at Ghent in the tenth century were quarried from Roman remains a few miles away. Moreover, the Roman roads were still viable routeways, and were again used long after the Roman danger had gone when commerce began to revive. They led, naturally enough, to the old crossing places and the old sites which would thus be used again. But, as suggested above, where there is little more than the juxtaposition of Roman remains and traces of early medieval abbeys, churches or castles on a site which is mainly obscured by later building, it is frequently impossible to be certain.

Rural settlement in the Roman West

In the medieval world which followed and in the prehistoric world which preceded the Roman Empire, colonisation and settlement sprang from a variety of motives, but they were essentially processes which involved the work of pioneer farmers, sometimes clearing new land afresh from the forest, sometimes reclaiming old cultivated land from the waste, but always with the primary aim, even the sole aim, of assuring their own subsistence. But it is a characteristic of much Roman colonisation and villa settlement that it was located with an eye on production for the market, even if it later developed into a more subsistence economy from the third century A.D.

The forms which were taken by rural settlement fall into two groups which reflect the very nature of Roman imperialism and romanisation. On the one hand there was the villa of the great land-owner, Roman or romanised, but in either case equipped with at least a veneer of the Latin language and Roman culture and with material wealth which marked him off profoundly from his labourers and peasants. On the other hand were the settlements of the indigenous peasants, often showing little influence of Roman occupation at all, and leaving much less trace in the archaeological record precisely because of their poverty in material goods. A picture such as this of a dual society akin to that of the British in India or the Japanese in Manchuria before 1945 may be overdrawn, for there were many gradations between ruler and ruled, landowner and peasant, native Celt and cultured Roman, but it helps rather than hinders, perhaps, the understanding of the problems of rural settlement.

It is impossible to generalise about the character of rural settlement among the native populations of the west, partly because there appears to have been so much variation, partly because so little is known. In southern Gaul there were nucleated settlements in the lower Rhône around Nîmes, near Narbonne, Marseilles and Aix-en-Provence, and Strabo mentions grouped villages in the Alps. But scattered settlement appears to have predominated.[34] In Italy itself, dispersed hamlet and village settlements have all been traced, but in northern Gaul hamlet and scattered settlements appear to have been normal and there are few traces of strongly nucleated settlements. In the silt fen of the English Fenland scattered farmhouses and loose aggregations of settlements in villages have both been traced. In England and Gaul there are possibilities that nucleated settlement occurred as a result of the creation of a dependent settlement adjacent to a villa. But it is also suggested that peripheral scattering of settlement may have occurred at a distance from the central villa. It seems difficult and perhaps rather unprofitable to generalise about the distribution of each type, particularly since there is no evident relationship with contemporary field systems. Traces of common-field farming with the light plough have been discovered in Italy and Gaul, and contemporary society in Belgium and perhaps the Rhineland may have been using a common-field system (see later, p. 227). In England, there are at least three forms of field system to be associated with the villa—centuriated lands, Celtic fields and 'long strip' cultivation,[35] but enclosure of compact farms from common field or directly from the waste on reclaimed land probably took place in many areas and much centuriated land was certainly cultivated in severalty.

Compared with the great variety of forms deriving from indigenous traditions, the Roman villa represents an institution and a settlement form of considerable uniformity. Normally consisting of buildings grouped around a courtyard, preferably on a slight rise so as to make it possible to supervise the work of the estate, the villa was the headquarters of a unit which included not only residence and farm buildings but also workshops, weaving sheds, kilns and even furnaces, particularly at a later stage in imperial development. Yet there was great variation in the character of the villa from the modest timber and thatch dwelling of a Gallo-Roman chief acquiring a veneer of Roman culture to the elaborate luxury villa such as that at St Uhlrich in the Moselle area which covered 100,000 square feet and contained 125 rooms. Excavations at Mayen revealed, indeed, building and rebuilding in no less than five phases, progressing from modest hut to palatial luxury villa. At least in early times many villas were the property of large landowners who preferred to live in the towns, and were often worked by slave labour. When new conquests ceased, slave labour became expensive and began to prove less efficient than free labour. It was replaced by the contractual labour services of free men, and in addition parts of the estates were often let out for a rent to peasant farmers. The headquarters of the villa, then, like modern plantations in tropical regions, which in some respects they resemble, possessed nearby a compact settlement of slave quarters or, at a later date, a village of peasant families tributary to the estate, sometimes, as is noted in the work of a Roman surveyor, at some distance from the villa itself.

Whereas it would be virtually impossible to attempt to characterise in any detail the distribution of new peasant settlement during the Roman period, the material remains of stone- or brick-built villas have been more frequently charted. In Gaul there was a high frequency of villas near the Rhine frontier: luxury villas near Trier reflect its importance as capital city for a time, but there were very many modest villas in the Meuse and Moselle valleys, the Rhine rift valley, and the lower Main (Fig. 2:3). Around Lyon, again, villas were common, particularly in the valleys of the Ain and the Doubs and between the Saône and the Loire. Along the routeways across Burgundy to Reims and the Seine, villas were again frequent. Aquitaine, like south-eastern Gaul is rich in the remains of villas, and so too are those parts of the western coasts where land and sea routes met.

Compared with the undistinguished remains of peasant settlement, villas are easily identifiable, and so also are certain other types of settlement on state-owned or public land. Over much of Western Europe, and particularly in North Africa, air photography has yielded abundant traces of field boundaries and agricultural service roads which were laid out by Roman surveyors in regular chessboard fashion (Fig. 2:8). These centuriated lands, as they are called, may be identified simply because they conform to standard surveyors' practice, built up of units of 20 by 20 *actus* (776 yards square). These centuriated lands were divided up as a result of acts of state and were frequently allocated to veteran soldiers or new settlers in frontier districts.[36] They have long been known from topographical maps in northern Italy where they dominate the modern landscape for mile upon mile of naturally well-drained land in the Po valley. But careful measurements of air photographs have yielded traces of centuriated lands in Kent, Sussex, Hertfordshire and perhaps in Essex and Middlesex, in the neighbourhood of Aix-en-Provence, near Orange and Avignon and Béziers among other examples in southern France,[37] in Austria, the Istrian peninsula and Dalmatia. The existence of centuriated land in Spain, near Valencia, has also recently come to light.[38]

In the geography of Roman and romanised settlement, in so far as it is revealed in archaeological traces and fragmentary literary evidence, it is possible to see several processes operating. First, and most obviously, the distribution of villa settlements tends to reflect en-

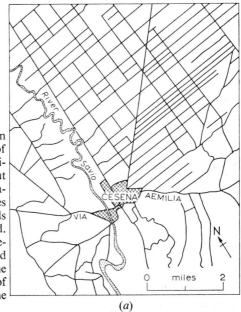

Fig. 2:8 Roman centuriation in modern rural landscapes.

(a) North Italian Plain: Cesena. Modern rural roads, many of which follow a rectilinear pattern, pick out the Roman grid. Occasional complete squares of 20 *actus* (776 yards square) can be identified. The contrast is clear between the centuriated zone in the plain and the irregular network of roads at the edge of the Apennines.

(*a*)

(b) Southern France: Valence. Modern rural roads and field boundaries occasionally follow the lines of a Roman pattern of centuriation, but the network is much less completely preserved than in the case of Cesena.

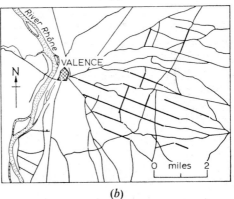

(*b*)

vironmental conditions. In a general sense, villas were most common in those areas of dense settlement and farming which were productive in terms of the crops most highly valued in Roman trade. Thus south-eastern Gaul, Aquitaine and southern and eastern Iberia were most highly romanised. These were the areas in which indigenous economy was most closely akin to the Roman, and in which climate and soils permitted the spread of Roman methods and Roman crops with the minimum of modification. The early limits of the vine in the Cevennes and the limit of the olive may have been significant. Further north, differences of soil became much more significant. In Lorraine there is a striking contrast between the distribution of villas on the richer valley soils, and the occurrence of crude timber structures built in shallow pits (*mardelles*) in forest clearings on poor soils. In the Loire valley, villas occupied sites which combined flood-plain meadow, well-drained loams on river terraces, and south-facing slopes of the incised valley sides which provided (and still provide) good land for vines (Fig. 2:9). The plateau surface, fertile enough when cleared but more limited in its range of soils and local climates and with a more difficult water supply, has left little trace of contemporary settlement; what there is (chiefly place-name evidence of dedication to St Martin, suggesting very early settlement of the fourth or fifth century) seems to indicate settlement by an under-privileged peasantry who embraced the promise of Christianity more eagerly than did the richer pagans of the villas.[39] In Britain, villas are to be found chiefly on easily cultivated light soils and there is relatively little evidence of new expansion by Roman villa owners on to the heavy clays.

It has already been suggested that the essential instruments of Roman colonisation in Western Europe were the town, the road and the frontier, and the distribution of the villas and of centuriated lands, the chief expression of romanised rural settlement, was related to these features quite as much as to the character of soil and climate. The concentration of villas along the routes through Burgundy and Champagne linking the Rhône–Saône trough to the Channel at

Fig. 2:9 The settlement of Touraine.

(a) The distribution of Roman *villae* and other substantial remains of settlement in the area around Tours. Note the concentration in the valleys and the avoidance of the forested plateau surface (after Boussard).

(b) Frankish settlement in the area around Tours. The extension of settlement on the plateau is evident and this is the area in which the headquarters of Frankish *vicariae* were located. But most of the Frankish settlement was on or near Roman sites, though very early Christian dedications are frequently near rather than on, the sites of Roman *villae* (after Boussard).

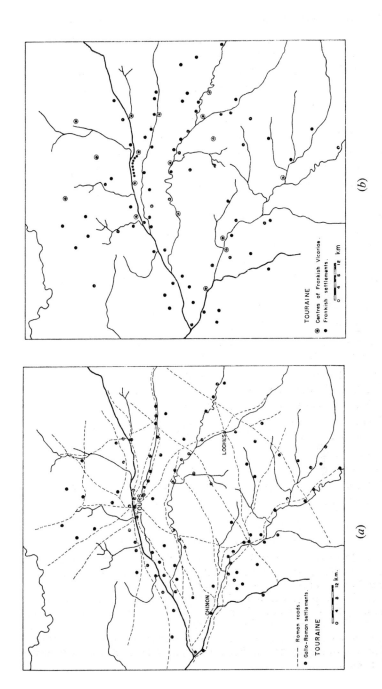

TOURAINE

--- Roman roads.
• Gallo-Roman settlements.

0 4 8 12 km.

(a)

TOURAINE

◉ Centres of Frankish Vicariae.
• Frankish settlements.

0 4 6 12 km

(b)

Boulogne have already been noted. In northern Belgium villa settlement had involved new inroads into the forest in order to be near the frontier road from Boulogne to Bavai and Tongres. Settlements derived from Roman villas are more frequent near the *Via Domitia* in the Midi. Particularly in the later stages of the Empire, proximity to the road system may have meant security to the Roman just as much as it meant danger to the barbarian. In Etruria, the modern revival of road traffic has generated recent settlement along main roads which follow the Roman line very closely. This recent settlement has frequently duplicated former Roman settlement patterns governed by proximity to the road, so that there is a very marked contrast between Roman and modern patterns of settlement on the one hand and on the other the medieval or Iron Age villages of subsistence farmers laid out with reference to soil quality and water supply rather than accessibility.[40]

The town played an especially important rôle in the distribution of Roman rural settlement. It is true that many towns, perhaps most, were predominantly agricultural in character; but it is also true for much of the empire that they contained the residences of prosperous landowners in the area. It was here that Roman and romanised landowners alike aspired to the cultural and material amenities, as well as to the political influence and prestige of urban life. Absentee landlords, officials, tax-collectors and military garrisons congregating in the towns helped to increase the demand for agricultural goods. Commercial agriculture was therefore stimulated, and the towns became profitable markets for the surpluses produced on the estates of the villas nearby. The towns became nuclei of economic growth in a world of underdeveloped indigenous, subsistence economies. The concentration of villas near urban centres may be seen very clearly in various areas; for instance in the neighbourhood of Bath; in the Loire valley there is a concentration of villas around Tours, a Roman centre large enough to build an amphitheatre with a capacity for 25,000 people. The villas near Lyon were more numerous and those near Trier more luxurious than those of other regions nearby.

No less than the towns the frontier stimulated the expansion of villa settlement and was a major sphere for the colonisation which went with the creation of centuriated land. Like the town, the frontier zone as a whole was a major market for agricultural produce, mainly through the presence of the army but also because of the concentration of industry and trade in the general area. Above all, the frontier supplied not only markets but also manpower for agricultural development. Veteran soldiers were settled in the centuriated lands; villas were set up by the families of officers, officials and merchants. The state participated directly in the colonisation of the *Agri Decumates* between the Rhine and the frontier in southwest Germany. New lands were cleared and occupied on the eastern slopes of the Black Forest and on the lower slopes of the Swabian Jura (Fig. 2:3). In the north, in the Wetterau, there are still traces of Roman centuriation to bear witness to this colonising activity. In the Alps and northwards to the Danube frontier soldiers and veterans were conspicuous among those who received grants of land from the state, frequently paying rent for small villas and employing native and imported labour.[41] Indeed, one of the most striking features in the development of settlement in the Roman frontier areas is the way in which German immigrants were allowed and even encouraged to settle as farmers and labourers within the frontier. It has been argued that much of Alsace and Lorraine may well have been strongly Germanised even before the fall of the Empire.

A number of difficulties surround the problem of how far the cultivated area of Western Europe was extended during the years of the Roman Empire in the West. In Iberia and southern Gaul it seems certain that the peace and order of the Empire, natural conditions similar to those of Italy, and a native population already accustomed to many of the features of Roman methods of farming and society made possible considerable development of commercial agriculture to supply the Roman market and also facilitated a much more massive colonisation from Italy than was ever possible in more northerly latitudes and at a later period. The clearing of woodland in classical times in the Mediterranean area seems to be indicated by the references in Strabo, Pliny and others to the existence of woodland in areas which were cleared by Arab times or by early medieval times.[42] In the frontier regions of Gaul there was an appreciable development of new colonisation on virgin land, particularly in southwest Germany in the *Agri Decumates* though it is sometimes difficult to say how far this was new and how far it represented a reoccupation of formerly cleared land. In Britain there was little extension of cultivation outside the areas of light soils and easily cultivable loams already cleared and settled in Iron Age times. In the English Fenland the northern silt area was very densely settled by a Romano-British population, and there was, similarly, a new expansion on reclaimed land in Holland. Yet it seems generally accepted that the Romans made little headway against the heavy clays and their damp oakwood forests. The reluctance of Roman settlement to expand against the northern forests stands in marked and significant contrast to the enormous and successful effort that went into the extension of farming into arid and semi-arid areas in Spain and North Africa, both areas suited to Roman knowledge and technology.

In Mediterranean lands, it has been suggested, limits were set to the expansion of farming by soil erosion on the one hand and by the spread of malaria on the other. It seems that malaria was introduced into Sicily in the fourth century B.C. and into Italy in the third, probably from North Africa. From then on it became an endemic disease and may have been responsible for the abandonment of the Maremma marshes of Etruria and the Pontine marshes of the Romagna after this period, but much of Italy seems not to have been affected by malaria until the Middle Ages. Excessive soil erosion produced by unwise clearing of forests for timber, grazing, fuel and farming has been held responsible for the decline of the Roman Empire. The decline has also been seen as a result of bad land-use methods developing as a result of the internal social and economic problems which were themselves the real causes of decline. Truth is more likely to be with the latter interpretation, but the extent of serious soil erosion has also been called into question. Air photographs of Italy, taken during the second world war, have revealed intact so many traces of ancient agriculture in which the effects of soil erosion cannot be seen that the universality of soil erosion has been very much doubted. Moreover it has been said[43] that the ploughs in use were not strong enough to cause much damage, and only where the hillside terraces had been abandoned and steep slopes cleared was there much creation of barren wastes. Right up to the end of the Middle Ages, Apulia and other parts of southern Italy and Sicily which are now desolate were probably still fertile and productive.

It is extremely difficult to assess the legacy of rural settlement in Roman times from the modern map. Centuriated fields are usually known only by their survival and air photography has revealed that they cover areas unsuspectedly large and varied. Roman villas are widely known and many have been excavated but the relationships between the villas, their dependent settlements and modern villages is difficult to assess, partly because archaeological evidence of peasant settlement may at best be minimal. There may be little evidence to find and what there is may be obscured by the buildings of present villages. Thus it has been argued that in the *Agri Decumates* the Alemanni who reconquered the province after A.D. 260 settled in areas previously occupied by the Romans and cultivated soils they had worked, but that they did not occupy the sites of the villas themselves.[44] In Britain few cases have been traced in which modern villages rest on the foundations of Roman villas or contemporary peasant settlement. It has commonly been argued that the hiatus between Roman withdrawal and Anglo-Saxon invasions was decisive and that the overwhelming majority of settlements in lowland Britain were founded afresh by Anglo-Saxon or even later by Scandinavian invaders. But there are some indications of continuity from Roman villa to medieval village in the Darenth valley, Kent, and in Withington in Wessex.[45] Moreover, the whole question of continuity of settlement from Romano-British to Anglo-Saxon times and of Celtic 'survival' has been reopened.[46] A study of the Loire valley suggests that some twenty-six out of forty-one Frankish domains were centred on old Roman sites (Fig. 2:9), and in Gaul as a whole it has been generally accepted that many modern villages carry place-names which were originally given to Gallo-Roman estates.

In Gaul place-names offer widespread evidence of rural settlement at the time of the Roman Empire and of the essential continuity from classical to medieval times in many places, but they are a source of evidence which is much less easily handled or dated than the archaeological material. A few pre-Celtic elements have been identified, particularly in the mountainous or upland regions where archaic forms have always tended to survive, as in the Massif Central, the Alps or Pyrenees. Most of such names are attributed to the Iberians or Ligurians who were pushed south and south-west by the invading Iron Age Celts. In Auvergne and Velay they tend to occur most frequently in the area south of the Puy de Dôme and in the Allier valley (Fig. 2:10). Superimposed upon this archaic stratum of place-names, there are widely scattered elements which are associated with the Celtic occupation of Gaul, and which reveal considerable activity in the clearing of new land for settlement, though it was still land which was for the most part on easily tilled and well-drained soils and in easily accessible areas. The suffix -*ialos*, frequently becoming -*euil* in modern forms, as in *Argenteuil*, is a clearing name of this period, but many are topographical names: -*nant*, valley (and similar to Welsh) appears in *Dinant*; -*briga*, height or mountain; -*dunos*, originally a hill or hilltop, came to mean fortress or fortification or even town as a result of its early association with hilltop forts, and it is a very common element, appearing for example in *Lugdunum*, Lyon and also Leyden, in the Netherlands; *Noviodunos*, Noyon; *Melodunos*, Melun. Market or -*magus* appears in names such as *Noviomagus* (new market), Nogent and Nijmegen. Other elements such as -*duros* (fortification) and -*ritum*, (crossing) are also common. Not all of these elements, however, are good indicators of Celtic or Gallic settlement, for some of them continued to be used during and after the Roman conquest. For example, -*ialos* long continued in use during the Roman period, and so probably did -*dunos* as well.

Auvergne and Velay were regions in which Celtic settlement was considerable. The predecessors of the Gauls had 'picked out the eyes' of the land and had settled on the terraces of the Allier valley and also at the edges of the plateaus below the basalt-capped escarpments (Fig. 2:10). Sites such as these were not only sheltered and well drained, but they were at spring-lines and on soils renewed and re-fertilised by downwash from the basic volcanic rocks above. The Gauls had, indeed, almost completed the colonisation of the larger valleys in the area, had developed new clearings in the forest and had settled along routes which they had pioneered and near bridges they had built, for trade and movement were beginning to be important enough to warrant new terms like 'market' and 'crossing-point'.

In general, the expansion of the Gauls through France is fairly clearly revealed by a comparison of names, notably those ending in -*duros*, which disappeared quickly and early during the conquest, and those ending in -*ialos*, which represent later expansion. The areas of maximum density in both cases lie in the Paris basin, but the later distribution would show an extension to the south and south-west, taking place at the expense of the Iberians and Ligurians. It would, indeed, seem that the Celtic unity of Gaul was only completed under the Roman aegis, for much of this extension must have taken place after the south had been conquered by Rome. To the north-east there are few of the later Celtic names, a fact which may well be associated with the pressure of Germanic peoples.

Long after the conquest, however, Gallic terms continued to be used in the naming of the many Gallo-Roman domains which were everywhere being founded within the Empire. Suffixes -*acus* and

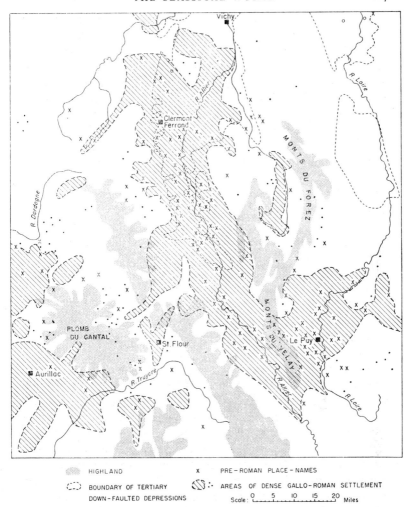

HIGHLAND
BOUNDARY OF TERTIARY
DOWN-FAULTED DEPRESSIONS

x PRE-ROMAN PLACE-NAMES
AREAS OF DENSE GALLO-ROMAN SETTLEMENT
Scale: 0 5 10 15 20 Miles

Fig. 2:10 Roman and pre-Roman settlement in Limagne. The concentration on rich and varied soils of limestone and volcanic origin is evident (after Derruau).

-*iacus* attached to a personal name refer to the rural estates of which the headquarters were the *villae*. But the suffixes themselves are Gallic indicators of possession (e.g. *fundus pauliacus* = Paul's estate). Place-names ending in -*acus* are therefore generally indicators of Gallo-Roman settlement, though two qualifications must be made.

First, it has been pointed out in a study of Aveyron that many -*ac* names of single farms or small hamlets are late medieval foundations taking the names of families who were themselves named from villages of genuine Gallo-Roman foundation. Secondly, Gallic and Latin personal names suggest early foundation during the period of Roman occupation, but the occurrence of Germanic names (as in *Carliacus, Charly*) also suggests that the habit of using -*acus* as a suffix certainly survived into the period of the late Empire and may even have persisted until early Frankish times. But in Provence, where the expansion of rural settlement in the Roman period was intense and early, the Gallic forms are supplemented by purely Latin suffixes such as -*anus* and -*anicus*.

The -*acus* names have been altered in various ways in different parts of the Roman Empire. In the southern half of France, including the centre-west, and also in Brittany they have formed the very abundant class of names which end in -ac, -at, or -as. In the northern half of France, approximately, the alterations have been towards -ay, -y, or -é and -ieu east of the Rhône. In German, -*acus* has become -ach or -ich (*Juliacum* = Julich, for example). In the Netherlands it has become -ijk, as in Doornijk, (= Tournai). In Italy it has often become -iago (Brissago = *Bruttiacum*) and in Spain -ique, a transformation which occurred before Arab times and before the softening of the c to forms such as -iche.

The distribution of -*acus* names in areas where studies have been made tend on the whole to show patterns which certainly stress the location of soils, relief and drainage suitable for early settlement, but they also tend to show concentrations along the axes of easy movement either by water or by the Roman roads, or they show the importance of the proximity of the towns. It is, of course, the importance of the town and the roads as centres from which rural colonisation was taking place which marks this period most clearly from those which follow. Names ending -*acum* are noticeably frequent in the neighbourhood of Lyon and Toulouse, for example. In Hérault they tend to concentrate on areas of well-drained loam terraces away from the danger of floods; they are frequent around Narbonne and Montpellier, and also in the neighbourhood of the *Via Domitia*, the great axis of movement from Italy to northern Spain. They avoid the poor soils to the west of Montpellier which still carry a sparse population and are covered by *garrigue*, and they avoid also the cold, thin soils of the Causses and the mountains of

Espinouse. Further north, Gallo-Roman domains were very densely packed on the fertile soils of the Allier valley and on the fertile loams which mantle the varied relief of the Pays des Buttes. The high land, the marshlands of central Limagne and the poor sandy soils of eastern Limagne were left uncultivated.

Place-names around Paris and in the middle Loire show signs of widespread clearing and settlement, but some areas, such as central Beauce, with fertile and easily cultivated soils, well away from the river routes by which Gallic settlement had begun to penetrate the area, were not seriously exploited except near the Roman roads (Fig. 3:7). Areas of poor or heavy soil, unsuitable climate or mountainous relief were largely unsettled during the Roman period but it is also evident that there were many areas of good soil and easily cleared woodland which were still unoccupied and which remained for clearing and settlement in later centuries.

The combination of evidence provided by archaeology and place-names points much more conclusively in Gaul than in England to the essential continuity of rural settlement and, of course, of language, and this has long been recognised. Nevertheless, as in the towns, the relationship between Roman villa and subsequent village settlement can only be understood in the light of drastic changes which took place in the late Roman Empire. The decline of the towns in the third century and the reversion to a much more local or regional economy in the Western Empire as a whole was accompanied by a flight to the countryside. Social and financial pressures worked together to increase the importance of the rural estates, which often became almost self-sufficient units for the production of everyday necessities. Just as artisans found themselves and their sons bound to their occupation so also the peasant became bound to the soil. Unrest, civil war and threat of barbarian invasions drove many to seek the protection of the large landowners whose villas were now often fortified. Many more peasants, however, were led by the burden of taxation to seek protection from the tax-collector, commending themselves and their lands to a powerful landowner who would make himself responsible for the payment of some taxes and who himself was frequently exempt from others. Estate, villa and dependent peasantry were thus unified in the *fundus* whose boundaries, at least in Gaul, were frequently identical with those of the Frankish domain and even with the medieval parish. Jullian has cited the large number of cases in which a parish church was founded directly on the site of the Roman villa as evidence of a very strong degree of continuity in Gaul from Roman villa to medieval village.[47] By the fourth century the villa was perhaps much closer to a manorial and feudalistic structure than it was to the plantation-style economy of the first century A.D.

Roads and the legacy of Rome

The Roman roads have proved so valuable to subsequent generations that they are still clearly visible in the modern road pattern of Western Europe. Roman roads were classified into public roads and military roads both of which, at least in principle, were paid for by the state; the vicinal routes were constructed and maintained by the *pagi* in which they lay; and private roads were built on the great rural estates. But it is as difficult to identify these by archaeological means as it would be to distinguish between British modern class A and B roads on a similar basis. Road widths and methods of construction varied independently of the roads' classifications. Some, notably in the south of Gaul, but also the road from Bavai to Tongres, were paved; others had a raised bank (the *agger*) to bear the weight of traffic and were drained by culverts at the side. These included most of the roads of eastern France. Others again were much more lightly constructed, as for example many of the roads in the military provinces of Germany and also in western France. Many bear the marks of being laid out by surveyors: their straightness, in general, is well known, and the sharp single or double angles produced by the alignment of independently surveyed sections of a road can frequently be traced. Roman roads were often the basis from which surveyors laid out the framework of centuriated lands or from which property boundaries were set out. It has been suggested for Gaul that the use of Roman roads by parish boundaries may not only reflect the existence of suitable landmarks, but that it may also reflect a progression from Gallo-Roman estate to Frankish domain and thus to medieval parish, the road continuing to define the property boundary, though the frequency with which Roman roads define parish boundaries in England, in an area where there is much less likelihood of any identity between Roman villa, Anglo-Saxon domain and medieval parish, would seem to argue against this view.

The Roman roads are known by very varied fragments of evidence besides archaeological remains and their coincidence with ancient parish boundaries.[48] Place-names may help: in England hamlets or villages with the element *strat-* (e.g. Stony Stratford) or *street* (e.g. Chilton Street) may be an indication of the line of a Roman road, as, for example, in the continuation of the Roman road south-east from Cambridge towards Colchester. On the continent such name evidence is abundant: *straten* in Belgium, *estrée* or *estrade* in France, *strada* in Spain, represent cases like that of the English *street*; other names recall milestones, boundaries, or features of the road itself, like Flé = *flexus*, bend; or Chambord = *Camboritum*, from *cambo* = bend; or Trèves from *trivium* = fork. Ancient salt roads, such as those leading away from salt-producing areas in Lorraine and Franche-Comté, may follow the line of Roman roads, e.g. between Metz and Strasbourg; so also do some of the older transhumance routes and drove roads, keeping, like many Roman roads, to watershed rather than valley routes. Literary evidence such as the Antonine itinerary, Ptolemy, the Peutinger Table and even post-Roman sources like the writings of Gregory of Tours are of major importance, of course, and give a sure indication of the best known and most travelled routes of the time.

Although the Roman network of roads in Western Europe was not conceived as a whole and was built piecemeal over a period of centuries, the pattern that emerged has a large-scale coherence (Fig. 2:5). In Italy the dominance of Rome is obvious and striking; in Spain the peripheral quadrilateral, supplemented by the grand diagonal route from Zaragoza to Mérida is perhaps the most economical way of linking the peripheral regions which were the best developed parts of Spain, while the diagonal represented a line of rapid movement to the far south-west and a military axis for the subjugation of the Meseta and the north-west. In Gaul, the focal position enjoyed by Lyon is stressed by the radiation of routes from it, no less than three crossing the Massif Central itself. To the north, it is on Reims rather than on Paris that roads converge, and Paris itself seems to lie in a transitional zone between a poorly developed west, sparsely provided with roads, and a more intensively developed east, towards the Rhine frontier. In the Rhine and Danube area the pattern is one of roads radiating from military camps well behind the frontier to join the road which ran parallel to and along the frontier itself.

Although the Roman road surveyors sometimes ignored local and parochial details of relief, soil or drainage in their concern for a direct route, the broader strategy of road location often reveals a very shrewd appreciation of natural features. In Gaul, high roads along watersheds often involved much less concern with drainage, bridging and steep gradients than a low-level valley route would have done. The use of the Alpine passes, the Gate of Carcassonne, the St Étienne corridor and the Swiss plateau from Geneva to the Rhine betrays a careful preoccupation with economy in building and with the time of the traveller. Modern lines of communication may follow the Roman roads for the same reasons but it is also evident that where the focus of movement has shifted, there has been less survival of the Roman routes into modern patterns. Paris replaced Lyon as the focus of French traffic and of its roads, so that much less of the Roman network is clearly visible in France than it is in Britain, where London is at the centre of both modern and Roman patterns.

REFERENCES

Abbreviations:

C.A.M.   *La Citta nell'alto medioevo.* Settimane di studio del centro Italiano di studi sull' alto medioevo, Spoleto, vol. 6, 1959.

C.E.H.E.   *Cambridge Economic History of Europe.* Vol. 1, *Agrarian Life of the Middle Ages,* ed. J. H. Clapham and E. Power, Cambridge, 1942; vol. 2, *Trade and Industry in the Middle Ages,* ed. M. M. Postan and E. E. Rich, Cambridge, 1952.

1. H. C. L. HAMMOND, *A History of Greece,* Oxford, 1950, pp. 109 ff.
2. E. C. SEMPLE, *The Geography of the Mediterranean Region: Its Relation to Ancient History,* London, 1932, pp. 16 ff.
3. R. HARTSHORNE, 'A functional approach to political geography', *Ann. Assoc. Amer. Geogr.,* vol. 40, 1950, pp. 95–130.
4. J. N. L. MYRES, *Geographical History in Greek Lands,* Oxford, 1949, especially chapters 6 and 7, pp. 133–71.
5. M. E. WHITE, 'Greek colonisation', *Journ. Econ. History,* vol. 21, 1961, pp. 443–54.
6. R. BLOCH, *The Origins of Rome,* London, 1960, p. 30.
7. J. WARD-PERKINS, 'Etruscan towns, Roman roads and medieval villages in the historical geography of southern Etruria', *Geogr. Journ.,* vol. 128, 1962, pp. 389–405.
8. R. BLOCH, *The Etruscans,* London, 1958, p. 135.
9. Bloch, *Origins of Rome,* p. 270.
10. M. CARY, *The Geographic Background to Greek and Roman History,* Oxford, 1949, p. 277.
11. L. HARMAND, *L'Occident Romain,* Paris, 1962, pp. 67 ff.
12. F. W. WALBANK, 'Trade and industry in the later Roman Empire in the west', *C.E.H.E.,* vol. 2, pp. 33–86.

13. STRABO. *The Geography of Strabo*, ed. H. L. Jones, 8 vols., London, 1917-26, vol. 4, ch. 1, pp. 1-2.
14. C. E. STEVENS, 'Agriculture and rural life in the later Roman Empire', *C.E.H.E.*, vol. 1, pp. 89-117.
15. Ibid., p. 95; also F. M. HEICHELHEIM, 'Effects of classical antiquity on the land', *Man's Rôle in Changing the Face of the Earth*, ed. W. L. Thomas, Chicago, 1956, pp. 165-82.
16. Stevens, *C.E.H.E.*, vol. 1, pp. 89-117.
17. R. DION, 'Introduction à l'histoire de la viticulture française', *L'Eventail de l'histoire vivante, hommage à L. Febvre*, Paris (See ch. 4-19) 1953' pp. 111-20.
18. Strabo, *Geography*, vol. 4, ch. 1, pp. 2-3.
19. Ibid., vol. 3, ch. 2, pp. 5-6.
20. Cary, *Geogr. Background to Greek and Roman History*, pp. 231-43.
21. O. DAVIES, *Roman Mines in Europe*, Oxford, 1935, p. 291.
22. Strabo, *Geography*, vol. 3, ch. 2, pp. 7-8.
23. Davies, *Roman Mines in Europe*, p. 99.
24. Walbank, *C.E.H.E.*, vol. 2, p. 35.
25. A. GRENIER, *Archéologie Gallo-Romaine*, 4 parts, 1931-1960, part 3, *L'architecture*, Paris, 1958, p. 85.
26. Ibid., p. 56.
27. Ibid., pp. 93-8.
28. Grenier, *Archéologie Gallo-Romaine*, part 2, *Les routes*, Paris, 1934, pp. 270 ff.
29. R. E. DICKINSON, *The West European City*, London, 1951, pp. 342-5.
30. J. BRADFORD, *Ancient Landscapes*, London, 1957, pp. 256-63.
31. Grenier, *Archéologie Gallo-Romaine*, part 2—*Navigation, Occupation du sol*, Paris, 1934, chapters 10-12.
32. J. HUBERT, 'Evolution de la topographie et de l'aspect des villes de Gaule du 5ᵉ au 10ᵉ siècles', *C.A.M.* 1959, vol. 6, pp. 529-58.
33. Y. DOLLINGER-LEONARD, 'De la cité romaine à la ville medievale dans la région de la Moselle et la haute Meuse', *Studien zu den Anfangen des Europäischen Stadtwesens*, ed. T. Mayer, Lindau, 1959, pp. 195-226.
34. Grenier, *Archéologie Gallo-Romaine* part 2, chapter 19.
35. S. APPLEBAUM, 'The pattern of settlement in Roman Britain', *Agric. Hist. Rev.*, vol. 11, 1963, pp. 1-14.
36. Bradford, *Ancient Landscapes*, pp. 143-217.
37. R. CHEVALLIER, 'Un document fondamental pour l'histoire de la géographie agraire: la photographie aérienne', *Etudes Rurales*, no. 1, 1961, pp. 70-'80.
38. Chevallier, 'La centuriation et les problèmes de la colonisation romaine', *Etudes Rurales*, no. 3, 1961, pp. 54-79.
39. R. BOUSSARD, 'Le peuplement de Touraine du 1ᵉʳ au 8ᵉ siècle', *Le Moyen Âge*, vol. 9, 1954, p. 261.
40. Ward-Perkins, *Geogr. Journ.*, vol. 128, 1962, pp. 389-405.
41. R. KOEBNER, 'The settlement and colonisation of Europe', *C.E.H.E.*, vol. 1, pp. 1-88.

42. H. C. DARBY, 'The clearing of the woodland in Europe', *Man's Rôle in Changing the Face of the Earth*, ed. W. L. Thomas, Chicago, 1956, pp. 183–195.

43. F. M. Heichelheim, *Man's Rôle in Changing the Face of the Earth* pp. 165–82.

44. Koebner, *C.E.H.E.*, vol. 1, p. 31.

45. H. P. R. FINBERG, *Roman and Saxon Withington*, Leicester, 1955.

46. G. R. J. JONES, 'Settlement patterns in Anglo-Saxon England', *Antiquity*, vol. 35, 1961, pp. 221–32; and Applebaum, *Agric. Hist. Rev.*, vol. 11, 1963.

47. C. JULLIAN, *La Gaule Romaine*, 8 vols, Paris, 1908–26, vol. 4, p. 375.

48. Grenier, *Archéologie Gallo-Romaine*, part 2, occupation du sol.

Part II
Evolution of Urban and Rural Settlement

CHAPTER 3

THE PEOPLING OF WESTERN EUROPE

Much had already been achieved towards the settlement of Europe even by the end of classical times. The major physical strains were already present in most Western European populations, but the modern languages and language distributions of Western Europe had still to take shape. The extent to which the modern villages and farms of Western Europe have their origin in prehistory is largely unknown, and although rural settlements in Mediterranean regions can sometimes be traced to classical origins they are, particularly in north-western Europe, more often to be traced to the pioneer farmers of a later age.

For Western Europe as a whole the period from the fall of the Roman Empire to the end of the Middle Ages was by far the most formative in terms of either the geography of language or the origins of rural settlement. On the broad canvas, the movement of whole peoples created new ethnic and linguistic patterns and profoundly modified the old ones. The age of the great migrations of the Germanic peoples—the *Völkerwanderung*—which completed the disintegration of the Roman Empire, was followed in turn by the expansion of the Slavs and by the continuation of those impulses from the east across the south Russian steppes which had had such great importance in the prehistoric movements of population. From the eighth to the tenth centuries the people of Europe were again on the move, prodded by the meteoric descent of the Scandinavians from the north and by Arab invasions in the Western Mediterranean.

It seems important to stress that populations in much of north-western Europe were still so sparsely scattered that ethnic migrations involving perhaps no more than tens of thousands of people could permanently alter the languages spoken over wide tracts of Western Europe. But after the great demographic expansion between the eleventh and the fourteenth centuries and the great age of clearing in France, the colonisation of east Germany and the Reconquista in Spain, such large-scale modifications of language distributions could not again so easily be brought about. Nor was it thought particularly desirable or politically important that they should be, until very much later times, when the identification of language with nationality began to give language distributions important political implications.

Quite apart from its intrinsic interest, the peopling of Europe in this critical period has very considerable significance in terms of political geography in providing a part of the essential background for the understanding of nationalism and the evolution of state frameworks. But, on a much more modest and local scale, the spasmodic growth and movement of population from the end of the Roman Empire to the end of the Middle Ages also involved the creation of new farms, hamlets and villages on an unprecedented scale. By 1320 the vast majority of the villages of Western Europe had been founded. Some that were founded then have since disappeared; some have been created since; and in many of those that were already founded the pattern of farms and houses has changed a great deal. But the extent of the medieval achievement and its importance in the development of the rural landscape should not be underestimated.

Before proceeding to a discussion of the evolution of settlement, it is necessary to comment briefly on the nature of the evidence from which conclusions about settlement have been reached. Basically, the evidence is of four kinds. A geographer may give prior place to the ground itself. The interpretation of site, water supply, relief, vegetation and soils in the light of what is known of contemporary societies and their equipment is of vital importance to an understanding of settlement and its development. Study of modern village patterns and their field systems on the ground frequently gives a lead to the age and conditions of initial settlement (see Chapter 5). Secondly, as in prehistory, settlement sites, cemeteries, pottery, ornaments, tools and other artefacts provide incontrovertible material evidence.[1] Once these material objects are identified and precisely located with respect to place and time (the latter a process which often involves considerable difficulty and problems), there still remains the problem of interpreting the human significance which attaches to them. Information about settlement, colonisation, economies and societies is acquired, not directly, but by inference from the nature and distribution of material objects. It is also worth noting that as more modern times are approached, the material remains of ancient societies increase in range and variety. Field boundaries, roads, marks of ancient cultivation in the form, for example, of ridge and furrow, the fabric of churches and other buildings which are still extant, all these are forms of evidence which pose problems of interpretation similar to those presented by a Bronze Age urn or piece of pottery.

Written or historical evidence has long been the mainstay of the traditional histories of the Dark Ages and of medieval settlement. The general movements of whole peoples and their battles, conquests and defeats are, of course, outlined in the chronicles, sagas and epics of more or less contemporary origin. But such accounts suffer, like all such historical sources, from the fact that they are accounts not of what actually happened, but of what the author thought happened, or, more accurately, what the author wishes to make his audience think happened. It is obvious, then, that such literary accounts are limited by the knowledge, accuracy, ideals, prejudices and attitudes of their authors even when they are more or less contemporary witnesses and even when historians have succeeded in unravelling the problems posed by a variety of texts in different versions and of different dates. Moreover, it was most often the dramatic, unusual and sudden events about which they wrote. Slow colonisation, movements of population which were part of normal everyday experience were rarely regarded as noteworthy and were therefore ignored. Conscious and unconscious selection or distortion of data is a charge which does not apply in the same way, however, to other forms of historical evidence which are very valuable for the reconstruction of the settlement history of smaller areas: charters, deeds, leases, laws and custumals, manorial accounts and surveys and other such documents of humdrum affairs. Such documents as these, frequently aristocratic or monastic in origin, and relating to land and dwellings, usually deal with the *minutiae* of a small area field by field or village by village. But the survival of detailed information of this kind is relatively rare and widely scattered, particularly for early periods.

The fourth type of evidence is place-names, frequently relict of an early age and richly informative of conditions at the time of settlement. They are a source so widely used and so important in understanding the geography of settlement that some comments must be made about their value and limitations. Compared with historical and even archaeological evidence they have one enormous advantage to the geographer, that they are widely distributed and evenly scattered. By the very nature of their survival they are, like charters, rentals or accounts, less likely to have been consciously distorted or biased by the interested witness of an author. They have mostly arisen spontaneously and probably without conscious intention.[2] But it must be remembered that, like the historical evidence, they have been filtered through men's minds, so that they are an indication of how men described a place, not necessarily how it actually was. Moreover, the interpretation and translation of place-names is a task for the philologist for it is obvious that the earliest and then the successive forms of names must be sought out and interpreted in the light of linguistic forms and laws.

With these initial qualifications in mind, however, much is to be gained from their study concerning the history and conditions of settlement and its relationship to routes and physical environment. First, the language and linguistic characteristics of the original place-name may give a valuable indication of the ethnic composition and provenance of those who settled it. Secondly, place-names may give a useful indication of the chronology of settlement and although it may frequently be impossible to pin down the origin of place-names to absolute dates, the *relative* chronology of settlement as given by them may yield invaluable conclusions about the progress of settlement in an area in relation to its accessibility or its physical conditions. Thirdly, the nature of an economy or society may be revealed in names given, and fourthly they may very often reveal a great deal of the land use of an area and the agricultural function it performed. Finally it is obvious that place-names, then as now, may be descriptive of the physical character of the places they designate and may thus characterise vegetation or soils as well as features of relief, aspect and drainage. Nevertheless, the evidence of place-names must be handled very cautiously. It is essentially linguistic evidence, and although philology may bring to bear a considerable body of linguistic rules on the elucidation of place-names and their successive forms, the extent to which place-names can be used as a basis for extrapolation to non-linguistic conclusions must necessarily be limited.

Until modern times, places would generally be given names, not by their own inhabitants, but by their neighbours. Names like Grimston or Trouville, with Scandinavian personal names plus Anglo-Saxon -*tun* or French -*ville* are thus given by a predominantly

Anglo-Saxon or French speaking population and need imply no more than one inhabitant, albeit a powerful one, with a Danish name (and he too need *not* be a Danish speaker). On the other hand, a name such as Skipton or Kirkham, which preserves evidence of a modification of the sounds of a language (*skip-*, as a Scandinavianised form of Anglo-Saxon *scīp*, sheep: *Kirk-* as a typically Scandinavianised form of Anglo-Saxon church) gives a much stronger indication of linguistic influence. So also does a name like Osmotherley, similar to Grimston, mentioned above, in that it is made up of Scandinavian personal names plus Anglo-Saxon suffix, but with the significant difference that the Scandinavian genitival *-ar* is preserved, telling us that the people who named Osmotherley retained and therefore used the Scandinavian grammatical form even though they also used the Anglo-Saxon ending *-ley* or *-leah* (clearing). Some conclusions may be reached in this way about the linguistic habits of a mixed population, but it is necessary to stress that considerable complications may exist in areas where bilingualism was normal. Place-names may have existed in two forms from very early times, and the selection of one or other of them as a normal form may be a relatively late development. This may well have been true of many places, for example, on the linguistic frontier between German and French in Alsace-Lorraine or between Walloon and Flemish in the area of modern Belgium. A British example of this kind of complication may be taken from Herefordshire, in the Golden Valley in the Black Mountains, where a large number of the Welsh names are a translation into Welsh of English names, and where the Golden Valley represents a mistranslation into English of a Welsh name.

Secondly, place-name elements associated initially with an invading group may pass into the language or the dialect of the resultant population and may thus go on to be used long after it has become irrelevant to try to distinguish between the component elements of a population on this sort of linguistic basis. Thus the suffix *-by*, frequently a good indicator of early Danish settlement of the period of the invasion in the Midlands and eastern England, is less reliable in north-western England, where suffixes in *-by* attached to Norman-French names show that the suffix *-by* had currency long after the invasion period. Similarly in Iberia, some Arabic elements passed into common usage in the Spanish language and it is thus impossible to use them as indicators of Arab settlement. Names containing words such as *atalaya* (watch-tower) or *acequia* (irrigation canal) or *noria* (irrigation wheel) are examples of this kind. Two other notes of caution must be sounded. It is also obvious, where place-names involving two linguistic components are concerned, that the dominance in place-names of one language over another does not imply a proportional superiority in numbers or a political dominance. Secondly, the survival of linguistic elements from a former population does not necessarily imply that a population speaking that language survived in that area in any considerable strength. If this were so, Indian languages would be much more commonly spoken in the U.S.A. or aborigine in Australia. Indigenous names are commonly taken over and used, often uncomprehendingly, by an immigrant population. Tautological constructions often result, as, for example in a name like *Rio Guadal*quivir, in which both Spanish and Arabic words for river occur (*guadal* from the same word as *wadi*, for river).

The dating of place-names is, obviously, fundamental to a full interpretation of settlement history, but this is very often a matter of difficulty and hazard. Surviving place-names may or may not indicate the initial settlement of an area, and in the absence of other evidence it is an assumption that places which carry Danish or Anglo-Saxon or Frankish names, for example, were first settled by Danes or Anglo-Saxons, etc. Some place-name elements were commonly used only for a relatively short period, coming into vogue and passing out of use fairly soon. In eastern England and the Midlands, -*by* is probably a case in point; -*ing* names have long been used as a touchstone of early Anglo-Saxon settlement, though it is important to distinguish the -*ingas* form, meaning 'clan of,' from other and often later forms. In Europe, -*ingen* names perform a similar function; -*lar* (as in Goslar) is regarded as a good indicator of early Germanic settlement at or before the time of the invasions. Arabic elements in Iberia and Visigothic or Burgundian elements in Iberia and France give fairly close chronological limits in their respective areas of settlement. For particular regions in eastern Germany a chronology of fashionable colonial names and clearing names can sometimes be worked out, with some indication of the provenance of immigrants. The date at which settlements are first mentioned may sometimes be a useful guide to the date of their foundation but there is a necessary condition that documents must be sufficiently numerous for it to be likely that a new settlement will be mentioned within a few years of its foundation and this is by no means always satisfied. It is, for example, only from the twelfth century in England that one can attach some weight to the date of first mention. But chronological precision is not always possible and there may remain a large residuum, perhaps including a majority of names, which cannot be assigned to a particular period with any confidence: in Germany, endings such as *-heim* and *-dorf*; in France, *-ville* or *-court*; in England *-ham* and *-ton*. Even where an absolute chronology is wanting, however, it may be possible to piece together a relative chronology of settlement within an area by using various criteria. Names of dependent hamlets or daughter settlements (such as names ending in *-thorpe*, *-cote*, *-dene*, *-wick*), sometimes implying a specialised function within a larger community (like the term *-dene*, swine pasture, or *-wick*, dairy farm) give a fairly direct implication of their secondary origin from a primary village. So also do many descriptive names such as Great and Little; Easton, Weston, Newton. Other names which are probably late in origin are those which give a direct indication of new clearing (names in *-ley* or *-field* for example).

THE GERMANIC INVASIONS

In the fateful year A.D. 410 Rome was sacked by the Visigoths only four years after a mixed band of Germanic peoples had crossed the Rhine and invaded Gaul. A generation before, the Danube frontier had been successfully pierced by Goths and Huns who had settled within the boundaries of the Empire; and in 395 in order to make its defence a more feasible task the Empire had been finally divided along a very important line through what is now Yugoslavia into Eastern and Western sections. A rump state persisted in northern Gaul, and it was not until 476 that the last Roman Emperor was deposed; but this was long after effective rule had ceased.

This is not the place for yet another inquest on the decline and fall of the Roman Empire and internal conditions within the Empire need not further concern us. But it is important to an understanding of the peopling of Europe to comment briefly on the development of new pressures of population outside the Empire.

The appearance of the Huns on the Danube frontier and in southern Russia was one of the new pressures pushing the German peoples west and south and directly threatening the frontiers of the Empire. Predominantly sheep and cattle herders, nomadic and mobile, and masters of the horse and the art of cavalry warfare, the Huns had shifted their attention westwards in the third and fourth centuries A.D. after having been thrown back from the frontiers of China about A.D. 170. To classical writers their Mongoloid characteristics represented a new physical type and the extent to which their habits and methods of war were governed by the horse was also something new. It had been the Huns who broke the frontier of the Danube in the fourth century, and in the fifth, already mingled with Germanic and probably Slav stock, they had established a short-lived but extensive empire in central Europe. As an element in the peopling of Europe, their contribution was, however, negligible.

It was quite otherwise, of course, with the Germanic peoples, pressed into movement by the pressure of the Huns from the east and attracted by the splendour and material wealth of the Empire. First identifiable as a linguistic group about 700–600 B.C. in the west Baltic area of Scania, Bornholm, Gothland and north Germany between the Rhine and the Oder, the Germans spread slowly southwards, helped on, perhaps, by the wetter and cooler conditions of the sub-Atlantic period from 500 B.C. or thereabouts. By 200 B.C. they had reached the river Main and by 114 B.C. they had appeared on the Italian frontiers of Rome. From then on, their culture and economy had been gradually and profoundly affected by their contacts with the Roman Empire, particularly on or near the frontier regions. Trade had revealed the wealth of material goods to be had within the Empire and a network of trade routes had developed over the whole of central Europe.[3] The copper and tin of Bohemia nourished trade over the Brenner pass and the Julian Alps from Italy; Baltic amber and probably German slaves moved south by way of the Oder or the Vistula to the Danube frontier. Thuringian tribes flourished through their trade in Roman bronze, pottery and glass at a junction of routes which led northwards, to the sources of Baltic amber, westwards to the Rhine frontier either by way of the Ruhr, Sieg and Lippe valleys, or by way of the Wetterau and the Main. In the later days of the Empire the western routes seem to have been less important than more easterly routes passing from the Baltic to Hercynian Poland and then by way of the Tisza to the Danube, or by way of the Dniester to the Black Sea. Gold, metals and amber thus bypassed Western Europe altogether along this easterly route, by which the Goths also were moving south-east in the third century and by which the Runic alphabet probably spread in south-east Europe and Scandinavia. Sir Mortimer Wheeler sums up the significance of this penetration of Roman goods into barbarian Europe: 'They are milestones on the barbarian road to Eldorado'.[4] The external pressures from the Huns and the internal pressure of population, all the more acutely felt because of German reluctance to win new land for farming from the sacred virgin forest, were pressing the Germans forward; the Empire, on the other hand, was a world of luxury and plenty to be taken over and enjoyed.

Archaeology and place-names suggest that the movements of peoples and the ways in which they settled were much more complex and confused than the simplified accounts of the chroniclers make out. Tribal confederacies were formed and broken up; tribal groupings were unstable and inconstant, and most groups were probably mixed. Nevertheless, it is to some extent useful to distinguish between eastern and western groups among the German peoples. The eastern groups have been characterised as predominantly pastoral, more concerned with warfare and more mobile than the western Germans. It was into the hands of these eastern Germans that the trade routes from eastern Europe to the Baltic had fallen. These, then, were peoples who were, because of their economy and society, fewer in numbers and more mobile than their western counterparts, and who were able to move rapidly over long distances into the wealthiest and most densely populated parts of the Roman Empire. It was, perhaps, because of these characteristics that they tended to constitute a minority among the populations they invaded, establishing new kingdoms, laws and lordships but making relatively little permanent impression on rural settlement and customs or on language.

The Goths, who are first heard of in the west Baltic and who were later to be found located both to the east and west of the lower Dniester (the eastern or Ostrogoths, and the western or Visigoths), are perhaps the best known of the east German groups. Pushed on by the Huns they invaded the frontier in the fourth century. It was the Visigoths who sacked Rome in 410, but only a few years later they had been replaced in Italy by an Ostrogothic kingdom and they themselves had established a Visigothic kingdom in Iberia and Aquitaine. Yet their numbers were small, estimated at 100,000 or so, and their impact on settlement was relatively slight, confined chiefly to a few areas in Aquitaine and north-western Iberia where place-names in -*ville* or -*villa* with Gothic personal name give an indication of minority groups of Suevi and Visigoths among a dominantly romanised population.[5] (see Fig. 3:8). The Suevi, who gave their name to Swabia, also followed the Vandals across the Rhine in 406, and settled, like the Visigoths in north-western Iberia. The brief sojourn of The Vandals, yet another group of east German people, stayed briefly in south-west Spain before they moved on in 429 to the conquest of North Africa and their stay is recalled in the name of Andalusia. They, too, attracted by the wealth of a province renowned for its grain, were no more than a small minority, perhaps 80,000 in all, and they have left little trace. The Burgundians carved out a short-lived kingdom in the upper Saône which lasted till 534, gave their name to a province of France and left a few place-names. The Lombards similarly left a mark on the north Italian plain, establishing an important kingdom with its capital at Pavia, and settling in sufficient numbers to leave place-names characteristically ending in -*fara* (= kinship group). Other groups of the eastern Germans, the Gepids in central Europe, or the Herules, pirates and raiders with the Saxons in the Channel, have left even slighter traces.

The so-called western group of Germanic peoples shared rather different characteristics. They had long been in contact with the Rhine–Danube frontier of the Empire, had supplied settlers and recruits for the frontier regions of the Empire, and had succeeded in wresting the *Agri Decumates* from the Romans. On the whole they were more concerned with agriculture and their economy was more intensive than that of the eastern Germans. Population densities were probably higher than further east. The western Germans were able to build on an economy and culture already well developed by the strong Celtic substratum in south-west Germany which is well attested archaeologically and represented by a fairly large number of place-names.

In northern Germany west of the Weser and in the whole of south and south-west Germany, the Celts and even earlier peoples have left some traces in the form of place-names: in river and hill names, as they did much later in England; in the form of names like *Wal-* and *-walchen*, which have in south Germany roughly the same significance of 'foreigner' as did the term 'Welsh' and some place-names in *wal-* in England; and in the form of Celtic suffixes in *-dunum, -duros, -magnos, -ritum* etc. discussed above. These latter forms are, however, often as much Romano-Celtic as purely Celtic in origin. In the Rhineland and the south-west the extent of Roman influence is felt in the form of Romano-Celtic elements in place-names as well as in the abundant archaeological wealth of the region. Indeed, the wealth of *-acum* and *-anum* names points to a considerable degree of continuity in the rural settlement of the area from the Gallo-Roman or Romano-Celtic estate to the medieval village.

In the Rhineland, Celt and German probably had some form of the heavy plough, practised common-field farming, perhaps with a two-course, crop-fallow rotation or, as seems more likely, a form of infield-outfield farming. Yet although arable farming was becoming increasingly important, cattle were valued more than anything else and religious taboos prevented much clearing of the forest. For this reason they preferred expansion and conquest to the extension of cultivation around existing settlements. The western Germans, then, were more sedentary and more numerous than the eastern groups. And they moved into parts of the Roman Empire which were less intensively developed and less densely peopled than the Mediterranean regions. They moved slowly and over short distances across the Rhine and Danube, but they affected settlement and linguistic distributions much more profoundly.

Of the west German groups the relatively cultured and advanced Alemanni, most highly romanised of the German peoples since their home had been in the *Agri Decumates*, moved into Switzerland, Alsace and Burgundy; the Bavarians spread southwards across the Danube. From north-west Germany the Saxons raided, traded and then settled round the shores of the Channel in the Pas de Calais as well as south-east England. In the Rhineland area the Salian Franks moved across the lower Rhine towards the Lys basin, reaching the Somme by A.D. 431. To the south the Ripuarian Franks conquered Cologne by 463 and inflicted a final defeat on the rump Gallo-Roman state of northern Gaul at Soissons in 483. A Frankish state was established which came, in the sixth century, to include all Gaul and most of what is now western and southern Germany. To the west and north the repercussions of German movement reached Brittany and Scandinavia.

In the west, Celtic groups from Britain migrated to Brittany and even set up a colony in north-west Spain which sent its bishops to Visigothic councils. In the sixth century, too, Scandinavian peoples were moving west and south-west. Angles invaded eastern and midland England from what is now Schleswig-Holstein; Swedish groups moved from Uppland into the Danish area and into western Norway across the central depression of Sweden. And in the wake of this generally westward movement of Celt, German and Scandinavian came the steady expansion of the Slav peoples and the more dramatic and also more ephemeral occupation of central Europe by the Avars.

Place-names are the major source for the reconstruction of the geography of early settlement[6] but there is one factor which makes for greater difficulty in Germany than further west. It is simply that in central Germany at least the Germans had been in occupation for a very long period, so that the identification or dating of various place-name strata is more difficult than in Britain or France where in many regions Germanic or Scandinavian peoples followed Roman and Celtic groups. The oldest stratum of Germanic names occurs within the core area of settlement in north Germany and usually on light, easily cleared and easily tilled soils which were also well drained. They include a few names in -ide or -ithi, now represented by some endings in -de; -mar and -lar elements as in Weimar or Goslar are also characteristically North German, occurring only in the area from Thuringia to Westphalia and Hesse. These are early and in Thuringia they have been ascribed to a period roughly contemporary with the Roman Empire. Early names ending in -leben in Thuringia have been associated with the Anglian settlement of the area in the fourth century A.D. since they are related to the element -lev found in Sweden and also in Jutland. Yet the fact that -lev or -leben does not occur in England may be interpreted as throwing doubt upon this identification and some have thought of it as a later place-name characteristic of the seventh or the eighth century. It is also possible that it may be an early naming habit which passed out of fashion by the time of the Anglian invasion of England.

Further controversy surrounds the much more important problems presented by Germanic names in -ingen and -heim (Fig. 3:1). Names deriving from ingas (folk) are widespread in Germany, northeastern France, Burgundy, Italy, the Low Countries, Scandinavia and England, though in various forms. In Germany they are first associated with descriptive elements and only later with personal names or folk names at the time of the invasions. They are most common in north-west Germany. Another early form is represented by -heim, starting at the time of the invasions but with a longer period of fashion lasting to the seventh or eighth century. This, too, is found outside Germany. In Scandinavia it is widespread (in Denmark alone there are over 200), and as -ham it is one of the most common endings in England and the Low Countries. The interpretation of these two forms has caused difficulty, however. In south Germany names in *-ingen* and names in *-heim* show distinct distributions. In the Rhine rift valley *-ingen* names are on the best soils of the terraces or the scarpfoot zone of the Black Forest; *-heim* names are on slightly less favourable sites. This led some

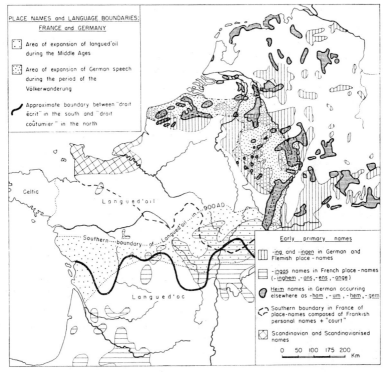

Fig. 3:1 Settlement and linguistic boundaries in France and Germany (after Bach, Schwarz, Brunhes).

authors to conclude that *-ingen* must be characteristic of settlement by the Alemanni, the first Germanic occupants of the area, and *-heim* of Frankish settlement, since they followed and conquered the Alemanni. But in France, *-ingen* occurs where the Alemanni never settled; *-heim* occurs widely in parts of Germany where the Franks never settled, and is rare in France where they did. In England *-ingas* is regarded as essentially a folk name, and this is probably true of many Germanic forms, the folk-name being commonly used at an earlier time than personal names of individual leaders.

It has been very shrewdly suggested that at a time of instability and movement a place might well be known by the folk-name of its occupants, and that it would only be at a later stage of permanence and stability that a place would be known by its farm buildings and its houses, and thus by the name -*heim*. There are, indeed, records of changes from -*ingen* to -*ingheim*, and in England it is generally agreed that -*ingham* forms tend to be later than -*ing* alone. This, indeed, is the view which fits the evidence best. In south Germany -*ingen* belongs, then, to the period of the invasions and is frequently to be found on the best and most easily worked soils. Villages on them tended to become large at an early date and to have remained larger than their neighbours. Other scraps of evidence point also to an early origin. Names with -*ingen* are found to correspond more frequently than other names to early church dedications such as those to St Martin; they are more often associated with mother parishes than with daughter chapelries. Niemeier has shown that in Württemberg, 188 out of 526 places with Frankish archaeological remains had names in -*ingen* and 80 in -*heim*, but that no other single place-name ending occurred more than 32 times.[7] Further north in an area of rare -*ingen* names, -*heim* was the most common place-name ending associated with the early form of field system known as the *eschflur* (see below p. 226).

In western Germany and parts of France, -*ingen* and -*heim* are useful indicators of early German settlement at the time of the invasion period or soon after it. As in England, village settlement subsequently expanded in the seventh to the ninth centuries, and its spread is indicated by the occurrence of different place-name forms, frequently grouped for the sake of convenience as 'late primary' names. Their distribution over the face of the land portrays graphically the expansion of settlement from the most favourable areas of settlement to slightly remoter regions, higher latitudes, and more difficult or less fertile soils, and they bear witness, too, to the great movement of clearing and expansion that went on quietly in much of western Europe long before the final exuberant phase of clearing from the eleventh to the thirteenth centuries. In Germany late primary names throw light on the recolonisation of southern Germany by the Germans at the expense of the Slavs and on the beginnings of that push to the east which culminated centuries later in the great drive of the Germans across the North German Plain.

The later primary names are in some ways less easy to use than

either the early -*ingen* forms or the late clearing names of the eleventh
to the thirteenth centuries, for they often stayed in fashion for many
years in different parts of the area. A fashionable form during the
German readvance across Bavaria to the east in the eighth century
was -*hausen* which occurs on good soils, while further north in the
Rhineland it occurs long after the period of earliest occupation and
occurs on poorer soils. Another such late primary name is -*hofen*,
occurring in south Germany and in Westphalia, common from the
eighth century but most frequent and fashionable in the ninth.
One of the most common village names in much of central Germany
is -*dorf*, occurring quite early in the southern Rhineland, but associated also with the eastward expansion of settlement by the Germans
to the eleventh century and even the first half of the twelfth century in Upper Austria (Fig. 3:2). It thus overlaps the names characteristic of the great age of clearing and German eastward expansion
which will be dealt with later. Because of this the distribution
of -*dorf* names is especially interesting. In the whole of western
Germany, where the best soils were already taken up by the ninth
century, -*dorf* names are relatively rare except between the Meuse
and Moselle, and they seem to represent an infilling of new subsidiary
settlements in the interstices of the existing pattern. But to the east
of a line parallel to the Triassic scarplands of Franconia and running
roughly from Würzburg to Ulm, -*dorf* villages increase dramatically
in frequency. A similar increase in the frequency of -*dorf* names
occurs also in the moraine and outwash country of the Bavarian
Foreland, and in the Danube valley below Regensburg it seems clear
that -*dorf* names represent primary settlement. Indeed, it seems
reasonable to conclude that although in western Germany -*dorf*
names even in the ninth century are characteristic of secondary
settlement, in central and eastern Germany -*dorf* was a name, like
-*ton* in England, which was applied for a long period and was
characteristic of primary settlement on good and mediocre soils
alike. It was a name repeated again and again in the process of east
German colonisation in the Danube valley, Upper Austria, Carinthia,
Silesia and the margins of the Bohemian massif. It frequently occurs
in association with settlement forms which are undoubtedly late.

   Place-names in -*weiler*, most common in south-western Germany
in old romanised country, were once thought to be a Germanisation
of Latin *villa* and thus indicative of former Roman settlement continued into German times, but -*weiler* villages show little corres-

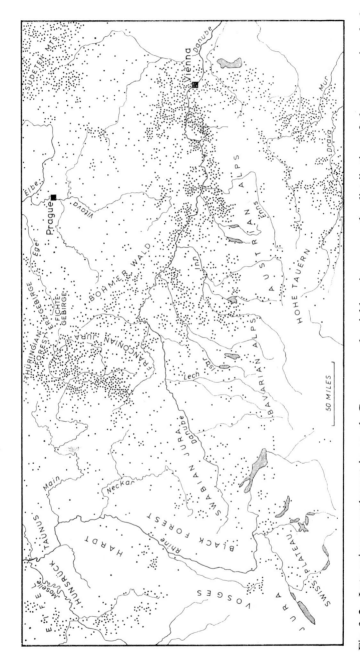

Fig. 3:2 Late primary settlement in south Germany and neighbouring areas: the distribution of place-names in -*dorf* (after Bach).

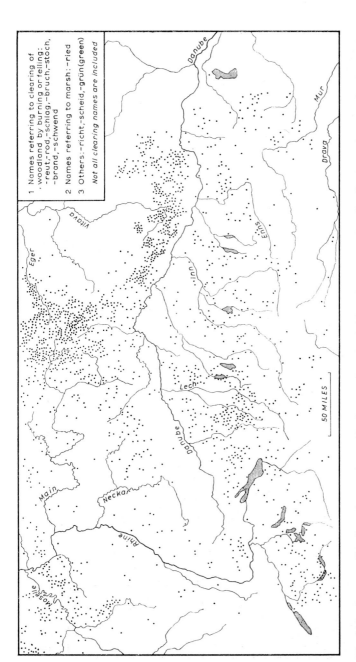

Fig. 3:3 Late medieval settlement in south Germany and neighbouring areas: the distribution of some clearing names (after Bach).

pondence to Roman archaeological sites and are so frequently on less favourable soils that they are now thought to be of much later origin, comparable with the French place-name ending *villiers* in being a derivation from medieval Latin and in representing late primary settlement.

The participation of western Germany in the great age of clearing which swept western Europe in the eleventh to the thirteenth centuries is abundantly illustrated in a great range of place-names which characteristically bear witness to the methods of clearing that were used and frequently to the type of vegetation that had been cleared (Fig. 3:3). Names in *-scheid* or *-schlag*, some names in *-au, -stock* (stump), names in *-reut* and *-rod* refer to the cutting down and clearing of woodland; names such as *-brand* and *-bronn* show that the burning of woodland was widely practised; topographical names, such as those ending in *-ried* (marshy place), *-hurst* (hill) or *-hagen* (heath) become much more common in this late phase. There is

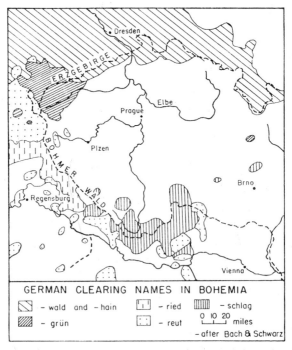

Fig. 3:4 The distribution of German clearing names in Bohemia (after Bach and Schwarz).

indeed a regional variation in the distribution of such names which has suggested, in east Germany at least, the possibility of discovering significant groupings and directions of colonial movement by plotting the forms of clearing names. For example, the distribution of names in -*schlag* suggests that the clearing of the southern Böhmerwald was from Austria and Bavaria (Fig. 3:4). In western and southern Germany, too, fashionable clearing names varied from place to place. West of the Rhine in Luxemburg, the Palatinate and the Eifel, -*scheid* is a name which is widely distributed and gives a hint of population pressure leading to a concerted attack upon the marginal soils and sites where it chiefly occurs. In the margins of the Black Forest the sequence from Roman remains and early place-names in the Rhine rift valley to the late clearing names at the very margins of woodland which is still uncleared provides a textbook example of the progress of settlement from productive soils and favourable sites to the most marginal of settlement sites by the end of the Middle Ages (Fig. 3:5). The colonisation of the

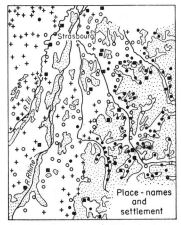
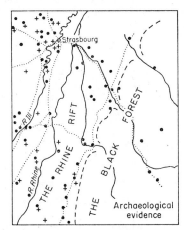

Early primary: + -ingen,-heim,-stedt,-lar.
Late primary: 6th to 9th century
o -weiler,-ach,-kirch,-zell,-hausen,
  -dorf, '-hofen,-hurst.
Clearing & secondary: 9th to 12th century
• -bach,-tal,-berg.
■ -au,-brunn,-brand,-wald,-reute,
  -schwanden,-bühl,-sand.

• Roman archaeological remains
  and settlement
⋯ Roman roads
  Alemannic and Frankish
+ archaeological finds

Fig. 3:5   Settlement in south-west Germany

Taunus massif is very graphically summed up in the pattern of its place-names on the modern map (Fig. 3:6). The block-faulted massif of the Taunus, rising 2000–2600 feet above sea-level, presents a steep scarp to the south but drops more gently to the Lahn valley in the north. Its metamorphic rocks, chiefly quartzites, sandstones and slates, have yielded thin poor soils, much of which are still forested, but on its flanks and especially to the south are patches of fertile loam soils. These are remarkably well picked out by the

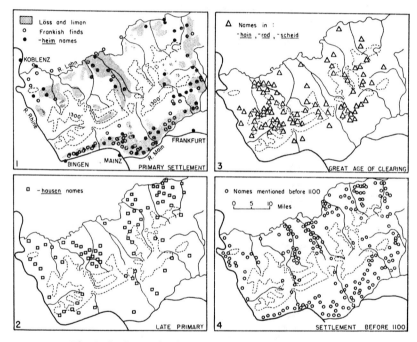

Fig. 3:6   Stages in the settlement of the Taunus region

distribution of Frankish finds and early place-names in -*heim*. Late primary names in -*hausen* suggest a filling in of settlement on the fertile loams of the lowland areas in the south below the scarp, and the beginnings of settlement on the more easily accessible northern slopes. The upper valleys and the watersheds were still left, however, and it was not until the age of clearing that these relatively unattractive areas were tackled.

In western Germany and Switzerland as a whole only the poorest lands remained for settlement by the eleventh century and almost all the better sites had been taken up. Further east this was less true, so that many lowland locations were still available in, for example, southern Bavaria, where only the best valley sites had been taken up. Marshy places in the poorly drained outwash plains and moraines of the interfluves were left for new settlement in the age of clearing, and many of these villages carry the name *-ried*, a 'marshy place'. In the whole of central Germany the approach of the German tide of immigration to the Böhmerwald and the Erzgebirge is very clearly evident, and many of these clearing villages are still characterised by settlement forms typical of the eastern German colonisation movement see Chapter 5).

In France, too, the history of settlement in the Dark Ages can be read to some extent in place-names.[8] German invaders brought with them names in *-ingas* or *-ingos* which have evolved into very different forms in different areas. In Lorraine they have become *-ange* or *anges*; in Franche-Comte *-anges* or *-ans*; in Picardy *-ingues*; in Savoy and Burgundy *inges*, and in Switzerland *-ens*. German names in *-heim* have counterparts in *-ham* in England, *-hjem* in Denmark and Norway, *-gem* in Flanders and *-um* in other parts of the Low Countries (Fig. 3:1).

In addition to these wholly Germanic names, two other forms are associated with the period of invasions and the period of consolidation which followed. They are names compounded of a personal name plus *-ville* or *-court*, very common in France north of the Loire and particularly thick in the eastern part of the Paris basin. Again, their significance is disputed. The personal names are frequently Germanic: Frankish in northern Gaul, Gothic in the south-west, and Burgundian in the Saône basin. Their distribution and their occasional association with the grave goods of Germanic warriors argue that they represent the establishment of a personal dominion by a minority of Germanic settlers over a predominantly Gallo-Roman population. It is possible, of course, that the fashion of giving Germanic personal names spread rapidly among a purely Gallo-Roman population and there is no way of disproving this possibility, yet it seems likely that Frankish settlers in the Paris area, for example, frequently split old Gallo-Roman domains and settled on one part of them, thus producing place-names in *-ville* or *-court* side by side with older names in *-acum*. Thus, Billancourt would be formed from a part of the Gallo-Roman domain represented by the nearby village of Passy, both now absorbed in the spread of Paris.

In general, archaeology, place-names and dialect study suggest a progressive diminution of Germanic influence in Merovingian Gaul from north-east to south and south-west. Immediately beyond what are now the German-speaking areas of Alsace and Lorraine there is a wide zone in which -*ingen* names represent a settlement of German family groups moving slowly and perhaps even relatively peacefully, occupying old cultivated land and also clearing new lands. In the Jura the Burgundian folk settled in the valley of the Doubs, and very soon after their establishment nibbled at the edge of the forests which had been left uncleared by Gallo-Roman settlement, leaving place-names in -*anges* (*ingas*) as their witness. Beyond the zone of fairly dense and almost contiguous Frankish settlement in north-eastern France, -*ville* and -*court* names tend to predominate in the old settled areas and as late as A.D. 900 there were also traces of Frankish modes of speech in the area. In the equivalent zone of Franche-Comté and Burgundy, dialect words of Alemannic and Burgundian origin occur. Beyond the Seine the frequency of Frankish personal names with -*ville* and -*court* (Fig. 3:1), suggesting the presence of a small Frankish minority, falls off considerably and there is also a corresponding thinning out of the archaeological evidence of cemeteries and grave goods. It is true that Frankish settlers, probably at a period later than that of the initial invasion, seem to have cleared and cultivated much of the forested lands of central Beauce, potentially fertile but still untouched by the Romans (see Fig. 3:7), yet it is not far to the south of this area that Frankish place-name evidence becomes very rare indeed. South of the Loire Frankish words are no longer to be found in the speech of the tenth century.

To the west, Frankish influence in settlement, like that of the Romans before them, faded away towards the margins of Brittany, giving place to a different cultural tradition which had much in common with south-west England in speech, place-names (in, for example, the frequency of *pen*-, *tre*- and -*pol*) and Dark Age Christianity. The limit of Breton speech, like that of Cornish, contracted to the west during the Middle Ages, but some indication of the extent of former Breton influence seems to be given by evidence which suggests the existence in Frankish times of a line of fortified settlements which separated Frank from Breton and Frank from Visigoth to the south. Such evidence is largely in the form of place-names incorporating the term *guerche*, etymologically similar to German *werke* and English *work* but indicating fortification. Place-names of this kind do not always occur in naturally defensible places, however, and only rarely on hilltops, and the fact that they are more commonly found on fertile soils near Roman roads seems to suggest that they may have been essentially fortified Frankish agricultural settlements.

In the southern half of France, Germanic settlement has left very few traces, least of all in Provence and Languedoc where continuity from classical times was most complete. A few groups of *-ingas* names (ending now in *-ens*) amounting to no more than a fifth of the total of Gallo-Roman names in the area of Toulouse bear witness to Gothic and Vandal settlement. Visigothic settlement in the Garonne basin, Basque settlement in the south-west and Visigothic or even, perhaps, Saxon settlement in the Charente basin were never able to predominate against the great weight of established Gallo-Roman tradition. Clearing and cultivation had in general already gone much further in the south and cultivable land was much more fully exploited, as for example the distribution of place-names in *-acum* and *-anum* around Albi shows.

The impact of the Germanic invasions on France and the Low Countries and the subsequent period of consolidation and expansion in Merovingian Gaul has been discussed very largely in terms of place-names. In a more general way it is clear that the various boundaries associated with Germanic influence sweep across the country, fanning out from the north and east in a great series of arcs pivoted like a military movement on the bastion of the Swiss Alps. Two of these boundary zones and their evolution seem to warrant further comment: the cultural contrast between northern and southern France, and the linguistic boundary in the east between French and German or Flemish and French, of which the latter will be chosen here because of the greater intensity with which it has been studied.

The cultural contrast between northern and southern France, which is one of the most important features of the historical geography of that country and one which is still very strongly impressed upon its landscapes, is clearly related to the persistence of Roman tradition in the south and the superimposition of Frankish traits in the north, though these are by no means the only factors involved. Many traits have been used to define various aspects of the transitional zone between these northern and southern cultural provinces

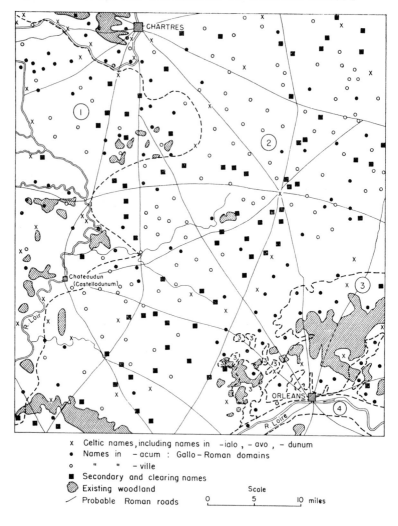

x   Celtic names, including names in   – ialo , – avo , – dunum
●   Names in   – acum : Gallo – Roman domains
○   "   "   – ville
■   Secondary and clearing names
◗   Existing woodland   Scale
╱   Probable   Roman roads   0   5   10 miles

of France (Fig. 3:1). The most obvious is the contrast in dialect and
linguistic usage between the *langue d'oc* of southern France and the
langue d'oil of the north, the former more closely related to classical
Latin, the latter more strongly affected by Frankish and Celtic elements. The boundary between them has fluctuated since the early
Middle Ages and the time of primary settlement, and there has been
a general tendency for the *langue d'oil* to expand southwards at the

Fig. 3:7 The settlement of Beauce (after Dauzat). Key to the numbers given on the map: 1. Plateau limon capping watersheds and clay-with-flints exposed on slopes. 2. Plateau limon capping watersheds with clays and limestones exposed on slopes. 3. Sands of Sologne and Orléannais, overlying limestones. 4. Loire valley, moderately incised into the plateau surface, and consisting of a wide flood plain and well-drained low terraces. Early settlement was sparse, but Roman clearing had made some inroads onto the plateau as well as the river valley. Yet it is evident in the neighbourhood of Orléans that proximity to the town was sometimes preferred to the richer soils on the limon. Frankish settlement, indicated by names in -*ville*, does, however, show a marked preference for the light soils and both clay-with-flints and sandy soils tended to be avoided. Secondary and clearing names of the later middle ages occur in the central zone of the plateau which had been least accessible from the river valleys and from both Chartres and Orléans.

expense of *langue d'oc*, partly because of the predominance of northern France and Paris in the history of the country.

Brunhes and other geographers of the French school drew attention early in this century to a second contrast, that between *droit écrit* and *droit coutoumier*. In the south, written law based on Roman foundations survived to the end of the *ancien régime*, whereas legal practice in the north depended on the customary law of precedent in a way similar to that of England and Germany. Thirdly, the boundary zone follows approximately two important political boundaries of the Dark Ages: that of the residual Gallo-Roman state, focused on the Paris basin, which survived until 486; and that of the Frankish kingdom which succeeded it and which for a time marched with the Visigothic kingdom to the south. It would be difficult, however, to find much justification in the later political history of France for these north–south divisions, for they disappeared with the Frankish conquest of the south in 507, and it is, indeed, the later political history of France which has done most to obscure and minimise them. Yet another type of contrast developed during the Middle Ages. The architecture of the southern area, more accomplished during the Dark Ages than that of the north because of its retention of the classical tradition, remained faithful to Romanesque practice even when a new and youthful mode had spread widely to the south and south-west from the area between the Loire and Rhine, the original home of the Gothic arch and the perpendicular emphasis in building which is so expressive of the new spiritual values and aspirations of the northern area in the eleventh, twelfth and thirteenth centuries.

A further symptom of the cultural contrast between north and south is the retention of older farming traditions in the south at a time when a new agricultural technology, more suited to soil and weather conditions and permitting a more intensive use of the land was developing in and spreading from the north. To the end of the eighteenth century the light plough was still widely used in the south (see p. 203), compact fields were normal and open-field farming weakly developed. In the north, open-field farming, the wheeled plough and stronger manorial organisation represent another and very important facet of this cultural complex. Many minor features of the landscape express other cultural differences: the style of farmhouses, the pitch of roofs, and the contrast between the retention of the hollow Roman tiles in the south and the use of flat tiles in the north.

The roots of this cultural division must surely lie in prehistory, though historians have disagreed as to the relative contribution to it of various cultural elements. The continuing importance of Celtic tradition in the north and the relatively high degree of romanisation in the Mediterranean south of France is very evident and so also is the greater intensity of settlement and development in the south long

7 *Nucleated settlement*, irregular open fields and enclosures in western France between Cognac and Jarnac. The concentration on vines is evident and has been important here from the seventeenth century.

VALLISOLETVM.

8 *Valladolid, Old Castile*. This view, by Hoefnagel (1563–7), shows suburban expansion beyond the medieval walls. Walled and irrigated gardens contain vines and fruits. The rural scene depicts a *noria* irrigation wheel and contemporary methods of threshing and winnowing (from Braun and Hogenberg, *Civitates, Orbis Terrarum*, 1572–1618).

9 *Rural landscape near Cavaillon, east of Avignon.* Intensive cultivation with irrigation on small peasant farms in the lower Rhône. Dense rural settlement and dispersion of farmsteads are characteristic, though much of this dispersion has taken place since the end of the eighteenth century.

before the Germanic invasions. Frankish settlement in the north undoubtedly served to accentuate the contrast, bringing new differences in language, dialects and customs, but it does seem likely that there has been too much of a tendency to see this cultural contrast emerging ready-made by the end of Roman or Frankish times. The great medieval surge of activity which was shared by Britain, Germany and the Low Countries as well as northern France was responsible for many of the new developments in rural settlement, architecture, manorial organisation and agrarian systems. Older divisions may have been accentuated in the process but new ones were certainly created. Indeed, the locations of many of the cultural boundaries mentioned above seem to have been a product of new agricultural expansion and rural settlement in areas which had been largely waste and forest when they divided Frank from Visigoth.

The transitional zone between *langue d'oc* and *langue d'oïl* stretches across a part of France in which regions of poor soil and difficult terrain are separated only occasionally by lowland zones of easily worked, fertile soils and early settlement. The Charente basin in the centre-west is one such area, all but surrounded by regions of heavy, acid soils on the ancient rocks of Armorica and the Massif Central, or by the light, sandy soils flanking the alluvial gravels of the Gironde to the south. Within the Massif itself, there are the two downfaulted basins of the upper Loire and the Allier valleys with richer soils and milder climates. Eastwards again the Saône and the Doubs follow a fertile lowland corridor between the Massif Central and the Alps. As a whole, then, this is a zone in which much late clearing and settlement was to be expected except for the narrow corridors of precocious early settlement in the Allier valley and in Burgundy. When it occurred, however, clearing tended to be more active from the north than from the south, perhaps because of a stronger manorial organisation, a greater pressure of population, and the possession of more efficient means for the exploitation of resources.[9] New northern traits were sometimes imposed upon the older settled southern areas in the process, blurring the transition from north to south in culture and economy. Thus, in Limagne, the basin of the Allier valley, the Gothic architecture of the town churches contrasts with the Romanesque tradition of the countryside. Strong manorial organisation, inspired by northern practice, succeeded in imposing upon an area which was otherwise characterised by southern traits in its agriculture, a regular division of agricultural lands into long, narrow strips organised into furlongs and open fields. Yet this was not an area in which the heavy plough was used at this time.

The problem of the origin of the linguistic frontier in Belgium has called forth a large bibliography and much controversy, which has sometimes generated more heat than light. The study of G. des Marez, still important as a pioneer study in settlement, relying as it did on evidence drawn from archaeology, customary law, dialect, and place-names as well as the available chronicles, took the view that the creation of the linguistic frontier was more or less complete by the eighth or ninth century, and that the most formative phase was in the late fourth century.[10] Des Marez concluded that even in the fourth century the Romans had abandoned the Rhine frontier for a defensive system of forward posts reaching into the Lys basin from a base defined by the line of the Roman road from Cologne through Tongres and Bavai to Arras and the neighbourhood of Boulogne. The Salian Franks, allowed to settle in the heaths and marshes of Toxandria in North Brabant, slowly filtered south-westwards along the valleys of the Scheldt and Lys, reoccupying formerly cultivated lands in a movement of pioneer farming families. Settlement was channelled in this direcion by the attraction of light, easily cultivated soils, abundant meadow in the river valleys and by the barriers presented by the existence of forest to the north, and to the south by the presence of the Roman frontier posts, uncleared forests, and Roman-occupied lands beyond. It was not a wave of invaders 'sweeping the Romans and their institutions before them, but a slow infiltration of groups of families', which was said to have left its mark by place-names in -*selle* and variants.

It now seems likely, however, that this interpretation is too simple, and is insufficiently critical of the evidence. Verlinden points out that there is no real evidence that the Romans abandoned their Rhine frontier or that the Tongres-Bavai-Arras road ever carried more than the kind of defences normal on major roads in the neighbourhood of the Rhine frontier.[11] The documentary evidence certainly supports the argument that the Salian Franks penetrated Roman defences in mid-fifth century, but they were conquerors who established themselves, not in the poorly developed and unattractive marsh, forest and heath of the north, which indeed they left deserted, but in the developed and populated lands of the south, to which they came as a ruling minority soon assimilated to the Belgo-Roman population and their language.

According to Verlinden it was not until the Ripuarian Franks began to settle in this deserted area in the seventh and eighth centuries that it received a definitively Flemish population and only between the ninth and eleventh centuries that the reclamation of marsh and the foundation of urban settlement helped to fill the many gaps in primary settlement. The sparsity of archaeological evidence of pagan Frankish settlement in the north compared with its relative abundance in Walloon Flanders argues in favour of Verlinden's thesis, and so does the discovery that many of the place-names in -*selle* are of much later origin than des Marez thought.

THE ARABS

The age of ferment in which so much of the ancient, classical world was lost but in which so much of the foundations of modern Europe were laid continued almost without break until the tenth century. The movement of the Germans overlapped the expansion of the Slavs; the expansion of the Slavs was cut across by new incursions from the south Russian steppes of nomadic, mobile warrior peoples —first the Avars, then the Bulgars with whom the Slavs were inextricably mixed, and then the Magyars in the late ninth and tenth centuries. These movements laid the foundations of modern linguistic and ethnic distributions in east-central Europe and eastern Europe, but they concerned Western Europe only marginally.[12] The Arab and Scandinavian expansions were both, however, fundamentally important for the settlement of Western Europe. The settlement of the Moors in Iberia and of the Scandinavians in the British Isles and Normandy added new and important elements to the populations of these areas. And almost everywhere in the west, piracy, raiding and looting by peoples who had supremacy at sea in the western Mediterranean and the marginal seas of northern Europe created conditions of permanent insecurity and uncertainty. One effect of these new threats and the new need for defence and security was to reinforce other changes which were profoundly affecting the social structure of society towards military feudalism. Insecurity also acted as a brake on trade to an extent which cannot yet be ascertained (see below pp. 347–350). The need for defence also affected the character and pattern of both urban and rural settlement, especially perhaps in Mediterranean lands, creating traditions of urban building and defence which were important for the future of the city in Western Europe as a whole.[13]

Unique among the migrant, conquering peoples of the Dark Ages, the Arabs were highly organised politically and they attained levels of knowledge, literacy and culture to a degree undreamt of by Scandinavian, Magyar or Slav contemporaries. The religious ideal of Islam, the stimulating and unifying force in the Arab conquest of an empire which stretched from Gibraltar to the oases of central Asia and the Thar desert, was without counterpart as a motivating force among barbarian invaders of western Europe. Political unity was rarely achieved and social unity not to be looked for in an empire of such vast extent and with so sparse a population density, in which great distances separated the nuclei of well-watered and fertile land. Fragmentation of religious sects, the inadequacy of techniques of political control, political rivalries and jealousies and resentment of Arab supremacy by Moor or Syrian or Egyptian provided the occasion for political fragmentation, which was also, however, encouraged by the inherent geographical separatism of component regions. Communication within the Arab Empire was clearly, therefore, an important matter politically and it was so also from an economic or a religious point of view. Pilgrimage to Mecca was an important aspect of the faith. The trader was more highly regarded among Muslims than among Christians and long-distance trade in luxuries had an important part to play in supplying the needs of wealthy officials and nobility made aware of the great variety of products which their subtropical world had to offer by travel, pilgrims, story-tellers and even well-written and informative Arab geographies. In addition to long-distance movement of commodities within the empire, there was also a long-distance diffusion of industrial technology, of new crops and agricultural practices, and also of knowledge, literature and science. It is a commonplace that much of classical and particularly Greek literature and science was preserved in the Arab world to be transmitted to the west in the later Middle Ages, but advances made in the T'ang dynasty also reached the west, slowly and hesitantly, through the intermediacy of the Arab trading world in the Indian Ocean.

The direct impact of the Arabs on Western Europe was felt mainly by Spain and Sicily. In Spain, Moors and Arabs replaced a decadent Visigothic kingdom, sweeping across the peninsula between 711 and 718, the western arm of a pincer movement on the Christian Mediterranean which was repulsed only at Poitiers in 732 by Charles Martel some fourteen years after the eastern movement had been defeated at Constantinople. The Byzantine Empire still maintained naval supremacy, thanks to its more highly organised provincial and imperial fleets, its control over the islands and peninsulas of the northern shores of the Mediterranean, and its possession of Greek Fire and superior resources in timber, iron and other naval stores. The Arabs were dominant on land, and the locations of their early capitals, well inland and away from the sea, clearly reflect this— Damascus and Baghdad in Syria and Mesopotamia for example. Fustat on the Nile opposite the ancient site of Memphis, and later Cairo both avoided the obvious port location of Alexandria. In North Africa, Kairouan was the capital of Afriqiya (approximately Tunisia), some thirty miles inland and awkwardly placed compared with Tunis. The positions of Fez in Morocco and Cordoba in Spain are similarly inland. Arab maritime rivalry with the Byzantines and then supremacy over them came later.[14] Indeed, the conquest of Sicily piecemeal from 800 to 902 was a part of the process by which the Arabs assured their brief dominance at sea, capturing many of the island bases of the Mediterranean. From Egypt and Syria, Cyprus, Rhodes and Crete were conquered; from Afriqiya, Sicily (800–902), Pantelleria (835), Malta (869) and Sardinia; from Spain the Balearic Islands. Arab maritime supremacy was short-lived and was quite soon challenged in the tenth and eleventh centuries by Normans and Italians so that Arab occupation of the islands they had conquered was often brief and superficial compared with the deeper mark they left on southern Spain, most of which was in Moorish hands for five centuries and possibly longer. The islands and the northernmost outposts of the Arab world were early recovered for Christendom, but by then they had performed two important and quite different functions.

On the one hand they were points of intellectual and economic contact at which ideas, techniques and new crops as well as commodities were exchanged. Palermo was perhaps the greatest of such centres where Western Europe learnt of Arab knowledge and through the Arabs of Greek science and astronomy, but the Balearic islands were another, where Arab traditions and techniques of navigation and particularly cartography were handed on to the west.

On the other hand the islands and even a few strongholds on the mainland, such as Garde Freinet in the heart of Provence itself, were also the bases from which raiders ravaged the coasts and hinterlands of Italy and southern France, conducting forays up the Rhône to

Arles or well into the Alps by way of the Durance, for example. The collapse of trade in this part of the western Mediterranean was one result of their efforts, and so also was the recoil of rural settlement from the coast and its contraction to those impregnable but inconvenient hilltop village sites so characteristic of central Italy or southern France.

In Spain the Moors replaced a Visigothic kingdom in which there seems to have been little change from the time of the late Roman Empire. Trade had declined, particularly the trade in wine and oil to Rome, and the towns had contracted still further[15] but it seems likely that much of the Roman achievement in irrigation still survived. True Arab immigrants to Spain were relatively few, constituting a ruling aristocracy, mainly in the towns, though there were a few in frontier military settlements. Most of the immigrant population were Berbers from North Africa, pastoralists, farmers and olive planters whose influence in the peopling of Spain was felt chiefly in Granada, which remained in Muslim hands until 1492, and in eastern Spain, where a large proportion of the population in some areas still spoke Arabic in the sixteenth century. Elsewhere their influence was much less. The north was reconquered early by the Christians; the centre was always sparsely populated and it too was reconquered early. The Berbers made less impact on the Guadalquivir basin than might be expected, perhaps because of the pre-existing density of the population. Place-names, which reveal many more nuances in the influence of the Moors in Spain, will be considered shortly below, but it is important to stress that the Christian population (Mozarabs), some of whom were later recruited to Islam, constituted the bulk of the population which also included a significant Jewish element, chiefly in the towns. Indeed, the Moorish invasions of Spain exemplify the general point that the conquest of relatively well-watered and densely populated lands in the Mediterranean peninsulas of Europe by peoples like the Arabs and later the Turks emanating from the arid lands and oases of North Africa and south-west Asia tended to produce a minority rule which assured its narrowly based authority, at least in the initial stages of conquest, by according religious toleration.[16]

The intensity of Arab settlement in Spain can be gauged by the distribution and density of place-names.[17] A distinction must be made between purely Arab and arabised names. Personal names containing, for example, the element *ibn* or *ben* (e.g. Bentarique =

Ibn Tariq) or locative and descriptive names, such as Trafalgar (Cape Hell), Gibraltar (mountain of Tariq), or La Mancha (table-land) are characteristic. River and stream names such as Guadala-jara, Guadalquivir, often include the element *guada*, identical to *wadi* in meaning. Many others, however, are hybrids of various kinds: arabised names of Greek, Carthaginian, Celt-Iberian or Roman origin, such as Zaragoza, which is derived from *Caesarea Augusta* by way of the arabised version, *Zarakusta*; and hybrids such as those which include an Arab prefix: *Al*muro, *Al*ponte, for example.

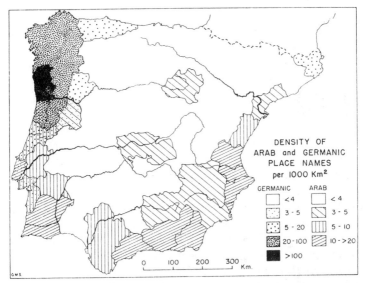

DENSITY OF
ARAB and GERMANIC
PLACE NAMES
per 1000 Km²

GERMANIC   ARAB

< 4   < 4
3 - 5   3 - 5
5 - 20   5 - 10
20 - 100   10 - >20
>100

0   100   200   300   Km.

Fig. 3:8   Arab and Germanic place-names in Iberia (after Lautensach).

Some Arabic words, however, entered into Spanish and Portuguese so that names containing them may be later than the Reconquista, such as Las Vegas (fertile acres); some irrigation terms, like *noria*, or *acequia*, and others such as *atalaya* or *aldea* (watchtower, village) are of the same kind. These must clearly be excluded from a study of Arabic place-names. The distribution of truly Arab and arabised names is plotted by density in Fig. 3:8. Altogether there are close on 3,000 and their distribution is to a large extent indicative of Arab influence in the peninsula as a whole. As may be expected, they are most numerous in the south, which was held longest until 1492; they are dense in the Guadalquivir and in the irrigated *huertas* of the east, particularly in the hinterlands of Cartagena and Valencia. There is a noticeable thickening of Arab place-names in the upper Tagus around Toledo, the upper Duero and the Ebro, where most of the names are arabised rather than pure Arab. To some extent the crude distribution of Arab names is misleading, since the density of all place-names varies considerably from one part of Iberia to another. Much of the north has its population in hamlets and scattered farms so that all place-names are abundant. The same is true of much of Portugal. But in Estremadura and La Mancha names are thin on the ground, partly because population density is low, but also because it tends to be concentrated in large and widely spaced villages so that the importance of Arab names is minimised. Lautensach attempted to correct this bias by plotting the density of Arab names by area and in other ways, thus revealing even more clearly than a dot map that the importance of the Arab settlement as measured by place-names varied proportionately with the length of time the area was in Arab hands (Fig. 3:9). River names give a further clue. In the area occupied the shortest time, in the Ebro and the Duero valleys, arabised names occur only for the main streams and for a few of the tributaries. Further south more of the major tributaries of the Tagus and the Guadiana show Arab influence, and in the southern zone of the Guadalquivir and Granada, quite minor streams carry Arabic names. The extent of Arab influence was therefore considerable and roughly proportional to the length of their stay, particularly in the irrigable lands of the eastern and southern periphery.

Whether in the context of the whole Arab Empire, or in the context of that regional unity in the western Mediterranean which is constituted by North Africa and Iberia, the irrigable lowlands of southern and eastern Spain and the Guadalquivir basin were potentially rich and populous areas, which could be developed with the help of the irrigation techniques and the same repertoire of crops with which the Arabs were familiar in the Maghreb, Egypt, Syria or even Mesopotamia. How much the Arabs contributed to irrigation in Spain that was new it is difficult to say, for much may have survived from classical times. The Arabs preserved and extended existing systems, introduced new methods of developing branch canals to conserve water, and the method of lifting water by an endless chain of buckets driven by wind or animal power, known as the *noria*. Their water tribunals, developed to administer supplies of irrigation water, have survived, for example, at Valencia and much of the termin-

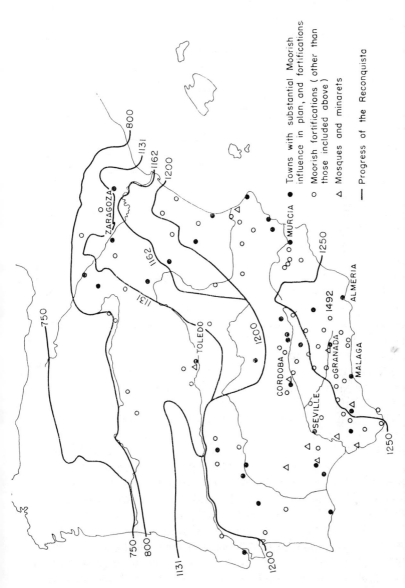

Fig. 3:9 Moorish features in Iberia, other than place-names, and the progress of the Reconquista in Spain. The wealth of Moorish elements in the south and east, coinciding with the evidence of place-names to a large extent, is quite evident.

ology of irrigation is of Arab origin. New irrigation works were put into effect in the Guadalquivir basin; round Málaga and Almería, itself a new Arab foundation of A.D. 825 on the lowland plains of Murcia; and at Alicante and Valencia, where the Turia canals were built between 911 and 976; and in the Ebro basin where some 25,000 acres were irrigated round Zaragoza. On the semi-arid plain of La Mancha, with less than 15 inches of rain a year, well irrigation was also developed by the Arabs.[18] On irrigated land, crops newly introduced into Western Europe were among those cultivated: rice near Valencia where water from the Turia was abundant; sugar, cotton, and even bananas in the lower Guadalquivir near Seville; and sugar in Granada and Valencia. Lucerne was reintroduced. Intensive, horticultural methods of cultivation were used for new fruits and vegetables such as oranges, lemons, peaches and apricots and strawberries, yet there was, it seems, relatively little trade in such commodities, and studies of the Valencia basin[19] suggest that the commercial production of luxury crops was very limited indeed, and that most were grown on the irrigated *huerta* land of large landowners and wealthy merchants near their urban or next to their suburban houses.

On unirrigated land olive cultivation was important, but viticulture suffered to the extent that the Muslims heeded the exhortations of their religion not to drink alcoholic liquor. The mulberry was introduced from Syria together with the silkworm and the new skills involved in silk production, and it was grown in southern Spain chiefly around the major cities in which silk cloths were woven: chiefly Cordoba, Almería and Valencia. The carob nut was introduced widely into southern Spain and Portugal, and the date palm was brought to arid areas such as Elche where it still exists. The pastoral traditions of the North African Berbers were established in the semi-arid meseta of Spain. They introduced their techniques of handling sheep and horses, their terminology, and new strains of animals, thus laying the foundations for the pre-eminence and the individuality of Spanish stock-rearing in the later Middle Ages.

Moorish development of mineral resources recalls the intensity of Roman exploitation, on which much of their effort still depended: the steel of Toledo, the silver and copper of the Sierra Morena, the mercury of Almadén (itself an Arabic place-name meaning 'the mine') and the tin of the Algarve and Galicia were all worked. Industry and crafts were primarily urban in location, depending again like the cultivation of luxury foodstuffs on the urban-dwelling official or landowner for patronage. Cordoba the capital had the greatest repertoire of crafts: silk, pottery, glass, leather, gold and silver are mentioned by Arab travellers and geographers such as Ibn Haukal or El Idrisi. Paper-making at Játiva near Valencia represented the first introduction into Western Europe of this type of manufacture, which had found its way originally from China.

Thus, in general, the effect of the Arab conquest of Spain was to develop the potential wealth of the southern and eastern sectors of the Spanish periphery at a time when the Christian countries of the west were backward or 'underdeveloped'. But the potential wealth of the periphery was realised in the context of a society which remained very largely oriented to local self-sufficiency, for trade in agricultural products was still relatively slight, and it is easy to exaggerate, from the glowing accounts of Arab geographers, the amount of commercial production which was taking place.

In the region of la Jara cacerena, some ninety miles west of Toledo between the Tagus and the Guadiana, most of the modern parishes give some indication of Roman settlement, and some of earlier Celt-Iberian settlement, as for example in the suffix given to the major town, *Augustobriva*. Visigothic settlement, limited to one place-name, was negligible in spite of the proximity of Toledo, capital and stronghold of the Visigoths. Settlement of Arab origin was also negligible in the first period of occupation and it is only from the tenth century that the Moors threw up castles and watch-towers on hilltop sites and shifted the site of the major town of the area from the lowland location of *Augustobriva* to a higher and more easily defensible site at Alija, a town which still has the haphazard, ir-regular arrangement of houses and streets characteristic of Arab settlements. Villages carrying late Arab place-names still show a similar pattern. The conditions of insecurity which provoked this defensive reaction in a frontier area of central Spain lasted for many years, for the area changed hands several times, and so much of the population fled, indeed, that it was renamed by the Moslems as la Jara—the deserted place.[20]

Once the Arabs were installed on the North African coast, as they were by 698, it was as natural that the conquest of Sicily should be as inviting for them as it had been for the Carthaginians and the Phoenicians long before them. The conquest of Sicily was begun in 708, but it was not until 831 that Palermo fell and 902 before the last

Christian stronghold fell. Immigration from North Africa was chiefly of soldiers, officials and the new landowners who introduced new irrigation techniques and new crops into Sicily as they had into Spain, in an effort to intensify agricultural production. Wheat continued to be important and the interior became renowned for its pastoral farming and for the rearing of pack animals, but the irrigated coastal valleys were most radically transformed by the intensive cultivation of rice, cotton, oranges, sugar and dates. Mulberry nourished silkworms for the manufacture of silks and brocades in Palermo where other cloths, tooled leather, gold, silver and inlaid woods were worked. Ibn Haukal estimated in 960–70 that there were some 200 mosques in the city and commented in glowing terms on its size and wealth. Arab rule in Sicily was, however, relatively short-lived. Messina, conquered by the Normans in their struggles for southern Italy, served as a base from which Sicily was attacked; Palermo was taken and Syracuse followed in the year before Domesday was being compiled in Norman England. It was after this period that Sicily entered its golden age, for the Moslems were allowed to retain their customs, laws, language and religion under the Normans, and Sicily became a notorious intermediary for trade between Christian and Muslim worlds, and the Normans and intellectual contacts flourished on an important scale, though Arabic influences gradually died out, leaving very little permanent trace.

THE SCANDINAVIANS

The expansion of the Scandinavian peoples over northern Europe is one of the most dramatic and even heroic episodes in the settlement of Europe and, although one may attempt to assess its effects, the circumstances of this sudden eruption are more difficult to elucidate.[21] For two hundred years after their first piratical raid on Holy Island off the coast of Northumbria in 793, the Scandinavians dominate the history of much of north and north-western Europe. Raiding, looting, and burning along all the coasts of Western Europe and far up its major rivers, the Rhine, the Meuse, the Seine, the Loire and even the Rhône—they spread uncertainty and insecurity wherever they went, producing a new emphasis on defence and protection which was to be so important in the organisation of feudalism and in the creation or revival of those walled, defended enclosures which were to become the nuclei of so many medieval towns.

In general, it was the Norse who moved to the far west. They settled first in the Orkneys and Shetlands, and then raided much further south in Ireland and northern France. They settled in strength in Ireland and north-western England and left their mark on the place-names of Wales. In 843 they were raiding Nantes, Arab Spain a few years later, and in 859–862 they were in the western Mediterranean. But the most remarkable achievements of the Norse were in the North Atlantic. From northern Britain, the Norse turned their attention to Iceland, and were responsible for its systematic colonisation and settlement, unusually well-known because of the survival of a document, the Landnamabøk, giving details of land occupation. As many as 30,000 to 35,000 men went out to Iceland from western Norway in a great wave of spontaneous emigration by individual families, taking their own boats with perhaps a score of men and probably slaves from Ireland or Scotland. And it was the Norse who led the first tentative European expansion to the New World. In 982 Erik the Red, banned from Iceland as a punishment for murder, discovered Greenland and established a Scandinavian settlement which persisted till the climatic deterioration of the fourteenth century finally eliminated it. In 1000 Leif, the son of Erik, sailed still further west, discovering and reporting on the new land of Vinland which lay to the south-west of Greenland and which can be no other than North America. Indeed, recent discoveries now suggest a definite landfall and settlement in Newfoundland.

In the east, the Swedes reached across to lake Ladoga and were established there from the early ninth to the mid-eleventh century. Exploring, trading and raiding to the south and south-west along the navigable rivers and across the low easy portages, Swedish groups, known as Varangians or Rus were in Novgorod and Kiev by 900 and had established contacts with the Arabs on the Volga and with the Byzantine Empire at Constantinople. Sweden itself had become a powerful and prosperous kingdom.

The Danes confined their attention more completely to home waters in the North Sea and the Channel. It was they who plundered and raided the ports and ships of the Frisian traders in the Low Countries (Dorestad, the Frisian port on the Rhine was plundered in 834 and then flooded and lost by 864). They occupied the island of Walcheren, and after raiding and plundering their way up the Seine and into Paris they were able to occupy and settle in Normandy under their leader Rollo after 911. In the North Sea it was the great achievement of the Danes, of course, that after a period of raiding and harrying, they carried out the large-scale invasion and settlement of eastern and midland England from the middle of the ninth century. Although the association of Norse, Swedes and Danes with these respective movements is in general valid, there was considerable ethnic mixture in them. Danes and Norse were both present in Ireland; and there was even a strong Celtic, probably Irish, element in the settlement of Iceland. The great Danish armies which invaded England contained Norse settlers; most of the Scandinavian settlers in Normandy were Danish, but Rollo and his immediate followers were Norse; and Danes and Norse were involved with the Swedes in the eastern expeditions.

The characteristic features of the Scandinavian expansion varied. It has often been pointed out that raiding and piracy by individual ships gradually became less random and more systematic. Relatively permanent winter headquarters were often set up from which raiding parties went forth systematically looting in their shallow-draught boats up the navigable rivers. These rivers still linked many of the important towns and citadels and passed through the wealthiest and largest agricultural settlements precisely because of the frequent association of navigable rivers with meadow on their flood-plains and easily tilled arable on low terraces. It is difficult to see any sharp distinction between raiding, piracy and looting on the one hand, and on the other, commerce in the form of primitive exchange and barter, or between raiding and organised military campaigns such as those of the Danes against the Frisian traders. Settlement, too, at least in the first instance, may have been to some extent a by-product and a concomitant of conquest, and a result, perhaps, of the disbanding of an army; only later may it have became the large-scale affair represented by the Danish settlement in Lincolnshire or East Anglia. Even so, the scale on which the settlement of the Danes in England took place has recently been called into question.[22]

In general, then, the Scandinavian expansion was one which took many forms according to the opportunities that were offered by the areas reached, the societies with which they came into contact and the degree of organisation of the Scandinavians themselves. It is clear that the opportunity for Scandinavian expansion was provided by the political weakness of Western Europe on the break-up of the Carolingian Empire in 814 and the subsequent disturbances. It is also clear that expansion was greatly facilitated by the superiority of Scandinavian shipping and navigation, for their clinker-built and half-decked ships built with a strong keel and a sturdy mast for the great square woollen sails were seaworthy and manoeuvrable. Navigation over open sea was possible and a variety of types of ship had been developed for specific purposes. The Oseberg ship, famous as the grave of a queen, was quite different in structure from the sturdy, ocean-going Gokstad ship.

But why should this great eruption of Scandinavian activity suddenly take place in the ninth century? The pressure of population on resources is always a convenient cause to invoke for such otherwise inexplicable migrations, but in the absence of any direct evidence of numbers, it is impossible to say. The practice of polygamy and the exposure of unwanted infants, both quoted as evidence, do not necessarily lead to or indicate overpopulation. Nor does modern evidence of pollen analysis and climatic change support the alternative concept of a migration due to deteriorating environmental conditions. Indeed, conditions in Greenland were unusually favourable for settlement. Internal discontent and the migration of large minorities as a result is a possible explanation, though there is again little evidence. There was certainly a search for wealth, loot and even trade, activities which in general preceded colonisation and settlement except in the Shetlands and the Orkneys, but this is not an unusual motive for raiding and piracy! Recent suggestions as to why Scandinavian activity increased so suddenly in these years are, nevertheless, inclined to stress the importance of trade to a degree which seems surprising for the period in question.[23]

One of the most outstanding features in the geography of early medieval trade is the overwhelming importance of the Byzantine and Arab Empires in controlling the trade routes to the spices, silks and luxuries of the East. The routes and the intermediaries by which these products reached northern and north-western Europe, and the quantities in which they moved, have been the subject of never-ending controversy, provoked above all by the lack of evidence. Mediterranean routes were blocked, at least to the merchants of the Carolingian Empire, and the western routes across the European isthmuses seem to have handled little of the trade. But there is increasing evidence, chiefly archaeological, of the use of routes linking Byzantium with the Baltic by way of the Dvina and the Dnieper and of the use, too, of routes by way of the Dvina-Oka-Volga to the Caspian and thence to the Muslim oases of Samarkand and Tashkent and so to the sources in the Pamir mountains of that silver money which has been left like a trail along the routes from the Black and the Caspian Seas to the Baltic and even to Denmark.[24] For a brief phase, while the obvious and cheapest route to the west by way of the Mediterranean was blocked, the Baltic became the gateway through which north-western Europe had contact with the wealth of the Arab world.[25] It was this wealth which nourished new ports on the Baltic such as Hedeby and Birka, new entrepôts such as Bornholm and the trade of the Varangians to the east. It may have been this wealth which financed the expansion of the Norse and the Danes. Or, it has been suggested, the sudden deprivation of wealth brought about by the stoppage of this eastern trade from about 840 to 880 may have stimulated the Scandinavians to take by force what they had only just learnt to acquire by exchange with their new-found wealth in Arab silver.[26]

Whatever the circumstances which surround the expansion of the Scandinavians, however, there is no doubt that their effects on the historical geography of Europe were profound. First, the exploration and colonization of Iceland and Greenland and the discovery of Vinland represented achievements which rival those of the fifteenth-century travellers in the Atlantic. Secondly, whereas Frisian and possibly Anglo-Saxon seamen and merchants had been familiar with the navigation of the North Sea and the Channel, the Scandinavians acquired a body of knowledge about navigation along the whole coast of north-western Europe from Iberia to the east Baltic and northern Norway. It is worth comment, perhaps, that much of the maritime vocabulary of French is of Scandinavian origin. For the first time, sea routes along the whole of this coast were possible. In spite of the disruption they caused the Scandinavians helped to lay the foundations of maritime commerce in north-western Europe which were built upon chiefly by Flemish and German from the eleventh century. Thirdly, their destruction and looting throughout Western Europe disrupted the old ecclesiastical estates and by the emphasis on defence which they made necessary helped to bring into being a new nobility whose task it was to protect rural society from the ravages of the Scandinavians, and indeed from each other. The origins of some of the noble families of France is to be found among such men; and in the countryside, a proliferation of new castles and strongpoints at defensible sites appeared, some of them acting as nuclei around which the 'protected' and subordinate peasantry grouped themselves in newly formed villages. The towns, too, gained a new identity in solving the problems posed by the need for defence, not least by their physical separation from the countryside by new or rebuilt walls. Old towns were changed and the nuclei of many new ones created by the settlement of merchants and traders in the shelter of fortifications created by powerful men at strategic points.

Finally the contribution of the Scandinavians to the rural settlement of western Europe in their age of expansion was very considerable. The greatest achievements were in the settlement of Scandinavia itself.[27] In Norway the expansion of the Viking Age is associated with scattered settlement and place-names ending in *-stadir, -heimr* and *-setr*. The first is a frequent element in the primary settlement of Iceland, but *-heim* is an element that seems to have been passing out of use even when Iceland was being settled, for it is fairly rare. In Denmark, Scania, and many of the islands of the west Baltic, including Öland, Viking settlement was in nucleated villages, loosely and irregularly grouped. And it seems to have been in this more southerly and more fertile area that much of the colonisation of this period was concentrated. The clearing and settlement of the central depression in Sweden was by no means complete even by the end of the Viking period; only a beginning had been made in the settlement of such areas as the Siljan depression; and the forests of northern Hälsingland were hardly touched. In Denmark and Sweden, names ending in *-by* are characteristic of the Viking period, and they were, of course, exported to England. In Denmark primary names in *-by* are very strongly concentrated in the islands and in eastern Jutland on the more productive boulder clay soils.

Place-names in *-torp* are a very clear indication of the expansion of secondary settlement in Denmark, overlapping in time from the Viking age to the eleventh and twelfth centuries. The word is the same as that which appears in many English place-names as *-thorpe* and is linguistically similar to the German *-dorf*, usually known, however, as a late primary rather than a secondary place-name. In Denmark alone there are some 3,500 *-torp* names and in Gothland and Scania a further 1,200, witness to the strength of this expansive movement of rural settlement. They were usually founded on uncleared, forested land, frequently intercalated between older settlements. They were co-operative ventures initiated by a mother village on which they were dependent from the beginning. Customary laws gave precedence to the mother village and they were often smaller in area and population than their founders. In England they are sometimes chapelries of their mother settlements and parish boundaries may occasionally show how they had been allotted a corner of the original parish from which they had been carved.

In Normandy, the Scandinavians left a deep impression on the map of place-names, in the Pays de Caux, the neighbourhood of Rouen, on the northern coast of Normandy and in the Cotentin peninsula.[28] The presence of a minority of powerful men is indicated by names such as Trouville (Scandinavian personal name plus -*ville*), but a deeper Scandinavian influence is reflected by a very large number of wholly Scandinavian names, many of which have their counterpart in England: *bekkr* (stream) as -*bec* in French and *beck* in English (e.g. Bolbec); *dal* (valley) as -*dalle* in French and *dale* in English (e.g. Becdalle); *thveit* (clearing) as -*tuit* in French and -*thwaite* in English (e.g. Satterthwaite); *toft* as -*tot* in French as in *Yvetot;* -*flodh* (bay) appears in Honfleur; and *ness* (headland) in Cap Gris Nez. There is little doubt that the Scandinavians contributed profoundly to the settlement of Normandy, clearing new lands for the first time, as in the Cotentin peninsula, where they settled in areas near the sea which had been untouched by Gallo-Roman or Merovingian settlement.

With two important exceptions, represented by the eastward settlement and colonisation of the German peoples and the southward expansion of Christian kingdoms against the Moors in Iberia the major lineaments of modern language distributions had been established by the end of the Arab, Scandinavian and Magyar invasions. For over five hundred years after the fall of the Roman Empire the ethnic patterns of some part or other of Western Europe had been in a state of flux. But this fluidity can have been the result only in part of an unusual mobility of the peoples concerned, and it was as much the result, from one point of view, of a relatively sparse population thinly scattered on the ground and thus capable of being more profoundly altered by the piecemeal infiltration of new settlers, the settlement of an army, depopulation by enslavement, murder or flight, and by the simpler process of inter-marriage and cultural assimilation. The sparsity of population recorded in the Domesday Book for the vills of north-western England and parts of the Midlands laid waste by King William suggests that a very small number of immigrant farming families could make great alterations in linguistic distributions in a very short time. Nevertheless, the failure of Arab and Scandinavian settlement in Iberia, Normandy and Britain to impose their languages completely, and the extent to which their settlement is known by names and dialectal characteristics which suggest a minority of newcomers among a much larger indigenous population, indicate, perhaps, that modification of the ethnic pattern was becoming more difficult to achieve.

It seems likely that there was a considerable net growth of population during the course of the Dark Ages from the fifth to the end of the tenth centuries, but it would be very hazardous indeed to attempt an estimate. Carolingian Europe was almost certainly sparsely populated as a whole, yet in certain regions of light, easily tilled fertile soils which had long been intensively settled, population densities could be quite high. In France the witness of very occasional monastic documents giving lists of tenants or taxpayers shows, for example, that eight villages in the neighbourhood of Paris could count some 4,100 peasants in the early ninth century compared with a total of 5,700 in the eighteenth. Evidence from the Pyrenees and Burgundy suggest surprisingly high densities, and a village of the Ardennes seems to have suffered already from overpopulation, for some 232 families were established on holdings (*mansi*) intended for sixty households. But it also seems very clear that economic and demographic pressures were still insufficient to allow great inroads to be made on poorer or heavier soils and there are, indeed, surprisingly few indications of new clearing and assarting in the admittedly rare documentary evidence. There were also very many areas in which settlement had not yet begun to take place. Average densities of population may have been low but it is more important, perhaps, that numbers were very unevenly distributed. Dense populations were often divided by great tracts of uninhabited waste. One may conclude, with Duby[29]: 'Here there were overpopulated islands where biological growth stimulated by agricultural prosperity pushed men to the edge of famine; in other places there were empty areas poorly exploited.'

Conclusions relating to population, in the absence of figures, are apt to rely on the number of burials counted in cemeteries, the number of villages or the extent of cultivated land. Little is known about the first and last of these criteria and it is clearly begging some important questions if the increasing number of place-names attributable to the period is held to indicate a proportional increase in the population. To put forward only three objections, a new place-name does not necessarily indicate a new place. Some at least of the Scandinavian place-names in eastern England may represent Anglo-Saxon villages which have been renamed. A change in rural habitat from strongly nucleated village to a scattered settlement pattern of hamlets or isolated farms may involve a multiplication of place-names without involving a single additional inhabitant. Over a period of disturbance and dislocation, new place-names may frequently represent no more than the reoccupation of a place formerly tenanted. Yet it cannot be gainsaid that the vast number of 'late primary' place-names all over Western Europe which have been attributed to the period between the Germanic invasions and the 'Great Age of Clearing' after 1050 seem to point to a parallel growth of total populations. And in England, where the remarkable and unique witness of Domesday Book is available, the number of vills recorded frequently approaches the modern total of settlement. In the English Midlands, for example (Bedfordshire, Buckinghamshire, Leicestershire, Staffordshire, and Northamptonshire) the Domesday vills number 1,288, a total which is surprisingly similar to the 1,311 parishes, townships, liberties, etc., recorded for the same area in the 1801 census. The settlements enumerated are not, of course, strictly comparable, but they suggest an order of magnitude. It has also been claimed that the parochial organisation of the church and the territorial delimitation of medieval parishes were taking shape from the eleventh to the thirteenth centuries. If this is so, then the map of parish boundaries in England indicates quite conclusively that over much of lowland England, village settlement had begun to approach the modern pattern very closely indeed by that time, and that much of the land must already have been cleared for farming. Large parishes and a multiplicity of chapelries and townships subsequently carved from great areas of waste suggest, on the other hand, that colonisation and settlement were yet far from complete in the uplands and highlands of Britain or on soils and terrain which were still unattractive for farming either because, like the heavy clays, they were difficult to clear and cultivate or because they were light, hungry and unproductive: the Breckland, the Weald, Charnwood Forest, or the light soils of Sherwood Forest are examples of such areas in England.

Settlement in England may have developed more precociously than on the continent, which was more disturbed politically and socially in the tenth and eleventh centuries; documents such as Domesday

Book are absent. But the map of the boundaries of French communes, near enough for our purposes to the map of parishes, would show essentially similar features to the English map and some of the un-cleared forest areas were still so large as to escape division into parish territories. In southern Germany and particularly in the southern Rhineland the frequency of place-names attributed to the period before 1050 is very high indeed. Estimates of the population of the Rhine rift valley have been made which suggest a growth from Carolingian times to the eleventh century, and in Iberia and Britain, Arab and Scandinavian place-names afford some evidence of the expansion in rural settlement which was taking place during the ninth and particularly the tenth centuries, even though it may give an uncertain indication of the proportions of Arabs or Scandi-navians.

THE GREAT EXPANSION: THE AGE OF CLEARING

The central feature of the historical geography of Western Europe in the later Middle Ages is undoubtedly the expansion, at a quickening pace, of population and economic activity from about 1050 to about 1300. In Italy and the western Mediterranean it was the age of the commercial revival and commercial revolution; it was the age of the counter-offensive against Islam, of crusades in the Near East and then, much later, of the opening up of routes across Asia to the Far East by European travellers and missionaries. In Flanders and in Britain, economic historians have uncovered contemporary industrial revolutions. And a new conception of urban society was nurtured, which grew from early beginnings of the tenth and eleventh centuries to be embodied in the magnificence of late medieval Venice, Florence, Bruges or Paris. And by 1300 even the more intricate patterns of the small market towns were beginning to take shape.

Over thirty years ago, Marc Bloch labelled this the Great Age of Clearing in France, a name that has also stuck in England and Germany simply because of its aptness.[30] Recent studies, particularly in England, have tended to stress that the extension of cultivated land reached its maximum in these years and that much marginal land was cultivated, particularly on light soils and in upland regions, which was later allowed to revert to pasture or waste. In Alpine and Mediterranean France, too, the clearing of land for farming reached a point at which excessively steep slopes were being cleared and thin, easily erodible soils were ploughed up to the permanent detriment of soil and vegetation. The colonisation of the Rhineland massifs extended further and further onto thin, cold, upland soils to the point at which the retention of the forest cover became the obvious and indeed the only possible economic use of the land. In many places the edge of the forest has since retreated no further. In Scandinavia the primary settlement of the lowland areas in the central depression was completed and secondary settlement filled out the network of villages in the more fertile southern lands of Denmark, Scania and southern Norway.

This, then, was the age in which the internal colonisation of Western Europe was virtually completed. Settlements have frequently been reorganised since this time but there are few areas where much potentially cultivable land was still uncleared and unsettled by the end of the Middle Ages. The chief exceptions were in Scandinavia; and in forested land preserved for hunting; fen and marshland; arid lands which needed irrigation. Hand in hand with this internal settlement went the great colonial movements: to the north pioneer settlement at the northern margins of cultivation; to the east, the expansion of German rural settlement and of German dominion from the line of the Elbe-Saale eastwards to beyond the Oder; to the south, the Reconquista in Iberia, dominantly a political, military and crusading movement, but also a great movement of colonisation and settlement.

More is known about the great age of clearing than of previous rural settlement partly because of the greater abundance of documents, but other forms of evidence are quite indispensable to an understanding of the progress of colonisation in these years. Place-name evidence is extremely important and gives valuable indications of the clearing of woodland, the drainage of marsh and the reclamation of heath, as well as the kind of economy and land use which followed new settlement. But there are also other types of evidence: pollen analysis at occasional sites (e.g. in the Rhöngebirge in Germany) has revealed the steady replacement of tree vegetation by plants and particularly by cultivated grains from Carolingian times onwards, and the proportion of herbaceous pollen and corn pollens increases rapidly from the eleventh century in the Rhöngebirge, and from the twelfth century in Mecklenburg. The analysis of the shape and plan of villages, as they appear at the earliest time for which reliable plans can be drawn up, can yield conclusions about the dating of village settlement or its expansion. Such analysis, which has been most profitably and systematically carried out by German geographers, also necessitates careful assessment of field systems and their organisation. Fuller discussion of both of these topics must come in a later chapter, and only their contribution to studies of the peopling of Europe need be mentioned here.

The expansion of settlement in the earlier period is known but dimly and sketchily from the rare documentary evidence of the period, but the great age of clearing from the eleventh to the end of the thirteenth century is also an age of increasingly informative data. Agrarian organisation was becoming sufficiently advanced and complex on monastic and lay estates to warrant the introduction of accounting methods and the account rolls themselves are thus evidence of an agrarian revolution. Charters, deeds, leases, custumals and the records of the tax-collector may all throw new light on processes of settlement and they begin to be abundant from about the middle of the twelfth century. The availability of evidence varies greatly from place to place. Some areas, more advanced or more tightly administered, such as northern Italy, southern France and England, generated more documents; their survival has varied from place to place as a result of the accidents of war and revolution or social change, and their availability varies with the efficiency of local archives. Moreover treatment has varied according to national trends in scholarship: historical geographers have pioneered the study of village plans and field systems in Germany; and social and economic historians have reaped a rich harvest from the wealth of English resources in documents.

There is sufficient evidence to make it clear that the movement of expansion was widespread in Western Europe even though its timing may have varied from place to place. In Burgundy, remote from Arabs, Scandinavians and Magyars alike, expansion seems to have begun in the tenth century. It appears to have begun early in the Paris basin, and to have been virtually complete in many parts of it by the middle of the thirteenth century. In south-eastern Britain, so much had been accomplished by Domesday times that relatively little remained to be done, though there were still areas of heavy or unattractive soils such as the Weald, Arden in Warwickshire and Charnwood Forest, which were cleared and settled chiefly in the twelfth and thirteenth centuries; and a very great deal was still to be done in northern England. In north-western Europe as a whole, new expansion seems to have gone on longest in areas most remote from northern France, western Germany and southern England, which had been most active at an early date: northern England, Scandinavia and east Germany were late frontiers of settlement. Many circumstances contributed to favour the expansion of settlement at this time.[31] Government and society were becoming more highly organised and more stable; both the clergy and the lay lords stood to gain from the more intensive use of the waste lands they had in their control. The church gained from the increase in tithe, and all gained from additional rents, from the proceeds of dispensing justice, and from the taxes levied on an increasing population, and they also gained in prestige and power from the increased number of men who owed allegiance to them and who could be called upon to defend the lordly estates.

The rôle of the monasteries has frequently been discussed in this connection, but the view that the new orders of the eleventh and twelfth centuries led the movement into the waste ought not to be emphasised too much. It is true that grants of land to the church and the monasteries tended to be of undeveloped land so that it was in the interest of the church to encourage its more intensive exploitation, but those orders like the Cistercians which deliberately chose remote places for the establishment of their monasteries and which regarded isolation as a part of their spiritual function did not actively encourage large-scale settlement as long as their spiritual values counted for something. Although they may have engaged extensively in pastoral activities such as the grazing of sheep, the exploitation of the wool trade and the rearing of cattle, the fact that so many of their abbeys remain still in the remote corners of the countryside well away from villages does suggest that their rôle as the nuclei round which rural settlement expanded in Western Europe may be easy to exaggerate.

Land hunger was a sufficient reason for the peasant to co-operate in the peopling of new settlements set up by the initiative of his superiors, and the prospect of exchanging a holding of 5–10 acres or even less in the old overcrowded villages for a holding of up to 50 or 60 acres in the new lands must have been enticing. Moreover, in the larger areas of frontier colonisation there was frequently the additional and important incentive that rents and dues, labour services and fines were lighter, and his personal freedom was often greater.

The vast bulk of the new settlements undoubtedly subsisted by their own efforts and traded little with the outside world but economic motives for the expansion of rural settlement into new areas became increasingly powerful at a time when agrarian technology in Western Europe had been profoundly altered by the spread of the heavy plough, the development of the three-course rotation, the horseshoe, and a more effective means of using horse power by the invention of the shoulder harness. The cultivation of the heavier soils, hard to work but once cleared productive of good yields, was now practicable and profitable. The reclamation of heathland could be entertained when deep-cutting ploughs were available to assist in the process of turning in the leached horizon of podzolised soils.

None of these factors encouraging or facilitating expansion would have been fully effective, however, without a growing population, evidence of which is increasingly being identified in very many scattered areas of Western Europe. Population figures of any accuracy are, of course, lacking for this period, but occasional and widely scattered rentals, poll taxes, hearth taxes and lists of tenants seem to point more or less unanimously to an increase of population from the eleventh to the end of the thirteenth century. Growth of population by a factor of two and a half from Domesday times to the early fourteenth century seems likely to be an underestimate for England. In France substantial local increases are revealed by monastic records for individual places, and by 1328 the total population of France may have been of the order of ten to twelve millions. In the Rhineland, population may have doubled between about 850 and 1150, and in the Moselle region it may have quadrupled between 900 and 1200 in an area in which initial population was thin and medieval clearing of mediocre soils was considerable. Such evidence as there is also suggests that the increase was greatest in those areas which had been least well developed at an earlier date. In England, for example, increase was less marked in those areas of south-east England and the Midlands which had been fully settled in Domesday times, and it was much higher in those areas, such as the Fenland, west Leicestershire, or north-west Warwickshire, in which the Domesday population had been sparse.

The forms taken by expansion into the wastelands varied from place to place and from time to time. In most areas considerable expansion undoubtedly went on unrecorded and unnoticed by a simple extension of the cultivated area round old settlements. Co-operative clearing of woodland by peasant villagers, perhaps with a certain degree of organisation and control by the manorial lords, led in many cases to the creation of a new pattern of furlongs on the edge of the old open fields. In other places, where manorial constraints were less marked or where individual peasants had the capital equipment or the time for the task, individually owned enclosures were created. Dependent farms or dependent hamlets sprung up at a suitable distance from the older villages, and it is often a difference only of degree which separates these from the fully fledged daughter village established with its own field system and customary arrangements, but carved from the territory of its parent village and sometimes still discernible as a chapelry of it. In the older settled areas of France, England and western Germany, new daughter villages were often intercalated between existing primary settlements as the pressure towards cereal farming led to the ploughing up of wastes and pastures. But in many parts of Western Europe a change occurred during the period in the ways in which this expansion of settlements was accomplished.

In the late twelfth and thirteenth centuries the creation of scattered farms lying amid fields enclosed individually from the waste became much more common. Sometimes they were the small, scattered farms of squatters, sometimes the larger, compact holding of a prosperous man whose migration to the confines of a village territory may have reflected his pretensions to keep a distance socially as well as physically from his fellows in the village. The association between late clearing and scattered settlement in northern France, England and western Germany is clear, but since the areas in which settlement expanded late were also those areas which were agriculturally marginal and therefore lent themselves more easily to scattered settlement associated with pastoral farming, it is impossible to generalise too sweepingly. Moreover, it has also been pointed out that towards the end of the great wave of medieval expansion, exchange economies had begun to spread sufficiently widely for some regions to concentrate on pastoral or dairy pursuits, to which scattered settlement was frequently more suited, especially in hilly terrain.

The distribution of new settlement in time and space between the eleventh and the thirteenth centuries has yet to be fully worked out. In the Île de France the process of clearing was complete before 1060; in Limagne, much remained still to do only on the hungry, light soils of the Varennes region; in the Toulouse area most of the *sauvetés* had been founded by 1100; in England Domesday reveals a surprisingly complete settlement pattern even by 1086 in much of southeast England. In Normandy a sample of settlement shows the creation of 11 places before 1066; 32 before the end of the eleventh century, 46 before 1200 and 47 at the end of the thirteenth century. In the Paris basin the process was more or less complete by the middle of the thirteenth century and forested areas like eastern Brie lying between the open and early cleared landscapes of the Île de France and Champagne had been cleared by this time.[33] In general it was the heavy clays and the thinner soils of higher lands which were now tackled: the Argonne, the higher lands of Lorraine; central Beauce was now reached and in the Massif Central and the Alps the upper limits of settlement were attained. In south-western France the pattern of new settlement is revealed by the frequency of place-names containing the element *artigues*, and these show the extension of settlement away from the accessible and well-drained terraces towards areas of lighter and less productive soils.

In much of Gascony and Aquitaine, the development of new settlement is revealed less systematically by characteristic place-names than by the settlement forms associated with the planned settlement of the *sauvetés* or the *villeneuves* organised by the French and English crowns on either side of the disputed frontiers in Gascony, Aquitaine and Toulouse in order to protect a peasantry formerly scattered vulnerably in hamlets. Frequently founded on easily defended or strategic locations such as hilltops, they were strongly fortified, and usually had a regular plan of streets. These *bastides* were widely spread in the region between the Massif Central and the foothills of the Pyrenees. Proclaimed by heralds who toured in Languedoc and elsewhere, the foundation of the *bastides* was accompanied by measures aimed at stimulating migration to them, but it is difficult to be sure that their creation represented a net increase to the rural population of the area, and it has been suggested that they often involved no more than a regrouping of population from hamlets to nucleated villages and small towns.

In western Germany late clearing names show again how expansion was reaching to the margins of cultivation in the Rhineland massif and elsewhere (see above). In the Low Countries expansion is so closely associated with the draining of marsh and the reclamation of heath that it warrants fuller discussion in a later section, but it is important to notice here that this was one of the areas, like northern Italy, where the proximity of urban markets seems to have been an important factor in the generation of new settlement.

In Scandinavia great inroads were made into the forest and many new settlements were founded during the great expansion of population from the eleventh to the thirteenth centuries. More still remained to be done, however, in Scandinavia and even by the end of the thirteenth century by no means all of the potentially cultivable land had been cleared, particularly in central Sweden. The movement started earlier in Denmark and Scania than in the central depression of Sweden or in Norway but it continued longer in these latter areas. Indeed, Scandinavia departs from the normal Western European pattern of settlement in that considerable numbers of villages were not founded until the sixteenth and seventeenth centuries and even later (see below). In Norway, scattered settlement characteristic of the age of Viking expansion continued to multiply, though it is often difficult to distinguish early from later settlement. Nevertheless, some 3,000 new settlements, many of them in south-east Norway, can be identified as having been created during this period by the form of their place-names, which combine a clearing element such as -rød or rud with a Christian personal name.[34]

In Denmark clearing names in -rød occur particularly in Scania and Sjaelland; in south Jutland names in -bølle are common and names in -holt and -hult are also clearing names. In Sweden names in -bøda, -holt, -mala, -ryd, and -torp characterise the age of clearing. By the end of the thirteenth century the population of Scandinavia may have been of the order of two millions: Denmark possessing about one million, Norway 400,000 and Sweden 600,000.[35]

In most of Western Europe the process of rural expansion filled in the waste places which had been left by earlier settlers able to concentrate on the fertile soils and more accessible regions. But in two areas particularly the process of rural settlement in the great age of clearing took place along an expanding frontier of colonisation. The boundaries of Western Christendom were being extended in both Spain and Germany as much by the efforts of modest peasants exploiting the soil and settling new lands as by the sword of the nobility and the clergy conquering territories from the Arabs in the west and from the Slavs in the east.

In Spain the progress of the Reconquista against the Moors took place by well-defined stages, which are summed up in Fig. 3:9. Slow at first and held up by the quarrels and dissensions among the Christian princes, the Reconquista made important progress in north-eastern Spain and on the central meseta by the end of the eleventh century, but the grand sweep of Portugal, Castile and

Aragon across the greater part of the peninsula was not accomplished until the thirteenth century, when all but the territory of Moorish Granada was reconquered with the Castilian acquisition of the Guadalquivir basin, and Murcia in 1266, and the conquest by Aragon of Valencia in 1238. The progress of the Reconquista southwards was accompanied by the foundation of new villages of Christian peasants grouped in large easily defended nucleated settlements. They were granted charters by which their privileges were defined and guaranteed. The agricultural settlement of much of the meseta began to take its modern shape only with the creation of these villages and the subsequent clearing of great open fields around them. The creation of new daughter settlements at the margins of village territories was often known, as in the case of so many clearing settlements of this date elsewhere in Western Europe, by the occurrence of woodland and clearing elements in their place-names. This was particularly true of Catalonia where settlements in the pre-littoral depression and along the coast were carrying southwards the distinctiveness of speech and custom brought by an immigrant population from southern France. Analysis of twelfth-century surnames shows how important migration across the eastern Pyrenees from southern France was in the settlement of Catalonia, an area which seemed to have more in common at this date with the area of Franco-Provençal speech than it did with the rest of the Iberian peninsula. In Castile as a whole the aridity of the meseta, combined with the insecurity of conditions along the frontier zone against the Moors, seem to have put a premium from the beginning on the development of a stock-rearing economy since cattle and sheep represented a mobile form of wealth which might be moved out of harm's way in the event of raiding and war. In the wake of the Reconquista transhumant flocks pushed south to extensive new pastures in the centre and south of the peninsula thus adding a new element to the stock-rearing economy which was to dominate Spain in the later Middle Ages.

THE COLONISATION OF EAST GERMANY

The colonisation of East Germany represents one of the greatest achievements of the later Middle Ages.[36] It was a genuine colonial movement taking place in a thoroughly medieval context, involving problems, processes and patterns similar to those associated with later movements of the expansion of pioneer farming on the 'frontier' in Siberia, the U.S.A. or the Argentine pampa. The settlement of eastern Germany changed the ethnic map of central Europe and laid the foundations of modern Germany, and the centre of gravity of German political development was pushed eastwards towards the new marchland states of Austria and Prussia. New rural settlement patterns, new towns and new routes were all created by the waves of immigrants who moved across the continent between the eleventh and fourteenth centuries. New problems emerged in the relationship of German to Slav, and although the linguistic patterns of east-central Europe, reorganised as they were by settlement and colonisation in these years, were to be reversed again much later and much more quickly in the twentieth century, nevertheless the legacy of this medieval colonial settlement still remains one of the most profoundly important aspects of the political geography of this area.

The colonisation and settlement of east Germany met many problems similar to those which were later faced by other pioneer movements. It would be a mistake to attempt to compare too closely the progress of settlement in this area with that of the Middle West in the nineteenth century, as did James Westfall Thompson, but it is of considerable interest to examine the solutions which were found in east Germany to the kind of problem common to all settlement movements of this character. They may indeed be listed. First the relationship of settlers to the indigenous inhabitants was a more pressing and urgent problem in east Germany than among many of the colonial movements of a later age. Secondly it has always been one of the major problems of migration to stimulate, organise and handle the movement of peasants from their old homes, channelling them along suitable routes and installing them on suitable sites chosen and prepared according to accepted and organised standards of land allocation and land tenure. The sheer scale of the tasks represented by these aspects of settlement and by the clearing of forest, the provision of tools, seed, equipment and housing called into being in medieval Germany a specialised class of colonising agent, the *locator*. The size of the movement and the numbers involved made some degree of planning and standardisation necessary and it is this that differentiates it from the smaller scale and more random movements of earlier generations.

Thirdly, like other movements of settlement, that of east Germany required the development of a suitable economic basis for settlement. Although the east German settlement was adjusted more completely than most later movements to a self-subsistence economy, it nevertheless required the production of surpluses by which trading links with the older and more developed lands could be forged and strengthened and by which imports of salt, wine, cloth, spices and

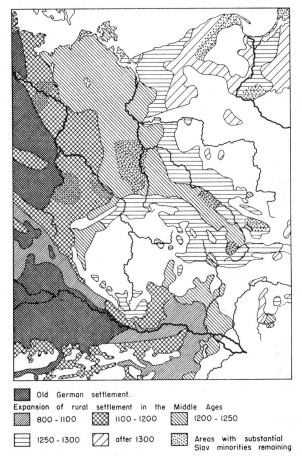

Old German settlement.

Expansion of rural settlement in the Middle Ages

800 - 1100   1100 - 1200   1200 - 1250

1250 - 1300   after 1300   Areas with substantial Slav minorities remaining

3:10   The progress of east German colonization (after Kuhn).

so on, could be assured. With the development of the North German Plain an economic revolution was brought to the Baltic. Finally, in economic terms, settlement in new and sparsely populated lands meant a revolution in the ratio of labour to land as in other parts of the world in other times. Land was cheap and abundant; labour was scarce and expensive; and these facts involved important social as well as economic implications for the status of the peasant. The movement in south Germany and Austria began and ended earlier than the movement in the north (Fig. 3:10). From the end of the seventh century the threat of the Avars had been removed and the routes to the east were opened up with the establishment of Frankish political supremacy to the Böhmerwald. Conquest was followed up by the foundation of new bishoprics at Würzburg on the Main, Passau and Regensburg on the Danube, and Freising on the Isar—all strategic locations for fortresses from which the Slavs could be converted, conquest could be assured and settlement protected. War and defence continued to be important aspects of the occupation of the south. Disturbed conditions occurred between 803 and 811 during Charlemagne's campaigns against Slav and Avar and the foundation of his East March recognised the insecurity and instability of this marchland region. From 896 the incursions of the Magyars represented a new threat, not brought to an end until their decisive defeat at Lechfeld, near Augsburg, in 955.

Settlement of German peasants, nobles and clergy pushed ahead in spite of these interruptions. From 791 settlers from the Rhineland had been driven on by the pressure of famine. By the end of the ninth century the banks of the river Raab had been temporarily reached, but lost again with the advance of the Magyars. After Lechfeld settlement was resumed on a larger scale. Bavarian and Franconian settlers moved eastwards to the margins of the Böhmerwald and to the Wienerwald by 994, and in the south to the valley of the river Enns. The distribution of place-names in -dorf characterises the areas affected by this early wave of movement (see Fig. 3:2). By 1018 Vienna had been founded, later to be made the capital of the Ostmark and of the powerful frontier dynasty of the Babenbergers. From Vienna settlement pushed even further east to the margins of the mid-Danube plains in Burgenland and to the banks of the Morava valley by the end of the eleventh century. In Hungary forward movement was brought to an early end by the growing power of the Hungarian state, and German settlers were diverted north and south to penetrate more deeply into Moravia on the one hand and into the Alps on the other. In Styria the Drave valley was reached, and parts of Slovenia and Carinthia were thinly settled by a minority of German peasants amid pre-existing Slav populations. But in the Böhmerwald and on the margins of the Erzgebirge settlers from the south-east

10 *Fredeburg, Sauerland, West Germany*. A regular, nucleated village with neatly spaced farms on each side of the main road. A street village of the *Angerdorf* type.

11 *Schwarzenborn, north of Marburg, West Germany*. A regular nucleated village laid out in an oval, elongated along the axis of the main road.

12 *Cordes, Tarn,* a hill-top settlement in the Causses on an easily defended site overlooking the river Córou, a tributary of the Aveyron.

13 *A terp, Netherlands.* Small settlements on artificially raised mounds above the marshland are characteristic of early settlement in parts of the Netherlands, especially in Groningen.

were, by the end of the thirteenth century, meeting and mingling with a stream of migrants who belonged to a different tradition of German settlement and had penetrated from Saxony. By this later date, planned and highly organised settlement forms had been adopted and place-names in -*dorf* had been replaced by clearing names. And the distribution of these late names makes it clear (see Fig. 3:3) that the frontier behind settlement was expanding towards less favourable sites and more marginal soils.

The character of the southern expansion differed considerably from the later expansion of the north. Perhaps because the movement took place at an early date and because the southern expansion was accompanied by conditions of insecurity and war, the initiative in settlement lay with the nobility and the clergy. The peasant needed the protection of his lord, just as the lord needed the peasant as a reserve of manpower and as a supplier of food. Serfdom, military service, and labour dues, the feudal apparatus of the old Rhineland estates were all reproduced in the new lands of the south-east. There was little need for organised recruiting or for the granting of new privileges to new tenants; there was the same grading of peasants and property as in old Germany; there was no uniform colonists' law; and there was little planning in the creation of new villages until a later stage when southern colonisation had begun to benefit from the experience of the north. Settlement forms in the lowlands recall those of the old west and in the upland zone, more fitted by climate and soils to pastoral farming, hamlets and scattered farms were normal. The similarity of geographical conditions as well as the similarity of social conditions in the lands of new settlement assisted in the duplication of old forms. The scarplands of Franconia, the margins of the Böhmerwald, the moraines, outwash plains and marsh of Bavaria and the Alpine valleys were all types of environment familiar in the old west, and there was no significant difference in climatic conditions.

In northern and central Germany the eastward movement of the farming frontier had necessarily to await political control over the area, which was not finally assured until the twelfth century, and a pressure of population on the land in the old north-west which was sufficiently heavy to make the prospect of migration an attractive proposition. And it must be emphasised that the Germans were moving into a region which was already occupied.

Various groups of Slavs, collectively known to the Germans as the

Wends, occupied the territory westward of the Poles in the Vistula basin to the Elbe–Saale line, the eastern frontier of Charlemagne's empire and the eastern limit of effective German farming settlement. The Wends were never so well organised as the Poles, Czechs and Magyars. Their political organisation was weak, their paganism made them legitimate prey to the German crusader and their economy relative to that of the Germans, was backward. Fishing and fowling played a large part in their economy. Hunting and stock-rearing were important, but arable farming was poorly developed. They used a crude form of the light plough and practised temporary cultivation by which fields were cleared by burning and then abandoned when fertility had declined. Their characteristic contributions to trade reflect this balance of their economy, for they were known chiefly for their honey, furs and wax, all products of a forest-collecting economy, besides their contribution to the slave trade. Yet two points deserve stress: their extensive economy supported no more than a sparse population except in areas of very fertile and easily worked löss soils which were sometimes more intensively farmed. There was still, therefore, plenty of room for the German immigration. Secondly, the Slav economy was to some extent complementary to rather than competitive with the German economy. The German immigrants were equipped with the heavy, wheeled plough with coulter and mouldboard and they had heavy felling axes with which they could clear the thicker forests in order to cultivate the heavier soils. The interest of the Slav in hunting and fowling could to some extent fit in with German settlement, particularly in the marshland areas. There is, indeed, some evidence that German colonisation was frequently accomplished by a peaceful symbiosis and welcomed by the Slav.

Yet the first phase of German expansion demonstrates clearly how important it was for the German to be able to support political conquest with a steady flow of German settlers such as demographic pressures later supplied. Between 919 and 932 the Sorbenland, lying between the Elbe and the Saale was conquered by the Germans. This was clearly a strategic area lying as it did near the headwaters of the Main and the Weser, controlling the routes across the Thuringian Forest to the south. It was also an area of dense Slav population in an area where the löss zone widens out. Further expansion took place along the Baltic coast into Mecklenburg and along the löss soils across the Elbe towards Magdeburg. But here, however, conquest was not followed up by the expansion of German rural settlement, and after the Wendish rebellion of 983 much of the German position east of the Elbe collapsed. Churches and monasteries fell into decay and German dominion over Slav populations persisted only in part of Holstein and the Sorbenland. It was, however, in these areas in western Mecklenburg that Slav settlement forms persisted. These are still areas in which Slav elements survive in the place-names and in which villages are frequently in the form of the *Rundling*, a Slav frontier form adjusted to the needs of defence (see Chapter 5).

It was not, however, until the middle of the twelfth century that the forward movement of German conquest was resumed, and this time, with the backing of a massive movement of migration. New conquests were made from the Slavs by 1143 in Holstein, Mecklenburg and Brandenburg. The success of the Wendish Crusade in the north from 1147 assured more land for settlement. Planned villages were being created in Holstein in a very few years after this; Lübeck was founded in 1143; and the conquest of Mecklenburg set in motion a forward movement all along the line of the Elbe. By the end of the twelfth century the settlement frontier had advanced by 50 to 70 miles (see Fig. 3:10) and in the process the planning of villages had become established practice; fields and houses were being more regularly grouped as the new villages became larger and more standardised in lay-out. Peasant holdings on the new lands were beginning to be standardised, so that in the south, on the margins of Hercynian Germany the norm was the Frankish *hufe* at about 60 acres and in the north the Flemish *hufe* of 42 acres.

In the south, the Franks were clearing new lands to the east of the Franconian scarplands on the margins of the Erzgebirge; and they were already using a new type of colonisation village known as the *Waldhufendorf*, distinctive in lay-out and neatly adapted to the problem of settling new immigrants in hilly wooded terrain (see Chapter 5 and Fig. 4:13). North of the Franks, the Thuringians were active, and to the north of them the Saxons were advancing rapidly along the Baltic coast, settling on the heathlands as well as on the heavier boulder clay soils. And the work of reclaiming the marshlands of the lower Elbe, the Oder and the *urstromtäler* of Brandenburg was left to the Dutch and the Flemish who had created a reputation for themselves as good colonists and who were particularly active in the marchland state of Brandenburg.

In the first half of the thirteenth century the movement reached its maximum activity. From 1220 the Dukes of Silesia had begun to encourage German immigration to their lands in order to stimulate their economic development and to increase the manpower under their rule, and movement was rapid, particularly to the zone of löss soils between the Oder and the foothills of the Sudeten Mountains. Further north the Oder had been reached by 1240 and the Neumark was organised beyond it with a new capital at Frankfurt-on-Oder. In the next 50 years settlement in the north advanced along the Pomeranian coast and a beginning was made in the settlement of East Prussia; while in the south the crestlines of the Erzgebirge and the Sudeten Mountains were overrun and German settlement reached its maximum extent in the Oder valley, constituting that great salient of German-speaking peoples in Silesia which coincides with the areas of most attractive soils and which has been so great a source of political discord. By 1300, however, the rate of movement had slowed down considerably, and new expansion on a large scale was limited to eastern Pomerania and the still advancing territories of the Teutonic Knights. Nothing more was achieved, for the high mortality of the Black Death of 1348 reduced the pressure on land and the flow of migrants stopped. Expansion eastwards ceased long before the German defeat at the Battle of Tannenberg (1410) put an end to their aspirations in Poland for the time being.

The process of colonial settlement in eastern Germany and the flow of migration eastwards had been geared partly to the demographic pressures which were at the root of increasing land hunger and deteriorating social conditions in the old west. It was also due to the desire of princes, dukes, counts and clergy to develop their newly acquired lands as sources of revenue. The lay nobility were always prominent but the monastic orders played an important part. The growth of the Cistercian and Praemonstratensian orders coincided with the great days of colonisation in the twelfth and thirteenth centuries, but the mobile military orders not bound to the sites of particular monasteries, could make the most of the great land grants that they received. The Knights of St John, the Knights Templars and above all, the Teutonic Knights, acquired very extensive lands in the east. The vigour, ruthlessness and organisation of the settlement of East Prussia bear witness to the activity of this latter order.

From 1150, as settlement became more complex and developed on an increasingly larger scale, its organisation fell into the hands of a specialised class of land agents or locators. They varied in function, status and wealth from the modest agent, content to lay out a few villages in a small estate, to the agent who acted on a much larger scale for prince or bishop; some were able to buy land for speculation or in order to settle it themselves. Their very existence is evidence of the scale of the migration. The locators supplied the floating capital to the migrants while they settled; and it was the locator or his men who recruited settlers and brought them to the site already chosen and prepared. They allocated lands and made themselves responsible for the supply of equipment, seed and even food for the period of initial settlement. In return they received a holding of land in the village which was often twice the size of the normal peasant allocation, and they received it free of tithe or rent. They usually received certain of the village monopolies and the highly valued right to two-thirds of the proceeds of dispensing justice in the village court.

'Go east, young man!' was advice commonly given in the lands of the old west, particularly at an early stage in the colonisation process, when the new lands were being advertised by such proclamations as that of the Bishop of Bremen as early as 1108: 'The Slavs are an abominable people, but their land is rich in flesh, honey, grain and birds and abounding in all the products of the fertility of the earth when cultivated, so that none can compare with it. So they say who know. Saxons, Franks, Lotharingians, men of Flanders most famous—here you can both save your souls and if it please you acquire the best of land to live in.'

Encouragements such as this, with the slight air of misrepresentation, flattery and dissimulation, such as one associates with so much advertising, may have been needed to encourage migration from the old west in the early stages of colonisation, but it has been pointed out that it was only in the early stages that migration was chiefly from the old west. Once colonisation was under way, new colonists were supplied from lands that had themselves been colonial. After the first waves of settlement had pushed out, long-distance movement of migrants was probably relatively slight. Indeed the distribution and grouping of place-names suggest this.

The most outstanding feature (and the one most obvious to the geographer) which resulted from the high degree of organisation and planning of the east German colonial movement was the repetition over much of this area of villages which were standardised in terms of size, lay-out and field system (see Chapter 5, p. 267). The same place-name element may occur commonly in groups of newly settled places, and names already well established in the east were sometimes repeated. For example, late clearing names are very significantly grouped in the margins of the Bohemian Massif (see Fig. 3:4). Names in *-schlag* occur north of the Danube between Linz and Vienna to the Czech side of the Böhmerwald, suggesting a sphere of settlement different from that which links the Regensburg section of the Danube with the northern part of the Böhmerwald by way of the distribution of names in *-ried*. *-Grün* is another place-name which links the sphere of the Elbe–Saale, rich in the little 'green villages' of the *Rundling* type, with the *-grün* forms of the Erzgebirge, where many of the villages carrying this name appear never to have possessed a green at all. In the upper Elbe and the Sudeten Mountains, however, settled later and from Saxony, the most commonly occurring names are those in *-hain* and *-wald*, both suggesting the clearing activity from which the *Waldhufendörfer* of the area were born.

The foundation of towns went hand in hand with the processes of rural colonisation, and burgesses no less than miners and peasants were among those who went east. Indeed the dates at which towns were founded frequently gives a clue to the timing of settlement as a whole. Like the villages, towns were also founded to standardised patterns, fairly simple in form and often involving no more than a rectangular or oval wall encircling a grid-iron pattern of streets. Many of these plans, like those of the villages, still survive in what is now eastern Germany and Poland. The urban laws of important towns in the old west were also frequently reproduced in the new lands. The laws of Lübeck, Magdeburg, Nürnberg and Vienna were the most commonly reproduced. The planning of towns went further than this, however, since even by the end of the twelfth century it was becoming apparent that efficient planning required the foundation of groups of villages in association with a town to serve them. Organised town and country planning became characteristic of the settlement of Silesia and was clearly a guiding principle in the settlement of East Prussia.

The foundation of towns and their success depended to a large extent on the production of agricultural surpluses. Pastoral farming seems to have been emphasised on the larger holdings and on the lands which were left in the hands of the lords. Little is known of the extent of cattle rearing, but sheep were being reared for their wool and were supplying the growing textile industry of Saxony as early as 1300. From the peasant farms of newly colonised lands grain surpluses began to flow north along navigable rivers to the Baltic ports; Brandenburg was beginning to export grain to England and Flanders by 1250. The foundations were being laid of German merchant activity in the Baltic which led to the pre-eminence of the Hanseatic League at a later date. Indeed, one aspect of the economic revolution brought about in the Baltic as a result of the success of German settlement is the participation by German merchants in the foundation of new towns in the east Baltic by which the Russian trade could be tapped. Novgorod acquired by 1250 an important colony of German merchants who were soon able to supersede the Scandinavians.

From 1186 a German expedition conquered Livonia and Courland, and in 1201 Riga was founded, but the most important of these moves in the Baltic was the conquest of East Prussia by the Military Order of the Teutonic Knights from 1231. In that year the Vistula was crossed and the town of Thorn founded; twenty years later Königsberg was established and Memel followed soon after. The subjugation of the Slav, the crushing of the Masurian and Prussian rebellions and their enforced conversion to Christianity were followed by a Germanisation more ruthless and thorough than elsewhere in the North German Plain. From 1280 German immigrants were imported, and 93 towns and 1,400 villages were founded between 1280 and 1410. Yet in spite of the scale of this movement settlement of the whole territory was never completed by the time that the loss of population in the Black Death and subsequent plagues brought the supply of settlers to an end.

The effect of the German movement was felt far beyond the boundaries reached by German conquest or even by German migrants. The economic development which was assured by the application of German techniques in mining, agriculture and trade stimulated many a Slav lord or prince to attract German immigrants. The Dukes of Silesia had done so from 1220, and so did the Czechs. Unlike the Slavs of northern Germany the Czechs were early organised into a strong and powerful state which was generating its own movement of internal colonisation in the thirteenth century, yet Prague had its quarter of privileged German merchants and German miners were working the silver of the Erzgebirge. German farmers were clearing the more gentle slopes of the outer margins of the Bohemian massif from Austria to the Böhmerwald, from Saxony to the Erzgebirge and from Silesia into the Sudeten Mountains. Czech expansion may have been discouraged by the greater barrier to movement and expansion presented by the steeper fault-line scarps which face inwards towards the Bohemian Plain. German minorities were already entrenched in the whole region of the Sudetenland by the end of the thirteenth century. Movement even further afield occurred to the south-east. Twenty-four German towns had been founded by German miners in the south of the Tatra Mountains in the thirteenth century, and in the twelfth century a movement as far as Transylvania sought to defend the frontiers of the Empire against nomadic invaders from southern Russia by settling German peasants.

In Poland, too, German immigration occurred at the invitation of Slav nobles who hoped to see their lands more efficiently developed. German settlement took place in the area of löss soils and in Hercynian Poland, especially along the route to Cracow and Kiev. But in this area particularly it is difficult to say exactly how far German villages and field systems or the adoption of German laws was a product of German immigration or of successful imitation by Slav landowners of German practices. 'Economic germanisation' of this kind took place far beyond the limits of German immigration but the extent of German settlement was often exaggerated by nationalistic German historians before the second world war.

Postscript

A neat and tidy linguistic boundary marking the progress of a linear farming frontier across the North German Plain was never the product of east German colonisation, whatever may have occurred in the Middle West of North America in the nineteenth century. Great areas remained in Germany in which Slav dialects continued to be spoken, long after the end of the Middle Ages (in Pomerania, Sorbenland, between the Elbe and the Saale, in Lusatia and Upper Silesia) and in which Slav settlement patterns and field systems continued to exist (in Mecklenburg and Sorbenland, for example). Beyond the margins of continuous German settlement there were sporadic islands of German settlement and small German minorities of peasant farmers. Even beyond these areas there were regions in which German forms of settlement had been adopted by Slav populations. German miners constituted exclaves of German-speakers far beyond the area of German rural settlement in the upland metalliferous regions of south-east Europe. And all over east central Europe important and influential German minorities of merchants and craftsmen were responsible for the foundation and prosperity of many of the new towns that were springing up.

The effect of German settlement was to create a zone in which there were many gradations between the areas of solid German settlement and the areas untouched by German influence. In medieval times the linguistic differences thus produced mattered much less than religion as a generator of passion and prejudice. But at a later date when nationality came to be important and was identified by the touchstone of language, the confusion of the linguistic map of the North German Plain, together with the absence of 'natural' frontiers in an area in which physical features trend on the whole from east to west, made the creation of satisfactory political boundaries an impossible task.

The conditions which affected German settlement in the east changed considerably after the end of the Middle Ages.[37] It was a gross anachronism to suggest, as Bismarck did that 'the Germans were consciously fulfilling their historic mission in central Europe'. But during the seventeenth and eighteenth centuries the dynastic policies of the Habsburgs, of Brandenburg-Prussia and particularly of Frederick II, put a new and different emphasis on rural colonisation in the lands which had been acquired from the Slavs. In 1618 Ducal Prussia fell to the Hohenzollerns, and some time later Polish suzerainty was brought to an end. In 1648 Pomerania was acquired at the Treaty of Westphalia. German settlers from Brandenburg, western Pomerania and Silesia were established in these areas in an unsuccessful attempt to produce German-speaking majorities in the new territories. This seventeenth-century expansion was associated with the introduction—an important one—of the potato on a large scale as a new staple.

Meanwhile in the Vistula delta Dutch settlers were responsible for the draining of marshes in the neighbourhood of Danzig, where their compatriots were already playing a prominent part in the trade of the area. Here too, new settlers brought new techniques to the exploitation of resources, as they did in the most successful of all new German settlement of the fifteenth and sixteenth centuries, namely the revival and extension of silver-mining in the Erzgebirge, responsible for the creation of new towns and villages on a large scale. But the germanisation of Bohemia was given a new impetus from a completely different direction after Czech national aspirations were suppressed in the events which assisted in the precipitation of the Thirty Years' War. This new movement was from Austria rather than Saxony and affected Moravia rather than Bohemia. It involved the confiscation of Czech estates for the benefit of Austrian landowners and a germanisation of the administration.

The most important of the movements to extend German settlement eastwards prior to the industrial revolution took place, however, in the time of Frederick the Great of Prussia, particularly after the acquisition of Silesia in 1740.[38] German farmers, miners and metal-workers were settled in an effort to develop the area as a Prussian arsenal on the basis of local resources: lead, silver, calamine, iron and charcoal. Coal could be used to work up the wrought iron of which the area was producing large quantities by the end of the eighteenth century.

Legislation aimed at securing a majority of German speakers and at reducing the use of Polish pointed the way also to means other than colonisation by which the language map of Europe might be changed, and it indicates also the new political importance which was attached to the geography of language by contemporaries. The acquisition of Polish territory by Prussia in the first partition of 1772 was followed up by an active settlement policy. Some of the Polish owned land was confiscated for redistribution to a German peasantry. New attempts at German settlement were concentrated particularly in the marshes of the Netze (Notec) valley. The difficulties of securing sufficient outfall had tended to restrain the drainage of interior marshes in the Middle Ages, and Flemish attention had been confined to the simpler problems of marsh drainage in coastal areas such as the Lower Elbe or interior marshes and parts of Brandenberg. The marshes of the Netze valley thus remained as a great salient of Slav populations which it was felt had to be reduced, all the more so since this was an important route linking the Oder and Vistula. Planned settlements, even more regular than those of the Middle Ages and bearing the marks of the surveyors' rod in the rectilinearity of their boundaries, were the product of this new process of settlement, but it is interesting that the compact nuclear form was preferred even at this late date, when much of the new or reorganised settlement of England, Denmark or Sweden was in the more obviously economic form of the scattered farmhouse set in the middle of its fields.

During the nineteenth century the growing importance of the concept that nationality was to be identified with language gave a new political importance to linguistic geography in central Europe, particularly after the unification of Germany in 1870. The germanisation of the regions of western Poland acquired by the Partition of 1815 became an important part of the programme by which national unity was to be created. Yet Polish nationality was also being forged by similar tools, and there developed before the first world war a struggle for the majority allegiance in which language played an important part. The weapons on the German side of the scales were various: German farming was given financial assistance and the provision of easy credit facilities; measures were directed to reduce the use of the Polish language in schools and in administration. Measures were directed against the Catholic religion, identified increasingly in this area with the Polish nationalism of the Polish clergy. The prestige of German as a *lingua franca* in east-central Europe and as a key to social and economic progress also helped on the German side. State legislation consistently aimed at securing a German-speaking majority and a colonisation commission was set up in 1886 'to strengthen German elements against the encroachment of Polonisation in the provinces of Posen and West Prussia, and to establish German peasants and German workers'. In 1894 the *Ostmarkenverein* was founded 'to complete the historic duty of Prussia in the eastern marches'. Both aimed at encouraging German and penalising Polish settlement in the area. But other items weighed heavily on the Polish side of the balance, chiefly the growth of Polish nationalism among the peasantry as well as the intellectuals, the bourgeoisie and the landowners. The Polish position was strengthened, too, by the movement of Polish landowners to settle a Polish peasantry on their lands. The relatively high birth rate among the Polish population worked in their favour and so did the increasing tendency of the German landless labourer to move westwards, attracted by the higher wages and the opportunities of the towns and of expanding industry. His place was filled by Polish immigrants and seasonal labour. By 1913 the map produced by the *Ostmarkenverein* to show the extent of germanisation in the lower Vistula displayed how little new territory had been won by these German policies, and could, indeed, be used by the Allies at Versailles to justify the creation of a Polish corridor on the grounds, then sacrosanct, of the linguistic affiliations of the majority.

The principles by which the boundaries of the new succession states were created after 1918 gave pride of place to national self-determination, but in the welter of boundary-making other factors became relevant: the creation of economically or strategically viable frontiers, the recognition of historic boundaries and a tendency to punish the Central Powers and reward the Allies and their supporters. Needless to say, these aims proved incompatible, for linguistic majorities, held to be a reasonable substitute for democratic expression of national loyalties, were taken as the basis of the new frontiers between Germany and Poland, but further south it was the historic boundary of Bohemia which separated Germany and Czechoslovakia, thus putting the large German-speaking population of Sudetenland in the new Slav state.

From the end of the Middle Ages geographical and economic considerations in the planning of new settlements had been increasingly replaced by dynastic and nationalistic considerations. After 1918 it was accepted in principle, though not always in practice, that boundaries should follow the national predilections of the populations on each side. Minority problems were an inevitable result. But in the years that followed a new solution to minority problems seemed to offer itself: to adjust the people to the boundary instead of the boundary to the people. In the seventeenth century the Spaniards had attempted a form of demographic surgery to excise from the body politic the impurity of a Moorish minority. After the first world war a similar policy resulted in the expulsion of 348,000 Turks from Greece, and of 1,400,000 Greeks from Turkey, resettled chiefly in Macedonia and Thrace. During the second world war German urban minorities were removed from the Baltic states when these fell to Russia in the 1939–40 Agreement. Hitler attempted to germanise the Polish corridor by expelling 1,500,000 Poles from the area in the early stages of the war.

The acceptance of the need to give Czechoslovakia its 1937 boundaries, and the acceptance by the Allies of a western boundary for Poland which was to consist of the Oder–Neisse line, necessarily involved the elimination of minority populations of Germans on the wrong side of the boundaries. Sir Winston Churchill stated in the House of Commons in 1944, 'Such an offer [of new frontiers] would have to be accompanied by the disentanglement of populations to the east and north. The expulsion of the Germans is a method which, so far as we have been able to see, would be the most satisfying and lasting. I am not alarmed by the disentanglement of populations, nor

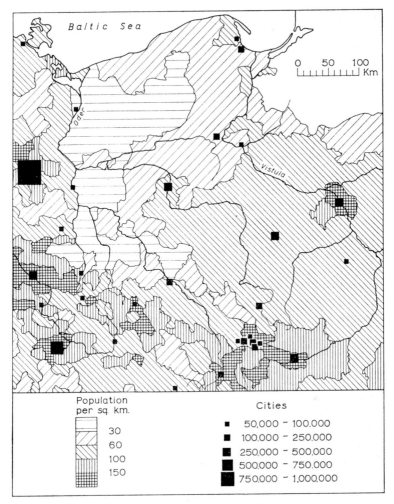

3.11 Population density in central Europe, 1959. The striking contrast between the emptiness of the 'lost areas' and the dense population of the post-war German state is evident.

even by these large transferences, which are more possible in modern conditions than they ever were before.'

In the postwar years the transference of these populations added to the chaos already produced by the flight of so many Germans from the east in the face of the Russian offensive. In 1947 the Allied Control Council was made responsible for carrying these plans into effect. Of the 3½ million Germans who were all that remained of a pre-war German population of 9 million within that territory now transferred to Poland, 2 million were transferred to the Russian zone and 1½ million to the British zone of north-west Germany. Of the 3,150,000 Germans who lived in Austria, Hungary and within 1937 boundaries of Czechoslovakia, 1,750,000 went to the Russian zone of east Germany. Other German populations were transferred from Hungary and Austria to south Germany and the Rhineland. By early 1947 only 250,000 Germans remained within the pre-war area of Czechoslovakia, chiefly skilled craftsmen and a few communists.[39]

Thus it was that a movement which represented one of the first colonial expansions from Western Europe was reversed in a single decade. Millions were now displaced where once pioneer farmers had moved forward in their tens of thousands, over a period of two centuries or more. The map of population density in 1959 shows a part of the gap they left (Fig. 3:11); the field systems and the village forms to a large extent remain as evidence and relics of a medieval expansion even if place-names are now Czech or Polish.[40] But the memory and the traditions remain among the German people.

REFERENCES

Abbreviations:

C.A.M.　　La Citta nell'alto medioevo. Settimane di studio del centro Italiano di studi sull' alto medioevo, Spoleto, vol. 6, 1959.
C.E.H.E.　　Cambridge Economic History of Europe. Vol. 1, Agrarian Life of the Middle Ages, ed. J. H. Clapham and E. Power, Cambridge, 1942.

1. F. T. WAINWRIGHT, Archaeology and Place-names and History, London, 1962.
2. Ibid., pp. 38–56.
3. SIR MORTIMER WHEELER, Rome beyond the Imperial Frontiers, London, 1954, pp. 1–119.
4. Ibid., p. 116.
5. R. KOEBNER, 'The settlement and colonisation of Europe', C.E.H.E., vol. 1, pp. 1–88.
   J. M. LACARRA, 'La historia urbana en España', C.A.M., vol. 6, 1959, pp. 319–58.
6. A. BACH, 'Deutsche Namenkunde', Ortsnamen, vol. 2, part 2, Heidelburg, 1956.
   E. SCHWARZ, Deutsche Namenforschung, 2 vols., Göttingen, 1949–50, especially vol. 1, chapters 4–7.

7. G. NIEMEIER, 'Gewannfluren, ihre Gliederungen und die Eschkern-theorie', *Petermanns Geogr. Mitteilungen*, vol. 90, 1944, pp. 57–74.

8. The following works contain very useful accounts of settlement in France, summarising many regional studies or providing basic information about place-names and the problems of using them:

E. SALIN, *La Civilisation Mérovingienne*, 4 vols, Paris, 1949, especially vol. 2;

A. DAUZAT, *Les Noms de Lieux*, Paris, 1944 and *La Toponymie française*, Paris, 1946;

E. NÈGRE, *Les Noms de Lieux de France*, Paris, 1964. The *Transactions* of the Third Congress of Toponymy and Anthroponymy at Brussels, 1949, publ. Louvain, 1951, contain much regional and specific detail relating particularly to France and the Low Countries.

9. M. DERRUAU, *La Grande Limagne*, Clermont Ferrand, 1949, pp. 463–92.

10. G. DES MAREZ, *Le Problème de la Colonisation franque et du Régime agraire en Belgique*, Brussels, 1926.

11. C. VERLINDEN, *Les Origines de la Frontière linguistique en Belgique*, Brussels, 1958.

12. F. LOT, *Les Invasions barbares*, Paris, 1925, 2 vols.

13. R. LATOUCHE, *The Birth of Western Economy*, London, 1961, pp. 211–34. See also, R. W. SOUTHERN, *The Making of the Middle Ages*, London, 1953.

14. A. R. LEWIS, *Naval Power and Trade in the Mediterranean, 500–1100*, Princeton, 1951.

15. Lacarra, *C.A.M.*, vol. 6, 1959, pp. 319–580.

16. F. BRAUDEL, *La Méditerranée et le Monde méditerranéen à l'Epoque de Philippe II*, Paris, 1949, pp. 185–8.

17. H. LAUTENSACH, 'Über die topographischen Namen arabischen Ursprungs in Spanien und Portugal', *Die Erde*, vol. 6, 1954, p. 219, and 'Maurischen Züge im geographischen Bild der iberischen Halbinsel', *Bonner Geographischen Abhandlungen*, vol. 28, 1960.

18. E. LEVI-PROVENCAL, *Mussulman Spain in the tenth century*, Paris, 1931.

R. S. SMITH, 'Medieval agrarian society in its prime: Spain', *C.E.H.E.*, vol. 1, pp. 344–60.

19. V. F. GONZALEZ, 'La evolución de los cultivos en las huertas levantinas de España', 16th International Geographical Congress, Lisbon, 1949, *Comptes Rendus*, vol. 3, pp. 286–306.

20. F. JIMENEZ DE GREGORIO, 'La población en la Jara cacereña', *Estudios Geograficos*, vol. 20, 1959, pp. 21–79; vol. 21, 1960, pp. 313–70; vol. 22, 1961, pp. 251–88.

21. J. BRØNSTED, *The Vikings*, London, 1960. See also H. SHETELIG, *Scandinavian Archaeology*, Oxford, 1937.

22. P. H. SAWYER, 'The density of the Danish settlement in England' *Univ. of Birmingham Hist. Journ.*, vol. 10, 1957, pp. 1–18.

23. A. R. LEWIS, *The Northern Seas, 300–1100*, Princeton, 1958, especially chapters 5–7.

24. W. HEYD, *Histoire du Commerce du Levant*, Paris, 1911.
25. S. BOLIN, 'Mohammed, Charlemagne and Ruric', *Scand. Econ. Hist.*, vol. 1, 1953, pp. 1–45.
26. Lewis, *Northern Seas*, chapters 5 and 7.
27. L. MUSSET, *Les Peuples scandinaves au moyen âge*, Paris, 1951.
28. Dauzat, *Noms de Lieux*, and Nègre, *Noms de Lieux de France*.
29. G. DUBY, *L'Economie rurale et la Vie des campagnes dans l'Occident mediéval*, 2 vols, Paris, 1962, vol. 1, p. 69.
30. M. BLOCH, *Les Caractères originaux de l'histoire rurale française*, Paris, first edition 1931, pp. 5–17. See also additions and comments in revised edition, ed. R. Dauvergne, 2 vols, 1956 and 1960, Paris.
31. Koebner, *C.E.H.E.*, vol. 1, pp. 63–88.
32. J. C. RUSSELL, *British medieval Population*, New Mexico, 1948, pp. 235–82.
33. Duby, *L'Economie rurale*, vol. 1, pp. 500–37.
34. Musset, *Les Peuples scandinaves*, p. 174.
35. Ibid., p. 175.
36. The most convenient and most stimulating accounts of German colonisation eastwards are:
H. AUBIN, 'German colonisation eastwards', *C.E.H.E.*, vol. 1, pp. 361–97;
J. W. THOMPSON, *Feudal Germany*, Chicago, 1928;
R. KÖTSCHKE and W. EBERT, *Geschichte der ostdeutschen Kolonisation*, Leipzig, 1937;
W. KUHN, *Geschichte der deutschen Ostsiedlung in der Neuzeit*, 2 vols., Cologne, 1955.
37. Kuhn, op. cit., vol. 2.
38. J. ANCEL, *Slaves et Germains*, Paris, 1946.
39. E. WISKEMANN, *Germany's eastern Neighbours*, London, 1956.
40. Z. WOJCIECHOWSKI, *Poland's place in Europe*, Poznan, 1947.

CHAPTER 4

AGRARIAN STRUCTURES AND
FIELD SYSTEMS BEFORE 1800

NORTH-WESTERN EUROPE

In his journeys across France, Arthur Young repeatedly noted the contrast between enclosed fields (which so delighted his eye in England but which so disappointed him in France as to the quality of the farming practised on them) and the open fields of the *champagne* country which he abominated.[1] In England the Parliamentary enclosure movement, which Arthur Young himself did so much to encourage, was largely responsible for sweeping away almost all that remained of similar open-field landscapes in England, except for a few isolated examples such as Yaxley in Lincolnshire, or Laxton in Nottinghamshire. In Scandinavia, north-west Germany and probably in some Mediterranean areas enclosure has removed most vestiges of the open fields that existed in Arthur Young's time, but in many areas, ancient contrasts between open field and enclosures still persist. One can travel west or south from the Paris basin with a copy of Arthur Young's travels in hand and still find the differences about which he wrote. In western Germany, too, the open landscapes and distant horizons of open-field country are characteristic of many parts. But the difference between compact, enclosed fields and open, hedgeless landscapes, often varied by a pattern of strips carrying different crops, is but one of the very many differences in the layout of fields and farms which are to be found in Europe and which are the product of a long history.

The layout of fields is, however, a legacy which seriously hinders modern methods of farming. In Brittany and Cornwall, for example, high banks crowned by thick hedges and surrounding small enclosed fields of a few acres were inconvenient during the period of agricultural improvement in the eighteenth century, and they still are today. Fields are too small for the deployment of mechanised implements. Hedges may harbour pests and diseases but the solid banks are also expensive to level down. In regions of open-field agriculture the sub-division of holdings into scattered parcels, of which there may be hundreds in a single commune or parish, may on the one hand provide a farmer with a variety of soils and therefore with a prospect of a balanced yield, but, much more often in the modern world where yields may be related more closely to the application of artificial fertilisers than slight local differences in soil fertility, this advantage may be greatly outweighed by the disadvantage of having to make long journeys to scattered strips, by the inability to use modern machine methods efficiently, or by the difficulty of organizing subsoil drainage in areas where heavy soils may require it. One of the necessary concomitants of the contemporary agricultural revolution in France and Germany or the Low Countries, has in fact been a close attention to, and official subsidy for, the consolidation of scattered parcels into compact blocks.

After the great wave of practical interest in field systems and farming efficiency which arose in the eighteenth and early nineteenth centuries in England and Scandinavia, academic interest in this topic was aroused in the late nineteenth century when pioneer studies were made, comparable to those of Meitzen for rural settlement. In England Seebohm studied the village community and pioneered the investigation of the structure and origins of the open fields in England[2] and this was followed by studies of the enclosure movement such as that of E. C. K. Gonner[3] and that of G. Slater.[4] By 1915, H. L. Gray had produced his monumental work on English field systems.[5] In France Marc Bloch outlined the major features of agrarian history, with considerable attention to settlement and field systems, in his book on *Les caractères originaux de l'histoire rurale francaise*, published in 1930.[6] Like Gray's work on England, this has necessarily been revised in the light of more recent knowledge, but it remains one of the classics.

In Scandinavia, Germany, France and England, much of the pioneer work in the study of settlement and field systems was done by economic and social historians. In England, where a long history of enclosure movements had eliminated most of the obvious evidence in the landscape of former open-field systems, this was not, perhaps, surprising. The quality and strength of the English school of economic and social history and the enormous wealth of medieval documentation made it natural that this should be so. In France and Germany, however, the interest of geographers was equally aroused. Vestiges of early field systems, still prominent on the ground and still presenting problems to the modern farmer, were still so much a part of the regional make-up of Western Europe, that they naturally attracted the interest of geographers who had been schooled in the conception of geography as the study of landscapes or as the study of differences between places. Other circumstances may have contributed to an interest in field systems and settlement patterns, such as the close academic relationship between the study of history and geography in France, and the willingness of continental geographers to approach regional geography through the study of past conditions. Such work as that of Roger Dion on *La formation du paysage rural français*[7] and the pioneer work of Niemeier on the analysis of field systems in Germany[8] converged on the same field of study as that already tilled by agrarian historians.

Since the second world war the interest of British geographers in this topic has been aroused, and there has been a parallel interest in the study of landscape history by local and social historians. New emphasis on the study of local geography in the field and enquiry into the history of places have also contributed greatly to the accumulation of detailed studies. The availability of new aids to research such as air photographs and the cataloguing and photographing of rare manuscript maps has clearly helped. Detailed regional studies have tended to emphasise the complexities which underlie the patterns of ancient field systems and have led to the abandonment of the relatively simple generalisations reached by some at least of the pioneer studies. Much of this modern work has been done by geographers as well as historians and much of it is the fruit of a preoccupation with the land and its use rather than with societies and their development.

The field systems of Western Europe
The pattern of fields and their relationship to rural settlement may be seen as one aspect of a complex set of relationships by which farming is adjusted to its physical, social and economic environment. The patterns of fields, in this sense, could be seen as the arrangements adopted on the ground to make the best use of a particular physical environment with a given range of farming equipment and within the context of a particular structure of society. The best use might be defined as the use which yields a maximum income consistent with the need to maintain fertility or, alternatively, the use which

assures an adequate and balanced means of subsistence from the resources available within the village territory.

In many communities before 1600, and perhaps in most, agriculture had to provide food, drink and the hides, skins and wool which formed the raw material for much equipment as well as clothing. In most areas, then, stock were an essential part of village economy, providing meat, milk and dairy products as well as leather, wool and fats. Cereals provided not only the staple bread crops and some animal fodder but, in northern Europe, barley also provided the drink crop for the brewing of ale and beer. Protein foods could be derived from beans and peas as well as meat, milk or eggs; fats were provided by the olive as well as by stock products; and in some areas wine or cider provided an alternative drink. In general, therefore, although most villages kept some stock, there was great flexibility in the ways by which stock products, grains and fruits or vegetables could be combined to produce a satisfactory diet. It is evident that a vegetarian diet could enable a greater density of population to be maintained than one in which stock products played a larger part, and therefore that a growing population would tend to be accompanied by a decrease in pasture and stock and an increase in arable and grain cultivation, but there were limits to this process which were set, not so much by diet, as by the need to maintain fertility in the arable fields by manuring them, and above all by the need for stock as power for the plough. The information which is given in Domesday about stock is chiefly that which concerns the number of ploughteams.

The balance between stock and arable farming is largely reflected, in pre-industrial communities, by the proportion of arable to pasture. Domesday is again witness that the village woodland was frequently important as a source of pannage for swine as well as faggots for fuel, charcoal for various purposes and timber for construction. To a very considerable extent therefore, arable, pasture, woodland and waste, meadow, commons and heath were all used and in many ways complemented each other. And it is obviously a corollary that where population grew and consumption of stock products declined in favour of a greater concentration on grain, the areas of woodland, heath and rough grazing would also contract as they were reclaimed for arable.[9]

Field systems are clearly adjusted to the demands made upon the land; and they must also be adjusted to farming practice, involving not only methods of ploughing but also the rotation of crops, pasturing arrangements, maintenance of fertility, and the seasonal rhythm of the farming calendar. The social organisation of the rural community is also of fundamental importance, for it is evident that communal restraints and obligations have always been very intimately related to the structure of open-field systems. Field systems may also vary according to the degree to which landholding is concentrated or according to the social and economic gradations from large landowner to unfree peasant. The strength of the manor and the power of the manorial lords have also proved to be an important factor in the structure and layout of field systems. Defence played an important rôle in village types in many areas.

Terrain, climate and soils directly affect the details of field patterns in relation to slope, soil quality or drainage, for example. Elements of the physical environment clearly affect types of crop grown on the open fields (e.g. the choice between bread grains such as wheat, rye, barley or oats), but perhaps the most important ways in which the physical environment is related to field systems are indirect. Thus, for example, hilly terrain may limit the extension of arable farming in relation to pasture; this may in turn greatly affect the balance of stock in relation to arable and therefore the supply of manure, and through this the rotation of crops and the structure of the field system. Similarly soil characteristics such as the proportion of sand, silt and clay, freedom of drainage, and the upward or downward movement of soil minerals may affect the problems and methods of ploughing or even the choice of plough, and these facts in turn will affect the characteristics of the field system. These examples may serve to illustrate the complex network of relationships extending through the social and economic as well as the physical environment, and it may clearly be necessary at a later stage to re-examine some of these strands in greater detail.

The classic studies of field systems in Western Europe have almost all attempted to reduce a great variety of individual cases and variations to simple generalisations in order to facilitate their systematisation and comprehension. H. L. Gray divided the field systems of England into four types: the so-called 'Celtic' system of western Britain and Ireland, the Midland system of lowland England, and two areas of important variations from it in East Anglia and Kent. Marc Bloch divided the field systems of France into three types and went so far as to dignify them as *régimes agraires*. He distinguished the area of open-field farming in the north and north-east; the area of enclosures in the west, and the area of enclosures and irregular open fields in the south. Flatrès in recent times has sought to identify common traits in the farming systems of the maritime fringes of Western Europe from Norway to western Britain, Ireland and Brittany, and the existence of common traits can easily be identified in the open-field farming of midland England, Denmark, southern Sweden, much of Germany, and northern France. Similarly, the pattern which Marc Bloch identified in the south of France has much in common with the farming of Italy and the unirrigated arable lands of *secano* (dry) farming in Spain. Roger Dion made only a two-fold distinction where others have seen three, in that he distinguishes in France only between the area of open field in the north and the areas of the south, west and centre in which he regarded enclosure as the essential characteristic and open fields as unusual and abnormal.

These 'systems' represent a very considerable advance on earlier monocausal explanations since they stress the functional relationships involved in the structure of field systems rather than the search for causes.

Except for Dion's insistence on a two-fold division in France there has been a general measure of agreement in identifying a major three-fold division of the field systems of Western Europe: (1) an 'Atlantic' or 'Celtic' system in the upland maritime western fringes; (2) the 'open-field', 'Midland', or 'champion' system of the areas bordering the North Sea and as far south as the Massif Central and the Alps; and (3) the so-called 'Mediterranean' system. In the modern idiom, one may regard them as models against which the actual arrangements of individual villages may be compared.

Champion farming. Champion farming prevailed in the English Midlands, northern and eastern France, much of western Germany and in Denmark and southern Sweden. Sufficient common traits exist for all these regions to be grouped and described under one heading, yet there is a problem of terminology. Gray's use of the term 'Midland system' is clearly applicable only to England. To speak of 'two-' or 'three-field systems' is inapplicable in the many cases in which open fields were more numerous, and confuses the open fields with the rotations practised on them. And to use the term 'open-field' is to invite confusion with other types of field system in which joint cultivation of common fields was practised.

Many French authors have, indeed, adopted the English phrase *'open-field'* to represent the equivalent of the English 'Midland' system, but there is, however, much to be said for the English term *champion* which is used so much in the early literature to contrast open-field landscapes with enclosure, and it is a term which carries few irrelevant or misleading connotations.

The open fields of champion country were very varied in the arrangement of their component elements. In northern France, western Germany, southern Scandinavia and lowland Britain, the simplest unit was the strip, land or selion (*lanière* in France, *Flur* in Germany) (Plates 3, 4 and 5). They are long in relation to their width; they form the smallest unit of cultivation and they are frequently units also in the subdivision of property. Strips of up to a kilometre in length are known in north-western Germany in certain special cases and on light soils, but most tend to be shorter. Indeed the furlong is related to their length (furrow-long), but in no systematic way, for strips varied greatly in actual size. It has been suggested that the usual length was related to the distance which a ploughteam, pulling a heavy, wheeled plough with a fixed mouldboard, could conveniently work without a rest. Thus the length of the furrow and the strip would vary according to the ease with which soils could be ploughed and the slope to be tilled. Slopes appear also to have affected the shape of the strips and the gentle sweeping curves of ridge-and-furrow in a reversed-S form give a pleasing line to many an English landscape of rolling hills. The width of strips was variable, but very often it was of the order of five to twelve yards.

Strips, or fractions of strips, were the units out of which holdings in the arable fields were made up, and the means by which they were separated therefore had importance (Figs. 4:1 and 4:2 provide examples). In many cases this was done by grassy balks, by boundary stones, or by the disposition of land in 'ridge-and-furrow', which also assured surface drainage, much needed before modern methods of subsoil drainage in areas of heavy clays. Such ridge-and-furrow is still identifiable in many parts of the midland England where land has remained in pasture since it was taken out of open-field cultivation and features similar to ridge-and-furrow exist in France, Germany and Scandinavia, where they are also regarded as important traces of former open-field arrangements. In England and on the continent there has been much difference of opinion about the extent to which grass balks were left between strips and the extent to which ridge-and-furrow was normal. Practice seems to have varied: in the Midlands, ridge-and-furrow was common; in Cambridgeshire and other parts of eastern England as well as in Scandinavia there is evidence of the existence of grass balks at one period or another, and

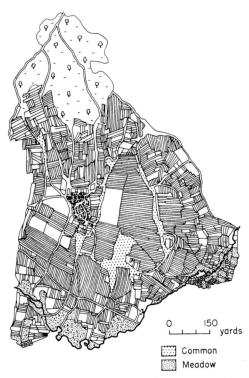

Fig. 4:1 An open-field, nucleated village in west Germany near Hanover, in its fully developed form in the eighteenth century. A complex example in which the fragmentation of strips, the multiplicity of fur-longs and the patches of waste and common are well seen. The contrast between the long strips near the village and the short strips and small furlongs near the bound-aries of the village terri-tory suggest the evolution of a *Gewanndorf* from a much smaller settlement by the accretion of fur-longs on an early nucleus of long strips (*Langstrei-fenflur*).

0   150 yards

Common
Meadow

in much of the limestone country of northern France, property divisions were marked by boundary stones. Although there has been disagreement it seems that ridge-and-furrow, wisely interpreted, provides important clues to the arrangement of open fields and their working. But it must be borne in mind that it exists outside the area of the champion system in regions of 'infield' farming; it may occa-sionally exist in enclosed lands; it is not necessarily diagnostic of the use of the heavy plough; and the absence of ridge-and-furrow can never be taken as evidence that open-field farming did not exist in an area.

Individual strips were grouped into furlongs (*quartiers* in France, *Gewanne* in Germany), and they were often the basic units in terms of ploughing and harrowing and the cultivation of the soil. Over all of Western Europe, the furlong varied greatly in size and in ways which seem to suggest conclusions about the ways in which they originated. Thus small furlongs on the edge of village territory have frequently been interpreted as being the result of collective clearing from the waste, occurring at a later date than the clearing of the much larger units which were the initial nucleus of cultivation. In some areas, peasants had a share in each furlong, as examples from eighteenth-century Denmark show, but this does not appear to have been normal or necessary.

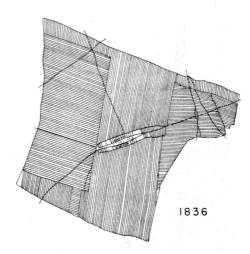

Fig. 4:2 A planned open-field village of the Angerdorf type which shows the organisation of strips in a planned system laid out during the colonisation of east Germany (after Krenzlin and Schwarz).

1836

The furlongs were grouped into larger units, which were the great open fields proper of England (*soles* in France, *Zelgen* in Germany). These large open fields, of which there were commonly two, three or four, were usually units with respect to the type of crop grown, the timing of fallow and the timing also of the season at which fallow or stubble was thrown open to the village flocks and herds. There were many variations, however, in the number of fields and in their combination with enclosed fields, and the rigidity of the system has been much overstressed in the past, particularly by authors who have based their accounts on the witness of advocates of enclosure. In particular, the bundles of strips or furlongs from which the open fields were made up could be regrouped from time to time if changes in rotations and cropping programmes suggested it. Such regroupings are evident in Alsace in the sixteenth century and in Cambridgeshire before enclosure, and it may well have been a common practice elsewhere.

Techniques of ploughing are very clearly related to the formation of strips and their combination into furlongs as the units of cultivation in the open fields. It has, indeed, been argued that the heavy plough equipped with coulter and fixed mouldboard, and drawn by a team of eight or possibly six oxen, was an instrument whose use necessitated the arrangement of land in strips. The turning of the plough-team at the end of each furrow, that is, at the headlands, would clearly be a cumbersome, time-consuming process and thus one to be avoided as far as possible. Furrows could be as long as the teams could manage without a rest. But if holdings were to be equitably shared in different fields and on different soils, properties would be inconveniently long and narrow unless strips were combined in hedgeless open fields. Yet the association of long, narrow strips with the use of the heavy plough is by no means an exact one. In central France and in Sweden lands divided into long, narrow strips were worked by the light plough in many areas. Similarly in Spain, North Africa and Turkey, arable lands divided into similar long strips occur far outside the region in which the heavy plough was normal.[10] The fact that strip cultivation is found far outside the area in which the heavy plough was used suggests that this type of technological determinism may have less to recommend it than was once thought.

The plough, however, and the ox-teams which pulled it represented a burden of capital investment too great even for many substantial free peasants to bear in the Middle Ages at the time when new lands were being cleared and new furlongs created. In its developed form, the heavy plough differed considerably from the light plough which continued to be used in the Mediterranean lands and in other regions of Western Europe (Fig. 4:3). It was distinguished by name, the heavy plough being known as the *caruca* in medieval Latin, the *charrue* in French and the *pflug* in German. The light plough or Latin *aratrum* was the French *araire*, Spanish *arado*, Slav *aralo* and Celtic *ard*. The heavy plough was equipped not only with a metal share but also with a coulter (a knife which could cut vertically through turf and soil). Each slice of turf cut by the coulter and the ploughshare was then thrust aside and pushed over by a fixed mouldboard, usually of wood in medieval times. The weight of the plough was thus greatly increased, so that another feature of the heavy plough developed, the wheeled carriage or foretrain which helped to take the weight. Each of these features could be independently attached to the older light plough, and it has been stressed that the coulter, for example, could be, and probably was, attached to the light plough. The mouldboard could be attached once a coulter had been devised, but both could and often did exist without the need for the wheeled foretrain on light soils. It has therefore been argued that the wheeled plough represented an instrument that was developed slowly over a long period and by a series of adaptations rather than something invented whole at a particular point in time (Fig. 4:3). Thus although wheeled ploughs and coulters were separately known in Iron Age times, particularly among the Belgae, it was not until much later that the last stage in the development of the heavy plough was reached with the design of an asymmetrical frame to balance the unequal drag of the mouldboard lying to one side of the central axis of the whole structure.[11]

The equipment of the heavy plough performed two functions which were either less important or which were not required in the light plough of Mediterranean lands. The coulter was designed to cut through a thick mat of weed, turf or stubble as well as soil. It could be useful on a light plough in friable soils with a sparse cover of vegetation in regions of pronounced summer drought, but it was clearly very useful on heavy soils and in more humid climates. The practice of deeper ploughing was also permitted by the use of the coulter, and the mouldboard was an obvious corollary to it since it turned over the slab of earth produced by coulter and share. Deep ploughing was also more important in north-western Europe than further south, since surface soil horizons were usually more leached and it was therefore an important function of ploughing to turn in surface soil and to bring up the lower mineral-rich horizons. Finally, the wheeled foretrain not only helped to take the weight, but it also assisted in the maintenance of an even depth of ploughing. It is thus clear that the heavy plough was devised for and also made possible the cultivation of heavy clays and strong loams, but it is also obvious that this was a cumbersome piece of equipment requiring a strong team of six to eight oxen or up to four horses, and that it would be of little use in accidented terrain and on steep slopes. The light plough was thus often retained even outside the area of the Mediterranean in hilly country, on thin, immature soils and in some areas of light soils (Fig. 4:4).

LIGHT PLOUGHS

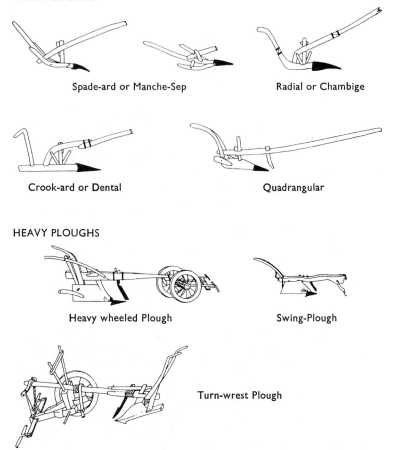

Spade-ard or Manche-Sep   Radial or Chambige

Crook-ard or Dental   Quadrangular

HEAVY PLOUGHS

Heavy wheeled Plough   Swing-Plough

Turn-wrest Plough

Fig. 4:3   Plough types in Western Europe *ca* 1800 (after Aitken, Haudricourt and Foster)

Heavy ploughs. (a) The heavy wheeled plough with coulter, fixed mouldboard and two handles (example from Denmark). This was the major developed form of the heavy plough and formerly widespread over much of
north-west Europe. (b) Swing-plough with coulter, mouldboard and two
handles (example from Norfolk), and formerly distributed mainly in
England. (c) Turn-wrest plough with wheels, adjustable coulter, mouldboard and two handles (example from northern France), formerly distributed chiefly in north-eastern France, the Low Countries and the Rhineland.

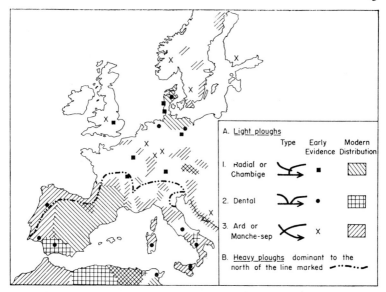

Fig. 4:4   The distribution of plough types in Western Europe (after Haudricourt and Delamarre).

The plough alone obviously represented a substantial investment of capital and effort but it also required the rearing and maintenance of a team of oxen and, since the maintenance of plough and team was beyond the means of most peasants, their provision had either to be co-operative and collective or it became the function of manorial lord or large landowner. In Domesday times there were far more peasant farmers than there were ploughteams, roughly in a ratio of 3·4 in south-east England (Kent and Sussex), and in a ratio of 2·3 to 3·5 in counties of the English Midlands. Communal ploughing with an instrument such as this, however, would clearly encourage open-field farming and it becomes easy to envisage the co-operation of villagers, not only in the clearing of new land from forest or heath but also in the cultivation of the furlongs so created.

The enclosure of large and individually worked arable fields from the waste or even from previously open-field arable in regions where the heavy plough was used were both processes which seem to have become increasingly common from the twelfth century and they seem to imply several possibilities: either that such enclosures were made by substantial peasants or manorial lords who could afford a plough of their own, or that there was an improvement from early times in the real wealth of the peasantry, or that ploughing techniques were developed which were less expensive in materials, craftsmanship and animal power than the traditional heavy, wheeled plough. There has, however, been very little work done on the relationship between ploughs and the cost of investment in them and the trend towards enclosure and farming in severalty.

The arable fields were only one part of the use to which the land of a village was put in the regions characterised by the champion type of farming. Woodland, meadow, commons and wastes, and the gardens or crofts which were appendages of farms and cottages constituted other essential elements of village life, and their exploitation was closely interwoven with that of the arable fields. This is not the place to enlarge upon the nature of village land use in any detail, but it is important to stress the interdependence of arable fields and the pasturing capacity of common wastes, pastures and meadows. Stock were pastured on the arable during the fallow year and on the stubble and the aftermath when harvests had been cleared. Hence during these times the stock manured the arable lands and thus helped to maintain fertility. But for most of the time stock were nourished on the communal pastures and meadows. The extent of the commons and their stock-carrying capacity therefore represented a limiting factor in relation to the supply of manure for the arable fields and in relation also to the number of animals that could be raised for draught purposes. Under this system, then, the extent to which arable land could be increased was limited until the circle was broken and dependence on common pasture reduced by the cultivation of fodder crops in the open arable fields. It also follows that considerable importance attached, not merely to a peasant's holding of arable land, but also to his 'stint', or the number of animals he was allowed to pasture on the open fields, and to his holding of meadow (since the supply of winter fodder, mainly hay, was traditionally one of the most important limiting factors on the number of stock that could be held over the winter months).

The problem of securing an adequate balance between stock and grain, or between pasture and arable was thus intricately bound up with another feature of the champion system which was, perhaps, its most characteristic element—the network of communal rights and restraints. And if the communal restraints tended on the one hand to reinforce the social bonds which held together the village community, they also influenced the appearance of the landscape in a number of important ways. It has already been seen that the use of the heavy plough encouraged co-operation in farming and communal cultivation of large open fields rather than individual cultivation of enclosures. The pasturing of stock at random after harvests and in the fallow years also meant that there had to be control over the types of crops to be grown, when they were to be sown and reaped, and when the open fields were to be thrown open to village flocks and herds. Arable land and meadow were therefore subject to common rights of pasture once the grain or hay harvest had been taken. Common rights thus existed normally over most of the village territory except where a lord of the manor or some other powerful owner had managed to extract lands from these communal obligations. Communal rights made it difficult to contract out of the arrangements for cropping and to grow what each wished on his strips in the open fields. They made it difficult for any individual farmer to extract his lands from the intermingled strips of others and to reorganise them into a compact holding. And the extent of communal rights also made it equally difficult to build a house or a farmstead in any other area than that normally devoted to gardens and crofts in and around the village. In the whole area characterised by champion farming, therefore, settlement patterns were related to the organisation of open fields.

In this classic form the champion system constituted a delicately balanced, but a fairly rigid system by which both stock and grain could be produced and by which fertility could be maintained. The major linkages in this structure are outlined diagrammatically in Fig. 4:5. The arrangements of fields and farmhouses were adjusted to the technological demands of the heavy plough, to agricultural practice and to the structure of manorial organisation or communal obligations. But there were very many ways in which major variations could and did occur. Where land was abundant and population sparse, cultivation of temporary and then permanent fields could be undertaken by individuals or by groups, cropping as they wished. Where land was abundant, scattered buildings and dispersed farms could be established on newly cultivated land, often at the margins of existing arable. Where manorial controls or collective restraints were weak there could be similar variation. Temporary wattle hurdles could be used to control the pasturing of stock or stubble or fallow of open fields as in the East Anglian variation of the open-

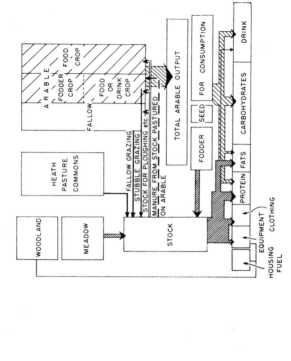

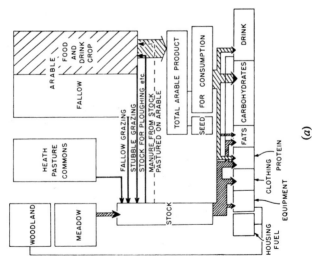

(a)

(b)

field systems described by Gray. This could mean greater flexibility of cropping arrangements, since individuals, or a part of the village community, could be emancipated from the rigours of a communal field system.

In the structure of champion farming in north-western Europe, the arrangement of arable fields was certainly related to the rotation of crops, but the two should not be confused as they sometimes are in descriptions of champion farming as the 'three-field system'. The three-course rotation, with which division into three large open fields was associated, was characteristically a rotation of winter grain, spring grain and then fallow. Winter grains were commonly wheat or rye; spring-sown grains were commonly barley or oats; pasturing on the fallow prepared the ground for the autumn-sown grain, which was normally the important bread grain. There were, however, variations, particularly on heavy clays, where beans sometimes replaced barley, and could be used as a fodder crop to fatten stock. Buckwheat, chickpeas, other pulse crops and even millet sometimes found their way into rotations elsewhere.

Each of the three fields was devoted wholly to a single crop or to fallow, so that individual farmers needed to have their holdings in three roughly equal portions so that they could take a representative share of total village crop production in each year. Indeed, this characteristic was taken by H. L. Gray as a diagnostic trait of the three-field system in midland England, since information about the location of holdings in particular fields is much more abundant than

Fig. 4:5   A diagrammatic representation of the relationships involved in two- and three-course rotations and open-field agriculture, assuming seed-yield ratios of 6.

(a) Two-course crop-fallow rotation. Arbitrary assumptions are made about seed-yield ratios (6:1) the pasturing capacity of meadow, common-lands, fallow and stubble grazings.
(b) Three-course winter corn, spring corn, fallow rotation. The same assumptions are made as in Fig. 4:5(a) and an arbitrary allocation of arable and fodder crops and food/drink crops is made. On the assumptions made, however, stock production is doubled with resultant benefits in diet and a further benefit for arable production in terms of manure supply and availability of stock for draught purposes. Just as the proportion of arable crops used for seed declines with increasing yields, so the proportion of stock used for draught purposes must decline with increasing stock population.

direct information about rotations. Similarly the implications of the three-field system for the balance of production of particular grain crops have also been used to derive conclusions about rotations from information about crop production. It is evident, for example, that a three-course rotation should produce winter and spring grains in roughly equal proportions. This fact is one of the most important that distinguishes the champion farming of north-western Europe from the two-course rotations further south. But it was by no means universal, for within the area in which it predominated there were many areas where it was replaced by other forms of rotation. In the Rhineland massifs, central Germany, and in Western France there were areas in which heavy manuring by abundant stock pastured on extensive wastelands could support almost continuous cultivation, frequently on poor soils and in marginal climates where rye, oats or buckwheat were the chief crops. Rotations were thus virtually indistinguishable from those of the infield system of the 'Atlantic' type.

Continuous cultivation dispensing with fallow also appears as a product of advanced agricultural techniques developed particularly in the Rhineland and the Low Countries by the end of the Middle Ages. Various types of rotation have been described, including alternations of rye, buckwheat, oats and short leys in the *Dreesch* system of Germany. In Flanders the precursors of rotations publicised in the agrarian revolution in England in the eighteenth century were being developed towards the end of the Middle Ages, using leguminous crops such as clover and lucerne (thus increasing the nitrogen content of the soils and also improving its organic content as well as supplying fodder for a greater herd of stock). The effect was thus to dispense completely with the fallow year and to increase agricultural productivity.

Two-course rotations in which a crop year alternated with a fallow year persisted in many areas of light, thin or poor soils or in areas where liability to drought in late summer prejudiced satisfactory yields from spring-sown crops. Thus the two-course rotation persisted during the *ancien régime* in Maine and Anjou, northern Brittany, the Jura and in parts of Lorraine, Alsace and the Rhineland massifs. It predominated in central Sweden and Jutland; and in England the two-course rotation was found by H. L. Gray to be most frequent on light soils overlying limestones and sandstones in the midland zone of the Jurassic scarplands.

Yet there were anomalous areas of fertile and productive soils, notably in the Rhine rift valley and chiefly in Alsace, in which the two-course rotation was characteristic in the *ancien régime*.[12] In these areas, closely linked to expanding urban markets by the navigable waterway of the Rhine, there was an early stimulus to produce grain for sale. Under these circumstances a system which could produce one good saleable grain crop every two years might be preferable to a system under which total production of crops might be greater but which produced a saleable wheat crop only one year in three. Indeed there is evidence from Alsace of conversion from three-field systems to two fields by the rearrangement of furlongs. During the seventeenth century, hops, tobacco, fodder crops and industrial crops replaced fallow and represented a much greater intensification of farming. Now, in distinguishing this from other parts of Alsace in which the normal three-course rotation was practised, it is not the quality of soil but the type of land tenure which is the differentiating element. In areas where customary tenants held from the larger landowners, peasants continued to produce spring grains for fodder for the lord's stock, so that the balance of advantage in these areas continued to lie with the three-course rotation.

Changes such as those exemplified in Alsace appear to have been very rare. In general, the three-course rotation represented an intensification of farming for most of the areas in which it was adopted since it produced four crops in six years compared with the three in six produced under the two-course system. The implications of this change were far-reaching.[13] When yields were low at 4, 5 or 6-fold on seed sown, the effect of an increase of one-sixth in the arable yield would lead to a more than proportionate increase in the amount of grain available for consumption.* Secondly, it often became possible to use part of the spring crop as fodder for stock as well as for a bread grain or for the brewing of ale or beer. Indeed, it seems possible that it was the additional production of fodder under the three-course rotation which may have made it possible to meet the more exacting food requirements of the horse on a larger scale than ever before,

---

* Thus, the produce of six years, assuming a yield of sixfold and a total cultivable area of x, would be 18x under a two-course rotation and 24x under a three-course rotation. If the amount of grain needed for seed is deducted, however, comprising 3x in the first instance and 4x in the second, the amount available for consumption is 15x in the first case and 20x in the second, an increase of 33 per cent with the three-course rotation.

and thus to make a greater use of more efficient horse-power in farm operations and general transport. In Germany, the introduction of the three-course rotation has been equated with the occurrence of larger holdings and the use of the horse in ploughing, whereas the two-course rotation continued to be practised with ploughteams of oxen on peasant holdings.

It is difficult, however, to pin down with any confidence the period at which transition took place in Western Europe to a three-course rotation from earlier field systems involving temporary cultivation, irregular rotations or the two-course rotation.it had been unknown in the time of Tacitus, but seems to have been known in the Paris basin in Carolingian times. But from the Paris basin it spread slowly to Britain, Germany and Scandinavia. Some English and French villages have left evidence of the alteration of their open fields from two to three in the twelfth and thirteenth centuries or even later, and it has, indeed, been suggested that the majority of the conversions are to be placed in this period.

If this is so, the three-course rotation represents an adjustment of farming and an intensification of agriculture in the face of the growing pressure of population in north-western Europe during the great age of clearing. The first and most widespread reaction to the growth of population was, of course, the expansion of secondary settlement and the colonisation of new areas, the drainage of marshland and the reclamation of heath and woodland. But after this stage had been completed, the arable land could only be increased at the expense of pasture and meadow, and would be restricted by the need to retain a minimum stock population for ploughing, manure, clothing and equipment as well as food. Beyond a certain point, as is evident from Fig. 4:5, the extension of arable at the expense of pasture, meadow and woodland grazings would lead to progressive impoverishment of the village community and a vicious circle of declining yields as draught-power and supplies of manure were prejudiced by shortage of stock. Conversion to the three-course rotation represented a way in which this situation could be evaded or at least postponed. And it may be that the greater discipline needed to operate the three-course rotation efficiently, to reorganise field systems and groupings of furlongs, and to supervise grazing also led to the development of restraints. Thus the elaboration of communal restraints affecting the grazing of common land, stubbles and fallows, or affecting the cultivation, sowing, and harvesting of open fields at agreed dates and according to agreed practices, may well have been a relatively late development brought into being by demographic pressures as well as by lordly power and initiative.[14]

The maritime west: 'Atlantic' or 'Celtic' systems. In his analysis of English field systems, H. L. Gray distinguished clearly between the open-field system of the Midlands and another type of agricultural practice, to be found in Wales and Scotland, the south-west peninsula and in north-western England. Gray regarded these western practices, which can also be shown to have much in common with the agrarian structures of Ireland and the Isle of Man, as characteristic of the Celtic west, and he seems to echo Meitzen in attributing these western field systems no less than the settlement patterns generally found with them to a Celtic origin. In France, Marc Bloch distinguished a western region characterised by enclosures and by scattered settlement in dispersed farms and hamlets. Open fields of a kind occurred, but they were not quite comparable with those of the champion country further east. Similarly in Scandinavia, Norwegian and Swedish authors have distinguished clearly between the favoured regions of Denmark and Scania, in which systems very similar to champion farming occurred, and other regions to the north where very different structures prevailed. Flatrès has drawn attention to the common features of all these regions, and these will be described below.[15] But it must be said at the outset, that although common features may exist, they do not point to a common Celtic origin such as that hinted at in Gray's discussion nor, indeed, can it be said that they point, necessarily, to any common origin at all.

Among the common features which are to be found in the field systems of the western regions perhaps the most obvious is the predominance of pasture over arable land. Pastures were generally held in common, usually by the village community, but sometimes by groups of neighbouring parishes. In the hilly terrains of maritime western Europe, common hill pastures were often so extensive, and arable land so scarce that temporary or seasonal quarters were established. Such summer settlements for stock were common for example in north-western England and frequently enter into place-names, as in the *booths* of Lancashire; but where seasonal movement was regular and over a greater altitudinal range to pastures which were only usable in the summer months, transhumance often developed on a larger scale. In Norway it has persisted to this day, and in Sweden the development of the summer settlements, the *saeters*, and the larger and more complex settlements of the *boothlands*, with some arable lands, can be traced. The system was expanding through the sixteenth century and flourished in the seventeenth but its full development came only in the nineteenth. Scotland had its summer *shielings* to which transhumant herds were taken; and in Wales the former existence of transhumance is expressed in the distinction between the permanent winter valley settlement, the *hendref*, and the temporary summer settlement, the *hafod*. Most mountain areas nourish forms of transhumance, and nothing unique or original can be claimed for maritime Western Europe in this respect. Switzerland or the Pyrenees can show far more developed and complex examples, but it is a trait which helps to mark off the west from the regions of champion farming.

A second important feature of the western areas, and perhaps the most characteristic feature, is the arrangement of the arable lands in patterns which have been generally labelled as 'infield-outfield'. Infield farming is usually characterised by intensive and continuous crop rotations which concentrate, sometimes exclusively, on grain production. In general, the cereals grown conformed to the damp but equable climates of the maritime margins of Western Europe. Oats, barley and even rye were more common than wheat except perhaps in Brittany and neighbouring parts of western France. In Britain, agricultural writers of the eighteenth century inveighed against rotations in which oats were grown year after year, with perhaps an occasional year of potatoes (not of course, available in the Middle Ages and spreading only slowly in the west in the seventeenth and eighteenth centuries). In many areas, however, there were good reasons for this type of practice. Arable land was scarce in relation to the amount of pasture and even to the meadow available in wet valley bottoms. The maximum use had therefore to be made of arable land for cereals rather than for fodder crops, which figure so largely in rotations of the champion areas at this later time. Moreover, the abundance of pasture and of stock meant that there was enough manure to maintain the fertility of intensively cultivated infields. Moreover, since the infield was cultivated and cropped every year, the need for rotation of fields was absent so that this was often also a 'one-field' system, containing a single large open field. Where open-field agriculture was practised in the western regions, the infield was usually surrounded by a hedge to keep stock away, but within it common forms of agriculture were practised and the land was often divided into strips as in champion areas. In Norway and in Ireland, the annual redistribution of strips was practised until very late— indeed, within living memory. In Cumberland the term 'changedale', appears to refer to the periodic redistribution of the *dales* or strips. In Brittany and in much of England strips were individually owned by peasant households, however, and in Scotland and Wales the joint cultivation of the infield by related groups of families was a very common feature. 'Runrig' in Scotland and 'rundale' in Cumberland are terms given to this practice in the literature. As in the champion regions, strips were separated by grass balks or were laid in ridge-and-furrow.

The types of plough used in the regions of infield farming varied considerably, as did also the type of strip cultivation. In Brittany, long narrow strips and the wheeled plough were used. In northwestern England, Scotland and Wales, ridge-and-furrow fossilised by conversion to pasture of former arable fields is much shorter in 'wave-length' than the ridge-and-furrow of champion country. And in many parts of the region as a whole, the light plough was preferred because of its greater flexibility on sloping land and on confined pieces of arable land.

Intensive cultivation and virtually continuous rotations on the infields were frequently combined with temporary cultivation of outfields. Waste, common or pasture was ploughed up, fenced off from the rest of the village lands, and cultivated for several years without benefit of intensive manuring until fertility dropped away to a point at which the land was allowed to revert to pasture, or in some areas to secondary scrub and woodland. Occasionally, temporary cultivation existed with very little permanent cultivation of the infield, and Finnish settlement in Sweden was well known for its entire reliance on temporary cultivation virtually indistinguishable from shifting cultivation. Forest lands were cleared by burning and planting turnips or rye in the ash which was left. Heavy crops were produced in the first few years after clearing in this system of *svedjebruk*, but as yields fell away the land was allowed to revert to pasture and new forest lands elsewhere were opened up.[16] At the other extreme socalled temporary fields were fairly regularly cultivated on a rotation basis, so that a system was approached which was identical with ley farming in that a few years of wheat, oats or barley were followed by several years grass before ploughing took place again.

In western regions, infield-outfield systems are or have been fairly widespread. They were common in many parts of northern and central Sweden until enclosure in the nineteenth century and they have been the usual type of field system in Norway. Indeed, temporary cultivation for rye or turnips still exists in parts of eastern Norway and the Trondelag. In western Britain and Ireland it was also normal until the nineteenth century and examples still survive in Brittany, particularly in coastal areas. In Brittany, Maine and Poitou, and also in parts of the Massif Central, infield-outfield systems and variations on them were once much more widespread than they now are, and French agricultural writers have indeed long drawn a distinction between the *terres chaudes* which were permanently cultivated, and the *terres froides* which were taken in for temporary cultivation. But it is also important to recognise that field systems of the same type also existed widely at the end of the eighteenth century in regions fairly well removed from the truly maritime margins of Western Europe. The Breckland in East Anglia and the light soil regions of Nottinghamshire, for example, were areas in which temporary cultivation of 'brakes' taken in from the waste were a normal feature of agriculture, and complex arrangements of more and less intensively used brakes have been identified. In continental Europe, the infield-outfield system was to be found in the Netherlands, where it was best developed in areas of light soils. In western Germany it was also to be found on the thin soils of the Rhineland massifs, where there was in the eighteenth century a transition from purely temporary cultivation on remote and high regions of poor soil to a combination of temporary cultivation with the champion system and the three-course rotation in the proximity of fertile lowland loam soils. In Belgium, Alsace, Lorraine and further south in the Alps, similar field systems existed. Thus, like transhumance, infield-outfield farming was never unique to maritime Western Europe. Enclaves of infield-outfield farming existed in regions of poor soils and abundant pasture within the general context of champion farming. Moreover, temporary cultivation of intakes from the waste merged gradually, as temporary fields became permanent and rotations more intensive, towards more or less continuous crop rotations with or without fallow but containing several years of grass ley. Rotations of this kind were indeed normal in western Britain before the agricultural revolution, and are also quoted for western France, south-western Germany and the Rhineland.

Although the patterns and problems of rural settlement will be taken up in a subsequent chapter, it should here be said that the distinctiveness of rural settlement in the maritime fringes of Western Europe was one of the starting points of Meitzen's analysis. Large nucleated villages are rare, hamlets of two to ten farmsteads are normal and dispersed farms and dwellings are common in the area as a whole. Yet it is obviously the case that this form of settlement, like transhumance and temporary cultivation, is not restricted to maritime Western Europe alone, and is not uniquely characteristic of this area.

Enclosures have also been a much more characteristic feature of the landscapes and agrarian history of the western lands. Indeed, in France the distinction between the enclosed lands of the *bocage* in western France and the *champagne* or open fields of the north and east was recognised long before Arthur Young publicised it for English readers. In much of western Britain piecemeal enclosure of new lands from the waste was normal from very early times. All over Western Europe the transition from temporary cultivation of occasional intakes to their permanent use for agriculture may have been followed by individual appropriation and enclosure. Where pasture land was abundant, as it was in much of these damp and hilly western regions, common rights of grazing were perhaps not quite so jealously guarded as in the arable regions further east, so that piecemeal intakes were possible either on payment of rent to the lord or by payment of a nominal fine or simply by right of occupation. In Rossendale, Lancashire, and in North Wales in the sixteenth century expansion took place by processes of this kind.

In central and northern Sweden expansion of settlement and of cultivated land took place around the summer *boothlands* and *saeters*. Meadow lands were supplemented by patches of arable land; these arable plots, which can be traced in various stages of evolution on the invaluable Swedish cadastral surveys of the seventeenth century, were organised in various ways around the little hamlets which were emerging first as temporary settlements and later as permanent village sites (see Figs 4:15 and 4:16). Where convenient, arable land was organised in rough and irregular open fields, but in many other settlements the arable was held in severalty and separately enclosed. Open field and enclosures existed side by side in the same village within only a few generations of the initial settlement of the area.[17] With its marginal climate for agriculture, with cool summers and a short growing season, northern Sweden was one of the last major frontiers of colonisation in Western Europe. New pioneer settlement was taking place from the sixteenth to the nineteenth centuries in ways that were not very different from those by which much expansion must have taken place hundreds of years earlier in more favoured parts of Western Europe. The apparently haphazard combination of irregular open field, similar to the infields of maritime Western Europe, and piecemeal primary enclosures from the waste bears comparison with conditions in more developed western lands in the twelfth and thirteenth centuries; it also warns against too simple or dogmatic a view about the evolution of the agrarian landscapes of the maritime fringes of north-western Europe.

In western Britain the enclosure of the open 'town' lands or infields began to occur from a fairly early period and much of it was already complete by the time that Parliamentary enclosure was introduced in the eighteenth century. In Brittany, the origin of the bocage has been surrounded by considerable controversy, though the main features of the bocage and its evolution are now becoming a little clearer. The enclosed bocage landscape of Brittany normally consists of small fields surrounded by a ditch and a high hedge or earthen banks themselves carrying a hedgerow with occasional fruit trees (Plates 1 and 6). Only in the windswept coastal zones, particularly in the west, or at higher altitudes, are the hedges absent. The hedgerow timber traditionally provided a source of litter, timber and fruit.[18] Brunet describes different shapes and sizes of typical bocage fields in Normandy and Cotentin, distinguishing between regular and irregular shapes, and among the former, between bocage with square or broadly rectangular fields of not more than about 150 metres or 500 feet, and large squarish divisions, usually of meadow, of about 850 feet (see Fig. 4:6).

Some have regarded the bocage as simply a sign of the early development of individual property among the Breton peasantry and thus as a confirmation of his rugged individuality and independence; others have stressed the need for enclosures either to defend the arable lands from grazing stock or to protect stock from the winds and gales characteristic of at least the coastal zones; yet others have suggested that hedgerow fruit and timber were important local resources. Serious discussion has made use of the ninth-century cartulary of Redon and of the Very Ancient Custom of Brittany of 1312 and 1325. On the basis of this documentary evidence, Chaumeil suggests several stages in development.[19] Even by the tenth century gardens or crofts were enclosed for vegetables, fruits etc.; enclosure of accommodation pastures for the winter and overnight maintenance of stock was the next step but general enclosure was still forbidden and arable and rough grazings were as yet open. At a later stage towards the end of the Middle Ages, enclosure began to take place on a larger scale from both the large unenclosed estates of the lords, and from the open fields worked by commoners. But it is important to stress that at the end of the Middle Ages arable lands were still small islands of cultivation in a sea of heathland and rough pasture. While the expansion of population further east led to the fully developed village with its obligatory rotations and the rest, the growth of population in much of Brittany and western France was still concerned with the creation of clearings by small groups of related families, often enclosing their lands as they were cleared, and naming their settlements by such suffixes as '-ière', '-ais' and '-ker', demonstrating an origin not earlier than the eleventh or twelfth century. Yet even by the end of the eighteenth century it was estimated that two-fifths to two-thirds of Brittany were heathland and waste and there seems to be little doubt that there was a much greater expansion of enclosures when the peasantry, growing rapidly in numbers and confirmed in its proprietorship of the land, began to reap the advantage of Brittany's proximity to the sea and therefore to outlets for wheat, potatoes, stock and dairy produce. It was not perhaps until after 1850 that the bocage reached its maximum extent and by then the disadvantage of small fields for mechanised farming and of hedges, harbouring pests and diseases and hampering the full development of arable crops, had already begun to be apparent. It was during this phase, undoubtedly, that the larger and more regular pattern of the bocage enclosures was created.

Further south, in the Gâtine vendéenne, terriers and notarial documents have told a slightly different story, at least for the earlier period.[20] This, too, was a region in which hamlets and open fields existed before 1350, and in which a peasant holding might consist of some 15 to 20 acres fragmented into a dozen open strips. But it was a region badly ravaged by the Hundred Years' War and by the plagues of the fourteenth and fifteenth centuries. When redevelopment began, the nobility were able to consolidate their ownership of large properties and began to lease parts of them out to share-croppers or métayers, charged with the duty of laying out and maintaining the hedges of their new compact holdings in which farm buildings were centrally placed. A few old hamlets survived, but the product of the fifteenth- and sixteenth-century redevelopment was a dispersed settlement pattern subsequently further developed during the nineteenth century.

The evolution of agrarian landscapes

Northern France. The contrasts in rural landscapes between eastern and western France have inevitably attracted studies of the distribution of bocage and open field and of the boundary zones in which open field gives way to enclosures. Studies of this kind are also closely associated with comparable analysis of settlement patterns and distribution. As in England, open field of the champion type has

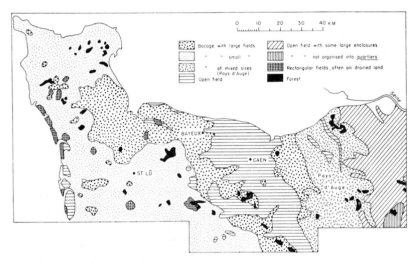

Fig. 4:6   The field patterns of Normandy (after Brunet)

been found to extend far to the west and south of the boundaries described by the pioneer authors on agrarian systems (Gray, Bloch and Dion); and in France enclaves of champion farming exist in regions of bocage and *vice versa*. Brunet has analysed in detail the field patterns of Normandy to show that open field and signs of former open field are characteristic of the Pays de Caen, Roumois and Liévin (Fig. 4:6). Now it is true that the champion of Caen coincides approximately with patches of limon overlying Lias and Jurassic limestones but it is probably the relief that provides the clearest correlation, and the champion farming zone coincides more exactly with an area identified as an exhumed post-Hercynian erosion surface. Dion showed in 1934 that the boundary in the Paris basin between champion farming and nucleated settlement coincided strikingly in Beauce and Perche with an important transition in soil type (Fig. 4:7). In the area characterised by bocage to the south and

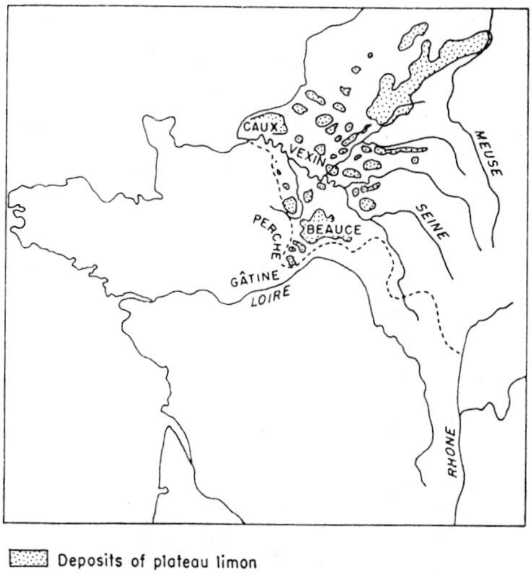

Fig. 4:7 The boundary in northern France between open-field and enclosures according to Arthur Young.

Deposits of plateau limon

west, soils are derived from sands and gravels with ferruginous concretions, originating largely as alluvial debris brought down from the Massif Central in the Tertiary period. Acid, leached and intractable or infertile soils are characteristic of the zone as a whole. To the north and east, however, in the zone of champion farming, soils are largely derived from a limon cover, thickening to the northeast, and overlying Tertiary and Cretaceous limestones. Thirdly, in the centre west there is a region which appears to have been essentially similar to the champion complex of northern France in late medieval times, but subsequent changes in field system and settlement patterns have so obscured this identity that it was unmentioned in this connection by Dion or Bloch.[21] In this region, too, the limits of the champion complex may be seen in terms of relief and soil and its distribution coincides, in general, with that of light, easily cultivated soils on Jurassic or Cretaceous limestones (Fig. 4:8). To the north the limit is the southern margin of the Armorican massif; to the north-east and east it is the thick deposits of red clays overlying Jurassic limestones. Beyond lie the bocage and the dispersed settlement of Poitou and Limousin. To the south there is a more gradual transition to the hamlets and enclosures characteristic of the Aquitaine basin. Within this area as a whole there is minor differentiation

CTS – 92

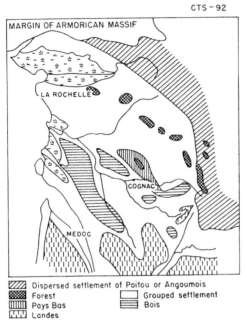

Fig. 4:8 Settlement, open-field and terrain in the centre west of France (after Enjalbert). The association of open-field and nucleated village settlement has been greatly obscured by dispersion of settlement consequent upon the expansion of viticulture from the seventeenth century.

▨ Dispersed settlement of Poitou or Angoumois
▩ Forest   ☐ Grouped settlement
▥ Pays Bas   ☰ Bois
▨ Landes

according to soil and relief, for the clay facies of the Portlandian stage at the top of the Jurassics was a region of thick woodland, late clearing and dispersed settlement. Similarly the Bois was cleared late. It is a region of sands and clays overlying limestones which was largely cleared on monastic initiative in the later Middle Ages or devoted to viticulture because of its proximity to the navigable Charente and thus to foreign markets. Indeed at a later date, from the seventeenth century, viticulture became so important as to bring about the destruction of the open field and the dispersion of settlement from the old village centres to the new vineyards.

Finally, Limagne is another region in which the transition from champion farming to other types of agrarian structure has been closely studied.[22] Limagne as a whole consists of a downfaulted basin in the Massif Central, drained by the Allier, partially filled with

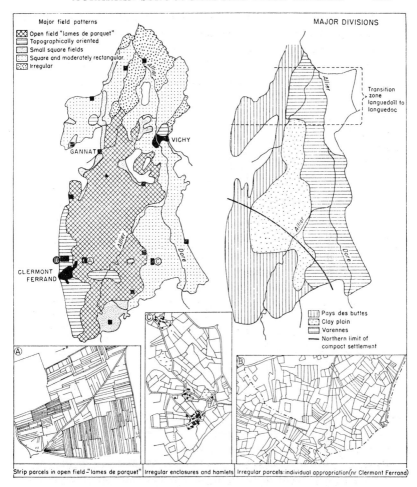

Fig. 4:9 Grande Limagne: field patterns and terrain (after Derruau).

Tertiary and Quaternary sediments, and strongly affected by former volcanic activity in the south. It thus lies across one of the most important cultural boundaries of France, that between the Langued'oc to the south and the Langued'oil to the north (see pp. 140–3 above). This north–south transition zone is transected by three natural divisions of quite different characteristics in terms of relief, soils and drainage (Fig. 4:9). In the western zone is the Pays des Buttes, an area of highly accidented relief based on limestones in the north and on volcanic rocks in the south. Soils and slopes are very varied over small areas and the older lavas in particular carry excellent soils for cultivation. In the south especially, downwash from volcanic sills has increased the fertility of lowland marls and rendzinas, so that suitable conditions exist for a very varied repertoire of crops with pasture on the plateaus, forest and viticulture on the slopes and arable on the flatter lands. In general this was a zone of early clearing and dense settlement even by Gallo-Roman times and it was in the medieval period a zone in which a productive and varied agriculture supported the precocious development of a local exchange economy organised in the large, nucleated and semi-urban settlements of the area. Open field was here rare and field patterns are controlled to a great extent by relief. There are also irregular enclosures produced by individual appropriation, quasi-regular divisions of pre-eighteenth-century division of common lands, and the rectangular field patterns produced by nineteenth-century divisions.

The central zone, however, is one in which drained marshland carries the distinctive stamp of Dutch drainage methods and field layout, but in which the older arable on the better drained land is still in open field, divided into very regular and long, narrow strips. Derruau labels this as a field pattern of *lames de parquet*, so regular are the divisions. In the eastern zone, the Varennes, dry, hungry acid soils are developed on Pliocene and Quaternary sands, and these were cleared late from the twelfth to the fourteenth century and worked from the beginning in enclosed fields round hamlets and scattered farmsteads frequently held in *métayage*, the most common form of tenure. The enclosures and the scattered settlement of the area are thus explicable in terms of late clearing or in terms of the spread of *métayage* tenures on large estates in much the same way as the comparable development in the Gâtine. The ancient enclosures of the south and west are more easily explicable in terms of very early settlement and kinship with the systems of the Mediterranean lands. The open-field zone of the central area, however, appears as an outlier of the champion zone of north-eastern France but it is a zone in which the organisation of arable into strips, furlongs and open fields appears to have taken place as a result of the initiative of manorial lords seeking accurate land assessments for rents and dues, for this was an area in which the light plough and the agricultural methods of the southern 'sub-Mediterranean' area continued to be practised.

Several conclusions emerge from this discussion of the distribution of field systems in France. It is obvious that the boundary zones between champion and bocage, and that between grouped, nucleated settlement and hamlet or dispersed settlement are frequently to be correlated with a distinction in soils and relief. In all of the cases here described it is the champion system, better adjusted, perhaps, to the predominance of arable farming, which is to be found on the more productive soils and in the areas of gentle relief. The second feature, however, is that the boundary between one type of system and another is not a simple one. There are outliers of the champion type of open-field farming in Brittany and Normandy, Devon and Cornwall, and further south in the French Alps as well as in Poitou, Aunis and Saintonge. But when due account is taken of the existence of so many enclaves and outliers and of the fact that the distribution of the so-called *régimes agraires* is by no means continuous within any one province, the whole concept must be called into question and re-examined.

There are, indeed, several other difficulties. The division of the agrarian systems of Western Europe before the industrial and agricultural revolutions of the nineteenth century into three major categories here described is to a large extent an intellectual one, and it is very important indeed to recognise this. The fact that field systems and settlement patterns of the medieval and early modern period were very closely interrelated with each other and with rotations, agricultural technology, tenurial conditions and inheritance practices demands consideration of the nature of these interrelationships, and this is best done through a very general classification of the field systems and settlement patterns of Europe. But it is first a classification and then a working model of the functional relationships involved. Individual examples may or may not conform, and many indeed do not, but the model provides a norm against which variations may be judged.

There is, however, a great temptation to forget that Atlantic, Mediterranean, and champion 'systems' represent idealised types or models and to assume that they represent distinct systems which originated independently, grew differently and spread separately into their respective provinces, each to be identified with a particular group of people. It may be too readily assumed, indeed, that they are distinctive and alternative rural economies introduced almost ready-made by a particular culture in prehistory or in the Dark Ages by Celtic, Gallo-Roman or Teutonic influence.

With this danger is associated another problem. Much of the evidence used in reconstructing ancient field systems is of relatively late date. The estate maps and plans, the land terriers and manorial surveys which provide the most abundant sources of material are of the sixteenth century or later, and very frequently date no further back than the eighteenth. Evidence from medieval documents has been used in abundance for the English material and much greater use has been made of it in recent years in France and Germany. But information about the development and changes of agrarian systems through the Middle Ages and in the early modern period is scarce for many parts of Western Europe, especially, of course, for the period up to the end of the thirteenth century, a particularly formative period. Growth and change have sometimes been too much neglected, with a resultant tendency to assume that the systems which appear fully fledged in the later Middle Ages had remained static for centuries and had been introduced in their main essentials at the time of initial settlement in the Dark Ages. Neglect of change through time has thus led to an undue concentration on an unprofitable and unverifiable search for origins.

Growth and change are, on the other hand, the central theme of a different method of study developed particularly in Germany and Sweden and given the clumsy but expressive name of the 'morphogenetic analysis' of the rural agrarian landscape.[23] Attention is focused on the form of field patterns at the earliest date at which the patterns of fields and strips can be established. In the absence of detailed medieval surveys, this must frequently mean a concentration on cadastral maps and surveys of the eighteenth century or, in more fortunate areas, notably in Sweden, on plans of the seventeenth century. Full use is made, too, of course, of air photographs and modern medium- and large-scale maps with full topographical information. The relationship of field patterns to settlement, relief, soils and drainage must obviously be examined closely, and so also must the archaeological evidence. Then an attempt is made to establish the most likely relative order in which various elements of the field pattern were introduced. Thus, for example, small furlongs at the edge of village territory may be thought to be later in origin than a large nucleus of arable land on more easily accessible and fertile, well-drained soils nearer to the centre of settlement. Comparison of many cases may confirm a hypothesis about the relative order in which particular elements have been introduced. In many ways the procedure is similar to that of the genetic geomorphologist in so far as it depends on the morphology of landscape for its evidence and proceeds by placing the formation of various elements or facets of the landscape in a chronological order in the light of knowledge about processes and about conditions in areas other than that which is being studied. Just as the geomorphologist may appeal to the content and analysis of geological deposits for a greater chronological precision and to other sources of evidence to reconstruct the climatic and ecological conditions at the time of formation, so also must the historian of the cultural landscape appeal to documentary evidence for greater precision and understanding of social, economic and technological change affecting field systems.

Germany and the Low Countries. The most profitable conclusions about the development of field systems have been reached as a result of intensive analysis in north-west Germany.[24] On parts of the *geest* lands of this area relict forms of ancient origin are to be found. The *Geest* itself consists of heathland degraded from a former oak-birch forest and occurs on sandy, podzolised soils developed on sandy glacial and fluvioglacial deposits which alternate with marshland. The heathlands have long been devoted to grazing but there occur small islands of slightly elevated and better drained sandy loams suited to arable cultivation. These potentially arable soils were known as *esch* lands, i.e. good land for cereals, and most of them were, in fact, the first lands to be cultivated and settled.[25] The characteristic field pattern to develop on the *esch* lands was that which has become known as the *Langstreifenflur* (formerly known as *esch*, but a term now recognised as a misnomer as applied to the field structure itself). The *Langstreifenflur* consisted of a single large open field of very long, parallel strips, some 5 to 15 metres wide and from 200 to 1,000 metres or more in length. It seems likely that it was cultivated like an infield with intensive manuring to permit continuous cultivation of rye. It may be that these 'islands' of arable land in the surrounding sea of pasture represent a stage in the shift from temporary and shifting cultivation to permanent, sedentary settlement. Perhaps the 'cattle-proud old European peasant' changed over to permanent arable as a result of the onset of colder and wetter conditions with the sub-Atlantic period during the late Iron Age. Carbon 14 dates give the first to the third centuries B.C. for the approximate time of earliest cultivation in this area. In parts of north-western Germany archaic survivals exist in a clearer form than in many areas because of the persistence of tenures through undivided inheritance. The long strips had originally been the arable held by the community of free farmers (*Vollerben*) who together formed a small hamlet of between three and ten farms, located at the margin between arable and pasture perhaps because of the need to stall-feed the cattle over the winter with hay and fodder drawn from the arable fields. This type of hamlet has been called the *Drubbel* to distinguish it from the clearing hamlets of the later Middle Ages. Place-names confirm that the hamlets associated with *Langstreifenflur* field patterns were of an early date, for in one area examined, thirty-three out of fifty-one places with '*-heim*' names had traces of *Langstreifenflur*, and names in other early forms, such as '*-mar*', '*-loh*' and '*-drup*' were found, but not late medieval forms such as '*-hagen*', '*-heide*' etc.

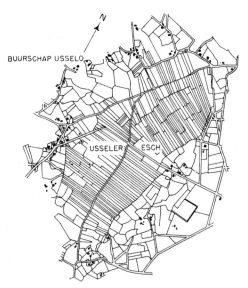

Fig. 4:10 An *esch* form with *Langstreifenflur* in the eastern Netherlands on light, sandy soils accompanied by hamlet groupings around the margins. Note that the reclamation of additional land for cultivation has been made by the addition of irregular enclosed fields (*Kämpe*) (after Keuning).

The *Langstreifenflur* and its associated hamlet survives in its purest form in parts of the Hümmling and Lüneberg Heaths and in the eastern Netherlands (Figs. 4:10 and 4:11), but in other areas, this nucleus has been greatly modified in various ways. In some parts of the north-west, even the original nucleus of arable has been converted to pasture and the old heathlands have been to varying degrees improved as pastures, so that only indirect traces of former field patterns exist and the hamlet settlements have been dispersed. In other parts of the north-west, subsequent accretion of new arable has very often taken the form of small irregular fields, individually enclosed from the waste, often by small holders or cottars who did

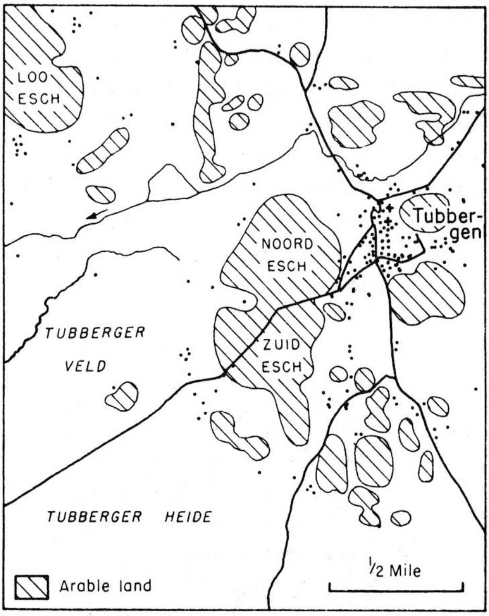

Fig. 4:11 Examples of *esch* types and associated settlement forms from the eastern Netherlands (after Keuning).

LOO ESCH

NOORD ESCH

Tubber-gen

TUBBERGER VELD

ZUID ESCH

TUBBERGER HEIDE

Arable land

½ Mile

not have rights in the *Langstreifenflur*. Further south, and particularly on the löss soils of the Börde, new arable fields were carved from the waste from an early time, but they were organised as new furlongs and eventually incorporated within the larger open fields of a three-course or similar rotation. In such cases a fully developed nucleated village with a champion type of field system replaced the earlier hamlet and only fragments are discernible of the original long strips (Fig. 4:1).

From Belgium there is evidence of a completely different kind, suggesting that an early form of field system rather like that of a 'western' infield existed at the time of the Roman Empire or soon afterwards. Using records of the abbey of St Pierre in Ghent, which include the *Liber Traditionum* dating back to the seventh century, A. Verhulst[26] has shown that a number of communities to the northeast of Ghent cultivated the sandy loam terraces above the river Lys in single open fields, which were still recognisable on eighteenth-century maps because of a very clear distinction between the surviving open field and small enclosures dating from the twelfth to fourteenth centuries which replaced an earlier heath and woodland vegetation on the light sandy soils which rise above the terraces of the Lys. Two other features help to make it clear that these single-field systems were already well established by the seventh century and almost certainly long before it. Their occurrence coincides with that of early place-names in -gem (e.g. Ledergem, Singem, Herlegem), a suffix comparable with German -heim and English -ham. Secondly, the arable lands are known as kouter, a term derived in the vernacular from Roman cultura, and in all likelihood so named at the time of the Roman occupation. If this is correct, then this would have been arable land already cleared by the time of the German occupation of the area and German settlement would thus have taken over existing cleared and fertile lands. If these -kouter names do in fact represent areas which were arable in Gallo-Roman times, then their distribution in Flanders, notably in the valleys of the Lys and Scheldt, may be significant.

The Belgian example relies on documentary evidence combined with place-names and eighteenth-century plans to establish early forms very similar to those deduced very largely by morphogenetic analysis in north-west Germany. Attempts have been made to find examples of similar field systems in other parts of Western Europe, and claims have been made for Mâconnais and for much of Germany, though there is, indeed, little evidence of Langstreifenflur to the south of the Rhineland. The most obvious and striking similarity is, however, between the single-field cultivation of an arable nucleus of the German type and the infield cultivation and hamlet settlement of the maritime fringes of Western Europe, though most of the infields of this western zone show no trace of the long strips so characteristic of north-western Germany. Yet Uhlig has been able to show examples in Brittany of permanently cultivated infields composed of bundles of very long narrow strips, usually on light soils (Fig. 4:12). Several hamlets or kers located at the edge of such a group of long strips may have properties scattered throughout them. Surrounding heathland pastures are often in the common ownership of the whole group of kers, suggesting that they represent an original community which has been split into component hamlets.[27]

In general, then, the continuous cultivation of infields represents a very ancient form of farming, developed at a time when pasture on uncultivated waste was abundant and perhaps when stock were a much more important part of rural economy than they became during the later Middle Ages. The long strips of the *Langstreifenflur* may have been preceded by more compact fields less systematically organised and cultivated by a light plough.

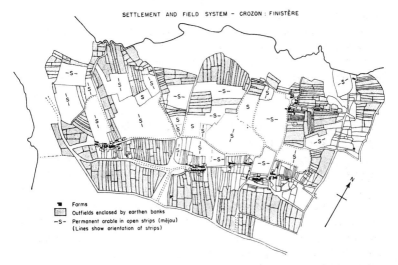

SETTLEMENT AND FIELD SYSTEM – CROZON : FINISTÈRE

■ Farms
▦ Outfields enclosed by earthen banks
–S– Permanent arable in open strips (mèjou)
(Lines show orientation of strips)

Fig. 4:12 Open-field *méjous* with hamlet settlement in Brittany (after Uhlig).

Alternative patterns of evolution have been suggested for southern Germany, though there is as yet little general agreement.[28] There is little trace of the *Langstreifenflur* in forms as readily identifiable as those of the north-west, and the irregular groupings of furlongs of varying sizes into open-field systems is much more like that of eastern France or midland England than the field systems of north-western Germany. The dating of the open-field pattern of *Gewannflur* has been much discussed and although some interpretations of early medieval texts suggest the existence of open-field organisation in the eighth or ninth centuries, it has also been very strongly urged, notably by Mortensen, that the *Gewannflur* in its developed form is a product of late medieval organisation. Others have followed Gradmann in the less revolutionary view that the *Gewannflur* is probably a secondary form developed from an earlier and simpler system.[29] In southern Germany much more than in the north-west the fragmentation of peasant holdings by equal division of inheritances, programmes of consolidation, and changes in land tenure and society have made early forms much less easily recognisable than in some other parts of Germany, so that it is particularly important to make full use of early documentary information as well as relict forms in the landscape in the reconstruction of early field systems.

Krenzlin's studies of lower Franconia suggest that two major types of field pattern preceded the development of the champion or *Gewannflur* of the later Middle Ages. Some villages show signs of having been arranged in some 5 to 12 large, rectangular open fields or *Blockflur* divided into pieces of some 2 to 5 hectares, and initially supporting relatively small hamlets rather than the large, compact villages which now exist. This appears to be the older form and occurred on the earliest settled land occupied before A.D. 800. The second and later form appears to have consisted of broad strips of up to 80 metres (or 90 yards) in width and up to 2 or 3 kilometres long ($1\frac{1}{4}$ to 2 miles). A peasant-holding (*Hufe*) might contain 2 to 4 such strips. This is a form clearly similar in some respects to that of the *Waldhufe* though the farmbuildings were not on the strips, and there were several to each holding. This type is characterised as the *Breitstreifenflur*, somewhat similar to the *Gelängeflur* of central and eastern Germany. These are to be found in lower Franconia on lands settled before A.D. 1000 in the neighbourhood, for example, of the Rhöngebirge. In northern Hesse the *Langstreifenflur* begins to make its appearance,[30] but in this area, too, there are traces of *Breitstreifenfluren* or *Gelängefluren* which are closely associated with clearing names in -*hain* and -*rode* which are of the later Middle Ages, and they are also closely associated with villages organised at an early date under heath-law.

A number of problems arise from these ideas about the development of German field systems. First, a plea has been entered for the extension of intensive geographical and historical studies to other parts of the country in order to avoid the unwarranted extension of ideas with local validity but of doubtful general application.[31] Studies of the German equivalents of lynchets have shown them to consist of two types: the squarish small fields similar to the Celtic fields of Britain, and known as *Kammerflur*; and the equivalent of strip lynchets or *Ackerterrassen*. The latter have sometimes been superimposed on the former on the same site, but where this has occurred it seems more likely that the two periods of occupation were separated by a period of disuse and contraction of settlement and that the earlier system appears not to have *evolved* into the later by any process of reorganisation or fragmentation.[32] But it should be said that by their very location and character these are on marginal lands, most likely to show less continuity of use in periods of fluctuating prosperity.

The creation of the *Langstreifenflur* on newly cultivated land or from existing *Blockflur* types presents another problem, for although it has been suggested that the *Langstreifenflur* may be associated with the Frankish conquest and settlement of the Rhineland, it would be difficult to see a reasonable relationship between this and the development of similar field patterns in other parts of Germany and in Brittany. Finally, it is true that long strips are *sometimes* associated with the light plough and that large compact fields may be the product of using the heavy plough, but it may be possible that the various stages in the evolution of the *Gewannflur* may be related fairly closely to the equally slow evolution and spread of the heavy plough. Thus the division of *Blockflur* fields with the growth of population and the fragmentation of holdings would be adjusted to the needs of the heavy plough, perhaps recently introduced, and therefore took on strip-like forms. The medieval development of the *Gewannflur* from earlier forms, whether from *Langstreifenflur* or other types, is a relatively uncharted process. Krenzlin has suggested that a degree of parcelling and fragmentation similar in scale to that which occurred in the nineteenth century in south-west Germany as a result of the increase of population would also have accompanied the growth of population in the twelfth and thirteenth centuries. In support of this view Krenzlin notes that it was in the upper Rhineland along the Bergstrasse and in the Wetterau, where population growth and economic development was stimulated by proximity to routes and towns, that the transformation of early settled hamlets into large, compact villages with *Gewannfluren* was most complete. Indeed, some of the early settled areas in lower Franconia which were off the main routes and which had little potential for development are still modest hamlets with a *Blockflur* field system.

Difficulties of interpretation which arise in part through the scarcity of documents and the ambiguity of the evidence in the landscape add to the problems of resolving the great variety of field patterns which exist in western Germany, but in the colonial East field systems have a greater simplicity, partly as a result of the recurrence of a fairly small number of standardised types which were the result of conscious planning and organisation over a relatively short period. Original forms and patterns have frequently been preserved through the practice of undivided inheritance. In much of the North German

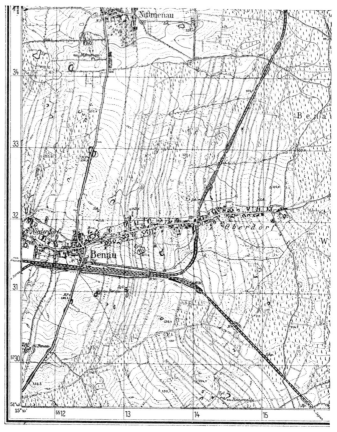

Fig. 4:13 A *Waldhufendorf* or forest-clearing village in east Germany near Frankfurt-on-Oder (after the German topographical 1:25,000, 1933, reduced to 1:50,000)

Plain open-field systems were established with regular arrangements of strips in large open fields (see Fig. 4:2); but in many areas where Slav settlement persisted, as in parts of Mecklenburg, Pomerania and Meissen, the irregular, small and compact fields of a *Blockflur* type were often retained. Further south in Hercynian Germany from eastern Franconia to Silesia, the Sudeten margins and beyond, one of the most common forms of field pattern was the *Waldhufen*, closely associated with a particular settlement form, since each peasant holding consisted of a single long narrow strip flanked by

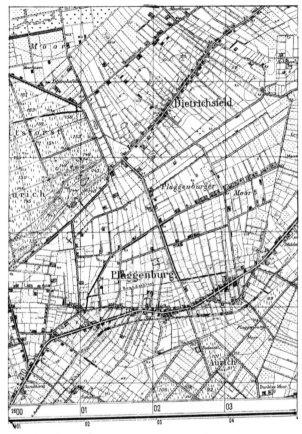

Fig. 4:14   A *Hagenhufendorf* or heath village in Hanover (after German topographical survey 1:25,000, 1942, reduced to 1:50,000).

access ways and leading away from the farmstead through the arable land to uncleared forest (see Fig. 4:13). Similar types of holding were developed in the reclamation of heathland and of marshland (Fig. 4:14).

Scandinavia. The study of early field systems in Sweden and Denmark has presented special problems and opportunities to the historical geographer. There is, in general, much less survival in the landscape of pre-industrial field systems and settlement patterns, since in both countries enclosure movements more radical even than those of England revolutionised the appearance of the agrarian landscape and the distribution of rural settlement. Yet in Sweden particularly there has been available a wealth of evidence in the form of provincial laws which codified rules and practices relating to the colonisation of new land, customary usage and the organisation of settlement and field systems. These often provide detailed evidence of the layout of fields and villages. Research by Swedish historical geographers has also revealed relict features of ridge-and-furrow, field-walls and ancient enclosures which have greatly assisted the interpretation of early field patterns. So too has the intensive study of ancient systems of mensuration and their application to house plots and field boundaries. From the later Middle Ages and especially after the introduction of Gustavus Vasa's public land registers and census lists in the 1530s there is detailed information about the grouping and location of individual farms and settlements. From 1630–50 the newly established Land Survey Office began to draw up that remarkable series of cadastral maps which provide rich detail at an unusually early date and for quite large areas of Sweden. Finally, relict features of archaic field systems have survived in some relatively remote and inaccessible areas where arable farming has been poor and marginal, and the intensive study of these has helped to throw light on former practices.

Early forms of settlement and field system have been most clearly traced in the seventeenth-century survey maps of the western margins of Sweden from Västergotland northwards through Värmland to Härjedalen and Jämtland.[33] A continuous gradation is apparent from the dispersed farmstead to joint villages which consisted of a loosely organised grouping of farms. Within these groupings, individual farms contained enclosures which had the chief function of keeping cattle away from the arable, the garden plots and the hay fields. From the earliest times, then, hay plots, arable, and small pastures for winter feeding and overnight accommodation were individually enclosed within each farm. Pastures beyond were open and grazed in common. It was only at a later stage, with the expansion of settlement and the development of larger and more continuous zones of arable that fences were thrown down and some form of joint rotation and cultivation adopted on the open field thus created. Erixon's conclusion that the infield type of open field was derived from the amalgamation of fields formerly cultivated independently

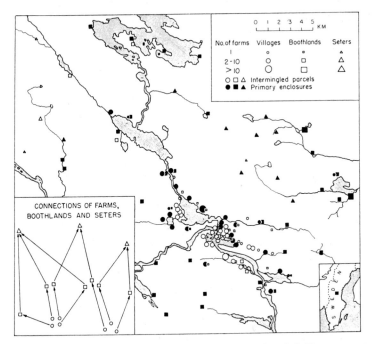

Fig. 4:15   The expansion of settlement and associated field systems in northern Hälsingland, Sweden (after Bodvall).

is one which receives support from the study by Gunnar Bodvall[34] of the way in which settlement developed in northern Hälsingland from temporarily occupied summer pastures to permanent villages with arable land (Figs. 4:15 and 4:16). In western Sweden villages with an infield and similar in some respects to those of Norway or western Britain preceded the growth of larger nucleated settlements with more highly organised field systems. And here, too, occasional cultivation of temporary outfields supplemented the product of the continuously cultivated infield (Fig. 4:17). Danish villages of northern Jutland, for which the land register of 1688 gives details, exemplify very clearly the decreasing intensity of cultivation towards the margins of village territory.[35]

In all of these cases, a separate and important identity attached to the village site, consisting of a much larger area than that which was needed for buildings, gardens, pens, and roads. Indeed, the village site was large enough for the accommodation and pasturing of stock and also contained a watering point for them at a stream, spring,

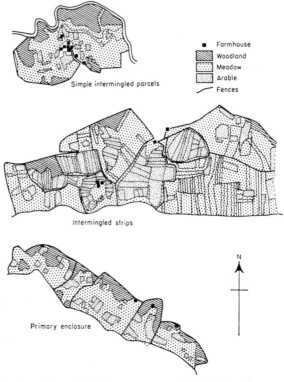

Fig. 4:16 Examples of field patterns associated with the expansion of settlement in the boothlands of Hälsingland (after Bodvall).

well or pond. Studies of relict field-walls in eastern Sweden[36] also stress the importance of this 'village-area' or *inmark* and the way in which it was marked off by walls from the arable and meadow, but linked by wide corridors to the pastures of the *utmark* beyond.

In a large part of eastern Sweden, Denmark and southern Finland, the unorganised and irregular field and settlement patterns of early times were replaced towards the end of the Middle Ages by a planned and highly organised system imposed from above. This systematic

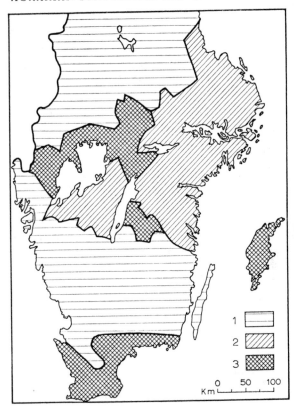

Fig. 4:17 Distribution of field systems in southern Sweden in the early nineteenth century. 1. One-field system of the forest regions and Öland. 2. Two-field system of the eastern plains and the Västergötland plain. 3. Three-field system of the southernmost plains, Gotland and parts of the Central Swedish plains (after Atlas of Sweden).

regulation and reorganisation took two major forms: in southern Finland and Eastern Sweden reorganisation occurred according to the *solskifte* system; in Denmark and Scania a variant known as the *bolskifte* was introduced.[37] *Solskifte* involved a total reorganisation of land and was in most cases followed or accompanied by a reorganisation of settlement as well (Fig. 4:18). The village was given a legal layout with measured house plots equivalent to the English messuage or toft, and called *tomt* in Sweden. This involved the creation of new settlement patterns which will be discussed later, but it was also accompanied by the division of fields in a new way. Large, open fields were organised, divided into very regular and squarish furlongs (*deld* or *skifte*) composed of strips (*teg*) with a measured width which varied according to the width of the messuages in the village. Each fully fledged farmer would have strips in each furlong. The location of his strip within the furlong would be constant in relation to that of other farmers and was determined according to the sequence of

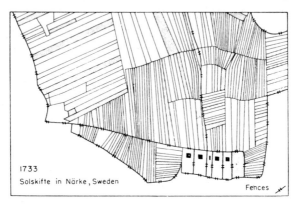

1733
Solskifte in Närke, Sweden
Fences

Fig. 4:18 A village organised under *solskifte* in eighteenth-century Sweden. The strips of one farmer are shown by the shaded areas. Note the regular position of his strips in each furlong and the systematic relationship to the position of his house in the village.

houses in the village, counting with reference to the apparent course of the sun across the sky and beginning in the east. Danish *bolskifte* differed in that strips were allocated according to the location of farms in particular groups within the village rather than with respect to the apparent course of the sun, but other aspects of the Danish reorganisation were very similar. Görannson has shown that much of this reorganisation in the island of Öland was done according to a unit of measurement, the ell of 47 cm., which was common by the twelfth and thirteenth centuries and was normal in churches built during that period. A major replanning of rural settlement took place later, however, in the thirteenth century and it was then that a more modern unit of 52 cm. was used as the standard.

Two implications of the *solskifte* reorganisation are worthy of comment. It is evident that a basic feature of reorganisation was to create a standardised division of holdings for greater ease of taxation. Görannson stresses that the new definition of strips, furlongs,

14 *Villeneuve-sur-Lot, S.W. France.* Founded in 1253 by Alphonse de Poitiers at the boundary between Perigord and Guyenne, and with a characteristically regular plan, Villeneuve-sur-Lot was one of the largest and strongest *bastides* of south-western France. The lower bridge is medieval, and the line of the medieval wall is traced by the boulevard at the bottom of the photograph.

15 *Bram, west of Carcassonne.* A small circular bastide with the church at the centre.

16 An example of planned marshland settlement or *veenkolonien* in Drenthe. Peat stacked for drying may be seen on the left.

17 *Aigues Mortes, Rhône delta.* "La ville de Saint Louis", and an excellent example of the planned town of the thirteenth century with rectangular street plan and almost perfect medieval ramparts. The town was built on the Rhône delta on land acquired by the Crown from a monastery in 1240 as a base for Royal participation in the Crusades. It prospered to mid-fourteenth century, when it had a population of 15,000, but its life as a port was limited by silting, in spite of canal-building and dredging. In the eighteenth century what remained of its trade passed to the new port of Sète.

fields and settlement was associated very closely with land assessments (the *attung*) similar in character to the English *hide* and the German *Hufe*. Assessed farms gathered into aggregates of 8 to 16 *attungar* constituted an important aspect of the reorganisation of settlement into nucleated villages. It is important, too, that the organisation of strips into furlongs and open fields took place independently of the introduction of the heavy plough, for although the heavy plough was a basic part of agricultural equipment in Denmark and Scania, the heavy plough was not known over much of the area in which Swedish *solskifte* was introduced and the light plough continued to be used. In Sweden and Finland as in Limagne on a smaller scale, methods of land apportionment involving furlongs and strips were adopted without the introduction of the heavy plough, fixed mouldboard and large ploughteam which had provided the technical *raison d'être* for this arrangement in midland England or the Paris basin.

A system such as this, established over a large part of Sweden, must have been imposed from above at the initiative of nobility or clergy long before the time when *solskifte* was made the legal basis for land division in the first laws of Sweden, about 1350. Although some have suggested that *solskifte* was imported from Germany or that it was a system exported to England where it left a few traces of 'sun-division',[38] there is better reason for thinking that the origin of the Scandinavian land division of the later Middle Ages was to be found in England. Görannson has brought to light much more evidence for the former existence of sun-division than was formerly thought to exist,[39] and although traces of it are much less clear than in Scandinavia as a result of the precocious development of a land market, growth of population, and the resultant obliteration of ordered divisions, there is a stronger case to be made out for the export of an English system to Scandinavia during the eleventh century, perhaps, than there is for movement of ideas in the other direction as suggested by Homans.

In some respects the field systems of Sweden and Denmark conform easily to those found elsewhere in Western Europe. On poor land such as the sandy heaths of Jutland and western Denmark, or in the uplands of Småland and at the northern margins of cultivation from Värmland to Jämtland infield farming with a single common field under more or less continuous cultivation was normal, sometimes combined with temporary cultivation as in the outfields of western Britain (see Fig. 4:17); on the more fertile lowlands of the central depression and particularly on the boulder-clay covered arable soils of Scania or eastern Denmark champion farming was normal and very similar to that of midland England or the Paris basin in essentials. In Scania and Denmark the heavy plough was normal and the two- or three-course rotation fairly common; in central Sweden the light plough continued to be used and although there were some areas in which the three-course rotation held sway, a two-course rotation of crop-fallow was more frequent.

In other respects the Scandinavian field systems yield conclusions important, perhaps, for the study of other areas in Europe. First, the evolution of village settlement from dispersed farms through a continuous gradation of loose hamlet to nucleated village is strikingly displayed as a part of a normal process of colonisation and intensification of farming from temporary summer grazing to permanent cultivation. Although this theme belongs to that of rural settlement, it is so closely associated with the development of enclosures and the emergence of a simply organised system of joint cultivation and single open-field cultivation, that it is worth stressing at this point. Secondly the idea of joint cultivation emerging out of a primary system of individual enclosures as settlement developed is logical and simple, and again commends itself as an analogy to be used in reconstructing the progress of settlement in areas less well endowed with documentary and cartographical evidence. Thirdly, the extent to which medieval field systems were here a result of planning and conscious reorganisation needs stress. Planning and organisation are implicit in the regularities and repetitions of the North German Plain, but that was an area of colonisation and frontier settlement, and Scandinavia was, relatively speaking, a long-settled land. Finally, the link with England, not one that can here be pursued, is one which may well be worth further analysis and research.

In general the field systems of north-western Europe have been discussed in the light of two complementary methods of approach, each with its own merits and its own pitfalls. The functional interrelationships which characterise the farming systems of medieval and early modern Western Europe described above must clearly be understood in so far as they demonstrate the delicate interdependence of man and land in a subsistence economy. These interrelationships can only be demonstrated, however, for broadly 'normal' or average situations. The retrospective analysis of documentary and map evidence, coupled with a morphogenetic approach stresses, on the other hand, the changing patterns of adjustment to new conditions from the time of early settlement to the end of the Middle Ages.

MEDITERRANEAN FARMING AND FIELD SYSTEMS

Arable farming

In the southern half of France, in Spain and Italy, patterns of fields and farms were much more varied than in north-western Europe. Cadastral surveys of the eighteenth century indicate a variety so great as to allow considerable disagreement between the views of Roger Dion and Marc Bloch not only about the origins but also about the essential characteristics of the system. Roger Dion considered that the liberty to enclose and to plant trees and shrubs in fields and hedges constituted one of the essential principles governing the structure of farming in southern France.[40] Fruit was an important and integral part of Mediterranean farming and diet, whether as wine, olives, plums, cherries, nuts, apples or pears. Their cultivation in fields normally devoted to arable farming was usual, a practice militating against common-field organisation. Collective practices, communal restraints and the maintenance of a delicate balance between stock and arable farming were, he thought, uncharacteristic of the region. Dion was inclined to interpret the surviving areas of open field to the excessive subdivision of properties originally organised in compact fields held in severalty, or as anomalous cases in which tenacious communal organisation has persisted from a very early time. The emphasis on enclosure and on the individualisation of farming was, Dion thought, to be derived from classical tradition, and indeed it was in the classical authors and particularly in the works of agronomists such as Columella or Varro and natural historians like Pliny that Dion sought much of his material, tending to ignore the great mass of medieval evidence.

Marc Bloch, on the other hand, recognised that enclosed fields were frequent in this area but he regarded them as a development subsequent to and later than the irregular open fields which, like those of the north, were to be associated with collective rights and restraints on the use of pasture, arable and commons (see Plate 7). Common pasture on the waste was normal and uniformity of cropping may also have existed, but for a variety of reasons, open fields decayed more easily and sooner than those of north-western Europe.

In modern France the distinction between open-field farming and enclosed lands is still frequently to be encountered though there are fewer clear regional distinctions than in the agriculture of the north. Indeed, regional studies show great variety over short distances. Corsica, for example, has many large communal pastures but arable fields are enclosed and individually held. Central Sardinia, on the other hand, has open-field farming in which the communal organisation of both arable and pasture is well developed. This difference between the two areas has been interpreted as the result of an early need to co-operate in defence against the Saracen and Italian raiders in Sardinia. In the lower Rhône, in Perigord and in parts of the French Alps attention has been drawn to the recurrence of a particular pattern: regularly divided open fields on low floodplains are the result of recent property divisions on land newly drained or irrigated; irregular open fields on dry, well-drained terraces may be the result of early settlement; and irregular enclosures on upper slopes represent early clearing in the Middle Ages of initially wooded slopes.

In Spain, patterns of field and farm in unirrigated areas vary between the 'humid crescent' of the north and west and the dry farming of the semi-arid meseta. In the former region, small properties and enclosed fields are normal; in the latter much open-field farming and many collective arrangements for pasture and cropping still survive on a large scale. Examples such as these may serve to illustrate the variety of Mediterranean practice. Strips exist and are often grouped into furlongs; open fields occur, but they are irregular in type and fairly rare; enclosures are common and widespread.

In so far as generalisations can be made, it seems necessary to stress that Mediterranean farming continued to use extensive rotations long after the north was turning over to the three-course rotations described above. A two-course rotation of winter grain followed by a year of fallow was normal, though in some dry areas such as central Spain a three-course rotation was often practised which was even more extensive.[41] Winter grain was here followed by a year of uncultivated weed fallow during which the fallowed ground was pastured by stock and manured. This was in turn followed by a year of clean fallow during which the aim was to maintain a fine surface mulch and to retain moisture in the soil for the next year's crops. Thus only one crop was taken in three years and that was often one of poor yield, giving no more than a marginal return on the seed sown.

The three-course rotation of central Spain illustrates, in an extreme form, the fact that conversion to the more intensive system of north-western Europe was frequently impossible because of the limits which were set by the Mediterranean climate. Classical writers had recognised that one of the most important aims in farming must be to maintain a carry-over of soil moisture from the fallow year to that in which the grain crop was to be grown.[42] This involved keeping the soil in a high pulverised state to reduce evaporation and run-off and to secure a high rate of percolation. Clean cultivation during fallow years was often recommended and, it seems, less frequently practised. The aim here, too, was to reduce the loss of soil moisture by reducing transpiration from unwanted weeds and vegetation, which would involve frequent ploughings and harrowing. Pliny had recommended that land should be ploughed five times a year and thought that the normal was three. Measures such as these represented a necessary concession to the summer drought of the Mediterranean climates and they were made chiefly in areas where summer drought was regular and prolonged. It was in the marginal areas such as southern France or northern Italy that deviations were most common. In the former region, fallow was commonly pastured and frequent fallow ploughings were unnecessary. In the latter region the inclusion of a spring crop recalled the northern three-course system, and it was here too that the practice of cultivating green crops for fodder or even for ploughing in, seems to have survived from Roman times into the Middle Ages.

One effect, however, of the insistence on clean cultivation was that stock were not so often pastured on fallow lands or the stubble grazings after harvests. This situation implied a lack of manure on arable lands and indeed, since rough grazings tended to have a low carrying capacity, there was a general lack of manure which in itself would prevent a more intensive use of the land. The close link between arable farming and stock farming which so commonly obtained further north was lacking in the Mediterranean, where rough grazings in the mountainous areas or in the marshlands and floodplains were sometimes so far removed from village arable lands as to favour transhumance on a large scale. Also grazing rights and the ownership of stock were more often divorced from ownership of arable than they were further north. Clean cultivation, shortage of stock and lack of manure for arable lands implied low yields. The whole system constituted a vicious circle which even now has not been completely broken in some of the drier and least well-developed parts of the area, as in parts of the central meseta where yields may be as low as 6 cwt per acre.

Yet the way out had been suggested in classical times by such measures as the replacement of the fallow by a green crop which could be ploughed in to maintain organic content of the soil and to increase its moisture-retaining capacity. Nitrogen content would also be increased if it were a leguminous crop. An alternative solution was to combine unirrigated farming of the traditional type with the cultivation of lucerne or other fodder crops under irrigation. This again was a classical solution advocated by agricultural writers of the time; it was a system used by the Arabs in Spain; but its most important development took place in the north Italian plain in the later Middle Ages, where it was an important part of an agricultural revolution associated with an ebullient urban demand.

The field systems of the Mediterranean, though varied, commonly used the light plough or *ard*. Several varieties have been noted each with its distinctive distribution in Europe (see Figs. 4:3 and 4:4). Compared with the heavy plough all varieties of the light plough merely scratched the surface of the soil and for this reason drew upon themselves the strictures of northern agricultural writers of the eighteenth century who often misunderstood their purpose. Mediterranean soils are on the whole lighter and more friable than those of northern Europe and surface soil horizons are also less leached, so that it was not normally important to bring the deeper horizons of the soil to the surface. The aim of ploughing was, indeed, to work the soil finely and frequently and this the light plough was designed to do efficiently and economically with the minimum draught power. Economy in the use of scarce stock gave it a distinct advantage over the heavy plough since it required no more than two oxen. This fact and the simplicity of its construction made it possible for peasants of only modest wealth to possess their own plough, and this in turn was one of the factors, perhaps, which assisted in the emancipation of the southern peasant and his fields from collective restraint or which obviated the need for collective obligations. Finally one other advantage of the light plough is the ease with which it could be carried about from one plot to another. Where parcels of land were widely scattered and in tiny patches on hilly land, the light plough could be used with little trouble in places completely inaccessible for the cumbersome wheeled plough of the northern plains.

Arable crops were supplemented in Mediterranean lands to a much greater extent than further north by the planted crops: perennial shrubs, trees and particularly vines. The olive played a fundamentally important part in diet since it provided the fats which were supplied in north-west Europe by stock products. Similarly wine from the grape fulfilled a rôle for which the northern equivalent—beer brewed from barley and hops—was largely a product of the arable lands. Other fruits and nuts were important: almonds, reintroduced by the Arabs; the carob nut in Iberia; chestnuts, a staple at times in parts of southern and central France. In some areas nuts may have contributed significantly to the intake of fats and proteins, particularly in areas where fish and meat or cheese were lacking. Apples, cherries, pears and plums were planted in small orchards by many villages and traditional fruits were supplemented by the exotic introductions of the Arabs: oranges, lemons, bananas, sugar, strawberries and new varieties of melon, for example.

Small fruits, vegetables and even arable crops were frequently intercalated with vines and olives or other tree crops in a type of farming which was very intensive and, indeed, almost horticultural in the detailed attention which was given to weeding, planting and manuring. It was this type of farming which was described as late as the beginning of this century by geographers such as Vidal de la Blache and Jean Brunhes as 'typically' Mediterranean, and is, indeed, still to be found in many areas.[43] And it had been the same contrast between the varied, garden-like farming of parts of Italy or southern France and the relative monotony of land use in the north which seized the imagination of classical writers such as Tacitus. The emphasis on perennial crops of various kinds and the cultivation of shrubs and trees in the hedgerows and in the arable itself made it necessary, or at least advantageous that peasants should till their own lands completely in severalty. The fact that vines and olives helped to supply drink and fats also helped to free the Mediterranean farmer from that complex interdependence of arable and stock which was so much a part of northern European farming.

Transhumance

One other aspect of the divorce between arable and pasture in Mediterranean lands is the widespread development during the

Middle Ages of transhumance. Its maximum development was in Castile, where there were as many as 3,450,000 transhumant sheep in the 1520s. Long-distance routes connected the summer pastures of the Pyrenees and the Cantabrian mountains with the winter pastures of the central meseta and the basin of the Guadalquivir. From the Middle Ages until the coming of the railway the sheep followed well-defined tracks, known as *cañadas*, a term which strictly referred to the segments of sheep-walks adjoining stretches of cultivated land, but generally extended to refer to the whole route. Klein[44] has described three principal systems: (i) a western group of routes, the *Leonesa* system, which collected sheep from gathering grounds north of León and went by way of Zamora, Salamanca and Béjar to winter pastures in Extremadura and the Guadiana valley; (ii) the most commonly used routes were those collectively known as the *Segoviana* system serving pastures in the Cantabrian mountains and going by way of Burgos, a most important centre, to Segovia, the southern slopes of the Guadarrama and then south to the Guadalquivir basin; (iii) the shortest system was that of *La Mancha*, connecting the highlands of Cuenca across La Mancha with the upper Guadalquivir and the lowlands of Murcia. There were many alternative routes, variously preferred according to the availability of grazing *en route*, or of sustenance for the drovers, the frequency of banditry and sheep-stealing or simply the weight of taxes.[45] The important fixed points were, indeed, the bridges and fords across major streams, the toll points at which taxes were collected on the number of sheep going through, or the collecting points for wool and lambs, for the clip was often taken *en route*. About mid-September preparations for the move south would begin and flocks were then collected, branded and started on their way south so as to take advantage of autumn rains and the revival of parched summer grazing in the brief period before the harsh winter set in on the meseta. Lambing took place soon after arrival on winter pastures in October, and it was not until April that the journey north would begin. From the thirteenth century to the days of decline in the eighteenth and nineteenth centuries, the transhumant sheep industry constituted a most important aspect of Castilian and indeed Spanish economy. In the fifteenth and sixteenth centuries numbers of sheep averaged about 2½ to 3 million, falling to 2 million during the second half of the sixteenth century, but still numbering about 1½ million in 1910, when the *transhumantes* were numerically overshadowed by a

Spanish sedentary flock of 12½ million, and when they were moved largely by rail.

In southern France there were transhumant routes followed by sheep and goats from the Alps and the Massif Central to the winter pastures of the Crau and Camargue and the plains of Languedoc. From the Cevennes, movement was to the Rhône delta; from Navarre to the basin of Aquitaine; from the Montagne Noire to the region of Toulouse; from the French Alps by way of the Durance valley through the gap at Sisteron to Arles and thence to the delta area. Much of the traffic in sheep was channelled twice a year at points where the Rhône was crossed and Arles in particular had a strategic position in relation to the movement of flocks. It was in such towns that the tolls were levied and that textile industries flourished, as at Arles, Nîmes and Beaucaire. In Haute Provence, the monasteries were very active in the organisation of grazing from the eleventh century onwards and the flocks constituted the essential element in the economic life of the area.[46] Wool, hides and leather provided revenues, sustained the periodic fairs and nourished a cloth industry which made use of local water power in scattered fulling mills. Conflict with alien sheepmasters from the lowlands was common, but medieval pressure on grazings had not been great enough to lead to excessive deforestation and soil erosion. A flourishing economy existed, based on transhumant sheep and oriented southwards towards the markets for wool, cloth, skins and timber in the towns, the fairs and the Papal court at Avignon. There were winter pastures in the Rhône valley, but many preferred grazings nearer at hand in the foothills of the Maritime Alps. Badly hit by the plagues and emigration of the late fourteenth century, the pastoral industries recovered in the fifteenth. By 1470 transhumance was again well organised, and many a village had far more stock then than it had in the 1950s.

In Italy, too, transhumance on a regional scale was highly developed and may occasionally have arisen from regular flock movements within the great *latifundia* of late Roman times. In general, undrained coastal marshes provided the winter pastures, upland slopes in the Apennines the summer grazings. In the south the chief movements were from the plain of Tavioliere through Foggia to the mountains of Abruzzi and Molise; and in central Italy the marshlands of the Tuscan Maremma and of the Roman Campagna were linked with the uplands of the central Apennines.

Mediterranean transhumance was certainly of very ancient origin, for settlements on the site of Rome itself have been interpreted, for example, as stages on a Bronze Age route of transhumance. It has been suggested that the breakdown of irrigation systems in the lower alluvial lands of peninsular Italy and their degeneration into marshland in the late Roman Empire and afterwards made such lands available for extensive grazing. Other forces were also working towards extensive forms of land use. Falling population and contracting markets towards the end of the Roman Empire tended in this direction and so also did the inefficiency and shortages of servile labour on the very big estates. Everywhere in the Mediterranean lands of Western Europe during the Dark Ages, low or falling population may have suggested transhumance as a way of exploiting distant pastures with a minimum use of labour. Moreover, flocks and herds were a mobile form of wealth which could be moved out of the way of invading bands of Teutonic barbarians and of marauding Saracens.

Sheep grazing had been important in Iberia in Iron Age times and during the Roman period and it may well have extended under Visigothic rule, for the Visigothic code of laws gave flocks unrestricted access to unenclosed commons and waste. The Arab conquest brought Berber immigrants from North Africa, accustomed to graze their flocks in environments very similar to that of the meseta, and it is certain that the later development of pastoralism in Spain owed a great deal to North African influence, for the methods and terminology of handling sheep were derived from North Africa. From 1154 there is evidence to suggest that precursors of the merino sheep, characterised by long, fine, white wools, were also imported from there. Finally, instability on the fluctuating frontier between Christian and Arab encouraged pastoral mobility rather than sedentary arable farming, and when the Reconquista began to push the Arabs southwards, grazing routes were also extended to make use of the new lands. In 1273, a generation after the great advances into the Guadalquivir and to the Levante, Castilian sheepmasters formed the association of the *Mesta* to organise and control the movements of sheep. It was named after traditional local meetings to sort out and claim stray sheep, but it became one of the most powerful organisations of late medieval Castile. Always important in central Spain at least, the grazing of sheep and the transhumance of stock came to dominate the whole agrarian economy of Castile in the fifteenth century.

An unusual combination of circumstances conspired in the late thirteenth century and again in the fifteenth to stimulate the development of pastoralism in Castile and Aragon. Wool was one of the few raw materials of the Middle Ages sufficiently durable and valuable to stand the cost of transport over long distances, and the cloth industry was one of few medieval industries to be highly localised. The demand for Spanish raw wool was increasing rapidly during the late thirteenth century, not only because of a rising demand from a flourishing cloth industry but for other reasons as well. In the late thirteenth century Italian manufacturers turned to weaving their own cloth instead of relying, as formerly, on semi-finished northern cloth from England and Flanders. Demand for Spanish wool was increasing in Italy and also in Flanders, for supplies of English raw wool were becoming increasingly difficult in the fourteenth century. During the course of the fourteenth century new techniques of cloth production were being adopted in order to make full use of the qualities of this long, fine wool in place of the very different traditional English wools. Exports of wool were also easy to tax, so that it was in the interest of the Crown as well as profitable to the merchants and the economy of Castile that exports should be encouraged. And the transhumant sheep themselves provided a profitable source of revenue at toll points on the major routes.

From the mid-fourteenth century a general change in the economic climate of Western Europe also favoured transhumance and the Mesta. Depopulation, low grain prices and the contraction of arable farming, together with an increase in the cost of labour once again favoured extensive forms of land use. In Spain as in England arable land was being converted to pasture or allowed to fall down to rough grazings. In this process there was a contraction of settlement in which many a village was abandoned, leaving only the headquarters of a sheep ranch as the surviving settlement. Laborde estimated in the early nineteenth century that there were 1,141 deserted villages in Spain, many of them represented in his time by 'the ruins of gothic castle . . . delapidated chapels, situated in the midst of fields or uncultivated lands'.

Finally, Castilian transhumance enjoyed the encouragement of the Crown, especially from the time of Isabella and Ferdinand. Standard grades and weights for wool were established; the activities of middlemen were controlled; the dispensation of justice was made more rapid and efficient by the establishment of the Consulado at Burgos in 1494; and privileges were given to Spanish merchants abroad to encourage the expansion of wool exports. Above all the interests of the Mesta were favoured, often at the expense of the peasantry. 'Every possible device of the new government was turned to the task of concentrating the rural energies and resources of Castile on the sheep industry.'[47] Imports of wheat were permitted to reduce the pressure towards the extension of arable farming; parts of the royal domain and then the estates of the Military Orders were leased to the Mesta for sheep grazing. And by the Law of Posesión members of the Mesta were granted permanent tenancies at low rents of grazings that were in their occupation. It was under circumstances such as these that the transhumant flock reached its maximum numbers in the early sixteenth century, to fall away later as the revival of population put new pressure on arable farming and as the balance of prices tended to shift away from wool and stock to the advantage of grain production. Yet the Mesta persisted, its privileges less and less effective, until its final dissolution in 1836. Sedentary flocks, moving within the confines of village and township territories, increased at the expense of the transhumant sheep.

The conflict of interest between shepherd and farmer is a part of ancient Mediterranean tradition, and in Castile a state of coexistence was maintained to the end of the Middle Ages between the interests of the towns and the Mesta. The Mesta officials prevented the enclosure of *cañadas* and secured the right of way for their flocks. The towns were able to keep the migrant sheep away from meadows, arable crops, vineyards, orchards and enclosed pastures for the stock of the township, though there was sometimes conflict for the use of unenclosed wastes. It was during the sixteenth century when the support of the Crown was given to the interests of the Mesta that arable farming tended to suffer. Village communities complained that they had been deprived of rough grazings to support their sedentary flocks; the expansion of arable was hindered by the grazing rights of the *transhumantes*, and the migrant sheep assisted in the deforestation of land on which soil erosion was subsequently severe. The extent of such devastation may have been exaggerated in the past except where graziers deliberately burned over forest lands to secure a good growth of grass in the following spring, but there were many other causes of friction between peasant and grazier. The damage done to growing crops by the surreptitious widening of the drovers' ways was complained of by the farmers; the graziers complained of the enclosure of their rights of way.

Many of these features of transhumance were common to France and Italy as well as Spain, and within Spain itself the privileges of the Mesta were echoed in the similar though less powerful organisation of the sheepmasters of Aragon. Even in Catalonia transhumance was important, though less well organised.[48]

The development of cattle ranching in southern Spain also took a form which was unique in Western Europe, and although transhumant routes were much less well organised, cattle were driven long distances to summer grazings. It seems appropriate therefore to include a comment under this heading, for although sheep were undoubtedly of greater economic significance in Spain as a whole in the later Middle Ages, the traditions of cattle rearing were, above all, exported to the New World to flourish abundantly in the grasslands of the western hemisphere. Just as shepherds pushed south in the van of the Reconquista, so also the cattle herders followed, establishing themselves in New Castile, Estremadura and Alentejo in the twelfth century, and later ousting sheep-raising in the Guadalquivir basin. 'The Andalusian Plain became in the later Middle Ages the one region of the peninsula where pastoral life and indeed agricultural life in general were dominated by the thriving, highly organised cattle-ranching economy.'[49]

On the extensive semi-arid rough grazings of southern Spain and the meseta, methods were needed quite different from those which were involved in the cultivated pastures and arable farms of the 'humid crescent.' And the methods which were evolved and even the stock which was reared were very similar indeed to those which were passed on by Mexican stockmen to the cowboy of the American West in the nineteenth century. The cattle breed of late medieval Andalusia was unique in Europe—a long-horned, long-legged and hardy animal, semi-wild and free-ranging, suited more to the production of hides and tough, stringy beef than to the production of dairy produce and the pulling of the plough. In the eyes of an American author, the stock-rearers were compelled 'to abandon their cosy little cow pastures for the open range, to take to their horses for herding, to perfect systematic methods of long distance grazing, and periodical round-ups for the branding of calves and the cutting out of beef cattle in the autumn for slaughter'.[50] Branding was practised in the tenth century and brands were codified and registered. The larger herds of up to 1,000 cattle were often in the ownership of the nobility, the military orders and the monasteries, but most were smaller township herds, rarely more than a hundred. The sheep routes were used by transhumant cattle, but movement was on a smaller scale and sedentary herds were more important from the beginning.

To a large extent, cattle ranching was a regional characteristic of southern Spain, and it was from southern Spain and particularly Andalusia that the great majority of the earliest emigrants went to the New World, taking with them the techniques of a ranching industry. In Spain itself, the Spanish hides and leathers gained a European reputation and were exported to Italy, France and the Low Countries. Meat consumption appears to have been high. Castile was one of the few areas in which horsemanship, needed by the common herdsman, was not restricted to the nobility.

Irrigation

Like transhumance, but for very different reasons, irrigation represented another branch of Mediterranean farming more or less independent of unirrigated arable farming and quite differently conducted. In many of the larger irrigated areas, farm buildings were usually scattered, fields individually held and 'enclosed' by irrigation ditches. Plots of irrigated arable or orchard demanded careful and intensive hand labour, and land was too valuable to be thrown open to common rights of grazing. Although water control demanded agreement and co-operative action, rights in water were usually individually held. There are, in general, few traces of open-field arrangements in the farming of irrigated lands and the cultivation of specialised crops was often quite independent of other branches of farming on neighbouring unirrigated land, except in the later Middle Ages when irrigated fodder crops were introduced into northern Italy.

Many of the irrigation systems which had been established in classical times in Western Europe and particularly in Italy fell into disuse with the contraction of markets and the breakdown of ordered government from the late Roman Empire to the Dark Ages. Perhaps more than any other form of agriculture, irrigation demands ordered rule and co-operation for its maintenance. The distribution of water must be carried out regularly and carefully or crops will not survive. Farms dependent on perennial crops which represent considerable investment in labour, capital and time, since they may take years to come into fruition, are particularly vulnerable to the temporary breakdown of water distribution. The main channels which take off water from rivers must be constantly maintained and cleared of weed and silt. Dams and impounded waters must similarly be carefully tended and constantly repaired, for serious breachings, once started, are very difficult indeed to repair with simple techniques. Moreover irrigation implies intensive land use if scarce water supplies are to be used to their best advantage. And the careful labour in water control, weeding, hoeing and planting which irrigation and drainage demand would scarcely repay the effort unless the crops could be sold or unless these methods were necessary to maintain the food supply of a dense population which could not otherwise be sustained.

After the fall of the Roman Empire and perhaps to some extent even before it, the conditions necessary for the maintenance of irrigation were no longer satisfied. Trade and urban markets were contracting; population was stagnant or declining, and the general tendency was to a more extensive use of land. Peace and order were too often lacking and Mediterranean lands were periodically over-run by invading barbarians for whom the niceties of irrigated agri-culture meant nothing. Many, but by no means all, of the classical irrigation schemes therefore fell into disuse, including the irrigation of the Tuscan Maremma and the Pontine marshes. The practice of irrigation survived precisely where the disruption and decline of the Empire was least, in Byzantine Syria, and perhaps in part of Iberia. In both of these areas irrigation continued to the time of the Arab conquest, when they were incorporated within an empire in which irrigation was essential and the knowledge of irrigation techniques widely diffused.

Western Europe had much to gain from its contacts with the Arab world in Iberia, Sicily and elsewhere during the renaissance of the later Middle Ages, but it has never been very clear how much was truly innovation from the Arab world of the Middle East, and how much was knowledge common to the classical world which had simply persisted through the Dark Ages from Roman times.

Methods of irrigation involved the use of simple gravity take-off canals or the impounding of streams by small dams of earth. Ditches were earth- or clay-lined and losses by percolation were inevitable. Although it may be difficult to assess confidently how much the Arabs contributed to irrigation in Western Europe, they certainly seem to have been responsible for the introduction of the *noria* as a better method of lifting water from wells and irrigation channels into the fields. The *noria*, which consisted essentially of earthenware buckets attached to a wheel or endless belt worked by animal power, is still to be seen in use in Iberia (Plate 8). The Arabs also introduced better methods of distributing water by means of branch canals guiding water to the furrows themselves; and they probably introduced new methods of collective water control, exemplified by the Water Tribunal of Valencia. Above all, however, it was the function of the Arabs to introduce into Western Europe new crops which could make irrigation productive and profitable: cotton, sugar, rice, citrus fruits, a number of soft fruits and vegetables; they also reintroduced lucerne.

The establishment or renewal of irrigation in southern France or Italy therefore depended to some extent on Arab inspiration, but it also awaited the economic expansion of the twelfth and thirteenth centuries which accompanied the growth of rural population, and the growth of new cities from which capital for investment in irrigation was sometimes forthcoming, and from which came also an increased demand for the products of irrigation. In Italy, in the neighbourhood of Milan, needs for irrigation and water supply were linked with the construction of canals for navigation. The growth in scale of operations with the elaboration of more complex organisation is also evident.

In southern France beginnings were made with the construction of irrigation works from the river Durance rather than the Rhône. perhaps because the Durance was a much easier source to manage. It has a relatively steep gradient, falling 750 feet in 55 miles to its junction with the Rhône, and short take-off canals were enough to bring water to the surface of the fairly low and level terraces into which the river is incised. Here, too, the first irrigation works were built in the twelfth century, in 1171, to be followed by new constructions in 1229, when the Durançole canal was built, and again in 1303 and 1356. In the sixteenth century Adam de Craponne built the first canal to water the Crau, again using the waters of the Durance. The fact that the water so provided was not fully used until much later illustrates the importance of demand and of accessibility to a vigorous market. In the Alps, particularly to the south of the upper Rhône–Rhine trough, the systems of irrigation designed for lowland farming were adapted to the pastoral life of the High Alps, and from the fourteenth century irrigation channels carried surplus water to

Alpine meadows. Channels cut almost parallel to the contours along upper slopes still form an intricate network on the map, crossing natural streams by means of wooden troughs constructed with difficulty in precipitous places. These troughs or *bisses*, miles long in places, were built by the communal investment and effort of individual parishes, and responsibility for their maintenance was also a collective task.

Most of the medieval irrigation works were local and small-scale, conducted within the framework of a limited society and local jurisdiction as well as a modest technology. Larger scale effort awaited the organisation of coherent territorial political units, the technical command of Dutch or Dutch-inspired hydraulic engineers and the availability of capital resources for a type of investment which had, for technical reasons, necessarily to be on a large scale. It also had to await demand for the products of irrigated farming, frequently luxury fruits for a wealthy market. Thus, there was a revival of interest in new irrigation works in the seventeenth century which owed much to the Dutch pioneer work in drainage and reclamation in north-western Europe and which was represented by efforts to drain marshland in the Mediterranean world, such as the interior marshes of the Arno, the Tiber valley or the delta lands of the Rhône. But it was not until the nineteenth century that irrigation works were planned on a truly large scale in a context of rising demand and standards of living in north-western Europe, and with a new conception of what was possible from an engineering point of view. Indeed it is only in the last hundred and fifty years that serious efforts have been made to drain, reclaim and irrigate the great deltas of the Mediterranean: the Ebro, the Rhône, the Tiber and the Po.

Although characteristic of Mediterranean farming, irrigation was by no means widespread in the Middle Ages. Where it did exist, it sometimes made important contributions to rural economy through an expanded production of fodder crops and a greater stock-carrying capacity, which in turn affected the whole structure of arable farming. But this close interdependence of 'dry' arable farming and irrigation was uncommon until a later date, and irrigated lands were often devoted to tree and shrub crops rather than to cereals or fodder. Like transhumance, irrigation was part of Mediterranean farming, but could be and frequently was relatively independent of other branches of farming. Arable was not so closely bound to grazing and stock as it was in the regions of the heavy plough and the large ploughteams of northern Europe. The whole system of farming was more flexible than that of north-western Europe, and could produce a much greater variety of crops (see Fig. 4:19). Be-

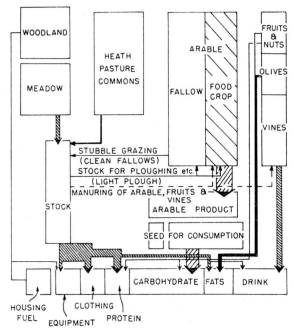

Fig. 4:19   A diagrammatic representation of the relationships involved in 'Mediterranean' farming systems. Similar assumptions are made as in Fig. 4:5(a) but a part of the area cultivated is attributed to fruits, olives and vines. Pasture, arable crops, vines, olives and fruits show much less interdependence than do the major categories of land use in north-western Europe.

cause of these features, Mediterranean farmers were more freely able to concentrate attention on the production of a single, particularly profitable crop. As a result, crop cycles of expanding production, boom and failure were much more a feature of Mediterranean farming than of northern agriculture. (See below, p. 529ff.)

REFERENCES

Abbreviations:

Ann. E.S.C.   *Annales, Economies, Sociétés, Civilisations*, Paris.
C.E.H.E.   *Cambridge Economic History of Europe*. Vol. 1, *Agrarian Life of the Middle Ages*, ed. J. H. Clapham and E. Power, Cambridge, 1942.

1. A. YOUNG, *Travels in France during the years 1787, 1788, 1789*, ed. J. Bentham-Edwards, London, 1905.
2. F. SEEBOHM, *The English Village Community*, Cambridge, 1883.
3. E. C. K. GONNER, *Common Land and Inclosure*, London, 1912.
4. G. SLATER, *The English Peasantry and the Enclosure of Common Fields*, London, 1907.
5. H. L. GRAY, *English Field Systems*, Cambridge, Mass., 1915.
6. M. BLOCH, *Les Caractères originaux de l'histoire rurale française*, Paris, 1st edition 1931; see also additions and comments in revised edition, ed. R. Dauvergne, 2 vols, 1956 and 1960, Paris.
7. R. DION, *La Formation du Paysage rural français*, Tours, 1934.
8. G. NIEMEIER, 'Eschprobleme in Nordwestdeutschland und in den ostlichen Niederlanden', 14th International Geographical Congress, Amsterdam, 1938, *Comptes Rendus*, vol. 2, pp. 27–40.
——, 'Gewannfluren, ihre Gliederungen und die Eschkerntheorie', *Petermanns Georgr. Mitteilungen*, vol. 90, 1944, pp. 57–74.
9. B. H. SLICHER VAN BATH, *The Agrarian History of Western Europe, A.D. 500–1850*, London, 1963.
10. E. JUILLARD, A. MEYNIER, X. DE PLANHOL, and D. FAUCHER, *Structures agraires et paysages ruraux*, Paris, 1956.
11. A. G. HAUDRICOURT and M. JEAN-BRUNHES DELAMARE. 'L'homme et la charrue', *Geographie Humaine*, vol. 25, Paris, 1955.
12. E. JUILLARD, 'L'assolement biennial dans l'agriculture septentrionale, Basse Alsace', *Annales de Géographie*, vol. 61, 1952, pp. 34–45.
13. Slicher van Bath, *Agrarian History of Western Europe*, pp. 18–21.
14. D. FAUCHER, 'L'assolement triennial en France', *Études Rurales*, no. 1, 1961, pp. 7–17;
A. KRENZLIN, 'Zur Genese der Gewannflur in Deutschland', Vadstena Symposium, *Geogr. Annaler*, vol. 43, 1961, pp. 190–204.
15. P. FLATRÈS, *Géographie rurale de quatre contrées Celtiques: Irlande, Galles, Cornwall and Man*, Rennes, 1957.
——, 'Paysages ruraux de pays atlantiques', *Ann. E.S.C.*, vol. 12, 1957, pp. 602–12.
16. S. MONTELIUS, 'The burning of forest land for the cultivation of crops', *Geogr. Annaler*, vol. 35, 1953, pp. 47–54.
17. G. BODVALL, 'Expansion of the permanently settled area in Northern Hälsingland', Siljan Symposium, *Geogr. Annaler*, vol. 42, 1960, pp. 244–9.
H. ALDSKOGIUS, 'Changing land use and settlement development in

the Siljan region', Siljan Symposium, *Geogr. Annaler*, vol. 42, 1960, pp. 250–61.

18. P. BRUNET, 'Problèmes relatifs aux structures agraires de la Basse-Normandie', *Ann. de Normandie*, vol. 5, 1955, pp. 115–34.

19. L. CHAUMEIL, 'L'Origine du bocage en Bretagne', *L'Eventail de l'histoire vivante, hommage à L. Febvre*, Paris, 1953, pp. 163–85.

20. L. MERLE, 'Les origines du bocage de la Gâtine poitevine', *Ann. E.S.C.*, vol. 12, 1957, pp. 613–18.

21. H. ENJALBERT, 'L'habitat groupe dans les pays du centre-ouest', *France méridionale et pays ibériques, Mélanges en hommage à D. Faucher*. 2 vols, Toulouse, 1948, vol. 1, pp. 217–40.

22. M. DERRUAU, *La Grande Limagne*, Clermont Ferrand, 1949.

23. 'Morphogenesis of the agrarian cultural landscape', Papers of the Vadstena Symposium presented at the 19th Int. Geogr. Congress, Stockholm, 1960, *Geogr. Annaler*, vol. 43, 1961, nos. 1 and 2.

24. Niemeier, 14th Int. Geogr. Congress, 1938, op. cit.

25. H. UHLIG, 'Old hamlets with infield and outfield in western and central Europe', Vadstena Symposium, *Geogr. Annaler*, vol. 43, 1961, pp. 285–312.

26. A. VERHULST, 'Historiographische studie over het oudste domein der Sint-Baafsabij te Gent', *Bull. de la Soc. Belge d'Etudes Géogr.*, vol. 22, 1953, pp. 321–54.

——, 'Les types différents de l'organisation domainiale et structures agraires en Belgique au moyen âge', *Ann. E.S.C.*, vol. 11, 1956, pp. 61–70.

27. Uhlig, *Geogr. Annaler*, vol. 43, 1961, p. 299.

28. Krenzlin, *Geogr. Annaler*, vol. 43, 1961, pp. 190–204.

29. Kolloquium über Fragen der Flurgenese, *Berichte zur deutschen Landeskunde*, Band 29, Heft 2, 1962, pp. 200–347.

30. Ibid., pp. 342–4: M. BORN, 'Schriftliche Discussionsbemerkungen'.

31. Ibid., p. 235: E. OTREMBA, 'Probleme der kollektiven Landnahme'; pp. 205–15: H. MORTENSEN, 'Die Arbeitsmethoden der deutschen Flurforschung und ihre Beweiskraft'.

32. M. BORN, 'Frühgeschichtliche Flurrelikte in den deutschen Mittelgebirgen', Vadstena Symposium, *Geogr. Annaler*, vol. 43, 1961, pp. 17–25.

33. S. ERIXON, 'Swedish villages without sytematic regulation', Vadstena Symposium, *Geogr. Annaler*, vol. 43, 1961, pp. 57–75.

34. G. BODVALL, 'Periodic settlement, land-clearing and cultivation', *Geogr. Annaler*, vol. 39, 1957, pp. 212–56.

35. V. HANSEN, 'The Danish village: its age and form', *Denmark*, Guidebook for the 19th Int. Geogr. Congress, Stockholm, 1960, pp. 238–53.

36. S.-O. LINDQUIST, 'Some investigations of field-wall areas in Ostergötland and Uppland', Vadstena Symposium, *Geogr. Annaler*, vol. 43, 1961, pp. 205–20.

37. S. GORÄNSSON, 'Field and village on the island of Öland', *Geogr. Annaler*, vol. 40, 1958, pp. 101–58.

——, 'Regular open-field patterns in England and Scandinavian *solskifte*', Vadstena Symposium, *Geogr. Annaler*, vol. 43, 1961, pp. 80–104.

38. G. C. HOMANS, *English Villagers of the thirteenth century*, Cambridge, Mass., 1941.
39. Goränsson, *Geogr. Annaler*, vol. 43, 1961, pp. 101–58.
40. Dion, *Formation du Paysage rural français*, pp. 14–33.
41. A. CABO ALONSO, 'Colectivismo agrario en tierra de Sayago', *Estudios Geograficos*, vol. 16, 1956, pp. 593–624.
42. C. PARAIN, 'Evolution of agricultural technique', *C.E.H.E.*, vol. 1, pp. 118–68.
43. J. M. HOUSTON, *The Western Mediterranean World*, London, 1964, pp. 125–34.
44. J. KLEIN, *The Mesta*, Harvard, 1920.
45. R. AITKEN, 'Routes of transhumance on the Spanish meseta', *Geogr. Journ.*, vol. 106, 1945, pp. 59–62.
46. T. SCLAFERT, *Cultures et Déboisement en Haute Provence*, Paris, 1959.
47. Klein, *The Mesta*, p. 223.
48. S. LLOBET and J. V. VALENTI, 'La trashumancia en Cataluña', 16th Int. Geogr. Congress, Lisbon, 1949, *Comptes Rendus*, vol. 3, pp. 36–49.
49. J. BISHKO, 'The peninsular background of Latin American cattle-ranching', *Hispanic American Hist. Rev.*, vol. 32, 1952, pp. 491–515.
50. Ibid., p. 498.

CHAPTER 5

RURAL SETTLEMENT BEFORE 1800

Anyone who has travelled in Western Europe or who has studied large-scale maps of almost any part of it must have been struck by the differences which occur from one region to another in the distribution of farms and villages and in the appearance of the rural landscape (see Plates 3–11). In much of western France—Brittany, Maine and La Vendée, for example—farms are scattered more or less evenly over the cultivated area. Each farmhouse stands more or less centrally in its fields and there is a dense and bewildering network of lanes or tracks linking one farm with another. Occasional hamlets contain church, post office, shop and café or inn, but other hamlets also exist which are no more than a collection of some three to a dozen farmhouses with their dependent buildings. But to the north-east of a fairly sharp line of division which cuts across the Paris basin from the lower Seine across Beauce to Perche, farms are almost entirely concentrated in compact villages which may contain from a hundred to a thousand people or more. Arthur Young, travelling in France in 1787 to 1789 noticed this fact, though he was much more interested in the division, roughly along the same line, between open field and enclosures. Of Picardy he wrote that there were 'No scattered farmhouses in this part of Picardy, all being collected into villages, which is as unfortunate for the beauty of the country as it is inconvenient for the population'.[1] Scattered houses and farms do exist in north-eastern France but they are fairly rare. Within the village, church, café or inn, shops, school and post office add to the strength and size of the village community.

Similar differences are to be found in Britain, where in the south-west peninsula, Wales, Lancashire and Cumberland as well as much of Scotland and Ireland, patterns of settlement approach much more closely to those of western France than they do to those of the English Midlands, where compact villages are very similar to those of northern France. In other parts of Europe similar contrasts are to be found. The scattered farms of north-west Germany and of

Flanders or of upland regions of Bavaria, Austria and other parts of the Alps contrast with the compact villages of most of the rest of Germany. Similar differences exist in the Mediterranean world between the great compact villages sparsely scattered over the central meseta of Spain and the thick spread of dispersed farmsteads in the 'humid crescent' of western and northern Iberia. In Italy too there are many local and regional differences between the massed hilltop villages of southern Italy and the scattered farmsteads of the north.

The differences in the form of rural settlement, so important a part of the rural landscape of Europe and so obviously a heritage from the past, are important in modern rural life. In areas of scattered farms it may be difficult or expensive to provide public services such as electricity, domestic water supply or telephones; expenditure on the provision of roads may be high and transport costly. Rural communities may lack a focus for their activities, and the cost of transporting children to school, of going to church, or of distributing commodities will be necessarily higher than in villages, where the concentration of population makes for greater abundance of services and communal relationships and greater economy in providing them. On the other hand farm buildings are usually at or near the centre of the lands they serve, so that journeys to work in the fields are shorter and the distances moved in taking equipment, carrying crops or manure or in herding cattle and sheep are less. Farm buildings in villages may be more than a mile from the fields to be visited and there may be much wasted time and labour in travelling to and fro. It is interesting that the balance of advantage still seems to vary from one place to another even in modern circumstances. In some areas, particularly in southern France and Italy, farmers have moved out from ancient and inconvenient hilltop villages to the centres of their intensively cultivated holdings, or to be nearer to modern roads and available water supplies in the valleys. This is particularly evident, for example, in the lower Rhône and the Durance valleys, but it is a common trend in many parts of the Mediterranean. Investment in new farm buildings (often with the help of loans) as in modern Bavaria or nineteenth-century Sweden and Denmark may tip the balance of advantage towards a location in the centre of a consolidated farm, though this is not always so. Recent colonisation schemes in southern Italy have favoured the creation of farmsteads located in the centres of holdings, but colonisation schemes in south-western Spain in Badajoz have provided for the concentration of settlement in large, newly planned villages.

From the late nineteenth century historians and geographers, aware of such differences in the pattern of rural settlement, have attempted to classify them and to explain the circumstances of their creation. The pioneer work in this particular field was that of Meitzen[2] who attempted to demonstrate an ethnic explanation for the contrasts which existed in France and Germany. In his view, village settlement was to be associated with Teutonic expansion after the fall of the Roman Empire. The way in which grouped, village settlement was characteristic of western Germany, Alsace and Lorraine and north-eastern France suggested this explanation. Similarly in England the difference between village settlement in the Midlands and the scattered farmsteads of western Britain might be thought to confirm this. On closer analysis, the equivalence of German influence with village settlement and of scattered settlement with other ethnic groups cannot be seriously maintained. North-west Germany and much of Flanders, parts of East Anglia and Kent, parts of Denmark and much of Sweden, are regions of scattered settlement but are obviously within the area of Teutonic occupation. The same is true in southern Germany and Austria. Village settlement also occurs widely in areas in which German influence cannot easily be traced in any way, such as parts of western France in Aunis and Saintonge or in the basins of Rennes and Caen.

Meitzen's hypothesis was followed by attempts to interpret the distribution of rural settlement in terms either of defence (a factor which finds its most obvious expression in the massed hilltop villages of the Mediterranean) or of water supply. On impervious rocks where run-off was immediate and streams frequent, farms could be as scattered as the availability of water would permit. Where water supply was restricted either by the existence of well-defined spring lines or by the need to sink wells, settlement would be grouped in villages. Again, this is an argument which is not difficult to refute, for there are many areas in which wells must be sunk but farms are scattered, as in parts of the Chilterns or in the limestone Causses. Equally, many areas of abundant surface water are also regions of strongly grouped settlement, as in the English Midlands, the Plain of Woëvre in Lorraine, or on the boulder clays of the North German Plain. Finally, among these monocausal explanations of the distribution of rural settlement, one may note an obvious tendency, sometimes too much neglected in modern literature, for the size of village settlement to vary with the nature of the terrain. Thus, where arable land is narrowly restricted to valley bottoms or to small patches of level or well-drained land on terraces, or dissected plateau surfaces and the like, there may be insufficient land for more than a single isolated farm or a small hamlet. On marginal land where population is sparse and pasture the optimum use, farms may be so large that anything other than scattered settlement may be excessively inconvenient. Nevertheless, while this tendency may be borne in mind, there are many areas in which arable land is abundant yet farms are scattered.

No single cause can be found which will explain the distribution of grouped and scattered settlement or the differences which exist in the form and size of villages. Defence, water supply and terrain may play their part, but they do so in the general context of the social framework of rural society and in the particular context of the relationship of settlement to agriculture. It is therefore clearly necessary to consider the pattern of rural settlement in relation to field systems and agrarian structures and with particular reference to the movement of men, animals and equipment between farm buildings and the fields that are cultivated or grazed from them.

The first step in interpreting rural settlement should obviously be the classification of types and forms in order to reduce a very considerable variety to some form of order. A number of classifications have been suggested, most of them more or less strictly morphological. Demangeon divided settlement into *agglomerated* and *dispersed* types,[3] and in the first group made the following subdivisions: (a) villages with champion or open-field systems; (b) villages with contiguous fields, chiefly the marsh villages and forest villages to be found in the Low Countries and central Europe; and (c) the village with dissociated fields, chiefly in Mediterranean areas. His *dispersed* group was divided into four categories: (a) primary dispersion of ancient origin, as in western France or highland Britain; (b) intercalated dispersion, as in parts of western France in which scattered farmsteads of medieval foundation are intercalated between villages. Many midland villages of England with post-enclosure farmsteads standing apart from the villages would also fall into this category; (c) secondary dispersion, by which an originally nucleated village has become dispersed, as in parts of Mediterranean France, the Swiss plateau, Flanders, or in Sweden following enclosure; and finally,

(d) recent and primary dispersion, as in the settlement of the U.S.A. in the nineteenth century. Demangeon's classification has considerable merit from a European point of view in that it stresses the association of settlement with field systems, and a sequential order of dispersion in relation to village settlement. Yet it is evident that a different method is used to categorise each of the two major divisions—one functional, the other genetic. Demangeon later made a different division of the grouped settlements of France in terms of their morphology,[4] recognising among his *agglomerated* settlements (a) the *long or linear villages* of eastern and northern France, many of them oriented by reference to roads, rivers, or relief; (b) the *massed villages of* the Midi; and (c) the *star villages* scattered throughout France, in which commercial functions and trade had brought about expansion along the line of the main roads. *Dispersed* settlement was now divided into *linear, nebular, hamlet* and completely *scattered* types.

In Germany, Ebert, an authority on East German colonisation, classified settlement forms into five major groups:

(*a*) dispersed

(*b*) estate settlements

(*c*) small villages, frequently with central green (*Gassen, Sackgassen, Weiler, Rundling*)

(*d*) large, compact villages

(*e*) linear villages

    i. with one or two rows

    ii. with one or two rows (marsh village type)

    iii. with one or two rows (forest village type)

    iv. chain villages (*Kettendörfer*)

Christaller's classification, which is one of the most satisfactory and on which Fig. 5:1 is based, has particular reference to the German situation but would hardly be applicable elsewhere:[5]

1. Isolated farms	*Einzelhöfe*	
irregularly scattered		Münsterland
scattered around a village		
nucleus	*Schwarmensiedlung*	Osnabrück
arranged in a linear fashion	*Kettendörfer*	
2. Hamlets	*Weiler*	
forest clearing hamlets		Munich area
grouped round estate		
farms (Gutshöfe)		Mecklenburg
subdivision of dispersed		
farms		

3. Villages

(a) irregular clustered villages	$\begin{cases} Haufendörfer \\ Gewanndörfer \end{cases}$	Rhineland
(b) regular clustered villages		
i. place villages, with greens	$\begin{cases} Platzdörfer \\ Rundlinge \end{cases}$	Sorbenland
ii. linear and compact grouped about an elongated green	Angerdörfer	East Germany
iii. street villages, compact	Strassendörfer	East Germany
iv. linear villages		
marsh	Marschhufendörfer	Schleswig
forest	Waldhufendörfer	Silesia
heath	Hagenhufendörfer	North-west Germany
fen	$\begin{cases} Moorkolonien \\ Fehnkolonien \end{cases}$	North-west Germany North-west Germany
v. estate settlements	Gutskolonien	
4. Estates (with or without villages)	Gutshöfe	Mecklenburg

Perhaps because of the part played in the development of German settlement by regular, planned colonisation carried out during a relatively short space of time, German settlement forms are more easily classified into types than the amorphous and complex combinations found in England or much of France. Indeed, as soon as attempts are made to classify on a larger scale and without particular reference to a single area or to presumptions about the way in which the settlements have evolved, difficulties appear. G. Schwarz, for example, groups settlement on a general basis into dispersed and grouped settlement.[6] Within the first group distinction may be made between degrees of dispersion in terms of (a) the nuclear family (b) the extended family (c) the 'lordly' settlement or estate house and farm. Grouped settlement may be divided on various characteristics: size, distinguishing between small villages or hamlets of, say, 3 to 10 houses; medium (10–25) and large villages (over 25 houses); compactness of settlement, simply distinguishing tight and loose clusters; shape, distinguishing chiefly clustered, linear villages, green villages and other shapes; regularity, distinguishing regular and irregular forms. Clearly, combinations of these various features with dispersed farmsteads or with hamlets may occur within a single parish or commune, yet already we have some 48 categories into which a village may fall. Moreover, the point at which a division is made between 'regular' and 'irregular', or 'tight' and 'loose' is

A   B   C

☐ 1   ▦ 2   ▤ 3   ▨ 4   ▦ 5   ▤ 6   ▦ 7   ☐ 8   ■ 9   ▦ 10

usually an arbitrary one. Most classifications must make more or less arbitrary 'steps' where the raw data are fairly continuously graduated, however, and settlement types are no exception. Demangeon's index of concentration or agglomeration represents one way of assessing the extent to which settlement is nucleated in terms of a formula: $K = \dfrac{E \times N}{T}$, where K is the index of agglomeration, E the population of the commune excluding that of the chief nucleated

Fig. 5:1   Rural settlement types in Germany and adjacent areas
A. Irregular forms
   1. Irregular villages (*Haufendörfer, Kettendörfer*).
   2. Hamlets (*Weiler, Drubbel*).
   3. Scattered farmsteads.
B. Regular forms of medieval eastern colonisation
   4. Small villages and hamlets, including *Gassendörfer, Rundlinge* and *Gutssiedlungen*.
   5. Areas with particularly strong development of *Rundling* forms.
   6. Large street villages and villages with elongated greens (*Angerdörfer* and *Strassendörfer*).
   7. Forest clearing and heath villages (*Waldhufendörfer* and *Hagenhufendörfer*).
   8. Marsh villages (*Marschhufendörfer*).
C. Post-medieval planned forms
   9. Geometrically laid-out villages of the eighteenth century.
   10. *Moorkolonien*.

settlement; N the number of settlements, excluding the chief centre; and T the total population of the commune. The major limitations of this method are, however, that it cannot measure different types of dispersion, and there are few censuses other than the French for which suitable population data exist. Other formulae have been developed, and are summarised by Houston.[7]

Classification alone is not enough and may, perhaps, be regarded as a preliminary step towards analysis of rural settlement forms as a function of agrarian, social and economic relationships in a particular environment both at the present time and at the time when the settlement pattern took shape. A functional approach to the historical geography of rural settlement is therefore needed. This may be conceived in terms of those forces which tend towards the concentration or dispersion of settlement. They may be internal to the community itself or they may be external. Of the internal factors, the major groups are those which involve agrarian organisation, social structure, social organisation and the provision of local services. External factors would be chiefly those of an economic character, relating to the regional relationships of a particular community both as a consumer of goods and services externally produced and as a producer of 'exported' agricultural goods. Or they may relate to the defence of the community from external attack, administrative pressures associated with government, feudal or ecclesiastical power.

GROUPED SETTLEMENT

Nucleated and linear villages. The close association between champion farming and village settlement has already been noted above, but before this association is examined in detail, it may be useful to put forward a theoretical consideration based on the principle of economy of movement in farming operations. One of the prime considerations of any farmer in the location of his farmstead must be to minimise the distances he needs to travel to the site of labour, or the distances over which he needs to herd stock, to take farm implements or to gather in crops. The relationship that this factor may have to the distribution of land use around a farm or village has been discussed by Chisholm[8] in the light of the concept that those forms of land use which are least demanding of regular attention, care or carriage of goods will tend to occur, *ceteris paribus*, at distances furthest removed from the farmstead. But economy of movement is also important in the relationship between village settlement and open-field agriculture. Wherever farming was organised in open fields, individual peasants had a number of strips which were scattered about the furlongs. Strips were often numerous and small as a result of the fragmentation of inheritances, purchase, subtenancies and so on. And in the classic three-field system, each peasant would have more or less the same area in each of the large open fields, in order to give him a crop of winter corn and spring corn and a fallow each year.

Now, if we assume that a peasant has, say, three strips in each of three fields, it should follow that the location for his farmstead which would minimise his movements would be at the 'centre of gravity' of the three points which in turn represent the 'centre of gravity' of the sets of strips in each field. Since his strips could be located anywhere within each of the three fields, it is clear that the optimum location for all farmers would be approximately the same and that an optimum location for the village would lie at the centre of gravity of the three component fields. If the three component fields were roughly equal in area, this would in fact be at the centre of gravity for the arable taken as a whole. This argument would also hold for a two-field arrangement in which each farmer had roughly equal parts of his holding in each of the two fields, each part consisting of a large number of scattered strips, though it may be that a linear village, roughly along the junction of the two fields, may be a valid alternative to a compact settlement in this case.

The purpose of this discussion is to show that, given the organisation of an open-field system with compulsory rotation of crops and widely scattered strips more or less evenly distributed in each of the open fields, the optimum pattern of settlement would be a nucleated village. It must be stressed, however, that this argument is not intended to imply that the organisation of the fields occurred *before* nucleation but simply that, whatever causes are involved in the chronological development of both, a nucleated village would have a functional relationship with a working open-field system.

In the East Anglian variation of the open-field system, foldcourses were superimposed on the open fields and neighbouring heaths. Regular cropping shifts occurred within the open arable with a system of rotation in the furlongs of each foldcourse in order to facilitate the folding of stock during the fallow and from Michaelmas to March.[9] Peasant holdings were thus much less regularly dispersed over the whole open fields of a parish and tended to be grouped within the area of a particular fold-course and its accompanying system of rotation. Within any parish of this type, there may well be many possible farm locations which would minimise movement to and from the fields and there would not necessarily be much advantage in a nucleated village. It is therefore interesting, though of course not conclusive, to find that the settlement patterns associated with the East Anglian variant on open-field systems are quite different from those of the English Midlands or north-eastern

France and provide many examples of villages with several dependent hamlets. It should also be pointed out that this was also an area in which manorial control was relatively weak and therefore an area in which deviations from a 'normal' village pattern may be expected on other grounds. In the areas of 'Mediterranean' farming systems, similar considerations applied where open-field arable existed, but it should also be remembered that the variety of natural conditions and of land-use types was reflected in a greater flexibility of settlement, which responded sensitively to other considerations, chiefly defence.

It has frequently been observed that farmsteads are located at the junction of different zones of land use. In north-western Europe this is often the contact between arable on the one hand and pasture, heath, meadow or rough grazing on the other, and it is clearly a way of minimising the movement of stock and men while retaining easy access to both. The land-use pattern itself is often related to differences in terrain or soils and the junction between zones of land use is thus a linear one along a break of slope, the edge of river terraces or a soil boundary. The location of each separate farmstead may be determined quite independently by such considerations so as to produce a roughly linear grouping midway between a conventional linear village and dispersed settlement. In the hill lands of western Britain, Scandinavia or Germany examples of such arrangements of settlement are common. In many cases independent farms constitute a pattern that must still be regarded as dispersed in spite of a linear arrangement, but given some other stimulus towards concentration, such as the division of farms by inheritance, the existence of a church, or a constricted water supply, a more closely knit linear village or a group of hamlets may result. The forest villages or heath or fen villages of Germany constitute a special case of this type in which the farmstead is located near the edge of the holding but also near to a route, a river, the rich meadowlands of a valley bottom or the dry site of an embankment.

Where the extent of the arable is small in relation to the amount of pasture and stock carried, conditions favour the intensive cultivation of an infield type, and the location of settlement at the junction between the island of arable and a surrounding environment of heath, scrub or hill pasture. This is the type of situation represented by the necklace of small hamlets surrounding the *méjous* of Brittany described by Uhlig[10] (Fig. 4:12), and it is very well portrayed in the *annular* village of Morley St Peter in Norfolk,[11] in which houses lie

18 *Ile de la Cité, Paris.* The defensible site in the Seine which constituted the early medieval pre-urban core of Paris.

19 *Magdeburg,* 1560–70 (Braun and Hogenberg). See also p. 321 and Figure 6.4.
The Ottonian town, with the cathedral and the site of the former Carolingian castle, lies to the
left. Later medieval building of the twelfth and thirteenth centuries, with a more regular plan
of streets, lies below the main street axis of the old town and in the "new town" to the left
of the moat surrounding the old walled area. Note also the windmills, tethered watermills
in the river, fish traps, and some evidence of the river trade in timber.

at the edge of heathland (now reclaimed) and the former island of arable, but the church is centrally located in isolation at the heart of the arable lands (Fig. 5:2). Similar *annular* settlement patterns surrounding islands of early arable lands have been described in the Netherlands in Overijssel and Gelderland. (See Figs. 4:10 and 4:11.)[12] But this is a point in classification at which the distinction between nucleated, hamlet and dispersed settlement has ceased to be a useful one. Scandinavian studies suggest that a linear arrangement of farms between pasture and arable may develop into a nucleated village of the 'green' type by a natural process as growth of population, arable land and communal organisation of open fields took place.[13] Thus the extension of arable into former pasture lands may engulf the settlement sites, leading to the establishment of a corridor of pasture providing access for animals through the arable to the accommodation pasture and protection of the village green.

Social factors encouraging concentration of settlement may fall into several categories. First of all, the collective obligations and restraints of champion farming worked very strongly indeed towards the creation and persistence of nucleated settlement. They made it difficult for any individual farmer to extract his lands from the intermingled strips of others and to reorganise them into a compact holding. The extent of common rights also made it equally difficult to build a house or a farmstead in any other area than that normally devoted to gardens and crofts in and around the village. Social considerations or the need for defence may at one time have encouraged families to group themselves together in nucleated villages, and communal restraints and obligations would reinforce that trend. In particular, the strength of manorial organisation or the vigour with which common rights of pasture were protected by the village community would also be reflected in the degree to which farms were grouped in villages.

The exercise or maintenance of authority over land and peasant seems often to have been important in the creation of compact settlement. Indeed, at one extreme of this spectrum is the plantation system in which the living quarters of slaves or labourers were organised in 'lines' or 'compounds' or some other compact form, sometimes walled in times of slavery in order to prevent escapes rather than for defence.

Discipline and supervision are thus the motives for nucleation of settlement in cases such as these. It has been suggested that the de-

ANNULAR SETTLEMENT : MORLEY ST. PETER, NORFOLK.

······ Parish boundary
━━━ Boundary between common meadow or pasture and arable as shown on map of 1629
━ ━ ━ Unfenced tracks across common meadow or pasture as shown on map of 1629
⬜ Arable land in open field strips in 1629
⬜ Early enclosures shown in 1629
·········· Late enclosures of commons and arable
⬜ Common land
⬜ Neighbouring parishes

¼ mile

Fig. 5:2 Old arable and *annular* settlement, Morley St Peter, Norfolk.
Note the centrally placed but isolated position of the church (after A.
Cartwright). Note the regularity of field boundaries and of roads in the
newly laid out portions. Roads here have verges of standard width.

pendent peasants of the late Roman villas may have been organised in similar compact groups. With the development of the manorial system a dependent relationship was established in which the lord's ability to provide security and protection would have been conditional upon the grouping of his villeins within a fairly confined location and the supervision and exaction of labour services would also be facilitated by a grouping of settlement within villages.

In medieval Europe the strength of manorial organisation was one of the most important factors affecting settlement patterns. In northeastern France, the Rhineland, southern Germany and much of England manorial organisation was strong and village settlement and open-field agriculture normal. Indeed, the creation of regular, planned villages grouped about a street or a green is often an indication of organised colonisation and settlement on virgin land, as in many parts of East Germany, but it may also be the product of a reorganisation of settlement superimposed from above, as in parts of Sweden (see above p. 236). In the *solskifte* arrangements of Denmark and Sweden, the grouping of strips in the open fields was in the same order as the order of farmhouses in the village. Houses were counted clockwise round the village green or the village street, following the same direction as the sun's apparent course above the horizon; first east, then south, and then west. Measurements of the frontages of farm crofts on the green or street suggest a standardised layout and the traces of a less regular and more scattered arrangement of houses and fields suggest that *solskifte* represented a wholesale reorganisation of settlement probably carried out in order to effect new changes in taxation and assessments.[14]

The importance of initiative and organisation from above at the hands of feudal lords, monasteries, or even, as in Germany, of settlement agents and entrepreneurs, is well exemplified in the period of the great age of clearing. Large-scale settlement under standardised social and economic circumstances produced a whole series of regular, planned village layouts which were conceived as a whole and which were often laid out in the space of a fairly short time as new settlers were brought in. The colonial settlement of east Germany provides the best example. In the early period of expansion into the lands east of the Elbe and in the areas between the Elbe and the Saale, Slav settlement forms of a defensive character were frequently reorganised or taken over by the German conquerors. These were the small nucleated green villages or hamlets known as *Rundlinge*, often with a *Blockflur* type of field system emphasising their association with Slav methods of cultivation. In the south, new settlement forms were being created as a means of colonising forest land. The forest clearing villages (*Waldhufendörfer*), with each holding independent and stretching away from road or valley bottom through

Fig. 5:3   *Strassendorf* villages associated with the colonisation of east Germany (and with late clearing names) (after German topographical survey 1:25,000, 1912, Finsterwalde, reduced to 1:50,000)

meadow and arable to uncleared forest (see Fig. 4:13 and p. 233), allowed for expansion as each new group of settlers moved in. Marsh or heath villages of a similar structure were repeated over wide areas in appropriate environments (*Hagen-* and *Marschhufendörfer*). In the northern plains on boulder clays and in the löss *Bördeland*, open-field forms of various types were developed. Standard village types were associated with the new regular field systems, and many of them were either street villages (*Strassendörfer*: Fig. 5:3) or grouped about a long, narrow rectangular or roughly oval green (*Angerdörfer*) (see Plates 10 and 11 and Fig. 4:2). Other forms were of compact green village types (*Platzdörfer*). In general these nucleated villages became larger towards the east as the colonisation movement developed. Similar standardised types based on German examples were to be found in Poland and even further afield; and examples are also to be found in France and the Low Countries in areas of late settlement and new development at the hands of powerful lords. In south-west France and in central Spain large-scale organisation of settlement also occurred during the great age of clearing and planned forms were frequently repeated here, too (see p. 281).

Planned colonisation in Silesia in the eighteenth century at the hands of Frederick the Great followed even more regular patterns, for by then the art of the surveyor imposed a truly geometrical pattern on the land. In the Low Countries and especially in Drenthe, the *Moorkolonien* and *Veen-* or *Fehnkolonien* were similar to the older marsh villages in plan (Plate 16) but they too now tended to be much more rectilinear and many were laid out as a result of the operations of reclamation companies (Fig. 5:4).

In many areas, however, where manorial organisation was weak or where villages contained several manors the simplicity and the unity of the compact village was lost (Fig. 5:5). Where land was available and common rights not too jealously guarded, squatting took place; and the new cottages that were built were usually placed at the edges of waste or common ground, e.g. above the level of cultivation and at the edge of hill pastures in upland areas where small lots could be carved out without too much hindrance. Some of the more amorphous and large 'green' villages may have originated in this way. Some squatters, of course, settled on the village green itself and others in the broad strips of uncultivated land that constituted rights of way. Settlement patterns in the regions of champion farming bear witness in many areas to this type of process where the control of manorial lords was weak, or where commons were abundant and encroachments not so much a heinous offence as a source of income for the lords of the manor through the fines that could be levied.

The provision of services at the lowest level of the rural-urban hierarchy was an additional function of the nucleated village. In East Anglia in the sixteenth and seventeenth centuries, the larger villages had their miller, their baker, butcher, carpenters, smiths and

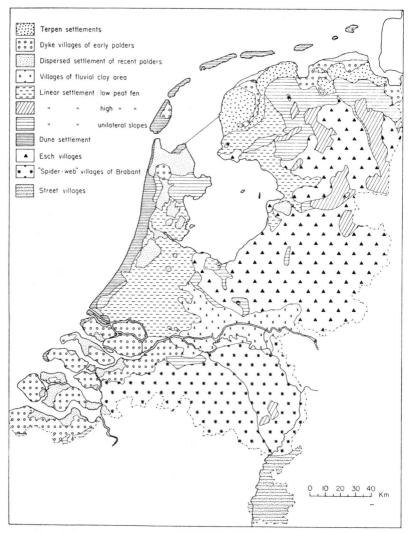

Terpen settlements

Dyke villages of early polders

Dispersed settlement of recent polders

Villages of fluvial clay area

Linear settlement : low peat fen

     "   "   high " "

     "   "   unilateral slopes

Dune settlement

Esch villages

"Spider-web" villages of Brabant

Street villages

Fig. 5:4   Rural settlement types in the Netherlands (after Keuning).

carters besides the priest and the innkeeper. Many also had a tailor and a shoemaker as well. The general tendency was towards further growth in those villages which were already large.

Defence and security represented a distinct and powerful element which usually worked towards the concentration of settlement during the Middle Ages, and in Mediterranean lands it has usually been the importance of defence which has been stressed rather than the relationships of rural settlement to agricultural activities. Instability has been a normal feature of Mediterranean life until relatively

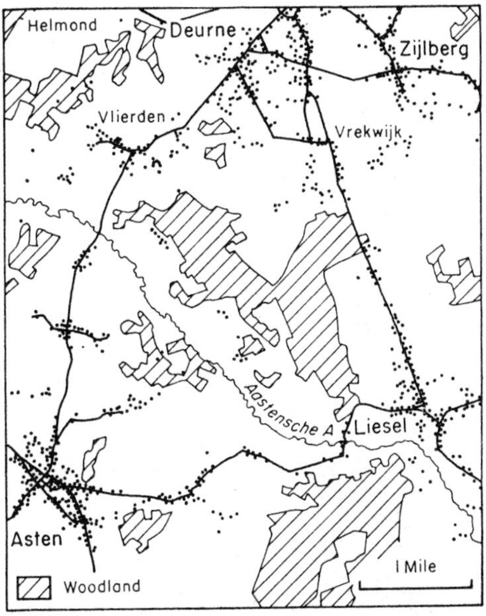

Fig. 5:5   An example of the 'spider-web' villages of Brabant, resulting from the extension of settlement along roads from originally compact nucleated settlement.

recent times. Villages and small towns still show traces of walling and many still huddle within their medieval defences. Indeed, it is commonly the case that agricultural demands have been ignored in the selection of settlement sites, for defensive hilltop positions are frequently inconvenient with respect to the cultivated lands and even to water supply.

In parts of central and northern Italy, the hilltop village is common, fortified in the early Middle Ages with *castellos* and walled where natural defences were inadequate (Fig. 5:6). Some may date from foundations in the sixth and seventh centuries, when Lombard invasions threatened the rural stability that had survived earlier Gothic invaders, but most may date from the ninth to eleventh centuries, a period of great uncertainty and Saracen piracy in the western Mediterranean. Many others may be a product of feudal instability and local internecine warfare. Indeed, some of the showpieces of rural settlement in Italy such as San Gimignano contain within their walled perimeters the high fortified towers which were the urban refuges of landowners and lesser nobility.[15] Medieval rural settlement in Etruria provides an excellent example of the way

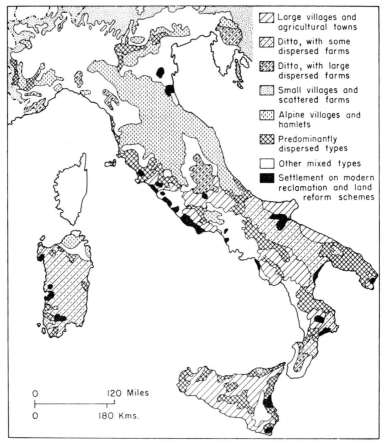

Fig. 5:6   Rural settlement types of Italy (after Houston and others).

in which defensive values were stressed in medieval times rather than accessibility to towns and routes or to good agricultural land, qualities which were sought out both in classical times and in the modern period.[16] In eastern Italy, too, defence rather than everyday convenience appears to have been an important element in the creation of great massed settlements which have been called agro-towns. The concentration of labourer, peasant, artisan and nobility in large nucleated villages, much greater in size than the normal village of north-western Europe, has made an enduring impact on the rural landscape of Italy, but it had important economic effects during the period of the Middle Ages itself. The urban-dwelling tradition of landowners and nobility may well have encouraged a much closer relationship than in north-western Europe between agriculture and urban commerce or industry, and it may well have facilitated a flow of capital between agriculture and industry which was important in mobilising capital for the commercial and industrial development of central Italy in the eleventh and twelfth centuries, and which was also important later in assisting the diversion of capital from industry and commerce to agriculture in the fifteenth century.[17]

In southern Italy the persistence of large nucleated villages has been associated with the continued dominance of the *latifundia* and a large population of poverty-stricken landless labourers, much too poor to invest in the building of new houses whether in or out of the village and reluctant to abandon the social contacts which the village affords. Similarly in the large estates of Andalusia, the large, compact village has been preserved. But in both of these areas, the persistence of the village is also associated with strong social cohesion and sense of community which is often a defence against, or a compensation for, the power of the landlord. It is, perhaps, significant that the modern agrarian reforms of southern Italy introduce dispersed farmsteads on newly created peasant holdings in a way which rightly emphasises the social as well as economic changes which are expected to occur.

In southern France rural settlement displays very similar contrasts to those of Italy. Provence is one of the classic areas of grouped settlement and as late as the end of the nineteenth century the degree to which population was concentrated in villages compared with that of north-eastern France. In the Durance valley there is a striking transition from the massed hilltop settlement of the lower valley to much more loosely grouped settlement and dispersed farms of the upper valley.

In Aquitaine, Toulouse and Languedoc, massed rural settlement is associated not only with local feudal instability and with Saracen raiding but also with successive military campaigns in disputed border regions. The Albigensian wars, the campaigns of the King of France and the Counts of Toulouse and, most important of all, the English wars created a context in which defence dominated the development of rural settlement over wide areas. The creation of walled and newly planned towns, the *bastides* of south-western France, went hand in hand with the colonisation of new land and

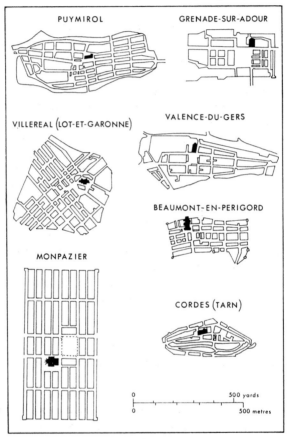

Fig. 5:7 Planned towns of south-western France—the *bastides* (after Dickinson).

with campaigns to attract new settlers who would form an essential part of the armies levied to defend the disputed frontier regions (Fig. 5:7). *Bastides* (such as Montflanquin) in Gascony and Aquitaine and planned border towns (such as Ludlow) in Britain were thus founded for very similar reasons and by very similar men, and their plans have much in common. Many of the *bastides* were no larger than villages, and had few truly urban functions; many of them were *sauvetés* in the sense that they represented a regrouping of existing population for the better defence of an area; many others were truly *villeneuves*, and did indeed represent new rural colonisation and settlement (Plates 14 and 15).

Finally the patterns of settlement in medieval and early modern Spain, though not so well known as those of France and Italy, show essentially similar features. North and north-western Spain were areas of hamlet settlement, but as the Reconquista got under way, new colonisation and the unstable conditions of a frontier zone against the Arab impelled a concentration of settlement which took place in fairly small villages and hamlets in León and Old Castile, but in larger and larger units as the reconquest moved south. Open-field farming was organised beyond the enclosed lands in the immediate neighbourhood of the village as population increased and although this was in a two-course rotation wherever possible, the aridity of central Spain often demanded a three-course shift of weed-fallow, clean fallow and grain. In León small towns spawned new hamlets in the eleventh century, often with monastic encouragement to new clearing and colonisation. In Castile hamlets were frequently grouped around the lord's castle.

As the reconquest reached southern Aragon, New Castile and Estremadura, and the area south of the Tagus in Portugal a different pattern of settlement was adopted. Widely spaced but very large villages were founded. Their spacing represents an adjustment to the aridity of the meseta, but the increasing size of these new villages of the thirteenth century is comparable with the trend in east Germany; it also reflects a change in the military conditions of the reconquest, for the new settlement was more highly organised and planned.[19] Guerilla warfare and spontaneous peasant colonisation had been the normal process of settlement in the tenth and eleventh century but the new movement was on a large scale and more highly organised. The crown granted conquered land in large estates notably to the military orders: the Hospitallers, the Knights of St John, the Order of Santiago and that of Calatrava, and here as in East Prussia massed villages were organised, often under the protection of elaborate fortresses. The impact of the Reconquista on the settlement of Spain is still fundamental: 'It is impossible to consider the varying patterns of settlement in the Peninsula without some reference to the stages and imprints made by the reconquest, still apparent on the landscapes'.[20]

In general, the patterns of rural settlement in the lands of the western Mediterranean are complex in structure and origin. Massed, defensively sited and walled villages were very frequently the result of village settlement or rebuilding at a time of instability and warfare, and other factors, notably land tenure, poverty and strong social bonds, have combined to perpetuate anachronistic structures which are picturesque but often insanitary and inconvenient and for these reasons alone they are often abandoned when opportunity offers. In other areas accessibility to arable lands, water and markets has long encouraged downward movement to scattered farms.

Compared with the regions of champion farming in north-western Europe, however, the most striking feature is that settlement forms in the Mediterranean have been much less closely integrated with the agrarian system. Agrarian restraints on settlement seem to have been fewer for, although open-field farming did exist, enclosure and isolated settlement were more easily achieved. A greater range of produce from closely settled and intensively cultivated lands may well have encouraged a greater degree of local trade and exchange which further helped to nourish the large, semi-urban semi-rural community. In central France, in the region of Limagne, Max Derruau places emphasis on this factor as a 'southern' trait in the settlement of the south-western part of the region.[21]

Hamlet settlement

There is obviously no sudden transition from rural settlement characterised by the dispersion of farmsteads to that in which the massed village or the agro-town is normal. Individual farmsteads may be surrounded by the cottages of labourers dependent upon the major unit, and each cottage may have a garden or a slightly larger piece of land cultivated by the labourer in his spare time. And from this situation there is no break to the semi-urban, semi-rural settlement to be found in Mediterranean areas. Yet many authors have made a distinction between the dispersed and isolated farmstead, the hamlet and the village. At one end of the scale the hamlet may frequently be the simple result of dividing an originally single unit; and its upper limit of size is often arbitrarily given as 10 to 15 farms. It may represent a loose grouping of small holdings scattered about a green, or untidily disposed along the margin of arable and pasture, but the hamlet in Western Europe has so frequently had significance as the unit with respect to which a field system has been organised that it is worth classifying as a separate division, intermediate between the individualism of the dispersed farmstead within its own compact holding and the collective functions and obligations frequently associated with the nucleated village.

In the regions of 'Atlantic' farming described above, temporary cultivation, pastoral activity, and relatively small areas of intensively cultivated infields are usually accompanied by hamlet settlement. In Norway, highland Britain, Ireland and Brittany, large compact nucleated villages are rare, hamlets are normal and dispersed farmsteads common in the region as a whole. Hamlets of between one and ten farms are very common indeed, usually irregularly arranged and often clearly the product of the subdivision of an initially individual farm. Indeed, little distinction is made in some of the languages of Western Europe between the single farm and the subdivided hamlet. In Norway the *gard* and in Brittany the *ker* mean either 'isolated farm' or 'group of farms', yet in both areas and also in Wales, a distinction is made between the farm and its steadings and the houses of the cottagers.[22] The location of farms and hamlets between the infield and the outlying pastures is a very common pattern in Norway, Ireland and Scotland. The occurrence in Brittany of several hamlets at the margin of a great island of arable land, in which each hamlet had a share of strips, has been noted, and here again the settlement lies at the margin between arable and meadow or pasture. Finally, one other aspect of the settlement of the western lands may be stressed: that is the extent to which the kinship group retained importance as the unit of settlement in hamlets and farms. Common links in customary usages have also been noted by Flatrès, but one hesitates to deduce from them any firm conclusion. For the non-Scandinavian parts of the area it has seemed feasible to some to associate common social features with a common Celtic origin. Yet the same features are commonly found in Norway in which there can be no question of Celtic origin. It has also been argued that many of the social features, expressed in settlement habits, and many of the agrarian structures, too, may reflect adjustments made to a society in which population densities were low because of the nature of the terrain and the climate, and in which agrarian systems had necessarily to be adjusted both to more difficult soils and terrain and to a greater predominance of stock-rearing. Yet very similar agrarian structures are to be found in the lowland regions of Cornwall and Devon, South Wales and Lancastria as well as in the hill regions of the same areas; and they are to be found equally on the lowland coastal fringes of Brittany and the level terrains of Maine or Poitou as well as in the accidented regions of Norwegian fiords, Brittany or the Massif Central. It has already been shown above that in north-west Germany, the nucleus of arable land or *esch* was supplemented in different ways as cultivation was extended and as infield/outfield cultivation gave way to regular two- or three-course rotations or to other systems (see p. 229). Similarly, there was evolution in settlement forms from the initial hamlets of fully privileged free farmers to the nucleated village or to the creation of subsidiary hamlets (perhaps of squatters or cottars) or to a more dispersed pattern. Thus, the contrasts between the hamlets of 'Atlantic' Europe and the nucleated forms of the area of champion farming are better seen as reflecting differential growth or different stages in development rather than basic differences between *civilisations agraires*.

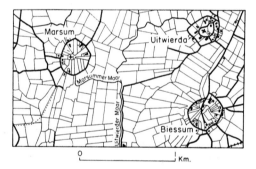

Fig. 5:8 *Terpen* hamlets and associated irregular enclosures in the northern Netherlands

Hamlets associated with the *esch* and the *Langstreifenflur* survive to the present in many parts of north-west Germany in which light sandy soils have hindered substantial expansion of population. In the eastern Netherlands, hamlet settlement associated with *esch* forms are still dominant on light sandy soils of former outwash plains and fluvioglacial sands, though there has been much secondary dispersion.[23] In Friesland hamlets occur on the artificial refuge mounds or *terpen* erected from the fifth century onwards as a defence against the encroaching sea (Figs. 5:8, 5:9 and Plate 13).

In France, hamlets are characteristic of settlement in Maine and
La Vendée. In interior Brittany there is a multitude of small hamlets
of two to five houses with occasional larger settlements. A single
commune may contain many such units and the valid rural unit is
not, in fact, the parish or the commune but the *quartier* composed of
a hamlet and several other localities, often possessing its own share

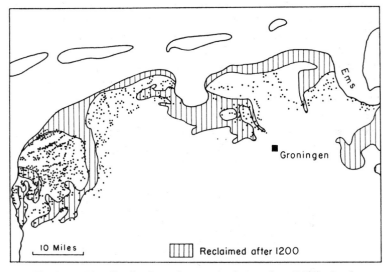

Fig. 5:9   The distribution of *terpen* in the northern Netherlands

of the heathland and distinguished from its neighbours by its customs
and its distinct festivals.[24] In western Britain, too, it was the township rather than the parish with respect to which field systems were
organised, and the centre of the township was a single hamlet. In
Maine and Gâtinais small hamlets coexist with scattered farmsteads,
and the naming of many in -*ière* and -*erie* indicates their origin as
single farms, founded in the great age of clearing in the later Middle
Ages. In the Massif Central and in many parts of the Alps, the predominance of hamlet forms is clearly related to the restricted arable
lands available in hilly terrain, setting limits to the growth of large
nucleated villages with highly organised field systems. In other areas
the predominance of hamlets may well result from the fact that the
extension of cultivation and growth of population, which elsewhere
made for the creation of nucleated villages of open-field cultivation,
were for some reason delayed until a period in which social and

economic change had made the dispersed farmstead a normal means of extending settlement. This may well have been the case in East Anglia, Brittany and La Vendée.

DISPERSED SETTLEMENTS

Although very frequently found mingled with hamlet and village settlement, the isolated farmstead often arises from different circumstances and requires separate study.

In the later Middle Ages dispersed settlement was often to be found in areas in which champion farming did not exist or was weakly developed. In Norway and much of Sweden, in highland Britain and western France, northern Spain and much of Portugal, scattered farms and small hamlets are the rule. In the Mediterranean lands there is frequently a combination of scattered settlement and massed villages or agro-towns. Within the areas of champion farming, past or present, there are great enclaves of irregular hamlets or dispersed settlement often associated with poor soils and upland terrain, as in the Massif Central or the Alps, or with a secondary dispersion which has followed the enclosure of former open-field systems, as in Denmark, Sweden, north-west Germany, and parts of midland England.

Wherever holdings are compact it would seem logical to place the farmstead more or less centrally in order to minimise movement of men and animals. Location may be drawn towards main routes away from the centre of the unit of exploitation if farming is highly commercialised and the provision of access roads expensive, as for example in reclaimed marshland; and similarly farm buildings may be drawn towards that part of an exploitation which requires more intensive or continuous labour than others. For example in Mediterranean lands, farms have often been relocated from inconvenient village sites towards the fields in which the polyculture or *coltura promiscua* of cereals, vines and tree crops is practised, or farmsteads have been moved from villages to the intensively cultivated irrigated parts of peasant holdings on the plains. Pressures towards the dispersion of settlement are very obvious indeed under certain circumstances: first, among large estates, whether for the cultivation of cereal crops, extensive pasture or for emparking and ornamental use; second, in terrain suitable only for extensive forms of farming and large-scale units and occupation—for example on semi-arid pastures in Spain or in hill lands with restricted possibilities for arable farming; and thirdly, where social considerations have been important. In the last case, the development of social differentiation and the social ambitions of newly established landowners may have contributed to the decision to establish farmsteads of some pretension away from the village, as, possibly, in the movement towards the creation of new isolated and moated farmsteads in East Anglia. Finally, it has often been the case in the past that the growth of individual responsibility for farming and the decay of communal obligations and restraints or the end of a need for defence and collective security have been sufficient to set in motion a trend towards the dispersion of farming and farmsteads.

The distinction between primary and secondary dispersed settlement made by Demangeon is a useful one to follow in any attempt at classification. Primary dispersion of settlement falls conveniently into three groups in Western Europe as a whole, though it should be pointed out that 'primary' is being used here in a sense rather different from that in which it is used to distinguish 'primary' and 'secondary' settlement during the early Middle Ages (see Chapter 3, p. 130). First, in England, France and western Germany the expansion of settlement into areas of poorer soil or hilly relief, even some of the later clearing in thick damp oak woodland, was accomplished by way of piecemeal clearing and the creation of enclosures rather than the formation of new furlongs later organised in open field. Many of these newly colonised areas, the product of pioneer farming by individual peasants rather than of organised clearing at the hands of the lord, were areas in which dispersed settlement appears to have been of primary origin. The Forest of Arden in Warwickshire is an excellent English example; the scattered farmsteads and tiny hamlets on heavy boulder clay soils of the watershed zones between the Stour and Cam systems in East Anglia, or on the boulder clays of northeast Hertfordshire and the Chalk soils and Clay-with-Flints of the Chilterns are others. But examples could be multiplied from England of many cases in which relatively late settlement tended towards a greater degree of dispersion. And some of this settlement had been accomplished by Domesday times. In France dispersed settlement of a similar origin in the later Middle Ages is to be found in the Argonne, the Pays de Caux, west of Paris on formerly wooded plateaus between the Seine and the Eure, or between the Seine and Beauce on the site of the former forest of Yveline, the forest of Othe, and the Wet Champagne.[25] In the Rhineland dispersed settlement accompanied late medieval clearing in the Black Forest and the Vosges; small hamlets and dispersed farms multiplied in the Swiss and Austrian Alps and Bavaria as temporary summer settlement gradually became permanent, and dispersion of settlement was characteristic, too, where dairy economies began to prevail.

A second type of primary dispersion is that which has followed the extension of the cultivated area by irrigation or drainage. In the English Fenland the drainage works of the seventeenth century were slowly and hesitantly followed by the creation of new settlements on dykes and embankments. In the Netherlands, the reclamation of the interior lakes from the seventeenth century to the nineteenth has been followed by the creation of dispersed farmsteads, and the same patterns have also developed on some of the more recently drained clays of the delta area (Fig. 5:4). In the irrigated lands of northern Italy dispersed farmsteads were built on intensively cultivated land (Fig. 5:6). In Spain, the irrigation systems established or maintained by the Arabs and sometimes extended after the Conquest were also settled by dispersed farmsteads. In Valencia the country houses and gardens of officials and wealthy merchants became the nuclei from which hamlets and then villages often sprung as population grew and the commercialisation of agriculture developed.

A third type of primary scattered settlement is associated with frontier colonisation in central and northern Sweden from the sixteenth to the nineteenth centuries. In this climatically marginal region, expansion of settlement continued into a period in which maps and records are abundant, and it may perhaps provide some sort of guide to the processes of expansion that must have gone on many centuries earlier in better favoured parts of Europe. In the Siljan region of central Sweden village settlement and permanent cultivation were established on relatively fertile soils derived from Silurian rocks or fluvioglacial sediments.[26] In the surrounding wastes and woodlands stock were pastured and grazing lands gradually extended so that organised grazing schedules had to be established and temporarily occupied summer settlements or *seters* created (Fig. 5:10 and 5:11). Around these *seters* grazing was improved by the burning of forest; fodder was collected and hay cut to ensure feed for the winter stall-feeding period; hay meadows were improved by irrigation; and the *seters* also became centres for hunting, fishing, lumbering, charcoal-burning and the distillation of tar. With the expansion of settlement and of commercial pressures towards stock-raising and forest exploitation, new *seters* were founded deeper in the forest. Distinctions emerged between home and distant *seters* and by the eighteenth and nineteenth centuries multi-*seter* systems had become highly regulated. Many of the early *seters* had become established as permanent settlements and some had grown into fully fledged villages. But with the increasing specialisation of forestry and fishing, the complex grazing systems have tended to decline from the mid-nineteenth century and are now rapidly disappearing.

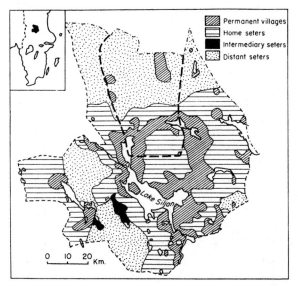

Fig. 5:10   Settlement in the Siljan region of Sweden

In northern Hälsingland a roughly similar sequence in the development of settlement has been traced (Fig. 4:15).[27] Here there were three types of settlement which are evident in the cadastral surveys of the seventeenth century, and it is clear that settlement was then expanding very rapidly. First, there was the permanently settled village with its well-developed arable farming, usually organised into a two- or three-field system. Secondly there were the *seters*, or *fäbodar*, the summer settlements for grazing, hay-making and other forest occupations, and thirdly there was a transitional form, the boothland or *bødland*, from which grazing was organised but which also possessed some arable land and usually produced a substantial hay harvest. Farmers normally moved to their boothland settlement with their cattle after the sowing of their seed on the home farm, and then stayed there after sowing boothland crops until after the hay harvest. Meanwhile a proportion of the labour moved up to the *seter*, and would return in time for harvest. The extension of cultivation in the boothland settlements was carefully governed by regula-

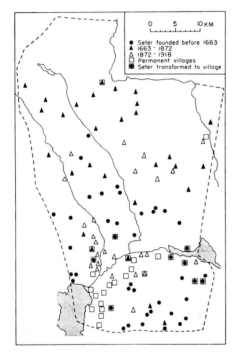

Fig. 5:11 The progress of colonisation north of Siljan, Sweden

tions which make it apparent that there was still plenty of potential arable for newcomers without undue risk of restricting available pasture. Considerable latitude in the location and arrangement of arable or of new settlement was permitted, and there were, indeed, many variations. Some farms were wholly enclosed and arable lands were quite distinct from those of neighbouring farms. In other cases there was some open field and it was the arable which was collectively fenced off from the pasture. Both enclosures and open field existed in the same settlement.[28] Farms were equally variable in location; dispersed farms in compact holdings were common, but so too were loose groupings of farms around a green. Here, as in so many other areas it is difficult to draw clear distinctions between grouped and dispersed settlement.

The evolution from summer settlements to permanently occupied sites is evident in the place-names of many Welsh farms and hamlets, for the permanent settlement of many *hafody* or summer dwellings certainly took place. In Lancashire there were the summer settlements of the booths in Rossendale, reflected in a number of place-names, and many Scottish shielings similarly became permanently occupied. But it is also likely that in many lowland areas of thick woodland a similar progression may also have occurred at much earlier dates from temporary summer grazing settlements to permanent farmsteads and then to hamlets and villages. And if later conditions in Sweden are truly analogous to such earlier sequences, then they offer confirmation of two conclusions stressed above: first that many villages may have grown slowly from individual dispersed farms; and second that when new land was abundant there could be much greater freedom both for settlement and for the organisation of arable. Only when pressure on land was strong need communal obligations become stringent.

Dispersion of settlement which has occurred through the existence of the large estate is a common feature everywhere in Europe, though the chronology and method of evolution has varied a great deal. In Italy, the large estate farm with barrack-like quarters for several families at the centre of the estate occurs widely in the centre and the south: they are the *casale* of the Roman Campagna, the *baglio* of Sicily and the *masseria* of southern Italy.[29] In northern Italy, on land newly reclaimed and irrigated between the fourteenth century and the nineteenth, large highly capitalised commercial farming has been accompanied by the spread of large and imposing farmsteads. In Germany the *Gutshof*, often with a dependent hamlet of estate workers, represented a similar feature.

The type of dispersed settlement associated with the large estate and the 'big house' was sometimes, in Western Europe, the product of a contraction of settlement and even the desertion of villages. During the fifteenth and sixteenth centuries in midland England and East Anglia, the conversion of land from arable to pasture and the depopulation of former villages affected as much as 10 to 15 per cent of the settlements in some areas such as east Leicestershire. Isolated and ruined churches, bereft of the cottages and farmsteads that once stood nearby; tracks that converge on a bumpy field in which there are now no more than house platforms; parish names and civil boundaries for a handful of scattered farmhouses: these are all signs of this kind of contraction of settlement. In England, too, some of these consolidated estates were later emparked as suitable surroundings for the 'big house'.

In Germany a similar evolution occurred: a contraction of settlement followed a decline in population and price structures that favoured a shift from arable to pastoral farming, later reinforced by the disturbances and losses of population that occurred in the period of the Thirty Years War. In Spain, the desertion of villages and their conversion to the ranch headquarters from which cattle were raised or sheep grazed is a most important aspect of late medieval history. The process was here encouraged, as in England, by the emphasis on wool production and sheep grazing, but in Spain other factors also worked in favour of conversion to pasture: both the political power of the Mesta and the royal encouragement accorded to it, and the semi-aridity of much of central and southern Spain. English travellers of the eighteenth century repeatedly commented on the existence in Spain of isolated and deserted chapels and abandoned villages, some of them the product of seventeenth-century decline as well as fifteenth-century depopulation. In Guadalajara a quarter of all settlements were depopulated at this period and by the end of the eighteenth century there were 169 deserted villages near Salamanca.[30] Laborde estimated that there were some 1,141 depopulated places in Spain about 1805, and many of these were represented only by scattered ranches and estate farms. Finally, one other mechanism peculiar to England was the creation of new estates and a dispersed settlement pattern as a result of the dissolution of the monasteries from 1538.

Secondary dispersion from an existing centre of population into nearby lands is, perhaps, the most common way in which isolated farmsteads have been created. During the age of clearing, the extension of cultivation was frequently accomplished by individual rather than collective action and farmsteads were located centrally within new compact farms. Where manorial control was weak, squatting on the wastelands produced a scatter of modest farmhouses; where land was still abundant, as in many parts of the Massif Central, western France and Scandinavia, the creation of new farms in the later Middle Ages and in subsequent new waves of expansion in the seventeenth and nineteenth centuries came to dominate the map of settlement.

The fundamental changes in the economy and society of Western

Europe during the later Middle Ages involved the decay of manorial organisation, the commutation of labour services, the decline of demesne farming and then the losses of population and contraction in arable farming of the fourteenth and fifteenth centuries; they also led in other ways to the dispersion of settlement. New forms of tenancy made their appearance with the decay of customary and villein tenures, and in parts of France and Italy share-cropping tenures were evolved which were designed to encourage the occupation and exploitation of estates which were short of labour or which had fallen out of cultivation during the fourteenth and fifteenth centuries.[31] Since the owner provided tools, seed, draught animals, and often the materials for the building of the farmhouse, the new tenures were a way both of attracting peasants who were not equipped with their own implements and of securing that land was occupied and cultivated. Rents took the form of a share of the produce rather than a fixed cash sum. The new tenants were allotted compact holdings; and in western France, at least, they were often charged with the requirement to enclose with a fence or hedge; they were often made responsible for the construction of the farmhouse.

In the Alps and much of northern and central Italy this form of share-cropping tenancy, known as *mezzadria*, was associated with the development of a scattered settlement pattern of modest farmsteads (see Fig. 5:6); in France, the equivalent form of tenancy was *métayage*, developed from the end of the Middle Ages in western and south-western France. Dispersion of settlement and the creation of the bocage landscape of Gâtinais and La Vendée are associated with it.[32]

Dispersed settlement was frequently a result of changes in land use or in the economic structure of farming which made the persistence of the nucleated village intolerable. In principle, it is obvious that changes which demanded more intensive labour on crops grown at a distance from the nucleated village would make dispersion highly desirable. In the centre-west of France, for example, an ancient landscape of open fields and nucleated villages was profoundly modified in the seventeenth century through the investment in viticulture to meet the growing demand for wines and brandy by Dutch merchants in particular. In the Mediterranean lands the growing of vines, mulberry, olives or citrus fruits on a commercial scale from the fifteenth century onwards provided such a stimulus to the relocation of farms from inconvenient hilltop sites.

But in many parts of Italy and southern France other factors have been working towards the dispersion of settlement from the later Middle Ages. The stimulus to the creation of massed, hilltop villages and semi-rural, semi-urban towns had frequently been the need for defence. Instability continued in many parts of the western Mediterranean to the sixteenth century with the hostilities of city states, internal strife, the French wars in Italy, and the threats of the Barbary corsairs. It was not until the nineteenth century and recent times that old villages have been deserted on a large scale. In the Durance valley, for example, inconvenient hilltop villages have sometimes been completely abandoned for sites nearer to newly irrigated fruit crops in the valley bottoms or on low terraces. Deserted villages are to be seen elsewhere, near Valréas in the western Alps, for example, and settlement is now predominantly scattered in the northern part of the Bouches-du-Rhône between the Alpilles and the Durance. Much of this dispersion represents an adjustment to the growth of very intensive land use for market-gardening and fruits with irrigation since 1870, but scattered farms are shown on maps of the early eighteenth century and even in the fifteenth century conditions were sufficiently peaceful to entice a few large landholders and some peasants to settle on isolated farms, and squatting settlement on formerly unoccupied land was also taking place. In the neighbourhood of Chateaurenard, for example, scattered settlement of this kind was recorded in the 1540s.[33]

Finally, the dispersion of settlement often followed the enclosure of open field and the abolition of communal practices and customary restraints. In England, the erection after Parliamentary enclosure of new and often substantial farmsteads away from the old is often betrayed by names which had a topical interest: Botany Bay, Bunkers Hill, New York, Waterloo and many other names and places famous towards the end of the eighteenth century or early nineteenth recur frequently on Ordnance Survey maps.

In Flanders and Brabant a similar process had occurred much earlier, for the enclosure of old open fields, the dispersion of settlement and even the decay of old village centres had been taking place in the fifteenth century in conjunction with an agrarian revolution by which fodder crops and commercial crops had begun to replace fallow (see below, p. 520) and intensive mixed farming systems with emphasis on stock production had made it profitable to rebuild. In the late eighteenth century the enclosure of fragmented holdings into consolidated blocks was beginning to spread in Denmark and Sweden, where the process culminated in a dispersion of settlement much more complete than in England. But the full development of this theme, as of the downward movement of peasant farms from their hilltop villages in the Mediterranean lands, belongs properly to the nineteenth century.

REFERENCES

Abbreviations:
Ann. E.S.C.   *Annales, Economies, Sociétés, Civilisations*, Paris.
C.E.H.E.   *Cambridge Economic History of Europe*. Vol. 1, *Agrarian Life of the Middle Ages*, ed. J. H. Clapham and E. Power, Cambridge, 1942. Vol. 2, *Trade and Industry in the Middle Ages*, ed. M. M. Postan and E. E. Rich, Cambridge, 1952.

1. A. YOUNG, *Travels in France 1792*, ed. M. Betham-Edwards, London, 1905, p. 8.
2. A. MEITZEN, *Siedlungen und Agrarwesen der Westgermanen und Ostgermanen, der Kelten, Römer, Finnen und Slawen*, Berlin, 1895.
3. A. DEMANGEON, *La Géographie de l'Habitat rurale*, Report of the Commission on types of rural settlement, Int. Geogr. Union, Newtown, Montgomeryshire, 1928, pp. 41–80.
4. A. DEMANGEON, 'Types de villages en France', *Annales de Géographie*, vol. 48, 1939, pp. 1–21.
5. R. E. DICKINSON, *Germany*, London, 1961, pp. 144–8.
6. G. SCHWARZ, *Allgemeine Siedlungsgeographie*, Berlin, 1959, pp. 79–83.
7. J. M. HOUSTON, *A Social Geography of Europe*, London, 1953, pp. 80–5.
8. M. CHISHOLM, *Rural Settlement and Land Use*, London, 1962.
9. K. J. ALLISON, 'The sheep-corn husbandry of Norfolk in the sixteenth and seventeenth centuries', *Agric. Hist. Rev.*, vol. 5, 1957, pp. 12–30.
10. H. UHLIG, 'Old hamlets with infield and outfield systems in western and central Europe', Vadstena Symposium, *Geogr. Annaler*, vol. 43, 1961, pp. 285–312.
11. I am indebted to A. Cartwright for unpublished information concerning Morley St. Peter.
12. H. J. KEUNING, 'L'habitat rural aux Pays-Bas', *La Néerlande*, ed. J. van Hinte, Leyden, 1938, pp. 93–119.
13. S. BOLIN, 'Medieval agrarian society in its prime: Scandinavia', *C.E.H.E.*, chapter 7, p. 474.
14. S. GORÄNNSON, 'Regular open-field patterns in England and Scandinavian *solskifte*', Vadstena Symposium, *Geogr. Annaler*, vol. 43, 1961, pp. 80–104.
15. F. L. HIORNS, *Town Building in History*, London, 1956.

16. J. WARD-PERKINS, 'Etruscan towns, Roman roads and medieval villages in the historical geography of southern Etruria', *Geogr. Journ.*, vol. 128, 1962, pp. 389–405.
17. R. S. LOPEZ, 'The trade of medieval Europe: the South', *C.E.H.E.*, vol. 2, pp. 257–354.
18. J. A. L. PITT-RIVERS, *People of the Sierra*, London, 1954.
19. J. M. HOUSTON, *The Western Mediterranean World*, London, 1964, p. 244.
20. Ibid., p. 245.
21. M. DERRUAU, *La Grande Limagne*, Clermont Ferrand, 1949, p. 103.
22. P. FLATRÈS, 'Paysages ruraux de pays atlantiques', *Ann. E.S.C.*, vol. 12, 1957, pp. 602–12.
23. Keuning, *La Néerlande*, pp. 96–104.
24. A. DEMANGEON, *La France*, part 2, *Geographie Universelle*, vol. 6, Paris, 1946, pp. 196–8.
25. Ibid., pp. 199–201.
26. H. ALDSKOGIUS, 'Changing land use and settlement development in the Siljan region', Siljan Symposium, *Geogr. Annaler*, vol. 42, 1960, pp. 250–61.
27. G. BODVALL, 'The expansion of the permanently settled area in northern Hälsingland', *Geogr. Annaler*, vol. 42, 1960, pp. 244–9.
28. G. BODVALL, 'Periodic settlement, land-clearing and cultivation', *Geogr. Annaler*, vol. 39, 1957, pp. 213–56.
29. Houston, *W. Mediterranean World*, p. 462.
30. Ibid., p. 242.
31. G. LUZATTO, *Economic History of Italy to the beginning of the sixteenth century*, London, 1961, p. 100.
32. L. MERLE, 'Les origines du bocage de la Gâtine poitevine', *Ann. E.S.C.*, vol. 12, 1957, pp. 613–18.
33. R. LIVET, 'Quelques origines de l'habitat rural dispersé en Provence', *Ann. E.S.C.*, vol. 9, 1954, pp. 101–18.

CHAPTER 6

MEDIEVAL AND EARLY MODERN TOWNS

Perhaps one of the most remarkable features in the historical geography of Western Europe is the extent to which modern towns are the heirs of medieval foundations. Indeed, almost all of the towns of Western Europe were founded or reshaped during the Middle Ages. The major exceptions—and they are relatively few in number—are the towns which were the result of state planning in the Renaissance and Baroque periods (for example, capitals, fortress towns, naval bases); some Scandinavian towns; towns which grew as a result of new factory industry on the coalfields in the nineteenth century; seaside resorts and spas; and modern new towns which are the result of deliberate planning or of sprawling suburban growth.

Secondly, many of the places which grew substantially or were refounded during the Middle Ages were on Roman sites and some of these in turn rested on even older Celtic or Iron Age foundations. Indeed, the antiquity and stability of town foundations is a striking paradox in the light of their rôle as the centres and even initiators of change in ideas, institutions, trade and industry. One of the major problems in a historical geography of towns in Western Europe is to establish the ways in which this continuity was achieved from Roman to medieval times.

Thirdly, it is an axiom of modern geography that towns and cities are fairly regularly scattered over the land, each acting to some degree as a centre for the surrounding countryside, at which goods and services are exchanged. Mining settlements, some industrial towns, seaside resorts and other specialised settlements may have relatively little regional function to perform, but most serve an urban sphere of influence or an urban hinterland. These hinterlands are relatively fluid and their 'watersheds' with those of neighbouring towns may vary with the type of service involved; yet it has been shown that there is often considerable stability in the extent, if not in the functions, of these urban hinterlands, from at least the early nineteenth century to the present. It is also evident that there exists a hierarchy of urban centres, each rank endowed with more complex and elaborate functions, from the village and its shop to the market towns, often some 12–20 miles apart, the county town, the regional capital and the metropolitan capital. The normal sphere of influence associated with each rank in the hierarchy is correspondingly greater, for while the market towns may draw on an area of about 6 to 10 miles radius the regional capital may act as a centre for the provision of more specialised services for towns and villages to a wider radius of 50 to 100 miles.

Such relationships have been worked out for contemporary situations, and similar patterns have been shown to exist for areas with such disparate histories as Wiltshire and Wisconsin. Christaller's studies in south Germany are of towns in which the survival of the medieval fabric is so complete that some, like Nördlingen, or Rothenburg have built their modern wealth and fortunes on a tourist trade.

Two further introductory comments may be made. First, the concepts of central place theory, concerning the relationships between town and country, the network of urban spheres of influence and the hierarchies of size and function, offer a method of approach to the historical study of towns which has by no means been fully explored or properly integrated into the existing literature on urban history. The nature of the urban hierarchy in the past and certainly the criteria by which it should be measured appear to be quite different from those used at the present time. The growth of the retail trade is a relatively recent phenomenon, and many of the functions which are now performed by separate industries concerned with processing, packaging and distribution were once performed by the local brewer, baker, butcher, carpenter, tailor or smith. When transport was unmechanised and farming less highly organised and specialised, the weekly visits to the market had a more important commercial and social funtion than they now have. There is then, a considerable need for the application of central place theory to the occupational structures, sizes and regional relations of pre-industrial and medieval towns.

Secondly, in the preoccupation of many urban geographers with contemporary functional relationships of towns, there is a danger that two apparently alternative and mutually exclusive types of approach to the study of towns may develop. One would be concerned solely with their present functional relationships and the degree of 'fit' to theoretical patterns, the other historical and concerned with the complexities of change and development, seeking to establish unsuspected relationships of general application through intensive study of a few cases or a particular period. It is also clear that the theoretical networks are so coarse and established hierarchies so imprecise that there is still a wide zone of indifference and much scope for choice. Within the limits of a coarsely regular spacing towns may well be sited with respect to defensive considerations, relief, navigable water, or the previous existence of fortified walls. If the regular patterns of size and spacing which are established were created in medieval times, then understanding will be enhanced if hinterland and function are examined in a medieval as well as a modern context.

CHARTER, MARKET AND WALL

The definition of a town has always presented problems. Size alone (difficult in modern times, with 1,000 or even 10,000 population as a minimum) is even less satisfactory to the historical geographer than to others, not only because many large villages with only agricultural functions may be greater than places generally accepted as towns, but also because size, at least in terms of population, is difficult to establish before censuses were taken. Economic functions in trade, crafts, industry or marketing have generally been regarded as fundamental components of town life and it could be argued that agricultural occupations should be in a minority. For urban historians, as for modern census-takers, definition is important, for controversy has raged in the past as to whether the earliest stages in the generation of towns were associated with defence and administration or commerce and industry. For our purposes it would be enough, perhaps, to adopt a wide view and to regard a town as 'a concentration of population larger than neighbouring agricultural settlements' in which there is a substantial non-agricultural population, which may be concerned with defence, administration, religion, commerce and/or industry, though not necessarily, of course, in that order.[1]

Many historians have seen the urban values of the bourgeoisie as the fundamental and radical source of modern society rather than the agricultural and territorial values of medieval nobility. The special concern of urban society for equitable and rapid justice, especially in civil disputes, for local government, for the protection and encouragement of trade and industry, financial honesty and the accumulation of wealth in goods and money rather than in land has sometimes seemed to set medieval urban and rural society quite apart. Henri Pirenne regarded the medieval city as a remarkable institution, as indeed it was.[2] He, too, was concerned to establish the distinctiveness and identity of towns as compared with the countryside, stressing not only their economic and defensive functions but also their legal entity. The three essential attributes of the fully developed medieval city were, he thought, summed up in: the market, the charter and the wall.

The medieval curtain walls which defended the population from attack before the wider use of gunpowder and artillery were major items of investment which required public taxation and collective arrangements for the manning of the walls, though they also facilitated the levying of tolls, the proceeds of which were partly devoted to the building, maintenance and repair of the wall. As towns grew, from the eleventh to the fourteenth centuries, new walls and the date of their building sometimes give important clues to the chronology and pattern of growth, as in the Flemish cloth towns. The wall, therefore, constituted one of the fundamental elements in the structure of the medieval town even though suburban settlements and parishes were often allowed to develop outside the walls.

The market is, in Pirenne's graphic description, symbolic of the economic function of the town as a whole, and the granting of rights to markets and fairs constituted an important part of urban privileges everywhere in Western Europe. Yet it is important to distinguish carefully the functions of markets and fairs.

At a period when the volume of business might not warrant permanent residence of merchants and their agents, the coming together of buyers and sellers at a known and predictable time and place was an important lubricant of exchange. The fair of St Denis at Paris existed from A.D. 634–5 and was widely known by A.D. 709; fairs at a number of Flemish towns are mentioned in the eleventh century, and those of Champagne were already highly organised by 1114.[3] At later dates, international importance attached to other fairs, such as those at Chalon-sur-Saône from the end of the twelfth-century; Geneva in the fourteenth century and Lyon in the fifteenth. In Germany the growth of the Frankfurt fair to international importance in the fourteenth century was linked with the development of the Rhine as an avenue of exchange between the Mediterranean and the north in the fourteenth century. Many other places on the international routes across Austria, Germany and Switzerland had fairs of much more than local importance in the fourteenth and fifteenth centuries: Nördlingen at the junction of the Frankfurt–Augsburg road with that from Nürnberg to Lake Constance; Zurzach near the junction of the Aar and the Rhine; Linz in Austria; Bolzano in northern Italy at the threshold of the Brenner pass; Leipzig; Zwolle, Zutphen and Arnhem in the Netherlands; and the great fair of Scania in Scandinavia are examples. But in addition to these greater fairs there were also the locally important gatherings which took place all over Europe at which regional products were exchanged, exotic products were available, and, as well as business, social contacts, pleasure and amusements were to be had. The medieval fair was thus of fundamental importance in bringing merchants together and in the distribution of goods carried over long distances. Verlinden goes so far as to conclude that 'the fairs were as important for medieval long-distance trade as were, for example, first the development of navigation in the Mediterranean and the North Sea, and, subsequently, the sea-route link between these two major areas.'[4]

Market law and the privilege of holding markets weekly or daily were granted by higher feudal authority. It seems likely that such legal institutions preceded the development of the market place as a physical feature of urban settlement,[5] for the market place was not necessarily a concomitant of market privileges, though most thriving market towns did in fact set aside some open space for the erection of temporary stalls and booths. In Germany the market settlement appeared later than the granting of market rights, and did not have a clearly defined functional and topographical entity until the early twelfth century, by which time it usually did involve the creation of a market place, the appurtenances relating to it and regular division of land into urban house lots or burgage tenements, as well as freedom for permanent settlers within the town walls and some degree of urban self-government.[6]

It has also been suggested that the market place and market privileges were not necessarily associated with early merchant settlement on long-distance trade routes.[7] The activity of the market centred mainly around the exchange of goods and services generated within the region served by the town and consisting of both the town itself and the villages or smaller towns of the surrounding countryside. Daily or weekly markets were, quite naturally, for the petty trade of a kind which involves frequent purchases of goods rather than the occasional and specialised trading such as that involving long-distance trade and exotic commodities. It is true that some travelled goods were sold by the petty traders of the market—salt, fish, spices, even some dyestuffs—but hardly on a scale likely to be of interest to the long-distance merchant. Settlements without a *portus* or a *wik* and thus lacking, presumably, a settlement of long-distance merchants, but which had market rights, were fairly common in eleventh-century Germany.[8]

Nevertheless, the earliest of the German towns with merchant communities did in fact usually possess markets oriented along the major trade routes entering the town.[9] Where river routes were involved the preferred sites were often on the low-lying but firm and well-drained ground of low terraces near the river banks, fords, bridges or the head of navigable water, and below the fortifications of the *burg* on spur, high terrace or meander core. But during the eleventh and twelfth centuries the amount of local exchange increased, following upon the rise of specialised urban handicrafts and the urban artisan, and also upon the growth of rural population and the expansion of agricultural surpluses from newly cultivated land. With this growth in local exchanges a shift took place in the location and function of the market place in the town as a whole. From the second half of the twelfth century the market place in developing German towns abandoned the major long-distance routes for a more central position in relation to the built-up area of the town, and were very often placed near to the major churches or other public buildings of the town.[10]

The importance which Pirenne attached to the charter is indicative of a whole range of legal and institutional characteristics which guaranteed the medieval town at least a certain degree of autonomy and which differentiated urban society clearly from the predominantly feudal and manorial countryside. Although grants of charters guaranteeing urban liberties and privileges frequently initiated the foundation of new towns in the twelfth and thirteenth centuries and later, it is clear that the legal differentiation of the medieval town was a secondary characteristic which developed subsequently to the rise of the merchant class and the permanent settlement of merchant communities in the new towns. Nevertheless, as a contributory element in the areal differentiation of town and country it is important to consider first the *raison d'être* of this distinction, the status of the individual in the towns, the differentiation of urban from rural land

20 *Meissen*, 1560–70 (Braun and Hogenberg). See p. 321 and Figure 6.5. The site of the early burg lies to the right and late medieval expansion was towards the small stream on the left. The towered houses stand out, especially on the skyline. Note also the covered and towered bridge, the suburban horticulture and the indications of an important timber trade.

21 *Siena*, c. 1570 (Braun and Hogenberg). An important centre of banking, commerce and the silk industry in the thirteenth century, on the route from Rome to Florence and the north Italian Plain. The towered houses of the patricians are of course exaggerated, but constitute an important element in the urban structure. The contrast between the medieval curtain wall and the growing complexity of urban defences against artillery in the sixteenth century is also apparent.

in terms of tenure, ownership, and seigneurial rights and the degree of legal, fiscal and political autonomy. The royal or imperial charter embodied many of these privileges and was regarded as the fundamental safeguard of urban liberties. Changes of dynasty brought forth a great crop of confirmed charters, and the documents themselves were locked away with maximum security and the essential contents often engraved for all to see in guildhalls and cathedrals. The new merchant class which emerged in the eleventh and twelfth centuries, often to a commanding position in the new urban communities, could not function smoothly or easily under the rules of agricultural feudalism. Serfdom, villeinage and personal unfreedom in general were, to say the least, a hindrance to the mobility a merchant needed for the exercise of personal initiative in trade; manorial and seigneurial jurisdiction over transactions in land must be unfettered if considerable investment in urban building on small plots were to be undertaken; the administration of justice had to be made quick and equitable, with a civil law adapted to the needs of merchants in settling disputes; relics of seigneurial monopolies sometimes persisted, but in most towns they were gradually eliminated. Above all, the city had a degree of autonomy, and it was recognised as a distinct legal territory. The city authorities were responsible for government, they were empowered to levy taxes and market tolls for the finances of city government, the carrying out of public works and public services, and they were also responsible for the execution of a distinctive economic or political policy.

SIZE, SPACING AND SITE

Even the largest of medieval European towns hardly approached the size or population of a modest English town of the present time, and barely topped 100,000. Growth and size are, however, very difficult to establish with any accuracy, for tallage rolls and hearth taxes, the chief sources, give at best an indirect indication and have only rarely survived.[11] The building of new fortifications may give a hint: in the Low Countries new walls were being built towards the end of the eleventh and in the twelfth centuries in the growing cloth towns, and new extensions were planned or carried out between 1250 and 1300, though in some cases anticipated growth never took place and for centuries the medieval walls still enclosed gardens and orchards (as, for example at Bruges). Before 1350, Milan and Venice may have had about 100,000 and were, like Naples and Florence, certainly over 50,000. In Flanders and Brabant, at the other end from northern Italy of the main European axis of urban growth, Ghent was the largest town with some 56,000 in mid-fourteenth century, but Bruges had about 35,000 and Louvain, Brussels and Ypres between 20,000 and 40,000. In Spain, Barcelona, Cordoba, Seville and Granada may have had some 35,000 or more, but elsewhere in Western Europe, Paris (about 80,000), London (35,000 to 45,000 in 1377) and Cologne (40,000) were the only large towns. In the German area Cologne and Lübeck probably led; Strasbourg, Nürnberg, Augsburg, Venice, Prague, Magdeburg and Danzig may have had about 20,000. Six other German towns had about 10,000 and in England and Holland, Leiden, Amsterdam, Delft, Haarlem, York, Bristol and perhaps Norwich were of the same order of magnitude. But most towns had far less than 10,000 and the normal size for regional centres such as Cambridge, Leicester, or Coventry was of the order of 1,000 to 3,000; in Germany there were some 200 places with populations of about 2,000 to 10,000. Medieval towns were, then, fairly small, and although populations were limited by disease, periodic famine and difficulties of assuring food supply, this was perhaps the result of a general economic and political tendency towards decentralisation rather than of absolute physical limitations on growth, for Rome, Peking, Baghdad and Constantinople had grown much larger under conditions otherwise no more technologically or demographically favourable.

In general, medieval towns approximated to the rank–size relationship to which some modern urban patterns conform, though at a much lower magnitude. J. C. Russell has fitted a formula to the figures for English towns that he has derived from the 1377 poll tax returns:

$$n_r = \frac{C\left(1 + \dfrac{\sqrt{r-1}}{10}\right)}{r}$$

where r = rank of city by size, n_r = the population of the city of r rank in the region, and C = the size of the largest city.[12] London, with 35,000, had about 1·5 per cent of the total population. York and Bristol with 11,000 and 9,500 were both below the anticipated sizes of the second and third largest cities, which should have had about 20,000 and 13,000 respectively. Russell, therefore, is inclined to include with these towns the populations of nearby places such as Beverley and Hull in the case of York and even Cardiff and Newport in the case of Bristol. The validity of this grouping is very doubtful, however, and his comment seems more reasonable that perhaps the larger towns were already relatively stunted by the centralisation of administration and government as well as trade on London. The sixty-five largest towns, containing about 9 per cent of the total population, probably represented the urban population of the period fairly well.

Estimates of the urban population of Germany about 1500 yield, in a general way, conformable results, though the estimates are less complete and precise than those for England in the fourteenth century. In Germany, however, the most striking deviation from the general pattern of rank–size correlation is the absence of a single leading city. Cologne and Lübeck shared the leadership but both were relatively small compared with the high populations of the remaining towns which lay among the ten to fifteen most important in the whole country. If these middle-ranking towns are taken as the norm by which the largest towns should be estimated rather than the other way round, the first ranking city should have been of the order of 100,000 and thus comparable with the capital cities of France or England at this time. The second city would have had about 55,000. The next four towns, with actual populations of 20–30,000 would be expected to have 20,000 to 38,000 using Russell's formula and assuming a leading city of 100,000. And that group which had 10,000 to 20,000, (including Augsburg, Hamburg, Frankfurt and Zürich) could have been expected to have about the populations they possessed. Thus in Germany in 1500 the disintegration of central government and the lack of urban leadership, no less than political leadership, is evident in the estimates of town sizes. But by 1500 Germany was nevertheless endowed with a fairly large group of substantial towns of the second order.

The spacing of medieval towns has not, perhaps, received the attention it deserves. Karl Bücher made estimates for medieval Germany in the late nineteenth century, and in view of his importance as a pioneer of the concept of the urban region, it seems worth quoting his remarks: 'If we take a map of the old German Empire and mark upon it the places which up to the end of the Middle Ages had received grants of municipal rights (and there were in all about 3,000 of them), we see the country dotted with towns at an average distance of four to five hours journey in the south and west and in the north and east of seven to eight. All were not of equal importance and the majority of them were or tried to be the economic centres of their territories.'[13] He went on to the calculation that each town in south-west Germany served an average of 40 to 50 square miles; in central and east Germany 60 to 85, and in east Germany 100 to 170 square miles. J. C. Russell's calculations for Leicestershire suggest that places with more than 100 people were on the average 4·2 miles apart and that those with more than 200 people were 8·8 miles apart. The average distance from Leicester to its surrounding boroughs was 13 miles. The calculation is an interesting one to have made, but it should be borne in mind that there were very many places in 1377 which had more than 100 people or even 200, and were nevertheless purely agricultural and supported no truly urban functions at all.

Much more rigorous studies are needed of the spacing of medieval urban centres with relation to their chronological development and also to the hierarchy of non-agricultural functions which they display. It seemed obvious to Karl Bücher that the spacing of medieval towns was related to the ability of a peasant from the most distant rural settlement to reach the town market in one day and be home again by nightfall. Major market towns in England, for example, tend to be at a distance of 20 to 30 miles apart (e.g. in East Anglia and the south-east Midlands) and smaller centres at distances of some 12 to 17 miles apart. Yet it is clear that the smaller and nearer market centres arose long after the major market towns, often the county towns, had been well established. Most of the major towns had some urban functions in Domesday times but many of the smaller ones were products of growth in the twelfth and thirteenth centuries, or they were the result of successful speculation in the planning of new town foundations. The conditions under which this secondary growth of small towns occurred need examination, for the rapidity and cost of transport changed little during the period.

Finally, the siting of medieval towns in Western Europe may be briefly considered in relation to the qualities of soil and terrain. The distinction between military and mercantile needs is obvious and important. Medieval towns which were based on Roman foundations clearly enjoyed the advantages, and suffered the handicaps, of the Roman choice made, perhaps, in the first or second centuries B.C. It has already been shown that the Roman appreciation of urban sites was governed by various considerations (see p. 89), and accessibility by road or river was frequently of prime importance. Impregnable defences were of little account if the sites were excessively difficult of access and earlier Celtic sites were sometimes for this reason abandoned. In the late Roman Empire considerations changed, however, and when walled citadels were established in the third century or later, defensive sites were valued and locations were even shifted to take advantage of such qualities. These locations were, therefore, inherited with the Roman walls which were so important in the pre-urban cores of the early Middle Ages when defence was a paramount consideration. Defensive sites on spurs, hilltops, incised meander cores and island sites in braided rivers (as at Paris) were commonly chosen, where natural defences could assist or replace the earthworks and palisades of the castle builders. Or for the wider defence and control of an area other types of site with military advantages were favoured, at gaps in escarpments, for example, the junction of mountain valley and open plain, the confluences of rivers, or the entry to a river gorge.

Merchant communities were, however, interested in a different set of qualities which only partially coincided with those of the castle builders. They needed accessibility to their routes above all, whether these were the navigable rivers, the sea or overland roads. Overland routes still often followed Roman roads, or they favoured naturally well-drained soils which provided hard, dry going for most of the year. Gravel terraces, sandy heaths, watershed routes on chalk or limestone were all favourable, but marsh, alluvium, clays and shales were to be avoided. Bridges, fords and passes were important keypoints restricting overland routes, which otherwise often followed very 'braided' and ramifying courses.

Out of the many types of site favoured by the castle builders, then, the merchants selected those which either combined defensibility and accessibility or which provided a suitably accessible site nearby. Thus, while hilltop sites were often subsequently neglected, those on meander cores near navigable rivers where hard ground provided crossing places were very much favoured (e.g. Cambridge, Leicester, Durham). Stable island sites in braided rivers which also provided crossing places were also promising (e.g. at Paris, Plate 18). Bridging points and heads of navigation have also been commonly used. Gap towns and those at junction of mountain valley and lowland plain have been particularly important at the margins of the north Italian plain or the Swiss plateau, especially where lake or river navigation was also possible.

The siting of many Dutch towns presents an interesting case since many had necessarily to be placed on artificially heightened sites on embankments in reclaimed land. Burke has distinguished various types which developed from the twelfth and thirteenth centuries:[14] the simple dike town, such as Sloten; the dike-and-dam town, of which Amsterdam itself is the outstanding example; the harbour town such as Enkhuisen; the military bastides of which Naarden is the most famous and photographed example; the water town or *grachtenstad*, most common on reclaimed land in Holland, and represented by Delft or Gouda; and finally the compound towns or *geestgrond* towns such as Haarlem or Alkmaar, part built on high ground and part constructed on drained and reclaimed land. It is a particular feature of the Dutch towns on reclaimed land that they involved a good deal of planning: a preliminary assessment of the land needed, the construction of an encircling moat, parallel internal drainage ditches, canals, sluices and windmill pumps to lift water to the surrounding levels, the integration of internal and external water transport, the artificial raising and consolidation of the ground and piling for many of the major buildings such as the gild hall, churches, weighing halls, quays and so on. The foundation or extension of a town was thus a matter requiring careful planning and forethought and considerable public investment.

ORIGINS, REVIVAL AND GROWTH
OF THE MEDIEVAL CITY

The origin of the medieval town has engaged the interest of urban historians from the late nineteenth century and should certainly engage that of historical geographers, since it is in the period of creation and early growth that the siting, spacing and basic sphere of influence of most European towns developed. Theories of urban origins have tended to centre about the relative importance of various ingredients in urban functions: administrative, defensive, religious, commercial, industrial and even agricultural. There would be little point in summarising these views but several general points may be made. First, the viewpoint and the definition of the town adopted by the student is fundamental. An economic definition of a town implies a search for mercantile origins; and the legal and constitutional origins or the topographical origins of towns may require quite different emphasis on different facets of growth. Agricultural origins have been stressed and it is evident that many of the smallest towns clearly arose because the largest agricultural villages were the obvious centres at which crafts and traders would settle, but agriculture was in a sense ubiquitous, so that although early towns (in Domesday times, for example) may have had a large agricultural component, this does not help to explain origins; similarly, studies of Slav towns based on archaeological excavations have emphasised the importance of crafts and artisans[15] as a component in the tenth-century towns of Russia and Poland, but it is hard to see these occupations as anything more than of secondary importance in relation to the growth of the great cities. Yet there is a moderately large area of agreement that many medieval towns bear witness in their early functions and certainly in their plans and topographical structures to the combination of two major elements: defence and administration, which have their physical expression in the fortifications surrounding a 'pre-urban core'; and the mercantile element, which normally has its physical expression in the market place. In the classic view of Pirenne, this new merchant class was unlikely to have emerged from the local agricultural populations or from the unfree servitors of the abbeys and monasteries, but was more probably associated with the spread of the Italian merchant from southern Europe and the example he set for surplus, displaced populations of the north who had lost their roots in the soil and became the itinerant traders. It was thus a class of men essentially engaged in long-distance trade who were the mainsprings, according to Pirenne, of the new merchant colonies which began to make permanent headquarters under the shelter of the fortified pre-urban cores.

One of the enduring problems in the growth of the medieval town still remains, however, the question of continuity from Roman times. It is here convenient to distinguish simply two aspects of the general problem: whether there was a continuous tradition of trading activity and of merchant settlement; and in what ways topographical continuity was maintained from the Roman to the medieval site and plan. Continuity of urban institutions and government is very rare; continuity of industry and trade doubtful and often controversial; but continuity of religious function is extremely significant all over continental Western Europe; topographical continuity of site is very evident.

Pirenne directed attention many years ago to the idea of an essential continuity in the trading sphere of the classical world through Merovingian times. Papyrus and gold continued to be used in the west, and Greek, Jewish or Syrian merchants continued to trade in the west and certainly as far to the north as Tours right up to the eighth century. But his contention that the true break between the ancient and the medieval world, the reversion to a natural economy and the decay of urban life, occurred in Carolingian times when Arab and Scandinavian invasions effectively blocked long-distance commerce, must be re-examined from a regional point of view.

Edith Ennen recognised three divisions in her consideration of urban origins of Western Europe[16]: first, northern Germany and Scandinavia, in which the Roman tradition had no significance; second, England, northern France, the Low Countries, Switzerland, the Rhineland, southern Germany and Austria, all regions in which Roman urban life substantially disappeared with the fall of the Empire, but in which, nevertheless, medieval towns show the imprint of Roman activity to a varying degree and in different ways; and third, Spain, Italy and southern France, in which there was an essential continuity not only in the occupation of the soil, agriculture, population and language but also in the existence of the towns.

In the Mediterranean lands of the west, Roman town life had been more advanced and mature than that of the north; the Ostrogoths and Lombards in Italy caused less destruction and disturbance than the Franks or Anglo-Saxons did further north; and many coastal cities retained some contact with the advanced commercial world of the eastern Mediterranean and continued to trade in Byzantine luxuries. In the north Italian plain a merchant class (the *negotiantes*) constituted a distinct social order, and the highest class of merchants was on an equal footing with the middle group of landowners. Among the town-dwelling artisans, jewellers, painters, coppersmiths, shoemakers, tailors and soapmakers are mentioned, probably living around the market place.[17] It may be that the early medieval gilds of Lombardy represent some continuous thread with the late Roman gilds, and other municipal institutions may have a link with the Empire. Pavia was certainly of continuous importance, for although no more than a Roman *municipium*, it became capital for Ostrogoth and Lombard and therefore a centre of consumption as well as a trading town in its own right, at a commanding position on the lower Ticino near its junction with the Po and with main roads converging from the Alps and Apennines. Frequented by the merchants of Venice, Genoa and Amalfi, and linked by a flourishing river trade to the developing towns of the Po basin and to the passes of the western Alps, Pavia led a precocious urban development in northern Italy until its position was challenged by Milan from about A.D. 1000. Customs stations at the foot of principal Alpine valleys (Susa, Bard, Bellinzona, Chiavenna, Bolzano and Valorgne) were placed to collect dues from merchants and pilgrims coming from the north. New urban growth flourished during the ninth century at Asti, Vercelli, Milan, Pavia, Verona, Cremona, Piacenza and Lucca.[18]

It is in the towns of northern Italy in particular (at Turin, Piacenza, Verona or Pavia, for example) that the topographical identity of modern towns with their Roman forebears extends even to the layout of blocks and streets (see pp. 90–2 above). Such evidence of topographical continuity is in itself a powerful argument for the continuity of an urban, non-agricultural population concerned with crafts and trade. It was also in northern Italy that the concept of the town survived as the centre from which the government of a province or *civitas* was exercised, whereas in other parts of the west it was only through the boundaries of the bishops' dioceses that these districts were preserved. The medieval *suburb* of the Italian towns[19] represented a much wider region than the very local meaning the word came to have further north and included a large area of the surrounding countryside in which the town claimed to have some influence. The integration of town and country was also associated with much greater geographical and social mobility as between town and countryside, or between merchant and landowner. Free merchants were already acquiring land in the *contadi* in the ninth century; the rural nobility were living in the towns and their towered, fortified houses grouped within medieval urban walls (see Plate 21) became a characteristic feature not only of Italy, but also of some towns in Spain and even southern Germany (see below, pp. 321–2).

In Spain the evolution of the towns from the fall of the Roman Empire was more complex.[20] In the north-west there was relatively little survival of urban life: this was the area in which the Suevi had occupied and looted the towns after having first settled in the countryside but it was also an area in which Roman town life had been very weakly developed (see p. 90). The Goths went to the south and east, and much that was Roman was preserved in, for example, Tarragona, for the Goths had long been in contact with the Roman Empire and were more highly romanised than the Suevi.

Eastern trade routes were to some extent maintained during the Visigothic kingdom and Syrian, Jewish and Greek merchants still visited the ports and the capital, Toledo, but most towns declined to little more than agricultural status during the sixth and seventh centuries. The individuality of Spanish towns lay, of course, in the long occupation by the Moors and in the process of the Reconquista which followed. All of the important cities fell into Muslim hands in the eighth century. They continued to be occupied by a Christian population which at first remained numerically dominant and relatively free but which was later reduced to a minority as conversion to Islam increased. At this later period the Christian population was often allotted special quarters in the towns, except at Cordoba and Toledo. Some new towns were founded, such as Murcia in 831, but for the most part urban expansion took place by the addition of new Arab quarters to old centres, distinguished frequently by the haphazard and tortuous streets as well as by their characteristic architecture. Urban densities of building were high and populations were far larger than any in contemporary Christian Europe, for totals of well over 20,000 are mentioned for Toledo, Almería, Granada and even 100,000 for Cordoba itself.

A new pattern emerged with the reconquest, however. Even in the ninth and tenth centuries trade between Christian and Arab Spain brought Byzantine silks and Persian woollens to the north in exchange for Frankish arms and cloth. León, Zamora and Oviedo flourished on this type of trade, but from about 1030 an urban revival began which owed less to Muslim trade than to exchanges within Christian Europe. In the whole of the north, from Galicia through Navarre to León, Aragon and Catalonia new urban growth was linked with the rise of pilgrimage to the shrine of Santiago de Compostella. Finally, in the central zone between the Guadiana and the Duero there were the old fortress cities which had military and ecclesiastical rather than commercial functions: Salamanca, Segovia and Avila, for example.

In southern France, where Roman cities had been as deeply rooted as anywhere in the west, instability and insecurity were constant threats to the survival of economic life.[21] Muslim bands from Spain were raiding the area in 713 and Narbonne was still worth looting in 793. But with quiescence on the Spanish front in the ninth century, sea raids by Saracen and Scandinavians threatened the whole of the coast, and for a time the Saracens settled in the Camargue and in eastern Provence. Urban life suffered disastrously, especially in eastern Provence where Fréjus and Toulon were destroyed, but perhaps the main result was to convert urban life to military purposes, so that the defended towns and their walls largely fulfilled the rôle that was played by rural castles further north. As a result, the wealth and possessions of the lesser nobility and the church were also concentrated within the security of urban walls, so that, as in Italy, investment in trade was facilitated when revival came. Nevertheless, some long-distance commerce and coastal trade persisted. At the contact between Islam and Christianity the traffic in slaves and eastern luxury goods was never completely broken in the ninth and tenth centuries. The merchants' routes through the southern towns to Spain carried Cordovan leathers and eastern cloths as well as slaves and money, notably from Lyon through Vienne to Arles or through Uzès and Nîmes to Béziers, Narbonne and overland to the Spanish march. The salt trade from the coast inland persisted too. Yet it was, in general, only in the eleventh and twelfth centuries that revival got under way.

Northern France, the Low Countries and the Rhineland form the greater part of the intermediate zone described by Edith Ennen. This was the area in which essential features of classical urban life were lost, but in which traces of Roman urbanism survive in many ways.[22] Ancient municipal organisation disappeared everywhere and the town ceased to be the centre of administration of a wide area around it. The term *civitas* increasingly referred not to a wide area of government but to the town and then later to the fortified citadel which was often all that remained in the late Roman Empire and the fifth to the ninth centuries. The main outlines of these changes by which the classical towns were altered have already been traced (see above pp. 91–6). Some of the ancient *civitates* became the residences of officials or kings; the fortifications of the late Roman Empire served as defences for princes and officials; but it was the Christian church which was the decisive element in continuity. Between the Meuse and the Loire some thirty *civitates* were the centres of bishoprics from the fourth or fifth centuries.[23] If bishoprics were moved, the classical towns frequently either disappeared or barely survived—*Civitas Boiorum* in Aquitaine disappeared; Cimiez was abandoned for Nice, and Apt for Viviers. At Xanten, Cologne, Trier and Bonn, however, there was a complete continuity from Roman times.

As the power and wealth of the bishops increased so also did the status of the ancient centres. Early Christian cemeteries outside the walls of the Roman towns sometimes became holy centres at which abbeys were founded, which themselves were sometimes the nucleus of urban revival at a later date.

The extent to which economic functions survived in the ancient Roman centres has been much discussed and in the absence of documentary evidence much doubt is likely to remain. Between the Meuse and the Loire there were certainly still merchants in the sixth and seventh centuries, buying wine in Orleans and selling spices. Franks, Syrians, Greeks and Jews were mentioned, and there were clearly still contacts with the Mediterranean world and also an artisan population. But during the eighth and ninth centuries southern commerce contracted, perhaps as a result of the difficulties affecting southern France at this time, and the trade of the area between the Meuse and the Loire became more strongly oriented towards the Seine basin and the Channel.[24] Navigation on the Seine and the shipment of wine, quite probably through the newly established fairs of St Denis at Paris, represented a new concern. Rouen, Amiens and Quentovic became important; Tournai remained important but mention was also made of Ghent and Valenciennes. There were merchant colonies or *portus* at Huy, Namur and Maastricht in the eighth century, suggesting a revival of trade along the Meuse.

In eastern France and the Rhineland, several ancient Roman centres retained economic as well as ecclesiastical importance through the critical period of the seventh and eighth centuries. Metz, on its commanding spur at the confluence of Moselle and Seille had been a Celtic tribal centre and a highly romanised town with temples, baths, amphitheatre and aqueduct. The regularities of Roman streets and notably the *cardo maximus* are still evident. But it was as centre of a bishopric, monastery and some twenty churches that it was known in the eighth century between the disappearance of Syrian and Oriental merchants in the fifth century and the settlement of a Jewish colony of merchants by A.D. 888. By A.D. 1000, however, it had established three fairs a year and was a place of some consequence.[25] Verdun on the navigable Meuse had been centre of a bishopric from A.D. 346 but it was notorious from the sixth to the tenth centuries as a centre of the slave trade and of a traffic in furs also deriving from the Slav regions. Trier had been the late Roman capital of the Empire and its wall had enclosed some 675 acres at a time when it was said to have 'drained the commerce of the world'. It, too, had Syrian merchants and devotees of oriental religions as well as Christianity in the fourth century and a bishop from A.D. 314. Town life here continued fairly vigorously into the sixth century and there were Frisian merchants there in the eighth and ninth. By the end of the tenth century the town began to take shape from four different nuclei: (a) the *Domstadt*, the walled and defended cathedral; (b) the abbeys and the two markets; (c) the agricultural settlement nearby; and (d) the new suburb established around the new market founded by the archbishop in A.D. 958 outside the Domstadt and cited even by A.D. 1000 as one of the most important on the Rhine.

In the Low Countries the towns of Flanders provided Pirenne with the strongest support for his view that the recrudescence of urban life from the tenth century owed almost nothing to Roman tradition and Roman foundations, and that the Flemish towns were *par excellence*, the product of a fusion between two different elements: the fortifications of church, abbey or count on the one hand, and on the other the communities of far-travelled merchants who sought protection and safe winter quarters in an area where trade routes converged near the shores of the North Sea from Champagne and the Rhineland. Of the late Roman *civitates*, Tongres can show little more than a continuity in the use of its site; Bavai was destroyed in the fourth century; but Cambrai continued to have contact with the Mediterranean to the seventh century and Tournai shows much more evidence of continuity: the bishop's *castrum* followed part of the Roman wall and even the ninth-century *portus* was within Roman walls; the Roman cloth industry may have faded, but Tournai's cloths of wool and linen were known in the ninth century.[26] In the area of southern Flanders there was, then, some continuity from Roman to early medieval times, but it was, on the whole, limited and tenuous.

In the Rhineland and northern Gaul or the Low Countries, many Roman sites certainly continued in use, but there is relatively little evidence that trade continued to function except in a favoured few. The nature of the link which connected the classical with the medieval town was frequently ecclesiastical, through the existence of a bishop's residence or the foundation of an abbey or a monastery on the site of an early Christian temple or cemetery. It is also evident that the link must frequently have been simply that late-Roman, heavily walled, fortress sites were still useful in the fifth and sixth centuries.

Moreover, the existence of fortifications at sites which were already well located with respect to navigable water, Roman roads or natural defences afforded by scarps, meander cores and the like, must often have coincided with a litter of ancient ruins which provided a quarry of building materials. Reports of the decay of old Roman walls

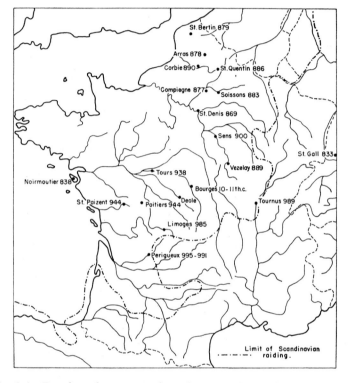

Fig. 6:1   Repair and reconstruction of town walls in Gaul in the ninth and tenth centuries (after Hubert).

around the *civitates* of the eighth century have been interpreted to mean not only that urban life continued to decline during this period, but also that a relative peace had brought conditions under which the walls could reasonably be allowed to decay.[27]

All this was changed by the Scandinavian invasions. Old walls were hurriedly repaired and new ones built (Fig. 6:1). Fortifications were built around monasteries and abbeys as well as the residences of bishops in old Roman *civitates* (Fig. 6:2). Above all, the new in-securities of the ninth and tenth centuries in north-western Europe had the effect of ushering in a new age of castle building by the new feudality. It may not have been until the eleventh century that most of the early wooden palisades and earthen mounds were replaced by

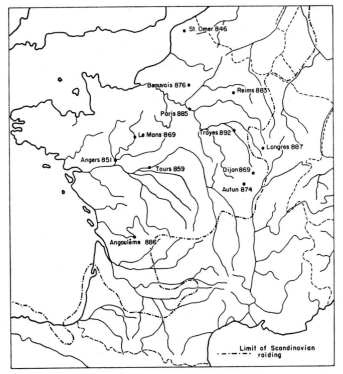

Fig. 6:2   Fortifications of monasteries in the ninth century (after Hubert).

solid stone-built walls, but these new fortifications of counts and princes in strategically chosen locations constituted another type of 'pre-urban' core besides that of ancient Roman origin around which the merchant colonies later began to cluster.

In the Low Countries and north-western Germany, the existence of the early merchant communities is thought to be indicated by the terms *portus* and *wik*, or *wijk*.[28] Dorestad, one of the Frisian ports of the eighth century, is referred to as a *wik*; Utrecht had its *Oudwijk* labelling the early site of the merchant community. Namur was named as a *portus* in A.D. 866 and Valenciennes in 875. Antwerp and Bruges were *wiks* at the end of the ninth. Now the use of the term *wik*, derived from the Latin *vicus*, may have a restricted usefulness as an indication of merchant activity. Its English counterpart, the -*wick* or -*wich* that appears in names like Northwich, Middlewich or Norwich, means simply a settlement that is not concerned with arable farming; it turns up in Essex, for example, as indicating 'outlying dairy farm', in Cheshire as a salt-producing settlement, or a trading place as in Norwich. As an indication of mercantile activity -*wik* may be of similarly limited value in north-west Germany (e.g. Brunswick) and the Low Countries. But, as Petri points out, although the existence of -*wik* and *portus* names may be an indication of early trade in the basin of the North Sea, this does not necessarily provide support for Pirenne's view of a revival of trade completely independent of old patterns, for some of the old Roman foundations, such as Liège and Tournai contained an early *portus*. What is, however, important is the evidence to support the idea that trade around the North Sea, in north-west Germany and the south-west Baltic was adequate to sustain permanent trading and non-agricultural settlements.

In Germany the influence of the Roman frontier had been strong in the Rhineland and the Danube valley, and many of the Roman foundations, particularly those which had become the seats of the bishops, formed the nuclei of medieval cities in ways similar to those of northern Gaul. But in much of Germany the Roman tradition had no meaning and the formation of the pre-urban core took various forms. In Carolingian times fortresses and trading posts had been set up on the frontier with the Slavs along the Elbe and the Saale and on the routes leading from the Rhineland eastwards. Many of the *wik* names and other evidence of merchant settlements are on the major trade routes of the time: along the Rhine, the Danube and the Elbe, on the Meuse and the Saale and even on less important rivers such as the Weser, the Fulde, the Main, Moselle and Neckar. Other precocious merchant settlements have been identified on the North Sea coast and on the more important overland routes, notably along the Hellweg from Dortmund towards Goslar. In detail, too, the location of the early merchant communities seems to confirm the importance of long-distance trade, for they were frequently located along the flanks of the long-distance routes leading away from the pre-urban nucleus or from the nodal points represented by fords, bridges, gaps and the like. This was the case, for example, at early Magdeburg. The merchant communities settled around the fortifications of a pre-urban core, but the component elements of the pre-urban core

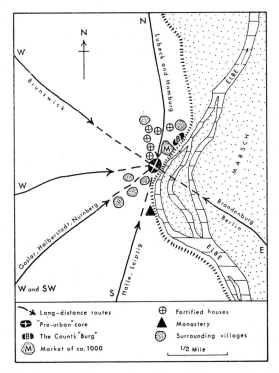

Fig. 6:3 Magdeburg. The context of early urban development at Magdeburg. The pre-urban core consisted of the Carolingian castle on the site of a Saxon house, the Saxon royal palace, a monastery and the Cathedral. The Count's fortified burg was another centre of early growth (after Mrusek).

were of various origin. In Germany they were, basically, the residences of king or emperor, princes, dukes and counts; ecclesiastical institutions, whether the seats of bishops or the sites of abbeys and monasteries; agricultural villages; and the individual defences of the lesser nobility.[29] Initially these all existed independently, perhaps, as at Magdeburg, each element disposed on adjacent sites which were appropriate for defence, trade or agriculture (Fig. 6:3). At Magde-

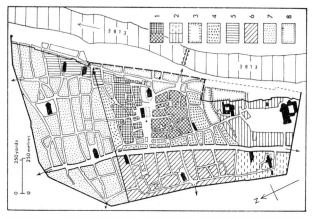

(c)

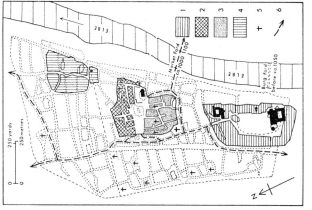

(b)

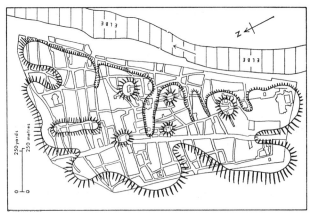

(a)

burg the royal palace and the cathedral comprised one nucleus on a commanding spur over the river, the count's burg another and the market a third, lying between them and in a better position for the river crossing (Fig. 6:4).[30] Several villages lay nearby and there also developed a scatter of fortified strongholds or towered houses. Further expansion occurred in the eleventh and twelfth centuries and a new extension to the north was quite distinct, as seen in the sixteenth-century map (Plate 19). Meissen had a basically similar structure of disparate nuclei which were linked at a relatively late date (Fig. 6:5 and Plate 20). Brunswick consisted of five such nuclei brought together only in 1269; Rostock consisted of three, organised as a unit from 1265. Common interests may serve to explain why disparate nuclei were established fairly closely to each other. Counts, bishops, monks and landed nobility would seek proximity to centres of royal government, for example, and farmers and traders would seek to supply and to be protected by their lay and ecclesiastical lords.

The occurrence of fortified tower-houses is a particularly illumina-

Fig. 6:4   Magdeburg: the urban plan.

(a) Magdeburg. The fortifications which constituted separate early nuclei took clear advantage of the spurs and heights overlooking the Elbe (after Mrusek).

(b) Magdeburg ca 1000 A.D.

1. The Carolingian castle-site (805) on the probable site of a Saxon lord's house; the Saxon royal palace: the monastery of St Moritz (937).
2. Cathedral (968) and the earlier and irregularly laid out part of the Ottonian town.
3. The later and regular Ottonian town with market place of ca 1200.
4. The Count's burg.
5. Towered houses of urban merchants and officials.
6. Long-distance routes (after Mrusek).

(c) Magdeburg ca 1250.

1. The Ottonian town.
2. The Immunity of the Cathedral.
3. Monastic land.
4. Gradual spread of settlement in the eleventh and twelfth centuries.
5. Area of the former Count's burg, subsequently used for ecclesiastical building in the thirteenth century.
6. Expansion of the town 1152–1192
7. Planned urban expansion 1213–1236.
8. Spread of settlement along the river bank in the twelfth and thirteenth centuries (after Mrusek).

ting feature of some German towns in this respect, recalling similar structures in Italy (e.g. at Siena, see Plate 21) and with similar functions. They consisted of tall multi-storied stone-built houses with living rooms in the upper quarters and substantial storage space

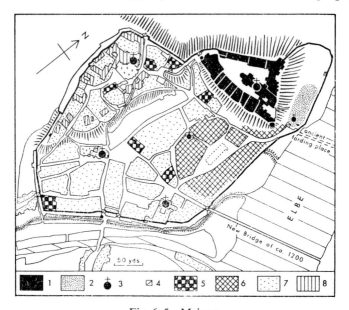

Fig. 6:5   Meissen

1. The early burg.
2. Merchants' settlement *ca* 1000 A.D.
3. Cathedral and churches.
4. Towers.
5. Fortified dwelling houses of higher officials and nobles.
6. Other settlement of the early middle ages.
7. Late medieval expansion.
8. Larger buildings associated with late medieval expansion (after Mrusek).

in cellars and lower rooms.[31] Thirteen such examples existed in Magdeburg, eight in Meissen, and as many as sixty to eighty in Regensburg, a town made wealthy from the eastern trade in the tenth and eleventh centuries. In southern Germany as in Italy, these individual defences appear to bridge a gap between the agglomeration of an urban settlement and the building of the collective city walls in the eleventh century or later.

Fig. 6:6 Halle

A River crossing to the eleventh century merchant settlement.

B River crossing to the market extension north of the early settlement.

C Twelfth century market.

+ Towered houses (after Mrusek).

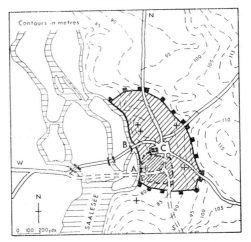

Of about 120 towns identified in Germany in the eleventh century, about 40 were on the sites of bishops' seats, 20 were near monasteries, and no less than 60 grew around royal foundations, including some 12 near the sites of royal palaces.[32] Cologne, Mainz and Magdeburg were the most important of the last. The predominance of royal and

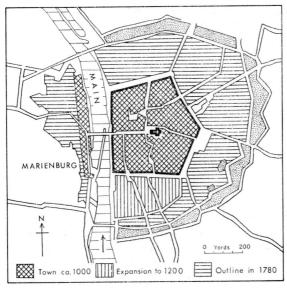

Fig. 6:7 Würzburg

ecclesiastical nuclei among the earliest of the German towns is associated with conditions which contrasted greatly with those of France and England. The influence of Rome had been largely absent, the Scandinavian expansion failed to have such widespread effects as in

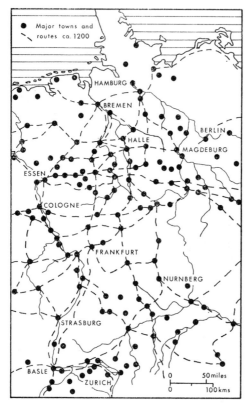

Fig. 6:8 Early medieval towns and routes in Germany before 1200. The clustering of important towns on major routes is apparent, particularly in central Germany along the axis of the *Hellweg* (after Dickinson).

France or England, and there was in the tenth and eleventh centuries a strong political unity in Germany just at the time when feudal disintegration was leading to the widespread creation, in England and France, of new fortified castles and strong points around which many new urban settlements grew up. The great age of castle building in Germany came later in the twelfth and thirteenth centuries with the disintegration of royal power, and it was then that many new towns found the castle as their nucleus.[33]

By the middle of the twelfth century there were perhaps some 200 towns of significance in the German area and many of these were on important trade routes (Fig. 6:8). But during the twelfth and thirteenth centuries there was a much more widespread proliferation of new towns in the old west as well as in the new colonial east (see Fig. 6:9). Some of these grew around castles and monasteries; some,

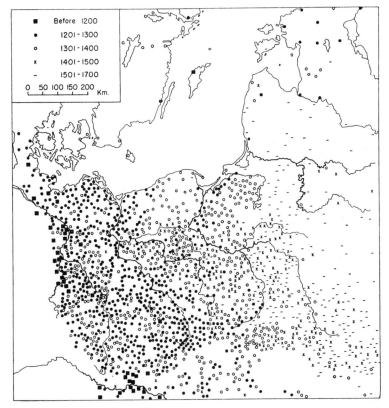

Fig. 6:9 Urban foundation in east central Europe (after Kötzschke, Ebert).

particularly in the new east, were founded on virgin ground; but perhaps the majority were towns which developed from agricultural villages in the same way as many of the small market towns of England.[34] Their place-names often bear witness to a village origin, for names ending in '-ingen', 'heim', '-dorf', '-hausen', and so on are very common.

The new towns arose with a different balance of economic functions from that of the early trading towns, and most of them were not, indeed, located on or near major routes but were more widely and regularly scattered (see Fig. 6:9). The growth of specialised urban crafts, the rise of the artisan and the generation of agricultural surpluses in the surrounding countryside served to increase the interchange of goods and services between town and country to the point at which new towns could be supported at closer intervals than in previous centuries. German economic historians have stressed that each town recognised a sphere of influence among the villages around it and regarded its sphere as a preserve within which it should have a monopoly of the provision of manufactured goods and services and a right to market its agricultural produce. The *Weichbild*, or municipal district, represented this sphere of influence. The possession of market rights was the essential feature of the new towns, and the market place tended to become more and more the focus of activity. Characteristically it ceased to be located at the widening of streets leading to the long-distance routes and was centrally placed within the walls, often near the main church or the castle, for it was important to facilitate the exchanges of the daily and weekly markets which were much more important to these new and modest towns than the operations of the long-distance merchants.

In the colonial east the new towns were planned deliberately in conjunction with the new villages, especially in the zones of later and large-scale colonisation.[35] Like the villages the new towns were standardised in plan and in their institutions, for both were often copied from the law and layout of older centres in central Germany: Magdeburg, Halle and Lübeck, for example, frequently provided the models for new charters. In the old west, as in England and France, the creation of a successful new town could be a profitable venture for the nobility on whose land it was built and by whose hand the market rights were granted and burgage tenements created. For success meant a development of urban land values, new sources of revenue and tolls from a growing population and growing agricultural incomes. In some areas, indeed, the speculative creation of new towns went too far, burgage tenements were not taken up and fair or market rights were little used. In Württemberg, particularly, there are many places that were given urban status but never acquired sufficient urban functions for them to prosper.

In the northern countries the spread of the town came later than in England and Germany, for although a few trading towns had developed in the Viking age, urban growth was slow until the twelfth century. In the area of modern Denmark, for example, there were no more than half a dozen urban foundations of importance before 1050 (Fig. 6:10). The major period of development, as in Norway

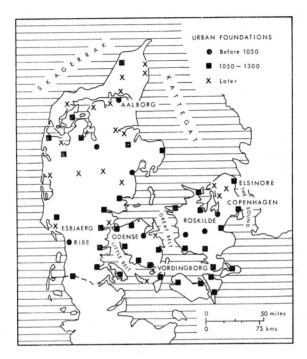

Fig. 6:10   Major urban foundations in Denmark. The concentration of early towns in eastern Denmark is apparent. Most of the urban foundations occur in the period 1050–1300.

and Sweden, did not come until 1050 to 1300, when many new foundations were created, strikingly concentrated in the eastern zones of fertile soil and on sites accessible from the sea. Ribe had become the principal centre for North Sea traffic; Aalborg and Aarhus exported grain; but it was Copenhagen which led, though its population was only some 3,000 in 1380.

In each of the three zones into which Edith Ennen divides the developing urban geography of early medieval Europe different processes were at work to produce characteristic features of urban topography and morphology. There is fairly general agreement that the earliest growth of the towns is to be associated with the addition of a merchant community to a pre-urban core concerned with government, religion or administration, but always important to the merchant community for the protection its walls could afford. In the Mediterranean zone, however, there were many more cases in which the merchant community survived the difficult periods from the fifth to the ninth centuries and topographical identity of Roman and medieval towns was maintained.

Beyond this point, however, it is difficult to find general agreement. Pirenne and others have argued that the early merchant communities were basically concerned with long-distance commerce and that the local exchanges of goods and services could not have been sufficient to sustain urban growth in the absence of substantial agricultural surpluses. Towered houses and merchant communities, according to Lehmann, were to be found on the routes of long-distance trade in southern Germany; and, indeed, given the modest bulk of early medieval commerce, one would suppose that long-distance merchants would be numerous enough to create significant communities only along the commonly frequented trade routes, and at major handling points, particularly at ports, heads of river navigation or bridging points.

Yet it is evident that towns were emerging here and there throughout Europe in the eleventh century and were not merely concentrated along the major trade routes. Ammann considers that the revival of towns on the basis of late Roman *civitates* began in western France in the tenth century.[36] By the eleventh there were very many urban foundations, many of them, it is true, very modest ones, all over England. From the ninth and tenth centuries local regional markets were the support of reviving towns in the Loire valley, according to Buttner. The ways in which Roman administrative centres and early medieval bishoprics became the framework of the reviving town in France suggest, too, that the mainspring for this type of development is to be sought in a more generalised process than the concentrations of long distance merchants along major trade routes.

In the relatively closed early medieval community with a predominantly subsistence economy, agricultural surpluses were relatively small, and most non-agricultural needs of the dependent peasantry were satisfied either by domestic production or by itinerant craftsmen and pedlars. But, nevertheless, agricultural surpluses did exist and were siphoned off from the countryside by way of the surplus production from demesne farms, by way of dues in labour, kind or money, and by way of carting and carriage services; and to the church went tithes, offerings and other dues. Some of this surplus went, of course, to local lords or priests domiciled in the village itself, but there was also a flow of agricultural surpluses or their equivalent in money to the abbey church, the bishops' seat, the castle of the count, and also to the royal administration. Castle and cathedral could be geographically separate, but they were, in fact, very often located close to each other, within the same pre-urban nucleus, as in the agglomerative cells of early German towns, or in the *cité* of Roman origin. It may be argued that relatively few commodities flowed in the return direction to be dispersed in the countryside but that in principle the rural peasantry and knighthood gained instead the feudal and military protection of the count and his men, or the spiritual protection of the bishop and the church. These are, indeed, functions which were geographically expressed in the size and boundaries of the effective units of administration—the county and its continental equivalents, the *contado*, *comté*, *Grafschaft*; or the bishoprics and archdeaconries. But the point to stress is that these were also economic regions to the extent that they were spheres within which taxes, surplus produce and so on were concentrated at the centre. Where the lesser rural nobility chose also to live in or near this central focus or pre-urban nucleus, as in Italy, southern Germany, southern France and Spain, correspondingly more of the surplus 'purchasing power' of the countryside would be focused at a point. The continuing residence of a garrison or of the nobility and their retainers was also important in focusing income at this early stage. (In Leicester, for example, the decay of the castle in the life of the town was a factor in the shift of trade away from its immediate proximity towards the meeting point of the routes through the town). Much of the concentrated surpluses or purchasing power concentrated in the nascent towns went towards the maintenance of garrisons, servants and so on, but the skills and services of artisans concerned with specialised trades were also required: armourers, fletchers, grocers, wheelwrights, sawyers, jewellers, drapers, cordwainers, saddlers and so on. And these artisans would provide for the needs of the countryside as well, though for the most part their services would be effectively available only to those, such as the manorial lords and the lesser nobility of the countryside, who rose above subsistence level.

Thus, even at a very low general level of productivity, the social and economic stratification of a feudal society would serve to concentrate purchasing power effectively over a wide area and to nourish a group of artisans and local merchants as well as a garrison and a priesthood. Growth of the external sector of this urban economy (i.e. the extent to which it traded with other towns and other regions) would thus depend upon the generation of demand for exotic products by the well-to-do and the ability to satisfy these demands by means of appropriate exports from the urban region or county-area. On the one hand the mobility of the new feudality, particularly with its participation in the Crusades from the eleventh century, ensured some acquaintance with the products available by long-distance commerce from the Mediterranean and elsewhere, and the internal growth of population and colonisation provided new sources of income and revenue for the regional lords. By the eleventh century a coarse regional network of towns was fairly well developed in England and France, and even in Domesday times merchants were beginning to settle in places that were more closely spaced than the county centres.

A further implication may be briefly considered. If the new towns of the tenth and eleventh centuries in Western Europe were the product of the long-distance merchant communities settling permanently, then the sources of this expansion may be sought in the revival of commerce and the influence of the Italian merchants spreading northwards. If, however, emphasis is put on the geographical concentration of purchasing power at focal points as the result of a developing feudal hierarchy and ecclesiastical centralisation, then the impetus to growth in the tenth and eleventh centuries must derive from internal sources, and therefore from an increase in agricultural production through the expansion of colonisation and settlement or through the beginnings of specialisation on wool, dairy produce, cloth, or wine. The development of feudal and manorial structures and resultant social and economic stratification may well have increased the efficiency with which surpluses were concentrated at the urban centres. The spread of commerce from Italy and the revival of long-distance trade could not, indeed, occur until a concentration of demand had begun to occur, both processes going hand in hand.

It is clear that the growth of long-distance commerce must be integrated with the developing network of urban centres all over Europe. The processes by which regional urban centres were developing must have operated relatively slowly over a long period and always at a modest scale so as to generate towns never much larger, in the absence of other stimuli, than 2,000 to 5,000 by the end of the Middle Ages. It was, however, the larger towns which had, perhaps, 10,000 or more by the end of the Middle Ages about which Pirenne was writing, located chiefly along the axis of the major trade routes liking Italy with the Low Countries and northern France through southern Germany, the Rhône valley, Switzerland and the Rhineland. The settlement of long-distance merchant communities by the side of pre-urban cores undoubtedly gave a much stronger impetus towards rapid growth from the eleventh century.

THE BAROQUE AND RENAISSANCE TOWN 1500-1800

Although most of the towns of Western Europe had been founded by the end of the Middle Ages, urban functions no less than the external characteristics of the towns were profoundly altered between 1500 and 1800. The urban hierarchy became much more articulated. A few new market centres appeared but the small market towns of the Middle Ages now became much larger than the villages around them and the largest towns, usually the great ports and capital cities, acquired populations of a new order of magnitude, creating new problems of communications and of urban–rural relations, and involving an impact on agricultural land use as well as a new differentiation of urban land usc. New types of town were created, too, and the most radical transformations of all were to be found in new forms of urban architecture and a completely new approach to town planning.

The most striking feature of the changing urban geography of the period was certainly the growth of the larger towns to a new order of magnitude. If one may attempt a generalisation, following that of Roger Mols,[37] the large towns of the Middle Ages had been of the order of 10,000 to 50,000; medium towns were of 2,000 to 10,000 and the small ones less than 2,000. By the end of the sixteenth century the upper limit of the small towns was 10,000 and that of the medium towns about 20,000, but there were still very few above 40,000. The following table gives some idea of the increase in the populations of the largest cities in Western Europe to 1800 (see below). Even in 1500 there were only four towns with over 100,000, but by 1800 there were sixteen. London was rapidly approaching a million and Paris half a million. All of the large towns were capital cities or ports (notably Barcelona, Marseilles and Amsterdam) with the exception of Lyon, the only large industrial and regional centre away from the coast and not a capital. In 1500 three out of the four largest towns had been Italian and even in 1600 eight out of the twelve largest towns were in Italy or Iberia. By 1800 ten out of sixteen were south of the Alps,

THE LARGE TOWNS OF WESTERN EUROPE

POPULATION	1400	1500	1600	1700	1800
over 400,000				London Paris	London (850,000) Paris Naples
200,000– 400,000			Naples Paris	Naples Amsterdam	Vienna Amsterdam
100,000– 200,000	Paris Naples	Paris Naples Venice Milan	London Venice Lisbon Milan Amsterdam Rome Palermo Messina Seville Antwerp	Rome Venice Milan Madrid Lisbon Vienna Seville Palermo	Madrid Lisbon Dublin Berlin Rome Barcelona Venice Milan Palermo Lyon Marseilles

but there was a new rank of large Atlantic ports and industrial towns which were close behind and growing rapidly: Bordeaux, population 91,000; Rouen, 87,000; Nantes, 77,000; Liverpool, 78,000; Manchester, 84,000; Bristol, 64,000; Birmingham, 74,000. In Germany Hamburg was perhaps the largest town other than Berlin with 85,000.

Mols has stressed that urban growth took place everywhere in Western Europe against a background of very heavy urban mortality until the later eighteenth century. The towns were rightly regarded by contemporaries as unhealthy places and most of the larger ones failed even to reproduce their numbers. Immigration from the countryside was a normal feature of the period even when relatively little overall growth was taking place.

While the capitals and the larger ports had grown most, two new and highly specialised types of town had also begun to develop, both expressive of the changes in society which had brought them into being. On the one hand were the military fortress towns, such as those which were built in southern Sweden in the seventeenth century or on the eastern frontier of France, and the new naval bases such as Brest, Lorient and Rochefort in France. On the other hand, the spas and the new sea-bathing places of the eighteenth century catered for new concepts of leisure activity and for a new preoccupation with health. Spas like Buxton, Bath, Karlsbad and Baden-Baden grew with an urbane dignity—which some still retain—but seaside resorts like Brighton and Ostend were still dependent on royal patronage or medical opinion for their popularity, and greater prosperity came only later, in the nineteenth century.

Many of the new features making for rapid urban growth, particularly of the capital cities, clearly stemmed from political, social and economic changes of the period. The growth of the nation state and the centralisation of government were obviously the dominant political trends. The absolute monarchies of France, Austria, Sweden, Spain and Prussia and the enlightened despotisms of the eighteenth century were the clearest expressions of this tendency, but the centralisation of government and administration was also characteristic of England and of the smaller states and principalities of Germany. The functions of the capital city as the seat of the court and of government generated the accumulation of industry and population to an unprecedented degree. Centralisation implied the existence of a bureaucracy located near the site of government. (Parkinson's famous law, that 'work expands to fill the time available to do it', was formulated, we are told, as a result of research into seventeenth-century administration). The maintenance of control over potentially dissident factions of a power-seeking nobility sometimes led, as in France, to the concentration of nobility at Court for a large part of the year. The institution of the aristocratic town house was an important feature of urban social life and urban planning in the eighteenth century, but the nobility also brought purchasing power and a veritable army of servants and retainers from the country. Physical proximity and access to the centres of power and decision making were highly desirable for the success of financial ventures as well as for the acquisition and retention of political power and social prestige.

Preoccupation with the power and wealth of the state had led to those economic policies summed up in the term 'mercantilist'. Industry and trade were encouraged or controlled by such means as quotas, tariffs, subsidies, the imposition of prohibitions, the granting of monopolies and privileges, and the import of foreign craftsmen to establish new industries or improve old ones. The emphasis on military and naval power and the development of the uniformed standing army were also features of the sixteenth and seventeenth centuries, and they too affected the urban geography of the period in several ways. In the Berlin of the early eighteenth century no less than 20 per cent of the total population consisted of the military garrison;[38] the capitals were very often the major arsenals and garrisons of the state as a whole. In many ways, therefore, the political trends of the time led to the concentration of purchasing power and population in the capital cities.

Economic change, too, favoured the rise of the larger centres and a degree of urbanisation greater than that which had characterised the medieval period as a whole. The most basic trend, perhaps, was that from local and urban markets to a national market for some agricultural as well as industrial products. Many of the new industries, monopoly companies and privileged manufactures found their obvious locations in close proximity to the seat of government or even, as in the case of some of the royal manufactures of France, in the royal palace itself. But the market was widened especially by the improvement of communications. Military and administrative needs, especially on the continent, combined with economic pressures to bring about new road building, river improvement and canal building, which helped to weld the nation states together. In France new roads constituted one of the major investments by the state during the eighteenth century and their concentration on Paris helped to strengthen the dominance of the capital. In England the turnpike roads sprang from economic rather than political or strategic needs, but it was the latter which inspired the road building of Scotland.

The rise in the standard of living, the increase in the social differentiation of classes and the proliferation of new crafts and industries also served to increase the number of urban-based activities even though some of the traditional and staple industries of the medieval towns were now dispersed in the countryside. Many of the new occupations, particularly the luxury trades for which the French were famous, were custom trades and therefore necessarily market-oriented. New skills and materials were involved in the clothing and textile industries as fashion changed and more ostentatious styles of dress and ornament were affected. Furnishings and furniture became

22 s'*Hertogenbosch*, (*Bois-le-Duc*), 1560–70 (Braun and Hogenberg). A varied scene of urban and suburban activity in the sixteenth century. Note the bleaching grounds for cloth.

23 *Palmanova*. A sixteenth century defence of the Venetian state in the north Italian plain, Palmanova exemplifies in a dramatic form the formal symmetry of Renaissance urban planning as well as the new conception of urban defence against artillery fire, and the work of the "sappers".

24 *Naarden*, near Amsterdam, also illustrates the importance of water defences to the United Provinces in the sixteenth and seventeenth centuries.

elaborate and luxurious and also demanded greater skills as well as new materials; the processing of foods and tobacco and the introduction of new beverages and foodstuffs created a new range of activities, many of which tended to concentrate either in the ports of entry for tropical raw materials, or in the capitals to which market-oriented industries were naturally drawn. Carriage building, clothing, quality furniture and musical instruments, fine metal working and particularly jewellery, gunmaking, paper, printing and, of course, banking tended to be associated with the specialised market of the capital cities.

Finally, the third major aspect of the period which played a dominant rôle in urban growth was its changing social character and values, particularly important in so far as it affected the nature of town planning and the urban architecture of the Baroque.[39] Prestige attached to birth and rank as well as wealth; the love of parade, ostentation and display reached a new height; and leisure and the pursuit of pleasure were expressed in new urban features: the pleasure parks and gardens; the parades and squares, the spas, theatres and assembly rooms.

The growth of the larger towns had important effects on the countryside. Many towns in Germany, France and the Low Countries lost much of their autonomy. The urban gilds were in decay or were resuscitated only as instruments of state policy rather than as urban societies. The territorial power of the state frequently overrode the privileges which the towns had enjoyed in the government and administration of the rural areas around them. But the towns, and especially the capital cities, were now much more substantial than they had been as markets for agricultural produce. The general tendency of price changes in the seventeenth and early eighteenth centuries was to favour industrial products at the expense of agricultural products, but within the agricultural sphere the shift was in favour of stock and dairy produce rather than grain. Butter and cheese markets, the stock fairs and the general-purpose markets flourished in the market towns of the period. Indeed, in the Low Countries, France and England the impact of the major towns on the agricultural geography of the period was fundamental: stock and dairy regions were emerging; the drove roads and the cattle trails were developing by which stock reared in remote and upland regions were driven to fattening pastures near to the big towns or to the urban markets such as Les Halles in Paris,[40] or Smithfield in

London. Local specialisations were developing, too, in poultry farming and in fruit and vegetable production (see Chapter 9).

Although urban trades and crafts were increasing steadily in variety and complexity during the period, a number of industries were characteristically dispersed in the countryside in many areas of Western Europe: the spinning and weaving of wool and linen; framework-knitting and lace manufacture; and processes concerned with straw and leather. But the dispersed industries continued to be controlled from the towns for it was the urban merchant who was often responsible for the supply and preparation of raw material, warehousing and storage, the financing of production and the marketing of the finished product, and the towns often remained important centres of manufacture.

Within the towns specialisation of urban land use began to be much more evident than it had been in Middle Ages. The localisation of crafts in particular streets had already taken place, and with new growth in the seventeenth and eighteenth centuries whole new quarters acquired their own specialisms, as for example at Birmingham, where gunsmiths and jewellers began to segregate from other crafts. But what was essentially new to the period was the beginning of separation of home and workplace.[41] The merchant no longer always lived near or over his warehouse; the merchant entrepreneurs who organised production on the basis of a putting-out system were also able to live elsewhere than at their place of work. Better quality residential housing began to be segregated in pleasant environments, near fashionable parades and near the centres of shopping and amusement. This was not, however, a trend which spread widely to other classes of society, for the craftsman remained near his workshop; the master and a few journeymen or apprentices formed the characteristic unit of production in most industries and all lived together near their work; the shopkeeper, too, lived with his goods.

Other features of the time that led to a greater degree of specialisation in urban land use were the growing division between retail and wholesale trade, and the multiplication of retail trades. The grocer took on new functions as the variety of foodstuffs increased; the tobacconist and vintner became much more common among the traders of moderately large towns such as Leicester or Norwich. Professional groups such as the lawyers and advocates increased in numbers and tended to live in fairly close proximity to each other and the courts. The fashionable shopping centres of the great towns began to emerge in a close relationship to the location of new theatres and assembly rooms.

The differentiation of urban land use, particularly in the large towns, and the growth of population also meant new problems of urban communications. Carriage and coach building were new and expanding industries connected with urban communications as well as for long-distance travel; the vast horse population created demands for hay and fodder from neighbouring agricultural regions and also supplied manure for use in the regions of intensive farming that were growing up near the towns, notably in the Netherlands, where canals made cheap bulk transport possible. Within the towns the street now became the focus of urban planning and individual houses were increasingly conceived as a part of the street rather than as the individual units from which the towns were agglomerated.

If the size and the functions of the Renaissance and Baroque towns altered during the period from 1500 to 1800, their external aspects changed in a much more obvious and dramatic way. Town planning and the control of urban building represented but one aspect of the new power assumed by the state in the *ancien régime*. The rediscovery of the classical tenets of architecture, codified in the work of Vitruvius and interpreted by such architects as Palladian wrought a profound revolution in ideas of town planning no less than in approaches to formal architecture.[42] The new classical ideals of order, symmetry, regularity and harmony were applied to urban building with the skill of a new class of cultured and professional architects, and they were applied to a society for which power, prestige and ostentation were important qualities. Wide boulevards and avenues for parade and pageantry were the basis of planning. Both appeared to demand the monumental piece or some architectural contrivance to 'close the vista'. Parks, gardens, squares and the great *places* of France used urban space in new and imposing ways.

Old capitals were remodelled and new ones built in conformity with the new ideas. Copenhagen was almost completely rebuilt. Oslo, like other Scandinavian towns, was replanned and rebuilt after devastation by fire. In Germany new capitals were constructed and old ones refurbished in accordance with the ambitions of the many rulers of the petty states into which the country had become fragmented. Karlsruhe, founded in 1715 on a rigid pattern in the area around a former hunting lodge, is one of the best examples, but Dresden, Munich and Hannover were remodelled, too. Paris,

Vienna, Berlin and London (after the Great Fire) were transformed. Old ports, made prosperous by the Atlantic trade, and new ports either created for it or built as naval bases, were planned on the regular and formal patterns of the period. Lorient, Brest, Rochefort in western France were created; Nantes, Bordeaux, Le Havre and Rouen felt the influence of the new planning and were able to carry it out with the wealth brought by the slave trade or the colonial trade.

Fortifications were still an integral part of urban planning and the elaboration of defences in depth by complex glacis and redoubts was particularly associated with the name of Vauban and the construction of some 150 fortress towns in eastern France. But most of the larger towns of continental Western Europe also took on a new outline as their defences were reorganised in the seventeenth century to afford a wide field of fire to the defenders and protection from enemy artillery and mining engineers. Some of these defence structures still survive, as at Palma Nova in Italy, a sixteenth-century example (Plate 23), or at Naarden in the Netherlands (Plate 24), but many of these wide zones devoted to urban defence were converted in the eighteenth century or later to wide boulevards which opened up the centre of the ancient towns to traffic, and which are still a great asset both for the open space they have provided and the potentialities of relieving modern traffic congestion.

The control of the urban plan implied conformity with the regulations of state or urban authority. The shape, size and scale of the streets were frequently laid down; the design of the façades was sometimes fixed so as to secure uniformity in external appearance if not in internal structure. Building lots were standardised and the quality and size of building predetermined. Architects and others drew up ideal designs for urban plans which frequently showed greater skill and ingenuity at the drawing board than appreciation and understanding of the needs of the community they were supposed to serve. Italian planners had laid stress particularly on military needs and were pioneers of sixteenth-century planning.[43] They had great influence on the development of towns in southern Germany and Austria. Dutch planning, however, was more functional and utilitarian, having acquired skill and experience through the need to plan towns on drained and reclaimed land. French planners of the late seventeenth and eighteenth century, however, gave greater stress to the social aspects of their urban plans, and tended to make liberal provision for internal open spaces.

REFERENCES

Abbreviations:
C.A.M.   *La Citta nell'alto medioevo.* Settimane di studio del centro
Italiano di studi sull' alto medioevo, Spoleto. vol 6, 1959.
C.E.H.E.   *Cambridge Economic History of Europe.* Vol. 3, *Economic
Organisation and Policies in the Middle Ages*, ed. M. M. Postan,
E. E. Rich and E. Miller, Cambridge, 1963.

1. J. H. MUNDY and P. RIESENBERG, *The Medieval Town*, Princeton,
   1958; the first chapter is devoted to a useful 'Definition of urbanism'.
2. H. PIRENNE, *Medieval Cities*, Princeton, 1949.
3. O. VERLINDEN, 'Markets and fairs', *C.E.H.E.*, vol. 3, pp. 119–53.
4. Ibid., p. 153.
5. H. PLANITZ, *Die deutsche Stadt im Mittelalter*, Graz-Köln, 1954,
   p. 82.
6. R. E. DICKINSON, *Germany*, London, 1961, p. 158.
7. K. BÜCHER, *Industrial Evolution* (1893), trans. S. M. Wickett, New
   York, 1907, pp. 115 ff.
8. Planitz, *Deutsche Stadt im Mittelalter*, p. 84.
9. Ibid., chapter 2.
10. E. A. GUTKIND, *Urban Development in Central Europe. International
    History of City Development*, vol. 1, London and New York, 1964, p.
    163.
11. H. VAN WERVEKE, 'The rise of the towns', *C.E.H.E.*, vol. 3, p. 37.
12. J. C. RUSSELL, 'The metropolitan city region of the Middle Ages',
    Journ. Regional Science, vol. 2, 1960, pp. 55–70.
13. Bücher, *Industrial Evolution*, p. 119.
14. G. L. BURKE, *The Making of the Dutch Towns*, London, 1956.
15. A. GIEYSZTOR, 'Les origines de la ville slave', *C.A.M.*, vol. 6, 1959,
    pp. 162–95.
16. E. ENNEN, 'Les différents types de formation des Villes Européennes',
    Le Moyen Age, vol. 11, 1956, pp. 399–411; see also idem. *Frühgeschichte
    der europäischen Stadt*, Bonn, 1953.
17. G. LUZATTO, *Economic History of Italy to the beginning of the sixteenth
    century*, London, 1961, p. 28.
18. Ibid., pp. 55–61.
19. Mundy and Riesenberg, *Medieval Town*.
20. J. M. LACARRA, 'La historia urbana en España', *C.A.M.*, vol. 6, 1959,
    pp. 319–58.
21. G. DUBY, 'Les villes de la Gaule sud-est', *C.A.M.*, vol. 6, 1959, pp.
    231–58.
22. F. L. GANSHOF, *Etude sur le Développement des Villes entre Loire et
    Rhin au Moyen Âge*, Paris and Brussels, 1943.
23. F. VERCAUTEREN, 'La vie urbaine du 6ᵉ au 9ᵉ siècle entre la Meuse
    et la Loire', *C.A.M.*, vol. 6, 1959, pp. 453–85.
24. Ibid.
25. Y. DOLLINGER-LEONARD, 'De la cité romaine à la ville mediévale

dans la région de la Moselle et la haute Meuse', *Studien zu den Anfangen des europäischen Stadtwesens*, ed. T. Mayer, Lindau, 1959, pp. 195–226.

26. W. PETRI, 'The medieval towns of the Netherlands and neighbouring parts of France', *Studien zu den Anfangen des europäischen Stadtwesens*, ed. T. Mayer, Lindau, 1959, pp. 227–96.

27. J. HUBERT, 'Evolution de la topographie et de l'aspect des villes de Gaule du 5ᵉ au 10ᵉ siècle', *C.A.M.*, vol. 6, 1959, pp. 529–58.

28. Petri, *Studien zu den Anfangen des eur. Stadtwesens*, p. 291.

29. E. LEHMANN, 'The beginnings of building in the German towns of the early Middle Ages', *C.A.M.*, vol. 6, 1959, pp. 559–90.

30. H.-J. MRUSEK, 'Zur städtebaulichen Entwicklung Magdeburgs im hohen Mittelalter', *Wissenschaftliche Zeitschrift der Martin-Luther-Universitäts*, Halle-Wittenberg, vol. 5, 1955–6, pp. 1219–1314.

31. Ibid., p. 1233.

32. Planitz, *Deutsche Stadt im Mittelalter*, p. 63.

33. Dickinson, *Germany*, p. 162.

34. Planitz, *Deutsche Stadt im Mittelalter*, p. 185.

35. Dickinson, *Germany*, p. 166.

36. C. HAASE, 'Neue untersuchungen zur frühen Geschichte der europäischen Stadt', *Vierteljahrschrifte für Sozial und Wirtschaftsgeschichte*, Wiesbaden, vol. 46, 1959, pp. 378–94.

37. R. MOLS, *Introduction à la Démographie historique des Villes européennes au 14ᵉ–18ᵉ siècle*, 3 vols, Louvain, 1954–6.

38. R. E. DICKINSON, *The West European City*, London, 1951.

39. L. MUMFORD, *The Culture of Cities*, London, 1940, chapter 2: 'Court, parade and capital', pp. 73–142.

40. H. VIDALENC, 'L'approvisionnement de Paris en viande sous *l'ancien régime*', *Rev. d'histoire économique et sociale*, vol. 30, 1952, pp. 116–32.

41. Gutkind, *Urban Development in Central Europe*, pp. 200–1.

42. F. L. HIORNS, *Town Building in History*, London, 1956.

43. Dickinson, *West European City* p. 44.

PART III

The Changing Economic
Geography of Western Europe

CHAPTER 7

TRADE AND INDUSTRY IN THE MIDDLE AGES

THE MEDITERRANEAN

So much could be written about the geography of trade and industry in the Middle Ages that it is possible here only to sketch out the main features very briefly indeed, pausing occasionally to treat some example in slightly greater detail. Geographical patterns of trade provide the basis for a comparative study of the space-relations of Europe under contrasting economic and locational situations and they also provide the essential framework for an understanding both of urban growth and of many aspects of industrial and even agricultural development. But the space-relations of Western Europe depend not only on the nature and source of their trade but also on the general conditions of transport and communications.

Of the major forms of transport, that by sea was relatively the cheapest, though it was still slow and hazardous. Navigation was still highly seasonal and not frequently undertaken during the winter months, even in the Mediterranean; it was slow, highly dependent on favourable winds, for square-rigged medieval shipping could not sail easily into the wind; it was risky, for natural hazards of rock and tempest were supplemented by the dangers of piracy and the wreckers. Ships hugged the coasts and preferred sheltered inland water (e.g. off the Low Countries) to the open sea, in spite of dangers of running aground. Methods of navigation were crude, especially before the introduction of the compass, and sailors had to rely on dead reckoning and good visibility. In north-western Europe, there were significant changes in ship design; ships were built larger and fully decked in order to carry the heavier cargoes demanded by the increase of the wine trade. The Hanseatic *cogge* represented an advance over earlier shipping just as the Mediterranean *carrack* or *nef* represented advances, at least for the carriage of cargo, over the long, narrow Mediterranean galley. The crews of the Mediterranean galleys required frequent stops for water and provisions at small coastal ports and the records of Mediterranean voyages from Venice to Corfu,

Ragusa or Constantinople in the sixteenth century show that for two-thirds of the time during such a journey, the ship was not actually moving, because of overnight stops, provisioning, bad weather or for other reasons.[1] Of the shipping that sought Levantine ports from Venice and Genoa in the twelfth or thirteenth centuries, probably no more than a third of the carrying capacity was available for cargo because of the space taken by crew and supplies.

River transport shared with maritime trade the advantage that a greater weight of cargo could be shifted with a smaller amount of energy than it could by land, and rivers were exploited for navigation to a degree which now seems difficult to comprehend, particularly since few rivers were regulated, tolls were collected frequently, and disputes about weirs and fishing rights were a permanent hazard, as well as part of the *raison d'être* of the gilds of watermen which flourished on the Seine and the Rhône and many other major rivers. Regions which had access to navigable water had a fundamental advantage in disposing of their surplus crops and thus in specialising for urban markets. The geography of viticulture in Western Europe still bears witness to this fact; the grain trade of the Rhineland, the Seine basin and of the Ouse and the Thames valleys grew in relation to the navigability of the rivers as well as to the productivity of valley terraces. Lake transport was also a useful asset on any long-distance route, as in northern Italy or Switzerland.

Overland trade is to be thought of in terms of packhorse transport as well as wheeled traffic, each with its own requirements and special facilities. For packhorse trade, steep gradients were less difficult than they were for wheeled traffic and the liability of soft clays to work into deep ruts was not so important. Roads were frequently rights-of-way and little more, and although Roman roads survived as major communications, many transport routes took one of several possible courses according to the season, the levying of tolls, obstructions in the road or the prevalence of unrest, brigandage and war. For wheeled traffic and packhorse alike, supplies of fodder and suitable resting places *en route* were very important. Yet road transport, like that by sea, could be highly organised, as it was, for example, to the Champagne Fairs in the thirteenth century or between Antwerp and Italy in the sixteenth.

There were also political obstacles to efficient transport. Tolls and prohibitions were common almost everywhere among Western European states, though they were only rarely harsh enough to strangle trade along a particular route: as, for example, when the Crown of France secured Champagne at the end of the thirteenth century. But war, brigandage and civil unrest were anathema to trade, and although routes often revived as soon as authority and peace were re-established, permanent damage was sometimes done, as in France during the Hundred Years' War or in Germany during the Thirty Years' War. In Germany, the absence of a central authority in the later Middle Ages called forth the urban leagues of Rhenish or Swabian towns, and above all, the Hanseatic League, which existed to defend the interests of traders and merchants and to provide conditions under which security of travel as well as urban autonomy and urban food supplies could be assured.

Thus, throughout the Middle Ages, water transport, particularly by sea, retained a clear advantage over land routes. Technological changes did little to alter this, and war, territorial fragmentation, tolls and internal insecurities probably strengthened the relative attraction of the sea trade. Perhaps the most important change was in the character and volume of the goods carried. As long as long-distance trade was essentially confined to the carriage of exotic, luxury goods with values extremely high in relation to their bulk— pepper, spices, furs, honey, cloths of gold and silver, silks and so on— cost of transport mattered much less than the arrival or non-arrival of the goods. Overland transport or the most devious routes could, if necessary, be employed for this type of trade. Breaks between land and water transport were a minor hindrance, so that lake or river transport for a few miles was worth using, and overland journeys across the necks of peninsulas were worth taking in order to avoid hazardous detours by water (as, for example, across the Jutland Peninsula).

The total volume of trade was often surprisingly small. Luzzatto comments: 'At Venice in the fourteenth century, the entire cargo of eastern wares could normally be carried by three state convoys travelling once a year to Constantinople, Beirut and Alexandria.'[2] Each convoy had two to four galleys, each probably of less than 500 tons, and with an effective carrying capacity of less than 166 tons. Thus even the Venetian shipping then carried home no more than 1,000 to 2,000 tons of eastern merchandise from the Levant. But the expansion of commerce in the twelfth and thirteenth centuries also began to involve the carriage of bulkier commodities such as cotton, woollen cloths, salt, herring and grain. For these commodities the level of transport costs mattered, and mattered a great deal, so that in the later Middle Ages, the relative advantage of water transport over land routes was increased; for example, the all-sea route by way of Gibraltar was preferred rather than the overland routes from Italy to north-west Europe, and the Sound route to the Baltic rather than that across the base of the Jutland peninsula in the hands of the Hanseatic merchants was increasing in importance.

For the geography of medieval trade, as for the peopling of Europe in prehistory, it is important to view the whole continent as a peninsula of Asia, and to view it, moreover, as a highly reticulated peninsula in which a series of inland seas penetrate so deeply into the very heart of the continent that there is no place in Western Europe, as it is here defined, which is more than about 320 miles from the sea. The configuration of the inland seas and the fact that navigable rivers drain into them at suitable locations also mean that trans-peninsular routes across the great isthmuses of Europe are relatively short and easy: first, from the Baltic to the Black Sea by way of various rivers; secondly, from the south-west Baltic by way of the Elbe towards the low passes in the eastern Alps and then to the head of the Adriatic; thirdly, from the North Sea basin and England to the Rhine and thus to the navigable Po basin, the Adriatic or to the Ligurian Sea, by way of the central passes of the Alps; fourthly, from the Rhône valley to the Channel by way of the Seine or to the North Sea across Champagne; and finally, the route across the Gate of Carcassonne from the Aude basin to the Garonne. Each of these routes has had a different rôle to play in relation to the ways in which Western Europe has reached external contacts and sources of trade. Each has had a different rôle in connecting the two great maritime spheres of activity: the Mediterranean and the marginal seas of north-western Europe. Some have had limited and local functions to perform, like the Gate of Carcassonne, for they lead to no great market or source of trade; but others converge so strongly and have so persistently led to areas productive of revenue and trade that they have nourished trade, industry and agricultural progress as well as precocious urban development: the Low Countries on the one hand, and Venice, Genoa and the north Italian plain on the other.

The changing geographical patterns of trade are, however, so complex that in order to present a coherent picture it has seemed most useful to consider first a brief outline of the successive geographies of Mediterranean trade: before and during the Arab conquest; during the great commercial revolution of the expansion of the eleventh to the thirteenth centuries; and then, finally, on the eve of new discovery overseas. Secondly, attention will be turned to north-western European trade, with particular reference to the industries of the Low Countries and the ports of Bruges and Antwerp.

Mediterranean trade to A.D. 1000

From the end of the Roman Empire to the eighth century ancient patterns of trade persisted, though everywhere there was decline. From the east Roman Empire, Greek, Syrian, Egyptian and Jewish merchants continued to bring produce from the Far East to the western towns. North Africa continued to ship grain and oil to Rome and Marseilles, Arles and Narbonne to act as entrepôts for the west sending slaves, timber and cloth eastwards in exchange for papyrus, dates, spices, silks and leather. Syria, Egypt and Constantinople handled an Asiatic trade which still flowed by several routes: the sea route in Chinese and Egyptian hands, the route by way of Trebizond to Persia and Turkestan, and from time to time, even the northern continental route by way of southern Russia.

But in Carolingian times a geographical revolution occurred in the trade routes of Western Europe. Pirenne's view of the collapse of western trade was perhaps exaggerated and his attribution of decline in the Mediterranean to the Arabs may need modification, but perhaps the important fact which may here be stressed is the revaluation of trade routes to Western Europe during the period. The western Mediterranean, it appears, became an economic backwater; Mediterranean goods and Levantine merchants ceased to penetrate as far north as the Loire; and the Christian ports of southern France withered for lack of commerce. It may be that this was due as much to the effect of Byzantine policies directed towards the channelling of trade to ports within the Empire such as Amalfi, Gaeta, Naples, Bari and above all Venice, as it was to the Arabs, for they lacked maritime power until the ninth century, possessed none of the strategic islands in the Mediterranean and carried little of its trade.[3] Conditions were different at a later stage, however, for during the ninth century the Arabs did gain supremacy at sea; Crete was taken in A.D. 827, then Pantelleria, Sicily and the Balearic Islands. The Saracen pirates of the western Mediterranean continued to hamper trade and commerce as well as to exert a profound effect on the pattern of rural settlement.

Amalfi was the only port in western Italy to carry on an appreciable trade in the ninth and tenth centuries. It had political links with the Byzantine Empire and trading privileges as well, but it had also been briefly occupied by the Arabs and it was able to maintain these Arab contacts in sustaining a trade in slaves, timber, iron and weapons to the Arab world in exchange for Levantine luxuries. Suspect by the rest of the Christian world, it is perhaps significant that the collapse of its trade came not through Arab intervention but through the blocking of its access into the eastern Mediterranean as a result of the Norman occupation of Sicily.

But if the western Mediterranean was an Arab lake in which the Christian ports were starved of trade, Venice at the head of the Adriatic was in a very different position, unique in Western Europe in its relations with the Arab east, Byzantium, and the Christian kingdoms of the west. As a distributing point into north-western Europe for goods from the eastern Mediterranean, the position of Venice is incomparable. The north Italian plain was itself one of the most flourishing of the markets of the west, and river navigation by the Po to Pavia carried salt, cloth and grain as well as spices. Pavia was the Lombard capital as well as a route centre for the passes over the western and central Alps to the Rhineland and Germany. The route by way of the Adige valley to Verona and the Brenner pass was probably little used, for the lands beyond the Brenner were still a region of frontier German settlement. The site of Venice, on lagoons and islands north of the Po delta, was magnificent for defence and had been occupied as a refuge from the mainland. Its isolation helped later not only to maintain its links with Byzantium but also to preserve some freedom from involvement with the mainland. Its lagoons and harbours gave it the resources for a salt-evaporating industry which in turn provided cargoes for trading ventures, and although it lacked any kind of agricultural base and was thus dependent from early times on trade for its subsistence, the absence of an agricultural and territorial nobility meant that the supremacy of trading and merchant interests in the government of the city went unchallenged.

Although virtually autonomous within the Byzantine Empire, Venice nevertheless drew valuable privileges from the link. Byzantine economic policies towards shipping and shipbuilding had tended to stunt development in Greece and Asia Minor to the advantage of merchants in the peripheral territories, and particularly to the advantage of the Venetians who rapidly became the chief carriers and shipbuilders of the Empire in the Mediterranean. By A.D. 1000 Venice had a quarter in Constantinople and preferential customs duties; by 1092 it had freedom to trade in all of the most important cities of the Empire; and it was able to inherit the Amalfitan privileges when that port was taken by the Normans. With the Arabs, too, the Venetians had direct contact in their trade with Alexandria, exporting arms, iron from Styria and Carinthia and shipbuilding timber from Dalmatia, as well as slaves. Well before the Crusades, then, Venice had flourished by reason of its intelligent exploitation of an intermediary position between western Christendom, the Arab world, and the Byzantine Empire.

In the Mediterranean, Venice at the head of the Adriatic survived as a window for north-western Europe on the rich world of the Levant and Far Eastern trade. But other routes had emerged which by-passed the Mediterranean completely. The chief of the trade routes from Europe to the Far East continued to be those which crossed the Fertile Crescent by caravan routes to new Arab ports on the Persian Gulf, or to new Red Sea ports and then by an Arab-dominated trade in the Indian Ocean to the Spice Islands, the entrepôt with Chinese traders at Kalah on the Malay peninsula, or even to China itself. But these routes, which were carrying new commodities such as camphor, aloes, coconuts, tin and sandalwood as well as spices, silks and precious stones, led to Arab territory, and little seeped through to the western world except indirectly through Amalfi, Venice, Moorish Spain and the Byzantine contacts, chiefly at Antioch, and Trebizond, to the Armenian routes across Persia and Afghanistan to the sea trade of the Indian Ocean.

But the Byzantine Empire had access also to the northern routes across Russia to the Caspian and to Turkestan, for the Khazar state, based on the lower Volga at Itil, converted to Judaism and tolerant of both Moslem and Christian merchants, acted as a go-between for trade with the east. The detailed examination of the trade in eastern Europe cannot here be discussed, but it was important for the west that at the time when the Arab conquests had closed the western Mediterranean, new routes could be opened up which took an unusual course, bringing eastern and northern Europe into the forefront of western contacts with the Arab world. The Scandinavian Varangians had established links across the eastern isthmus of Europe by way of the Dvina and the Dnieper to the Black Sea. Further east there was a trade from the caravan cities of central Asia, notably Tashkent, Bukhara and Samarkand, towards central Russia and the Baltic, and although this has left its traces chiefly in the form of archaeological finds of Arab money coined from newly discovered silver resources of the Pamir Mountains, it is certain that the Swedes had reached the Caspian by way of the Volga and that they had established contact with the Khazars at Itil. And there was, finally one other route which helped to fill the gap left by the decline of the Mediterranean trade; this was that complex of routes in central Europe which departed from Kiev and, largely in the hands of Jewish merchants, passed ultimately to Mainz by way of the upper Danube and Regensburg, one of the most flourishing of German towns in the eleventh century and well known as a depot for spices.

Thus, in general, the blocking of the western Mediterranean was accompanied by the virtual abandonment of trade along the western isthmuses across Europe and by the economic contraction felt within the Carolingian Empire. But the Adriatic link suffered much less, and there was, indeed, a revolutionary use of the eastern isthmuses from the Caspian and Black Seas to the Baltic. It was this which gave a new impetus to Scandinavian expansion.

The commercial revolution of the eleventh to the fourteenth centuries

'The greatest economic empire the world had ever seen.' So wrote R. S. Lopez of the achievements of Italian merchants in the thirteenth and fourteenth centuries when their activities reached from England to the Sahara, and across the oases of central Asia to China and the Far East.[4] It was an economic empire which involved the elaboration of sophisticated commercial techniques which gave the Italian merchant a lead of many years over his northern European counterpart; it involved the development of the great medieval cities of northern and central Italy of which Genoa and Pisa, Florence, Milan and Venice were the chief: and it was accompanied by investment in a great variety of industrial techniques and skills which made much of northern Italy a substantial source of trade in its own right, rather than simply the entrepôt for spices and eastern luxuries brought from afar. The ports of Italy were not the only ports to flourish with the revival of commerce in the western Mediterranean, for the Provençal ports led by Marseilles and the Catalans led by Barcelona shared in the general expansion of activity, yet it was the

Italian ports which remained the giants throughout. For the first time since the heyday of the Roman Empire Italy was again making full use of its central position in the Mediterranean to command the trade of both the eastern and western basins. And the balance of activity which had been in southern Italy and Sicily when the centre of gravity of Mediterranean trade was attracted southwards by the prosperity of Arab Spain, North Africa and the Levant and repelled by the poverty of northern Europe, was now beginning to shift to the north and centre of the peninsula, and so to create that imbalance between northern and southern Italy which still plagues the development of the country.

Three new conditions favoured the revival of trade. The first and undoubtedly the most important secular trend was the growth of population and production over the whole of north-western Europe. The organisation of the feudal hierarchy, coupled with the expansion of population and the renewal in very many places of pioneer agricultural colonisation, created an effective and growing demand from the clergy, the nobility and the new men of the towns for the kind of expensive goods produced by, or imported through, the Italian cities.

The second fact of importance was the rise of the Papacy, which affected economic growth in Italy in various ways: the number of pilgrims to Rome swelled the numbers passing along the routes to central Italy from the rest of Western Europe, and this alone acted as a stimulus to the wayside towns controlling, for example, the passes through the central Alps. The silk industry of Siena is said to have started from humble beginnings in the production of novelties for travellers approaching Rome itself. Further, the increase in the status of the Papacy also involved an increase in the flow of revenue to Rome from Western Europe as a whole, and this in turn stimulated the rise of the Italian banking houses and the trade of merchants whose responsibility it was to collect Papal revenues. And finally, the fact that Rome was becoming once again a centre of consumption and of demand for luxury products stimulated the growth of Italian industry and commerce.

The third new condition which favoured expansion was the counter-offensive against Islam, in itself an expression of the new-found confidence of Christendom. In Spain the Reconquista made great strides in the eleventh century; in Sicily the Moors were conquered by the Normans; and further east, Crete, Cyprus and Antioch were regained. But it was, above all the Crusades (1096–1291) which pushed back the frontier of Islam and opened the way for Christian and chiefly Italian commerce in the Mediterranean and beyond. The counter-offensive was fundamental in a number of ways: it cleared the western Mediterranean of Saracen pirates and made possible the reign of the Italian cities in the Mediterranean seaways; it opened up direct contacts in the Levant between Italian merchants and the Moslem merchants who handled the Far Eastern produce. The carriage of men and equipment in Genoese or Pisan ships stimulated shipbuilding and provided a source of revenue in itself; and the assistance of Italian shipping in successful campaigns on the Syrian coast was rewarded by agencies, revenues and quarters or colonies in the Levantine ports which were footholds from which to engage directly in the import of eastern goods. The loot from successful raiding of Saracen shipping provided capital for further expansion of shipping and trade; and finally, the participation of the western knights from England, France or Germany in the Crusades exposed them to new tastes and new products: sugar, citrus fruits, dates, figs, cotton textiles and fine leather work, for example.

The range of Italian commercial and industrial activity may, perhaps, best be reviewed here under three main headings: first, the expansion of Italian trade in and beyond the Mediterranean; secondly, the activity of Italian merchants overland in Western Europe and their impact on the development of exchange with northern and central Europe; and thirdly, the growth of Italian industry (Fig. 7:1).

It was Pisa and Genoa which led the revival of Italian commerce in the western Mediterranean in the late tenth and eleventh centuries. Pisa was a river port with a dependent seaport which had ceased to suffer from the Saracen raiders and pirates rather earlier than its northern neighbour, Genoa. It was also near to Lucca, and lay on the Via Francigena, the major pilgrim route to Rome, and it was from Pisa that the first substantial moves against the Arabs were made in the western Mediterranean. By 1016, Pisa was successful in securing a dominant position in Corsica, Elba and northern Sardinia, and in the eleventh century was trading with southern Italy, the Balearic Islands, Spain and North Africa, treating alike with Arabs and the Italo-Byzantine cities of Gaeta, Naples and Amalfi.[5]

Genoa was less favourably placed for an early recovery. The Genoese decline from Roman importance had been virtually complete; the Saracens were more strongly entrenched in western

Liguria, which they controlled from their base at Garde-Freinet, and the removal of their threat came later than further south. It may have been their harrying which brought about the abandonment of the

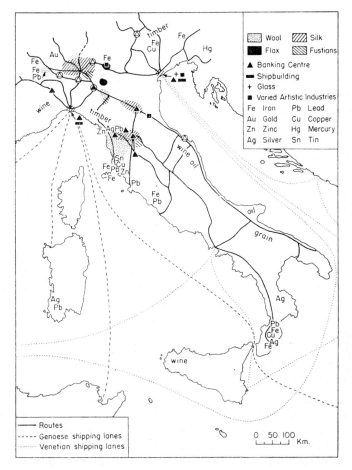

Fig. 7:1   Outstanding features in the economic geography of medieval Italy

Roman road across the Ligurian mountains and its replacement by a new and more easterly road to Piacenza. Yet from the mid-tenth century there was some revival, and with walls rebuilt and a new cathedral established, Genoa was soon joining Pisa in forays against the Arabs in the Tyrrhenian Sea, and then later in more ambitious ventures in the eastern Mediterranean.

Genoa, and then Pisa were the ports which shipped men, horses and equipment to the Holy Land in 1097–99. As a result they received privileges in the conquered towns—in Antioch, Genoa received thirty houses, a church and a bazaar in 1097; Pisa sent 120 ships to Syria in 1099 and got preferential rights in Jaffa. Other rights and privileges followed in later years as a result of similar services in subsequent Crusades, and although the Provençal cities and Venice itself followed a similar policy, Genoa and Pisa had by 1200 acquired more privileges than any other ports in the Syrian towns. The effect these concessions had on trade was not immediate, but they ultimately provided bases from which Italian merchants conducted trade directly with the Syrian traders and merchants who handled the products of Levantine industry and raw materials such as cotton or even wool. And the Crusaders' principalities in the Levant themselves demanded regular supplies and reinforcements which were often carried by the Genoese, the Pisans, the Venetians and then, later, Provençal or Catalan shipping.

Pisa's overseas trade with the Levant in spices, silks, fine cloths and other luxury products was backed by a more local trade in bulkier and cheaper commodities, chiefly iron, salt, grain and silver from the coastal regions of central Italy as well as cloth of Pisan manufacture. Until its final defeat and eclipse at the hands of the Genoese in 1284, Pisa also carried for the merchants of the developing towns of the Tuscan hinterland, notably Florence, Lucca and Prato. It was, indeed, to replace the rôle formerly played by Pisa that Florence developed Leghorn as its outport at a later date.

Although the revival of trade came later at Genoa than at Pisa, the Genoese had the advantage of a more favourable position in relation to the growing centres of trade in Lombardy across the Ligurian Alps and in Europe beyond the central Alpine passes. At first concerned with marketing the products of nearby towns such as Asti, Piacenza, Novi and Tortona immediately beyond the Ligurian Alps, Genoa soon attracted the merchants of Milan and their trade in cloth and metals. Like other Italian towns, Genoa had also established a cloth-finishing and dyeing industry even in the early thirteenth century. Thus, in spite of its restricted and infertile territorial base, Genoa had a wider hinterland than Pisa in north-western Europe with which to support the carrying trade it developed from

Gibraltar to the Crimea. The Genoese were pioneers in shipping and in maritime affairs, adopting the portolan charts and the compass as aids to navigation, developing the practice of winter navigation from the early thirteenth century, and pioneering new and unfamiliar sea routes beyond the Straits of Gibraltar.

For their assistance in restoring the Greek Empire in Constantinople in 1261, after its period under Venetian rule, the Genoese acquired substantial privileges in the trade of the Black Sea. The Genoese suburb of Pera across the Golden Horn from Constantinople pre-empted most of the latter's trade; and in the late thirteenth and fourteenth centuries the Genoese, from their colonies at Kaffa and Tana and with their preferential terms at Trebizond, participated directly in the trade with central Asia and China. In the eastern Mediterranean, the Aegean and the Black Sea the Genoese were worthy competitors of Venice. In the western Mediterranean the Genoese had acquired a special position in North Africa and they were the most important of the foreign merchants to develop the trade of Barcelona and of the newly reconquered territories of southern Spain in the early thirteenth century. Their success at Seville, Cadiz and Lisbon gradually tempted them further afield until by 1277 Genoese galleys had begun to sail direct to France, Flanders and England. Their use of the all-sea route to north-western Europe was one of the most important changes in the trade routes of the Middle Ages, though it was not until the fourteenth century that regular convoys were operated from both Genoa and Venice to England and Flanders. Northern cloth and English wool were henceforth brought directly to Italy; in return went southern spices and silks, together with wine and alum, a re-export from Genoa, derived from Phocea in Asia Minor, of which Genoa had a virtual monopoly in the late thirteenth and early fourteenth centuries.

Venice retained its early lead in Mediterranean trade and shipping, however, for it rapidly followed Genoa and Pisa in seeking privileges in the Syrian ports as a recompense for assistance to the Crusaders, and even by 1100 it had sent 200 ships to Jaffa in return for handsome privileges. Venetian colonies were, like those of its rivals, scattered through the Levantine coast from Egypt to Jaffa and when the alliance against the Byzantine Empire was organised as the so-called Fourth Crusade of 1204, Venice was able to triumph as leader, securing Crete, a number of strategically placed harbours in Greece, immunity from customs in the coastal areas of Greece and Marmora, and freedom to trade at any port in the Empire. It retained its quarter at Constantinople, where there was, indeed, a large Venetian community, and the Venetians were able to gain a lead over the Genoese in the exploitation of the Black Sea trade during the brief period when the Mongol dominance in Asia from southern Russia to China and Korea opened central Asia to European travellers and missionaries. But if Venice led in developing trade in the Black Sea colonies, it had to follow Genoa along the western sea routes to England and Flanders, and indeed was never able seriously to threaten the Genoese position in the western Mediterranean. Local trade continued, however, to be based on the bulk movements of salt either from the salt-pans in the neighbourhood of the Po delta and Istria, or from further south, as far as southern Italy and Cyprus. Wheat, too, was an essential article of trade from eastern Italy, Apulia and Sicily. As yet, Venetian prosperity was derived mainly from its carrying trade and industry was still restricted to a growing concern with cloth and the shipbuilding industry, part in public hands, part in private yards. The deforestation of Dalmatia for the shipyards of Venice was already beginning to take place on a serious scale.

From the eleventh century onwards Italian merchants spread overland through Western Europe, bringing their superior expertise in commerce and finance, as well as Mediterranean luxury goods, to the northern countries; by the end of the twelfth century they were to be found in almost every important town and city in Western Europe; but the major point of contact with the relatively unsophisticated northern merchants until the end of the thirteenth century was undoubtedly the Champagne Fairs (Fig. 7:2). At first, it was the northern Italians who were dominant, from Milan, Cremona, Piacenza and Asti, but during the thirteenth century the merchants of Florence, Siena and Lucca began to appear most frequently in the records. There were craftsmen, woollen textile workers, and petty traders among the Italians in Europe but by far the most significant were the merchants, traders and bankers who were not merely organising the sale of spices, silks, dyestuffs and southern luxuries, but were also responsible for the collection and transmission of ecclesiastical tithes and other dues to the Papacy. Through functions of this kind, many of the Italian merchants became deeply involved in the trade of other countries and turned also to providing loans for government, sometimes disastrously. The part played by Florentine merchants and bankers in the English wool trade is significant in this respect.

The routes which were followed by trade and traders were mainly those of the central and western Alps, for the Venetian merchants, dominant in the east, preferred to act as hosts to German merchants,

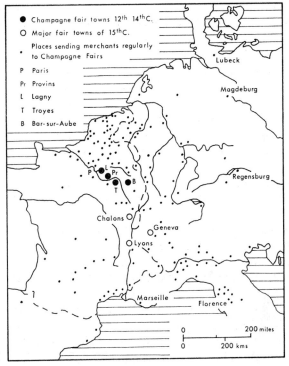

Fig. 7:2   The origins of merchants attending the Champagne Fairs

and as yet the traffic with southern Germany was hardly well developed. In the central Alps the Septimer, Splügen and Little St Bernard passes were perhaps the most commonly used, but by the early thirteenth century the bridging of the Schöllenen gorge had opened up the St Gotthard pass to international trade and for various reasons it gradually replaced the other central passes of the Alps in popularity (Plate 26). Firstly, it was directly on the route from Milan to the navigable Rhine at Basle, and did not, like some of the other passes, involve a detour round the Bernese Oberland or the Glarus

Alps; secondly, it involved but one high pass and steep climb, unlike some of the more westerly passes which involved a crossing of the Jura; and thirdly, it made full use of water navigation by the Ticino and Lake Maggiore to the south, and by Lake Lucerne in the north. But the St Gotthard, fundamentally important in assuring the position of the Free Cantons that were the core of an independent Switzerland, and important in nourishing the trade of Zürich and Basle as well as the southern Rhineland, was not nearly so important to the commerce of the twelfth and thirteenth centuries as more westerly routes, partly because of the high tolls and the inconvenient monopolies of the Swiss cantons.

The easy route along the Rhône–Saône trough was above all favoured by the Italian commerce of the twelfth and thirteenth centuries. Some went by sea from Genoa or other Ligurian ports to Provençal ports such as Arles, Nîmes, Beaucaire and Tarascon (Plate 25) for shipment up the Rhône by land route or by water to Chalon-sur-Saône and thence overland to the Champagne Fairs. But perhaps the bulk of the commerce to the Champagne Fairs was handled by professional carriers or *vectuarii*, who relied on caravans of pack animals and worked to a regular schedule; many of these carriers used passes in the western group, and chiefly the Mont Cenis route by way of Turin, and the Dora Riparia.[6]

The fairs of Champagne were highly organised on an unchanging schedule lasting throughout almost the whole of the year at four places, each fair lasting about six weeks: the winter fair at Lagny started on 2 January; the fair of Bar-sur-Aube on Shrove Tuesday; Provins on the Tuesday before Ascension Day; the Troyes 'hot fair' on the 24 June; Provins again on the 14 September; and the Troyes 'cold fair' on 2 November. Each fair followed the same order of business: 8 days for the period of entry, 10 days for the sale of cloth, 11 days for the sale of leathers, hides and skins, 19 days for the sale of goods by weight and for the settlement of accounts, and 4 days for the drawing up of the 'letters of the fair' (Plate 27). A variety of commerce was done: wines were brought for sale, dyestuffs from Albi, Montauban and Toulouse, or linens from Besançon and Lorraine, for example. Spanish, French, English and German merchants were present in strength, but these fairs were especially centres at which Mediterranean spices, silks, dyestuffs and manufactured luxuries were exchanged for Flemish and English semi-finished cloth or English raw wool. The organisation of the fairs was clearly phased to the advantage of the northern merchants who were able to sell their cloth and count their earnings before purchasing the Mediterranean goods which were sold mainly by weight, and it has been suggested that the organisation of the fairs was probably developed in order to make conditions easy for the relatively unsophisticated Flemish and other northern merchants at a time when the Italians were making full use of credit instruments and of fast courier services, taking no more than 20 days, in order to keep their agents at the Champagne Fairs informed and to despatch contracts and credit instruments if necessary.[7]

The four chief towns of the Champagne Fairs were tolerably well sited in relation to the relief and rivers of the area, though none was outstanding. All were on Roman routes or navigable rivers: Troyes occupied a hill site overlooking the Seine on Agrippa's road to the Saône; Bar-sur-Aube was at a junction of Roman roads; Lagny at a navigable point on the Marne; and Provins a gap town in the escarpment fringing the Île de France and on the road from Paris to Basle.[8] None was particularly well located to dominate the routes of Champagne and all four shared the prosperity that followed the fairs. What was, however, much more important than local site factors was the fact that the whole zone lay directly on the routes from the Saône valley towards Paris and the Seine on the one hand and towards Flanders on the other. The position of Champagne in relation to the trade routes of Western Europe as a whole was strengthened by the fact that the County was independent both of the Empire and of the Crown of France.

Yet, in spite of their organisation, or perhaps because of it, the trade of the Champagne Fairs declined rapidly from the end of the thirteenth century after the County of Champagne was absorbed into the Kingdom of France (1285) and became involved in war taxation, war with Flanders, and the crippling of its trade as a result of French measures directed against the cloth industry of Flanders and the wool trade of England. But by this time the use of more easterly routes was increasing and the Genoese had pioneered the all-sea route to Bruges.

The development of industry in Italy during this period derived to a great extent from its commercial supremacy. In return for the spices and luxuries which the Italian merchants shipped north of the Alps, the northern countries sent chiefly their cloth in the twelfth and thirteenth centuries. A Venetian tariff of 1265 lists over thirty different kinds of cloth from France, England and Flanders, but only ten from Italy and those were of the poorer qualities. Much of the northern cloth was ultimately exported by Italian merchants to North Africa, the Levant, Constantinople and Italy itself, and it was therefore the Italians who were best able to gauge the demands of an exacting Mediterranean market and who also imported many of the best and most expensive dyes—grain, brasilwood, or woad from southern France, for example—and also alum from Asia Minor.[9] Thus there developed during the twelfth and early thirteenth centuries an important finishing industry in Italy. Northern cloth was exported grey to Italian manufacturers who raised the felt, dyed the cloth and then completed the finishing processes to produce the very high quality scarlet, crimson and purple cloths much appreciated in the Levant. Many of the Italian towns active in the northern commerce participated in this finishing industry—Pisa, Lucca, Genoa, Milan and Venice, for example, but it was Florence which acquired the greatest reputation and the *Arte di Calimala*, the gild which controlled the dyeing and finishing industry, was founded in 1212.

The manufacture of cloth had been fairly widespread throughout Italy, as it was in most western countries before the revival of commerce, but the development of a specialised and highly organised cloth industry producing good quality cloths for export markets was a development which came to Italy after its reputation had been acquired for the finishing of foreign cloth. The list of 1265 mentions cloths from towns in Tuscany and the north Italian plain—Lucca, Florence, Milan, Como, Bergamo and Brescia. Pisa, too, had an early cloth industry of importance, but not until the end of the thirteenth century and the beginning of the fourteenth did Italian towns and above all, Florence, begin to acquire a reputation for the best quality cloths.

The circumstances which gave new impetus to Italian cloth production were to some extent bound up with the part played by Italian merchants in English trade towards the end of the thirteenth century when they replaced the Flemings and became so deeply involved in the English wool trade that by 1273 the Florentines alone were taking some 12 per cent of the exported English clip. Pegolotti's account gives a surprisingly detailed list of the major sources of English wool in the early fourteenth century, by which time the Italians were able to export the wool directly in Italian ships from London or Southampton by way of the newly opened sea route. By the end of the century unrest and shortages in Flanders provided not only an opportunity for expanding production, but also the occasion for the migration to Italy of skilled Flemish craftsmen. Florence was the major single producer of cloth, having organised its *Arte della Lana* for the control of an industry which was throughout capitalistic in organisation. By 1307 Florence was turning out some 100,000 pieces of cloth a year, and although output was down to 80,000 pieces by 1338, the value had doubled.

The silk industry was also concentrated to a large extent in Tuscany by the end of the thirteenth century. It had been introduced into Sicily by the Arabs and had later spread to a number of Italian towns. Genoa, Milan, and Venice had silk industries by the end of the thirteenth century but Lucca was the best known for its silks and silk cloths with gold and silver threads, until political strife encouraged its artisans to migrate elsewhere, taking with them their skills and capital—to Florence, Venice and Bologna in particular.

Finally, the other major industry, for which Milan had gained a European reputation, was that of arms and armour. Iron from the Alps and Lombardy provided the raw material and the advent of mercenary troops in the Italian cities together with the elaboration of heavy armour, provided the demand. This was essentially a workshop rather than a capitalistic industry, but it served to establish a reputation for metal working at Milan which has never been lost.

Mediterranean trade in the fourteenth and fifteenth centuries

This is not the place to enter deeply into the controversies of economic historians on the problems of interpreting this period as one of contraction and depression after the great boom years of the thirteenth century, but an understanding of the problems is essential to an interpretation of its geography. Postan adduced the evidence of population, prices and production to suggest contraction and his interpretation has been followed by R. S. Lopez, so far as the Mediterranean is concerned.[10] Such quantitative evidence as there is of urban expansion (by the building of town walls), of population movement, or of production and trade in cloth lends support to the idea of a generalised contraction in the level of trade and industrial or agricultural output. Before the years of plague, population had perhaps reached starvation level, but after the Black Death population fell and so did demand. As markets shrank, so there were tendencies towards the cutting of costs in industry and trade. In

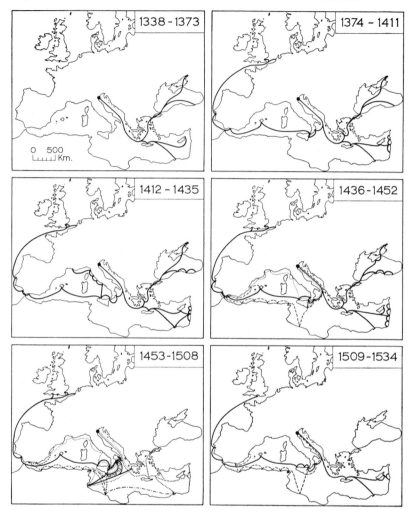

commerce, low profits prevailed, low rates of interest ruled since capital was relatively abundant, and the advantage lay with the large business house and the established shipping routes. Under such conditions, capital was sometimes more profitably invested in state loans, agricultural investment or even fine building and luxurious tapestries or works of art.

It was moreover, a period of political disintegration and change:

Fig. 7:3   Merchant galley fleets of the Venetian State, 1332–1534 (after
Tenenti and Vivanti)
The routes taken by the regular merchant fleets are generalised and
simplified. Additional coastal ports were called at for a number of years
and ports were often omitted. In occasional years fleets did not run on
particular routes. The eastern routes were the most important in the
fourteenth century and continued to the end, though the Black Sea route
ended abruptly in 1452. The Flanders and England routes were also of
continuing importance, to Bruges, Southampton and London. The North
African routes did not come into prominence before the mid-fifteenth
century.

Notes:
1338–1373: The Black Sea route was in operation in 1332–3 and 1336,
and the Flanders galleys ran in 1347 and 1357–8. The branch to Trebizond
operated mainly from 1338–1344 and from 1368.

1374–1411: Flanders galleys did not sail from 1377–1383; the branch to
Trebizond operated only occasionally.

1412–1435: The major change is the appearance of a new route to
southern France occasionally extended to the Spanish coast.

1436–1452: Former routes continued with the addition of a new route
to the North African coast.

1453–1508: The end of the Black Sea routes with the fall of Constantinople to the Turks; in general a much greater concentration of routes in
Southern Italy and the Western Mediterranean.

1509–1534: Atlantic galleys are destined for Southampton, but operate
only in a few years: 1516–17, 1519–20, 1530 and 1533; the North African
route functioned in only six out of the twenty-five years; and it was only
the routes to the eastern Mediterranean which survived regularly.

the Hundred Years' War in France and England; civil war in Spain
and southern Italy; long-term difficulties in the Low Countries. In the
Mediterranean, traditional patterns of trade were being forcefully
altered with the advent of the Ottoman Turks to the mainland of
Europe in the late fourteenth century and with their conquest of
Constantinople itself in 1453 (Fig. 7:3). It is true that Genoa and
Venice often transferred previous agreements with the Byzantines to

the new Turkish rulers, but Genoese trade at Pera declined drastically and there were constant frictions and difficulties in the Levant which gave a brief importance to Cyprus as a trading base, and which also tended to enhance the importance of trade through Alexandria and Egypt. Beyond Europe there were other difficulties, for the brief season for European travel to the Far East was ended by the break-up of the Mongol Empire in the fourteenth century and the replacement of the Yuan dynasty in China by the anti-foreign emperors.

Internal and external factors were therefore leading to contraction, but it has also been suggested that there were structural changes in society and a redistribution of income which of necessity affected the geography of trade; and there was also great regional variation in the impact of depression. The changes of the fourteenth century tended to cause a rise in the real wages of urban labourers and artisans and a relative rise in the prices of industrial as against agricultural prices.[11] Slicher van Bath and others have also pointed to a shift in agricultural prices which favoured stock and stock products as against grain.[12] The idea of a relative impoverishment of the lesser nobility has also been mooted, though this is controversial. These interpretations, if correct, would help to explain an important feature in the geography of trade at this time, which displays a tendency towards what has been called a 'democratisation' of trade, as the real incomes of artisans, some peasants, and even labourers increased. In the cloth industry there was a new and rising demand for middle and lower quality cloths; there was a tendency for a greater proportion of total trade to be in bulky and low-cost products rather than highly expensive luxuries. Older centres of trade and industry either declined or changed to face this new trend, but there was also a shift towards the development of new areas which had been peripheral to the former axis of trade linking northern and central Italy with Flanders by way of the Champagne Fairs and the Rhine: South Germany, Poland, Hungary and Bohemia; Iberia and North Africa; and in some respects the advance of the English cloth industry in the west.

South Germany was perhaps the chief area in which economic advance occurred on a large scale during the fifteenth century, and for several reasons (Fig. 7:4). The eastwards shift of trade routes from Flanders and Champagne towards Brabant and the Rhine also involved the development of new north–south links across southern Germany from the Rhineland, Saxony and Thuringia towards the

Main basin, the Swabian Jura and the upper Danube, and so to the eastern passes across the Alps, particularly the Brenner. The eastern passes converged ultimately on Venice, from which came the flow of luxury textiles, silks, brocades and velvets, mirrors, glass and Far Eastern goods which sustained the commerce of the south German

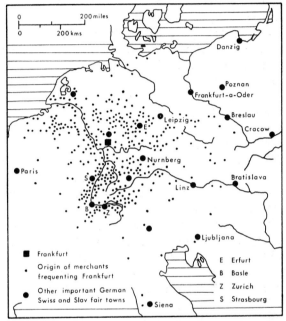

Fig. 7:4   The origin of merchants frequenting Frankfurt fairs in the fourteenth and fifteenth centuries

towns. In the west it had been the Italian merchants who had carried the overland trade into north-western Europe; in the east Venetian merchants had been reluctant to engage themselves north of the Alps and had preferred to concentrate on maritime activity, so that the Germans, based in Venice at the *Fondaco dei Tedeschi*, gained much of the profits of redistributing Venetian goods through central Europe and to the Rhine and the Low Countries. Italian industrial skills were introduced into the south German towns by German merchant entrepreneurs and Italian business and financial techniques were adopted to give the German merchants an advantage over their northern colleagues. Indeed, the south German banking families, such as the Welsers, Fuggers, Tuchers and Hochstetters of Augsburg played a very important rôle in the development of mining and trade in north-western Europe in the sixteenth century and in the finance of the Habsburg Empire.

South German commerce also reflected the growing importance of the Slav lands of east-central Europe for, while the west may have been in decline, the development of commercial agriculture in east Germany, Poland and the Baltic countries was a dominating feature of the fifteenth century. The commerce of Bohemia, Slovenia and the Austrian Alps was also expanding rapidly as a result of the renewed exploitation of metals, particularly silver.

The major regions of mining in central Europe in the fifteenth century were in the Ore Mountains of Bohemia, Styria and Carinthia, Neusohl in Hungary and in the neighbourhood of Mansfeld in Saxony.[13] From the mid-fourteenth century central European silver mining had been in a state of depression but from about 1460 the industry was revived, partly through the application of water power to the crushing of ores, the working of bellows, the driving of hammers and the use of improved means of drainage permitting deeper mining, but partly through the general rise in silver prices about this period which made such expensive innovations practicable and profitable.

According to Nef, the output of silver in central Europe increased very rapidly during the period 1460–1530, when there was a shortage of gold currency in the Mediterranean and new silver coins such as the Joachimsthaler, precursor of the dollar, represented an attempt to provide a silver substitute for gold. Bohemian and Saxon silver thus helped to fill a gap in the European supply of precious metals, until the arrival of new supplies from across the Atlantic in the sixteenth century. At a time when credit was founded on precious metals and when the availability of credit and money were by no means geographically uniform, the physical availability of silver or gold was an important commercial stimulus. It is likely that the rise of the south German banking houses, particularly at Augsburg, was closely dependent on the prosperity of silver mining in the area. Other minerals were also important: the calamine ores of Tyrol and Carinthia were being used for the manufacture of brass; the iron of Styria and Carinthia and of the south German towns themselves represented an important part of contemporary European output; the salt of Hallein and the copper of Austria and the Ore Mountains contributed to regional prosperity.

25 *Tarascon and Beaucaire*, twin towns of the Lower Rhône, handled the trade of the Rhône from the thirteenth century, but were also important towns on the routes of transhumance from the Alps to the Rhône delta. The fairs of Beaucaire had international significance in the middle ages, and still survive, though in an altered form. The terminus of the Rhône-Sète canal is also shown.

26 *Lucerne and the Vierwaldstätter See.* An important stage on the St. Gotthard route, of growing importance in the thirteenth century after the bridging of the Schöllenen gorge near Andermatt. The shortest route from the Milan area to the navigable Rhine, the single high ascent and the possibility of lake navigation over a substantial section on both Swiss and Italian flanks gave this route many advantages over its competitors.

27 *Bar-sur-Aube.* The wooden shelter was originally built for the merchants attending the Champagne fairs, of which Bar-sur-Aube was one of the centres.

Ravensburg, with its Great Merchant Company formed in 1380 and trading from Spain to Budapest, was one of the important towns; Regensburg, anciently important for its Danube trade, was another; route towns like Rothenburg or Nördlingen enjoyed their period of greatness. Ulm on the upper Danube had gained a wide reputation for its flax and linens, but it is typical of a general trend in south Germany that new skills were borrowed from Italy in order to assimilate new imports of raw cotton from the Levant to local traditions for the production of mixed cotton and linen or woollen goods. A cheap cloth was thus produced which competed well in Italian markets. Nürnberg's trade was still of local significance in the early fourteenth century but by the 1330s its sphere of activity had widened and already its arms industry was known in Spain, Italy and Flanders. The armourers' gild was the leading one of the city, and it came to compete very successfully with the industries of Milan and Ferrara which had given it inspiration. Although Nürnberg's metal products—its clocks, arms, armour and toys—were known throughout Europe, it too had local textile industries, based on local flax and linen production. During the fifteenth century its merchants were the most important single group at the Venetian *Fondaco dei Tedeschi*, and the range of its interests is symbolised in the pioneer globe of Martin Behaim, one of its citizens, which summarised European knowledge of the pre-Columbian world. Finally, Augsburg itself, well placed in relation to the Brenner and the routes to the silver of Bohemia and Saxony was chiefly renowned for the banking families to which it gave birth, though it was also concerned with the manufacture of metals, woollens and linens.

In Iberia, both Catalan and Portuguese trade made considerable advances, the former in the thirteenth and fourteenth century, the latter rather later in time. In the Reconquista, Catalonia and Aragon had made contact with Arab and Jewish traders in their conquest of Majorca in 1229 and Valencia in 1238. It is quite possible that the Catalan *portolani*, the first reasonably accurate navigators' charts of the Mediterranean, were derived from Arab examples. To this embryonic sea-state Sicily was added in 1282, then Malta, Sardinia, and in 1443 Naples itself. Even in the thirteenth century the Catalan cities had succeeded in establishing factories or agencies in Beirut, Damascus and Alexandria. They had, therefore, a foothold in the spice trade of the east but they also had an important hold over the grain and wool supplies of the western Mediterranean through their position in Sicily and southern Italy. To the west the Catalans followed the Genoese and Venetians to England and Flanders, and to the south the establishment of treaty relations and consulates in North Africa completed a trading sphere which dominated the western Mediterranean to the late fourteenth and early fifteenth centuries, when financial crisis, internal troubles and eventually the Catalan revolution of 1462–72 helped to bring about decline (Plate 30).

The Catalan position rested to some extent on the prosperity of North Africa and its trade with Europe. The fragmentation of Muslim territories in North Africa assisted penetration by European trading interests but the latter were attracted chiefly by the direct and indirect trade which was nourished by the trans-Saharan trade in gold dust from West Africa. Venice and Genoa had renewed their interest in the area in the fifteenth century; the Genoese organised an expedition overland which reached as far as the oasis of Tuat in 1457; and the Barbary states constituted a new market for English cloth, particularly poor and medium-quality cloths such as the kerseys of East Anglia. Like the silver of central Europe the gold dust of West Africa helped to finance Mediterranean trade at a time of general currency shortage, simultaneously stimulating the trade of areas through which it passed. By 1460 the Portuguese had reached the Gulf of Guinea by sea and the West African gold had begun to take a different route by sea to Europe in company with Guinea pepper, ivory and a few slaves.

From the end of the fourteenth century treaty links had given Portuguese traders a privileged position in England, particularly at times when Portuguese wine supplemented French during the Hundred Years' War. Olive oil, cork, dyestuffs, wine and salt were exchanged for English cloth by Portuguese merchants in western ports, of which Bristol was the chief. But with the Portuguese penetration along the coast of Africa, new sources of trade were tapped, not only in West African commodities but also in the sugar, wine and dyewoods that came from Madeira and the Azores during the fifteenth century.

Northern Italy undoubtedly retained its leadership in the commerce and industry of Western Europe during the period. The industries of Venice developed towards the greater refinements and luxuries of the fifteenth century in textiles, glass, building and the arts. But the advance of peripheral regions indicates three important features in the changing geography of trade and commerce. First, the importance of the 'demonstration' effect in the geographical spread of new advances in trading and industrial techniques outside Italy, particularly in south Germany, but also in Switzerland where the growth of the textile industries at St Gallen, for example, and the use of cotton in new fabrics, is similar to that at Ulm or Augsburg in its dependence on Italian traditions. The Genoese played a similar demonstrative rôle in the Catalan seaports and, perhaps, in Seville and Portuguese ports as well. Secondly, some have stressed the importance of currency supplies and the availability of precious metals, acting as a stimulant in the regions through which they pass—as in North Africa, southern Germany and, for a time, Portugal. Finally, perhaps, the shift towards trade in goods of slightly lower value and the greater competition in transport costs at a time of contracting trade may have shifted the balance a little further towards the advantage of water transport. For this is the period in which the all-sea route round the Iberian peninsula seemed preferable to the overland routes for many merchants; and further north the Sound route to the Baltic was beginning to revive at the expense of the Hanseatic monopoly over the transpeninsular route. But across Western Europe, war as well as economic factors also help to explain the shift of routes from the Rhône and the western isthmuses to the Rhine and south Germany.

FLANDERS AND THE SOUTHERN LOW COUNTRIES

In northern Europe, the Low Countries occupied an equivalent position to Italy in the south in relation to the great trade-routes of Europe. Henri Pirenne was perhaps more deterministic in his assessment of their positional value than most geographers would now dare to be: 'The great extent of its coastline, proximity to England, the three great rivers which cross it and which attach it by natural routes to Germany, Burgundy and central France, destined the Low Countries to play in the basin of the North Sea the same rôle that was played in the Mediterranean by Venice, Genoa and Pisa'.[14] The navigable Rhine, the Meuse and the Scheldt focus river trade from a wide area to the zone between the Zuider Zee and the Flemish coast; the sea route which in medieval times hugged the coasts and offshore islands from western France to the Jutland peninsula crossed the routes to southern England, the Thames and the East Anglian coast somewhere in this region; and finally this was the zone of easy transit which passes through the löss zone of productive agriculture and good food supplies that links the *Hellweg* in Germany to the routes of the Paris basin by way of the plains of Brabant or the Sambre–Meuse depression. There was a concentration of routes, but it was not, except on a continental scale, a *single* focus of routes. Positional value was fully realised at different times in history in different parts of the whole zone from the estuary of the Canche and the Somme to the Zuider Zee or even further afield.

Rotterdam and Antwerp now vie for the transit trade flowing through the Low Countries from the great industrial zones of the Ruhr and Lorraine as well as from the areas further upstream; Amsterdam is relegated to unimportance in this particular function and Dunkirk has been deliberately built up by the French to secure trade of north-eastern France which might otherwise be attracted to Antwerp. Ostend is a port of transit for passengers from Britain heading along the Belgian motorway towards Germany along a route travelled in early years by traffic heading from Bruges to Cologne; and the magnificent heritage that Bruges still preserves from its medieval prosperity as a port and industrial town for all Europe is now a tourist attraction on the self-same routes between England and the Continent that once carried English wool. Position has been of undoubted and continuing importance in the industrial and commercial prosperity of some part or other of the Low Countries, but it is commonly a factor whose weight is difficult to assess. Indeed, the interest in the historical geography of the Low Countries often lies in an assessment of the political, social, economic and technological circumstances under which this or that sector of the whole zone of the Low Countries has been able to use its positional value more effectively than the rest.

By the middle of the twelfth century Flanders had become the foremost, and possibly the only, compact and predominantly industrial area in north-west Europe. The chief centres of its cloth industry, Ypres, Ghent, Douai and Bruges, came to rank among the most important towns of northern Europe. The industry was scattered in the towns of a wide area extending to the Canche estuary in the west and to the basin of the Scheldt to the east (Fig. 7:5).[15] Many of the earliest major centres of the industry well known for the quality of their cloths were in the south and west of the area: Arras, St Omer, Douai, Tournai, Cambrai, Lille and Valenciennes. In Brabant, the rise of the cloth industry came later: Malines cloth was well known in the twelfth century, but it was not until much later that the cloths of Brussels and Louvain acquired an international reputation. The main centres of the industry came increasingly to be focused on the Lys basin, and it was the cloths of Bruges, Ghent and Ypres that were best known in the Mediterranean lands in the later Middle Ages. There was regional specialisation in the cloths marketed:

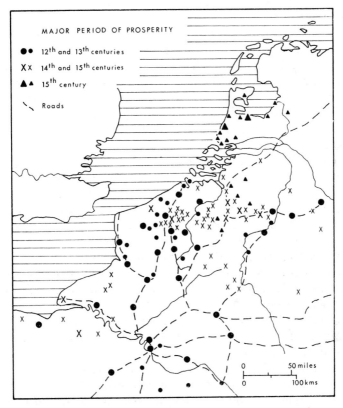

Fig. 7:5   The medieval cloth towns of the Low Countries

dyed cloths from Ypres, the blues of Lille and Douai, the scarlets of Douai, Ghent and Malines, the black cloths of Ypres and Ghent, the lighter cloths of Arras. Throughout Europe and on the routes to the Middle East Flemish cloth was held in high repute, and it is by such qualitative evidence that the significance of the industry must still be judged in the absence of quantitative evidence of production.[16]

The industry was highly organised and even by the end of the twelfth century the Flemish cloth towns had grouped themselves into a *Hanse* of seventeen towns to regulate their relations with the Champagne Fairs, the source of many dyestuffs and of alum for the cloth industry as well as markets for the finished product. Powerful gilds of merchant entrepreneurs controlled the industry in the twelfth and thirteenth century, and the processes have been described by which they had been able to extend their control, first selling work to the craftsmen and buying back the finished product, then later owning the raw material through all the stages of manufacture. Weavers, fullers, and dyers were reduced ultimately to dependence on the merchant entrepreneurs. Scrupulous control was probably a necessary condition for the maintenance of the high standards of quality which assured Flemish cloth its universal markets. Processes of production were regulated and inspection was regular, but it was perhaps the fact that the industry depended so much on distant sources of raw materials and distant markets, detailed knowledge of which constituted much of the expertise of the merchant entrepreneurs, that helped to put control of it into their hands.

The most important of the raw materials that were imported into Flanders was, of course, English wool. Local wools from the sheep pastures of Artois or from the drained marshes of the Flemish coastlands were insufficient to meet the needs of the industry even in the twelfth century, and local wools sufficed only for the medium-quality cloths. Spanish wool, too, was being increasingly used in the late thirteenth century. Many of the dyestuffs also came long distances, though it is true that a local specialisation on woad contributed to the wealth of Picardy and of Amiens. But woad was also a speciality of the Garonne basin; grain, the red dye from the kermes insect, came from Iberia and Asia Minor; true vermilion from the Red Sea; brasil from Ceylon. Alum was for a long period a monopoly of the Genoese from the coast of Asia Minor, and as an alternative mordant, the humble woodash came to the Low Countries from the Baltic. The merchants who controlled the sources of raw materials and knew the kinds of cloth needed in particular markets were in a strong position. It was an industry in which continuity of production depended on the tenuous links established over long distances at a time of slow and difficult transport.

The cloth industry in general was unique in medieval Europe in the extent to which it was a localised craft. It is true that mining and other extractive industries were necessarily highly concentrated, though the production of iron was very widely scattered in the Middle Ages, but most secondary manufacture was widely distributed in the towns, a few of which may have had an outstanding reputation for the quality of a particular product, the result perhaps of the possession of excellent raw materials of unusual character or quality. In some respects this also applies to the cloth industry, for poor-quality cloth was made for local use in most parts of Western Europe; the fact that differentiated the production of areas such as the Flemish towns was the concentration on a high-quality product for a fairly restricted market. It is also true that the raw materials for the cloth industry were not only able to stand the costs of transport over long distances but were also tough and durable enough to withstand the rigours and delays of long journeys. High-quality wool was a scarce and expensive commodity in which England had a European reputation; dyestuffs were rare and expensive enough to be grouped in the same class as the luxury spices and herbs carried from Asia by way of the Levant. It is evident, then, that almost any location might have been a viable one on the major routes from England to the towns in northern and central Italy from which the cloths were distributed to the distant markets of the Levant. Indeed, both termini possessed important cloth industries—England and Italy—and there were industries of more than local significance at the fair towns of Champagne. It is, however, more difficult to explain the need for localisation in the industry as a whole, except in terms of the concentration of the skill, care and technical knowledge required for the production of high-quality cloth, combined with the capital needed for the assembly of raw materials and the maintenance of stocks rather than investment in fixed capital. Thus although the migrant weavers who accompanied John Kemp to York in 1331 and the emigrant Flemish craftsmen who took their skills to Florence at the end of the thirteenth century may not have introduced the cloth industry to those areas, they took with them skills and technical knowledge which were of fundamental importance in the production of good-quality cloth.

The localisation of the cloth industry in Flanders has been attributed to a variety of circumstances. The attempt has been made, though necessarily unconvincingly, to trace a continuous preoccupation with the cloth industry from the time of the Roman Empire, when the armies of the Rhine frontier and then Rome itself constituted a market for cloths and mantles produced in the area of the Low Countries, at places such as Tournai, Metz, Reims and Trier. In the eighth and ninth centuries the activities of the Frisian merchants in the Rhineland and the southern basin of the North Sea included trade in cloth, for Frisian cloth was worn by Charlemagne and his court and was presented as a gift to an Arab caliph. It is very doubtful whether this was a production of the Frisian people themselves, for they lacked the resources for a substantial cloth industry, and the argument often suggested is that the Frisians merely carried cloth which was produced in the Low Countries, or possibly in England.

Whatever the link between medieval Flanders and the cloth handled by North Sea traders in the eighth and ninth centuries, there is certain evidence of a cloth industry of more than local importance by the early eleventh century. Market tolls of Arras in 1024 and 1036, and of St Omer in 1043 mention tolls on dyes, wool and cloth, and English wool was being imported to Bruges before the end of the eleventh century. Cloth was already a major commodity, together with wine and spices, to be handled at the cycle of five summer Flemish fairs at Lille, Ypres, Thourout, Douai and Messines by the end of the eleventh century, and from the mid-eleventh century cloth manufacture appears to have been a full-time occupation rather than a seasonal or part-time activity. Even by this time, production was regulated as to quality and size of cloths. There seems to be little doubt that the industry had become much larger in scale and in degree of specialisation at this period.

It is evident, then, that any explanation of the localisation of the industry in Flanders must take account of this formative period in the eleventh century or even earlier. Some authors have given prominence to the policy of the Counts of Flanders, independent of the Empire and untroubled by the rise of France during the period of expansion and consolidation. There seems to be little doubt that the Counts encouraged the Flemish merchants by privileges and concessions, but this may represent no more than a wise recognition of their established importance and, while a favourable political environment may have been a necessary condition for the localisation of an industry, alone it would hardly have been sufficient. An alternative and fairly commonly held view puts emphasis on the circumstances accompanying the growth of population in Flanders in the eleventh century and later. The consequences of population growth were to be seen in the creation of secondary settlements and perhaps in the effort that went into the drainage and reclamation of new land from marshland and heathland. It was more directly expressed in the extent of Flemish emigration to the new colonies of Germany, particularly as drainers and reclaimers, or their participation in the Sicilian campaigns of the Normans and in the Crusades. But one other response, according to this view, is the drift to the towns, the expansion of commerce, and participation in an industry which could use to the full the wool produced from the newly drained marshes as well as the sheep pastures of the chalk downs of Artois or the sandy heathlands of Flanders itself.

There are, however, difficulties in accepting this progression as an adequate one to explain the initial concentration of industry in the area, though it may well have been an essential aspect of the period of growth and development. Growth of population was common enough over Europe and the expansion of settlement and the reclamation of new land for cultivation was going on apace in many an area which could also support flocks of sheep on commons and wastes. Moreover, if industrial development took place as a part-time occupation taken up to supplement an inadequate income from farming and using whatever raw materials were to hand, there should have been an initial phase of rural production developing slowly to the kind of industry able to support the rich entrepreneur, to produce high-quality cloth, and to concentrate raw materials from a wide area. While there is much to be said about the transition at a later date from urban to rural industry, there is little to suggest how a localised and specialised industry was concentrated into the towns from what was presumably an initially rural location.[17]

The earliest evidence of the cloth industry in Flanders seems to indicate its urban importance, whilst a dependence on foreign sources for dyestuffs and even for wool stresses the rôle played in the industry by the merchant entrepreneur. Van Werveke considers that the localisation of a specialised industry was primarily the result of an increased demand for good-quality cloth by the Flemish merchants who were themselves pioneers of a rapidly developing interregional and international commerce in north-western Europe. It was, after all, Flemish merchants who did much to open up the trade links from the salt and wine of the Île d'Oléron and the Bay of Bourgneuf to the coastlands of the North Sea and the Baltic between the Scandinavian expansion and the rise of German commerce in the thirteenth century (Plate 28). And if in the process of establishing new trade links with the Italian merchants along overland routes such as those which met at the Champagne Fairs they themselves recognised the potential demand for high-quality cloth, they were well placed to provide the capital for financing its production and to command the sources of mordants, dyestuffs and, later, English wool. Local pressures of population and land hunger may have created conditions under which industrial expansion was possible, but the Flemish merchant entrepreneurs played the active rôle in initiating, financing and organising the industry, which for that reason was an urban one, under the personal control of the new urban-dwelling communities.

Recognition of the importance of the merchant entrepreneur in initiating the Flemish industry has followed the increasing awareness, since Pirenne wrote, of the important rôle that Flemish merchants played in the expansion of commerce and the carrying trade in north-western Europe.[18] It also makes it possible to interpret the foundation and early growth of the Flemish towns as essentially part of the *same* process of development as that which involved the expansion of commerce and the location of industry. Formerly it had been necessary to presume early development in two stages, the first involving the foundation of towns in the tenth century and the creation of new communities of merchants, the second consisting of a phase in which the cloth industry nourished the growth of a rich merchant class and the development of Flemish commerce in the eleventh and twelfth centuries. Finally, the interpretation of Van Werveke demands a review of the use made of position and resources in the Flemish region. The location of an industry which arose out of local wool supplies from drained marshes, chalk pastures and heathland, combined with the part-time labour of an over-populated countryside puts great emphasis on the quality of local resources, but if the stress is placed on the innovations made by merchant entrepreneurs, it is the positional qualities of the area in relation to the movement of commerce that should be stressed in the interpretation of the distribution of industry. And it is, indeed, the case that the list of towns known to be important includes many to the south and south-west of the area which were more or less aligned, like the Flemish fair towns themselves, on the routes which led from the English Channel to the Champagne Fairs and thence to the upper Saône (Fig. 7:5).

During the late thirteenth century and in the fourteenth, however, the expansion of the cloth industry of Flanders was halted; changes occurred in the structure and character of the industry, and there were important shifts in the location of the industry. There was a contraction of the urban cloth industry to Bruges, Ypres and Ghent, and it was largely in Brabantine towns that new growth was concentrated. Yet during the same period a different trend was beginning: the shift from urban to rural industry, and particularly from the towns of Flanders to the countryside of the south-west near Cassel, Hondschoote, Tourcoing and Armentières.[19] The origins of the modern distribution of industries may be traced as a result of these changes. And the processes which gave rise to the shifting location of industry illustrate not only the complexity of the circumstances surrounding these shifts but also the enduring significance of the nodal position of the Low Countries.

The combination of circumstances which affected the location and structure of the Flemish industry reached a critical stage in the late thirteenth century. Industrial unrest, growing among the artisans during the second half of the thirteenth century, reached a climax in the general revolt of 1280 which occurred in Bruges, Ypres, Ghent and Tournai. The craftsmen had found common interest with the Count of Flanders against the power of the merchant entrepreneurs who controlled the rich merchant gilds, and this alliance was sufficient to defeat the combination of the merchant gilds and the French Crown. The artisans were, in general, able to destroy the power of the merchant gilds and to win a share in the government of the major towns. But industrial disturbances continued, for the weavers, fullers and dyers found themselves in conflict with each other, and all remained dependent on the richer merchants for their supplies of raw wool and dyestuffs and also for their markets. Weavers and fullers rose at Ypres and Bruges in 1324, for example, and repeatedly during the fourteenth century there were urban risings and revolts such as that which racked Louvain in 1378–83 or Ypres in 1383.

One direct effect of urban discontent was that Flemish artisans were the more likely to respond to encouragements from abroad to migrate. Flemish weavers were offered protection and encouragement by the English crown from the late thirteenth century; Edward III repeated earlier encouragements in 1337, and in 1331 John Kemp had moved from Flanders with his weavers, fullers and dyers to York. There had been other migrations to Germany, to Austria and particularly to Italy, where the Flemish skills were used to good effect in the development of an industry that could compete successfully with that of Flanders itself. Migrant craftsmen may not have been responsible for introducing a cloth industry *de novo* in the lands to which they went but the importance of their migration should not be underrated, for the advantages of localisation by then enjoyed by the Flemish industry were largely residual ones: skill, care, organisation and technical knowledge, and it was these qualities which were now being dispersed over all Western Europe, but particularly to its chief competitors, Italy and England.

The second element affecting Flanders in the late thirteenth century was its unfortunate political and diplomatic position in the conflict between England and France. In France, there was a substantial market for Flemish woollens, and since the incorporation of Champagne and its fairs into the kingdom of France in 1285, there lay also the routes by which cloth was despatched to the Mediterranean, and by way of which many of its dyestuffs came. France countered Flemish alliance with England by confiscation of its cloth, by heavy taxation and by disabilities imposed on Flemish merchants. But England could threaten Flanders not only by banning the import of Flemish cloth but also by withholding supplies of raw wool or by imposing heavy taxation on its export, a factor which helped to raise Flemish costs substantially after 1303. Thus political difficulties were important in disrupting the tenous links by which Flanders was connected over long distances to its sources of raw materials and its markets, and therefore in creating the shortages, unemployment and distress which exacerbated industrial unrest.

A third aspect of this changing situation was the decreasing participation of Flemish merchants in active overseas trade and the loss of initiative to German and Italian traders. The disruption of established trade routes in the late thirteenth century by war and embargo accelerated a decline that was already evident. German merchants had replaced the Flemings in the Baltic trade from about 1250; in England the Italian merchants and bankers were replacing them in the trade of raw wool, and by 1314 it was, significantly, an Italian—Pegolotti—who codified the sources of English raw wool. The merchants of Cologne and the Hanseatic *cogges* were bringing their trade to Bruges itself, and the Flemish Hanse of the Seventeen Towns no longer had any real function during the fourteenth century. The abandonment of active trade to foreign merchants was also associated with internal struggles and the loss of control by the merchant entrepreneurs over the industry in the towns. Small employers arose to take their place, many of them master weavers buying wool and selling their cloth to fullers and dyers, later extending their operations to finance the fulling and dyeing by wage labour. The decline of active Flemish trade thus impinged on the organisation of the industry and on its internal troubles but decline was also very much a product of the changes in trade routes which profoundly affected the positional value of the Flemish towns.

The Champagne Fairs had been a stable zone of contact between the Flemish and Italian merchants from the eleventh and twelfth centuries, and the organisation of their trade and transport had made them a delicate and efficient instrument of exchange between north and south, between the experienced Italian merchants and their simpler northern counterparts. With the incorporation of Champagne by France from 1285, its involvement in war taxation, and the quarrels of France with Flanders, the rapid decline of the Champagne Fairs began. New routes avoided the Fairs: in the west, the Genoese had pioneered the all-sea route to Flanders by 1277, and Bruges rapidly increased in status as the port of entry for Italians using it. To the south-east, the most direct route of all from Milan and the north Italian plain to the Low Countries by way of the St Gotthard pass was being increasingly used. It was a route with a number of advantages in addition to its directness, for it crossed the Alps with only a single steep ascent, and it provided water transport for a good deal of its length: lake Como, the Vierwaldstättersee, and the Rhine. From Cologne, the overland route across Brabant reached Bruges and Ghent from the east by way of Brussels and Louvain or Malines.

The changes in the location of the cloth industry which followed its changing fortunes involved, first of all, the final decay of industry in the south-west of the area. Arras, at one time one of the best-known towns for its cloths and its merchants, had been most conveniently placed in relation to the Champagne. But the annexation of Artois by France as early as 1191 and its subsequent separation from the main cloth-producing region may have been one of the reasons why Arras had steadily lost importance. St Omer, also once an important cloth town and port, had turned to the wine trade. But after 1312, with the annexation of Walloon Flanders by France and its involvement in her wars and politics, this area too declined. Falling output, poor-quality production and high prices were characteristic of Douai, Lille, Béthune and Orchies in the fourteenth century. It is also evident, however, that the cloth trade had ceased to flourish in precisely those towns which had been nearest to the routes leading into Champagne. Indeed, the urban cloth industry of Flanders was contracting towards the maritime lands and particularly to Ypres, Bruges and Ghent, the largest towns and those now best placed to receive wool from Bruges and to sell the finished products to the traders who came by sea or from Brabant. From the end of the thirteenth century and in the fourteenth, it was primarily in the Brabant towns that the growth of the cloth industry occurred most rapidly. Textiles were of rising importance in Brussels, Malines, Louvain and other towns which lay on or near the routes from Bruges or Antwerp to the Rhine at Cologne (Fig. 7:5). As in an earlier age in Flanders, the growth of the cloth industry here seems to have been closely related to the enterprise of the merchants for the Brabanters participated equally with the German merchants of the Rhineland, in developing the Rhine trade as an alternative to the Champagne route to the south. The active development of Brabantine commerce and of a cloth industry was also assisted by the fact that the Duke of Brabant had been able to maintain a benevolent neutrality in the late thirteenth century so that Brabantine merchants had secured exemption from the English ban on wool exports from 1294–7 and was able to maintain a wool supply from England while securing privileges for Brabantine merchants in the markets of France. And in Brabant, too, the social conflict of artisans and merchants had been held in check by the Duke's support for the merchants.

The other major change which affected the area as a whole in the fourteenth century was the shift from an urban to a rural, domestic industry. Spinning had long been done in the countryside and the major cloth towns had been surrounded by satellite villages in which spinning had been a woman's occupation. But during the fourteenth century, following a similar trend in England, the rural weaver was able to enjoy much greater freedom from strict regulation and control by the urban gilds. Entrepreneurs could find cheaper and more tractable labour in the villages and the conditions of production were more flexible. These factors operated, too, in England, but the atmosphere of industrial strife of the towns was much more a positive factor in Flanders; there is, on the other hand, very little evidence that the fulling mill driven by water power was ever important in bringing about a rural drift of industry there. Fulling mills were used in the Artois industry, but they could never have been important in the low-lying lands of Flanders itself. Van Werveke has also suggested that the dispersion into the countryside of a highly organised industry such as cloth production was in medieval Flanders had necessarily to await the introduction and spread among the merchants and entrepreneurs of literacy and of elementary techniques of book-keeping, without which continued control over the industry would have been impossible.[20] But although this may have been an important factor, the spread of industry into the countryside seems also to have involved the rise of the small entrepreneur who made no attempt to establish control over all the processes of production, but who was content to sell his woven cloth to other entrepreneurs for fulling, dyeing and finishing.

The expansion of rural industry was, indeed, much resented by the urban gilds and friction developed between town and countryside which flared at times into open civil war. Ghent, Bruges, St Omer and Ypres were affected at one time or another in the fourteenth century, but it was important for the subsequent development of the textile industries of Flanders that Ghent and Bruges were sufficiently rich and powerful to enforce successfully the ban on rural weaving in their neighbourhoods. Ypres and other towns to the south and west were not, and this area the rural industry spread most widely. The cloth industry of Armentières, a town whose early sprawling growth betrays its village origins, was not mentioned until 1413; Cassel and Hondschoote are first mentioned in connection with the cloth industry only in the fourteenth century, and Tourcoing and Poperinghe were other centres of importance which began their growth as industrial villages. Thus, the rural cloth industry had been eliminated from the neighbourhood of Bruges and Ghent, but where the urban cloth industry had been less strongly entrenched, in Brabant and to the south-west, rural industry developed rapidly and remained to lay the foundations, much later, for the nineteenth-century industrialisation of a textile industry near to the coalfields of Nord and Pas-de-Calais.

There was one other feature which helped to differentiate the declining urban industry of the towns from the expanding production of the countryside. It was one which arose directly out of the English and Italian competition with Flanders in the production of cloth and for the supplies of raw wool. England and Italy had been able to compete successfully with the urban industry of Flanders in the production of traditional fine but heavy woollen cloths. One of the reasons for this success was the ease with which English and Italian producers could secure supplies of good-quality English wool, the English directly, the Italian merchants through the financial activities of their bankers and merchants. The traditional industry of the Flemish towns was thus tied to an expensive and an ever-dwindling supply of English raw wool. Rural producers, however, had been forced to rely from an early time on what were at first regarded as inferior wools from Spain. Faced with the problem of making good or even luxury cloths from the Spanish imports, the industrial villages turned to new techniques by which fine, light cloths were made, such as the *says* and *sayettes* which were mentioned at Cassel as early as the fourteenth century. Imports of Spanish wool were well able to keep pace with the growth of industry, and markets in the Mediterranean and North Africa prized the new light types of cloth now being made.

With the loss of the urban cloth trade to English competition, the old Flemish and Brabantine towns were left with a pool of skilled labour, a knowledge of textiles and unemployed craftsmen. It was under these circumstances that alternative occupations were sought, preferably in a replacement industry in which existing skills, equipment and knowledge of markets could best be used. The linen industry was the most important of the new industries to emerge.[21] A crude, domestic flax industry had already existed during the Middle Ages, but in the fifteenth century techniques were improved, linens were made of finer quality and the industry expanded. A number of the towns which had been worst hit by the depression in the cloth trade were the most prominent in the new one. By the sixteenth century linen had replaced the woollen industry at Ghent. It was a new, but growing industry at Courtrai in the sixteenth century; and although the linen gild was a new one in Brussels in 1421, some 2,500 were engaged in the industry by 1541. Like the woollen cloth industry in the south-west, the linen industry was very often a product of rural domestic organisation, the weavers beginning by using raw materials they themselves had grown and despatching the finished product through the urban merchants. It is true, as often quoted in this connection, that the water of the Lys basin was soft and eminently suitable for retting the flax, but it may be that more important factors facilitated the expansion of the industry in the later Middle Ages, notably that there was an abundance of cheap and skilled labour starved of the raw material for its traditional occupations, an available and experienced organisation for marketing the product, and the possibility of expanding the production of flax as a result of an agricultural revolution in which the collective rotations of the three-field system had been replaced by a greater individualism of cropping. The industry spread in Flanders, Brabant, Hainault and in Holland as well during these years, and domestic flax had to be supplemented by imports from the Baltic and particularly from Russia. Although the products of Flanders may have been overshadowed in some respects by the Dutch linen industry, Ghent and Courtrai continued in the seventeenth and eighteenth centuries to be the chief centres of a Flemish industry which had grown with the increasing demand for linen which followed the exuberant changes in fashion of the sixteenth and seventeenth century. Indeed, this was one of the few ways in which Flanders continued to benefit from its Spanish connection in the seventeenth century, for Spain and its subtropical colonies took increasing quantities of a textile more suited to a hotter climate than the traditional woollen cloth, and this connection with American export markets survived the Spanish political connection into the eighteenth century; production increased by some 75 per cent between 1762 and 1785, when the Dutch industry was declining. By the early nineteenth century there were some 330,000 workers involved in the linen industry, still largely a rural and domestic industry.

To the east of the Lys basin and in the neighbourhood of Bruges, linen yarn was used increasingly in the sixteenth century to make the lace which Flanders no less than Venice supplied to the fashionable demands of a newly rich bourgeoisie. From Bruges across Brabant to Brussels and Malines, lace-making was a rural occupation which provided supplementary earnings to a fairly large population. A third response to the failure of the cloth industry was, similarly, a concentration on luxury products, but of a different character. Tapestries and carpets were, like lace and linen, new luxuries which marked the rising material standard of living enjoyed by the well-to-do during the Renaissance, and these, too, provided occupation for redundant textile workers, becoming a rural industry directed and organised in a number of towns from Arras to Brussels. Some, however, turned to luxury cloth worked with gold and silver thread, as at Brussels; silk was used in the making of tapestries or 'Arras cloths' at Brussels, according to Guicciardini it had been introduced to Bruges by mid-sixteenth century. Cotton, too, was among these new raw materials, and cloths of linen and cotton or wool and cotton mixtures were being produced in the sixteenth century at Ghent. It was from the Low Countries that silk workers came to Canterbury in the sixteenth century and from Antwerp that cotton workers went to Manchester and Bolton during the same period.

PORTS OF THE LOW COUNTRIES

The changing location of the cloth industry in the Low Countries is a striking illustration of the general way in which the focus of prosperity shifted within the area as a whole. The advantages of position at the 'crossroads of Europe' are of no more than a general guide to the interpretation of why the prosperity of particular regions rose and fell *within* the whole zone from Flanders to Friesland. The tendency of the geographical concentration of trade, prosperity and capital to shift within this zone is even better demonstrated, however, by the successive importance of Bruges, Antwerp and Amsterdam as the great ports of north-western Europe. As in the shift of industry from Flanders to Brabant and then to Holland and Zeeland in the sixteenth and the seventeenth centuries, so in the changing fortunes of the ports, very many other circumstances besides positional values must be taken into account. Four elements in particular appear to have been of major importance: the position of ports in relation to changes in the trade routes most commonly used; the political environment, a factor of particular importance in the history of Antwerp; the economic development of the hinterlands; and physical circumstances affecting accessibility and navigation.

One other general point may also be made at this point: the circumstances which surround the rise and fall of individual ports in the Low Countries should, perhaps, be distinguished from the circumstances which were making for the concentration of trade in the great ports rather than its dispersion among a greater number of small ones. In some respects, Bruges was *primus inter pares* among the cloth towns of Flanders because of its participation in overseas trade, but it monopolised imports of English wool only for the relatively short periods when it was the staple, and it appears never to have been overwhelmingly greater in size than Ghent or Ypres. The cosmopolitan merchants of Antwerp, however, concentrated within their hands a much more complex and far-reaching network of trade and finance, and for fifty years it towered above the performance of its rivals in a fashion that Bruges had never done. But it was Amsterdam which carried this process of concentration to the greatest extent: 'The reign of Amsterdam was the last in which a veritable empire of credit could be held by a city in her own right,' according to Violet Barbour.[22]

Bruges 27.4.81

The increasing concentration of trade and commerce on an individual city seems to have been a characteristic evident in the development of Bruges from early times to the period of the early fourteenth century when it could be described as a 'world market of the Middle Ages'. Yet this concentration took place in spite of striking disadvantages in the nature of its site, and at a time when the active participation of Flemish merchants in overseas trade was declining. Indeed, the great days of Bruges occurred at a time when foreign merchants were handling much of its trade.[23]

Although the silting of the Zwin in the later Middle Ages has been much exaggerated as a factor in the decline of Bruges, physical changes had much to do with its early growth. The earliest settlement, named as a landing place or *bryggja* (O.N.) was founded at the junction between the sandy 'uplands' and the maritime plain, but it was not until the tenth century that settlement began to grow around the castle of the count. Its earliest fortifications (about 987) took place at about the same time that reclamation of land got under way. But it now appears from pedological evidence that in its earliest stages, Bruges had no direct waterway to the sea, and that the approaches to the town were covered by shallow waters navigable only at high tide by flat-bottomed boats. Indeed, it seems likely that the bay of the Zwin, on which Bruges depended for its navigation, was created only in 1134 as a result of marine flooding in that year.[24] It was on the shores of this bay that the outports of Bruges were successively founded as the progress of new reclamation threatened the access of Bruges to the sea, for reclamation by the creation of new polders was going on apace during the thirteenth century, much of it organised by the officials of the count or by the urban patriciate of Bruges itself. Damme, founded in 1180 and with a name symbolic of its relationship also to new drainage and reclamation, was the first of the outports, built to handle the new decked ships which were carrying the growing traffic in wine from the ports of western France. Sluys, founded in 1290 or thereabouts, was the last of the great outports, again with a name connected with reclamation and drainage, but providing a deep-water harbour for the larger ships of the Hanseatic league—the *cogges*—and also for the Italian galley fleets which had begun to anchor at Sluys before the end of the thirteenth century. But even in the greatest days of its commerce, the merchants of Bruges depended on transhipment for the carriage of goods up to the town itself, and it was certainly normal in the early fourteenth century, when Pegolotti, the Italian merchant, wrote at length on this point. It is thus difficult to see how the decline of Bruges can be attributed in any significant way to the silting of its rivers and canals, for the whole history of Bruges is a tale of its struggle to maintain water transport to the sea.

Two phases in the growth of Bruges may be distinguished, for its early development as a port was linked with the active participation of Flemish merchants in overseas commerce, just as its later stages were associated with the dominance of foreign merchants, particularly the Hanseatic League. And in each of these periods trade and trade routes differed significantly, and so did the rôle of Bruges. From the time when Flemish merchants were first mentioned in London between 991 and 1002, the English trade had been important. It was Flemish merchants who, from 1100, were exporting English wool from England, and tin, lead, and wheat at a later date; it was Flemish merchants who brought cloths, wine and Mediterranean goods to the fairs of Stamford, St Ives, Boston, Winchester and Northampton in the thirteenth century; and Flemish bankers preceded the Italians in the development of finance. But the route taken by English wool even in 1100 was usually by way of Dover to Wissant (between Calais and Boulogne) in the twelfth century, and later still, when the wool staple was organised, Bruges was at best only one of many towns to which wool could be brought. Up to the early thirteenth century the Flemish merchants involved in the English trade were drawn from the whole zone of Flanders and many were from interior towns such as Ghent or Ypres. Arras merchants played an important part, and the merchants of Bruges were but the leaders in the Flemish Hanse in London. Indeed, Bruges played little part at any time in the import of English wool, handled from 1313 by one staple port, sometimes in England, sometimes on the continent: St Omer in 1313 and 1320, Antwerp in 1313 and 1338, Bruges in 1325 and 1340, Calais from 1363 to 1558.

To the end of the thirteenth century the Champagne Fairs had been the major zone of contact between the northern and Italian merchants and it was here that the Flemish merchants had found raw materials and markets for the cloth industry that nourished their prosperity. But it had been Arras merchants who were most to the fore and in the cycle of Flemish fairs; Bruges was only one of five important centres. Indeed, until the end of the twelfth century St Omer seems to have been the chief of the ports in this flourishing western zone of Flanders in contact with the Champagne Fairs.

It had been with the south-west that the trade of Bruges had been dominant in developing the trade in wine and salt from western France that led to the interest of Portuguese merchants and then by the end of the thirteenth century to the pioneer voyages by Genoese merchants. And it was in this direction that the active commerce of the Flemish merchants persisted longest, for although they had begun to develop Bruges as an entrepôt for the transit of wine and salt further to the north-east towards the Weser basin and then to the Baltic itself, Bruges merchants were quickly eliminated from the Baltic in the thirteenth century by the growing strength of Lübeck and its allies.

But with the changes in the pattern of major trade routes that occurred at the end of the thirteenth century and which ultimately involved many new difficulties for the Flemish cloth industry, Bruges emerged with an enhanced status (Plate 29). The decline of Champagne Fairs after their incorporation into the domain of France was going on at a time when Italian shipping had begun to make greater use of the all-sea route. Italian galley fleets organised by the republics were calling regularly at Sluys, and soon afterwards were joined by the carracks, sailing ships perhaps modelled on the Hanseatic *cogges* and used for the northern trade by individual merchants. Italians themselves brought their commerce to the markets of Bruges in the fourteenth century, forming an important part of the foreign colony. Some, indeed, found accommodation in the house of the family of van der Buerse, in front of which developed a centre of international exchange commemorated still in the word *bourse*. The Italians also brought banking business to Bruges and were the great patrons of Flemish artists such as Jan van Eyck or Hugo van der Goes.[25]

The German merchants were also attracted to Bruges in strength, partly because of the very presence of the Italians, partly because Bruges retained its major function as an entrepôt between north-western European trade and the Baltic trade, partly because of its growing importance as a terminus for the trade to the Rhine at Cologne, and partly because of the continuing importance of the cloth industry in its hinterland. The *kontor* of the Hanseatic merchants at Bruges was perhaps the most important of their four chief centres outside the sphere of the German ports themselves, and it was the only one in which the German merchants were scattered through the city rather than concentrated in a particular quarter as they were in the Steelyard of London, in Bergen and in Novgorod. The *cogges* of the Hanseatic merchants made possible a larger volume of trade, embracing timber, wheat and salt, medium-quality as well as luxury cloths, and a greater trade in fish and wine. And it was on Bruges that much of the entrepôt trade was concentrated as long as the foreign merchants could be sure of meeting each other there in order to transact business.

But even during the course of the fourteenth century when the influence of the German merchants in Bruges was at its height, the cloth industry of Flanders was losing ground to that of Brabant and the rural industry of the south. The maintenance of Bruges as a focus of trade had already begun to depend not so much on the activity of its immediate hinterland as on its rôle as a meeting-place— and the meeting-place, as such, could well be in Ardenbourg, Dordrecht, Antwerp or elsewhere. The Italian merchants from time to time threatened to use Dordrecht; the Hanseatic merchants left Bruges for Ardenbourg in 1280 and 1307 and for Dordrecht in 1388, though they later returned, and even as late as 1478 felt confident enough in the future of Bruges, on the eve of its total eclipse as an important port, to build the magnificent house of the *Oosterlingen* (the eastern merchants). The policies of Bruges towards its foreign merchants may have been a little more rigid than those of its competitors in the fifteenth century, but the reasons for the transference of commercial activity to Antwerp seem more likely to rest in more positive advantages than this. And while it is true that Bruges lost its access to the sea during the course of the fifteenth century, this was more the result, perhaps, of human neglect than of acceleration in the rate of silting.

Antwerp

It is obvious that the changes in the routes to the south, now passing by way of Brabant to the Rhine rather than south to the Champagne fairs, would favour the Scheldt and the Brabantine port of Antwerp, but the rise of Antwerp was also closely related to changes in the physical and political geography of its estuary. Before the fifteenth century the area as a whole was shared by Brabant, Flanders and

Zeeland, each jealous of its tolls and the privileges of its merchants. In the fourteenth century Antwerp had suffered from the subordination of its interests to those of Flanders, and it was not until the early fifteenth century that political unity at the hands of the Burgundians changed the position of Antwerp from a location which was marginal and vulnerable, to a location which was central and had an outlet to the sea in friendly hands.

During the Middle Ages, the estuary of the Scheldt consisted of a maze of shallow channels in which there were three main routes for the shipping which used it.[26] The first, and for long the most important, was the Hanseatic route between the Baltic, Holland and Bruges, a route which avoided the open sea, seeking shelter as much as possible behind the dunes and offshore islands of Friesland, turning south through the Zuider Zee and then by way of natural streams and artificial water-courses to the delta area, following a route behind the shelter of Walcheren and Noord Beveland to Antwerp, or more commonly, to Bruges. The second of the delta routes was a more direct one to the Baltic lands, following a line roughly north from the Scheldt estuary between Tolen and Zuid Beveland; this carried most traffic in the later Middle Ages and saw the early rise of towns along its course, notably Bergen-op-Zoom. Finally the third route from Antwerp was the Honte-Wielingen route just to the north of the Flemish coast. All of these except the last are unrecognisable on modern maps, for drainage, reclamation and flooding have substantially changed the aspect of the delta area, as shown in Fig. 7:6. The shallowness of the approaches meant that from an early time the transhipment of goods going up to Antwerp was necessary at towns on the islands of the delta region. Middleburg, Bergen-op-Zoom and Zieriksee were the most important of several towns and villages which shared in this early trade.

Two important consequences followed. First, the trade and shipping which grew with the expansion of Brabant were stimulated through the whole of the delta rather than in a single port. Secondly, in the early stages of its growth, Antwerp failed to develop its own carrying trade on anything like the same scale that the great ports elsewhere had done in the active and vigorous stages of early growth. Tolls, revenues and dues had been collected in the delta towns, shipping and shipbuilding had been stimulated there and much of the carrying trade remained in the hands of alien merchants rather than those of Antwerp men.

From the late fourteenth century and in the early fifteenth, how-ever, physical conditions in the delta area changed significantly. Only a few feet were enough to make the difference between a channel that was navigable for ocean-going ships and a channel passable only

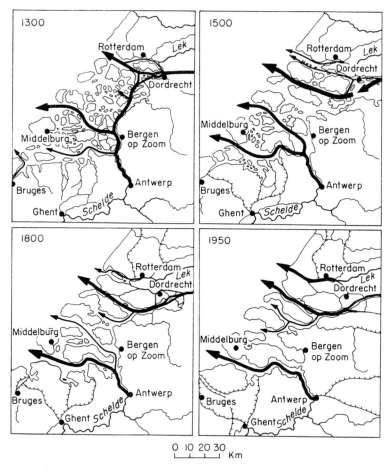

Fig. 7:6 Trade routes in the Low Countries and the approaches to Antwerp

by barges and lighters. Up to the fourteenth century the reclamation of new land from the sea had narrowed the tidal approaches to the Scheldt estuary, which led to an increase in tidal scour and the deep-ening of navigable channels. The great inundations of the period

1375–1425 which created so much devastation over all the Low Countries undoubtedly caused new changes, brought about by the tidal scour of the receding floods. At all events, the Honte-Weilingen route was navigable by ocean-going shipping during the second half of the fifteenth century. From 1450 ocean-going ships had new access to Antwerp itself. In the 1520s between six and thirty-six ships a year paid the anchorage money due on direct traffic, and in the 1530s these had increased to 200 to 300 ships a year. Transhipment did not die out, for several reasons: the Scheldt was a difficult passage for the sailing ships of the day and port facilities were still so limited as to delay traffic seriously on occasion. Moreover, it was often more convenient to unload partial cargoes for Antwerp at the delta ports rather than undergo the devious passage up the river. The physical changes which made it possible for ships to sail directly up to Antwerp were certainly not a prime cause of its growth but they must have greatly facilitated expansion at a critical period. It is worth noting that the new opportunities for direct passage to Antwerp were much resented by the delta ports and particularly Middleburg, which had benefited most from the need for transhipment. Bindoff has written of the ways in which the delta ports of Zeeland and Flanders attempted systematically during the fifteenth century to replace the physical need for ships to stop at their harbours by legal requirements to pay tolls or satisfy staple rights. Antwerp proved well able to hold its own against its neighbours in the battle of the tolls and of staple rights which followed. Traffic on the increasingly important Honte route was allowed to move unhindered; Middelburg succeeded in establishing itself as a wine staple, but the growth of Antwerp was never seriously affected. In the movement of trade and industry towards Brabant in the thirteenth and fourteenth centuries, Antwerp had acquired new significance in relation to the convergence of land routes. The overland road from Cologne to Antwerp was carrying more and more of the trade from the south, and it was a good route through an area of dry, well-drained sandy soils and country in which provisions were readily available and cheap.

The port expanded very rapidly to the point in mid-sixteenth century of which it has been said of it that 'Never since has there been a market which concentrated to such a degree the trade of all the important commercial nations of the world'.[27] Perhaps the most striking feature of its growth is the way in which the merchants who were attracted to it, sometimes by a relatively minor advantage, in turn drew other merchants there, so that by a cumulative process a population of alien merchants, bankers, financiers and entrepreneurs congregated to make of Antwerp the centre *par excellence* of north-western European trade at a time when the nature of trade was changing; when there was a greater range and variety of products associated with the rising standard of living of the Renaissance period; when financial functions were becoming important; and when above all, European trade was beginning to feel the impact of new discoveries overseas.

As long as Antwerp had been tied to Flanders in the fourteenth century its interests had sometimes been sacrificed to those of Bruges by the policy of the Count of Flanders but during the fifteenth century and after the advent of the house of Burgundy, Antwerp was able to compete with Bruges and its interests had the support of the administration. English merchants had been established there in 1338, but reappeared in greater numbers and on a more permanent basis in the early fifteenth century. The English Merchant Adventurers who used Antwerp after 1407 were at first a relatively unimportant group in the trade of north-west Europe, welcomed at smaller ports such as Bergen, Antwerp and Middelburg, but neglected at the larger ports. They were associated, however, with the rapidly rising export of English cloth during the fifteenth century and their initially modest association with Antwerp was of great benefit to its growth.[28]

Perhaps it was the presence of the English merchants and their cloth which attracted the German merchants from Cologne. This in turn implied the presence of the Hanseatic League which obtained privileges in 1490 though it was never as important politically as it was in Bruges and never dominated the trade of Antwerp. The connections with the Rhineland seem fairly quickly to have brought also the south German merchants, from about 1479. The south German merchants came from an area of expanding commerce associated not only with the growth of overland trade through Germany to the north Italian plain but also with the growing wealth of minerals and manufactured goods from that part of Europe: the cottons, fustians and arms of south Germany and the Swiss plateau; the copper and silver of the Erzgebirge and Styria. Antwerp thus became the centre from which the developing banking interests of the south German merchants from Frankfurt, Augsburg and Nürnburg were spread throughout north-western Europe. The Welsers, the Fuggers, the

Hochstätters and Tuchers, important in the finance of the House of Habsburg and in the development of mineral resources as far apart as the English Lake District, southern Spain and South America, all used Antwerp as a major centre of contact and exchange.

The overland routes from Antwerp by way of the Rhine or south to Trier and across Luxemburg to Basle, contributed in no small measure to the nodal position of Antwerp in relation to the routes of all Europe. The overland traffic is better known than most because records of the duty levied on merchandise exported from the Low Countries have survived. Overland routes were safer and more regular than the sea route and could be used during the winter.[29] They were becoming highly organised, too, as transport firms made themselves responsible for arranging relays of carriers on particular sections of the route. Sea routes were followed which could be varied according to the exigencies of war, but the major routes were those which went by way of the Rhine to Basle and the St Gotthard Pass to Milan or by way of Frankfurt and Nürnburg to the Brenner and to Venice, or even further east by way of Salzburg to Tarvisio. Italian, Flemish and German merchants were the most frequent on these routes, though Portuguese and the French were represented among the important firms. Over two-thirds of the goods travelling along these routes were not, however, of Low Country origin in the two years for which detailed studies have been made. Kerseys from East Anglia were the largest single item and it was a trade in which English cloth dominated the south-bound traffic. Venice, Ancona, Milan and Genoa were the chief destinations, Flemish and German merchants concentrating on Venice which itself re-exported to Mediterranean ports, Italian merchants often using Ancona, however, if they wished to handle the re-export trade themselves.

Although the overland traffic could move throughout the year, March to July were the busiest months.[30] Goods which were destined for the Levant had to arrive in Italian ports before the end of the Mediterranean sailing season. Since the overland journey could take up to three months, goods leaving in August would arrive in Italy too late for shipment. Indeed, the traffic for Venice and Ancona, much of which was destined for re-export showed much greater seasonal fluctuation than that for other Italian cities. Guicciardini may have exaggerated when he remarked that there were 500 ships in the river, 200 passenger coaches a day and 2,000 waggons a day of which 1,000 were bringing provisions, but the duties levied on overland trade record the departure of an average of some forty convoys per month from Antwerp, reaching a total of two a day in the busiest season.

Italian merchants who came by overland routes found their merchant seamen well established, for the Italian galleys had long been accustomed to use Antwerp as a possible alternative to Bruges. The Portuguese seamen had followed the Venetians along the western sea routes to Antwerp by 1460, and from 1488, when Maximilian called upon the nations to transfer themselves from Bruges to Antwerp following Brabantine support for his policy against the rebellious Flemings, the Portuguese trade moved much more completely to Antwerp, especially after they had transferred the wine staple there in 1499. The Portuguese contact had been built upon an initially modest trade of salt and wine in exchange for cloth and other northern products, but from the time of Portuguese penetration along the African coast in the 1460s they were also attracted by the south German and Austrian copper to be found in Antwerp, for copper rings and bracelets were among the chief of the commodities which the Portuguese were trading for ivory, gold, Guinea pepper and slaves along the African coasts. It was therefore a natural consequence that Portuguese pepper should be brought to Antwerp for distribution in 1501 after the rounding of the Cape and the establishment of direct contact with the Asiatic trade. The series of accidents which made Charles V ruler of the Low Countries as well as of Spain brought a political connection with Iberia which strengthened commercial links between Antwerp and Spain and helped to direct to it a flow of precious metals which was to become a flood of silver before the end of Antwerp's greatness.

Spanish bullion from the New World, like the silver resources of the south German banking houses, helped to nourish the development of Antwerp as a financial centre at a time when financial operations were being elaborated along more modern lines and were becoming a much more important adjunct to trade than ever before. Speculation in foreign exchanges was developing, marine insurance was being pioneered; the manipulation of interest rates, the refinement of arbitrage operations, dealings in futures and bills of exchange were all new developments which enhanced the importance of Antwerp as the centre of exchange in north-western Europe during the first half of the sixteenth century.

The trade of Antwerp grew very rapidly indeed during the great days of its pre-eminence in the first half of the sixteenth century, though there was a period of depression from 1520 to 1530 and a period of violent fluctuation during the 1540s and 1550s. In mid-century it was undoubtedly handling about 70 to 80 per cent of the total foreign trade of the country, and between 1543 and 1545 the volume of its trade was probably about three times that of London. The composition of its trade in the heyday of prosperity was described at length and in glowing terms by Guicciardini (see page 399). English cloth alone amounted to about a third of the total value of the import trade, and Italian luxury goods about a fifth. Baltic grain and German wine were worth about a tenth of the value of import trade; French wine and Portuguese spices each about a sixteenth. In all, the lists of commodities given in exuberant detail by Guicciardini provide a revealing comment on the pattern of trade in sixteenth-century Europe.

Commercial pre-eminence gave rise to industrial functions which were nourished by the abundance of capital and the congregation of skills and knowledge among a cosmopolitan merchant population. The import and re-export of English cloth was always an important function of the town, and as in Italy many years before or in Leiden later, there grew up a finishing industry of substantial importance, using alum imported from the Papal States, dyes from new colonial products such as indigo and cochineal as well as traditional sources. Arms from Liège and south Germany were imported but Antwerp developed an arms industry of its own, as it did a glass manufacture based on skills introduced by foreign artisans. It was the Italian merchants who brought the techniques of making up satins and cloths of gold. The manufacture of soap was introduced by foreigners, and Antwerp was also the first of the northern towns in which sugar-refining made its appearance—introduced through Portuguese contacts and involving at first imports of sugar from São Thomé, the Azores and Madeira—stepping stones on the way to the New World.

Population growth reflected the rapidity of Antwerp's expansion. In 1436 it had been as large as Brussels or the university town of Louvain, with some 3,480 houses. By 1526 it contained 8,500 houses compared with 5,950 at Brussels and 3,300 in Louvain. By 1566 Guicciardini claimed for it a population of 105,000 people, and a foreign community of some 15,000, and he was probably not very far from the truth (Plate 36).

The meteoric rise of Antwerp to a position of pre-eminence among the ports of Europe in the first half of the sixteenth century may be interpreted by the historical geographer in three ways. First, the growth of the port was clearly related to the fortunes of its site and situation. It was not until physical and political changes in the delta area had occurred that the more general advantages of Antwerp's situation could be realised. The prosperity of the Brabantine towns in its immediate hinterland, the revival of overland trade to the Rhine and the growth of trade on the sea routes of north-western Europe combined to favour the Scheldt estuary. But the growth of Antwerp was also associated with the rising fortune of new merchant groups— the English Merchant Adventurers, the south German merchants and bankers, the Portuguese and the Spaniards, who lifted Antwerp above the status of Bruges, the port which had identified itself with the declining Hanseatic League, and the now moribund Flemish cloth trade. Secondly, Antwerp was 'in the right place at the right time', for it happened to be the pre-eminent port in the late fifteenth century at a time when geographical horizons were suddenly to widen immeasurably, when trade was growing rapidly again and also becoming much more varied with the rising standards of living and luxury of the Renaissance. It was a time when financial operations were becoming more complex and potentially more profitable, and when the accumulation and mobilisation of capital were receiving new emphasis.

But there is a third consideration. Some have stressed that Antwerp may also be seen as the *fortuitous* meeting-place of a varied congregation of merchants and bankers drawn from all Europe, though it may be rightly objected that the circumstances underlying this state of affairs were by no means accidental, and that, for example, the congregation of alien merchants was a logical progression from the establishment there of the English connection in the fifteenth century. The circumstances which deprived the Antwerp merchants of an active participation in the carrying trade and overseas commerce as a result of the early need for transhipment were precisely those which placed the initiative for the development of trade into the hands of alien merchants, thus encouraged to assemble in Antwerp. However this may be, it could be argued that forces were at work to concentrate the trade of Europe at a single focal point. The need for a rapid and reliable exchange of news and information about trade and shipping, finance and foreign exchanges still required the close physical proximity of merchants and their agents in a single market which was the nearest possible approximation in the sixteenth century to the economic definition of Adam Smith of the perfect market. In terms of commodity trade, too, the entrepôt function was an important one. Even for products which did not require to be processed or finished, the entrepôt received whole cargoes from a variety of sources and broke them up into small parcels for particular destinations. Cargoes of eastern goods brought from Portugal were broken into smaller lots for dispersal to destinations all over north-western Europe. Many commodities were also graded and sorted, packed and finished. That this could be an important function is indicated by the fact that one-third of the wholesale cost of English cloth at Antwerp in the sixteenth century lay in the finishing processes. The agglomeration at Antwerp of the finishing and processing industries as well as banking and the transference of both the name and the institution of the *bourse* from Bruges help to illustrate the operation of the economies of localisation which applied in this period to the concentration of trade just as they applied so strikingly to the concentration of industry in the industrial revolution and later.

The collapse of Antwerp came in the last quarter of the sixteenth century with the revolt of the Dutch and the separation of Antwerp from the sea by territory controlled by the rebels. But even before the revolt, Antwerp's decline seems already to have begun. The links which had held together merchants from so great a variety of trading countries were beginning to loosen. The Portuguese discontinued their trade in 1549, for the German merchants were now contracting to deliver copper dirctly to the Portuguese for the African trade, and the structure of the silver trade from central Europe was changing radically with the advent of bullion in unprecedented quantity from the New World. It was more important, perhaps, that a critical stage had been reached in the expansion of English cloth exports. London's exports had doubled between 1500 and 1540 but after mid-sixteenth century the market for English cloth was flooded and English merchants were now seeking to unload cloth directly on to foreign markets to the detriment of Antwerp's middleman functions. Financial crisis followed in 1557 for the money market of Antwerp had involved itself too deeply in the provision of state loans and was excessively vulnerable to the bankruptcy of Spain and France.

These were, in the long run, relatively minor matters compared with the disasters of the late sixteenth century. In 1572 the Sea Beggars had taken Flushing on Walcheren and soon demonstrated by the capture of a Portuguese spice fleet worth half a million gulden that the control of the delta islands by a hostile power was enough to strangle the trade of Antwerp. After the final reconquest of Antwerp for Spain by Parma in 1585 the lower Scheldt remained politically divided, for just as the delta region was in the hands of the rebels who had the seapower, so the mainland was held by the military power of the Spaniards. The need for transhipment was revived by the Dutch, now in control of the outports, and this inconvenience, combined with the heavy taxation of traffic going up to Antwerp, meant the ruin of the place as an international port. Financial as well as commercial functions passed to Amsterdam; and the Bourse became first a library and then a carpet factory. By 1664 an attempt to reopen Antwerp to trade seemed worth while, but this could be done only by river and canal to Ghent and then to the sea by way of Bruges. But the closure of the Scheldt to sea trade, confirmed at the final settlement between the Dutch and the Spanish in 1648, crippled Antwerp until its re-opening at the hands of revolutionary France in 1792.

The continuing importance to Antwerp of freedom of navigation in the delta area has been demonstrated again and again during its recent history as well as in the circumstances of its early history. When the independence of Belgium was assured after 1839, Antwerp's access to the sea by way of the Honte channel was guaranteed, but the navigable route to the Rhine, which had once gone by way of natural channels between Zuid Beveland and Tholen on the one hand and the mainland on the other, continued to depend on Dutch goodwill, and on the building of a canal with two locks (in 1866) on Zuid Beveland. Modern proposals, made in conjunction with the Delta plan to reclaim much more of the estuary zone for agriculture, envisage the cutting of a new canal link between Antwerp and the Rhine which will reduce shipping time from Dordrecht to Antwerp from ten or eleven to six hours (Fig. 7:7).[31] It is to follow approximately the line of the ancient sea route of the Hanseatic League which went not merely to the Rhine but also by devious ways to the Baltic sea route itself. It is, however, interesting that this new link, like earlier routes which connect Antwerp to the sea, is the subject of much delicate and careful negotiation between the Belgian government, anxious to secure a competitive position for Antwerp in the lucrative Rhine trade, and the Dutch government, anxious that the

28 *Saltings behind La Baule, western France.* The evaporation of brine in shallow basins on the salt marshes of the Bay of Bourgneuf and its neighbourhood still continues, but it provided an essential and important commodity in the developing north-western European trade of the middle ages.

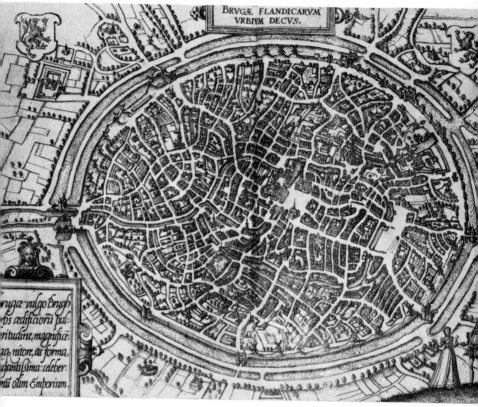

29 *Bruges* (published in Guicciardini, 1567). By the sixteenth century, Bruges had lost most of its medieval importance as a port and cloth-producing town, but the urban plan gives an indication of its size and defences, and of the importance of water transport in its interior communications.

Left. 3.30 p.m.

Belgians should pay for the construction of a canal which will, incidentally, assist in the communications network of the new lands to be reclaimed in the delta area, and also anxious to secure com-

Fig. 7:7 The proposed new Rhine – Antwerp canal

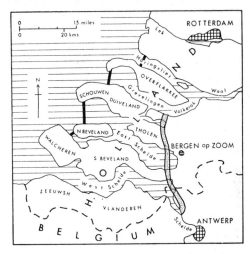

pensation for the hazard of introducing sea water from the Scheldt estuary into the reclaimed land and freshwater reservoirs to be constructed when the Delta plan is put into operation.

THE TRADE OF ANTWERP ABOUT 1566, ACCORDING TO GUICCIARDINI

With Denmark, Osterland, Livonia, Norway, Sweden, Poland and other Septentrional Countries
From: Wheat, rye, copper, brass, saltpetre, woad, madder. Austrian wools, timber, pitch, wood ash, amber, furs, leather, skins. Fish 'powdered and dried with smoake, the sunne and the wind, yea and the cold'.
To: Spices, drugs, sugar, salt. English and Flemish cloth, linens, jewels, silks, tapestry, Spanish sack and other wines.

With Germany
From: Silver, quicksilver, copper, saltpetre, armour, wools of Hesse, fustians, woad, madder, saffron, Rhenish wines.
To: Jewels, spices, drugs, sugar, English and Flemish cloth, tapestry, linen.

With France
From, by sea: Salt, woad of Toulouse, cloth of Brittany and Normandy, saffron. Wines, paper, glass.
By land: Fine woollens of Paris and Rouen, Tours and Champagne silks, silk yarn from Lyon.

To Jewels, silver, quicksilver, lead, tin, copper, brass, saltpetre. English and Flemish cloth, linens, tapestry. Austrian wool, soap, leather, furs.

With Spain
From: Jewels, gold, silver, dyes, drugs, silk, especially velvets and taffetas of Toledo. Salt, alum, wool, iron, leather, wines, oil, soap, fruits (oranges, lemons, olives, melons, dates, figs etc.), sugar and wine from Canaries.
To: Quicksilver, copper, brass, tin, lead. English and Flemish cloth, tapestry, linen, flax, corn, dried fish, butter, cheese. 'All munitions for the warres.' 'All things made with the hand of Artificers for the Spaniards, even of base condition, hate travail to the death.'

With Portugal
From: Jewels, spices, cotton, sugar, wines, oil.
To: Silver, copper, brass, lead, tin, armour.

With Barbary
From: Sugar, dyestuffs, leather.
To: Cloth, linen, metals.

With Italy and Italian States
From:
Florence—Cloth of gold and silver, brocades, satins, furs and other fine and curious works.
Naples—Satins, silks and saffron.
Sicily—Oranges, Malmsey wine.
Venice—Spices, drugs, silks and dyes.
Ancona—Spices, drugs, cotton, silk, dyes, velvets.
Genoa—Velvets, satin and coral.
To: English and Flemish cloth, linens, tin, lead, copper, brass, dyes, fish and sometimes corn.

With England
From: Over 80 per cent of imports from England were of woollen cloth, mostly undyed and unfinished. Tin, lead, fine wool sheepskins, rabbit-skins, fine furs, leather, cheese, beer, and Malmsey wine brought out of Candia to England.
To: Jewels, quicksilver, cloths of gold and silver, silks, spices, drugs, dyes, alum, cotton, linen goods, says, tapestries, hops, glass, fish, iron and copper, and 'all kinds of munitions for the warres'.

With Scotland
From: Furs and skins, leather, wool and cloths, 'but evil wrought'.

REFERENCES

Abbreviations:
Ann. E.S.C.   *Annales, Economies, Sociétés, Civilisations*, Paris.
C.E.H.E.   *Cambridge Economic History of Europe.* Vol. 2, *Trade and Industry in the Middle Ages*, ed. M. M. Postan and E. E. Rich, Cambridge, 1952.
E.H.R.   *Economic History Review.*

1. E. FASANO-GUARINI, 'Au 16ᵉ siècle: Comment naviguent les galères', *Ann. E.S.C.*, vol. 16, 1961, pp. 279–96.
2. F. LUZZATTO, *Economic History of Italy to the beginning of the sixteenth century*, London, 1961, p. 87.
3. A. R. LEWIS, *Naval Power and Trade in the Mediterranean, 500–1100*, Princeton, 1951.
4. R. S. LOPEZ, 'The trade of medieval Europe: the south', *C.E.H.E.*, vol. 2, p. 289.
5. Luzatto, *Economic History of Italy*, pp. 53–4.
6. R. D. FACE, 'The *vectuarii* in the overland commerce between Champagne and southern Europe', *E.H.R.*, second series, vol. 12, 1959–60, pp. 237–46.
7. R. D. FACE, 'Techniques of business in the trade between the fairs of Champagne and southern Europe', *E.H.R.*, second series, vol. 10, 1957–8, p. 427.
8. E. CHAPIN, *Les Villes de foires de Champagne*, Paris, 1935.
9. E. CARUS-WILSON, 'The woollen industry', *C.E.H.E.*, vol. 2, pp. 387–97.
10. M. M. POSTAN, 'Some economic evidence of declining population in the later Middle Ages', *E.H.R.*, second series, vol. 2, 1949–50, pp. 221–46.
    R. S. LOPEZ and H. A. MISKIMIN, 'The economic depression of the renaissance', *E.H.R.*, second series, vol. 14, 1961–2, pp. 408–26.
11. M. MALOWIST, 'Les mouvements d'expansion en Europe au 15ᵉ et 16ᵉ siècles', *Ann. E.S.C.*, vol. 17, 1962, pp. 923–1929.
12. B. H. SLICHER VAN BATH, *The Agrarian History of Western Europe, A.D. 500–1850*, London, 1963, pp. 137–43.
13. J. U. NEF, 'Mining and metallurgy in medieval civilisation', *C.E.H.E.*, vol. 2, pp. 469–73.
14. H. PIRENNE, *Histoire de Belgique*, 7 vols, Brussels, 1902–32.
15. Carus-Wilson, *C.E.H.E.*, vol. 2, pp. 355–428.
16. H. LAURENT, *Un grand Commerce d'exportation au moyen âge: la Draperie des Pays-Bas en France et dans les pays méditerranés, 12ᵉ–14ᵉ siècle*, Paris, 1935.
17. H. VAN WERVEKE, 'Industrial growth in the Middle Ages: the cloth industry of Flanders', *E.H.R.*, second series, vol. 6, 1953–4, pp. 237–54.
18. H. VAN WERVEKE, *Bruges et Anvers: huit siècles de commerce flamand*, Brussels, 1944.

402 AN HISTORICAL GEOGRAPHY OF WESTERN EUROPE

19. G. ESPINAS, *La Draperie dans la Frandre française au moyen âge*, 2 vols., Paris, 1923.
20. Werveke, *E.H.R.*, second series, vol. 6, 1953-4, pp. 237-54.
21. L. DECHESNE, *Histoire économique et sociale de la Belgique*, Liège, 1932, pp. 145-57.
22. V. BARBOUR, *Studies in the Development of Capitalism in Amsterdam in the seventeenth century*, John Hopkins Studies in Historical and Political Science, no. 67, New Haven, 1950, p. 13.
23. Werveke, *Bruges et Anvers*.
24. A. E. VERHULST, 'Les origines et l'histoire ancienne de la ville de Bruges', *Le Moyen Âge*, vol. 15, 1960, pp. 37-63.
25. M. VERKEST, *Bruges*, Bruges, 1952.
26. S. T. BINDOFF, *The Scheldt Question*, London, 1945.
27. S. T. BINDOFF, 'The greatness of Antwerp', *New Cambridge Modern History*, vol. 2: *The Reformation, 1520-59*, ed. G. R. Elton, Cambridge, 1958, p. 50.
28. J. VAN HOUTTE, 'Anvers au 15ᵉ et 16ᵉ siècle', *Ann. E.S.C.*, vol. 16, 1961, pp. 248-78.
29. W. BRULEZ, 'L'exportation des Pays-Bas vers l'Italie par voie de terre, au milieu du 16ᵉ siècle', *Ann. E.S.C.*, vol. 14, 1959, pp. 461-91.
30. L. GUICCIARDINI, *Description de tout le pais bas*, Antwerp, 1567, pp. 154-69.
31. *The Guardian*, 6 February 1965, p. 5.

CHAPTER 8

EXPANSION OVERSEAS AND ITS IMPACT ON THE ECONOMIC GEOGRAPHY OF EUROPE

It is a commonplace that the discovery of the New World and the use of the all-sea route by the Portuguese to the Far East revolutionised the geography of Europe. The Mediterranean, according to this time-honoured stereotype, was reduced from a main highway of trade and commerce to a landlocked backwater and the states of northern and central Italy, keystone of an older structure of commerce, lost the greater part of their transit function. Eastern Spain declined to the advantage of the great Atlantic ports: Seville, Cadiz and Lisbon. And the future was to lie with the Atlantic-facing ports which grew with the development of colonial commerce—Bordeaux, La Rochelle, Nantes, Lorient, St Malo, Bristol, Liverpool, Glasgow, Amsterdam, Hamburg and Bremen. Yet this was a change which took a very considerable time to work itself out, and even at the end of the sixteenth century or the early seventeenth the rosy future of the colonial trade and of those areas which participated in it were by no means evident. And there were many other factors besides the colonial trade which worked towards the expansion of western ports in France and England and towards the decline of northern and central Italy.

It would be wrong to overemphasise the impact of the overseas world as a factor making for fundamental geographical change in Western Europe between 1500 and 1800, and some attention must therefore be devoted briefly to other major trends of the period which were making for geographical change on a large scale. Moreover, the shifts in commercial prosperity which have been outlined above demand closer consideration of the mechanisms by which geographical changes were brought about, particularly in the absence of technological change and the revaluation of physical resources which this has frequently involved. It is abundantly clear, for example, that the time-lag between the decline of Mediterranean giants and the rise of the newcomers to international trade is a long one. It may thus be helpful to draw attention to the frictions that delayed rapid geographical adjustment, or, to put it another way, the inertia which operated to delay change. As the patterns of change are too complex to be discussed at adequate length for the whole period and for the whole area of Western Europe, it is necessary to concentrate on several aspects: the relationships of Spain and the New World in the sixteenth century as an example of the immediate impact of overseas discoveries on one major area, followed by a more general study of the Mediterranean and Italy in the sixteenth and early seventeenth century and the beginnings of decline. The reaction of France to the expansion of colonial trade will be very briefly outlined with respect to the western ports, but it has also seemed worth while to make a more detailed study of the Dutch Republic in order to integrate the overseas developments into the historical geography of intra-European trade.

In the most general of terms, the modern world was marked off from that of medieval times by basic movements, one of which was the expansion of Europe overseas. Others were the Renaissance, the Reformation, and the rise of the nation state and of centralised government. Each of these basic changes was very closely linked to the other and also to the dominant features of the economic history of the period, the rise of commercial capitalism and the participation of the state in economic affairs, especially through the policies collectively labelled as mercantilist. The political geography of contemporary Europe would be dominated by analysis of the distributions, strengths and interactions of Lutherans, Calvinists, Roman Catholics and others, and it would no doubt be concerned with the link between religion and the rising power of the nation state or, in central Europe, of the principalities under the Empire. It is always necessary to bear in mind the strength and vehemence of religious antipathies in, for example, the Wars of Religion in France, the Thirty Years' War, the Dutch revolt, or the expulsion of the Moors from Spain. But in terms of the developing economic geography of Europe two factors are important. One is the association between the Protestant ethic and the rise of capitalism,[1] for if motivations towards the exploitation of resources or the potential commercial value of particular locations and sites differed according to religious persuasion, then this would be a matter of importance. Among the Huguenots of France or the Calvinists of Holland and Zeeland, such regional variations of enterprise have been suspected, but it is often difficult to establish whether the religious affiliation is a primary element or not in the development of such places as La Rochelle or Amsterdam. Yet there was frequently, in France, for example, a tendency for the merchant and the artisan to embrace the reformed religion while the peasant and the landowner remained faithful to Rome. The second factor of importance is the diffusion of skills and techniques that followed the disruption of old faiths or the repression of new ones, and the migration of craftsmen and merchants to more favourable climates of opinion. Migrants from Antwerp and the Low Countries introduced the weaving of cotton and flax and the new draperies—worsteds, serges and baize—to England in the sixteenth century; French Huguenots took their skills in the manufacture of linens, silks, lace and other fine textiles to the United Provinces in the late seventeenth century after the revocation of the Edict of Nantes in 1685.[2] Examples could be multiplied, for the spread of skills and expertise, accomplished by a relatively small number of migrants, was nevertheless regarded as important by contemporary witnesses, particularly if it contributed to the establishment of a new industry or the greater perfection of an old one.

The intellectual revolution of the Renaissance need not here concern us, but one mundane aspect of the growth of interest in secular matters was the enormous and far-reaching increase in the range and variety of consumer goods: rich and voluminous clothing of silks as well as woollen cloth, of cottons and Indian muslins, linen and lace; great elaboration in the quality and abundance of household furnishings—carpets, tapestries, mirrors and glass, furniture and upholstery; the development of more complex arms and armour, carriages and coaches; and changes in food and drink that almost constitute a gastronomic revolution in the seventeenth and eighteenth centuries. Coffee, sugar, tea, chocolate, the potato, tobacco and the tomato are a few of the new imports from the New World, to which were added new developments in Europe itself—gin and brandies, the fortified wines of Portugal and Xerez; the vintage wines of Bordeaux. Most of these new products were luxuries and they were consumed by and produced for a small proportion of the total population. They implied the spread of new retail functions and new trades into the smaller towns as well as the metropolitan centres and thus they contributed in no small measure to the urbanisation of the period, particularly since many of the consumer goods were blended or 'tailor-made' by craftsmen to individual tastes. The provision of goods and services tended to become more centralised in the growing towns and also more specialised. Yet because of the absence of large-scale mass consumption, there were still relatively few pressures towards large-scale and standardised cheap production, least of all in societies like those of France, Spain or Austria which were so strongly differentiated in social as well as economic terms.

Thirdly, the rise of the nation state and of centralised government had most important geographical as well as economic implications. First of all, absolute monarchy and the centralisation of government involved the creation of a bureaucracy and the centralisation of decisions (to an absurd extent in the Spain of Philip II); it was frequently accompanied by the centralisation of the court and also of a military garrison. As described above (p. 333), this was a situation which led directly to the growth of the great capitals of Western Europe, swollen with populations whose demands for food and clothing were a considerable factor making for change in the countrysides around. The centralisation of bureaucracy, army, court and merchants also involved the creation of good internal communication so that the writ of authority could be delivered rapidly even to remoter regions. In France emphasis was put in the late sixteenth and seventeenth centuries on the creation of royal posts, the improvements of roads and the beginnings of canal-building (the Briare canal from the Seine to the Loire, completed in 1640). Sir William Temple was greatly appreciative of the facility of movement to any part of the United Provinces, by sea, river or inland waterway. Improved roads were often intended primarily for the rapid movement of troops, the rapid dissemination and collection of news and information by the state, the easy movement of nobility from their estates to the Court, or to maintain the supply of foodstuffs for the capital city, a matter of political as well as economic importance. The roads to the capitals and the frontiers tended to be favoured at the expense of those in other peripheral regions, as in France. But the improved communications of the eighteenth century were ultimately important in facilitating the development of commercial agriculture and localised industry on a wider basis, in spite of Arthur Young's protestations in southern France, for example, of their under-use.

In economic terms, good internal communications also assisted in the creation of a single internal market within which regional particularisms might be broken down and regional self-sufficiency ended. But the reduction and abolition of tolls, duties and local taxes often proved difficult or impossible, even in an absolute monarchy. France retained a complex system of customs areas even after Colbert's efforts; and Hamburg retained some privileges as a sign of its ancient autonomy even to 1939.

Externally, the centralised nation states were preoccupied by the maintenance of military, political and economic power and prestige. Agriculture, industry and trade were manipulated with the idea of increasing the strength of the state. Policies were aimed at building internal strength and revenue by stimulating the growth of population and by aiming at self-sufficiency as far as possible.[3] External trade should yield an export surplus which would bring in precious metals. Export industries were therefore encouraged, the export of money or precious metals discouraged or prohibited; the import of manufactured goods was also discouraged, especially if they could be produced at home. Thus encouragement was often offered to home industries and to the immigration of foreign craftsmen who might help in producing substitutes for imported manufactures. Economic policies varied from one state to another and depended greatly on the economic geography of the country itself and on its needs. But the general effect was obviously to favour the state with a large protected internal market at the expense of the small—to favour France, England, Prussia and Austria, for example, at the expense of Lombardy, Venetia, Tuscany, the United Provinces or the smaller German principalities.

The expansion of Europe overseas and its impact on Europe may, perhaps, be divided into two phases. During the sixteenth century the great empires of Spain and Portugal supplied commodities which were low in bulk and high in price, but even so, their contribution to the total trade of Europe was slight against the massive but unspectacular bulk of intra-European trade in wine, cloth, fish, salt, grain and timber. But during the seventeenth century conditions began to change, and by its end colonial trade was beginning to play a major part in the commerce of several West European countries and to compete in terms of value, if not in volume, with the intra-European trade. In the New World, the development of a plantation economy involved a highly speculative and occasionally lucrative trade in slaves which was part of the triangular trading systems of the North Atlantic; and a series of new commodities was added to the older staples of the colonial trade as plantations were developed and output expanded: sugar, tobacco, indigo, cotton, chocolate and later coffee. In the East Indian trade, spices and pepper were supplemented by sugar, coffee, tea, Japanese copper, Chinese tea, silk and porcelain, and Indian cottons. Tropical woods were added to the repertoire of the cabinet-maker and the coach-maker; furs, dyestuffs, and other products were hunted or collected. These new additions to the imports of Western Europe often had the important characteristic that they needed further processing and thus stimulated new manufacturing industries, while the traditional industries of Europe were in turn stimulated by the demands of wealthy planters in the New World for cloth, furniture, metal goods and so on. So too, the North American Indian and the merchant of southeast Asia, by their demands for cloth and metal goods, helped to generate industrial and commercial development based on the great ports. By mid-eighteenth century the ports of the western seaboards from Bordeaux to Glasgow were beginning to emerge as important centres of new expansion, but the full effects of this commercial revolution were not felt until the eighteenth century, on the very eve of industrial change in England.

OVERSEAS TRADE AND THE MEDITERRANEAN IN THE SIXTEENTH CENTURY

Spices and the Portuguese

Portuguese seamen and merchants had begun to penetrate northwards along the Atlantic coasts to the ports of England and Flanders in the fourteenth century, before turning their attention to more southerly shores where they were encouraged by the dreams of Prince Henry the Navigator[4] and by the conquest of the African foothold of Ceuta as the beginning, perhaps, of an even greater reconquest of Islam. The Portuguese had assimilated Arab and Mediterranean knowledge of cartography, astronomy and surveying and had borrowed from Arab and Asiatic tradition to construct their lateen-sailed caravels which could sail much closer to the wind than contemporary square-rigged northern ships. The caravels were limited in size and difficult to put about, but they were easy to work in oceanic conditions of regular winds. Astronomical methods of navigation which were of little use in the Mediterranean were more valuable in the Atlantic where approximations were often adequate, and where it was often more important to know latitude, which could be more accurately measured, than longitude, still very difficult to establish.

With ships such as these, and with the combined square- and lateen-sailed ships that spread eventually throughout Europe, the Portuguese had pushed slowly along the African coast in the fifteenth century, tapping first the gold, ivory and Guinea pepper of West Africa and then penetrating to the Cape of Good Hope in the voyage of Bartolomeu Dias in 1487. Vasco da Gama's successful voyage of 1497 to East Africa and to Calicut, a major spice port of the Indian Ocean, led the way to the organisation of regular annual fleets and to the establishment of Portuguese naval supremacy in the Indian Ocean. Cabral led the first of many such royal fleets and although only six of his thirteen ships returned to Lisbon in 1501, their cargoes of spices covered the cost of the whole expedition and Portuguese spices were being sold that year in Antwerp. In 1507 Sokotra was seized, and Hormuz occupied in the same year. In 1510 Goa was conquered and the Portuguese network of strategic points in the Indian Ocean successfully strangled the Muslim trade from India to the Levant and closed the waiting agencies of the Mediterranean ports. The early control of the spice trade was maintained for some time by the Portuguese naval supremacy, and by the royal monopoly of the trade, though this was being slowly undermined by the expansion of private trade in the East. Control of the trade was, indeed, greatly facilitated because the trade routes were strongly channelled either through the Sunda Straits or the Malacca Straits, and because the sources of the spices were highly localised. The pepper for the European trade came largely from Malabar, since the other sources, Kedah and western Java, supplied regions to the north and east. Ginger also came from Malabar, cinnamon from Ceylon, cloves from the Moluccas, and nutmeg and mace from the Banda Islands.[5]

The effect of the diversion of the spice trade from the Levant routes to the Atlantic and to Antwerp was immediate and disastrous. In 1504 the Venetian galleys arrived in Alexandria and Beirut to find no spices. England was buying Portuguese spices in Antwerp and south German merchants were buying there in preference to their traditional market in Venice. Castile and France were soon buying Portuguese spices, and so too were the Genoese and the Venetians themselves. Many of the Levantine firms suffered bankruptcy, and the Turks were able to occupy Egypt and Syria from 1517.

Yet the Portuguese hold on the Far Eastern trade depended on naval supremacy and control over the Muslim trade of the Indian Ocean and this was not completely maintained. The Portuguese stranglehold on the spices entering Europe was relaxed as a result of piracy, corruption, inefficiency and shipping losses, added to a divergence of interest between the private traders and the royal officials charged with maintaining the royal monopoly. Trade began to flow again along the old channels through the Persian Gulf and the Red Sea to the Levantine ports.[6] The Venetian fleets continued to visit the east Mediterranean ports and acquired new agencies under Turkish rule. In Egypt, Venice was established in Cairo and at Alexandria, where Genoa, Ragusa and France were also represented. In Syria the Venetians established a colony at Aleppo to be nearer to the route from Baghdad and Basra by which the spices came. By mid-sixteenth century the spice trade had revived so much that the annual movement of spices through the Levant was probably as great as it had ever been before 1500. It is true that very many strong and established trading interests were concerned in the revival of the old trades—the Venetians, the Turks in Egypt and Syria, the Arab traders of the Indian Ocean, but it is also clear that there was a very considerable expansion in the European demand for spices at a time of growing population and prosperity. Moreover, the other major contribution of the new European expansion overseas—the silver from the Americas—gave Europe the wherewithal to pay for an expansion of its imports in a trade that had traditionally been a deficit one. The spices and the other Far Eastern produce to enter Europe through the Levant were only a part of the trade which the Mediterranean ports had conducted in Syria and Egypt. Cotton, wool, leather, carpets and textiles, raisins, currants, dates and figs from the Levant itself were of substantial importance. Indeed, the final eclipse of the Mediterranean spice trade only came after 1600 when the Dutch were able to control the sources of the spices and the Indian Ocean trade as well as the link to Europe. But by then the English Levant company, the French and the Dutch had ousted the Italian ports completely from the remaining Levantine traffic and the Venetian fleets ceased altogether to visit the Levant after 1571. Thus, the impact of overseas discovery in the Far East on the Mediterranean was by no means catastrophic, and although the participants in the Mediterranean trade were changing, the end of the spice trade was certainly not so sudden as one might expect and its effects could easily be exaggerated.

Silver and the Spaniards

In the Americas, the voyage of Columbus in 1492 had been followed up by a flood of exploratory voyages which soon discovered the major lineaments of the American coastline. By 1513 Balboa had reached the Pacific and only a few years later Magellan set out on his voyage of circumnavigation. In 1519 Mexico was conquered and in 1532 Pizarro and his men brought about the downfall of the Inca Empire. By mid-sixteenth century all of the chief centres of population in tropical America were in Spanish hands.[7]

The impact of the New World on the economic geography of Spain and of the western Mediterranean may be examined under three headings: the ways in which the trade with the New World and its settlers affected the geography of industry and agriculture in Spain itself and to a lesser extent in other parts of Western Europe; secondly, the geographical effect of the import of bullion to Spain and Europe from the New World; and thirdly the ways in which the organisation of trade and economic relations with the New World posed a new geographical problem for the Spanish Crown.

Spain had been presented with a geographical problem. The sheer extent of the coastline which was to be preserved for a Spanish monopoly presented new problems of scale to Europeans accustomed to thinking in terms of the Mediterranean and its Levantine or North African agencies. Portugal faced a similar problem in the Far East, of course, but there was a further problem which was primarily Spain's. For whereas Portugal was concerned to make trading contacts with peoples on a comparable level of culture, and could therefore use the type of trading post and agency that had served well in the Mediterranean trade, Spain had to organise settlement and trade in a much more direct way among peoples whose level of culture was much lower than or completely different from that of Europe.

It was, of course, assumed that the trade with the New World should be a monopoly in precisely the same way that, for example, Venetian possessions in the eastern Mediterranean or Aragonese possessions in southern Italy and Sicily were regarded as the exclusive preserve of Venetian or Aragonese shipping. Since it was Isabella who had financed Columbus and who laid claim to that part of the New World to the west of the line laid down at the so-called Treaty of Tordesillas in 1494, it was Castile which organised relations with the New World and held the initial monopoly.[8] The Council of the Indies was set up under Isabella to control the affairs of the New World; the *Casa de Contratación* was set up in 1503, initially to deal with the trade of the Crown to the Indies, later becoming the organisation to deal with all the American trade. It inspected cargoes and shipping and arranged for their protection, collected customs duties and the protection tax, and controlled all of the trade to and from the Americas, concerning itself particularly, of course, with the imports of bullion. It was responsible also for a hydrographic bureau and a school of navigation and cartography which made important advances in knowledge and of which great explorers such as Amerigo Vespucci, Sebastian Cabot and Juan de Solis were pilots-major.

The *consulado* of Seville, a gild of merchants with a subsidiary organisation at Cadiz, held from 1543 the trading monopoly which was officially strictly confined to Spanish merchants, though this, like so many of the Spanish monopolistic devices, was undermined by the thinly disguised and indirect participation of foreign merchants. The Genoese in particular played a dominant rôle. There had been a Genoese colony in Seville from the fourteenth century, but their trade, number and importance increased enormously in the sixteenth century as they handled much of the growing export of foodstuffs, clothing and manufactured goods to the New World and took a leading part in credit and finance and in the new but expanding slave trade.[9] The ports trading direct to the Americas were mainly Seville and Cadiz. Between 1529 and 1573 trade was opened up through other ports in Castile and León though trade from the New World still had to come to the Guadalquivir, and only a few ships of Málaga and Corunna gained much advantage from this relaxation of the Sevillian monopoly. The shipping to the New World was further organised from 1537 into the two great treasure fleets a year sailing between Seville and Cadiz and the central American ports: the *Galleons* to Panama and the mainland, and the *Flota* to Mexico and the Caribbean. Vera Cruz in Mexico, Porto Bello, Cartagena and Havana were the great assembly points. The system reached a peak in mid-sixteenth century (when there were 874 sailings) and another at the end of the century, but the general average of sailings remained fairly constant from the 1520s to the early seventeenth century after which rapid decline set in.[10] The average size of shipping, however, increased from some 70 tons in 1504 to

391 in 1641–5, and gross tonnage entering and leaving the Andalusian ports increased from 15,680 tons in 1506–10 to 273,560 tons in 1606–10. But by the early seventeenth century the Spanish monopoly of the New World trade had long been ineffective. Foreign merchants participated illegally through the *Consulado*; some five-sixths of the cargoes of the legitimate shipping were estimated to be of foreign origin; there were losses by piracy and above all, English, French, and Dutch ships were trading directly and illicitly with the Spanish colonies, particularly from bases such as Curaçao, Jamaica or Buenos Aires.

Finally, emigration too was strictly controlled. With the aim of maintaining religious purity in the New World, heretics, Jews and infidels were to be strictly excluded. At first, Castilians only were allowed to go, then Spaniards, and then under Charles V any of his subjects were allowed to migrate, with permission, and provided they were faithful to the Catholic religion. Some non-Spaniards did migrate: a few Flemish and Genoese and some Portuguese after 1580. South German bankers such as the Fuggers and Welsers were allowed to participate in trading ventures and were granted concessions, notably in Venezuela.

For a time in the sixteenth century the impact of the New World appeared to generate a new and thriving regional development in agriculture and industry, but the initial impetus was lost and by the seventeenth century decline had intervened. Andalusia, the source of so many of the early emigrants and of many of the agricultural techniques exported to the New World, prospered in the sixteenth century, chiefly through the demands of the colonists for its fish, wines, grain, salt and olive oil. Seville itself was the town to benefit most, of course, and its soap, salt, cloth, pottery and silk industries were all of some significance. Its population increased from some 15,000 in the early sixteenth century to 90,000 by 1594. In northern Spain the iron industry of Bilbao was one of the most important in Western Europe, competing with Liège and Namur and only slightly less important than Styria as a supplier of high-quality iron, produced near tidewater from local supplies of good haematite ore and the abundant charcoal-timber of the Cantabrian Mountains. The industry had long exported iron to England and north-western Europe, but the growing demand for metals among the settlers of the New World and the requirements of the shipbuilding industry gave a new stimulus.

Shipbuilding emerged as the other major industry of northern Spain in the neighbourhood of Bilbao and Santander, where, rather than in Andalusia, Spanish ships for the Americas were produced. Like the Portuguese, northern Spanish seamen had gained experience in trade to north-western Europe concerned with wine, salt, wool and leather as well as iron. And their shipbuilding, like the iron industry, had good resources in the hardwood forests of the Cantabrian Mountains. In the shipyards of the Biscayan ports was developed the *galeoncete*, forerunner of the frigate and long, narrow, fast and seaworthy. Here, too, the great unwieldy *galleass* was developed, a ship of which it has been said that it combined the height and topheaviness of the galleon with the weight and lack of manoeuvrability of the galley.[11] Ships built in Biscay were often sent to Andalusia for fitting out, for the pine woods of the south made thin and poor shipbuilding material deemed suitable only for superstructures. Effort in shipbuilding was substantial, for it has been estimated that in 1585 Spanish shipping capacity was about as great as the Dutch and three times as great as the French. But by the end of the century rapid decline had set in, for many of the ships engaged in the trade of the New World were then built either in Holland or in Central America, notably at Cartagena.

For a time, industrial production also increased under the stimulus of colonial demand. Toledo's silk industry flourished and so too did the silk industries of Granada, where Málaga was the chief centre. The production of raw silk provided additional sources of rural income. Woollen textiles, linen, leather and arms industries were stimulated too by rising demand. An internal growth of population estimated at some 15 per cent between 1530 and 1594 helped to revive arable farming, which had suffered at the hands of the Mesta. Yet in industry, agriculture and population, the promise of the early sixteenth century was never fulfilled. First, like the Far Eastern spices coming through Portugal, the silver induced little secondary manufacture. Secondly, although European prices had already begun to rise, the imports of silver certainly induced a rapid inflation in Spain which kept its prices higher than those of other European countries and thus tended to put Spanish exports at a disadvantage compared with those of Northern Europe.[12] Thirdly the distribution of silver throughout Europe helped to spread inflationary pressures. Yet it has been cogently argued that inflation was by no means wholly or even perhaps mainly produced by the import of Spanish bullion and

30 *Barcelona*, 1563–7. (Braun and Hogenberg). Note the convoy of galleys approaching the harbour. Intensive horticulture and gardens are depicted within the outer wall as well as in the suburban area.

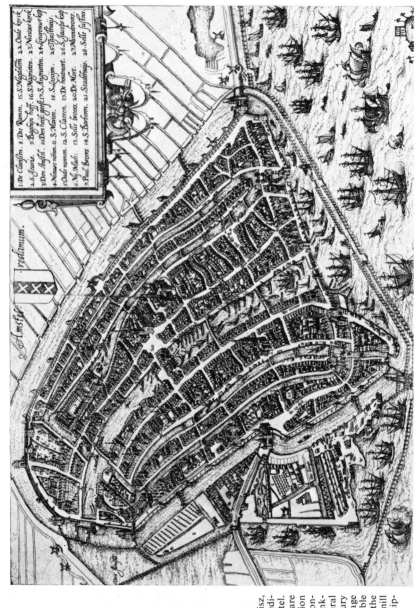

31 *Amsterdam, 1544* (C. Anthonisz, Braun and Hogenberg). The medieval town was built on the Amstel. The market place and Stadthuis are near the bridge, and the orientation of streets and buildings was controlled by the river, the embankments and the early peripheral drainage canal. By mid-16th century two other peripheral drainage canals had been dug to enable further urban expansion. Note the surrounding polders and windmill pumps, and the activity in the ship-building yards.

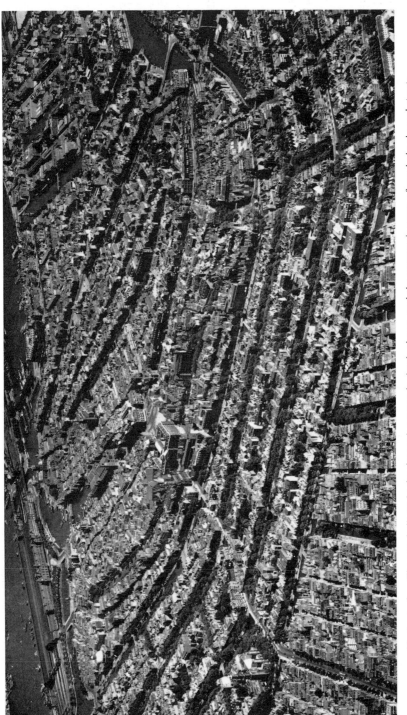

32 *Amsterdam*. The area built up in the sixteenth century is clearly shown, and the concentric zones of regularly planned streets and drainage canals built during the seventeenth century can be seen in the lower part of the photograph.

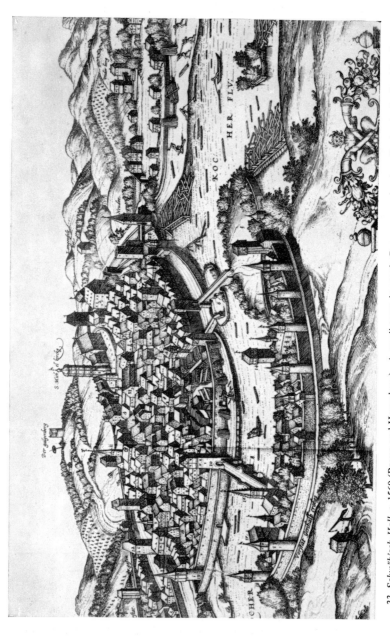

33 *Schwäbisch-Hall*, c. 1560 (Braun and Hogenberg). A small town in south Germany on the river Kocher in the Swabian Jura east of Heilbronn. Note the towered walls, the transpontine settlement and new suburban growth. The timber trade was a mainstay of the town and the region.

that there is indeed no clear correlation between the rate of import of American silver and the rate of inflation in England between 1550 and 1650. Other mechanisms were at work to produce inflationary trends, not least the growth of population and the rising demand for grain which was again putting pressure on food resources.[13]

Attention has also been focused on the routes by which Spanish bullion was distributed through Europe, for the availability of silver was an important stimulus to financial and banking activity and a lubricant for trade and industry through the credit facilities it made possible. London, Rouen, Amsterdam and Antwerp were the chief beneficiaries of smuggled bullion, but much was distributed from Spain through German and Genoese bankers towards the Low Countries, and it would seem that Spanish bullion nourished the revival of financial prosperity at Genoa in the last quarter of the sixteenth century when Spanish silver took an overland route to the Low Countries through Genoa, and through the fairs of Piacenza and Besançon.[14] Yet this, too, was short-lived, and the financial importance of Genoa appears to have lasted only until the rise of Amsterdam.

Thus, in the sixteenth century, the impact of the overseas discoveries and settlement on the old-established leadership of the Mediterranean was not, it seems, fundamental until after 1600. The silver from the New World, like the spices from the Far East, tended to by-pass the Mediterranean and Italy, but in both cases there was a temporary revival of prosperity. Neither spices nor silver induced industrial activity in the ports which handled them, whether in the Mediterranean or in north-western Europe, while the established Mediterranean trade in foodstuffs, raw materials, and manufactured goods or the trade generated within the Levant appears to have loomed larger in the sixteenth century that it ever had in earlier times. In Spain, economic decline has been attributed primarily to the currency inflation produced by New World silver, and although this effect may have been exaggerated, it was nevertheless important.

Change in the Mediterranean world

Overseas discovery and settlement produced some change in the Mediterranean world, but there were other less dramatic, and perhaps more fundamental changes in the economic and political geography of the Mediterranean which were not particularly strongly linked with the overseas expansion but which were ultimately to contribute to the decline of the Mediterranean world after 1600. The expansion of population during the sixteenth century was a universal phenomenon throughout Europe, but it was in the Mediterranean that renewed pressure on food resources appears to have reached a critical level. Secondly, the industrial leadership of Italy in certain types of manufacture was being steadily eroded during the sixteenth century by the cheaper and more efficiently produced goods of northern Europe and particularly of England, France and the Netherlands. Thirdly, changes in the geography of trade and shipping in Europe which were quite independent of overseas discoveries reduced the positional significance which had attached to northern and central Italy since the revival of trade in the eleventh century. And finally, changes in the political geography of Europe with the rise of the nation state and the opposition of the two great empires of the sixteenth century—the Ottoman Empire and the Empire of Charles V and then the empire of Philip II—worked to the disadvantage of the Mediterranean states and particularly of Italy.

Information about the growth of population in the Mediterranean in the sixteenth century is limited, but there is enough to suggest substantial growth, especially in the towns. Catalonian parish registers suggest a rapid expansion, partly through natural increase, but also through the immigration of French and Italians.[15] The population of Galicia grew from about 600,000 in 1490 to 900,000 in 1590 in spite of a constant drain by emigration. In Castile numbers may possibly have doubled from three million in 1530 to six million in 1594, though growth was less rapid in the north around Salamanca (by about one-third) while numbers tripled around Toledo. In the replies to the enquiry of Philip II about population in 1575–8 60–70 per cent of the places in Cuenca reported expansion in the recent past; 70 per cent of the places near Madrid did the same, and over a half of the places near Toledo. In Valencia growth was slow between 1527 and 1563, but numbers increased by 50 per cent from then to 1609. Lisbon grew from 65,000 to 100,000 in the second half of the sixteenth century, and Sicily from 600,000 to 1,100,000 between 1500 and 1600. Palermo's population quadrupled to 100,000 in this period, and even Catania and Messina had reached figures of 18,000 and 42,000 by the end of the century. Naples was certainly one of the largest towns in Europe by 1547 with a population of 212,000 in that year. Rome, too, was growing, rapidly doubling its population of 50,000 in 1526 by the end of the century. Rome and Naples grew very largely as a secondary result of the concentration of administration, justice and social life on the capital during the period rather than through industrial expansion, but the industrial towns of the north were also growing: Milan was over 100,000 by 1592; Pavia grew from 5,000 in 1529 to 17,000 in 1576; Venice grew from 115,000 to 168,000 in 1563 and reached its peak about 1576; Florence grew from 60,000 to 76,000 between 1551 and 1622 and Tuscany as a whole showed a modest increase.

The growth of population in the Mediterranean was probably no faster than among northern nations, but there is abundant evidence that this growth of numbers was putting considerable pressure on the food supplies available for urban populations, for grain shortages, famines and high prices were causes of recurrent crises in the Mediterranean at this time.[16] Security of grain supplies became one of the important political problems of the large cities and particularly of the extended city-states of northern and central Italy, for many of them lacked a territorial base large enough to assure sufficient food surpluses. State granaries were often organised. At Venice, imports of wheat and their sales in the city were strictly controlled. Wheat cargoes were commandeered in times of shortage and immigrants, newcomers or temporary populations were sometimes ejected from the cities if the security of grain supplies was threatened.[17] Marseilles ejected its Huguenots in 1562 at a time of grain shortage; Naples disbanded its university for a year for the same reason in 1591; rationing was sometimes instituted, but in general it was only the moderately well-to-do who could afford to accumulate stocks and pay the very high prices at times of extreme shortage. In spite of local irrigation agriculture and access to navigable water at the very gates of the town, Pavia suffered so much from the instability of its grain supplies that the grain trade was most rigorously controlled by public officials; compulsory purchases at fixed prices were made; elected officials controlled all grain and barley entering the town and compiled records, some of which survive; and public granaries were set up to store surpluses against time of need.[18]

Population growth necessarily involved an increasing demand for foodstuffs, but grain supplies were limited by the prohibitive cost of long-distance overland transport, which still meant that the effective areas of supply were those with easy access to the coasts or to navigable rivers. The potential areas of surplus grain were, therefore, limited in number: eastern Spain still had difficulty supporting its own population; North Africa too could hardly feed itself, but southern Italy and Sicily were still traditional exporters of wheat, though a Spanish administration could tie political strings to its exports. Further east most potential suppliers of wheat were in the hands of the Ottoman Turks and were either concerned to supply Constantinople, Cairo and Alexandria or were handicapped, in spite of active smuggling traffic, by the official ban on Turkish exports to Christian Europe: the Danube lands fed Constantinople, Egyptian surpluses were locally used, and the grain trade from Thrace, Macedonia and Thessaly was unstable and insecure.[19] The city-states of northern and central Italy were therefore particularly vulnerable to grain shortages, not only because of increasing population but also because of the contraction, for political reasons, of potential areas of supply. By the end of the century, indeed, the way was paved for substantial imports of northern European grain from the Baltic, and Dutch, Hanseatic and English shipping were bringing grain to Mediterranean ports from the 1580s. Lübeck was not only important in the trade of Cadiz and Seville in the sixteenth century but was also beginning to send grain to Leghorn. Hamburg had links with Cadiz, and the Dutch and English were developing their trade under the aegis of their monopoly companies. This new trend was symptomatic of the increasing dependence of the Mediterranean on northern Europe for foodstuffs as well as raw materials, and it also exemplified the invasion of the Mediterranean by northern European shipping and the decline in status of the ancient great ports of the Mediterranean.[20]

In the maritime trade and shipping of the Mediterranean, Venice, Genoa and the Catalan ports lost the pre-eminence they had formerly enjoyed in the fifteenth century, and although the northern Europeans were taking an increasing share of Mediterranean commerce by the end of the sixteenth century, Marseilles in the west (Plate 35) and Ragusa (Dubrovnik) or Ancona in the Adriatic were enjoying a new-found prosperity. There were various factors, some of general significance, some local to particular ports, which help to explain this shift.

It has been suggested that conditions had begun to favour smaller shipping of between 50 and 200 tons rather than the great ships which had become characteristic of Venice and Genoa, but which were also normal at Ragusa. The fifteenth-century pattern of commerce had depended on an organised and regular flow of traffic, much of it moving between assured markets and assured sources of supply.[21] The regular annual shipments of spices, silks, wines and luxuries from Venice and Genoa to England and Flanders is an example; and the regular lines established from Venice to the Black Sea until 1453, or from Venice to Aigues Mortes from 1402,[22] or from Venice to the Barbary states after 1436 represent other examples of a trade concerned not only with expensive luxuries but also with bulk goods: the grain trade, the salt trade from Languedoc, the wool trade from Spain and the cotton of the Levant. Moreover, naval warfare was still conceived in terms of military techniques and it was still thought that merchantmen should be convertible in time of war. Thus there was a premium on height, which gave an advantage in boarding, and on the manpower which could be carried. The ships of Venice, Genoa and Ragusa were enormous by standards of northern Europe. Ships of 600 tons were normal and there were some of over 1,000 tons at a time when the bulk of English and French shipping was considerably less than 100 tons. They were slow, heavy, and moderately seaworthy and they carried a substantial cargo.

But new conditions encouraged the small ships: the adaptation of artillery to naval use was beginning to change the character of naval warfare and to put a premium on speed and manoeuvrability; the piracy of the Barbary corsairs and the smuggling and interloping encouraged by the hostility between Christian and Turk again gave the advantage to speed and manoeuvrability; and economic changes, particularly the changes in the spice trade and the disintegration of the grain trade and of the old pattern of the wool trade, also favoured the small ship, able to pick up small cargoes from many ports. In modern terms, conditions had begun to favour the tramp ship rather than the cargo-liner. Even the Venetian and Ragusan ships were built much smaller by the end of the sixteenth century, for high initial costs and low returns discouraged investment in the large ship. In general, then, conditions favoured the newcomers to the Mediterranean trade—Marseilles, the English and the Dutch.

Marseilles in particular was assisted by the French agreement of 1535 with the Turks which gave Marseilles a foothold in the profitable North African trade and the Levant. At a time when English cloth exports were reaching a maximum and when English kerseys and other cheaper cloths were finding a substantial outlet in North Africa, Marseilles was well placed to handle re-exports at the overland terminus of the Rhône route, the use of which for international traffic increased during the first half of the sixteenth century until the decline of Antwerp and the disturbances of the French Wars of Religion. But Marseilles was also well placed to benefit from the expansion of French trade as a whole with the Levant. During the seventeenth century it was through Marseilles that imports came from the Levant of raw cotton (chiefly from Syria and Asia Minor), wool from Macedonia and Albania; raw silk of poor quality for the industry of Provence itself and particularly for the hosiery industry of Marseilles, Nimes and Aix, dyestuffs, hides and skins from North Africa, and olive oil, grain and coffee. Soap, silk, cotton and woollen industries provided a basis for the later expansion of industry in the eighteenth century, when trade between Marseilles and the Levant increased.[23]

The growth of Ragusa depended essentially on its position between Christian and Moslem Europe and also on the failure of Venice to adapt its carrying trade to the changed conditions of the sixteenth century or to exploit a potentially similar intermediary rôle in the Adriatic.[24] Although Ragusa was an early foundation of the seventh century and a fishing port which also had some early importance as an outlet for Bosnia and Serbia, it did not, until the fifteenth century, build ships capable of carrying 100 tons of wheat. But by the end of that century its fleet was the largest in the Adriatic and its merchants had contacts in all the important towns of the Mediterranean. Contrary to trends in Marseilles the size of Ragusan shipping was increasing, and its 180 ships of the decade 1560–70 had twice the gross tonnage of the average ship of that port of thirty years earlier (the great Ragusan ships *nave ragusea*, built from the abundant Bosnian timbers, gave the word 'argosy' to the English language). Trade was not only with the Adriatic ports of Italy but also to a wider sphere beyond. Ragusan ships took wine, spices and raisins to London in return for cloth and metal goods, and sailed regularly to eastern Spain and the Levant. The overland route from Ragusa to Constantinople was also of importance since it by-passed the dangerous waters of the Aegean, and Bosnian gold and wool as well as timber came by it from the immediate hinterland. As at Ancona, Ragusan merchants welcomed an increasing trade brought by German merchants who were led to use ports other than Venice by the exclusiveness and rigidity of Venetian policy.

The condition of Italy has always been crucial to the geography of Mediterranean trade and industry. Newcomers had pre-empted the ancient trade of Venice and Genoa. In the Levant, Venice had managed to retain relations with the Ottoman Empire in the fifteenth century in order to preserve its trading position and privileges, but in the sixteenth century it was drawn into hostilities with Turkey which were as disastrous to its privileges as the *rapprochement* of Francis I was advantageous to Marseilles. Venetian economic policy had lacked flexibility not only in the retention of the large ship but also in its continued reluctance to allow its clients to participate in the Levant trade, a policy which had helped to divert Lombard merchants to Ancona, and German merchants to Ragusa. By the end of the sixteenth century Venetian commerce was restricted to the Adriatic and its importance rested on its industrial expertise.

Genoa had lost its maritime empire in the Black Sea and the Levant with the advent of the Turks, and although this was to some extent compensated by its participation in the trade of Seville and the expansion of trade with the New World, or by its position in the trade of North Africa and Catalonia, Genoese shippers were reduced more and more to a relatively local and passive trade in the western Mediterranean. The Genoese silk industry had enjoyed prosperity in the sixteenth century, but the Genoese had shifted to banking and finance, in which they were of international importance until the fall of Antwerp and the rise of Amsterdam; but the ancient carrying trade had been almost entirely lost.

It was, indeed, by its industries and its manufactured goods that northern Italy was known in the sixteenth century. In the trade of Antwerp as reported by Guicciardini, for example (see p. 399), it was the silks, glass, woollen cloth, arms and munitions and luxury goods or works of art, that came from the Italian states. It has, indeed, been suggested that the industrial quadrilateral bounded by Genoa, Milan, Venice and Florence constituted a region of advanced industry in the late medieval world in the same relationship to Europe as industrial Western Europe was to the world as a whole between 1870 and 1914.[25] But in the sixteenth century this industrial quadrilateral was beginning to take second place to the new industrial centres of north-western Europe. Northern and central Italy was still one of the most advanced industrial regions, with a relatively high standard of living. But it was already obvious that the Italian cities were unable to compete with the new and lower-cost producers of northern Europe except in the highest-quality goods, and luxury products in which the advantages of skilled labour, artistic traditions and experienced management could still be exploited. But even these advantages proved to be wasting assets as France, England and the Netherlands learned to copy even the most extravagant Italian fripperies and to compete successfully with Italian industrial skills. By the end of the seventeenth century Italy had become an economically backward and depressed area and its industrial structure had almost collapsed.[26]

In the production of woollen cloths, Florence had continued to lead during much of the sixteenth century. In the 1560s Florence was still producing some 31,500 cloths a year and wool imports to its port at Leghorn remained high. But Florentine output had remained fairly constant at a time when English and Low Country cloth exports were increasing, and were invading the Mediterranean markets in strength. English poor-quality cloth sold well in North Africa, but the new draperies of England and the woollens of Holland were finding other new markets as fine, light cloths eminently suitable to warmer climates. English supplies of raw wool had long been devoted mainly to English industries, but during the sixteenth century both the Low Countries and England were importing fine, long wools of Spanish merino which were suited to the production of the combed wools and unfulled worsted cloths of which many of the new light cloths were made. Italian and Florentine producers were still importing wool from Málaga, Alicante and Cartagena but they were supplementing Spanish wool with poorer-quality wools from Algeria, Tunis, the Balkans and the Levant.

The Venetian cloth industry followed a course somewhat similar to that of Florence in that it survived the sixteenth century but declined rapidly after 1600. Indeed, production increased from some 2,000 cloths a year in 1518–20 to 20–25,000 in the period 1570–1620, though the subsequent fall to a level of less than 2,000 by 1710 was disastrous and unrelieved, and largely a product of inability to reduce prices or to adopt new techniques. In the north Italian plain the cloth industry had prospered in the fourteenth and fifteenth centuries as a result of the enterprise and initiative of merchants who maintained commercial contact with a wider world through the Alpine passes or by way of the main axes of east–west movement along the foothills of the Apennines and on the navigable waters of the Po and its tributaries. Here too the industry declined. Urban industry had already suffered the competition of rural domestic industries in which there had been growth during the fifteenth century, but even so, there were still some 60 cloth enterprises in Como in 1600 producing 8–10,000 cloths a year, and a similar number in Milan producing 15,000 cloths a year.

The decline of the woollen industry had to some extent been compensated by a retreat to more expensive and luxury cloths, and the silk industry continued to show vigour. Mulberry cultivation and the rearing of the silkworm, both rural occupations which involved intensive labour suitable for women and children, had spread widely in the north Italian plain in the sixteenth century, particularly around Milan. They flourished in Tuscany and the Kingdom of Naples, for in these areas the mulberry and its demands could be easily fitted into the complex interculture of tree and shrub crops which was already well established. Domestic production was supplemented by imports from Spain, Sicily and Syria. Italy's advantage lay primarily in its existing lead in the techniques of silk production as a result of its medieval industries, and the efforts of Francis I and Olivier de Serres to introduce the industry to France did not at first meet with unqualified success. Spanish silk had the reputation of being high in price and low in quality. Venice, Genoa, Como, the ancient centres of the industry in Tuscany, and Naples continued, therefore, to depend on the production and export of silk, and in spite of decline in the seventeenth and eighteenth centuries at the hands of French, Dutch and English competition, Italian silks retained a high reputation up to the revival of the nineteenth century.

In its major industries, then, Italian decline was postponed until the seventeenth century after a long period of stability and stagnant output during the sixteenth. Other industries followed a roughly similar pattern or retreated into producing fine luxuries: the Milanese arms and metal industries declined in the face of south German competition, particularly from Nürnberg, while the pre-eminence in jewellery, goldsmiths' work and fine glass was retained. Venice kept its fame for the production of fine lace like that other declining area of medieval textile production—Flanders; and the growth of the glass and crystal manufacture at Murano continued throughout the period.

A number of factors contributed to Italian industrial decline. The reduction of Italy to a marginal position in relation to the new alignment of trade routes does not appear to have been of major significance in the sixteenth century. Even in the Levantine trade for which Italy was still as well placed as ever, Italian cloths and manufactures were being outpriced by cheaper northern products. High wage levels reflected, perhaps, the erstwhile industrial leadership of Italy rather than sixteenth-century reality, and the losses of population in the plagues of the seventeenth century were sometimes followed by labour shortages which maintained uneconomically high wage levels. Similarly, complex gild regulations and the persistence of long-established business oligarchies were relics of the past which prevented or hindered innovation and required the production of goods which were out-of-date in fashion and of excellent quality but expensive. Traditional markets had been lost or disturbed by the decline of Spain, the Thirty Years' War, or hostilities in the Levant, but it was, above all, the loss of markets to the new and low-cost competitors of northern Europe, England, France and the Netherlands which challenged Italian industry. And while these countries relied on more efficient methods of production, and on the whole welcomed technical innovation, they also aimed at reducing imports from Italy and at producing for their own home markets the trivialities, fripperies and luxuries with which Italian trade was associated. In this application of mercantilist doctrines the rising nation states were ultimately successful, so that the silk of Lyon, Spitalfields, Amsterdam and eastern Spain replaced Italian products. But the political fragmentation of Italy in this new world of the rising nation state and mercantilist policies made it impossible to develop a large internal market to compensate for the loss of exports.

The last of the major themes in relation to the changing geography of the Mediterranean world in the sixteenth century arises from what has been said above and concerns the rôle of Italy in the political geography of Western Europe. During the later Middle Ages a division may be made between the area grouped around the axis of commercial and industrial expansion linking Italy with the Low Countries by way of the Rhineland and south Germany and, secondly, the area to the west of this axis: France, England and Iberia. In this western area the growth of territorial power and the centralisation of the state is a dominant theme and it was in this area, to one side of the major trade routes, that urban autonomy was least developed and the cities subordinated to the territorial power of the crown. In Germany, however, central authority was weak, in Italy absent altogether, so that the cities, especially where nourished by long-distance trade and commerce, were able to insist upon their autonomy *vis-à-vis* local territorial rulers.[27] But the pressures on the city-states were increasing, partly because of the necessary interdependence of town and country; partly because the scale and expense of warfare were increasing beyond the capacity of the relatively small city-states in revenue or manpower; and partly because of the vulnerability of overland trade routes. All of these factors may have contributed to the trend in the fourteenth century towards the creation of the urban leagues in Germany and the territorial expansion of the larger Italian city-states. The Italian cities, unlike those further north, were large enough and wealthy enough to dominate their surroundings in a way to which the German cities could not aspire. For example, Florence, which had no more than straddled the middle Arno in 1300, acquired Pisa and its territory in 1406, allowed it to decay before creating Leghorn as its new outlet, and then by the end of the fifteenth century pushed out the limits of its territory to the greater part of the Arno basin, with an extension beyond towards the north-eastern slopes of the Apennines. The ancient city-state of Florence had thus swollen into the state of Tuscany. Even Venice, isolated from the mainland within its lagoons, found it necessary to follow a similar course and after 1400 began a territorial expansion north of the Po and to the Alps which took it within twenty miles of Milan.

But the distended city-states were still too small for the conditions of the sixteenth century. In a military sense they fell easily to the artillery and the trained armies of Spain and France in the wars of the sixteenth century; they were vulnerable to the manipulation of grain supplies in the years of shortage during the sixteenth century; and their internal markets were too small to maintain industrial strength.

In sum, then, the relative decline of the Mediterranean in Western Europe is seen to be the product of a complex and changing situation in which many elements were very closely linked and in which there was a very considerable time-lag between the overseas discoveries, which may be said to mark an important stage in its relative decline, and the onset of an absolute decline in the late sixteenth or seventeenth century. The impact of the New World and the Far East in this changing geographical situation was, after all, not so fundamental as has often been claimed. Much more attention should be placed on internal long-term changes within Western Europe. Of these, the relative movement of population and associated agricultural change is clearly important. There is no reason to suppose that the increase of population in north-western Europe was any less than in the Mediterranean lands during the sixteenth century, and in England at least it may well have been much greater between the 1520s and the beginning of the seventeenth century. In north-western Europe, moreover, there was a period of heavy mortality from about 1600 which cut short the expansion of numbers. Yet the greater crisis in the Mediterranean lands may be associated, perhaps, with the inability of agriculture to support a substantially larger population. Rural densities of population appear already to have been high, and the Mediterranean farmers were less successful in their efforts to extend cultivation into new areas, or to intensify agricultural production by the use of new methods.

In northern Europe there still remained lands for the extension of farming, in central Sweden, for example, or at the upland margin of cultivation in Wales and Lancashire. The expansion of commercial cultivation of cereals near navigable water round the shores of the Baltic was a continuing process in the fifteenth and sixteenth centuries. Within north-western Europe there was still relatively little emphasis on the intensification of farming except near urban markets, though more complex rotations were being developed at a time when Mediterranean farming was still mainly restricted to its two-course rotation, and when the areas of commercial cereal farming for the markets of the western Mediterranean were contracting rather than expanding. Thirdly, industrial and urban growth were closely related to population trends and the availability of foodstuffs, but whereas Mediterranean Europe had reached a kind of maturity in the textile and metal industries of the Renaissance, England was making more use of coal in its humdrum concerns with brewing, salt, brick-making, distilling and a host of other industries. The new industries as well as the growing cloth industry in the north were frequently concerned with middle- or low-quality, cheap goods which were effectively raising the standards of housing, furnishing and diet of the yeoman farmer no less than the gentleman. The Netherlands shared or even led this trend, and although France may have lagged behind, Scandinavia shared in the general expansion as a result of the revival of pioneer settlement on its northern frontiers and the beginnings of expansion in its copper and iron production. Thus, in general, agricultural expansion and a movement which has been called a 'first industrial revolution' were changing the face of north-western Europe at a time when Italian industry was relatively stagnant and held back by the rigidities of a mature industrial structure.

Finally, the invasion of the Mediterranean by northern shipping: the success of the Dutch, the participation of the Hanseatic ships of Lübeck and Hamburg in the Mediterranean grain trade, and the intervention of the English Levant Company underline one other feature of the period, especially after the beginnings of Antwerp's decline. Even up to the second half of the sixteenth century, the position of Italy in relation to the trade routes of Europe and the Mediterranean was strongly maintained. The spice trade was reviving, but an increasing amount of the trade which went into the Mediterranean concerned the exports of northern as well as Italian cloths and luxuries to the Levant or North Africa. Much of this trade went overland across the isthmus of Europe from the Low Countries through France to the Rhône and Marseilles or Genoa or through the Rhineland and southern Germany to Venice, Ancona or Ragusa. But towards the end of the sixteenth century and in the seventeenth the insecurity of overland routes, the growing efficiency of maritime trade notably as a result of Dutch shipbuilding and commercial organisation, and the commercial advantages of an unbroken journey on which consignments could be fully controlled by the shipper or his agent had all tended to give a greater advantage once again to the all-sea route around the European peninsula than to the trans-peninsular routes. It was now northern European shipping, not the Italian fleets of the Middle Ages, which were making the journey, but the net effect was to make the Italian cities the termini of sea routes, not the vital and strategic transit-points between long-distance land and sea routes that they once had been.

The loss of Italy's central and strategic position in relation to the geography of trade was, therefore, not so much to be associated with the impact of the New World and the Cape route as with the development of maritime commerce in Europe itself.

One other general point should perhaps be made. From the revival of commerce in the eleventh century to the sixteenth century the bundle of routes connecting the Low Countries with northern Italy and the Mediterranean across eastern France, the Rhineland, southern Germany, the Alps and the Rhône had generated urban growth, industrial development and agricultural change which had been reflected in densities of population well above the average. This broad belt of Western Europe, linking the North Sea with the

Adriatic and the western Mediterranean across one of the great isthmuses of Europe, is greatly varied in relief and is crossed transversely by several major barriers through which passes, gaps, and gorges have constricted trade, but they have also offered many alternative routes, so that prosperity and wealth have been, from time to time, widely distributed in the zone as a whole rather than narrowly confined and channelled to one overwhelmingly dominant trade route. From the eleventh to the sixteenth century, then, this was a dominant axis in the development of urban, industrial and commercial activity (as it has become again in the modern world).

But this central axis of Western Europe was weakened after 1600 not only by the diversion of its commerce to the sea routes of the western coasts, but also by the defection of one of its two great terminals: northern and central Italy. In the new world of nation states commerce began to be more strongly oriented to capitals as well as to ports. The Thirty Years' War in Germany disrupted the flow of international traffic across this politically fragmented zone of Western Europe. And the transit trade by Rhine or by overland routes from the Low Countries was of very definitely secondary importance in the Dutch trade. For although the central axis of Western European trade was weakened, the concentration of activity at its northern end was enhanced by the rise of commercial activity, industrial progress and agricultural wealth in the Dutch Republic, and it is to this area that we must now turn.

TRADE AND INDUSTRY OF THE NETHERLANDS

The concentrations of trade, industry and prosperity which have persistently occurred in the Low Countries from the Middle Ages to the present time have not always occurred in the same zone. During the Middle Ages the favoured regions of the Low Countries were those where overland routes met the sea routes at Bruges and Antwerp. But in the late sixteenth century the success of the Sea-Beggars and the tenacity of the Dutch rebels heralded a new shift in the concentration of activity towards the Dutch area, which in the space of no more than fifty years acquired a reputation over all Europe for its success in trade, its high standards of living and the quality of its manufactures. The rich merchants set a new standard for all Europe in the richness and variety of their possessions no less than in the severity of their religion and the single-mindedness of their commerce.

The first half of the seventeenth century has been called the 'Dutch half-century', so completely outstanding were their supremacy in commerce and their leadership in so many other ways. Not only were Dutch engineers like Vermuyden active in the drainage of the Fenland or of Canvey Island but they were also draining the marshes of Europe from the Vistula delta to the marshes of the Sèvre-Niortaise in western France and they were organising the irrigation and drainage of Mediterranean lands in, for example, the valleys of the Arno and the Tiber. Dutch efficiency in the drainage of marshland was but one facet of a reputation which also involved the organisation of trade and shipping, new skills, the application of wind-power to industry, and a revolution in agriculture which was the envy and model of English agronomists and travellers. Contemporary accounts written in England and France attempted to describe the basis of Dutch prosperity and these are accounts which are singularly useful. They are all the more useful because they were written at a time when there was in England and France a great deal of new thinking about economic matters and a new awareness of geographical contrasts. One can see in some of them the outlines of an economic geography which attempted to explain and understand regional differences and the location of industrial and commercial activity. Sir William Temple's *Observations on the United Provinces* (1673) may serve as an English example,[28] and the Bishop Huet's *Memoir of the Dutch Trade*[29] exemplifies a French approach.

For the historical geographer three features of the Dutch half-century are particularly striking. The first is that it offers a further opportunity to examine the function of positional values at the cross-roads of Europe where the Rhine and Meuse met the sea lanes along the southern margins of the North Sea. Holland and Zeeland were the successors to Flanders and Brabant in the leadership of commerce, before the mantle passed in the eighteenth century to London.

Secondly, the reign of Amsterdam marks the culmination of a trend towards the concentration of commercial activity in single cities. Barbour comments: 'The reign of Amsterdam was the last in which a veritable empire of trade and credit could be held by one city in her own right.' The argument is developed that this was, indeed, the last century in which the trade of Europe was in great part intra-European and therefore susceptible of domination from a position commanding the crossroads of Europe. But, as in the study of Bruges and Antwerp, the concentration of activity is a process commanding attention in its own right quite apart from the factors peculiar to a particular site or position. In terms of the rapidity of its growth, its absolute size, the range of its industries or its control of the carrying trade, shipbuilding and the financial markets and banking of Europe, Amsterdam towered above Antwerp.[30] Yet it could also be said that the towns of Holland and Zeeland shared in the prosperity of Amsterdam much more than the towns of Brabant had participated in the activity of Antwerp in the sixteenth century.

Thirdly the historical geographer no less than the economist or the economic historian must also be attracted to the idea that the Dutch republic in the seventeenth century had almost all the requisities for rapid and continuous commercial development such as in fact occurred a century later in England during the industrial revolution. In all respects except one the Dutch area in the seventeenth century satisfied conditions of industrial growth such as those described by Rostow as the 'pre-conditions for take-off'. The rate of capital accumulation was high and the mobilisation of savings efficient. An economic climate existed in which savings were commonly devoted to further production and reinvestment in trade or industry rather than to ostentatious consumption or unprofitable investment in real estate. Acquisitive attitudes and incentives were widespread. Personal power and the ideals of a territorial aristocracy or religious piety were notoriously subordinate to the ideals of an acquisitive society. Education and literacy, advances in science, mathematics and philosophy were coupled with progress in printing, optics and cartography. Where appropriate, technological innovation was encouraged and stimulated and there was no lack of ingenuity in the use of wind power, in water control and in the development of new machines and processes in industry (e.g. the narrow 'Dutch' loom for making ribbons).

In almost all respects the Dutch republic in the seventeenth century satisfied the conditions for rapid progress which have since been postulated by economists writing of other places and of other times. The most outstanding deficiency was quite clearly the application of power to industry. Continuous expansion to a new scale of output, such as was achieved in the industrial revolution of later years, was severely limited by the impossibility of increasing the output of power at a sufficiently rapid rate. Wind-power, exploited to the limit by new technological advances, was insufficient and haphazard; water-power was not available; and although the peat re-

34 *Marseilles, c.* 1575 (Braun and Hogenberg). The growth of Marseilles and its trade had been rapid in the sixteenth century, and the harbour is filled with small sailing ships and Mediterranean galleys. Note the method of fishing used.

35 *Conil and Jerez*, 1563–7 (Hoefnagel, Braun and Hogenberg). Conil, south of Cadiz, was an important fishing town on the R. Salado. Nets are being mended on the further bank and the process of drying, salting, and packing fish is illustrated in the foreground.

Jerez de la Frontera had already created its reputation for its "sherris sack", and its vineyards and a mule train are prominent in the engraving.

sources of Holland were being thoroughly worked, the expansion of output was limited and transport expensive. In fact, Holland lacked the coal resources which were so important to England in permitting that rapid expansion of output which is possible from easily accessible mineral resources.

Contemporary writers were at one in stressing the extent to which the Dutch prosperity was based on trade. Guicciardini and Temple considered it a strange paradox that a country so lacking in natural resources and raw materials should nevertheless support flourishing industries, but they recognised clearly that industrial growth was, in their time, almost completely dependent on foreign trade even in essential raw materials. Guicciardini remarked with some exaggeration that 'Flax there is none growing in the country (sic): yet is more linen cloth made there than in any other country of the world. Their flax is brought out of Flanders, Liège and Osterland. Wool likewise they have none of their own breed (sic) yet make infinite number of cloths. Their wool cometh out of England, Scotland and Spain. They have no timber at all growing, and yet spend more timber in the building of ships and fencing their dikes and ramparts than any country doth. Their timber cometh to them out of Osterland.[31] Over a hundred years later, Temple was to write in similar terms: 'No country has been found in this present age or upon record where so vast a trade has been managed . . . yet they have no native commodities towards the building or rigging of the smallest vessel. Their flax, hemp, pitch, wood and iron, coming all from abroad, as wool does for clothing for their men and corn for feeding them. . . . Nor do I know of anything properly of their own growth that is considerable either for their own necessary use or for traffic with their neighbours, besides butter, cheese and earthenware.'[32]

Dependence on trade for essential foodstuffs and raw materials was, however, nothing new in Dutch experience; it arose out of the historical geography of the area at an early date. Four elements in the medieval geography of the Netherlands may be singled out as being of outstanding importance: the expansion of the fishing industry; the land-use patterns which followed reclamation and drainage; the location of medieval trade routes from the Baltic to the Rhineland and the Low Countries; and the relationship of Antwerp to the shipping and navigation of the delta area.

The fishing industry was accorded a strategic position in relation to the economic growth of the Netherlands by contemporary witnesses, notably Sir Walter Raleigh, or Bishop Huet of Avranches.[33] Huet considered that the herring fishery constituted the 'greatest traffic and the best gold mine of the United Provinces'; Sir Walter Raleigh held up the Dutch fishing industry as an example for England to follow, and was concerned with the fishing industry primarily as a nursery of sailors, a source of experience in navigation, a stimulus to shipbuilding and thus as a necessary basis of naval strength. De Witt regarded the fishing industry almost as a 'leading sector' in the growth of Dutch commerce, and calculated the effect of the fishing industry on a variety of other employments, such as shipbuilders, timber merchants, cordage makers, hemp buyers. There is no doubt that the herring fisheries stimulated activity in shipping and shipbuilding as well as the accumulation of maritime skills, but they also provided a valuable export, for herring and cod were dried and smoked or carefully packed with salt in barrels, a trade which in turn gave encouragement both to the salt trade from Portugal and France and to the local production of salt by the use of peat. The Baltic fisheries which had earlier brought revenue to Lübeck and the ports and creeks of Scania suffered a relative decline with the growth of the herring fisheries in the North Sea in the later Middle Ages, and although changes in the migration habits of the herring shoals have been held responsible for this change, it is likely that technical improvements in the packing of fish with salt which were pioneered in Flanders or Zeeland and certainly used in Biervliet from the fourteenth century made possible the supremacy of the Dutch industry. By the early seventeenth century Dutch fishing fleets of up to 3,000 vessels a year fished off the coasts of England and Scotland. Amsterdam and its villages had important fisheries, but Enkhuizen was the largest of the herring ports in the province of Holland, according to Huet. Rotterdam and Dordrecht were also important, and Schiedam, Delft, Brill and Maaslandsluis were also mentioned. The whale fisheries, which operated chiefly from Amsterdam to the coasts of Greenland and Spitzbergen and which owed much to the exploratory voyages of Arctic waters in search of north-west and north-east passages, required much larger-scale capital outlay both for equipment and for the fishing expeditions which were involved. Huet estimated that the whale fisheries involved some 200 ships of 200-250 tons, and it was a profitable trade producing a supply of oil for lighting, for the manufacture of soap and for the preparation of leathers and skins.[34]

Contemporary witnesses were fully aware of the stimulus which had been given to Dutch trade and shipping by the fishing industry, but they were less conscious of the ways in which the Dutch preoccupation with the drainage and reclamation of land from the sea provided favourable conditions for the expansion of trade. The fever to reclaim new land was spreading from Flanders to Zeeland in the twelfth and early thirteenth centuries, when great strides were being made in the piecemeal reclamation of islands in the delta area by the new techniques of poldering, mentioned at Middelburg on the island of Walcheren in 1219. In Holland, too, the early thirteenth century was a period of great activity in drainage and reclamation associated with the name of William the Diker, Count of Holland. Systems of dikes and canals were established to protect a fairly large zone around the Central Moor which was threatened by the advancing waters of the Zuider Zee to the north and inundations from the riverine lands to the south. In the expansion of settlement which followed reclamation, new places were founded on raised embankments and at sites where sluices controlled drainage to tidal water. They were often given names ending in -dijk and -dam (Amsterdam and Rotterdam are the outstanding examples). A ring of new towns was formed at the margins of the Great Moor which constituted the core of the province of Holland and which is given the name of *Randstadt-Holland*. From Dordrecht and Rotterdam in the south through Delft and Leyden to Amsterdam the ring was almost completed in the east by Hilversum and Utrecht.[35]

Rotterdam and Dordrecht were on important distributaries of the Rhine and, predictably, became important river ports in the later Middle Ages. But what is less obvious is that places like Utrecht and Gouda, and above all, Amsterdam, were also well placed to benefit from the flow of long-distance commerce. The new towns of those parts of Holland and Zeeland which were reclaimed from the sea grew up in a world dominated by the Hanseatic League and in which the shipping of the northern seas was slow, hazardous and insecure. Trade routes which made their way inside the shelter of the Frisian Islands from Hamburg to the Zuider Zee were preferred to the dangers of the open sea. And from the Zuider Zee quiet passages along the water links led in the east by way of Deventer towards Cologne and in the west by various routes to the islands of the delta and so to Bruges or Antwerp. Hanseatic merchants had already come to dominate the trade of the ports on the eastern side of the Zuider Zee which had been early established and which served the larger hinterland of the upland regions—Kampen, Stavoren and Zwolle, for example.[36] At first insignificant and serving the poor hinterlands of newly reclaimed marsh, the merchants of the western Zuider Zee, notably at Enkhuizen, Hoorn and Amsterdam, handled their own trade and, like the English Merchant Adventurers at a later date, took advantage of smaller trades and less profitable occupations. But these were the trades which expanded most when the agricultural wealth of the reclaimed lands was fully realised.

The circumstances under which drainage and reclamation of the Dutch area had been achieved were also important for its trading future, for an important distinction appeared at an early date between those lands which were reclaimed from peat and those which had been reclaimed from marine or riverine silts and clays. Provided the water table could be kept sufficiently low by the control of sluices and outfalls, the clays and silts could be made to yield good crops of cereals as well as pasture. But the peats of Holland, like those of the English fenland at a later date, proved more difficult to drain and they were therefore retained as pasture lands from very early times. Many of the new settlements on the reclaimed lands of Holland were therefore incapable of producing arable crops, and were dependent on exports of dairy produce to secure the imports of grain that were needed for sustenance. Fishing, too, was an early supplement to a predominantly stock-rearing economy. Thus from the thirteenth century Dutch ports were involved in the grain trade which was also newly developing with the export surpluses available from recently colonised German villages in the lands east of the Elbe.

A regional division in the functions of the Dutch ports was already beginning to be evident in the later Middle Ages. On the one hand, Amsterdam, Hoorn, Enkhuizen and other smaller ports of the province of Holland were drawn into the Baltic trade, partly because of the precocious development of the grain trade and the early demand for shipbuilding timber, and partly because they were so easily accessible from the major routes into the Baltic through the Zuider Zee. By about 1500, when more and more of the bulk trade to the Baltic was passing through the Skaggerak rather than across the Jutland peninsula from Hamburg to Lübeck, 70 per cent of all ships passing through the Sound and paying the Danish tolls were Dutch. But of the total Dutch shipping, 78 per cent came from the ports to the west of the Zuider Zee, 14 per cent from the old, declining, Hanseatic-controlled ports on the eastern side of the Zuider Zee, and only 8 per cent from the southern provinces in spite of the flourishing state of their maritime trade.[37] Indeed, by 1500 about a half of all Dutch voyages to the Baltic originated from Amsterdam and its satellite 'Skipper' towns.

The ports of Zeeland had followed quite a different progression, for their development had been very closely bound up with that of Antwerp. It has already been noted that in the early stages of its growth Antwerp was dependent upon the transhipment of its commerce in the delta ports because of the shallow character of its approaches. Middelburg, Bergen-op-Zoom and Zieriksee were the chief places to benefit from the expansion of Antwerp's trade, participating actively in shipbuilding and the carrying trade. The Zeelanders were led not merely to England for cloth, but also to the ports of France and south-western Europe for wine and salt and they came naturally to share Antwerp's interest in the Spanish and Portuguese trade. If the Baltic trade was the special province of Amsterdam and its neighbours, Zeeland acquired a special position in relation to the trade with England, Iberia, the Mediterranean and then the Americas.

Finally, Rotterdam and Dordrecht were the chief of the river ports. Dordrecht in particular had close contacts with England, for it was one of the major ports handling English cloth in the sixteenth and seventeenth centuries. Rotterdam shared in this transit trade along the Rhine, and both also served as entrepôts for the grain exports from the lower Rhineland, notably from Jülich and Cleves. Dordrecht was the staple for Rhenish wine in the sixteenth century and according to Guicciardini, it was, like Rotterdam, a rich and populous town. Sir William Temple echoed Guicciardini's assessment and that of Bishop Huet, stressing the importance of the Rhine transit trade, the wine trade from Cologne and the Moselle, the import of oak from the forested Rhineland massifs, the trade in flax and linen from Westphalia and the continuing importance of metals, armaments, and copper from south Germany through Nürnburg of Frankfurt.[38] The specialisation of function among the three major zones of the Dutch ports can be easily exaggerated, for Rotterdam and Dordrecht participated active in long distance trade, to south-west Europe and the Baltic, and so indeed did the ports of Holland itself, notably Amsterdam, but the tendency towards specialisation, and the contribution it could make to the efficiency of the Dutch, was appreciated by Sir William Temple, who observed with perspicacity 'the custom of every town affecting some particular commerce or staple, valuing itself thereupon, and so improving it to the greatest height, as Flushing by the trade of the West Indies, Middelburg of French wines, Terveer by the Scotch staple, Dort by the English staple and Rhenish wines, Rotterdam by the English and Scotch trade at large and by French wines'.[39]

It is convenient to divide the Dutch sphere of commerce in the sixteenth and seventeenth centuries into two fairly distinct zones of activity, each characterised, in general, by different techniques of commerce, shipping and finance.[40] On the one hand, there were the dramatic and spectacular achievements of the Dutch in long-distance trade overseas: in the East and West Indies; in North America and Brazil; in their temporary occupation of Ceylon and their monopoly of the Japanese trade; and nearer at home, in the trade with the Mediterranean and the Levant. On the other hand there was the trade of home waters in Western Europe, a trade which was assured of its safety by travelling in convoy and which involved quick turn-round of bulk cargoes. This was a trade characterised by low profits and competition on price and delivery rather than the combination of high risks, high profits and naval supremacy that was characteristic of the long-distance luxury trades in goods of low bulk and high price.

Among the home trades in the coastal waters of Europe it was the Baltic trade in which the Dutch retained their pre-eminence longest, and in which the efficiency of their shipping and commercial organisation was most evident to contemporaries in the seventeenth century. During the later Middle Ages the German merchants of the Hanseatic League and notably those of Hamburg and Lübeck had almost succeeded in monopolising the trade between the Baltic and the North Sea.

Much of the traffic had been carried across the base of the Jutland peninsula either by way of the Eider valley or by way of the Stecknitz canal, built in the early fifteenth century and the precursor of the Kiel Canal. Spices and silks, wine, fine textiles and Mediterranean produce had been the main imports to the Baltic and they were valuable commodities which could stand the cost of transhipment overland or by canal. The return trade from the Baltic to Hamburg still consisted to a large extent of furs, honey, wax, woodash and other products of a forest environment. But these were steadily yielding second place to the bulk trade in grain and timber which followed the more intensive

economic development of the Baltic lands in the later Middle
Ages.

After the Danish war of 1438–41 against the Hanseatic League,
in which the assistance of the Netherlands had been sought, the
Sound was opened to traffic using the circuitous but all-sea route from
the Baltic to the North Sea. Both the English Merchant Adventurers
and Dutch traders ventured into the Baltic trade during the mid-
fifteenth century, but where the English merchants were still no
match for the Hanseatic towns, the Dutch were able from the beginning to secure a dominating rôle. The traffic in bulky products such
as grain and timber, for which the Sound route was most advantageous, increased during the revival of activity in the late fifteenth
century and afterwards at the expense of other trade. The Hanseatic
League retained a large proportion of the dwindling trade in expensive and luxury goods, but the lower freight costs of the Dutch carriers
assured for them an increasingly strong position. Danzig merchants,
for example, began to prefer the Dutch carriers to the German
rivals because of their lower charges. Dutch competition on the
Sound route thus served to create and then to stress the divergence
of interest between the different geographical branches of the
Hanseatic League. Lübeck and Hamburg were primarily interested in
the carrying trade and in the maintenance of trade over the Jutland
peninsula; but the interest of the German merchants in the Baltic
ports was in finding a cheaper outlet for their bulkier trades.

The composition of the Baltic trade and the overwhelming importance of the Dutch in it is unusually well known because of the fact
that the Danes were able to levy tolls on almost all of the international shipping which passed through the only navigable passage
from the Baltic to the North Sea, by way of the Great Belt and the
Skaggerak. And the records of the tolls through the Sound have
survived in great detail from the end of the fifteenth century to the
late eighteenth.[41] It is true that there are difficulties in interpreting
the records in detail, notably because of unknown shortcomings such
as smuggling, differences in control, the freedom of Swedish shipping
from toll until 1710, and the ambiguities as to whether it is the ship's
home port or the shipmaster's port that is given, yet this remains an
incomparably important record of European trade in the early
modern period.

Of the 400,000 ships which passed through the Sound from 1497
to 1660, no less than 59 per cent came from the United Provinces,

and the remainder was shared among English, Scottish, German and Scandinavian shipping. Between 1661 and 1783 the Dutch share of a larger number of entries was much smaller, representing 35 per cent of a total of 520,885 ships, and after the 1760s the decline of the Dutch trade is reflected in a diminishing number of entries. During this period the trade of the English and Scottish merchants had increased to 19 per cent, and the trade of the Scandinavian countries themselves had grown most appreciably, for Danish trade amounted to 10 per cent, Norwegian 6 per cent and Swedish 13 per cent. It is also clear that very many of the westbound ships found Amsterdam as their destination. Of the relatively small proportion of shipping that went straight to Atlantic ports, most had destinations in France. Very few ships headed directly for the Mediterranean or Iberian ports from the Baltic.

Of the goods moving into the Baltic, salt, herring, wine, textiles skins and hides and colonial goods were the chief. Salt was the bulkiest commodity, and right up to 1720, except during the French wars, the Dutch retained their early lead, carrying 60 per cent or more of the salt taken into the Baltic. Nearly a half of this salt trade came from the Bay of Bourgneuf, supplier of salt to northern Europe from the Middle Ages, and the rest came chiefly from Portugal, Italy, and the Netherlands, the latter mostly a re-export. In the sixteenth and seventeenth centuries the predominance of Dutch sources for the herring imports into the Baltic bears out the aphorism that Amsterdam was 'built on herring-bones', for the Dutch share, at first over 80 per cent, was usually 60 per cent or more until the destruction of a great part of the Dutch herring fleet by the French in 1700. After this their share fell to less than a third in the eighteenth century with a corresponding rise in Scottish, Norwegian and Swedish trade. In the wine trade, Dutch ships took some 86 per cent of the Rhine wines imported into the Baltic between 1497 and 1660 and over two-thirds in the subsequent period to 1783, but their share was falling in the eighteenth century as Scandinavian countries and German ports carried more of their own trade. Trade in other wines followed a similar course, the Dutch share falling catastrophically from about two-thirds in the early seventeenth century to less than 10 per cent in the eighteenth century.

In the shipment of textiles, England and the Netherlands predominated, and although the English merchants took well over half of this trade up to 1629, the Dutch share rose rapidly after 1629 as the Dutch merchants captured about half of the English traffic. This was a very considerable trade, in terms of value, increasing substantially during the period, for the average shipment rose from 35,500 cloths a year between 1562 and 1567 to 50,200 between 1661 and 1783. And from 1630 to about 1740 the Dutch in general retained a slight lead on the English shippers of cloth, a change which corresponded to the success of the Dutch producers, especially of Leyden, during this period. There was some movement of other textiles into the Baltic, chiefly cotton, wools and silks. They were not quantitatively very important, but the Dutch were again able to retain their lead until well on in the eighteenth century. Hides and skins represented another significant item in the Baltic trade, but it was England and Scotland which led and the Dutch had never been much interested in the trade.

It was, however, otherwise with tropical and sub-tropical products, chiefly sugar, coffee, spices, indigo, chocolate, tropical woods and dyestuffs, that branch of the trade which was most valuable in relation to its bulk, and whose growth reflected the expansion of overseas settlement, slavery and plantation agriculture in the Americas as well as the commercial activities of Europe in Asia. The volume of this trade increased enormously, from 2 million pounds weight in 1642-8, to 10 million by 1739 and 35½ million in 1735. Up to 1720 the Dutch and the English merchants were a good second. But during the eighteenth century the rise of Scandinavian and German shipping cut down the share taken by Amsterdam and London. After 1740, Hamburg's expansion, particularly in the sugar trade, was most notable and it was competing with Amsterdam and London as an entrepôt for the Baltic traffic, taking a considerable proportion of its imports from the French colonial ports.

Of the exports from the Baltic to the west, corn was the major commodity, representing 65 per cent of the trade about 1565 and some 53 per cent of the total exports in 1635. It was the corn trade for which Amsterdam was, perhaps, best known in the sixteenth century, and its entrepôt function in the corn trade was already well developed. The fact that grain prices were persistently high during the sixteenth century relatively to prices of other agricultural products and in relation to industrial prices was, perhaps, one of the major factors making possible the rapidity of Amsterdam's growth through the ploughing back of high profits into trade, shipbuilding and urban investment. To 1660 the Dutch share of the Baltic corn trade was some 77 per cent of a total of 4·6 million lasts (of which 4 million were rye and the rest wheat). Even in the later period from 1660 to 1783 the Dutch handled 70 per cent of a slightly declining trade (total 4·7 million lasts, of which 3·3 million were rye and 1·4 million wheat). Fluctuations were considerable according to the condition of the harvests, the occurrence of war and the variations of price levels, and the Dutch were taking rather less after 1720 than they had earlier.

Danzig had been renowned as the centre of the Baltic grain trade and as the staple of a rapidly developing Polish output, handling the grain brought from the Vistula basin as well as more local trade. Up to 1660 it was responsible for some 60 to 70 per cent of the exports going through the Sound, and Danzig prices were the ruling prices throughout north-western Europe. The Bishop Huet, labelling it as one of the principal towns of Europe, commented: 'Its great store-houses of grain make it well-known throughout Europe, so that it is commonly called "The Germany of the Northern Kingdoms and of the United Provinces".'[42] The agencies of the Dutch merchants in Danzig and the activities of Dutch drainers and reclaimers in the lower Vistula constituted an important element in the total population of the city and its surroundings. Although the rye trade tended to shift eastwards in the eighteenth century towards Königsberg and east Baltic ports such as Riga, Danzig continued to handle the greater part of the wheat exports of the Baltic, though some also went from Stettin to which wheat from the löss lands of Silesia came by way of the Oder. The islands of Rügen and Zealand also had surpluses for export in most years.

The timber trade was one of the key trades in the expansion of Dutch commerce, and particularly that of Amsterdam, for quite apart from the entrepôt trade in timber, which was in itself important and profitable, the maintenance of a high level of cheap timber imports was fundamental in securing the efficiency of the Dutch shipbuilding industry and therefore of the carrying trade as well. Bishop Huet remarked:

'The traffic in timber is one of the most considerable after that in grain, for besides the great consumption of their Marine, they also use a great quantity to make barrels, pipes, kegs and other casks, without counting that which they use in buildings, foundations, boats, dykes, jetties and fortifications both by sea and land. They also sell it for great sums of money to the French, Italians and Spanish. All that, however, does not equal the prodigious quantity which they employ in the construction of vessels, ships and other boats which serve them for Navigation, either for their own use or for that of other nations. White wood and fir come principally from Norway and Sweden. Fine oak and oak staves come from the Baltic; ships' masts from Norway, Muscovy, Riga, Narva, Reval and Danzig. The Dutch still draw a great quantity of timber by the rivers Elbe, Weser and Rhine; in such a way that this commerce must be considered as one of the most important and necessary for the State of this Republic. It is only necessary to have seen the shipyards of Zaandam to be persuaded of it.'[43]

Tolls levied in the Sound excluded the important Swedish trade until the decade 1710–20, but after this period the figures of timber movement show a very rapid increase and timber exports surpassed those of any other commodity in volume.

During the seventeenth century the Dutch had been handling at least 60 per cent of this trade and even in the eighteenth century they were able to retain 47 per cent of it, compared with the 18 per cent taken by English ships. According to the tolls, Finland was the most important source of timber in the eighteenth century, followed by Livonia-Estonia and Sweden, though Finland's expansion had been very recent, developing on a large scale only after 1700. St Petersburg was handling some exports in the later period; Riga was well known as a source of large timber for masts; and Sweden for masts, planks, and beams of fir; but there was always a very considerable demand not only for the soft woods of the coniferous forests of Scandinavia, but also for the hardwoods drawn from central Europe by way of the river trade. Thus, Stettin tapped the oak forests of central Germany and Silesia by way of the Oder; and Danzig exported oak from the Vistula basin as well as firs from East Prussia. Finally, the timber trade of the Netherlands was by no means confined to the Baltic, for not only were hardwoods brought to the Netherlands by way of the Rhine, Elbe and Weser, but also the Norwegian timber trade and much of that which left Sweden by its western ports, including Göteborg, never passed through the Sound.

Timber exports were the major source of Norway's external revenue during the eighteenth century. Huet had said: 'The principal Merchandise and riches of the kingdom of Norway consist of Ships' Masts, of all sorts of wood, as much for the construction of vessels as for other Carpenters' materials; in iron and copper mines, tar, pitch, dried fish, hides and skins, ashes and butter.' Some 300 Dutch ships of 400 to 500 tons were engaged in the Norwegian trade, most of them coming from the Frisian islands or Amsterdam and its neighbourhood.

Corn and timber were the commodities which moved in greatest volume from the Baltic, but iron and non-ferrous metals followed in importance. Huet's description identifies Sweden with the bulk of this traffic in the late seventeenth and early eighteenth centuries: 'Sweden furnishes many more things than Denmark, and its Commerce is much more considerable. Red Copper, estimated the best in Europe, is principally drawn from this Country, Iron, Steel and a quantity of all sorts of Arms made of these metals, as Muskets, Pistolets, Canons for the armour of Ships, Ball, Pikes, Helmets, Armour and a quantity of other things, without mentioning other products, such as Brass wire. . . .'[44] Dutch capital and enterprise had been closely associated with the development of Swedish copper resources during the period of the Thirty Years' War, and the Dutch remained pre-eminent in the carrying trade until their replacement by Swedish shippers in the eighteenth century. In the iron trade the Dutch had played a similar rôle in the seventeenth century, when the growing exports of Swedish iron were handled through Dutch or Swedish shippers and were sent mainly to the United Provinces and England, but after 1720 the balance of the trade changed considerably, for England emerged as the greatest consumer in the European iron trade and Sweden's monopoly was threatened increasingly by competition from Russia.

Linen and canvas became important exports through the Sound during and after the second half of the seventeenth century and their volume far exceeded that of imports of woollen cloth into the Baltic. But the Dutch were always subordinate to the English merchants in both the marketing and carriage of linens from Danzig, Königsberg, Narva and later, after 1710, St Petersburg. In other commodities, however, the Dutch took a large share: hemp and flax, furs and skins, potash for the cloth and bleaching industries, pitch and tar for shipbuilding and construction.

The Baltic trade was certainly that in which the Dutch, and particularly the merchants of Amsterdam, were able to take full advantage of their early and fortunate alliance with the Danes, and to exploit the lead in the bulk trades, in which cheapness and efficiency of shipping mattered greatly. The Baltic trade was always the most highly organised of the Dutch trades, and in 1666, for example, it was estimated that some three-quarters of the capital of the Amsterdam bourse was tied up in the Baltic commerce. Contemporaries described it as the 'soul of all trade' and it clearly played a strategic rôle in the economic geography of Dutch commerce as a whole in the sixteenth and seventeenth centuries. The entrepôt functions of Amsterdam were important and profitable in salt, wine, and tropical or subtropical products re-exported after processing. Amsterdam was the entrepôt for the grain trade at a time when rising population and high grain prices had extended a profitable trade to destinations as far as the Mediterranean by the end of the sixteenth century. Timber was also re-exported, and it was as a source, for example, of wainscoting that Sir Thomas Gresham knew of Amsterdam.[45] The Baltic trade provided important markets for Dutch exports, notably herring, cloth, and the products of processing industries such as sugar-refining and tobacco manufacture. It provided raw materials for Dutch industry: corn for the distilling of spirits and the brewing of beer; potash and even some dyestuffs for the cloth industry; but by far the most important raw materials were those involved in the shipbuilding industry. Although hardwoods were still required for many purposes, the Dutch were the first to explore the uses of softwoods in their shipbuilding industry, and masts, planks, decking and an increasing proportion of the superstructure were of pine and fir, timbers which were much cheaper and more tractable than the oak which had formerly been used. But many other of the raw materials needed in shipbuilding were also provided by the Baltic countries: hemp and flax for cordage and sailcloth, linen canvas, tar and pitch, iron, brass and copper. Imports from the Baltic were therefore an element in the low capital cost of shipping which was in turn one of the factors in the low freight rates which the Dutch could offer, but they were also a strategic element in relation to naval power and armaments. The Dutch carriers could draw not only on their own arms industry and on that of Liège but also on the Swedish output; and control over the timber trade of the Baltic was of increasing importance during the seventeenth century as the shortage of large timber within access of navigable water slowly became evident in England and France to people like John Evelyn and Samuel Pepys.

Finally, it may be useful to recognise the Baltic trade as a 'colonial' trade in that most of it involved the exchange of raw materials for manufactured products. The corn for which the Baltic trade was famous came from areas which were by Western European standards still farmed extensively, but many other of the Baltic products were directly a reflection of the fresh exploitation of forest resources. Honey, wax and furs had been the products in medieval times of a forest hunting and collecting economy, but by the sixteenth and seventeenth centuries timber, pitch, tar, and potash could be exported as inroads on the virgin forests were made. Even the production of iron represented, from one point of view, a means of earning revenue from reserves of timber, which were converted into charcoal and used in smelting and refining. It has been said elsewhere that in the eighteenth century the iron industry underwent a 'flight to the wilderness' as producers sought new resources of charcoal to increase the production of iron, and Sweden provides an example on a European scale. Nevertheless, the rising exports of iron, armaments, copper and brass from Sweden, and of linen and iron from Russia are symptomatic of the growth of manufacturing industry in the Baltic countries.

To the end of the seventeenth century the Dutch had maintained their lead in most branches of the Baltic trade except cloth, but after 1720 they suffered a relative or even absolute decline. In cloth, iron, linen, salt and timber, and in sugar, spices and other tropical products, the Dutch lost ground to England, but it is also apparent that the Scandinavian countries were carrying more and more of their own goods, and German merchants from Hamburg, Danzig and the east Baltic ports were also more active than they had formerly been. With the decline of the Dutch as carriers, the concentration on Amsterdam of the old entrepôt trades was also brought to an end.

The complement to the Dutch Baltic trade was their carrying trade to France and Iberia and across the North Sea to England, and although this was a trade which cannot be so closely charted as that which passed through the Sound and paid its tolls, the Dutch here too were predominant in the seventeenth century. The English trade was overwhelmingly in cloth, for although the Dutch were able to compete most successfully with traditional English broadcloths; English serges, says, and other products of the new draperies were imported into Holland for resale and re-export, principally to Germany. Middelburg had been the earliest of the staple ports, but it had been replaced as the chief centre of the English cloth trade by Delft, then Rotterdam during the seventeenth century, and later still by Dordrecht. Tin, lead, coal, and vitriol reflected the wealth of English mineral resources but other important exports were of colonial products, chiefly Virginia tobacco and Barbados sugar. Dutch linens, sailcloths and silks were the chief return trades in a list that contained a great variety of manufactured products. In general terms the importance of the Dutch trade may be measured by the fact that in 1697 the Dutch took no less than 41 per cent of all England's exports and supplied nearly 15 per cent of its imports.

The French trade of the Dutch was described by Huet in some detail and he provides estimates for 1658 which suggest that of the imports from France, woollen cloths, velvets, satins, cloths of gold and silver, and taffetas, manufactures of Lyon, Paris and Tours, together with gloves, ribbons, lace and other haberdashery constituted about a quarter of all French exports to the United Provinces; other luxury products and furnishings or furniture such as clocks, mirrors, fans, beds, blankets and the like made up another fifth. Linens and paper were also among the manufactures which France could still market in Holland, but wines, brandies and vinegar, mainly from Bordeaux, western France, Champagne and Burgundy, made up 16 per cent. Bay salt, evaporated from the pans dug in the salt marshes of the west-centre, was one of the bulkiest commodities in the trade from western France and, together with wine, must have occupied most of the 500–600 ships which went to Brouage, La Rochelle, Maran and the Îles de Ré and Oléron. Grain had been an important export in the abundant years, but it was less in evidence in the hungry years of the late seventeenth century; and of other agricultural products, flax and hemp from Brittany, saffron, honey, almonds, olives, figs, plums and capers are mentioned, none of them of great importance and many of them from southern France. The French trade had been subjected to great fluctuations from midcentury as a result of the mercantilist tariffs of 1664 and 1667 and the wars and tariff revisions of later years. By the end of the century the Dutch had successfully established silk, ribbon, lace and paper industries to the detriment of French exports, but the strength of the Dutch position in the French trade and particularly in the salt, wine and brandy trade of the west, had not been seriously impaired. And the French remained dependent on Dutch re-exports either from the Baltic or from the East Indies and the Americas; spices, drugs, dyewoods, copper, steel, brass wire, armaments, Russian furs, flax hemp, tar, pitch and timber were all prominent among Dutch exports to France together with Dutch products, chiefly cloth, linens, dairy produce and the ubiquitous herring.

The Iberian trade flourished particularly at the time of the Franco-Dutch wars at the end of the seventeenth century. Spain took Dutch cloths and linens, particularly from Overijssel, Douai, Valenciennes, and Cambrai; cottons, ribbons, and fine silks; ironmongery from Liège and southern Germany; metals and armaments from Sweden; leather from Russia; and Baltic timber and timber products went from the Netherlands to Spain together with some colonial re-exports from the Far East. For the Dutch in Spain, Cadiz was the greatest attraction, and if there were normally some 30 ships engaged in the traffic at Cadiz and Seville, there were some 15 to 20 more at the arrival or departure of the *Flota* and the *Galeon*. Spanish wool was by far the most important of the Iberian products to enter the Dutch trade, for it was indispensable as a raw material for the cloth industries of the Low Countries; wines from the southern provinces were exported by way of Málaga and Alicante, but Xerez already had the lead in Spain. Dried fruits, almonds, figs and citrus fruits, olive oil from Seville and Majorca, together with soap and barilla all emphasise the environmental basis of exchange between the Netherlands and the Mediterranean lands. Northern Spain sent chiefly salt, iron and steel. But glamour, risk and profit still attached to the colonial trade of south-western Europe. Tobacco and sugar were now the Portuguese contributions to the Dutch warehouses, for the spice trade of former years had been pre-empted and the Dutch now sought Brazilian, not Asian, products at Lisbon. At Cadiz the Dutch were the principal carriers to the rest of Europe of a new variety of products which now diversified the ancient preoccupation with silver. Huet provides an impressive list: pearls from the Caribbean; emeralds from Bogotá; the wool of vicuña, and cinchona bark from Peru; cochineal and indigo from Guatemala; logwood, chocolate and vanilla from Mexico and central America; tobacco from Maracaibo, Havana and Santo Domingo and hides from many places in the New World.

In many ways the Mediterranean trade had more in common with the new long-distance trades of the overseas territories than it had with the bulk trades of north-west Europe. This, too, was a long-distance trade in relatively dangerous waters for which merchantmen had necessarily to be armed. It was primarily, though by no means entirely, a luxury trade and one in which both profits and risks were high. The corresponding English trade was handled by the Levant Company, established in 1570, but the Dutch relied heavily on the organisation of convoy systems to ensure the safety of their Mediterranean trade. By the end of the seventeenth century some thirty ships a year organised in three or four convoys made the round journey, stopping at Leghorn for provisions and also for supplies of currency in piastres. The cargo ships had twenty to twenty-five guns, but the danger of piracy in the Mediterranean also required the presence in each convoy of two escort vessels of fifty to sixty guns. For both Dutch and English, Smyrna was the chief port among many calling points in the eastern Mediterranean, for this was still the terminus of Persian caravans and the entrepôt for European cloth. The Egyptian trade was handled at Cairo and Alexandria, and there was still a trickle of commerce overland from the Red Sea. But the bulk of the trade with the Turkish Empire concerned local and Middle East produce, chiefly textiles and textile fibres such as raw cotton, cotton fabrics, angora wool, silk of poor quality, and wool. Cordovan leather, alum, coffee and dried fruits were also handled in return for cloth and colonial goods. Indeed, long before the end of the seventeenth century pepper, spices and drugs were being imported from the Netherlands into the Levant, reversing the earlier flow. The Italian trade of the Dutch was chiefly with Genoa and Leghorn, though Venice, Naples and Messina were also important, and it involved the exchange of colonial and Baltic goods for imports which consisted principally of silks and other fine textiles, glass, marble, and the fruits, wines and olives which Italy could also send. But the manufactured goods which had still been important in Italian production and trade in 1600 were no longer significant, with the single and outstanding exception of silk from Lombardy, Tuscany and southern Italy.

In the expansion of Europe overseas in the seventeenth century the Dutch themselves had played a most prominent part, of course, and had long ago taken over the mantle of Portugal in the Far East by the time that Huet or Temple wrote. From the moment when the Portuguese were brought under the Spanish crown in 1580 the Dutch could legitimately attack the crumbling structure of Portuguese power in the Indian Ocean. Van Linschoten had already shown the way by the publication of his *Itinerario*, a geographical account of the eastern countries which also contained detailed sailing instructions. Between 1595 and 1597 Cornelius de Houtman was sent on a reconnaissance tour in the east and the following year four Dutch fleets went by way of the Magellan Straits and the Cape of Good Hope to explore the possibilities of trade and conquest. They were overwhelmingly successful, so that by 1602 the Dutch were able to form an East India Company, organised on a more permanent basis than the corresponding English company and considerably more heavily capitalised. In the Far East the Dutch were often welcomed by Muslims as potential allies against the Portuguese and as offering an alternative trading outlet. The Dutch did not, like the Portuguese, mix business with religion, and were therefore welcome in some quarters on that account; for example, in Japan. They came offering more suitable merchandise than had the Portuguese: armour, weapons, glass, velvets, fine cloths, toys and metal goods. Above all, they were more numerous. In the early seventeenth century the Dutch company had a capital of £500,000 as against the English £30,000; between 1602 and 1610 the Dutch sent 60 ships as against the English 17. The Portuguese in the Far East had rapidly been crushed or their positions by-passed, so that the trade through the Sunda Straits was made the basis of the Dutch position and continued Portuguese occupation of the Malacca Straits became irrelevant. English competition for a dominant position in the spice trade was largely overcome after the Massacre of Amboina in 1623, and Dutch headquarters were established in Java at Batavia (Jakarta) in 1618 under the Governor-Generalship of Jan Pieterszoon Coen. From this strategic point control was extended over the Spice Islands themselves: the conquest of the Banda Islands in 1621 was followed by the absorption of Amboina in 1647, bringing with it control over the production of cloves. In twenty years the Dutch had succeeded in establishing a near-monopoly over the sources of the lucrative spice trade to Europe more completely than the Portuguese had ever done and they were subsequently successful in the larger aim, never attempted by the Portuguese, of dominating and effectively controlling not only the trade from Asia to Europe by the Cape of Good Hope, but also the inter-Asiatic trade and therefore the trade by way of the Indian Ocean and the Levant to the Mediterranean.[46] Between 1638 and 1658 they occupied Ceylon; Mauritius was occupied and the Cape of Good Hope was settled from 1652. From 1624 to 1661 they were in Formosa, and between 1638 and 1854 the Dutch colonists near Nagasaki were the only Europeans allowed to trade in Japan.

The extent of the Dutch monopoly over the spice trade to Europe in the seventeenth century may have been exaggerated, but it was an immensely profitable trade. The dividends of the Dutch East India company between 1605 and 1612 averaged 37½ per cent. For the republic as a whole it meant that a profitable entrepôt trade in colonial products was added to the existing functions of Amsterdam and Rotterdam. When the spice trade of the Far East lost its early predominance in the colonial trade as new products were introduced and new tastes were nurtured in the populations of Western Europe, the Dutch were very well placed as the rulers of Java, a densely peopled, fertile and productive land, to encourage or force the cultivation of new plantation crops. In the early eighteenth century sugar, coffee, indigo and tea loomed larger among the products of the Dutch East Indies than the pepper, nutmegs, cloves and camphor which had originally attracted their attention. From further afield Chinese silks, lacquer ware, paper, porcelain and tea or Japanese silk and copper were brought to European markets and became the source of immediate profit, inspiration of new ideas and even new industries such as the porcelain of Delft.

In the West Indies the Dutch effort was less spectacular but in many ways as profitable. The Dutch West India Company had been founded in 1621 and participated in the attempt to break open the Spanish monopoly of trade with the New World. Occasionally the Dutch achieved a rare and rich capture of America bullion convoys and for a time they succeeded in occupying Brazil in the 1640s, though they were later ejected from everywhere except the Guianas by the Brazilian colonists. In the Caribbean, Curaçao became the most important of a group of islands from which illicit trade with the Spanish settlers was conducted. Until the early eighteenth century the Dutch were predominant in the slave trade with West Africa, for they were able to secure the official Spanish permission for their slave-trading activity and had established a number of fortified posts on the West African coast. Finally, in North America the Dutch held a strong and valuable foothold through their patronage of Hudson's exploratory voyages and their settlement of Nieuw Amsterdam (New York) from 1623 to 1664. Indeed, in the first half of the seventeenth century the Dutch traders, penetrating inland by way of the Hudson valley, were well on the way to securing a major share of the North American fur trade in which English and French settlers were also competing for the favour of Indian tribes.

Maritime activity in Asia and the Americas contributed directly to the wealth and prosperity of the United Provinces, but the Dutch also led in the fields of exploration and discovery and in cartography. This is not the place to enlarge upon this theme, but it is an important aspect of the expansion of Europe overseas that the Dutch should have been responsible for the exploration of the North-east Passage, from which emerged new contacts with Russia and a greater knowledge of the Arctic waters in which Dutch whaling fleets were already beginning to operate. In the North-west Passage the Dutch had financed the exploits of Henry Hudson and thus the discovery of the Bay which bears his name. It was also the Dutch who made the early landfalls in western Australia: Janszoon in 1606, Hartogszoon and Houtman in 1616 and 1619, then Tasman in 1642, who succeeded in circumnavigating Australia and making a landfall in New Zealand.

The success of the Dutch carrying trade throughout the world rested on an astute appreciation of the problems presented by sea transport in the changing world of the seventeenth century at a time when the impact of overseas settlement was increasing. The Spanish and Portuguese in the sixteenth century had attempted to adapt late medieval institutions developed for the trade of the Mediterranean— an inland sea of limited access in which much of the trade originated in three relatively small and well-defined zones: the coast between Antioch and Alexandria, the northern Adriatic, and the coast between Barcelona and Leghorn. Monopolistic control of the major lines of trade had seemed a possible aim, particularly since so much hung on success in the spice trade. In the new world of the overseas empires, however, distances were greater, navigation was more hazardous, and security depended upon a much more complex structure of strongpoints and native alliances than were ever necessary in the Mediterranean world. The Dutch it was who recognised the existence of the two great geographical provinces of trade in which the aims and needs of commerce were essentially different. The coastal waters of north-west Europe from the Baltic to Lisbon and Cadiz constituted one of these provinces; the Atlantic, the Indian Ocean and the Pacific constituted the other; and the Mediterranean had something of the characteristics of both.

In overseas waters as in home waters the major aims of an efficient carrying trade were, of course, to ensure rapid and safe delivery at the lowest cost of transport, but the relative importance of these aims was different in the two spheres of commerce. The most obvious difference was distance, which necessarily meant that much greater amounts of capital were tied up for long periods in overseas shipping and in the purchase of commodities. For these reasons alone the long-distance trade was more heavily capitalised than the home trade and required more formal arrangements than the *ad hoc* and often small-scale co-operative investment by relatively small merchants and traders. The second major difference was that this was a commerce which, for the most part, was carried out with tropical lands and was concerned with commodities which were not produced at home, or indeed, in Europe; the imports of tropical produce could, in principle, be controlled and therefore monopoly profits could be secured. Thirdly, the fact that new trade routes over long distances brought merchantmen into contact with alien societies and also with European competitors in unpoliced waters made for uncertainty and insecurity, quite apart from the unknown hazards of navigation in unfamiliar waters and the inevitable risks of long-distance journeys. In the overseas province, therefore, effort had necessarily to be invested in the acquisition and protection of naval bases and in the maintenance, if necessary by force, bribery and intrigue, of commercial interests in alien territories. These functions also required capital investment on a large scale. A number of conditions therefore favoured the institution of chartered monopoly companies for this kind of trade in the Netherlands no less than in England and France. Large resources of capital were needed to finance long voyages; to finance military and naval action and the protection of strongpoints overseas; and to finance the purchase of expensive luxury goods. Risks were high and if they could be spread over several voyages the more could they be reduced; and a monopoly company was also able to maintain prices through control of supplies and sales. In terms of shipping, speed, manoeuvrability, manpower and firepower were the qualities which were needed. Carrying capacity had often to be sacrificed to such requirements. But since the cargoes handled were of high value in relation to their bulk, and could be expected to yield high profits provided that they could be safely delivered, low carrying costs were by no means always the most important desideratum, compared with the success of the voyage and the safe delivery of the cargo.

In the coastal waters of Europe the chief aims were also to ensure rapid and safe delivery and to reduce freight costs to the minimum. In general, home waters were so much better known and ports and harbours so much more accessible that shipping was certainly more secure than in the Atlantic or Indian Oceans; and except in the Mediterranean, in years of peace there was safety from piracy. Cost and speed of delivery were therefore much more critical factors in the coastal waters of Europe than in the overseas trade. It is true that competition from English, German, Scandinavian and French shippers served as a stimulus in keeping costs down, but it is also worth noting that much of the home trade depended on the bulk carriage of relatively cheap commodities such as grain, salt, timber and herring, for which the cost of transport was an important element in price and therefore a determinant of demand. Maintaining this bulk trade at a high level demanded the full use of shipping on frequent journeys over relatively small distances, giving a large turnover and low profits.

The Dutch recognised that there was an essential conflict between the aim of achieving maximum economy in freight costs on the one hand, and the double aim of achieving maximum security against attack and building ships which could be converted rapidly into naval ships in time of war. Speed, manoeuvrability and gunpower could only be achieved at the cost of carrying capacity or at the cost of the large crews needed to man complex rigging, for gunnery or for boarding duties. In time of war, or in unstable and insecure trades like the Levant trade, the convoy system assured security and the Dutch merchants could therefore concentrate singlemindedly on the reduction of freight costs to a minimum. This was achieved in various ways, which may be discussed briefly under three headings: first, the costs which varied directly with distance covered or time taken; secondly the overhead costs of fixed capital investment, chiefly, of course, in shipping; and thirdly, the intensity of use.

In the first group, it was time rather than distance that mattered in the age of the sailing ship, since wind-power was free and there were no important costs which varied directly with distance. The wages of the crew, their food supplies, insurance and interest charges on loans covering cargoes varied were the chief items of expense. Dutch rates of interest and insurance premiums were low, substantial economies were secured in wage costs by the development of types of cargo ship with simplified rigging which were easily handled by a small crew. The economies which were possible are hinted at in the comments of Huet on the Mediterranean trade that the ships in convoy with 20 to 25 guns had crews of 60 to 70 men, but the heavily-armed escort vessels with 50 to 60 guns required crews of 160 to 170 men.

Overhead costs were largely associated with interest, maintenance costs and depreciation of the fixed capital investment in shipping. Here again the low rates of interest and the effective machinery for the provision of loans and mobilisation of capital contributed to the cutting of transport costs, but great attention was also paid to maximising the carrying capacity of shipping in relation to the capital cost as well as in relation to the size of crews. New types of ship were built, including many specialised types for particular trades or areas; the most outstanding, known throughout Europe for its economy and efficiency, was the *flute* or fly-boat, a ship normally of 200 to 500 tons, flat-bottomed and with a broad beam to give maximum cargo space, rigged in such a way as to need only a small crew, and though slow, with good sailing qualities. Such ships were constructed at low cost by the highly organised shipbuilding industry concentrated chiefly at Zaandam near Amsterdam, renowned for the efficiency of its methods. Maximum use was made of machines and of windpower for the shifting of heavy timbers, and the operation of sawmills; stocks of parts, which were standardised, were kept in an organised fashion so that a number of ships could be assembled at once. Baltic timber was imported cheaply, thanks to the efficiency of the industry itself, and economies were made in materials by using pine and fir wherever possible in place of oak, and by eliminating ornament. The Baltic trade, of course, also supplied sailcloth, flax and hemp for cordage, pitch and tar. English ships of equivalent tonnage would cost half as much again or even twice as much as the Dutch-built product.

Thirdly the maximum utilisation of shipping capacity was achieved through both the efficiency with which trade was organised, and the concentration of trade on Amsterdam, perhaps the outstanding feature of the economic geography of the period. Maximum use of capacity depended mainly on the extent to which a full rather than a partial cargo was carried; whether return cargoes could be obtained; and a quick turn-round in the ports, which demanded availability of cargoes in the right place at the right time.

In a number of ways, the Dutch were better placed than any other group of traders to satisfy these conditions, partly because the very scale of their operations meant that there was a greater likelihood of cargoes being available. The entrepôt function performed by Amsterdam, and indeed by the Dutch ports as a group, was of fundamental importance. Sir William Temple commented on 'the lowness of their customs and easiness of paying with them, which with the freedom of their ports invite both stranger and natives to bring commodities hither not only as to a market but as to a magazine, where they lodge till they are invited abroad to other and better markets.[47] Violet Barbour quotes Pieter de la Court to the effect that 'a great commodity market, capable of buying up the cargoes of whole fleets, and of providing return cargoes as promptly, was an important factor in keeping down freight rates and in attracting shipping, both Dutch and foreign.' De la Court added, '. . . the English and Flemish merchants etc. do oft-times know no better way to transport their Goods to such Foreign Parts as they design, than to carry them first to Amsterdam, and from thence to other places.'[48]

Quick turn-round of ships and full cargoes both on outward and return journeys were also assured by the system of agencies and factors set up by the Dutch merchants in overseas ports, with the responsibility of arranging for cargoes to be available for shipment. It was the practice of Dutch agents, permanently stationed in overseas ports, to buy when conditions were favourable and also to buy in large quantities, frequently contracting for whole harvests or vintages. From Danzig and Amsterdam grain was available from the storehouses at any time; the French complained bitterly that the vintage of the Loire valley was largely in the hands of Dutch merchants. The large-scale purchases of the Dutch factors were certainly one of the means by which full cargoes were obtained and low prices secured for freight as well as for the commodity itself. Barbour commented that it was part of their advantage over their rivals in the Norway trade that they took off timber by the shipload, paying custom according to the ship's tonnage. They bought standing timber in Germany and almost the entire grain surplus from Denmark; and they contracted for cod supplies from English and French Atlantic fisheries. Finally, the Dutch merchants enjoyed one other advantage which tended to channel trade to their own ships, namely, the extent of capital investment abroad, both in private enterprise and in government loans. They held the concession for Austrian quicksilver and Hungarian copper; they were deeply involved in the investment and management of Swedish copper; they held the farm of the Tsar's export monopolies in tar, hemp, salmon and wool and they were deeply involved elsewhere in Russian development, notably, in shipbuilding, timber industries and metallurgy.

The industries of the Netherlands in the seventeeth century were renowned throughout Europe for their quality and variety. A basic division of the Dutch industries into the colonial *trafieken* industries and the traditional industries has been suggested more than once, and it is undoubtedly a useful guide; but there is less clarity in this classification than at first appears. Activity in overseas commerce introduced many new commodities into European trade and it is a characteristic of seventeenth-century colonial commerce that the new trades involved much more investment in processing and finishing industries than did the contributions of the overseas territories in the sixteenth. Sugar-refining was the most important, becoming one of Amsterdam's leading occupations after its introduction from Antwerp in the late sixteenth century. By 1662 there were some fifty sugar-bakeries. Tobacco-cutting and wrapping and the manufacture of snuff, diamond-cutting and polishing, the printing of East Indian calicoes, the refining of drugs, oils, and camphor were all industries which rested on the colonial trade. Other industries used new materials from tropical regions or traditional materials drawn indifferently from new and old sources: oriental woods and lacquers in the manufacture of furniture; soap-making; the dyeing, weaving and finishing of silk yarns drawn from Italian and Far Eastern sources, and depending originally on the skills of immigrants. Delft pottery was revitalised by the introduction of Chinese models and techniques. Yet another group of industries used raw materials or semi-finished products from other parts of Europe: the grain trade of Amsterdam was associated with malting, brewing and the distillation of spirits, particularly gin. Imported French wines and brandies were 'doctored' and cut. The bleaching, dyeing and finishing of imported woollen cloths from England and of linens from Westphalia, the southern Netherlands and the Baltic were particularly important industries which were also greatly stimulated by immigrations from Antwerp and the southern Netherlands in the sixteenth century and by the arrival of French Huguenots in the seventeenth. Ribbon, hat and paper manufactures also owed much to immigrant skills. But there is again little difference between these finishing industries and those which depended on the import of linens and linen yarn, not from Germany, but from the more local rural areas of Groningen, Friesland and Overijssel, where flax was widely grown. The Dutch cloth industry relied upon imports of Spanish wool, though wool of England, Germany and the Levant was also imported in smaller quantities. It was established at Amsterdam, Haarlem, Gouda and Utrecht, but it was particularly important at Leyden, a town of 63,000 in the seventeenth century and with an output equivalent to about a half of the total value of English exports at that time. Here too, immigrants from the south had brought new skills as they had done to England, and although there was an early expansion of worsted cloths similar to the bays and says of the new draperies in England, it was in the production of woollen cloths and camlets that the Dutch industry excelled.[49] Finally, one other group of industries should be mentioned, for they were closely associated with the development of the Netherlands as a centre of learning and scholarship: printing, paper manufacture, the Dutch school of cartography, and the manufacture of lenses, spectacles and scientific instruments.

Among the Dutch towns, several had acquired strong reputations for particular industries. Leyden had its printing and instrument-making as well as a great cloth production; Haarlem was renowned for the finishing of linens brought from Germany and the Netherlands, and also for its manufacture of silks and velvets. Delft's pottery and the cheeses of Edam and Gouda were famous. Amsterdam, however, was dominant. It was to Amsterdam, already well established as the centre of a flourishing Baltic trade in grain and timber, that the merchants of the southern Netherlands came to establish commercial houses and financial institutions. The Chamber of Assurance was founded there in 1598, a new bourse in 1608 and an exchange bank the following year. Its revenue doubled in twenty-two years at the turn of the century and its population, already substantial at some 30,000 in 1567, expanded to 105,000 in 1622 and was quite probably over 200,000 in 1675.

Urban growth was planned because of the need to organise careful reclamation and drainage and to sink deep piles to secure foundations, but the scale of the new expansion impressed contemporaries in the first half of the seventeenth century and, indeed, provided an urban framework which was still viable until well into the nineteenth century (Plates 31 and 32). The industries of Amsterdam, like those of the Netherlands as a whole, reflected very clearly the trade by which its merchants had made their fortunes, and depended on merchant capital and new or immigrant skills. Yet the town itself, founded upon a dyke-and-dam site on a minor stream, and with a position which was of strategic value mainly in terms of ancient Hanseatic routes from the Frisian islands to the Zeeland ports, was already inconvenient and difficult of access even in the days of its most rapid growth in the seventeenth century. Temple in particular remarked at length upon the site of Amsterdam:

'For havens they have not any good upon their whole coast. The best are at Helversluys which has no trade at all, and Flushing which has little. But Amsterdam, that triumphs in the spoils of Lisbon and Antwerp seems to be the most incommodious haven they have, being seated upon so shallow waters that ordinary ships cannot come up to it without the advantage of the tides; nor great ones without unloading. The entrance to the Tessel, and the passage over the Zuyder Zee is more dangerous than a voyage from thence to Spain, lying in all blind and narrow channels so that it easily appears that 'tis not an haven that draws trade, but trade that fills an haven and brings it into vogue.'[50]

An attempt has here been made to demonstrate the major features of the economic and commercial geography of the United Provinces in the seventeenth century, and it is clear that in the period of its greatest economic leadership its commercial activities were closely interwoven with its industrial development and the financial expertise which was so much the envy of all other western countries. The mainsprings of Dutch economic development are not by any means the primary concern of the historical geographer, but it may be useful to summarise briefly the stimuli to growth and to attempt to assess among them the value of geographical position and of the utilisation of the geographical environment. The relationship between the early rise of the Dutch ports and the routes of medieval Hanseatic shipping, and the importance of the delta ports of Zeeland in the early growth of Antwerp have already been discussed but it may here be stressed that these positional advantages were of no more than temporary importance; and though the major towns of the United Provinces continued to enjoy a waterside location, many of the routes which had been important in early growth were no better than inland waterways during the seventeenth century, when the geography of maritime trade in the area had changed out of recognition as the size and carrying capacity of shipping increased.

Secondly, the history of reclamation brought about a situation in which agricultural specialisation in dairy produce was forced upon the Dutch. Trade in bulk products and the import of grain were essential from the beginning. By the sixteenth century Amsterdam was a flourishing regional centre already dominating the Baltic trade in bulk products, and clearly the first choice as a metropolitan trading centre for merchants who were forced to flee Antwerp in the late sixteenth century.

The Revolt of the Netherlands was, perhaps, the major single formative influence in the growth of economic prosperity in the late sixteenth century. The immigration of merchants, artisans and capital from the southern Netherlands and particularly from Antwerp is a major chapter in the development of Amsterdam and it is difficult to overemphasise the impact of this sudden accession of wealth and population, commercial and financial expertise, and new trades and industries. The Revolt provided, too, the opportunity to expand horizons overseas in the Portuguese and Spanish empires and to accumulate profits and capital by supplying even the enemy Spanish forces. But what is also evident, though much less tangible, is that social and political structures and values were altered. The loose organisation of the States General was such that it gave a predominant interest to those commercial provinces which contributed most of the revenue; if it was the voices of Holland and Zeeland which were most strongly heard, these were also the very states in which the commercial interests of the rich merchants were most strongly represented. In the formulation of policy, and particularly of commercial policy, the rich merchants had much greater influence than their counterparts in any other country of Europe. The social climate of the United Provinces was also changed towards the attitudes of an acquisitive society rather than those of an agricultural and territorial nobility. Profits were more commonly ploughed back into trade and industry than elsewhere and the elevation of frugality to a virtue was a characteristic frequently noticed by contemporaries in France or England. Temple remarked, 'For never any country traded so much and consumed so little. They are the great masters of the Indian spices and of the Persian silks, but wear plain woollens and feed upon their own fish and roots. Nay, they sell the finest of their own cloth abroad and buy coarse out of England for their own use. . . .

In short, they furnish infinite luxury, which they never practise, and traffic in pleasures which they never taste except' (as he goes on to say), 'for French wine and brandy!'[51]

An upward spiral of development was set in motion at a time when the colonial trade was expanding rapidly and when, in England and France alike, colonial trade was beginning to generate new growth in the Atlantic ports. High rates of capital accumulation, low rates of interest, technological advances and the generation of new skills were all interrelated in the upward growth of the seventeenth century. One might, in some sense, agree with Temple that 'the trade of this country is discovered to be no effect of common contrivance, of natural dispositions or trivial accidents, but of a great concurrence of circumstances which never before met in the world to such a degree'.

By the end of the seventeenth century the Dutch leadership rested to a great extent upon its efficiency in the carrying trade, the maintenance of its colonial trade and its entrepôt functions, and an industrial structure which was to a large extent also based on entrepôt trade. During the eighteenth century the Dutch lost ground in the carrying trade in the Baltic and for many years during the eighteenth century trade was kept active to a very large extent as a result of its function as a neutral go-between for England and France in time of war.[52] After 1780 the Dutch position was irrevocably lost when the country finally abandoned this neutral position. Technical advantages in shipping and the organisation of the carrying trade had been successfully taken over by English, Scandinavian and French shipping, and mercantilistic policies directed against Dutch trade achieved results in the larger national markets of France and England. The loss of the carrying trade meant decline in entrepôt functions and consequently a loss of advantage in many of the Dutch entrepôt industries. Sugar-refining was developed in England, Hamburg and the French ports; distilling on the Elbe; sawmilling around the Baltic; and the finishing of linen and cloth in the areas in which they were manufactured rather than in Rotterdam, Amsterdam or Haarlem. In the colonial trade, too, the share of the Dutch colonies in the supply of spices, sugar, coffee and indigo was becoming smaller as the plantations of the New World increased their output and as the British and French position in India was established. Dutch supremacy remained only in its financial leadership until this too was swept away as a result of financial crisis at the end of the eighteenth century.

With the loss of prosperity in the eighteenth century, the rôle of position and resource had necessarily to be revalued. Formerly the richer profits of the carrying trade and overseas commerce greatly overshadowed the transit trade to the Rhine, but it was this last aspect of the position of the Netherlands which came increasingly to the fore in the eighteenth century. The hinterland of the Rhineland and the Meuse, ravaged by the Thirty Years' War, was recovering and developing afresh as a source of metals, linen, timber and woollen cloths as well as wine and grain. New attention was being paid to the creation of alternative outlets as Hamburg encouraged the diversion of trade to itself by low duties and the strength of the English connection. Bremen was competing for the trade of the Weser basin, and the Austrian Netherlands was also encouraging the use of overland routes from Cologne to Ghent and Ostend by new investment in roadbuilding and by offering low duties on transit trade. Indeed, a situation had arisen like that of the inter-war years, when Dunkirk, Antwerp, Rotterdam and Bremen competed for the transit trade of the Rhinelands, each supported by nationalistic economic policies. For the Netherlands in the early nineteenth century, however, the transit trade to the Rhine, together with the colonial connections with the East Indies, and the enduring wealth of its agriculture represented the chief assets with which the Dutch entered the period of the industrial revolution. In the age of iron and coal the initiative in development lay once again in the southern Netherlands, for the Dutch lacked the natural resources to benefit from the new industrial technology.

Reference has been made earlier to the process of concentration and dispersion in connection with the ports of the Low Countries (see pp. 384–399). It was argued in the case of Antwerp that the congregation of foreign merchants, perhaps as a result of fortuitous circumstances, was so important in facilitating the exchange of information as well as of money and commodities that a developing spiral of growth was generated in Antwerp itself during the first half of the sixteenth century. The very fact that so much of Antwerp's capital and so many of its merchants moved to Amsterdam suggests that the advantages of concentration continued to exert a considerable pull even at the time of the Revolt. But the Dutch carried the process of concentration much further than was ever possible at Antwerp, since they were able to add their supremacy in the carrying trade and a much greater emphasis on colonial and entrepôt functions and industries.

The internal economies of the localisation of trade and commercial functions in a single centre continued to develop in Amsterdam: specialised financial exchanges were founded, for example, specialised warehouses for particular commodities could be built, refining and processing industries developed. But in terms of the carrying trade, there were very positive advantages to be secured by the establishment of an entrepôt. The distribution and collection of partial cargoes at many small ports was more economically done through an entrepôt than by direct trade. Partial cargoes of high-priced commodities of low bulk could clearly be carried more economically in conjunction with bulk trades in low-priced goods than they could by themselves, and this factor must have assisted the grafting of the colonial trade to existing bulk trades. The colonial trade was necessarily an entrepôt trade, of course, not only because of the need for processing, refining and the breaking up of whole cargoes into smaller parcels, but also because of the way it was organised and financed.

As long as the colonial trade was still relatively small in scale, it could support only a few entrepôts, of which Amsterdam was the chief. But with the growth of the colonial trade and the expansion of industrial production in the eighteenth century, the scale of activity in relation to the size of cargoes and the number of ports may well have increased to the point at which direct trade links could be established at the expense of a central entrepôt. This is a hypothesis which might profitably be more rigorously formulated and tested. Yet it is evident that, for example, in mid-eighteenth century, English cloth was going directly from London or Topsham to Hamburg, Bilbao, Cadiz or Leghorn instead of going through Amsterdam or Rotterdam for finishing and dyeing. German linens were going through Altona, Hamburg or Bremen to England and elsewhere. And the expansion of the eighteenth century trade in sugar, tobacco, and coffee was so great as to permit a wide dispersal of refining, processing and blending in ports as far apart as Bordeaux and Danzig.

THE PORTS OF WESTERN FRANCE

The rise in importance of colonial and overseas trade is one of the dominant facts of the economic geography of Europe in the late seventeenth and eighteenth centuries. In North America the early fishing and the fur trades were supplemented by the trade that followed the settlement of substantial communities along the whole of the eastern seaboard; but the chief generator of new trade on an increasing scale was the development of the plantation system in north-east Brazil, Spanish America, the southern colonies of the eastern seaboard and, above all, the Caribbean islands. Tropical products were brought to European markets on an increasing scale; the slave trade represented a source of high profits and also of disastrous losses; and West Africa as well as the colonial territories of the New World supplied growing markets for European foodstuffs, wine, brandy and manufactured products.

The overseas colonial trade had been of small proportions in English commerce in 1600; by 1700 no less than 20 per cent of British exports went to colonial regions; but by 1784 some 50 per cent of British exports went to British colonies, which constituted a market for many of the manufactured goods that were particularly strategic in the changing character of British industry during the industrial revolution: cottons, woollen cloth, iron and copper wares, saddlery and arms. The shipbuilding industry was itself a consumer of many other products of industry.[53] The growth of colonial trade was bound to undermine the Dutch pre-eminence in the carrying trade of Europe even without the intervention of mercantilist policies aimed precisely to this end by England, France, Denmark and Sweden. The great strength of the Dutch had been in the efficiency with which they had organised the exchange and carriage of goods within Europe. Success in the colonial trade, however, required different qualities from those which were needed in the European trade, and Dutch leadership was less outstanding in this respect than in the commercially rigorous domestic trade. As the volume of trade expanded, entrepôt functions were performed by other ports besides Amsterdam, and processing industries became more widely disseminated over Western Europe.

It was a matter of policy that trade with the colonies should be a monopoly of the mother country, and chartered companies were frequently given monopolies of trade to particular areas. Thus, although the Dutch retained a dominant position in the East Indies, other and newly settled overseas territories were able to compete successfully with Java and the Spice Islands in the production of sugar, coffee, indigo and some spices.

36 *Antwerp*. Published by Guicciardini in 1567 at the period of Antwerp's commercial pre-eminence, the engraving gives an impression of bustling activity on the river Scheldt. The importance of small craft, transhipping goods from the delta ports, is evident The planning of defences has optimistically left space for new urban growth

37 *La Rochelle*, principal port of the Huguenots in the sixteenth and seventeenth centuries, and pioneer of the American trade, particularly with Canada, La Rochelle was also important in the wine trade. The old harbour and the fourteenth century Tour St. Nicolas is shown (right).

In Britain particularly, the western ports which came to handle much of the colonial trade—Bristol, Liverpool, Whitehaven and then Glasgow—were the foci of new growth during the eighteenth century. Hamburg, Bremen, Rouen, Le Havre, Marseilles, Copenhagen and Göteborg (a new town of the seventeenth century planned to give Sweden an outlet on the North Sea and to strengthen Swedish maritime interests in a wider world) shared in the expansion of colonial trade to a greater or lesser extent. But it was in western France that the growth of the colonial trade and its relationship to the changing economic geography of Western Europe can be most clearly charted. In Brittany, St Malo, Brest and Lorient were most affected, but it was Nantes, La Rochelle and Bordeaux among the Atlantic ports of France that were most obviously revitalised.

The development of the western ports of France took place in an economic environment much more strongly influenced by the hand of the state and by diplomatic and political conditions than was the case in Bristol and Liverpool. Periods of stability and expansion in the reigns of Henry IV, Louis XIV and Louis XV or during the administrations of Sully, Richelieu or Colbert alternated with periods of war and internal struggle which held up economic growth. The wars of religion, the Frondes, the Dutch wars, the war of the Spanish succession to 1713, the war of the Austrian succession and the Seven Years' War all interrupted the expansion of external French trade and maritime activity. Even the efforts of the state itself to stimulate colonial and naval activity were repeatedly jeopardised by military and territorial preoccupations on the eastern frontier.

Nevertheless, by 1750 the French had succeeded in winning a great empire. In the New World Breton and Norman sailors had established a leading position in the fishing of the Newfoundland Banks and explorers such as Cartier and Champlain had penetrated into the St Lawrence and paved the way for French participation in the fur trade and the exploration of the Great Lakes and the Mississippi. From 1632 settlement was pioneered in Canada, later to be planned on a larger scale by Colbert.

A whole series of monopoly companies had been founded by the state during the seventeenth century to further French overseas activity, and if some at least were not quite wholeheartedly backed by the merchants, they did, on the whole, succeed in breaking the monopoly of the Dutch and in making possible the great advances of French trade in the eighteenth century. The French East India

Company had been modelled by Colbert on the Dutch company, though French merchants had subscribed only about a third of its capital. Although it laid the foundations of the French position in India during the first half of the eighteenth century and was responsible for the creation of Lorient as a new port from which the eastern trade was to be handled, it was never a commercial success and it was wound up in 1769 after the collapse of the French position in India in the Seven Years' War. In 1635 the Company of St Christopher had begun the settlement of colonists in Guadeloupe, Martinique and St Christopher, and French pirates had already established themselves in some of the smaller islands of the Caribbean in order to participate illegally in the Spanish American trade. In 1664 French activity in the West Indies was reorganised under the auspices of Colbert's newly founded West Indian Company, and the basis was laid for that immense expansion of sugar, coffee, cotton and indigo which poured into the western French ports from these colonies after 1750. In 1716, French imports from the Antilles amounted to 16,700,000 livres tournois, but in 1788 the imports to France from this area alone amounted to some 185 million livres.

The continuing prosperity of the Breton ports from the sixteenth to the eighteenth century rested on the agricultural and industrial development of the peninsula as well as on its magnificent position both for small-scale coasting trade and for Atlantic commerce. Brest, St Malo, Lorient and Nantes were its major ports, but the little fishing villages along the coast collected local produce and also participated directly in overseas fishing in the Newfoundland Banks. Although its roads were notoriously poor and its access to Paris therefore mainly by river and coast, Brittany's many small harbours were well placed to export the grain and linens which were the major product of the area in this period. When harvests were adequate in the rest of France, Brittany could normally export its surplus grain to Spain and Portugal, but it also supplied some of the needs of Bordeaux and, as Paris grew in size, Breton grain was shipped to the capital by way of Rouen and the Seine or of Nantes and the Loire. Orléans, too, was constrained at times to search in Brittany for its grain supplies when the production of its normal hinterland in Beauce was earmarked for Paris.

By the end of the sixteenth century Brittany had also acquired a reputation for its linen and lace, industries based on local flax production and the availability of cheap labour and the prevalence of low standards of living. Rope, sails and nets for the fishing industry provided additional occupations. In the seventeenth century, when Breton lace and linens constituted an important source of revenue in Spanish markets, the problem of raising the quality and output of domestic linens received most attention from the state.

The Breton ports thus combined a number of advantages for overseas trade: an existing maritime tradition based on fishing and coastal trade; established contacts in Spain and Portugal; and marketable surpluses of grain and linen. The westerly position was perhaps a more questionable advantage, for although the northern coast of Brittany was an excellent base for privateering activities against Dutch or English shipping in times of war, legitimate trade was equally vulnerable to enemy naval action. St Malo had been a pioneer of Breton activity in the Atlantic fishing grounds off Newfoundland, and it was from St Malo that Jacques Cartier sailed in 1535 (Plate 38). Its merchants had been interested in the efforts of the French in the East Indies between 1600 and 1616 until they were discouraged by losses sustained at the hands of the Dutch. In seventeenth- and eighteenth-century England St Malo was best known for its piracy and privateering, and its interloping commerce with the Spanish colonies reached such proportions that the St Malo merchants formed a company to organise the trade in 1705. But this, too, collapsed after the grant to England of the *asiento* to trade slaves with the Spanish colonies after 1713.

In the late seventeenth and eighteenth centuries, therefore, it was the fishing of the Newfoundland Banks which constituted the chief source of St Malo's wealth.[54] Towards the end of the seventeenth century some 80 ships a year, averaging 130 tons, sailed from St Malo for the fishing on the Banks. A few of the ships came from other harbours, notably Granville, Barfleur, Binic or Cherbourg, but three-quarters were locally owned. Dried cod or salt fish were then carried back to Europe, but some 70 per cent of St Malo's ships returned indirectly, selling their fish at intermediate ports of call in Italy, Spain and Mediterranean France (chiefly Marseilles), and also in Bordeaux, Nantes and the Channel ports. Soap, olive oil, wine, sugar and spices were the chief imports to St Malo from this triangular movement.

Brest had the advantage of an excellent harbour on a ria coast, well sheltered from the dangers of hostile shipping in the Channel, but it has always had the disadvantage of a poor hinterland and difficulty of access to major markets by overland routes. At the end of the sixteenth century it was still a little fishing port of some 1,500 people, and although it was used as an official centre of the French East India Company, larger growth awaited the recognition of its value as a naval base. Replanned and fortified by Vauban in 1683, it also acquired shipyards and naval barracks, so that by 1776 it had reached a population of some 22,000. The creation of Lorient was also a result of deliberate planning, for its site had been selected, after a careful survey of the coasts of France made under the supervision of Colbert, by the directors of the East India Company as a base for its operations. Shipyards and warehouses were built and the town was planned. Its fortunes rose and fell with those of the French in India, but after the dissolution of the company it was handed over to the crown and subsequently used chiefly as a naval base. Arthur Young commented on it briefly, 'The buildings [of Lorient] are magnificent, but they want the vigour and vivacity of an active commerce'.

But of all the Breton ports Nantes was the most outstanding. The economic and strategic importance of its site had been recognised from Roman and Celtic times, when it had defended the crossing of the Loire and had been frontier fortress of Brittany as well as an important river port by which the produce of the Loire valley had been exported. Islands in the braided course of the Loire here made a river crossing practicable by relatively easy bridgebuilding. The river was tidal and accessible by sea-going ships, though shifting sands proved a constant source of difficulty; even before the industrial revolution large ships of over 180 tons had to use outports such as Coueron, Paimboeuf and Mindin.[55] The Loire itself was a corridor to the heart of the Massif Central, but it was also the route to Orleans and the Paris market, particularly after the completion of the canal in 1642. Yet, here, too, river navigation was hindered by occasional floods, but more frequently by shallow water and contrary winds, so that the construction of good roads in the eighteenth century was important in improving accessibility to Paris as well as to the hinterland of Nantes in Brittany and La Vendée.

During the Middle Ages and in the sixteenth century, however, Nantes had served primarily as a regional port for Brittany and had filled an international rôle in exporting salt from the Bay of Bourgneuf.[56] Up to 6,000 small ships a year were said to be involved in this trade towards the end of the fifteenth century, though it subsequently lost ground with the dislocations of the wars of religion and the operation of the tax on salt, which tended to turn the international trade towards Portugal and Andalusia. But the salt trade and the exports of wine from Touraine to the Low Countries and the Baltic had attracted the attentions of Dutch merchants who joined existing colonies of foreign merchants there, chiefly Spanish and Portuguese, and in the course of the seventeenth century came to dominate the foreign trade of Nantes. The wealth, the commercial and financial expertise of the Dutch, their wholesale purchase of Loire wines, and their import to France of sugar by way of Amsterdam rather than from the French colonies direct, were all much resented by the merchants of Nantes itself, so that Colbert's efforts to reduce dependence on the Dutch were given support and encouragement.

When the colonial trade began to develop in the seventeenth century, it rested upon solid achievements in local and interregional trade, so that there was available here, as at Bordeaux, Bristol or Liverpool, a reservoir of maritime skill in navigation and shipbuilding, commercial knowledge, local capital and also a great variety of goods for export. Salt, wine and brandy continued to be the local staples, the last rapidly gaining ground in West Africa as well as among the Dutch. Grain was exported at times of good harvests; iron and steel were imported from Spain and Sweden; coal from England and the St Étienne field (by way of the Loire navigation); tar and masts were brought from Bordeaux and Bayonne and masts from the forests of Nivernais by way of the Loire; oil and soap came coastwise from Marseilles; and salt beef for export to the colonies was drawn from Ireland; flax, hemp and linens were brought from the Loire valley as well as Brittany and during the course of the eighteenth century Nantes added also an interest in cotton printing and weaving.

The overseas trade of Nantes had been encouraged by the creation of the Company of Morbihan in 1626 for the purpose of developing the eastern trade; the Company of St Peter's Boat Bedecked with Lilies, which was aimed at stimulating long-distance voyages overseas, was subsequently also created with its headquarters at Nantes; the Common Bourse of 1643 was to engage in the Madagascar trade; and in 1665 Nantes was given a chamber of the East India Company, and also had relations with the Northern Company and the African and West Indian Companies.

Like St Malo, Nantes participated in the cod-fishing off the Newfoundland Banks, but it was with the West Indies that trade developed most vigorously from about 1630; contacts with the West African coast had aroused interest in the slave trade by the end of the century. Overseas trade was already well established by the end of the seventeenth century. It involved a triangular run from Nantes to West Africa with brandy, cloth, salt, metal pots and ornaments, slave ships to the West Indies, and imports of sugar, indigo, cacao and timber or dyewoods. In 1698 some 50 ships were occupied in the colonial trade; by 1738 there were about 88; and in 1743, 111. The volume of trade increased rapidly during the eighteenth century, particularly in the period from 1730 to 1750 and again after the Seven Years' War to 1789. The continuing importance of the colonial trade to Nantes is evident not only because it normally constituted between two-thirds and three-quarters of the total value of the import trade of the port, but also because of its importance in the re-export trade of the town and in developing industries there.[57]

IMPORTS TO NANTES IN THE EIGHTEENTH CENTURY
(*million livres tournois*)

YEAR	FROM EUROPE	FROM COLONIES	TOTAL	COLONIAL IMPORTS AS PERCENTAGE OF TOTAL
1729	3·3	7·1	10·4	68·3
1735	4·3	7·7	12·0	64·2
1743	4·7	9·8	14·5	67·6
1752	12·9	17·7	30·6	57·8
1777	10·0	24·3	34·3	70·9

EXPORTS FROM NANTES IN THE EIGHTEENTH CENTURY
(*million livres tournois*)

YEAR	TO EUROPE	TO INDIA AND GUINEA	TO W. INDIES AND N. AMERICA	TOTAL	EXPORTS TO COLONIES AS PERCENTAGE OF TOTAL
1729	9·2	1·2	6·3	16·8	44·6
1735	18·7	0·4	4·4	23·5	20·4
1743	11·7	2·4	5·4	19·6	39·1
1752	12·6	1·6	3·1	17·3	27·3
1777	20·0	2·8	7·2	30·1	33·2

Sugar was by far the most important import and refineries had been established at Nantes from 1670 producing both for domestic consumption and for re-export of refined sugar to Amsterdam, Scandinavia, Spain and the southern Netherlands. At the end of the seventeenth century 40 per cent of the re-exports of sugar from Nantes were taken by the Dutch alone. The total volume of imports of sugar from the West Indies increased rapidly during the eighteenth century from 6·35 million pounds in 1698 to 32·6 million in 1740. Coffee imports grew mainly after 1723, for until then the East India Company, based at Lorient, held the monopoly, but re-exports from Nantes to the Netherlands, Scandinavia and Germany increased rapidly in the second half of the eighteenth century. Indigo, cotton and dyewoods were also important imports, some of which were retained for the developing cotton textile and printing industries of the town itself. Cacao and tobacco showed considerable instability in the volume of imports, and tea, very important in the first half of the century, when even England was supplied from Nantes, ceased to be significant in trade at a later date.

For much of the eighteenth century, Nantes was also the largest French slave port. Growth of the West African slave trade had been particularly rapid in mid-eighteenth century up to 1754, after which it was severely curtailed during and after the Seven Years War.[58] In 1770 there were only 23 slavers out of a total complement of some 110 ships, but the industry revived very rapidly in subsequent years until 1792. An average of some 35 ships a year sailed to West Africa in the period 1783–92, and they were now larger ships of over 200 tons, many operating from outports in the lower Loire.

For Nantes, then, there is no doubt that the colonial trade was the 'keystone of its commerce'. In the years before 1730 it was the greatest port of France and, although it yielded to Bordeaux and Marseilles during much of the eighteenth century, it regained prime place at the end of the century with the development of its slave trade and West Indian traffic. Yet its rise to international importance was so closely bound up with colonial trade that the events of the Revolutionary and Napoleonic wars reduced it to the function of a regional port in the early nineteenth century.

The ancient provinces of Poitou, La Vendée, Aunis and Saintonge constitute a rather indefinite region, sometimes known as the *Centre-Ouest*, an area which has been relatively isolated from Paris, and which has lacked the identity and unity given to the Loire to the north and the Gironde to the south by the character of their valleys and the dominance of Nantes and Bordeaux. Lacking a single urban focus, the *Centre-Ouest* has been served by many ports and harbours, though in the *ancien régime*, La Rochelle especially began to add a new wealth derived from overseas maritime activity to the modest income that came from local, regional trade.

Like Brittany and Nantes, the *Centre-Ouest* had a tradition of maritime activity on which to base the more spectacular achievements of long-distance trade, for the coastal marshes which alternate with low limestone cliffs were very suitable sites for the evaporation of salt in the long, sunny summers of the region. The Île d'Oléron, Sables d'Olonne, La Rochelle and then Brouage had made their reputations on a salt and wine trade with the Low Countries and the Baltic. In the seventeenth century much of this trade, together with grain exports and the handling of the new and rapidly expanding brandy trade, had fallen into the hands of the Dutch.

By the early seventeenth century La Rochelle had become distinguished, not merely as the chief port of the area, but also as the strongest centre of Huguenot traders and craftsmen in the west (Plate 37). With a defensive site on a limestone ridge rising above the marshes, it had repulsed Catholic forces in 1573 during the wars of religion, and was only reduced by Richelieu in 1628 after a long and difficult siege. The Huguenot sailors of La Rochelle had already gained valuable experience in the interception of French Catholic shipping off the coast, so that La Rochelle, like St Malo, was well prepared to profit from an interloping trade in the Spanish colonies. It may be that its Protestant tradition helped to channel the best of its expertise towards commerce and industry rather than to government and political affairs, but it was certainly La Rochelle which most precociously developed trade with the West Indies. In the shipping census of 1664 it was revealed as possessing more ships of over 100 tons than either Bordeaux or Nantes, and it was already sending 27 ships a year to the West Indies in 1672 and 49 in 1685. Its sugar-refining and slave trades had begun to develop by the end of the century.

It was in the Canadian and Baltic trade, however, that La Rochelle was unique among the ports of western France. It became the chief port from which emigrants went out to the St Lawrence settlement, and it was also the chief beneficiary of the Canadian fur trade. The Baltic trade rested much more heavily on royal encouragement, however, for La Rochelle was made the base from which the operations of the Company of the North were directed after its re-formation by Colbert in 1670. The choice of La Rochelle was wiser than earlier efforts based on the Channel ports of Dieppe, Rouen and Calais, for the ports of western France had always had a closer link with the Baltic trade than the Channel ports, whose trade with England and the Low Countries was more important. The Northern Company had aimed at carrying the wine, brandy and salt of western France in French rather than Dutch ships, and it aimed moreover to return with naval stores and timber which would, it was planned, provide the materials for a shipbuilding industry to supply shipping for new colonial trades as well as for the French navy. A dockyard, with Dutch carpenters who were to train French craftsmen, was accordingly set up at La Rochelle. Dutch competition in the Baltic trade was still very strong in the seventeenth century and the war with Holland from 1672 put the carrying trade in the hands of Swedish.

The prosperity of La Rochelle was, however, relatively short-lived, for its commerce was severely affected by the dispersal of Huguenot merchants, sailors and craftsmen that followed the Revocation of the Edict of Nantes in 1685. Its West Indian trade fell at the end of the seventeenth century to the advantage of Nantes and Bordeaux; its Canadian trade was lost after 1763 to Britain; and La Rochelle, like other ports of this lowland, marshy coast, had begun to suffer from silting and shallow water.

Brouage, which now stands within its useless fortifications, surrounded by reclaimed marshes, was created as a salt-exporting port in mid-sixteenth century, in an area subject to silting (Plate 39). Its site amid the salt pans was at a place where incoming ships were accustomed to unload the ballast in which they arrived.[59] Refortified in 1628 by Richelieu during his campaign to reduce La Rochelle, the.port silted up rapidly and its population declined to a malaria-ridden forty souls, or thereabouts, towards the end of the eighteenth century. Colbert founded Rochefort to replace Brouage. Situated on the Charente and little more than a fortress in 1661, two years later it was laid out as a planned city, with all the shipbuilding yards and facilities needed by a major naval base. Dutch carpenters were brought in; an arsenal and a foundry were built; a naval school and a college of hydrography were established. During the late seventeenth century, the facilities it provided were instrumental in raising the French navy from some twenty to thirty ships in 1661 to a complement of 200 in 1677, but it had a difficult sea-approach up the winding course of the Charente and was abandoned as an important naval base after the Napoleonic wars.

The medieval prosperity of Bordeaux had been solidly based on the shipment of its wines to England in exchange for wool, cloth and metals, a trade that grew up after the political connection had been made between England and Gascony in the Angevin state. With the expansion of viticulture in the area the wine trade continued to be the chief preoccupation of the port and its bourgeoisie. There was a relative decline in the fifteenth century with the loss of the English political connection, and in the sixteenth and seventeenth centuries the expansion of trade was hindered by the interruptions of war and by customs regulations which worked against Bordeaux's commerce with the larger hinterland in France as a whole. Bordeaux wines were also out of favour in France during the period: for example, Colbert thought they were unhealthy and the Duc de Savigny disliked them. It was not until the end of the seventeenth century and the early eighteenth that they began to come back into favour in France, as a result partly of a renaissance in viticultural practices, partly of new-found favour among the French public, the aristocracy and even Louis XV himself. The American market was also taking increasing quantities of French wine during this period, and the English taste for claret survived the competition of Spanish and Portuguese wines at the turn of the century and later. Although the figures below are not exactly comparable, they appear to indicate a modest, but substantial increase at least in the wine exported out of France.[60]

WINES LOADED AT BORDEAUX IN 1729			OUTPUT OF WINE FROM THE AREA, 1789	
FOR:	NO. OF SHIPS	TONS	FOR:	TONS
Brittany, Normandy, Picardy and Flanders	710	17,000	Overseas colonies	30,000
England	175	5,000	Small white wines for foreign trade	50,000
Holland	275	22,500	Fine claret for England and Ireland	2,000
Hamburg and northern countries	210	18,000	Claret for northern countries for other French ports	8,000 25,000
American colonies	123	7,500	Fine wines to France	5,000
			Vin ordinaire for local consumption	75,000
			Waste and other loss	5,000
Total	1,493	70,000	Total	200,000
			Consumed in France	140,000
EXPORTS		53,000	EXPORTS	60,000

The success of the wine trade had attracted colonies of foreign merchants who were accorded favourable treatment, and although the Dutch led here as they did in other French ports, there was a German colony, particularly of Hamburg merchants interested in the re-export of colonial sugar in the eighteenth century, a group of Portuguese Jews who were given protection by Colbert in the seventeenth century, and Irish merchants whose presence reflected the importance of re-exports of Irish beef to the colonies.

For much of the seventeenth century Bordeaux had been slow to involve itself in the colonial trade, a fact possibly associated with the sluggishness of the market for the wines of the area, and with the predominance of foreign merchant enterprise in the shipment of its products overseas; but in the eighteenth century, and particularly after 1713, the Bordeaux merchants began to take a share of the colonial trade pioneered by other ports. In 1722, 120 ships were despatched from Bordeaux to the West Indies; in 1729, 123 ships went out to bring back cargoes of sugar and indigo worth 7 million livres. By 1782, however, 310 ships went from Bordeaux to the Antilles and the value of the West Indian import had risen to 130 million livres. The value of colonial imports increased by up to twelve times between 1730 and 1785. Sugar, indigo and later coffee were the chief imports; as at Nantes these commodities sustained a valuable re-export trade to the rest of France, and indeed, to continental Europe. From 1730 to 1789 was the great period of urban building during which the avenues and monumental buildings were laid out which still dignify the city. It had become the second city of France, enriched by the wealth of the sugar merchants and slave traders, and with a population which had grown from some 45,000 in 1580 and 58,000 in 1650 to about 80,000 in 1750 and about 100,000 in 1800.

As at Nantes, there developed industries connected with port activities as well as with the functions of Bordeaux as regional capital. The distillation of wines into brandy had been introduced in 1559, but it was not until mid-seventeenth century that rapid expansion of brandy production got under way for English, Dutch and Scandinavian markets, and in the eighteenth century for American markets. Perhaps because of the concern of the Bordeaux distillers for their reputation, they had in the early eighteenth century resisted the introduction of experimental liqueurs made from grain, sugar, pears and apples, and possibly it was as a result of this that they failed to develop the rum manufacture which became so important in the Americas and England. The manufacture of bottle glass was a second industry associated with wine and its export, though until the eighteenth century glass bottles had been of little importance compared with wooden barrels, also an article of local manufacture.

Sugar-refining emerged as the chief industry deriving from the colonial trade. It had been established in Bordeaux by a Flemish merchant about 1635 but expansion awaited the growth of colonial trade and grew during the eighteenth century with a protected market in southern France, Burgundy and Alsace, and with the right to re-export to Italy and the Levant. By 1740 some sixteen refineries consumed about fifty cargoes of raw sugar a year, each perhaps averaging 200 tons. By 1790 there were about twenty-six refineries, working on a larger scale and employing about 300 workers.

Shipbuilding was naturally dependent on the prosperity of Bordeaux's overseas trade. In the early seventeenth century the port had possessed no large ships of its own; in 1651 it had sent only eight ships to Newfoundland and had only sixty-two ships engaged in the coasting trade, most of them no more than ten to twelve tons. Even by 1730 very few of Bordeaux's growing merchant fleet were locally built; but by 1756 some sixteen ships of 34 to 480 tons were launched, and from 1763 to 1778 some 245 ships were launched—an average of sixteen ships with a total tonnage of 4,900 tons a year.

In the area of Atlantic France as a whole, as also in western Britain, the colonial trade was obviously of increasing importance during the seventeenth century, yet it is clear that the European trade was almost everywhere quantitatively more important and in the western French ports at least, it seemed to be on the whole more reliably productive of safe, though modest profits for the merchants involved. In France particularly, the colonial trade was artificially stimulated by state encouragement, by the formation of privileged companies, and by investment which was poured into the creation of new ports and harbours, shipyards and navigational schools. The acquisition of the First French Empire, the encouragement of the state and the attempts to reduce the predominance of Dutch enterprise constituted the essential preliminaries to the success of eighteenth-century trade.

In Britain, the shift of activity to her western ports during the seventeenth and eighteenth centuries helped to focus the growing prosperity of western and northern England and provided capital, markets and raw materials for the expanding industries which were emerging in the broader hinterlands of Bristol and Liverpool. The West Country cloth industry, the metal industries of the Midlands and the textile industries of Lancashire were all to some degree affected, as well as the industrial structures of Bristol and Liverpool themselves. This westward shift, combined with the existence of the coalfields of western England, made possible the rapid acceleration of industrial development though the very scale of this new growth has tended to obscure the substantial expansion which had already occurred in these areas in the first half of the eighteenth century.

In Atlantic France, however, a fortunate combination of a western maritime position and mineral resources suitable for industrial development did not exist, a lack which was never overcome; the French colonial trade, so promising at the end of the eighteenth century when the expansion of the West Indian trade had more than compensated for the territorial losses of 1763, was cut short by the revolutionary and Napoleonic wars. Brittany lacked a hinterland of industrial importance and its northern coast was strategically unsafe; St Malo was one of the first French ports to decline. Nantes had been much better placed in relation to the broad hinterland opened up by the Loire valley, but the difficulties of the Loire navigation and its distance from Paris and from the established domestic industries and the coal resources of the Massif Central placed it at a considerable disadvantage compared with, say, Liverpool or even Glasgow. The *Centre-Ouest* provided brandy, salt and wine for export but it lacked access to a large hinterland. Bordeaux flourished during the eighteenth century as a major regional capital as well as a colonial port, but its hinterland, well served by navigable rivers, remained one in which the rate of potential expansion in agriculture alone set the major limits to growth. In Atlantic France of the eighteenth century, colonial trade had become of fundamental importance, but the area lacked the mineral resources to carry it through to the nineteenth century as an effective competitor to its English neighbours.

REFERENCES

Abbreviations:
Ann. E.S.C.   *Annales, Economies, Sociétés, Civilisations,* Paris.
E.H.R.   *Economic History Review.*
1. R. H. TAWNEY, *Religion and the Rise of Capitalism*, London, 1922.
   M. WEBER, *The Spirit of Capitalism and the Protestant Ethic*, London, 1930.
2. R. C. SCOVILLE, *Huguenots and the Economic Development of France, 1680-1720*, Berkeley, 1960.
3. E. HECKSCHER, *Mercantilism*, 2 vols, London, 1935.
   C. H. WILSON, 'Mercantilism, some vicissitudes of an idea', *E.H.R.*, second series, vol. 10, 1957-8, pp. 181-8.
4. J. H. PARRY, *Europe and a wider World*, London, 1949, pp. 7-28.
5. I. A. MACGREGOR, 'Europe and the East', *New Cambridge Modern History*, vol. 2: *The Reformation, 1520-59*, ed. G. R. Elton, Cambridge, 1958, pp. 593-4.
6. F. C. LANE, 'The Mediterranean spice trade: evidence of its revival in the sixteenth century, *Amer. Hist. Rev.*, vol. 45, 1940, pp. 581-90.
7. Parry, *Europe and a wider World*, pp. 60-75.
8. C. H. HARING, *Trade and Navigation between Spain and the Indies*, Cambridge, Mass., 1918.
9. R. PIKE, 'The Genoese in Seville and the opening of the New World', *Journ. Econ. Hist.*, vol. 22, 1962, pp. 348-78.
10. H. and P. CHAUNU, *Séville et l'Atlantique*, 11 vols, Paris, 1950-9.
11. L'ABBE GARNIER, 'Galères et galleasses à la fin du moyen âge', *Le Navire et l'Economie maritime*, ed. M. Mollat, Paris, 1958, pp. 37-52.
12. E. J. HAMILTON, *American Treasure and the Price Revolution in Spain, 1501-1650*, Cambridge, Mass., 1934.
13. Y. S. BRENNER, 'The inflation of prices in England, 1550-1650', *E.H.R.*, second series, vol. 15, 1962-3, pp. 266-85.
    See also B. H. SLICHER VAN BATH, *The Agrarian History of Western Europe, A.D. 500-1850*, London, 1963, pp. 195-206.
14. F. BRAUDEL, *La Méditerranée et le Monde méditerranéen à l'Epoque de Philippe II*, Paris, 1949, pp. 385-97.
15. M. R. REINHARD and A. ARMENGAUD, *Histoire générale de la Population mondiale*, Paris, 1961.
16. Braudel, *La Méditerranée*, pp. 447-69.
17. Ibid., pp. 455-61.
18. D. ZANETTI, 'L'approvisionnement de Pavie au 16e siècle', *Ann. E.S.C.*, vol. 18, 1963, pp. 44-62.
19. Braudel, *La Méditerranée*, pp. 462-9.
20. Ibid., pp. 470-508.
21. Ibid., pp. 249-58.
22. A. TENENTI and others, 'Le film d'un grand système de navigation—les galères marchandes vénitiennes, 14e-16e siècles', *Ann. E.S.C.*, vol. 16, 1961, pp. 83-6.

23. P. MASSON, *Histoire de Commerce français dans le Levant au 18ᵉ siècle*, Paris, 1911.
24. M. J. TADIĆ, 'Le port de Raguse et sa flotte au 16ᵉ siècle', *Le Navire et l'Economie maritime*, ed. M. Mollat, Paris, 1958, pp. 9–26.
25. Braudel, *La Méditerranée*, pp. 349–56.
26. C. M. CIPOLLA, 'The decline of Italy: the case of a fully matured economy', *E.H.R.*, N.S., vol. 5, 1952–3, p. 178.
27. M. V. CLARKE, *The Medieval City State*, London, 1925.
28. SIR WILLIAM TEMPLE, *Observations on the United Provinces* (1673), repr. Cambridge, 1932.
29. BISHOP HUET, *Mémoires sur le Commerce des Hollandais*, Amsterdam, 1718.
30. V. BARBOUR, *Studies in the Development of Capitalism in Amsterdam in the seventeenth century*, John Hopkins Studies in Historical and Political Science, no. 67, New Haven, 1950.
31. L. GUICCIARDINI, *Description de tout le pais bas*, Antwerp, 1567, p. 239.
32. Temple, *Observations on the United Provinces*, p. 128.
33. Huet, *Mémoires*, pp. 43–4.
34. Ibid., pp. 45–6.
35. See chapter 9, section on Drainage and reclamation in the Low Countries.
36. G. L. BURKE, *The Making of the Dutch Towns*, London, 1956.
37. A. E. CHRISTENSEN, *Dutch Trade to the Baltic about 1600*, Copenhagen, 1961, p. 255.
38. Huet, *Mémoires*, pp. 73–6.
39. Temple, *Observations on the United Provinces*, p. 138.
40. V. BARBOUR, 'Dutch and English merchant shipping', *Essays in Economic History*, ed. E. M. Carus-Wilson, London, 1954, vol. 1, pp. 227–53.
41. W. S. UNGER, 'Trade through the Sound in the seventeenth and eighteenth centuries', *E.H.R.*, second series, vol. 12, 1959–60, pp. 206–21.
42. Huet, *Mémoires*, pp. 58–65.
43. Ibid., p. 68.
44. Ibid., p. 59.
45. Barbour, *Capitalism in Amsterdam*, p. 14.
46. Parry, *Europe and a wider World*, p. 56.
47. Temple, *Observations on the United Provinces*, p. 138.
48. Quoted by Barbour, *Capitalism in Amsterdam*, p. 20.
49. C. H. WILSON, 'Cloth production and international competition in the seventeenth century', *E.H.R.*, N.S. vol. 13, 1960–61, pp. 209–21.
50. Temple, *Observations on the United Provinces*, p. 128.
51. Ibid., p. 142.
52. C. H. WILSON, 'The economic decline of the Netherlands', *Essays in Economic History*, ed. E. M. Carus-Wilson, London, 1954, vol. 1, pp. 254–69.
53. E. J. HOBSBAWM, 'The general crisis of the European economy in the

seventeenth century', *Past and Present*, no. 5, 1954, pp. 33–53 and no. 6, 1954, pp. 44–63.

54. J. DELUMEAU, 'Les Terre-neuviers Malouins á la fin du XVIIᵉ, siècle', *Ann. E.S.C.*, vol. 16, 1961, pp. 665–85.
55. J. MEYER, 'Le commerce négrier nantais, 1774–92', *Ann. E.S.C.*, vol. 15, 1960, pp. 120–9.
56. A. DE WISMES, P. CAILLAUD, and J. S. GAUTHIER, *Nantes*, Nantes, n.d.
57. P. JEULIN, *L'évolution du port de Nantes*, Paris, 1929.
58. Meyer, *Ann. E.S.C.*, vol. 15, 1960, p. 121.
59. J. VIGE, *Brouage*, Saintes, 1960.
60. Municipalité Bordelais. *Bordeaux: aperçu historique*, vol. 1, Bordeaux, 1962.

CHAPTER 9

AGRICULTURAL AND REGIONAL CHANGE

INTRODUCTION

The agrarian structures of medieval Western Europe were largely geared to the provision of subsistence, either for the farmer and his family, or for the needs of a relatively local and circumscribed society in a fairly small area within which surplus crops were exchanged. In general, land use had to be a direct compromise between the needs of the population and the capacity of the land they lived on. On sandy soils rye was often grown in preference to wheat; in damp climates oats and barley were more reliable; and when growing seasons were short, barley was favoured. The balance of diet and the nature of the staple crops varied according to environmental possibilities. Yet trade was important at an early date in a number of regions where accessibility to navigable water offered opportunities of exchange for products which were more valuable and less bulky than grain or which were not too perishable for slow journeys to distant markets: wool, wine, some dairy products, olive oil, and a variety of Mediterranean fruits, for example. By the end of the Middle Ages the grain trade had also become a substantial source of income for Baltic countries; and the overland movement of livestock along organised drove-roads had already begun to reflect the divorce of cattle-rearing and cattle-fattening, by which land use could be adjusted to the extensive and intensive aspects of pastoral farming.

The economic stimulus of the market and the growth or decline of population are clearly two of the most basic stimuli towards agricultural change, though it may frequently be argued of particular cases in the past that population changes may themselves be a result of agricultural change (see below). The traditional agrarian structures and field systems sometimes placed certain limits on the concentration of farming on particular crops for sale. Beyond these limits the obligatory rotations of the open-field system were strained, often to a point at which breakdown or drastic modification had to occur.

For instance, where circumstances favoured pastoral farming as in midland England in the fifteenth century, conversion to pasture destroyed the open-field system and culminated in the depopulation of villages: 'Sheep are eating up men' in the well-used phrase of Sir Thomas More. In many parts of western Europe, however, the extent to which farming could be oriented to the production of a single product for the market was limited by the continuing need to assure a satisfactory output of subsistence crops as a primary aim of peasant farming, if not of large-scale and estate farming. In parts of France, Germany and Spain which were remote from easy communications, this point was a critical threshold not finally and irrevocably crossed until the nineteenth century. During the *ancien régime* in France, for example, the grain trade was hedged around with prohibitions and customs duties; price fluctuations in years of bad harvest were extreme; and the variability of yields was so great that few farmers were confident enough to dispense completely with the production of staple foodstuffs. Where they were minded so to do, as in southern France, intendants were greatly concerned that the extension of viticulture on former cereal land might threaten grain supplies in times of shortage.

Economic and demographic pressures towards a general expansion of agricultural output may be resolved, in principle, in two ways: either by bringing more land under cultivation or by making more intensive use of available resources. The great expansion of population and activity in Western Europe that came to a halt about 1300 to 1320 had been based very largely on the extension of the cultivated area. There had been changes which led to a greater output from existing arable land, and they should not be underrated. The development of the shoulder harness and the horseshoe had permitted more effective use of horse-power; and the shift from two-course to three-course rotations, or from temporary cultivation to permanent cultivation and regular rotations were great advances towards intensification. But, in general, greater output had been made possible by the clearing of the woodland, the reclamation of the heathlands, the drainage of marshes and the irrigation of dry lands. These are, indeed, the major themes in the transformation of the European landscape. The extension of the cultivated area represented a very heavy investment of capital or labour in the creation of new arable land, through irrigation, the drainage of marshes or the clearing of the thick oak woodlands on heavy clays in north-western Europe, but these categories of newly reclaimed land varied substantially in their subsequent productivity, and in the degree to which they continue to require investment. Once cleared, the heavy clays were good arable land but they continued to require intensive labour of men and animals in order to secure tolerable harvests; the heathlands were easy to clear but when a retreat from the margin of cultivation occurred it was often most rapid on the light, sandy, acid lands or on the uplands. The drainage of marshes, however, frequently brought into agricultural use land which was fertile and easy to cultivate, though initial investment in labour, capital and in organisation was heavy and considerable attention was needed for maintenance and repair. Much of the process of settlement during the great age of clearing coincided with the clearing of woodland, but the drainage of marshland and land reclamation from the sea is of such particular interest, in the way in which it illuminates the relationship between society, technology and the use of the physical environment, that a brief account has been given below of the history of drainage and reclamation in the Low Countries.

The intensification of farming on existing cultivable areas has most commonly occurred in close proximity to urban markets or within easy access of navigable water. The increase in productivity per acre implied by intensification may take place as a result of higher yields obtained from existing crops as a result of heavier application of labour or capital, or it may involve concentration on high-yielding crops of greater value per acre. It is axiomatic that up to a certain point, increased application of labour brings about an increase of output or reduces liability to crop failures in years of unfavourable weather. Deep digging or deep and frequent ploughing, hoeing, weeding, row cultivation, pruning and the tethering of stock are farming practices in which more labour could profitably be used on customary crops. But more intensive methods of farming may result from a transference to new uses of land: for example, from grazing to cereals or from grain to vines, each with very different demands on labour. Thus in southern and south-western France, the greater returns per acre to be gained from viticulture justified heavy investment of labour and made it possible to gain a modest living from much smaller holdings than those needed for grain farming. Similarly near Lyon, in northern Italy and eastern Spain, the concentration on mulberry cultivation and sericulture made use of the labour of women and children in the fields and combined it with a remunerative domestic industry so as to maintain the viability of small peasant holdings.

But intensification of agriculture resulted also from the investment of capital. Fixed capital was invested in irrigation, drainage and reclamation, the reorganisation and enclosure of fields, or the creation of new and more convenient farm buildings, and many such episodes of heavy investment in fixed capital installations have had enduring results on the landscapes of Western Europe: the drainage of the Fens or the creation of polders in the Low Countries, the irrigation of the north Italian plain in the late Middle Ages, the multiplication of dispersed settlement in central and northern Italy or western France as a result of the creation of share-cropping tenures and the creation of new compact holdings. Greater application of short-term capital—stock for draught purposes, implements, manuring, liming and marling—has also helped to produce higher yields. The cultivation of root and fodder crops has permitted an increase in stock population and led to the increase of grain yields by the more intensive manuring that was thus made possible. Measures such as these also resulted in the elimination of the fallow year by more or less complicated rotations involving a ley period of clover, lucerne, roots or other forage crops.

The increase in productivity in several branches of farming more or less simultaneously by such changing methods, in a manner reminiscent of the so-called agricultural revolution in England in the eighteenth century, took place in two areas of Western Europe in the period from the fourteenth to the eighteenth centuries, namely in northern Italy in the fifteenth and sixteenth centuries and in the Low Countries over a more extended period. Irrigation and the introduction of new crops, particularly rice and mulberry, were important in northern Italy, and in Flanders fodder crops, industrial and dye-producing crops played an important part. These were also areas of great commercial and industrial strength and of continuous urban demand, not only for staple grains but also for animal products, vegetables and industrial crops which commanded higher prices than grains. The principles of von Thünen's 'rings' operated to bring about a concentration on such crops in the proximity of the towns, but the commercialisation of farming near the towns also served to attract investment by the urban bourgeoisie, as for example in the great grain farms of Beauce or the rice plantations of the Po valley. Rising urban standards of living and more varied and interesting diet also played an important part in relation to the development of new farming systems, for many of the new techniques arose out of the spread of horticultural crops from orchards and market gardens to the larger context of general farming. In just the same way as viticulture spread from urban walled gardens into the open countryside in late medieval France, or as the garden pea has in recent years spread from market garden to general farming with modern methods of preparation and marketing, so also did turnips, rape and coleseed in the early modern period.

In many ways, therefore, the development of more intensive forms of farming was related to the proximity of the towns, not only as markets for food and raw materials but also as suppliers of capital. German authors speak of *Intensitätinseln*, islands of intensive and commercial farming in the neighbourhood of the great cities and the industrial centres of late medieval and early modern Europe. Flanders and Brabant, Zeeland and Holland constitute one of these areas; the north Italian plain in the orbit of Milan and Venice is another. The Rhine valley, particularly around the rift valley towns, was a third such region and Catalonia a fourth. Paris and London were also surrounded by areas of agriculture which were more commercially advanced than their neighbours in the later Middle Ages; increasingly so in the seventeenth and eighteenth centuries in the case of London when its urban influence became much more pronounced.

Population and agricultural change

Although the relevance of population movement for agricultural change is clear in general the precise nature of the relationship is difficult to establish. Between the eleventh century and the end of the thirteenth there is little doubt that populations at least doubled. Demographic expansion had many repercussions: the extension of the cultivated area, the decline in real incomes of the peasantry, the splitting up of holdings, increases in the price of land and of grain, a tendency to shift from extensive pastoral to arable farming, and new movements of colonisation in Spain, eastern Germany and Scandinavia.

There is also a growing body of opinion that a critical situation had been reached by the close of the thirteenth century in that, through population pressure on available resources, subsistence was threatened by harvest fluctuations that might have been unimportant in earlier times. Local famines and locally heavy mortality were common phenomena in an age of poor transport and inefficient marketing, but the widespread occurrence of food shortages, famines and even starvation which followed the poor harvests of 1315–17 almost everywhere in Western Europe signalled the closing of an era and the closing of the frontier of colonisation. Over much of France, Flanders and England a cool, wet summer followed by a disastrously wet autumn produced a miserable harvest. Grain prices rose beyond the capacity of many to pay. Bark, roots, seeds and the scavengings of the countryside were eaten, and a heavy mortality followed. At Ypres, 10 per cent of the population died in the summer and autumn of 1316. Banditry, theft and violence increased, and the effect of wars and royal taxation exacerbated the situation. Yet the famines of 1315–17 were but the prelude to the Black Death of 1348–9 and of the subsequent waves of plague which reduced the population of Western Europe by a proportion variously calculated at a third to a half. The bubonic plague, carried by rats, had been transmitted along one of the great caravan trade routes of the time from China to the Crimea and Constantinople where the disease appeared first in 1347. Soon afterwards, it appeared in Crete, Genoa and southern France. The following year it had spread more widely into the whole of Italy, North Africa, Spain and much of France. In 1349 Germany, Austria, Switzerland and Hungary were affected, and the plague was widespread in the Low Countries and Britain. By 1350 it had reached its maximum extent in east central Europe and Scandinavia. In England, numbers may have fallen from about 3·7 million in 1350 to 2 million in 1377; Italian towns lost from 30 to 60 per cent of their population. Towards the end of the fourteenth century occasional epidemic waves of plague were recorded, and the plague had become endemic in much of Western Europe.

The fall in numbers and the stagnation of population which continued well into the fifteenth century in many parts of Western Europe, created a new relationship of population to resources.[1] Grain prices tended to fall as demand declined and there was frequently a shift to pastoral products, notably wool. The cultivation of marginal land was abandoned in some areas, and in many regions of heavy clay soils which had been valued arable in the prosperous days of the thirteenth century, land was allowed to fall down to pasture and there was a shift to pastoral farming. Peasant holdings tended to be larger and, since labour was relatively scarce, real wages increased, involving a shift towards a larger consumption of animal products either as food or in manufactures.[2] There was a move towards the use of land in more extensive forms as pasture or rough grazings, a process which, in particular, was responsible for the contraction of rural settlement and the desertion of villages. The details are discussed elsewhere (pp. 291-3), for this process has contributed every· where to the development of modern rural settlement patterns and agrarian structures.

The revival of population growth was long delayed—until the fifteenth century in Artois and Hainault, for example, and until much later in the fifteenth century in Brabant. In the Low Countries as a whole, it tended to occur earlier in the towns than in the countryside. In Spain and Italy there was an earlier revival, though throughout the fifteenth century there were many individual years in which heavy mortality followed a recrudesence of disease or low levels of subsistence. In southern France, by-passed by international trade routes during the period, revival was later, and in much of Germany too, recovery was only under way towards the end of the fifteenth century, though the towns showed earlier and important signs of expanding economy and population.

During the sixteenth century, however, expansion was widespread, though still halted from time to time by poor harvests and occasional epidemics. Italian and French immigration, coupled with a high rate of natural increase, was responsible for the rapid expansion evident in Catalonian parish registers. The population of Galicia increased by 50 per cent between 1490 and 1590 in spite of losses due to emigration and migration.[3] Castilian population doubled from 3 million in 1530 to 6 million in 1594, and though numbers were increased by only a third in the Salamanca area they were much more than doubled round Madrid and Toledo. In Valencia there was moderate expansion between 1527 and 1563 and then an increase of 50 per cent in the next 45 years. In Italy there was rapid growth, especially in the towns (see pp. 416-17 above). It is difficult to reach a satisfactory estimate for France, though Paris had a population of 200,000 by 1590 and the total population was probably between 15 and 20 million. The population of Germany has been estimated at 12 million in 1500, rising to 20 million by 1600. The towns made substantial but unspectacular progress, but in the countryside new settlement in the eastern marches was resumed, especially in Pomerania and Brandenburg, and new mining towns and villages were established in Bohemia and round its margins. In England, too, there was rapid growth, especially in the second half of the sixteenth century, when the upper limits of cultivation were being forced back on a new scale in the north of England and in Wales, and when new dispersed farmsteads were being created in compact holdings. In Scandinavia the sixteenth century witnessed an advance of the frontier of settlement in the north and new summer settlements were being founded or had recently been founded at the time of Gustavus Vasa. These later became permanent nuclei from which further colonisation took place.

Like earlier phases of growth, that of the sixteenth century came to a halt. During the seventeenth century war became more frequent and destructive and climates may have become a little wetter and cooler. The period 1600–1850 has been characterised as a relatively cold one, during which glaciers were extending. Records of grape harvests, tree rings and available meteorological data substantiate this evidence. Grain production may well have suffered and it has even been suggested that the spread of maize into Western Europe was limited by the relatively unfavourable climate, just as the spread of the potato may have been facilitated. The chief sequences of poor years and bad harvests during the period were probably 1590–1602, 1606–09, 1639–44, 1672–77, 1691–1703 and 1709–16. Plague and epidemics once again became more frequent towards the end of the sixteenth century and remained a characteristic feature of mid-seventeenth century life in England. In Spain, Italy, France and Switzerland there were major epidemics in 1629–31 and in 1720. But plagues were not an entirely independent factor, for very often high mortality from plague was linked to bad harvests. War, too, had become more devastating with the increase in mercenary and professional armies. Living conditions in the field were abominable and the seizure of crops, looting and burning caused many more casualties than direct military action.

Germany suffered particularly badly in the seventeenth century, and it has been estimated that in Mecklenburg, Silesia, much of central Germany, Bavaria and the Palatinate, losses of population amounted to as much as two-thirds. Germany's population was probably lower in 1700 than in 1600 and recovery was delayed until the mid-eighteenth century. In Italy and Iberia plague was almost endemic in the seventeenth century and there were nine major occurrences of plague in the western Mediterranean from 1609 to 1654.

The population of Spain fell from 8 to 5½ million during the century and that of Italy was in decline.

For the whole of Scandinavia and Iceland very detailed sources of population data are available.[4] From the end of the seventeenth century parish registers give remarkably complete details of births, deaths, sex, marriage, age at death and suspected cause of death (see Fig. 9:1). Age pyramids for the eighteenth century display the broad base and sharply tapering apex associated with high birth rates and high mortality (Fig. 9:2), though Iceland is somewhat irregular and Finland displays a very high proportion of babies and a very high infant mortality. Scandinavian marriage rates were high and the mean age of marriage relatively low. Crude birth rates were high at about 31–33 per thousand, but lower than those of eighteenth-century France or Europe as a whole in the early nineteenth century. Mortality rates were also slightly lower than in much of Western Europe as late as 1800–20. Yet they were at about 26–28 per thousand (compared with a modern rate of 14·8 in Sweden in 1936–40). Infant mortality was then some five times as high as now and between 1 and 10 years of age it was ten times as high as it is now. The average expectation of life at birth in Scandinavia in the eighteenth century was 36 years for men and 39 for women, compared with 64 and 66 respectively in the 1930s. The general picture which emerges, then, is one of a relatively young population with few old people, and therefore one in which resilience to economic and social change was high. Birth and death rates were high, though not as high as in eighteenth-century France or much of Western Europe in the early part of the nineteenth century. For the period, Scandinavia was a relatively healthy area, and also one of relatively low fertility. The movement of total population shows a modest increase during the eighteenth century which was in general less than 1·2 per cent per year and in Sweden and Denmark only 0·5 and 0·3 per cent.

Yet these overall movements conceal dramatic short-term fluctuations which are summarised in Fig. 9:1, and it is also clear that there is a close, though by no means complete, correlation with poor harvests. Thus a very bad harvest such as that of 1742, which itself followed crop failures in 1740 and 1741, led to grain shortages and to high grain prices. Mortality was heavy, and there was a fall in conceptions which was reflected in the low birth rate of the following year. A similar combination of circumstances followed again in 1758, 1763, 1772, in the 1780s, 1790 and about 1800. A tendency for the marriage rate to fall at times of high prices and to rise again later is also apparent. But there were other years of bad harvests, such as 1748, which were not followed by heavy mortality and a lower number of births. These facts appear to suggest a cycle of population

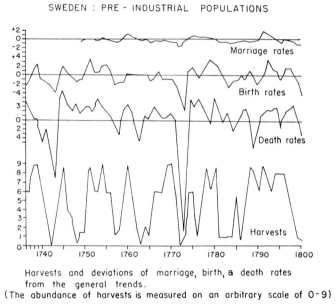

Harvests and deviations of marriage, birth, a death rates from the general trends.
(The abundance of harvests is measured on an arbitrary scale of 0-9)

Fig. 9:1   Pre-industrial population trends: Sweden, 1740–1800 (after Gille)

movement characteristic of pre-industrial populations. The famous concept of Malthus that population tended to press upon the means of subsistence seems to be vindicated by the evidence. For much of the cycle, population lived near the margin of subsistence. Crises were induced by high cereal prices and shortages brought about by war, civil disturbances, or more commonly by the failure of the harvest. Poorer peasants and wage labourers were sometimes reduced to a diet of bark, seeds, rotting grain, and whatever could be scavenged from village or field. Heavy mortality resulted, not perhaps so much from outright starvation as from intestinal diseases or other diseases such as typhoid, plague or influenza against which resistance was reduced by inadequate diet. Births and marriage rates also suffered and infant mortality was very high indeed. In the succeeding phase, however, population began rapidly to recover. Death rates were low, partly because standards of nutrition for a smaller population were greater, and partly because a large proportion of the very young and the aged had been already eliminated in the period of high mortality. Birth rates at this time were high: the age structure of the population was more centred around the fertile age groups; wages were relatively high and land for farming available. Sons were able

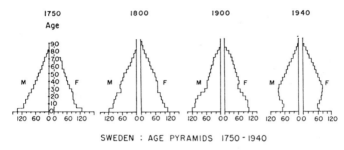

SWEDEN : AGE PYRAMIDS 1750 - 1940

Fig. 9:2   Sweden, age pyramids, 1750, 1800, 1900 and 1940 (after Gille)

to enter into family holdings at an early age because of the high mortality of older groups. Thus the marriage rate was high and the age of marriage low since many more could afford to support a wife at a younger age than formerly; and because of the lowering average age of marriage, birth rates tended to be high. Finally, cheaper food and higher standards of nutrition may have directly affected fertility. Thus, at this stage of the cycle, population growth would take place and would continue to occur until checked by another crisis brought on by war, bad harvests or epidemics. During the early stages of growth, moreover, devastation caused by war or poor harvests need not have had disastrous effects on population as long as there was a substantial margin of subsistence.

Now it is true that the Scandinavian countries lie very near to the northern margins of cultivation in Western Europe, and it may be supposed that this very fact might make their harvests more subject to disastrous fluctuations than those of more favoured countries further south and west. Yet there is a growing body of evidence that the mechanisms of population movement which can be statistically demonstrated in Scandinavia in the eighteenth century and which were described in England by Malthus obtained also in France and Germany. In France, very detailed studies have been made for the district around Beauvais in the Paris basin and are being made for other parts of France, and it is already apparent that very similar mechanisms were at work in the seventeenth and eighteenth centuries.[5] Professor Goubert has identified three types of recurrent demographic crisis in the Beauvais district of the Paris basin, due to pestilence, war and famine (Fig. 9:3). *Epidemic* crises show heavy

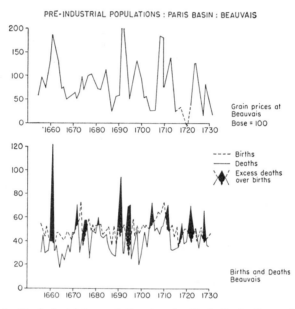

Fig. 9:3   Pre-industrial population trends: Paris Basin–Beauvais, 1660–1730 (after Goubert)

mortality, especially from June to October, but occur independently of grain price movements and are not accompanied by low marriage or birth rates. In crises resulting from *military* action, high mortality was less commonly the result of violence and fighting than of famine brought about by the seizure, looting and destruction of crops by passing armies (see Fig. 9:3). Of the three types *famine* was the most frequent visitor, though the poor harvests responsible for famines may often have been the consequence or riot, war and disturbance as well as the result of bad weather.

In France as a whole, however, there are hints of significant regional variations in the incidence of heavy mortality, especially in so far as this was due to poor harvests and the prevalence of high grain prices. Areas of relatively small holdings in peasant proprietorship suffered heavily, especially if there were few other resources than the cereal production of a predominantly arable economy. The domestic spinners of Picardy could survive the shortage of grain which followed the cold year of 1709 much more easily than the grain producers of Beauvais. Where there was a substantial pastoral side to local economy there were also greater possibilities of survival. Brittany appears to have been much less haunted by the spectre of famine in the seventeenth century than most other parts of France: the climate is equable and more reliable, and diet rested on a great variety of grains—wheat, rye, barley and the high-yielding and untithed buckwheat—so that there was less risk of crop failure. There was also a greater extent of uncultivated heaths and commons on which stock were reared, and Brittany's domestic textile production, its fishing and its participation in commerce helped to cushion the population from the worst severity of food shortages. Taxes and tithes were low compared with those of rest of France. Regional differences in the fluctuation of population may well have been substantial, though little study has yet been made of where and how this may have occurred.

Prices, agricultural change and regional specialisation

Economic historians have naturally paid much attention to the importance of price movements as a factor in agricultural development. Slicher van Bath has recently summarised most revealingly the relationships through time between agricultural and industrial prices, between wages and grain prices, and the relative movements of prices for cereals, meat, wool, hides and skins, butter and cheese and industrial crops.[6] During the great expansion of the Middle Ages grain prices rose rapidly, but in the years of depression that followed the demand for grain fell, grain prices declined and real wages rose, particularly in Germany and England. Industrial prices remained relatively high and butter, meat and fat prices fell much less steeply than grain prices.

To the historical geographer these shifts in the balance of prices are important in so far as they created new differentials in the opportunities of particular areas to make use of their resources of soil, climate and terrain. The fall in grain prices as well as the fall in population after 1320–50 brought new land reclamation to a halt, notably in the Low Countries; it helped to reduce the incentive to clear and settle in new villages in eastern Germany. Land reverted to pasture and rough grazing, and it is often hard to decide whether arable was being 'converted' to pasture or simply abandoned and allowed to 'fall down' to pasture. In England the 'deserted' villages represent extreme cases of this situation; in Germany this was the period of the *Wüstungen* when similar contraction of settlement took place. But the same process of contraction and desertion was going on in Spain, France, Scandinavia and in the Alps.

The shift of prices in favour of animal products obviously encouraged conversion to pasture, especially in those areas where because of soil or climate conditions pasture represented a more rational or profitable use of land than arable. Thus heavy clays in midland England were enclosed more commonly than areas of light and easily cultivated soil; upland margins of cultivation in the Alps and the Tyrol retreated, but new small dairy farms spread over the countryside. From Denmark store cattle were exported to the Low countries and to Lübeck and Hamburg.

The development of rural industry was also favoured by the shift in prices, not only because of the obvious and direct advantage of higher prices for manufactured goods and higher real wages in industry than in arable farming, but also because within agriculture itself price structures also favoured industrial crops such as flax and hemp, or dyestuffs such as woad and madder, as well as wool, leather and hides as against arable products.

But with the recovery of population in the sixteenth century and with a general tendency towards inflation, encouraged by a rising level of economic activity and the influx of bullion from the New World, agricultural prices again began to rise. In this new phase of growing demand, grain prices rose earlier and faster than prices of stock products while industrial prices remained relatively low. Land reclamation was revived in the Low Countries, irrigation was extended in the Po valley and trade in wine, olive oil, salt and also in new subtropical crops increased in other parts of the Mediterranean. Greater attention was paid in many areas to the ways in which grain yields could be increased by new cultivation methods, or by heavy manuring, marling and liming, but in the major towns and industrial areas and increasingly in the Mediterranean, local grain supplies were inadequate to support the population, which provided Hamburg,

Lübeck and Amsterdam especially with the opportunity to import Baltic grain, much to their financial advantage.

Just as the demographic expansion of the sixteenth century was one of the most important factors in the configuration of price structures during that period, so at a later stage from about 1650 to about 1750 the relative stagnation of population was one of the important elements which underlay new changes in the pattern of prices. Cereal prices again fell, real wages were relatively high, stock prices held up relatively well and the terms of trade as between agricultural and industrial prices moved to the disadvantage of the former. As in the fourteenth and fifteenth centuries there was a widespread tendency for the conversion of arable land to pasture, a shift from grain to stock, and encouragement to rural, domestic industry. But there were also new and important trends within arable farming from grain to fodder crops and ley farming and thus towards the evolution of a progressive and intensive arable farming oriented towards both stock-rearing and cereal production.

Seventeenth-century agricultural depression was, however, characteristic of Spain and Germany, the southern Netherlands and France. Rural depopulation was a result of the conversion of arable to pasture, a trend which was again common in areas of damp summers, heavy clays or hilly terrain such as Austria, Switzerland, Ireland, parts of midland England, the margins of the Ardennes and the Condroz depression in the Low Countries, Burgundy and Normandy. In the United Provinces little new land was reclaimed after 1665 though factors other than the balance of prices were certainly involved here.

As in the earlier period of low grain prices so in the seventeenth and early eighteenth centuries the shift towards industrial crops and stock-rearing provided the raw materials for rural domestic industry just when manufacture could offer a reasonable return to supplement earnings reduced by the fall of agricultural prices as a whole. Textile industries handling woollens and linen and, increasingly, cotton and silk were the chief ones to be developed.[7] Such widely diverse areas as Valencia, Alicante, Catalonia, the Massif Central and the Lyon area, the eastern Netherlands, Westphalia, Switzerland, Scotland, Ireland and the English Midlands were profoundly affected by the spread of rural industry (see Chapter 10).

The so-called depression of the seventeenth century was accompanied, therefore, by a very strongly marked geographical differentiation in land uses which has had enduring effects on the landscapes of many parts of western Europe. This was the case to an outstanding extent in those areas where the changes in the balance of prices and demand coincided with the growth of ports and capital cities on an unprecedented scale. In areas of easy accessibility and in the expanding regions of commercialised farming that were emerging round the great cities of the seventeenth and eighteenth centuries areas of specialised land use were beginning to crystallise out in response to the principles which were clarified and enunciated by von Thünen at the very end of the period here under review.

Around Paris the dairy farming of Brie and Normandy complemented the granaries of Beauce and the Île de France. The vines of the Île de France had to be protected from the competition of new and ordinary wines produced in bulk for the Paris population in the Loire and Yonne valleys. In the Low Countries the differentiation of pastoral and dairy areas devoted to stock-raising, dairying and fattening, industrial crops and horticulture or market gardening was taking a modern shape in the seventeenth century.

It was in England, however, that the new geographical specialisation of farming took place in a fairly clear relationship to the extension of the London food market, though no more than a thumb-nail sketch can be given here.[8] Dutch influence had been important in the location of market-gardening, fruit and hop cultivation, and it is noteworthy that in Norfolk, Essex and Kent the new emphasis on 'gardening' owed much to Dutch example. Yet these were areas in fairly close proximity to London, especially the most important of the new zones of horticulture, Kent. Essex and East Suffolk had concentrated on dairying since the late Middle Ages, but now in the seventeenth century new areas of dairy farming emerged a little further afield in Buckinghamshire, Hertfordshire and on the fringes of the West Country. Huntingdonshire and east Leicestershire were gaining a reputation for their cheeses, and so too was Cheshire. In the claylands of the Midlands, particularly in Leicestershire, and also in East Anglia, the fattening of cattle driven south or east on long-distance drove roads from the upland pastures of Wales, Scotland and northern England represented a new specialisation. On the claylands, the conversion of arable to pasture, often accompanied by enclosure and some rural depopulation has left discernible evidence in the rural landscapes of the area, but in areas of light soils or drier climates which were, in general, more committed to arable farming

38 *St. Malo*. Sited originally on an island, and defended by walls dating from the thirteenth and fourteenth centuries, but strengthened in the seventeenth, St. Malo had early contacts with the New World and the fishing grounds of the Newfoundland Banks, and had important early trade with the Spanish Empire, but it achieved notoriety in the seventeenth and eighteenth centuries as a port for privateers operating from the English Channel.

39 *Brouage*. A fragment of the sixteenth century walls which still surround this "fossil" port, isolated even from the sea as a result of silting and marsh drainage.

40 *Windmills at Leidsendam.* The use of windmills in the Dutch schemes of lake drainage in the sixteenth and seventeenth centuries is well known. The photo shows how banks of windmills lifted water from an inner ring dyke, draining the reclaimed land, to the higher level of an outer channel.

than the clays of the Midlands, this solution was not easily practicable. A. H. John has remarked upon the fact that the efforts of these regions to profit from the relative advantage of prices for animal products over grain prices led them to experiment with types of mixed farming involving the cultivation of fodder crops such as turnips, clover or lucerne.[9] Norfolk, Surrey and Hertfordshire, all areas in sufficient proximity to London to benefit from intensive methods of mixed farming, were certainly among the pioneers in this adaptation and reorganisation of Dutch ideas which constituted, in the seventeenth century, the prototype of techniques which were at the heart of the agricultural revolution in the eighteenth century.

Finally, one other point should be made before proceeding to a series of case studies. The impact of overseas competition on the agriculture of Western Europe is a dominant and well-known theme of the late nineteenth century, when the influx of Balkan, Russian and North American wheat changed the pattern of land use in England, forced a reappraisal of agricultural resources on the Danes, and hastened the raising of protective tariffs in Germany and France. Somewhat later, the import of frozen beef from the Argentine created a new crisis. But these were merely relatively recent episodes in a continuing history of the impact of overseas competition on European agriculture. In the nineteenth century the cultivation of the mulberry and the rearing of the silk-worm in southern France, northern Italy and eastern Spain was profoundly affected by Japanese and Chinese competition as well as by the ravages of disease. In the late seventeenth and eighteenth century it had been the European sugar producers of Spain and Sicily who had been hard hit by the competition of Java and the plantations of the New World.

It would be tedious to pursue in detail the changing geography of agriculture throughout Western Europe prior to the industrial revolution in order to illustrate further the principles and ideas so far outlined. Instead it is proposed to focus attention on four topics. The history of viticulture in France emphasises clearly the importance of ancient origins but it also illustrates the enduring effect of easy accessibility to northern markets in the location of viticultural areas near the northern boundary of cultivation. The advantages of water navigation are much less important than they once were, and the argument that a particular wine 'does not travel' may be a reflection, not of transport difficulties, but of the fact that it was in the past produced too far away from navigable water to warrant the kind of care and attention which has gone into the marketable wines nearer to easy transport links. Moreover, the location of the great vintage wines of France provides an excellent illustration of the ways in which invested capital, traditional skills, marketing organisation and commercial goodwill represent the central features of an 'agricultural inertia' as important as its industrial counterpart in maintaining highly localised agricultural specialities. A second study takes up one of the themes concerned with the extension of the cultivated area, with reference to the reclamation and drainage of land in the Low Countries. Both in northern Italy and in the Low Countries overriding interest attaches to the stimulus given by urban and commercial expansion to the reclamation of land, the intensification of land use, technical changes in agricultural structures, tenurial change and capital investment in farming. The linkages by which this stimulus was felt were, however, frequently complex and indirect, and they were also not by any means the only forces which operated to produce change and development. It is, indeed, this complexity which makes these two areas worthy of more detailed study. The third area, eastern Spain, shares in this process too, for Catalonia may be regarded as one of the *Intensitätinseln* of advanced agriculture which depended on commerical expansion and urban life. But eastern Spain also provides a case study of other elements of importance in agricultural and regional change: the limitations imposed by climate and water shortage; the acceptance and spread of new crops; and the competition between the Mediterranean world and the new plantations of a developing overseas world in the production of subtropical crops.

VITICULTURE IN FRANCE

The vine is one of the most strongly localised crops of all Western Europe *outside* the Mediterranean region itself. In Mediterranean lands, it is widely grown and, although there are nowadays large areas in which the vine is almost a monoculture, wine production for domestic consumption has always been fairly easy in southern regions and the vine has formed one element in varied local farming systems and its cultivation has been widely scattered. But away from the Mediterranean, viticulture has become very highly concentrated in a relatively small number of areas where intensive production is frequently associated with the production of vintage wines of good quality. It is also evident that the locations of all these areas are fairly well selected not only in relation to insolation and the occurrence of light, well-drained soils, preferably with a sunny, south-facing aspect in more northern areas, but also in relation to river valleys and water transport. Thus the Rhine, the Moselle, the Loire, the Marne, the Gironde and the Rhône–Saône trough are all regions in which the vine has flourished on escarpment slopes, on gravel terraces or on the flanks of deeply incised meanders. Although soil and aspect are important, particularly for drainage and insolation, the skill and care employed in the selection of the vines, the cultivation of the grape and its careful harvesting and processing are the important factors in ensuring excellent wines. High quality compensates for the lower yields and higher risks of these northerly and marginal areas. It is also clear that the original localisation of viticulture in these areas took place many centuries ago and that marginal locations have been preserved and perpetuated by the development of internal economies of localisation: skill, techniques, management and, above all, quality and reputation.

The introduction and spread of new, acclimatised varieties of vine into Gaul in the Roman period has already been briefly outlined, and it would appear that even by the fourth century A.D. the major areas later known for their wines were already producing and exporting wine: the Côte d'Or in Burgundy, the district of the Bituriges around Bordeaux, where Spanish varieties of vine had been acclimatised, near the Rhine frontier and in the Moselle valley, and especially in the neighbourhood of Trier; in the Loire valley near Tours and Nantes, and in the Seine basin near Paris (see above, pp. 80–1).

During the Dark Ages, viticultural traditions were kept alive partly through liturgical needs, but also through the prestige as well as the pleasure associated with the consumption of wine. It was in particular among the monasteries and at the bishops' seats that the viticultural traditions of the Roman Empire were preserved. In Burgundy viticulture was preserved in each of three dioceses. Macon and Chalons were dioceses which had easy access to the Rhône navigation and also plenty of potentially good land for viticulture. Here there was no problem in supplying the bishop and his needs. But Autun, the third bishopric, possessed only the eastern scarp of the Côte d'Or as potential wine-growing land and it was therefore on this section of the scarp that attention was concentrated and good yields secured by dint of terracing and careful cultivation (Fig. 9:4).[10] Here it is, indeed, that the fine quality wines of Beaune and

Nuits are still produced. (The locations of some of the vineyards on the Côte d'Or producing such well known burgundies as those of Gevrey-Chambertin are shown on Fig. 9:5). It is interesting also that the boundaries of the dioceses were based essentially on the limits of ancient Roman *civitates*. In this, as in the persistence of many town

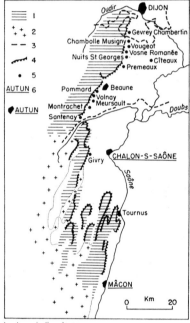

Fig. 9:4   The concentration of vintage wines within the limits of the ancient diocese of Autun (after Dion)

1. Jurassic limestones
2. Crystalline rocks and Palaeozoic schists
3. Boundaries of the Diocese of Autun
4. Escarpment of the Côte d'Or
5. Vintage wines
6. Bishops' seats

sites from Roman to medieval times, the link has been established through the continuity of the Christian tradition from late Roman times.

Even in Merovingian and Carolingian times there was still a northern European trade in wine. The wine of western Gaul was being exported, and in the late eighth and early ninth centuries sherds of Rhenish pottery found in southern Scandinavian sites suggest that Rhenish wines were being sent north-eastwards from Cologne to the Jutland peninsula. In Alsace vines were planted for

Frisian traders and the fairs of St Denis were celebrated for the exchange of wine, deriving, in all probability, from the Île de France.

The general reaction, however, to the contraction of trade and the shift towards subsistence farming everywhere in Western Europe during the Dark Ages was to grow vines far beyond what would now

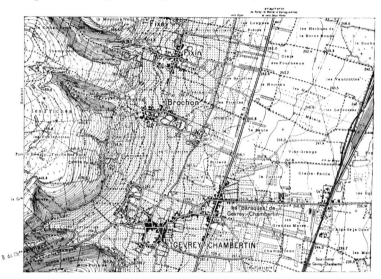

Fig. 9:5 Viticulture on the Côte d'Or. Note the location of the vineyards on the face of the escarpment (marked by dashed lines). Note also the open-field lay-out of the arable lands on the plain (Inst. Geog. Nat., 1:20,000, 1949, Gevrey-Chambertin 8, reduced to 1:50,000).

be regarded as a reasonable commercial limit. It must be remembered that the modern northern limit of viticulture is no fixed climatic limit, but a complex, arbitrary and transitional zone. A long, dry summer is required to ripen the vine and good drainage at the root is needed. At the northern margins of cultivation the best advantage must be taken of slope, aspect and soil conditions and of local climates. Nevertheless in more northerly latitudes vintages are irregular in quality and quantity as a result of variations in summer weather from one year to another, so that it is necessary to weigh carefully the chances of an adequate yield and a drinkable wine. But in the eleventh century, vines were grown in English monastery grounds, as at Malmesbury or Bury St Edmunds, for example, and there were many vineyards scattered about London in south-east England in the eleventh century.[11] Vines were grown, too, in Normandy, Flanders, and north-east France and viticulture was not abandoned in the Somme and in Normandy until the sixteenth century.[12] In many parts of northern France, of course, vines continued to be grown in the sheltered conditions of walled gardens in towns and their suburbs, and monasteries valued the acquisition of land suitable for viticulture, as in the Low Countries, where Flemish monasteries held vineyards in the Meuse and even further afield in order to secure their supplies.

But it was, above all, wine which provided the *raison d'être* for the revival of commerce in north-western Europe in the eleventh century and later. And although at first the movement of wine was over the shortest distances from the most northerly marginal areas of suitable summer climate, the range of commerce later tended to increase and to include those regions which are still renowned for quality wines. Thus in the early eleventh century wines were moving down the Seine to the Channel and to England, from such centres as Auxerre, Laon and Soissons. Similarly, merchants from Cologne and Flanders were taking Rhenish wines to the Low Countries and England in the twelfth century. In the west, Noirmoutier on Oléron and the Île de Ré were involved in the early trade, and the rise of the wine trade there was very closely associated with the expansion of the salt trade. Much of this trade, too, was in the hands of merchants from the Low Countries. In the twelfth and thirteenth centuries the exports of wine and salt from western France provided the major link in the axis of coastal trade that was being built up from Bordeaux and Bayonne to the Baltic. Indeed, it is with the appearance of large, fully decked ships that the expansion of this trade took place from La Rochelle, Île d'Oléron and Bayonne; the new port of Damme near Bruges may have been created for these larger vessels. By 1200 the wines of Poitou and Anjou had joined the 'French' wines from the Seine basin as the most important in the English market. Much of the early trade was in the hands of Flemish merchants and contributed to the expansion of Bruges and its commerce, but the importance of German merchants was growing in the thirteenth and fourteenth centuries as they superseded the Flemish in organising the exchange of wine and salt to the Low Countries and the Baltic in exchange for Flemish cloth, fish, furs and other northern goods.

The English merchants had also established themselves in strength in western France in the thirteenth century. The acquisition of

Aquitaine and Gascony by the English crown in 1152 threw open new opportunities for the Anglo-French trade in wine. From the thirteenth century, Bordeaux became of increasing significance, already supporting a colony of English merchants by 1300 when 170 ships a year were involved in the London trade and when approximately a quarter to a fifth of Bordeaux's trade was conducted with England, much of it in the hands of English shippers.[13] The towns in the hinterland of Bordeaux which were sending wines to England were all on navigable rivers. Wine from the further hinterland was certainly involved in the trade, but a distinction was made between the Bordelais, the area around Bordeaux which included Médoc and Graves, and which was permitted to export its wines before those of the further hinterland or Haut Pays were put on the market. The wines of the bourgeoisie, the nobility and clergy in the neighbourhood of Bordeaux had the additional advantage of freedom from customs duties. The wines of the Haut Pays, already at a disadvantage, were more drastically cut off from the English market during the political vicissitudes of the area during the Hundred Years' War, but vestiges of the ancient discrimination still survived when the privileges of Bordeaux were again codified and keenly defended in the sixteenth century. Though the limits of navigation and local variations in soils and climate had an important influence on the location of vineyards, the area of production of the Bordeaux wines was, therefore, defined rather by provincial boundaries.[14]

In north-western Europe wine played a rôle even greater than that of wool or salt in stimulating the expansion of commerce in fairly bulky commodities from the eleventh century. The maritime laws and customs codified in the Rôles d'Oléron, one of the chief of the early wine ports, were the source of much English and also Hanseatic sea law. The *tun*, the large cask for wine equivalent to two pipes or four hogsheads became a measure of ships' capacity, applied as the space occupied by a *tun*, and from there it was a relatively short step to the concept of the ton as a measure of weight.

In the area between the Rhine on the one hand and the western coast of France on the other there were several other regions in which medieval viticulture flourished during the twelfth and thirteenth centuries as a response to external demands from more northerly markets. In the Paris basin the wines of Laon, Soissons and Beauvais were known from the ninth and tenth centuries; Flemish abbeys coveted land here for viticulture and Laon wines were being exported to Flanders by overland routes in the eleventh and twelfth centuries. But it was always a very marginal area, and according to one medieval poet, the vintage of Beauvais was so poor that it deserved to be excommunicated,[15] and did in fact gradually disappear during the sixteenth century. The wines of France of this period, shipped by way of Rouen to England, came from the Île de France, not from the whole area of modern France. To the end of the Middle Ages, Paris, like Domesday London, was surrounded by vineyards in places which have long since been swallowed up by urban growth. Montmartre, Issy, Chaillot, Suresnes and Ivry are but a few of the well-known places which once had vintages.[16] To the east, Reims, Epernay and Châlons-sur-Marne were already established as wine producers, and commercial production on the Champagne scarp was in being by the fourteenth century, though the wine was not yet known as champagne. Although the Champagne Fairs provided a market, viticulture preceded their rise and survived their decline, for because of its bulk the overland movement of wine to the Low Countries took direct routes from the vineyards rather than an indirect course through the fair towns.

Towards the south the location of medieval viticulture in France is best considered as resulting from a compromise between the disadvantage of a lengthening route, and the advantage of a sunnier climate likely to produce a good, full-bodied and alcoholic vintage more often than the northern areas where white wines were normal and thin growths too common. Auxerre and Tonnerre both had a good early reputation for their quality and could ship down the Yonne to Paris and thence to Rouen and the Channel. These were the wines of Burgundy which most commonly reached Paris at this period, for the region of the modern great burgundies of the Côte d'Or lay away from navigable water on the scarps, and their nearest river led south to the regions of easy wine production. To some extent quality compensated for distance in securing a market in Paris, but it was not until the patronage of the Dukes of Burgundy and the Papacy at Avignon was extended to the wines of Beaune that the Côte d'Or revived in the fourteenth century. In the Jura the wines of Arbois also depended on noble patronage for their success just as, further west, in the Loire valley, the vines of Anjou were given an initial stimulus in the thirteenth century by the English crown and nobility in a frontier region of the Angevin kingdom.

Between the sixteenth and the eighteenth centuries, however, new changes occurred which profoundly affected the type as well as the distribution of viticulture in much of France. The period as a whole is one of great change in drinking habits throughout north-western Europe; many of these changes occurred first in Holland, and English and German consumers soon followed. In the sixteenth century beer brewed with hops had spread from the Low Countries to England, but in the seventeenth century new beverages were imported into Europe and as expensive and rare luxuries began to attract the taste of the aristocrats, the intelligentsia and the bourgeoisie. Tea, coffee and cocoa were the major new colonial contributions to European tables, but the Dutch also developed and propagated a taste for stronger drinks such as grain spirits and gin distilled in Holland from imported Baltic grain. Fortified wines with added brandy, sugar and spices were also introduced at this period, whilst artificially sweetened wines, 'cut wines' and mixed vintages were other features of a trade which shocked the integrity of many good Frenchmen. True brandies (of distilled wine or *vin brulé*, translated by the Dutch as *brand wijn* and corrupted by the English to brandy) were made of grape harvests that were surplus, or productive only of a weak, thin vintage, and the Dutch taste for sweet white wines was satisfied by the development of new vintage areas such as that of Sauternes.[17] Weak wines grown on peasant holdings rather than on noble or bourgeois estates were exported or doctored.

Dutch commercial expertise and capital made it possible for whole vintages to be bought up and even contracted for in advance, and although French merchants complained the area under vines was extended to new localities. In the Loire valley the wines of Touraine and Anjou were revived by Dutch enterprise operating from Nantes; from Bayonne viticulture spread up the Adour valley, and from La Rochelle the potentialities of the Charente valley were exploited and brandies supplemented white wines in a profitable export trade, particularly from the neighbourhood of Cognac. Further south in the area of the Haut Pays above Bordeaux brandy production allowed the area to overcome its continuing disadvantage as against the Bordelais and a new area of viticulture developed in the watershed area between the Adour and Garonne in the Armagnac district, and then further upstream near the newly constructed Canal des deux Mers, in the eighteenth century.

The expansion of northern markets, particularly in England, Scandinavia and the Baltic, stimulated the new viticulture, particularly in the west, but in much of northern France urban growth coupled with the spread of wine drinking among other classes than the bourgeoisie and the nobility brought equally far-reaching changes. The growth of the towns had already displaced many of the early vineyards from the gardens of urban houses to nearby suburban villages in which the bourgeoisie had acquired property for viticulture; but when artisans and even urban labourers began to take up the habit of wine-drinking, suburban viticulture spread with little regard for the finer characters which had given many of the northern marginal areas their reputation for quality wines. One response to this was the prohibition of urban wine-bibbing by the lower orders, who promptly resorted to cafés and drinking houses located just outside the town limits. Other old reputations were completely swamped, like that of the wines of Île de France, and new areas of viticulture concerned with the production of ordinary rather than vintage wine grew up beyond the regional ban around Paris in the Loire valley near Orléans and in the Seine and Yonne basins (Fig. 9:6).

Yet another solution to the need to protect the reputations of quality wines was to preserve the exclusiveness of a brand name, like Champagne, which became so known as late as the seventeenth century, or again, by new and meticulous attention to the quality of the stock, the picking of the grape at exactly the right moment and its most careful manufacture and storage to produce a true vintage wine. Among such new techniques was the process, developed in the eighteenth century, whereby the bubbles were put into champagne.

In the south-west of France a similar social evolution in the habit of wine-drinking may be traced, but there were complicating elements.[18] The viticulture of Bordeaux was badly hit by the war against the Dutch from 1672 and later hostilities with England. Both Dutch and English sought alternatives to the supplies from Bordeaux and found them in Portugal and Xerez in Spain. The English Methuen Treaty with Portugal (1703) provided for very favourable customs duties and the duty on Spanish sherry remained less punitive than that on French claret, so that in the first half of the eighteenth century England imported an average of 20–30,000 tuns of Portuguese wine, 10–15,000 of sherry and only 1–3,000 of claret. In the Bordeaux districts, however, more wine than ever was being produced on peasant holdings and on newly drained marshland as well as on the old vineyards of the châteaux. Thus the bourgeoisie and the *noblesse de*

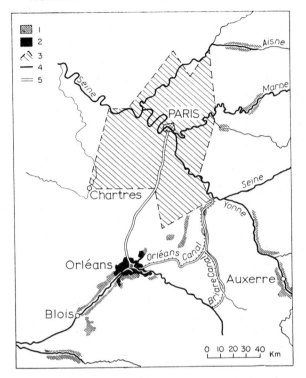

Fig. 9:6   Provisioning of Paris with cheap wine in the seventeenth and
eighteenth centuries (after Dion)

1. Vineyards producing cheap wine.
2. Parishes in the Orléans district indicated in 1709 as being 'all in
vineyards'.
3. Area round Paris in which wine production for sale to merchants and
innkeepers had been prohibited in 1577.
4. Rivers used for navigation.
5. Paris–Orléans road.

la robe were stimulated to experiment at their châteaux, frequently
on old settled sites on dry, well-drained gravels, with new methods
of stock selection, cultivation and harvesting as well as storage. The
effect was to create vintage wines as a prestige product which could
compete with the fortified ports and sherries. In a similar way the
house of Martell, from 1715, and that of Hennessy a little later, were
also experimenting to produce liqueur brandies quite different from

the *vin brulé* with which the Dutch had formerly been content in the seventeenth century.

From the fourteenth to the eighteenth century, but particularly from the end of the seventeenth, the habit of wine-drinking had spread down the social scale and a popular viticulture had developed around the towns in all of those parts of France where vines could easily be grown. After 1715 the spread of viticulture appeared to begin to threaten the area of land under cultivation for cereals, and, with persistent regional barriers to exchange as well as poor overland communications, this seemed to generate a real danger to the security of food supplies, so that in 1731 new plantings of vines were forbidden. The preamble to the decree of 1731 commented that there was 'too great an abundance of vines, which occupied a great quantity of lands suitable to carry grains or to make pastures . . . and they multiply the quantity of wine so much that they destroy their value and their reputation in many places'.[19] But after the middle of the century, the climate of opinion changed towards a greater degree of *laissez-faire* and freedom of trade so that this restrictive decree was repealed in 1759 and the way thus opened, particularly in the south of France for the great expansion of viticulture which was characteristic of the nineteenth century.

DRAINAGE AND RECLAMATION IN THE LOW COUNTRIES

It can be said of the Netherlands with more truth than of any other country that it is a creation of man, for it owes its existence to the long-continued struggle to drain and reclaim new land and to protect existing lands from the invasion of the sea. Forty per cent of the country lies under sea level and without constant attention to diking and draining the most productive agricultural regions, the most densely populated areas and many of the major cities would be under water or in grave danger of flooding. In terms of the area drained, the greater part of the Dutch achievement has, of course, taken place in the last hundred and fifty years with the aid of modern technology and hydraulic engineering. Even greater projects are in train with the progress of the plans to drain the Ijsselmeer (the former Zuider Zee) and the projects to reclaim the delta area and the Wadden Zee. But modern plans complete a process that has been going on since the natural ramparts of the dunes were threatened by the sea and the first hesitant steps were taken to protect hard-won agricultural land. Dutch and Flemish landscapes bear witness of this long struggle in many ways. Intricate networks of dikes, many of them now in the midst of an agricultural countryside, are far removed from the sea they formerly kept out; the shapes of fields and the patterns of drainage ditches no less than the form of villages and the pattern of settlement give a clue to the age of reclamation; and occasionally areas once settled and farmed are now marsh and lake, as in the Biesbosch, for reclamation has not always been a tale of success.

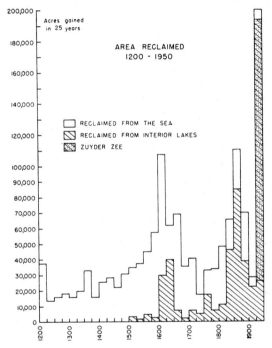

Fig. 9:7   The chronology of drainage and reclamation in the Netherlands

The rate of reclamation from the twelfth century to the twentieth is shown in Fig. 9:7, from which it may be seen that there have regularly been periods of great activity in the draining of new land followed by periods at which relatively little was done. First in Flanders, then in Zeeland and Holland, there was great activity in reclamation in the eleventh and twelfth centuries, a wave of development which was continued in the thirteenth. After these first efforts there was a period of relatively little activity until the area of new reclamations again steadily rose, particularly after 1500. The peak of development was reached in the period 1600–25, a brilliant time in many other aspects of Dutch history, but substantial new areas continued to be won until the last quarter of the seventeenth century. The eighteenth century as a whole is one of reduced activity, and renewal of expansion awaited the new techniques and heavy capital investment of the nineteenth century.[20]

Fig. 9:8 Areas gained by drainage and reclamation since 1200

In the geographical pattern of new reclamation several features are outstanding (Fig. 9:8). The first is that the *scale* of new reclamations increases, in general, through time. Medieval accomplishments, with the exception of the earliest schemes of the thirteenth century by the Count of Holland, tended to be on a small scale and piecemeal as new polders were added to old ones; the map of Zeeland illustrates this feature well (see Fig. 9:9).[21] Larger areas were tackled on a more co-ordinated basis with new techniques of drainage in the seventeenth century, but it was not, for example, until 1852 that earlier plans to drain an area as large as Haarlemmermeer were brought to fruition. Secondly, until 1600 almost all of the new reclamations were made from the sea, and it was not until the next period that serious advances were made in draining the great expanses of the interior lakes. It is only in the present century that new technologies have made possible the concept of even greater gain to be won by the reclamation of the Zuider Zee.

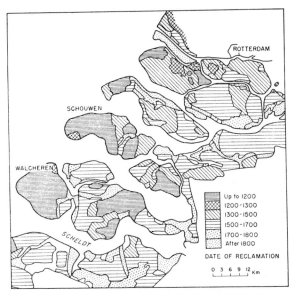

Fig. 9:9   The Netherlands: the sequence of polder-making in Zeeland
(after van Veen)

The conditions which most affected the location and timing of new reclamation may be briefly listed before going on to examine the history of drainage in greater detail. First of all, the geology of superficial deposits and the potential quality of the soils for agriculture have clearly helped to control the history of reclamation. The young marine clays of Zeeland and South Holland were attractive for early reclamation since they yielded fertile arable lands; they did not, like the peats, shrink on drainage; and dikes were easy to construct, using the clay itself. Further north the zone of young marine and fluvial deposits surrounding the central moor of Holland were also early reclaimed. In the Meuse and the Rhine distributaries, reclamation of fluvial clays in the Betuwe and in the Great Hollandse Waard was also accomplished during the Middle Ages. The lowland peats were being tackled in the Middle Ages but major advances there awaited the seventeenth and nineteenth centuries, for the problems of reclamation were often increased as a result of exploitation for fuel; shrinkage occurred on drainage; and, before the development of pumping machinery, the water table remained too high and the danger of flooding too great for widespread conversion into arable land. Acid moorland peats generally remained untouched until a later period when reclamation became worthwhile, as for example in the *Moorkolonien* of Drenthe and it was not until recently that advances against the sea have been so considerable that large areas of sandy off-shore deposits have begun to be reclaimed.

A second physical factor of great and continuing importance has always been the availability of an outfall. The easiest way of draining marshland at or below sea-level is by the use of tidal sluices, allowing drainage water to be released at low tide, which gives an advantage to those areas near to tidal water and where there is a high tidal range. Thus, since tidal range increases southwards from North Holland towards the estuary of the Scheldt (5 feet at the Texel, 12 feet at the mouth of the Scheldt), conditions have favoured early reclamation of Zeeland and Brabant rather than the northern areas. Moreover, proximity to outfall is also indirectly related to the occurrence of peat and clay soils; in general, in those areas near to present or past watercourses, marine or fluvial clays and silts are found, while the peat deposits tend to be located in the areas between the rivers (see Fig. 9:10).

The third important physical factor, affecting the chronology of reclamation rather than its distribution, has been the fluctuation in sea-level in historical time. Following the accumulation of peats in the Atlantic period at a time of relatively low sea-level, a number of transgressive phases have been associated with the deposition of the Young Marine Clays,[22] and although they have not always been strictly contemporaneous over the whole of the Netherlands, the following chronology is accepted: a sub-Atlantic, pre-Roman or Dunkirk I transgression beginning about 300 B.C., followed by the Roman regression during which occupation took place. The end of Roman occupation at about A.D. 270 may be associated with new flooding, and did, in fact, coincide with the post-Roman or Dunkirk II transgression. In Walcheren two phases of transgression are separated by traces of Merovingian occupation and are followed by

Carolingian settlement. In the north there was a transgression between the third and tenth centuries, and young marine clays were deposited and artificial mounds or *terpen* were erected as refuges for stock and people (see Plate 13). The onset of the post-Carolingian, Dunkirk III or late Medieval transgression began from the tenth or

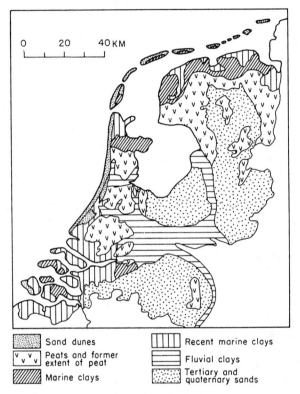

0   20   40 KM

Sand dunes

Peats and former extent of peat

Marine clays

Recent marine clays

Fluvial clays

Tertiary and quaternary sands

Fig. 9:10   Superficial deposits in the Netherlands

eleventh centuries. In Zeeland and South Holland existing islands were eroded and only the cores of present islands were left (from which reclamation was soon restarted). In North Holland thin clays were deposited, there was some erosion of peat deposits and a number of lakes were formed, including lake Beemster. In the Zuider Zee there is a sequence from the low deposits, which are fresh-water, to the silts laid down in brackish water during the period 1250 to 1480 when the Zuider Zee took its modern form. Between 1480 and 1600 salinity increased, and after 1600 deposits became fully marine. For other parts of the Netherlands it has been suggested that the period from 1250 to about 1500 was one of relatively high sea-level, and that after a period of relative regression between about 1650 and 1700 a rise of sea-level began which has continued up to the present time. It is obvious that fluctuations are due to general changes in sea-level or to tectonic movements. The former have been attributed to slight changes in climate and to the extension or contraction of glaciers. Thus the low sea-levels of the seventeenth century coincide with a cold period and the extension of Alpine glaciers. Changes in sea-level, together with the frequency of storminess in the North Sea and other factors, clearly affect the practicability of active land reclamation and drainage, and it may be no coincidence that the first great surge of medieval activity came at a time of relatively low sea-level and that the fourteenth and fifteenth centuries were periods of high sea-level and relatively little activity before the great days of the sixteenth and seventeenth centuries with their low sea-levels. Only in the nineteenth and twentieth centuries, with the development of modern technologies, has drainage and reclamation work taken place at periods of relatively high sea-levels. There are, however, many other factors at work in the chronology of reclamation and changing sea-level may not be the most important.

Demographic pressure and land hunger both stimulated medieval reclamation, and then at a later period the profitability of commercial farming attracted the necessary capital investment to larger-scale drainage works in the sixteenth and seventeenth centuries. Rapidly growing urban and industrial markets coupled with the relative abundance of capital and low rates of interest provided the stimulus, while the growing knowledge of hydraulic engineers such as Leeghwater and Vierlingh made larger-scale operations more feasible.[23] Technological advances in dike-building and drainage made possible the extension of new operations in various ways. The simple tidal sluice and the formation of the polders were enormously important in the Middle Ages. Techniques of river control, the shaping of sea defences, and above all, the improvement of the windmill to the point at which it became a useful machine for pumping water, also represented substantial technological advances, the last making possible the drainage of interior lakes during the sixteenth and seventeenth centuries. Finally, drainage and reclamation are almost always co-operative ventures which require joint organisation for the initial enterprise and then some form of corporate control to maintain dikes and drains, to pump water, to levy taxes and to maintain general repair and improvement. In medieval times the nobility and the monasteries often initiated drainage, but even from the eleventh century in Flanders communal organisations known as the *wateringues* existed for water control, and their Dutch counterparts, the *waterschappen* were later federated into larger organisations such as the *hoofdwaterschappen* of the Rhineland in 1255. The great schemes of the seventeenth century were necessarily conceived and carried out as a whole by the great engineers of the day, but the co-ordination of many bodies dealing with river and sea defences as well as windmill drainage and pumping did not develop until after the General Regulations on Diking of 1791 and the beginnings of provincial contributions for water control in 1779. It was not until the nineteenth century that co-ordinated state control was established and that the largest projects of all could thus be financed and developed.

The earliest reaction to the post-Roman transgression of the sea and the onset of flooding, was the building of artificial mounds of refuge known as *terpen*. Rising some twelve to thirty feet above the surrounding level, they are generally oval or round and from four to forty acres in area.[24] Many are still village sites and some carry early Frisian place-names ending in *-um* (as Winsum, Loppersum for example). Their use for arable farming was difficult, and fishing, salt production, cattle-rearing and trade appear to have been the major occupations. There are still traces of some 1,500 in the Netherlands alone (see Fig. 5:9). The reaction to subsequent transgressions further south in Flanders and Zeeland was, however, different, and here the first diking can be traced. Dike-building was aimed not so much at reclaiming new land from the sea as at protecting already claimed and cultivated land from flooding. Some of the land reclaimed in Flanders by A.D. 1000, for example, appears to have been inundated no earlier than 944, and it was in this area that pressure of population was felt earliest, and where reclamation could easily be accomplished on a small, piecemeal scale. New villages were being founded on drained land, and salt marshes and sheep pastures were made into arable land. As early as the tenth century the simple but effective device of the sluice made possible new reclamation on a larger scale, since it permitted water to be drained out at low tides without any need for pumping. From the eleventh century local associations or *wateringues* were being formed and in the east were being directed from the towns, notably Bruges. The lay nobility and the monasteries encouraged reclamation, for a dense population and the flourishing towns which were growing with the Flemish cloth industry provided markets for agricultural produce. As early as 1138 and 1153 the new term *polder* had appeared in documents relating to Flanders; it was first mentioned in Middelburg in 1219. It may be that this new term reflects a new stage of reclamation in which the offensive was first taken against the sea and diking ceased to be entirely defensive. In this new activity it was the clays which were first reclaimed. Peat had long been removed for fuel, litter and fertiliser and although a beginning had been made in the reclamation of peat land in eastern Flanders by mid-thirteenth century, its protection was more difficult and it was the first land to be lost in the great floods of the fourteenth century.[25]

In Zeeland there was a similar movement towards reclamation which began a little later than in Flanders and took a slightly different form, for the eroded islands of the delta were the nuclei around which polders were made, gradually extending and linking the islands in a piecemeal fashion, in general working from the easily reclaimed lands of the south and west to the inner areas of the delta (see Fig. 9:9).

In Holland proper the great achievements were those associated with William the Diker, Count of Holland in the early thirteenth century. At the heart of central Holland lay the Great Moor, an area of peat later extracted for fuel and other purposes and represented in historical times by peat bogs and lakes, of which the largest was the Haarlemmermeer. Around the Great Moor were the clays associated with the courses of the Vecht and the Oude Rijn; to the west lay the new and old dunes of the coast. It was in this fringe area that early reclamation took place on the largest scale in Holland, creating the agricultural foundation to support the great trading towns which emerged in the Golden Loop or the Randstadt: Leyden, Haarlem, Amsterdam and Utrecht. Further south on the river clays between the Rhine and the Meuse reclamation was also pushed forward by the creation of the Great Hollandse Waard. The effect of this thirteenth-century activity was to isolate the interior lakes and marshes from the sea, and, in a larger strategy, to defend the whole area of central Holland from the advancing waters in the delta area on the one hand, and from the increasingly saline waters of a growing Zuider Zee on the other.

Nevertheless, much was lost in the subsequent period of relatively high sea-level and increased storminess in the North Sea during the late thirteenth and fourteenth centuries. Floods became frequent and loss of life as well as of reclaimed land was often considerable. The rate of new reclamation declined; during the fourteenth century, the Zuider Zee reached roughly the form that it had until recently, and

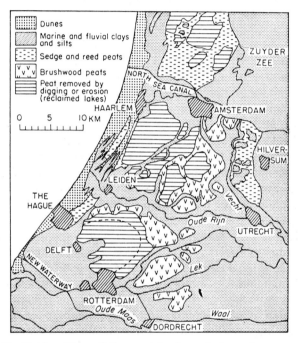

Fig. 9:11   Reclamation of the peat lands and river clays around the margins of the Great Moor. Note the location of the major towns around the fringes of the Great Moor (after Burke).

in certain years disaster overtook old reclamations: in 1287 for example, when flooding was also serious in eastern England; or in Flanders in the floods of 1375–6 and 1404 when reclaimed areas to the seaward of the modern coast were lost; or in the terrible year of the St Elizabeth flood in 1421 when some 42,000 acres were permanently lost, chiefly in the area between the Rhine and the Meuse where the Hollandse Diep was scoured out and the marshes of the Biesbosch created.

In the fourteenth and fifteenth centuries, at a time when population was stagnant or rising only slowly, the areas reclaimed were relatively small. Yet during the sixteenth century there was much new advance which coincided not only with a low sea-level but also with the revival of prosperity that accompanied the developing commercial function of the area as a whole. Between 1540 and 1715 some 80 per cent of new drainage and reclamation had been achieved by methods of water control which did not involve the artificial lifting of water by pumping or other means. Techniques of coastal diking, river control and polder-making and the placing of tidal sluices had been brought to a fine art by the accumulation of a great empirical body of information about hydraulic engineering which was codified in the work of Andries Vierlingh, the great dikemaster of the sixteenth century whose writings (about 1570) bear witness to the soundness of contemporary knowledge and methods.

The reclamation of the interior lakes of the peat lands presented greater difficulties. Deep-cutting of peat below—for fuel, and also for salt-manufacture by the process of *selberning*, later made illegal—created man-made lakes, the draining of which was added to the inherent problems of reclaiming peat land. The drainage of the interior lakes called for much larger-scale investment than that for individual coastal polders; and it required a means of pumping water from a low to a high level. Further, it pre-supposed satisfactory organisation, planning and co-operation. The first of these requirements was met by the availability of capital from merchants and bankers of Holland itself during the great period of economic expansion in the first half of the seventeenth century. Secondly, the improvement of the windmill for the pumping of water was only one of many innovations which presaged the Dutch inventiveness in the nineteenth and twentieth centuries in hydraulic engineering and earth-shifting machinery (Plate 40). The *krabelaar* or water harrow had been a fifteenth-century device which disturbed bottom muds so that they were removed on the ebb flow of tides; the mud-mill and the bucket dredge made possible the deepening of channels for navigation, and the idea of using tidal scouring as an aid in the deepening or maintenance of channels was well known. Windmills were beginning to replace horse-mills for the lifting of water in the early fifteenth century, but they had a lift of only six or seven feet. The introduction of the movable cap in place of the ancient post-mill made it more practicable to shift the mill sails into the wind, and simultaneously made it possible to build much higher mills carrying a greater sail and therefore both more powerful and more sensitive to lighter winds. Thus by the early seventeenth century windmills had a potential lift of some ten feet and if necessary could be built in banks of two or more at different levels. Thus water could be lifted from internal drainage channels across the ring dike which surrounded the newly drained area and into the peripheral canal at a higher level which drained ultimately into the sea.

The third condition for the drainage of interior lakes was fulfilled by the organising and engineering genius of men such as Jan Leeghwater, who was responsible for the successful drainage of lake Beemster in 1612. Lake Beemster was some thirteen feet deep and covered about twenty-five to thirty square miles, and its drainage, financed by a company of merchants, yielded 17,000 acres of agricultural land and required some forty-three windmills. It was Leeghwater who had ambitious and workable plans for the drainage of the Haarlemmermeer, to reclaim some 90,000 acres with the aid of 160 banked windmills, though this was a project which had to await the nineteenth century, state action and the steam engine.

By the early eighteenth century economic decline had begun in many branches of Dutch industry and trade. Moreover, from 1730 a new enemy,. the pile-worm, had begun to attack and seriously to undermine timber piles, dikes and other defences, so that costs of maintenance and replacements precluded much new development. The eighteenth century was, then, one of stability in which little new drainage was attempted, although future expansion was heralded in 1787 by the introduction near Rotterdam of an English steam pump for drainage purposes.

The achievements of the Flemish and the Dutch in the reclamation of land from sea and marsh were known, appreciated and imitated all over Europe in the Middle Ages, and later in the seventeenth and eighteenth centuries. In the eleventh and twelfth centuries the Flemings were prominent among the colonists of east Germany. They were reclaiming marshland along the Elbe and settling in the marshy *Urstromtäler* of Brandenburg; their prowess in the settlement of heath was recalled in place-names such as Fläming Heath. But the Dutch in the seventeenth century were the experts who were invited almost everywhere in Western Europe where there were marshes to be drained (Fig. 9:12). In Russia, Scandinavia and Italy, Dutch engineers were involved in the cutting of canals, the dredging of rivers and the draining of marshes. In England it was Cornelius Vermuyden who confidently laid out his master plan for the drainage of the southern Fenland which included not only the cuts that were made in his time but also plans for a peripheral cut-off channel to

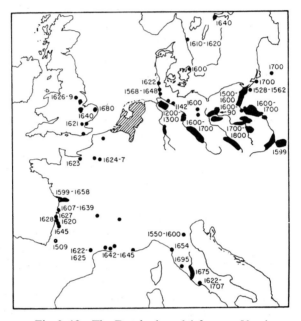

Fig. 9:12 The Dutch abroad (after van Veen)

carry upland drainage round the margin of the Fenland which has been established only in recent times. In the Isle of Axholme, at Canvey Island off the Essex coast and in the Norfolk Broads the Dutch engineers were busy using familiar techniques of drainage. In Germany, too, they continued work in Brandenburg-Prussia which had been started in the Middle Ages by their Flemish neighbours. Further east it was the Dutch who reclaimed the Vistula delta near Danzig. In France, too, Dutch commercial interests paved the way for Dutch hydraulic engineers. In the Médoc peninsula Dutch drainage engineers reclaimed land on which new *palus* wines were grown; and quite near to their sphere of interests in the salt and brandy trades of Aunis and Saintonge, Humphrey Bradley and others were deeply involved in the drainage of the Sèvre-Niortaise.

AGRICULTURAL CHANGE IN THE LOW COUNTRIES

As in so many other spheres, the Dutch had acquired an enviable reputation throughout Europe for the productivity of their agriculture. In England particularly, Dutch and Flemish methods were imitated and then improved, with far-reaching consequences for the progress of the agricultural revolution in the eighteenth century. From the end of the Middle Ages the advances made in Flanders, Brabant, Zeeland and Holland towards more intensive land use, a greater variety of production and higher yields were perhaps more clearly related than similar advances in other areas to three major factors, two geographical, the other historical: the proximity of large urban centres, soil and drainage conditions, and the impact through time of the changing balance of price structures.

The effects of the towns on land use changes were several. Urban populations were growing rapidly and standards of living were being raised, so that the towns were, above all, expanding markets for agricultural products. In accordance with the principles of von Thünen there was a discernible tendency for costs of transport to the towns to influence the use of land.[26] Those crops for which the cost of transporting the yield of a given unit of land was high tended to be grown near the towns, and products which were perishable must clearly be grown near to the towns. Thus the effect of lively urban demand is generally to be seen in several ways: a premium is put upon the use of land near to the towns for high-yielding or perishable products such as fruit and vegetables, milk and butter; a premium is also put upon intensity of land use and a high application of labour and capital. Extensive uses for fallow or rough grazings are discouraged. Rents and land values increase towards the towns as a result of the prevalence and profitability of intensive land use. The operation of these factors is a demonstrable feature of land use in the Low Countries from the end of the Middle Ages, and is expressed in the emergence of a fruit and market-garden industry near the towns, the concentration on peat production (a bulky and fragile commodity, costly to transport) in the neighbourhood of Amsterdam and other large towns, the trend towards intensive dairying near the urban markets of Holland and Zeeland and the relegation of stock-rearing and sheep-grazing to regions further afield in the Netherlands. Grain production, too, tended to be relegated to distant areas. Other arable products, notably commercial crops such as flax, oilseeds and dyestuffs were grown in the Netherlands as well as being imported. The towns affected the geography of agriculture in other ways too. They were suppliers of labour for the intensive hand methods used in horticultural enterprises; they were suppliers, too, of manure, and heavy manuring was one of the most essential features of the new agriculture in the Low Countries. Night soil from the towns, street sweepings, ashes and rags were used, and it is worth bearing in mind in this respect that the animal population of any large town before the age of the motor-car was a very large one. In a addition to a large horse population pigs, poultry and cattle were kept in large numbers in most pre-industrial towns. Moreover, the towns were suppliers of capital for farming through the investment of merchants and traders in land, and in much of the Netherlands, of course, the reclamation of land for agriculture involved a very heavy investment indeed.

The second major element in the agriculture of the Netherlands and which necessarily conditioned the form taken by agricultural change in the period from about 1400 to 1750 was, of course, the physical environment. In the east and south of the Netherlands and in Brabant and Flanders, light, sandy loams or leached podzolised sandy soils with or without a hard pan are commonly found. Light sandy soils also occur on and near the coastal dune belt. These soil conditions have clearly posed problems in the reclamation of arable, but they have also traditionally provided areas of rough grazings for cattle and sheep. Although the light soils have necessitated heavy manuring and have often been much improved by liming and marling, they were, nevertheless, soils which were easily cultivated and which, warming readily, therefore lent themselves to fruit and market-gardening. It was, indeed, the concentration of effort on the light soils which proved so important and valuable when the Flemish and Dutch techniques were transferred to English conditions. The other outstanding feature of the physical environment of the Netherlands which was important for agricultural change was the level of the water table in newly reclaimed areas. On the claylands and silts of the delta region and the lower valleys of the Rhine and Meuse, the height of the water table could be sufficiently well controlled to allow the growing of arable crops, but on peat lands this was less easy, because of the inadequacies of windmill pumps, the proximity of lakes formed in abandoned peat-cuttings, or the shrinkage of the peat. At all events, much of the peat lands had of necessity to be devoted to pasture and was primarily used for dairying. Edam, Gouda, Alkmaar and Hoorn had acquired a reputation for their cheeses before the end of the Middle Ages and Dutch or Frisian cattle were already known for their milking qualities.

Changes in the price structure of agricultural products were also fundamental in stimulating new adjustments of land use.[27] In the Low Countries grain prices were low relatively to those of stock products and industrial prices from 1310 to 1480, a period also of low or falling population. Between 1480 and 1620–50 prices for grain were high and population was rising. Circumstances favoured the reclamation of land for arable farming. Between 1620–50 and 1735–55 prices for grain were again relatively low in comparison with those for stock products and conditions once more favoured the production of fodder crops, grass, dairy products and meat rather than grain; it was under these conditions that agricultural advances were made most rapidly towards intensive production of both stock and grain. Finally, towards the end of the eighteenth century there occurred a new phase of rising population and rising grain prices. In general, therefore, periods of relatively low prices stimulated the shift to fodder crops, commercial and industrial crops, especially on small farms on which labour was intensive.

The agricultural advances which were made may be listed under five headings.[28] First and most important, fallow had been increasingly eliminated on better farms by growing pulse (a practice from 1328 in French Flanders) by using temporary leys of some three to six years (first identified south of Ghent about 1320) and by the cultivation of fodder crops such as clover, lucerne, burnet, timothy grass and turnips (from the early fifteenth century). Secondly, fertility was successfully maintained by the *leguminosae* among fodder crops, by the heavy manuring which was made possible as a result of the increased stock population supported by the new fodder crops, and by other methods, including the use of peat ashes, urban refuse, liming and marling. Thirdly, among new implements which were introduced (such as the winnowing machine inspired by Chinese tools), by far the most important improvement was the light, adaptable and efficient Brabant plough with no foretrain and with a sliding foot in place of the former cumbersome wheels. It was a plough eminently suitable for the light soils of the Netherlands and provided a model for the Rotherham plough in England at a later date. Fourth, new crops were introduced, many of them industrial crops which involved processing or which supplied new or growing industries: flax was spreading in Flanders in the fourteenth century in conjunction with the linen industry and involved deep cultivation and thorough manuring; coleseed spread from the northern Netherlands and was valued for its oil and also for the cattle-cake which could be made from it; buckwheat was important on poor soils and on newly cutover peat lands; madder and hops were new in the fourteenth century and some of the fodder crops appeared soon afterwards. Another wave of introductions followed the overseas expansion, notably tobacco, which made headway around Amersfoort, and potatoes, which became an important article of diet during the eighteenth century. By 1800 mangolds and sugar beet were also known. New crops increased the variety of farming, but many of them were valuable enough to warrant intensive cultivation, weeding and manuring.

The fifth, and in many ways the most important, development was that of horticulture. At one extreme this involved the extreme care and attention lavished on glasshouse crops—a branch of horticulture new in Western Europe—or on the new tulip and hyacinth bulbs imported from Turkey and central Asia, and the basis for the great tulip investment 'bubble' of 1636–7. Leyden and Delft were well known for their turnips, cabbage and carrots in the sixteenth century, but in the seventeenth there were many new market garden crops, particularly in the neighbourhood of Amsterdam and Haarlem: lettuce, cauliflower, beans, cucumbers, and strawberries were now being produced. Market-gardening clearly involved heavy and intensive labour and manuring, and it was generally carried out on small owner-occupied units, frequently of less than ten acres. What was particularly important for the development of arable farming in general was the transfer to general farming of crops and methods which had first been developed on the small market gardens. It is also evident that improved and intensive farming tended to spread first to the small farms, and only at a later stage to tenant farms and large estates. Turnips were first introduced into general agriculture long after they had been accepted as a market-garden crop, and the same was true of carrots and cabbages. Bed and row cultivation as well as deep digging and heavy manuring were also introduced by way of the market gardens.

An agricultural revolution had occurred in Flanders, Brabant and the Netherlands by mid-seventeenth century, and this fact was recognised by a number of English writers and publicists, notably Sir Richard Weston and Walter Blyth, who were the first of many to introduce Dutch and Flemish methods to English farming.[29] Immigrants from the Netherlands to East Anglia, Yorkshire and the southern counties introduced both market-gardening and new crops. Turnips and clover were being introduced widely in the seventeenth century; cole-seed became common in the Fenlands; Dutch cattle and the Brabant plough were also imported. Borrowing was selective, but nevertheless Dutch and Flemish techniques were extremely useful in the improvement of light soils in eastern England, where the stimuli of urban markets and changing price structures were also operating to encourage the adoption of new methods in order to increase dairy and fatstock production on light, relatively dry soils formerly devoted to arable and heath.

The regional geography of agriculture in the Netherlands in the seventeenth and eighteenth centuries clearly reflected the effect of the towns, the shift towards market-gardening, stock production and the cultivation of commercial crops as well as the history of drainage and reclamation and the nature of the soil. On sandy soils near the dune barrier of Holland, horticulture became established in its modern location. In the rest of Holland dairying was the chief land use. The drained peat lands were of necessity under permanent pasture. In the province of Holland new lakes were still forming on a fairly large scale to the south of Amsterdam as a result of the continued exploitation of peat; these are now lakes which provide open water for recreation like those other abandoned and flooded turf pits in the Norfolk Broads (Plate 42).

On the clays of South Holland and Utrecht, and on the delta lands of Zeeland intensive arable farming with emphasis on commercial crops had developed. Madder, flax and hemp were grown in addition to corn and pulse crops.

On sandy soils of the eastern and southern United Provinces, in areas far removed from the urban stimulus of Amsterdam, Rotterdam, Leyden, and other large towns, a different agrarian economy prevailed. These were the backward areas, in which sheep were raised on sandy heathlands or store cattle for droving to the richer fattening pastures of Holland or Friesland. North Brabant was underpopulated and underdeveloped, having greatly suffered in the Eighty Years' War, and its major concerns were sheep-rearing and flax production for the nascent industries of Eindhoven (linen), Tilburg and Oosterwijk (wool). On sandy heathlands in Drenthe and Overijssel a similar sheep-rearing economy existed with commercial flax production, and domestic textile industries, which had begun as a means of supplementing inadequate farming incomes and subsequently emerged as a major industry at Hengelo and Enschede. Rye and buckwheat were the chief crops. Temporary cultivation was often practised, but during the eighteenth century new efforts were being made to reclaim the acid, podzolised heath soils for permanent farming. The peat deposits of Friesland and Groningen were also the centre of much new expansion in the eighteenth century, partly as a source of fuel for the industries of Amsterdam, but also as the sites of new experiments in reclamation and of new village settlements, the *Moor-* and *Veenkolonien*.

AGRICULTURAL CHANGE IN THE NORTH ITALIAN PLAIN

By the end of the sixteenth century the north Italian plain was known throughout Europe as a region of intensive agriculture. Although maize had still to become established in the area, rice was already an important crop, mulberry cultivation was expanding and the area had a deservedly high reputation for its fruits and wines. Intensive production of lucerne, hay and other forage crops and a high stock population were fundamental in maintaining high grain yields but they depended on careful irrigation from systems which had been developed and extended from the twelfth century.

A clear regional distinction had emerged within the north Italian plain, picking out relatively minor differences in soil, relief and water supply which had formerly been expressed chiefly in terms of natural vegetation.[30] Below the foothills of the Alps and in front of the Alpine valleys there is a zone of moraines, composed of coarse fluvioglacial materials and solifluction deposits, the latter also flanking the northern Apennines. South of the moraines lies the zone of the *high terraces*, a dissected outwash plain of fluvioglacial materials which are coarser towards the Alps and finer towards the river Po. Rivers are fairly deeply incised, water tables are low, and soils acid. Many of the soils are dry, highly permeable sands and gravels, but there are also in places sticky infertile and impermeable clays (*ferreto* soils). Heath and pine forests are common now, but the area once carried mixed woods of elm, beech, chestnut and pubescent oak.[31] In a survey of Spanish origin made in the sixteenth century in

Lombardy only about a third of this kind of terrain was cultivated, and it was mainly under extensive pasture and arable for poor subsistence peasant farming.[32] In the western part of the zone of high terraces acid heaths persisted to the nineteenth century. Two-thirds of the land was owned by the church and the aristocracy in the early eighteenth century. Further east around Como, Brescia and Bergamo about 50 per cent of the land was under direct cultivation by small peasant farmers. About a third of this land was under grass but vines were of importance and mulberry cultivation increasing.

Greater changes had occurred by the sixteenth century in the region known as the *low plains*. With increasing distance from the Alps towards the river finer sediments are characteristic, producing soils retentive of moisture and formerly carrying damp oak forest of *Quercus cerris*, pedunculate oak and poplar. But the most important feature is the existence of the zone of springs (*fontanili* or *risorgive*) below the high terraces. These assure a constant and reliable water supply for irrigation. Even in the unirrigated areas 75 per cent of these fertile soils were cultivated in the sixteenth century, but in many areas irrigation works had been developed from the twelfth century onwards and about 85 per cent of the low plains were under crops, hay or lucerne. In the sixteenth century there was a distinction in tenure and settlement between this zone and the high terraces, for much of the old irrigated land was owned by lay lords or monasteries and was in share-cropping tenures (*mezzadria*) associated with a dense rural population, scattered settlement and a concentration on forage crops, grain and wine. The newly irrigated lands of the lower plains were devoted to the intensive production of lucerne, hay or sainfoin, cut seven to eight times a year, as well as to the new plantation crop of rice. This was an area much more completely oriented to commercial agriculture financed from the towns. Finally, the modern flood plain of the Po and its tributaries was largely waste and marsh until the great reclamation schemes of the nineteenth century. But in the neighbourhood of Mantua the northern shift of the course of the Po up to 1100 necessitated early diking and embanking, which was going on at the same time as active clearing and colonisation.[33] Much further west in Piedmont, the gentle gradients of the Ticino and the Sesia facilitated early irrigation of the flood plain from the rivers rather than from the *fontanili*. But although no more than a beginning had been made in the reclamation of the flood plains by the end of the Middle Ages, rice cultivation had made great headway from about 1460 and was already associated with the use of migrant, landless labour, fairly large-scale exploitations, and the large isolated farmsteads which are still characteristic of the area.

This agricultural landscape of the sixteenth century was the product of agrarian change which had involved development not only in farming practices and crops but also in irrigation and in landholding. Even in the twelfth century Cistercian monasteries were active pioneers of irrigation on a small scale, mainly to irrigate water meadows near Milan. A hundred years later the initiative had passed to the urban commune, and Milan's great irrigation canal, the *Muzza*, was built between 1220 and 1239.[34] Finally, ducal initiative was important in the building of the Martesana canal in 1457 both for irrigation and navigation. But side by side with the creation of the larger canals which took off from existing rivers to irrigate the low terraces and the flood plain, there was also much small-scale and piecemeal effort by which some 50,000 acres of land were eventually to be irrigated from the *risorgive* near Milan.

Changes in farming in Lombardy as a whole were linked to irrigation on the one hand and on the other to urban demand for food and raw materials in the context of industrial expansion, the growth of population and rising standards of consumption. The innovations and investment involved in this new commercial farming were facilitated by tenurial change, the availability of urban capital for farming and reclamation, and the success of ducal policies. The expanding industries of Milan in the fifteenth and sixteenth centuries, apart from building, were chiefly concerned with woollen cloth, fustians, arms, needles and other metal products, and above all, silk. Wool imports rather than local produce were used for the cloth industry, but the spread of woollen spinning and weaving into the countryside in the sixteenth century must have tended to strengthen the links of town and country. Woad and madder had been important in the Milanese area in the fourteenth century and woad was exported to England and Flanders in the fifteenth. The metal industries probably had least relationship with the countryside but the silk industry depended on a close association of town and country not only through the organisation of the industry but also through the spread of mulberry production, silkworm-rearing and silk spinning into the countryside around the cities.

The provisioning of the urban food market was the chief concern of agricultural development, however, and although of continuing

41 *"The country of the thousand isles."* A zone of early drainage in North Holland in a region much affected by former exploitation of turf, but now specialising in the production of fresh vegetables, chiefly cabbage. The linear settlement is characteristic of some of the drained peatlands of the Netherlands.

42 *Oud Loosdrecht*, near Hilversum, Netherlands. Now a holiday centre for fishing, boating and yachting near Amsterdam, Oud Loosdrecht is a linear settlement in a region formerly devoted to the large scale production of peat from the sixteenth century to the eighteenth. These lakes, like the Norfolk Broads, are a result of the flooding of abandoned turf-pits.

importance, grain cultivation was overshadowed by new developments. The intensive production of hay, lucerne and sainfoin on the irrigated water meadows of the region around Milan served to support a precocious dairy industry which involved investment, among other things, in new farm buildings equipped for stall-feeding. Green crops and animal manure raised the level of fertility of arable land in general, but for rice, and also for the market-gardening, fruit and vines which were so greatly encouraged in the area, night-soil from the towns was also important.

The commercialisation of farming in Milan also involved changes towards a structure of land ownership and tenure which provided a secure and suitable framework for the investment of capital. Economic stimuli coincided with the interest of ducal policy to reduce the power of the old nobility and the church and there seems to be little doubt that the extent of church lands in particular was substantially reduced, for by mid-sixteenth century they owned no more than 10–15 per cent of the land in this area compared with 65–70 per cent in southern Italy.[35] Substantial, commercially oriented tenant farmers had gradually replaced small, subsistence peasant farmers as lessees of the church lands, and it was this new class which was able to use local agrarian laws in order to secure possession. Dowd has explained the process by which this took place. If landlords did not fully reimburse outgoing tenants for improvements they had made during their tenure, landlords were obliged to renew their lease to the tenant if he so wished. The commercial farmers of the period, much better endowed with capital than their landlords, had frequently carried out improvements in irrigation, clearing, draining and building which some landowners and especially the church, usually short of liquid capital, could not reimburse. Rents were thus fixed and were of declining real value with the inflation of the period, so that control effectively passed to the tenants, who paid no more than nominal rents and retained undisturbed possession.

Finally, the political domination of the countryside by the town which has already been noted elsewhere as a characteristic of Italy in the later Middle Ages occurred also in Milan. The urban commune of the twelfth and thirteenth centuries gave way to the despotic regional state with the domination of the Visconti after 1277 and the extension of boundaries to the river Po by 1312 and to include Pavia, Piacenza, Bergamo and Brescia by 1339. Ducal policies to develop industry and improve navigation and irrigation works, and their support for the new bourgeoisie as a countervailing power against the church and the feudal oligarchy also operated to stimulate the interaction between town and country which was the outstanding characteristic of development in Lombardy in the later Middle Ages, and which laid the foundations for a new revival of activity in the late eighteenth and nineteenth centuries.

EASTERN SPAIN: CATALONIA AND THE LEVANTE

The changing land use of eastern Spain before 1800 is much less clearly related to urban growth and to the spheres of influence of major cities than is the case in Lombardy or the Low Countries. The agriculture of Catalonia represents the clearest example, occurring in a close and symbiotic relationship to the commercial and industrial expansion of Barcelona. But whereas the self-sustaining activity of Barcelona as metropolitan centre, great Mediterranean port and industrial centre was responsible for generating rural activity in the area around it, the development of Valencia, Alicante or Murcia gives the impression that the towns existed to serve the needs of the countryside, and even their industries before 1800 arose out of the opportunities presented by a rural concentration on mulberry cultivation and raw silk production.

But eastern Spain is an area of considerable geographical contrast and fragmentation. Lowland terrain suitable for cultivation and accessible from the coast occurs only in scattered basins separated by the mountain barriers and arid uplands which approach the shores of the Mediterranean. The narrow coastal plains and the pre-littoral depression of Catalonia represent one such area in the north. Beyond the delta of the Ebro, traditionally unhealthy and prograding rapidly during historical time, low-lying land and areas suitable for settlement are scarce as far as the plain of Valencia. Beyond Valencia and the difficult roads across the mountains which form the southern flank of the amphitheatre of hills there are the smaller and isolated basins of Alicante and Murcia. Physical fragmentation is paralleled by different traditional political connections and loyalties: the particularism of Catalonia, the Aragonese connection of Valencia and the Castilian association with Murcia and Alicante dating from the Reconquest. But the separate regional characteristics of the land uses of Catalonia, Valencia, Murcia and Alicante are determined above all by availability of water and the varying patterns of water control, which were most important before 1800.

Finally, if urban influence and adjustment to the availability of water constituted two of the leading elements in the land use of eastern Spain, they may perhaps be seen to work themselves out against a background of changing crop combinations which reflect the widening of European horizons through the introduction of new crops (particularly in the Arab period) or through the competition on European markets between Mediterranean and new, colonial producers of sub-tropical crops. In the changing agriculture of eastern Spain it seems possible to discern a series of crop booms, not wholly dissimilar from those which occurred in other sub-tropical or tropical areas, and in which the producers of eastern Spain took up a particular crop and profited from it until overseas producers were able to compete successfully and to undercut the Mediterranean producer.

Murcia and Alicante

The lowland basin of Murcia in the south is watered by the Segura river.[36] It was an area of dense Moorish settlement and the city of Murcia (A.D. 825) was one of the relatively few important towns of Spain founded by the Moors. Irrigation is necessary, for the low plain receives no more than 10 to 15 inches of rainfall, but because of the relatively small catchment area and its aridity there is a less stable and reliable régime than among more northern rivers in eastern Spain. Alexander de Laborde[37] commented that the bed of the Segura river was 'frequently too low to allow of the water being conveyed over the lands to any extent'. Irrigation was chiefly by *noria* since the reservoirs which had been constructed by the Moors had been allowed to fall into decay after the reconquest, when many Moriscos had migrated into the kingdom of Granada to avoid Castilian rule. Although laws relating to irrigation date back to 1277 only two of the ancient reservoirs with their irrigation canals still survived near Murcia in the late eighteenth century. Nothing new had been established in the intervening centuries. Water supply was clearly a limiting factor in the agriculture of the eighteenth century for contemporary travellers mention wheat, barley and fallow rotations on the irrigated lands, with *barilla* as a fallow crop on saline soils near the coast, grown for the potash content of its ashes, which were exported chiefly to England. Laborde remarked that vegetables and herbs were scarce and 'there was not a fruit tree', so that fruits and vegetables had to be imported. Wheat and rye, wine, esparto grass, saffron, olives and mulberries were the chief products.[38] In fact, the area was a problem region until the development of new irrigation schemes in the late nineteenth century, for the instability of the hydrological régime involved much greater risk of loss in the occasional dry year than was the case further north, with the result that farmers were less willing to invest in fruits or tree crops other than those which can resist a dry year, such as vines and olives.

In the basin of Alicante, on the other hand, a more reliable river régime results from the fact that a high proportion of rainfall is filtered through deep water tables in limestone country and acute fluctuations in river flow tend to be reduced. In the late eighteenth century, too, water supply was assured from a reservoir constructed in 1542 (El Pantano) which could supply irrigation water once in fifteen days to all irrigated land during the summer. *Norias* were also used in an intensive, terraced farming system, highly regarded by both Townsend and Laborde. 'The land never rests; for no sooner has it rewarded the farmer with one crop than he begins to prepare it for another.'[39] A typical calendar would involve barley, sown in September and harvested in April; maize from May to September, interplanted with melons; then wheat, sown in November and ready in early June. Grain yields were high, but fruits and nuts—citrus fruits, figs, olives, almonds, carobs and vines—were also interspersed in the arable plots. Mulberry plantations supported a flourishing silk industry at Alicante and in the coastal areas crops of *barilla* were grown on saline soils. Modern descriptions of the area show relatively little change, though there seems even to have been a relative decline in the early twentieth century when the silting up of the old dams made irrigation water scarce and unreliable, so that the chief crops in the 1920s were still wheat and barley interspersed with drought-resisting crops such as olives, nuts and vines;[40] some mulberry was still grown, though not *barilla*.

Valencia

The alluvial plain of Valencia, limited to the west by the faultline escarpment of the Iberian Mountains, is a much larger expanse of irrigable land, naturally better watered with a rainfall of about 17 inches in lowland areas, and fed by the larger catchment basins of several river systems, of which the chief are the Turia and the Júcar. Irrigation water during the dry season is assured as a result of the supply from spring rains and also from snow melt which together provide the source of maximum flow during late spring and early summer. But slow percolation through limestones delays the transmission of rainfall maxima and tends to ensure a steady flow.[41] Conditions therefore favour the extension of irrigation by simple means, easiest of all from the abundant springs near which some 118 villages in the area are sited. Towards the coast the alluvial deposits have recently been actively prograding. From the first century A.D. there has been a gain of some two and a half miles, though only a half mile or so of this has taken place since the fourteenth century. Alluviation was much more rapid before the river was checked by the complicated pattern of irrigation canals over the coastal plain. Yet this very fact, and the depth at which Roman artefacts occur, must indicate the extent to which irrigation has been responsible for spreading new and fertile alluvium on the irrigated land.

The present pattern is one in which the city of Valencia is dominant in an intensively cultivated region where population density reaches levels of over 1,000 to the square mile on agricultural land. The Water Tribunal for the dispensation of irrigation water and the settlement of disputes still meets in time-honoured fashion, but the farming systems are advanced and productive, concentrating on the cultivation of forage crops, such as lucerne and maize for dairy stock; on oranges and other fruits, market gardening, and on rice plantations near the coast. Intensive and highly productive farming in fairly small units has also been characteristic of the agriculture of the region in the past as well as in the present, and although the complete commercialisation of farming and the abandonment of subsistence crops did not take place until the nineteenth century, the agrarian history of the irrigated area is one of a succession of different cash crops for external trade: wine and olives, sugar, mulberry, oranges and, more recently, vegetables for northern markets, notably onions and potatoes.[42]

It is however necessary to make a distinction between the irrigated lands or *regadío* and the unirrigated *secano*. In the sixteenth century much of the *secano*, particularly in the northern mountainous areas, was still in the pines and oaks of natural evergreen forest, supplying shipbuilding timber in small quantities together with charcoal and pasture for swine.[43] At lower altitudes on the drier hills there was rough grazing for sheep and goats in the *matorral* or *monte bajo*, and some poor arable lands. Finally, on the unirrigated plains olives, figs, carobs and almonds were grown in the south and an increasing amount of mulberry for the thriving silk industry of Valencia itself. Grapes had been cultivated in Roman times for wine, but in Moorish times it was raisins for which the area had a reputation. In the sixteenth century wine production was again increasing. Interspersed among the dry upland pastures, however, there were also narrow strips of irrigated land in the middle courses of the rivers on which cultivation was intensive and where irrigated fodder crops such as lucerne were produced to supplement feeding for stock grazed on natural pastures, and also for mules bred for transport on the routes leading out from Valencia.

The irrigated lands carried a dense population from early times. During the Roman period wheat, olives and wine had been produced here; Valencia was a Roman foundation, and some of the irrigation canals in several of the modern *huertas* are of Roman origin. Flour, wine and olive oil were exported from the region. But it was during the Arab period that the famous irrigation canals of Turia were built between 911 and 976, later supplemented by new canals built soon after the reconquest in 1238. In the Turia systems, fed by simple gravity take-off from the main stream, water rights went with the possession of all land. In the Elche system, which depended on the construction of a reservoir, water rights went with the possession of shares in the barrage itself. The irrigation systems of the Lucar were of later origin, but the administrative mechanisms by which water was distributed have survived in their essentials to the present. During the Arab period settlement had taken place on the *rahales*, which consisted of irrigated gardens and orchards together with parcels of arable land. It was on these *huertas* that many of the new luxury crops were grown, such as cotton, sugar, rice, peaches, strawberries and citrus fruits. In addition to the *rahales* there were larger country houses and gardens or *ruzafas*, fulfilling mainly an ornamental and recreational rôle. On the reconquest, these often became part of the new lords' demesnes and the focus of new rural settlement.[44] Those near Valencia itself were incorporated into the suburbs of the town; further afield the *ruzafa* or *rahal* became the nucleus of villages which carry the original element in their place-names, such as *Rafelcofer* or *Real de Montroy*.

The new luxury crops were largely destined for local consumption in the town or, frequently, in the households of the officials and nobility on whose land they were grown. In general they appear to have played only a small rôle in the trade of the Arab world and it was not until the Christian period that commercial expansion began. Specialisation of crops for export was then stimulated by the general reorientation of trade to more northerly latitudes where the new crops were special luxuries or, for climatic reasons, could not be grown. The extent of Aragonese possessions in the Mediterranean and, in the sixteenth century, the close Spanish connection with the Low Countries and Germany was also a stimulus to trade. Rice was one of the first of such crops to be exported. It had been introduced by the Arabs and two rice-mills are mentioned in documents drawn up shortly after the reconquest, but expansion was nevertheless slow. From the beginning rice was grown on that part of the alluvial plain in which a high water table could be maintained, i.e. near the coastal zone. The periodic flooding needed for rice crops was here easy to achieve, but only at the expense of occasional dangers from saline infiltration into the water table at times of water shortage, and also of hazards to health, which were so serious that rice growing was frequently banned or discouraged to the end of the *ancien régime* because of the prevalence of malaria.

Sugar, however, was the boom crop of the sixteenth and seventeenth centuries. It had already become commercially significant in the fifteenth century, for a sugar mill was certainly established at Valencia in 1406–8 and by 1433 the *Cabildo* of the cathedral reported that 'To a few years previously sugar had been planted only in small quantities by occasional individuals for their own consumption, but since then it had extended into lands formerly producing wheat and other cereals . . . and therefore it ought to be liable for tithe'.[45] Sugar had the greatest success of all in the *huerta* of Gandía to the south where its cultivation persisted longest and where there were still plantations covering some ten square miles and supporting seven sugar mills even at the end of the eighteenth century. Throughout the sixteenth and seventeenth centuries sugar was still a great luxury in the rest of Europe, but until the plantations of South and Central America became significant producers of sugar towards the end of the seventeenth century, followed by Java in the eighteenth, Spain was one of very few European sources, together with Sicily, the Azores and Madeira. But Spanish production was soon eliminated by overseas competition. Laborde commented in 1807 that 'formerly sugar canes were cultivated in the south. They were given up on the introduction of West Indian sugar and are now only attended to in Gandía and places near it, where the canes succeed very well'.[46]

The expulsion of the Moors caused a setback from which the industry recovered in the seventeenth century, but at this northern margin of production yields were low and variable, while slave labour on tropical plantations was cheap. By 1754 several mills had been dismantled and in most areas of Spain, except near Gandía, sugar production died out by the end of the century. It had never, however, been a monoculture and vines, olives, and grain continued to be cultivated throughout the period of the sugar boom.

By the end of the eighteenth century mulberry had replaced sugar as the chief cash crop of the area, but whereas the distribution of sugar had been strictly limited to areas in which irrigation water was abundant, mulberry could be more widely grown on drier lands in the interior. Mulberry, like sugar, could not be integrated into the rotations on arable land, but it could be grown widespread in hedgerows and along ditches. It could be cultivated on a small scale and assimilated easily to the domestic economy of the small farm, for women and children supplied the labour for the collection of leaves, the rearing of the silkworms and the subsequent preparation of yarn from the cocoons. As in southern France and northern Italy mulberry cultivation and the preparation of silk yarn as a rural industry reached maximum proportions in the first half of the nineteenth century, until output was halted by silkworm diseases and prices were undercut by the expanding production of the Far East in the 1860s and 1870s. In spite of legal prohibitions much of the silk was exported as yarn in the eighteenth century, for it was estimated as being some 30 per cent cheaper than the yarn of Languedoc or northern Italy, though it was certainly of lower quality. But the manufacture of woven silk was also the chief industry of Valencia itself to the end of the eighteenth century and the number of looms had increased from some 800 in 1718 to 3,195 in 1769, including some 107 stocking frames. In the whole province there were then some 3,437 looms, using perhaps 600,000 lbs of raw silk. By 1786 the number of looms had again increased and Valencia itself had become a town of 82,000 and one of the larger towns of Western Europe.

Yet even during the silk boom, food supplies were never so assured that subsistence crops were not felt to be necessary, and wheat and maize were also intensively produced in a system of multiple cropping which was the admiration of Townsend and Laborde around 1800. Laborde thought it the 'best attended and richest agriculture in Spain'[47] and drew attention to the careful terracing for vines and raisins and the great variety of produce, while Townsend remarked upon the fact that up to three crops a year were being produced.

The end of the silk boom came in mid-nineteenth century and output was already declining when severe floods of the river Júcar brought about further serious losses in 1864. But already orange cultivation had begun to replace it. Rising standards of living in England and France, coupled with rapid transport and the growing demand for fruit and marmalade helped to give a new stimulus during the second half of the nineteenth century, but water supply was also reliable enough to encourage investment in perennial tree crops, unlike the situation further south in Murcia. It was the orange which was the great boom crop to 1914–18, after which a more diversified farming with onions and early potatoes reduced the vulnerability of the farmer, evident in overdependence on a single crop.

In some respects, the succession of cash crops in the basin of Valencia follows a pattern similar to that of the lower Rhône, a region in which Pierre George[48] identified successive preoccupations: pastoral farming during the Middle Ages, then olives in the eighteenth century, followed by mulberry and silk production. In the lower Rhône the failure of the mulberry from mid-nineteenth century coincided with the rapid expansion up to the 1860s and early 1870s of viticulture, catering for the growing demand in France for *vin ordinaire*. This specialisation too was brought to a halt by the phylloxera crisis and was succeeded by a diversification of production towards market-gardening, fruit cultivation and the production of irrigated fodder crops for dairying. Like sugar in Valencia, olives in southern France were a little too close to the northern boundary of production to be able to withstand competition when communications were improved and more distant and cheaper sources of supply could be more readily tapped. One of the underlying conditions for the flexibility in cropping systems shown by these Mediterranean producers is the greater freedom from the collective restraints and a less closely knit interdependence of stock and arable farming than were characteristic of open-field agriculture in northern Europe.

Catalonia

In many respects the agriculture of Catalonia points the contrast between the farming of the relatively advanced and commercially involved regions of Western Europe and those which remained faithful to a much greater degree to traditional subsistence farming. To contemporary observers Catalonia was clearly the most productive and technologically advanced area in Spain at the end of the eighteenth century. In 1807 Laborde remarked that 'of all the provinces of Spain, Catalonia is the most active and industrious, whether in commerce, manufactures or agriculture'.[49] Townsend remarked that 'all through Catalonia you admire at every step the industry of the inhabitants . . . who give fertility to a soil which naturally, except for vines, is most unproductive'.

Intensive farming for a variety of crops, and supporting a dense rural population even on unirrigated land, was characteristic of Catalonian agriculture. Compared with southern areas of Spain, a higher rainfall of 20 to 25 inches a year, together with a shorter period of summer drought, permitted a much more productive system of unirrigated arable farming. The accidented relief of Catalonia and the heavier precipitation of the upland regions nourish a dense stream network which allows small-scale irrigation from the relatively reliable water supply of small streams for the cultivation of fruits, vegetables and fodder crops. Catalan farming seemed backward to Arthur Young, always hypercritical and also travelling southwards from regions of more advanced farming, but other observers who had spent more time in Spain and who perhaps understood better than he the basic conditions of Mediterranean farming, noted a careful attention to farming implements and methods. Oxen, rather than mules, were the draught animals most commonly used; and an adjustable and improved light plough had been introduced for the heavier soils of the area. 'In the valleys,' wrote Townsend, 'we see the peasants engaged in tillage, and with two strong oxen breaking up their fallows; where, by means of a coulter and a mouldboard to a well-constructed plough, they turn deep furrows, such as I had never before remarked in Spain.'[50]

Wheat, barley, rye and maize were the chief cereals and the mainstay of subsistence, but vines for wine and brandy were the outstanding cash crop of Catalonia. Vegetables and *mestall* (wheat and rye) were intersown among the vines, and the practice of sowing winter crops in the vineyards was normal then, as it is now. Francisco de Zamora noted the production of early vegetables, particularly peas and beans for the Barcelona market, as early as 1789.[51] Oranges had begun to make headway in the south of Catalonia by the end of the century, having been introduced relatively recently. A wide repertoire of other crops was also grown: olives, carobs, almonds, figs, mulberry, clover, lucerne, sainfoin, flax and hemp. Transhumant sheep and sedentary flocks were supported by Pyrenean pastures and the lower slopes of the coastal and pre-littoral cordilleras of Catalonia itself, and dairy-farming with irrigated fodder crops was also beginning to develop near Barcelona. In sum, cadastral surveys and the accounts of travellers reveal a varied, intensive and small-scale agriculture almost akin to horticulture, and with the vine frequently occupying more land than cereals and as much as 50 per cent or more of the total cultivated land in each holding. There were none of the great under-used *latifundia* so characteristic of southern Spain, but holdings tended to be excessively small. In four areas of Catalonia, for example, average holdings in the late eighteenth century varied from 1·6 acres to 3 acres; only 3 per cent of the holdings were over 15 acres, and 75 per cent were less than 2·5 acres.[52]

Contemporaries were aware that land-tenure practices contributed to the intensity and productivity of agriculture by affording security to the tenant and by encouraging the most profitable use of the limited capital available. Although equal inheritance was the normal practice in Spain, in Catalonia it had become usual to hand over property intact to one of the sons, usually the eldest, thus putting a brake on the fragmentation of holdings. Townsend noted the relative security which was given by the emphyteutic lease, a tenure rather similar in general to the *mezzadria* types of lease common in northern Italy, and associated with a similar dispersed settlement pattern. Tenancies under the emphyteutic lease were for years or for lives, fines being paid on successions, but they were essentially sharecropping tenancies by which the landlord provided agreed items of working equipment, seed etc. as well as fixed capital. Finally, the tenure locally known as the *rabassa morta* had been developed to encourage new planting in vineyards. It allowed for a tenancy to last until the death of all or the larger part of the original vines planted in the land when first leased. Initially devised to encourage new planting and to protect a tenant's investment in viticulture at a time of expanding commercial horizons, the *rabassa morta* became a very common form of tenure in Catalonia and an influence making for stability and peasant security.

Viticulture was to Catalonia in the eighteenth century what sugar had been to Valencia. Tarragona, Mataro and other coastal centres had enjoyed a classical reputation for their wines, which was revived in the Middle Ages, but a far-reaching commerce in the wines of

Catalonia had only begun to develop in the late seventeenth century in association with a marked revival in the fortunes of Barcelona and Catalan trade in Spain and the western Mediterranean.[53] By 1702 the Governor of Cadiz was concerned about the increase in the import of Catalan wines and brandies. Depositions made in Panadés in 1757, indicated that over the previous thirty or forty years the area under vines had increased at the expense of forests and arable land. Woodland was being cleared and poorer land devoted to vines in other places, while at Tarragona, Townsend noted that olive trees had been cut down 'to make room for vines at a time when brandy happened to be in great request'.[54] Tarragona, Sitges and the Panadés areas appear to have been the most prosperous, but viti-culture occupied over half the cultivated area in places near Barcelona and was also important further north.

For the small peasantry of Catalonia, viticulture offered a profit-able crop and a possible use for poorer land at a time when the continued growth of population in the region during the eighteenth century was bringing about a reduction in the size of holdings that were already tiny. As in parts of southern France during the eighteenth and nineteenth centuries, the higher yields of viticulture made it possible for smallholders to make a living by intensive labour in weeding, pruning, manuring and in making terraces for vines. Although wines were shipped direct from coastal areas to Barcelona or consumers overseas, there was also a different kind of trade, noted by Townsend at Benicarlo: 'The soil is peculiarly favour-able for the cultivation of the vine, and produces a generous wine, much used for enriching the poorer wines in the neighbourhood of Bordeaux for the purpose of making claret. . . .' But brandy was also a major export, its production having been introduced and nourished by French merchants in the seventeenth century. Whereas wine tended to come from the coastal regions, brandies were more com-monly the product of the further hinterland from which communica-tions to the coast were poor and expensive.[55] Wines and brandy exports to Barcelona for reshipment elsewhere gave considerable impetus to the expansion of small coastal ports such as Sitges, Vendrell and Reus. Some shipped their wines direct to distant markets, and even the small town and port of Sitges had some 52 ships capable of making transatlantic voyages in 1775. Before the freedom of Atlantic commerce was granted to the Catalan ports, Barcelona and its satellites had to send wine to Cadiz for re-export, but after 1778 freedom of trade gave a new impetus to the export trade and to the Atlantic commerce of Barcelona.

In the marketing of wines and brandies no less than the fruits, vegetables and dairy products for which Catalonia had gained a reputation by the end of the eighteenth century, it was Barcelona which was the outstanding focus of activity. Townsend's remarks at the end of the century symbolise its rôle: 'As we approach Barcelona, all is in motion, and the whole road appears alive, with horses, mules, waggons, carts and people, thronging to the market with their wares. No such activity, no such appearance of business, is seen in any other of the provinces.'[56] During the late seventeenth and the eighteenth centuries the growth of industry and trade at Barcelona revived its medieval prosperity and re-emphasised the distinctiveness of Catalonia within Spain, of which the Catalans were insistently and acutely aware. It became the centre of a region of rural domestic textile industries concerned largely with wool, linen, cotton and lace, and was in the forefront of new urban industrial growth including the introduction of new factory industry. The population of Barcelona grew by leaps and bounds during the late eighteenth century, from 70,000 in 1760 to an estimated 130,000 in 1798.[57]

Like Milan or the towns of Holland in the seventeenth century, or those of Flanders in the Middle Ages, Barcelona was a pole of activity generating agricultural expansion through its function as a centre of consumption and as a market for commodities for export, and through its financial activities in supplying credit and capital for rural agricultural and industrial growth. It is, perhaps, significant of the influence of Barcelona on a larger region that the price movements of Catalonia and Valencia show general trends during the late seventeenth century which are parallel with those of Western Europe and quite unlike the characteristic trends of prices in Castile and much of the rest of Spain, a fact which may suggest a basically independent market area, and the commercial involvement of Catalan and Valencian farming in the general European sphere of commerce.

REFERENCES

Abbreviations:
Ann. E.S.C.   *Annales, Economies, Sociétés, Civilisations*, Paris.
C.E.H.E.   *Cambridge Economic History of Europe*. Vol. 1, *Agrarian Life of the Middle Ages*, ed. J. H. Clapham and E. Power, Cambridge, 1942.
E.H.R.   *Economic History Review*.

1. M. M. POSTAN, 'Some economic evidence of a declining population', *E.H.R.*, second series, vol. 2, 1949–50, pp. 221–46.
2. B. H. SLICHER VAN BATH, *The Agrarian History of Western Europe, A.D. 500–1850*, London, 1963.
3. M. R. REINHARD and A. ARMENGAUD, *Histoire générale de la Population mondiale*, Paris, 1961.
4. H. GILLE, 'Demographic history of the northern countries', *Population Studies*, vol. 3, 1949–50, pp. 1–54.
5. P. GOUBERT, *Beauvais et le Beauvaisis de 1600 à 1730*, Paris, 1961.
6. Slicher van Bath, *Agrarian History of Western Europe*, pp. 137–41.
7. Ibid., pp. 217–18.
8. F. J. FISHER, 'The development of the London food market 1540–1640', *Essays in Economic History*, ed. E. M. Carus-Wilson, London, 1954, vol. 1, pp. 135–51.
9. A. H. JOHN, 'The course of agricultural change in England 1650–1750', *Studies in the Industrial Revolution*, ed. L. S. Pressnell, London, 1960, pp. 125–55.
10. R. DION, *Histoire de la vigne et du vin en France des origines au 19ᵉ siècle*, Paris, 1959, p. 47.
11. H. C. DARBY, ed. *Domesday Geography of South-East England*, Cambridge, 1961, p. 609.
12. H. PIRENNE, 'Le vin et l'histoire française', *Ann. d'Histoire écon. et sociale*, vol. 5, 1933, pp. 225–43.
13. M. K. JAMES, 'Fluctuations in the Anglo-Gascon wine trade in the fourteenth century', *E.H.R.*, second series, vol. 4, 1951–2, pp. 170–96.
14. G. G. WEIGEND, 'The basis and significance of viticulture in south-west France', *Annals of the Association of American geographies*, vol. 44, 1954, pp. 75–101.
15. Dion, *Histoire de la vigne*, p. 209.
16. Ibid., p. 222.
17. Ibid., pp. 424–58.
18. H. ENJALBERT, 'Comment naissent les grands crus: Bordeaux, porto, cognac', *Ann. E.S.C.*, vol. 8, 1953, pp. 315–28 and 457–74.
19. Dion, *Histoire de la vigne*, p. 598.
20. P. WAGRET, *Les Polders*, Paris, 1959, pp. 66–114.
21. P. VAN VEEN, *Dredge, Drain, Reclaim*, The Hague, 1955, p. 58.
22. A. J. PANNEKOEK, ed., *Geological History of the Netherlands*, The Hague, 1956, pp. 114–29.

23. M. DENDERMONDE, *The Dutch and their Dikes*, Amsterdam, 1956, pp. 58–61.
24. J. B. L. HOL, 'La lutte contre les eaux et la mise en culture', *La Néerlande*, ed. J. van Hinte, Leyden, 1938, pp. 64–92.
25. M. K. E. GOTTSCHALK, *Historische geografie van Westlijke Eeuws Vlaanderen*, Assen, 1955.
26. M. CHISHOLM, *Rural Settlement and Land Use*, London, 1962.
27. B. H. SLICHER VAN BATH, 'The rise of intensive husbandry in the Low Countries', *Britain and the Netherlands*, ed. J. S. Bromley, London, 1960, pp. 130–53.
28. B. H. SLICHER VAN BATH, 'Agriculture in the Low Countries, 1600–1800', 10th Int. Congress of Historical Sciences, section IV, *Biblioteca Storica Sansoni*, new series, vol. 25–6, 1955, Florence, pp. 169–203.
29. G. E. FUSSELL, 'Low Countries influence on English farming', *English Historical Review*, vol. 74, 1959, pp. 611–22.
30. J. M. HOUSTON, *The Western Mediterranean World*, London, 1964, p. 485.
31. Ibid., pp. 472–98.
32. D. F. DOWD, 'The economic expansion of Lombardy, 1300–1500', *Journ. Econ. Hist.*, vol. 21, 1961, pp. 143–60.
33. G. LUZATTO, *Economic History of Italy to the beginning of the sixteenth century*, London, 1961, p. 93.
34. G. MICKWITZ, 'Medieval agrarian society in its prime: Italy', *C.E.H.E.*, vol. 1, p. 324.
35. Dowd, *Journ. Econ. Hist.*, vol. 21, 1961, pp. 143–60.
36. A. MONBEIG, 'Les transformations économiques dans les huertas et la région entre Alicante et Murcia', *Annales de Géographie*, vol. 39, 1930, pp. 597–607.
37. A. DE LABORDE, *A View of Spain*, 5 vols., London, 1809, vol. 2, pp. 215–17.
38. Ibid., vol. 2, pp. 215–17.
39. J. TOWNSEND, *A Journey through Spain in the years 1786 and 1787*, 3 vols, London, 1791, vol. 3, pp. 196–7.
40. Monbeig, *Annales de Géographie*, vol. 39, 1930, pp. 597–607.
41. V. F. GONZALEZ, 'La evolución de los cultivos en las huertas levantinas de España', 16th Int. Geographical Congress, Lisbon, 1949, *Comptes Rendus*, vol. 3, pp. 286–306.
42. Ibid., p. 288.
43. T. H. DONGHI, 'Moriscos of the kingdom of Valencia in the sixteenth century', *Ann. E.S.C.*, vol. 11, 1956, pp. 154–82.
44. Gonzalez, 'La evolución de los cultivos en las huertas levantinas de España', p. 301.
45. Ibid., p. 304.
46. Laborde, *A View of Spain*, vol. 1, p. 302.
47. Ibid., vol. 1, pp. 294–317.
48. P. GEORGE, *Le Bas Rhône*, Paris, 1925.
49. Laborde, *A View of Spain*, vol. 1, p. 107.
50. Townsend, *A Journey through Spain*, vol. 3, p. 317.

51. S. LLOBET, 'La geografía agraria de la comarca de Maresme', *Estudios Geograficos*, vol. 15, 1955, pp. 23–72.
52. Ibid., pp. 57 ff.
53. J. FONTANA LAZARO, 'The external trade of Barcelona in the second half of the seventeenth century', *Estudios de Historia Moderna*, vol. 5, 1955, pp. 199–214.
54. Townsend, *A Journey through Spain*, vol. 3, p. 311.
55. E. G. Y. REVENTOS, 'El cultivo de la vid y el comercio catalan del siglo 18', *Estudios de Historia Moderna*, vol. 2, 1952, pp. 159–78.
56. Townsend, *A Journey through Spain*, vol. 3, p. 317.
57. Laborde, *A View of Spain*, vol. 1, p. 29.

CHAPTER 10

INDUSTRY IN THE EARLY MODERN PERIOD

It was Karl Bücher, pioneer among German economic historians and one of the few early economic historians to give full weight to spatial elements in historical change, who characterised this as a period in which one of the dominant features was the shift from production for the urban region to production for the national market.[1] It would be easy to overemphasise this trend, for in the Middle Ages there had, of course, been highly localised industries producing for national and international markets, notably the woollen cloth industry; and well into the nineteenth century many industries continued to produce only for the towns in which they were located and for the surrounding countryside, particularly construction industries and some food processing. Yet it remains true that during the early modern period a number of industries ceased to be more or less ubiquitously distributed and became concentrated in favoured regions. Regional specialisation developed, for example, in hosiery, lace, metal manufactures such as edge tools, locks and nails, glass and pottery, as well as in textiles. During the period as a whole, a number of factors led towards regional specialisations in agriculture as well as in industry (see above, Ch. 9), a process which carried with it new opportunities for further specialisation and concentration in those industries which processed agricultural raw materials or made use of agricultural by-products. Malting, brewing and milling, wine-making, dairy industries, leather, woollens and linen manufacturing were obviously the major industries to be affected, each developing regional concentrations corresponding to agricultural changes and the orientation of trade to urban markets. In England, for example, dairy specialisation in Cheshire and Staffordshire created the need for coarse earthenware pottery for the export of butter and cheese, which gave an early impetus to the pottery industry of North Staffordshire; industries using wool and leather flourished in the Midlands, in Northamptonshire and Leicestershire; malting and milling were important industries in the grain-growing counties of the south Midlands, and particularly in the towns through which grain passed *en route* for London markets. The shifts of prices in favour of industrial products during the seventeenth century also helped to encourage agricultural industry and industrial employment in the countryside, for the wages of artisans in industry tended to be higher than those of agricultural labourers.

Changes in industrial organisation were clearly of profound importance for the location of industry. The so-called 'domestic' or 'putting-out system' has been regarded as typical of the period, though it was a form of industrial organisation mainly restricted to the textile industries and some metal-working trades. Raw materials were supplied by the entrepreneur to craftsmen working in their own homes. The tools and equipment used by workmen were usually their own, though this was not always the case and elaborate machinery such as the framework-knitting machine was often rented out. Completed goods were returned to the merchant for further processing, dyeing, sorting, finishing, storage and sale. The fact that the entrepreneur retained ownership of the raw materials has been regarded as a diagnostic trait of the system, a feature which enabled the craftsmen to work with the minimum of capital in raw materials which were expensive and not necessarily of local origin. It also enabled the entrepreneur to retain or acquire control over all stages of production without the need for heavy investment in the provision of workplaces in factories for his dependent workpeople.

Geographically the putting-out system facilitated the rural spread of industry on a much larger scale than ever before, though it must be remembered that many of the craftsmen thus organised did in fact live in the towns. Rural industry was emancipated from the need to work locally produced raw materials. The fact that detailed and continuous supervision and control could not easily be exercised by the entrepreneur tended to confine the putting-out system to the production of fairly standardised articles by methods which were labour-intensive. Independent craftsmen continued to flourish in the very many industries in which personal production for the individual customer prevailed, and in luxury industries demanding a high degree of skill.

Where heavy investment in fixed capital was required, as in coal-mining, smelting, shipbuilding, brewing and sugar-refining, direct employment of large numbers of workmen was more common in a capitalistic form of industrial organisation. The growth of the factory system was still unimportant compared with what it became in the nineteenth century, but in some areas and in some industries it was already developing. Nef and others have drawn attention to the increasing scale of investment in industrial plant which was necessitated in the sixteenth and seventeenth centuries by the increasing depth of mines and the development of new problems of drainage and transport. The use of coal as a fuel made possible much more rapid expansion in some English industries such as glass manufacturing, brewing or salt-refining.[2] In the metal industries the divorce of the blast furnace from the forge and the use of more powerful waterdriven blast permitted an increase in the size and scale of furnaces and thus demanded greater capital investment. The new colonial industries often required large investment if only to finance the purchase of costly raw materials and their processing through various stages of production. Finally, one effect of the state's concern for industrial production was sometimes to encourage the development of industry in large-scale units, as for example when the privileges granted to a new manufacture required the concentration of production in order to maintain a monopoly or to secure high standards of quality. Enterprises employing large numbers of workers and involving concentration in large-scale units, whether factories, mines or shipbuilding yards, were not uncommon in England even before the application of steam-power to industry at the end of the eighteenth century, and they had begun to make headway in France, as in the cloth manufactures of Abbeville, or the mining industry at Anzin.

In the emergent nation states of the period, industry was generally encouraged by the mercantilist policies of the time, sometimes because it provided employment for a surplus population, but more often to save or earn foreign currency by providing an article of export or a substitute for imported manufactures. Subsidies, privileges, monopolies and tax holidays were often given to establish new industries or to imitate industries and techniques pioneered or better developed in competing countries. Imports of foreign manufactured goods were prohibited or highly taxed in order to protect less efficient or 'infant' industries at home.

The encouragement of innovation is one of the most interesting features of state economic policy during the period, for the establishment of new techniques and industries depended greatly on the introduction and spread of new skills by immigrant craftsmen as well as on immigrant capital and entrepreneurship. The export of the new machinery and the emigration of skilled craftsmen were forbidden in England at the end of the eighteenth century, but the immigration of craftsmen was, on the other hand, welcomed and encouraged. In the sixteenth century, it was Italian and Flemish craftsmen who were most highly valued for their skills in the manufacture of fine cloths, linen and lace, jewellery and goldsmiths' work, glass, mirrors and printing; in the seventeenth it was the Dutch who were imitated, envied and encouraged to immigrate. Dutch weavers, shipbuilders, merchants and drainage experts were among those who migrated, often with royal or noble encouragement to France, England, Scandinavia, Germany, Poland and Russia. The Revocation of the Edict of Nantes in 1685 was followed by the emigration of many protestant Huguenots to many parts of Europe and especially perhaps to Germany, and they took with them the skills which had made European reputations for many French luxury products.[3] Ultimately, in the second half of the eighteenth century, it was English craftsmen who began to establish machine methods in France and the Low Countries, and thus gave some impetus to the beginning of industrial revolution on the continent.

THE GEOGRAPHICAL DISTRIBUTION OF INDUSTRY

In comparison with the earlier predominantly urban-industrial pattern of the Middle Ages and with the later urban concentrations of the nineteenth century, the main distinguishing feature of the early modern period was the spread of rural and semi-rural industries.[4] This trend, already apparent in the later Middle Ages, had always been characteristic of mining and smelting industries, but it now reached much greater proportions. Urban locations, of course, continued to be characteristic of many of the crafts and industries associated with the growth of the capital cities and the great ports. New luxury industries and colonial or entrepôt industries were oriented to the ports and capitals as well as many industries which continued to be predominantly market-oriented. A third feature of the period and clearly evident in the eighteenth century was the emergence of new 'industrial regions'—areas in which rural and semi-rural industry was the dynamic factor in bringing about major regional change and the growth of new large towns. The textile industries of Lancashire and Yorkshire or the metal industries of the West Midlands were the most obvious of such agglomerations by 1800; in France the textile industries of Nord and the metals, lace and silk industries around St Etienne; in Sweden the iron industries of Bergslagen; and in Germany the textile and metal industries of the Rhineland, Saxony and Silesia.

It may be useful to review briefly the factors mainly involved in the localisation of industry during the period. First, communications continued to be difficult and expensive, especially overland, and it was only towards the end of the eighteenth century that matters were greatly improved by the military road-building programmes of France, Spain and the Low Countries or the turnpike movement in England. Water transport, and especially the coastal trade, remained the most efficient and cheapest means of communication. River navigation was being improved in England and France in the eighteenth century, but weirs, fisheries and tolls were sometimes major problems. Canals had already proved their worth as a means of cheap and safe movement of bulk commodities in Italy, France and the Low Countries, but construction over long distances required a great deal of capital expenditure and it was only in England that they made a major contribution to transport by 1800. Provincial tolls, customs duties and prohibitions on trade continued to restrict the internal movement of goods within Europe.

The difficulties and uncertainties of transport tended naturally to reduce the extent to which specialisation could take place. Market areas for many products were small, especially for the cheap or bulky products of food-processing industries, construction industries or the work of everyday craftsmanship. But it is also a feature of the period that in a number of industries the production of expensive, high-quality or luxury goods could be strongly localised and specialised while low-quality products for mass consumption continued to be produced locally for nearby markets. Thus, many areas which had suitable resources continued to produce crude and homespun textiles in spite of the existence of long-distance trade in medium- and high-quality cloths and the concentration of production of good quality cloth in particular areas. Local building materials continued to be used for ordinary structures, but fine stone was taken long distances to enrich the streets of London, Paris and Berlin, just as it was in the Middle Ages for the building of cathedrals and churches. In France, difficulties of transport had led to a wide scatter of small-scale iron producers working for local markets, but high-quality malleable iron would be transported over long distances to its markets. The quality of the product was in many trades the characteristic which created a wider market and permitted concentration of production. Quality was partly a function of concentration and localisation itself in so far as greater scale permitted greater division of labour and the development of great skills, but it was skill that mattered, usually the empirical but often inarticulate knowledge of the craftsman, not easily communicated by word of mouth or by the printed word, and best learnt by long practice. It was for this reason, perhaps, that the skilled migrant craftsmen or the refugee protestants from France or the Low Countries were so important and so highly regarded as pioneers of industrial innovation. Quality was also a function of the availability of raw materials and the nature of resources was frequently a critical matter in the development of specialised industry, particularly at a time when the technological capacity to standardise raw materials of mineral or agricultural origin was very limited. Thus iron ores free from phosphorus, sulphur and silicon were highly prized. The peculiar natural quality of Shropshire coal was important in early coke smelting in England and the purity of the Bergslagen ores and of Swedish charcoal were fundamental in the high quality and therefore the 'merchantability' of Swedish iron. Similarly, much has been written of the variations in quality of wool as a factor in the location and fortunes of woollen cloth industries in England and the Low Countries.

High transport costs tended also to increase the attraction of an industrial location at the source of raw materials in industries where a significant loss of weight occurred in processing and manufacture, although no single resource had the outstanding pull of coal in the steam age. The refining and smelting of metals was necessarily carried on near the sources of ore; valuable constructional timber of oak or tall pines for ships' masts could be widely traded, but wood and charcoal for fuel was a limiting factor in the location of iron industries; coal played an important part in the manufacture of salt, glass and chemicals, in brewing and in many industries which involved the re-heating of metal; and the use of water-power obviously demanded location along the banks of suitable streams.

The orientation of industry to its markets was, however, still important in many industries which depended on close contact between producer and consumer and in which there was a large service element. The manufacture of clothing, shoes, carriages, furniture and furnishings, tapestries and works of art fall into this category, locating themselves characteristically in the capitals. Indeed, the line between 'service industries' or 'distributive trades' and manufacturing industries was often impossible to draw as long as many craftsmen produced tailor-made goods for particular clients according to their own specifications or even using their own raw materials. In many cases retail trade only began to be differentiated from production and wholesale trade in the eighteenth century.

The availability of capital was more significant in the attraction of industry to particular areas than it was later, for even within national territories it could not be assumed that capital or credit were ubiquitously available on the same terms. In the crudest sense the proximity of silver-mining and the availability of currency at ports helped in the finance of enterprises. But the general effect of the uneven geographical distribution of currency, credit, capital or rates of interest was in general to favour the great ports and the capital cities.

Labour supply and the conditions of labour exerted a very strong effect on the location of industry. The medieval urban gilds persisted into the modern period, and in many areas of Western Europe they were often resuscitated and used by the state as a means of imposing and enforcing regulations on quality or methods of production. In the later Middle Ages the cloth industries of the Low Countries had moved to the countryside, to escape the restrictions and rigidities of gild regulations as well as the social and political frictions which had emerged within the urban framework. In Prussia and France the state attempted to restrict the spread of unregulated industry into the countryside. In France these restrictions were brought to an end in 1762, though they had long been ineffective. It was to the advantage of rural industry in England, Saxony and Silesia that it was either quietly tolerated or actively encouraged. Rural labour was cheap and abundant, especially in areas of agricultural underemployment or overpopulation. It is true that foodstuffs were often cheaper than in the towns, but during the seventeenth and early eighteenth centuries agricultural wages tended to be at a disadvantage compared with industrial wages, and urban wages higher than rural.

Several factors, therefore, tended to encourage the expansion of rural industry in the period: the structure of the 'putting-out system'; the increasing use of water-power; the orientation of many industries to sources of raw materials; rural underemployment, gild restrictions in the towns; and the balance of prices for agricultural and industrial products. The use of local resources was obviously one of the most important conditions underlying the development of rural industry in particular areas: wool in Yorkshire, the West Country or the Low Countries, for example; flax and linen in Westphalia, Flanders, Silesia or Brittany; hides and skins for the leather industries of the Midlands; timber, ores and water-power in the metal-working areas: but it may be that the environmental basis for rural industry can be easily overemphasised. Many rural industries, such as the cotton industry of Germany, Switzerland, Catalonia or Lancashire, the lace and hosiery industries of the East Midlands in England or the silk and lace of the St Etienne areas, relied on raw materials that were imported from elsewhere, while many areas of important woollen or linen textile industries had come to rely on imported raw materials by the eighteenth century. The nature of the resources locally available may have helped to dictate the *kind* of industry taken up by rural populations, but the incentive to take up industrial occupations needed some other stimulus than simply the availability of a raw material. Consideration of the distribution of areas of rural industry in relation to agrarian conditions has frequently suggested that such industry tended to develop most, perhaps, in areas of rural underemployment; in areas where farms had been subdivided beyond the point at which agricultural activity alone could support the peasant household; or in areas of poverty-stricken, marginal farming on poor soils (as, for example in the sandy heathlands of the eastern Netherlands) or on the upland margins of farming in hilly and mountainous districts (as in northern England, Wales or the Rhineland massifs).

The distribution of rural industry was often located with respect to urban marketing centres. The towns were not only the places at which the finished products of rural domestic industry were marketed and the headquarters of merchant-entrepreneurs who organised industries, but they were also centres at which preparatory stages of production and finishing processes were often undertaken. The towns also became the centres of ancillary industries concerned with the manufacture of tools or the provision of other and more specialised products of the industry. For example, in the East Midlands, Nottingham, Derby and Leicester were the centres from which lace and hosiery industries were directed and the distribution of rural industry was clearly related to distance from these centres or from some of the smaller towns which also acted as market centres.[5] Similar patterns are to be found elsewhere in the relations of Manchester with the cotton-manufacturing area of Lancashire, in the relations of Birmingham and Wolverhampton with the metal industries of the Midlands; and in the relations of Barcelona, Milan and Lyon with the industrial areas that grew up around them.

It would be impossible to present a detailed survey of the industrial geography of Western Europe, and indeed, the general outlines of urban industrial growth have already been touched upon in connection with the development of towns and trade (see Chapters 7 and 8). It therefore seems appropriate to concentrate on several studies which may serve to illustrate the themes briefly touched upon above. The developing industries of southern Belgium and the iron industry of Sweden provide examples of the use made of natural resources in a period when the foundations of modern industrial distributions were being laid. France and Germany provide examples on a larger scale of the distribution of rural industry.

TEXTILE AND METAL INDUSTRIES IN SOUTHERN BELGIUM

Right up to modern times the major distinction in the industrial geography of Belgium has been that between the textiles of the Lys basin and the mining and metal industries of the south along the axis of the Sambre-Meuse depression and the coalfield. Even during the Middle Ages this distinction already existed, for Huy, Dinant and Namur had a very early reputation for their copper, brass and iron industries. North of the ancient massif of the Ardennes, Devonian and Carboniferous rocks have been much folded, faulted and mineralised. The strike of the country is oriented from west-southwest to east-north-east and is followed very clearly by the line of the structurally guided trough of the Sambre and Meuse rivers. Copper, calamine and iron ores were the raw materials used in the medieval industries, though the copper of Huy and Dinant appears to have declined at a fairly early date through the competition of more efficient German industries in the Harz Mountains and Bohemia. But Namur and Liège were medieval centres of iron-working of much more than local importance. The tectonic history of this area of old, hard rocks involved not only the deposition of valuable mineral ores, but also regional uplift and the incision of the Sambre-Meuse and their tributaries into the general level of the plateau. Thus there were available not only the mineral ores but also the water-power and the timber resources to work them, for many of the steep slopes and thin soils which had been worthless as arable land had been left under woodland.

The Walloon region of the southern Netherlands was, indeed, one of the major regions of technological advance in the iron industry of medieval times. In the thirteenth century the use of water-power to drive bellows for the heating of the furnace resulted in several important changes in the industry. Permanent installations became necessary for the manufacture of iron and it was no longer practical for temporary forges to be built wherever sources of iron ore and charcoal were to hand. The permanent sites had to be on the banks of streams big enough to generate adequate water-power. Secondly, greater blast from power-driven bellows made possible an increase in the size of the furnace, and this produced fuel economies, particularly after about 1500 when a change to the bee-hive shaped furnace ensured a better distribution of heat inside it. Moreover, the greater heat produced by the new process brought about complete fusion of the iron and the production of a pig iron in which there was a high proportion of carbon. Refining by reheating and beating in the forge was still necessary, so that the introduction of the power-driven bellows also caused the separation of the iron industry into the smelting process, carried on in the furnace, and the refining process, carried on in the forges.

By the sixteenth century the Sambre-Meuse depression, endowed with good resources of iron ore, water-power and timber for charcoal, and also easily accessible to the markets of the Rhine by way of the navigable Meuse, had become one of the most outstanding areas of iron production in Europe, ranking with a handful of areas internationally known for the quality and quantity of their output—Bilbao, Ferrara near Milan, Nürnberg and its surroundings, and Styria in the Austrian Alps. In the Namur district there were some 35 furnaces and 85 forges, occupying some 7,000 charcoal burners in mid-sixteenth century. Guicciardini wrote of the Namur district that 'forges of iron are so innumerable that the whole country seemeth to be Vulcan's forge'.[6] But it was in the Liège district that the greatest expansion seems to have taken place during the course of the sixteenth century, and iron and coal appear as industries playing a strategic rôle in the development of an industrial complex which also embraced glass, chemicals, iron-working industries and armaments. The location and character of each of these industries was very closely linked with the others through the use of local resources and skills, but perhaps the most important fact was the existence and use of coal on a much larger scale than before. Indeed, the principality of Liège provides an excellent example of the type of growth occurring in England in the sixteenth century and labelled by J. U. Nef as a 'first industrial revolution' in order to stress the new importance of coal and capital in the development of certain industries.

Of the sections of the Belgian coalfield where coal outcrops at the surface, Namur and Liège had the additional advantages for early exploitation that they were very near to navigable water and mining by adits as well as surface pits could be easily undertaken. Of these two areas the latter had some further advantage in being very near to the substantial urban market of Liège itself and in lying some way downstream from Namur and therefore nearer to the markets of the Low Countries. In the thirteenth and fourteenth centuries coal pits had been dug on the left bank of the Meuse, and in the sixteenth century the right bank, across the river from Liège itself, was opened up. A map of 1577 displays some 69 pits in the area, and after this expansion output increased fourfold during the first half of the sixteenth century, even though it stood at only some 90,000 tons even in a good year.[7]

Much of this coal went to the domestic hearths of Liège itself, a town which grew very rapidly in population—from some 4,000 in 1470 to 35,000 in 1550. Some was exported overland to the immediate hinterland of the town to the north, but most of the exports went by river down the Meuse to the ports of Holland and Zeeland where they competed with Newcastle coal, or up the Rhine, reaching as far as Frankfurt-on-Main, where a sixteenth-century salt manufacturer, for example, had a contract with a Liège mine owner for supplies. Finally, an increasing number of Liège industries made important use of coal: brewing, chemical and gunpowder industries, and above all, the metal-working industries and the nail makers. For although charcoal was necessary for the refining of iron, coal could be used in the work of the smithy and in foundry work.

As in England the increase of coal production was accompanied by a greater emphasis on capital investment and a more elaborate organisation of production. Capital was needed for the payment of land taxes, rents, payments for the right to dig pits and for the right of access to the pits, but more and more capital was needed, too, for the equipment needed in the digging and maintenance of deeper pits which required ventilation, drainage and haulage equipment.

Permanent working and maintenance were also needed, not only to make full use of capital invested but also to prevent deterioration and flooding. Part-time and seasonal labour in shallow diggings gave way to a permanent, wage-paid labour force. Thus, coal-mining became a more specialised industry, organised increasingly along capitalistic lines, and also much more productive than it had been before 1500.

By 1600 the iron industry of the Liège area had been localised in five main areas: around Liège itself, on the lower Ourthe, the Vesdre, scattered along the Sambre-Meuse towards Namur, and finally on the banks of the Eau Noire. Virtually all the individual sites had, by the end of the sixteenth century, a waterside location to provide the water-power needed for the bellows in the blast furnaces and the forges and for water-driven hammers, or for the rolling, slitting and stamping machines devised for the smithing and nail-making industries. The iron industry thrived on local ores, charcoal and water-power, and on local sales to the smiths, the nailmakers, and the sword and cannon makers who were able to use local coal resources. As in the English Midlands, there were advantages in the location of metal industries on the coalfields long before the classic changes of the industrial revolution enabled coal to be used in the blast furnaces and in the refining of pig iron. Nevertheless, the scale of the industry was still very small. Most of the iron-works, it has been said, were closed for much of the year because there was insufficient water, because the labourers had harvests to attend to or because of frost or flood. The forgers were craftsmen who could also turn their hands to the mining of ore, the smelting process or the burning of charcoal. In 1562 the output of iron from Liège was probably no greater than 1,000 tons of pig iron, yet this was an important part of one of the major areas of iron production in Western Europe.

Of the iron-using industries in southern Belgium which made full use of coal, the munitions and armaments industry was the most important and the most highly organised. Jean Curtius was internationally known in the second half of the sixteenth century as a great arms manufacturer, at a time when the principality of Liège, not yet incorporated into the Spanish Netherlands and politically neutral, exported its products impartially to the highest bidder, with Spain and the Empire as the best markets. Valenciennes, Tournai and Namur shared in this preoccupation with arms, which constituted one of the important exports of Antwerp, particularly to Spain. The arms industry included the manufacture of gunpowder, saltpetre and sulphuric acid, processes in which coal was used for distillation. Other industries introduced in the sixteenth century also made use of coal: the refining of alum for the cloth industry, and the manufacture of glass, an industry brought from Italy which used the local sands of the Sambre-Meuse valley before turning to the higher-quality silica sands of the Campine.

The cloth industry, too, flourished later in this area, for although coarse cloths were being produced in the fourteenth century in the valley of the Vesdre, a tributary of the Meuse, it was not until the seventeenth century that the region began to be important for the cloths that were marketed in Verviers, the chief centre.[8] The natural advantages for the location of a cloth industry are not entirely obvious. The local wool was coarse and insufficient for the industry once the first phase of expansion occurred; communications were bad, not only because of the lack of good roads and of navigable water, but also because of the marginal position of the area near a political frontier. Its advantages were its possession of soft and clean water, a factor perhaps much exaggerated in studies of the early growth of the industry, since in this respect the Vesdre was no better than any other stream draining north from the Ardennes;[9] cheap labour and freedom from gild regulation; and the regular and efficient water-power naturally available in this hilly region. Like the textile districts of northern England Verviers seems to have been a poor and remote area where cloth was initially a domestic industry using locally available raw materials to supplement inadequate incomes from marginal farming in a region of small, independent farmers. It began, and long remained as a rural and domestic industry, marketing its products in Verviers. But it was in the right area to benefit from the abundance of local water-power and also, much later, from its proximity to the coalfield. It is, perhaps, of interest that in the interwar years the woollen industry of Belgium showed a distinctive tendency to shift from the Verviers district to Flanders, partly because of an abundance of labour, made redundant through the decline of the cotton industry, and partly, it is said, because of the higher wages and better labour conditions resulting from trade union organisation in the Verviers district. The wheel had turned full circle from the time when the medieval cloth industry had begun to shift, for similar reasons, from the irksome regulations and conditions of the towns.

By the end of the eighteenth century the industrial geography of

Belgium had begun to show a pattern which is still traceable in spite of the changes of the industrial revolution: concentration on linen in Flanders and Brabant; coal-mining, iron, metal industries, chemicals and glass in the Sambre-Meuse depression; and textiles in the Verviers district. In detail, much of this industry was rural and domestic in organisation, sustaining a dense rural population for which the Belgian area was already renowned in the sixteenth century, but, like the industries of England, those of Belgium were industries which catered for a mass consumption and which were much more easily capable of mass production and machine methods than the luxury products for which, for example, French industry was best known. And if these industries happened to be well located with respect to navigable water and to coal resources, this was not so much a happy coincidence as a product of locational advantages already operating long before the industrial revolution.

THE SWEDISH IRON INDUSTRY BEFORE 1800

One of the striking features of the period between the sixteenth and eighteenth centuries was the rapidity of Swedish economic development. From a place of poverty at the margin of cultivation and settlement in northern Europe, barely touched by a money economy and largely free from the trammels of a feudal order, Sweden rose to a remarkable position of political unity, military power and economic prosperity in the seventeenth and early eighteenth centuries. Several characteristics are outstanding in Swedish historical geography, and never more so than during this period of growth: a continuing history of pioneer colonisation and settlement on the northern climatic margin of temperate crop cultivation; a wealth of natural resources in timber, minerals and water-power; the importance of innovation in technology, commerce and finance introduced from the more advanced economies of Western Europe; and the continuing interest and importance of the state in economic affairs.

From the thirteenth to the sixteenth centuries, the economy was local and largely concerned with subsistence production, and such external trade as there was had fallen largely into the hands of the Hanseatic league, exporting Swedish iron, copper, tar, wood-ash and other timber products to European markets.[10] The herring fisheries of Scania were in Danish hands, but they were of declining importance in the later Middle Ages. The Hanseatic monopoly of Swedish trade was, however, broken open in the fifteenth century by the rising prosperity of the Dutch and their participation in the trade through the Sound rather than across the Hanseatic-held routes across the base of the Jutland peninsula. Moreover it was largely through Dutch commercial and financial expertise, Dutch or Walloon technology and Dutch capital investment that Sweden began to enter significantly into the European economic scene in the seventeenth century.

Copper was the first of the Swedish resources to play an important rôle in European trade, and it was indeed the revenues from copper exports that helped to sustain Swedish political ambitions in the Thirty Years' War and after. The copper resources of Stora Kopparberg, near Falun, had been exploited from the thirteenth century and mining methods had been reorganised on advanced German lines, but the new expansion of the seventeenth century was inspired by Dutch capital and by the initiative of the Swedish state. Copper exports were deliberately exploited as a source of revenue and for the foreign currency that could be acquired, at first to pay a Danish indemnity after 1613. The state owned a large interest in the mine; demand was rising rapidly with the increasing use all over Europe of brass and bronze, of cooking utensils made of these metals and of copper currency. For a time Swedish copper dominated European markets, between the decline of copper production in England and Saxony and the rise of Japanese imports in the late seventeenth century. Transylvania was the only major competitor, but excessive and predatory exploitation led to the great cave-in of the Stora Kopparberg mine in 1687, and levels of production never recovered from this disaster. In spite of its one-time importance to the economy Swedish copper has left relatively little trace on the industrial geography of Sweden, except for the mine and its attendant settlement.

It was otherwise with the exploitation of Swedish iron resources, which have continued from the end of the Middle Ages to be a major prop of the external economy, and have continued to generate those multiplier effects which are most obviously evident in the growth of industrial regions in areas of former iron production and refining. The iron ores of northern Sweden were beyond the margin of effective settlement and were not within reasonable access of settlement or of charcoal supplies, and like the Grängesberg ores of central Sweden were unusable by reason of their phosphorus content. It was the pure ores of Bergslagen and above all of Dannemora that provided the raw material for the high-quality pig iron and malleable iron for which Sweden was famous throughout Europe in the eighteenth century. Water-power was abundant, regular and reliable and also widely distributed in the region of the iron ore deposits; water transport was used wherever possible; and Sweden had in abundance suitable forest resources for the manufacture of charcoal. In many areas of Western Europe endowed with more fertile soils and a more productive climate, the clearing of forests for farming, building or fuel had meant that a reduced charcoal supply was often a limiting factor in the expansion of iron industries despite the practice of coppicing. Swedish coniferous timber also had the advantage that it burned to a charcoal with a lower phosphoric content than that obtained from the deciduous trees used by most Western European producers.[11] High-quality ore combined with pure charcoal made possible the production of soft malleable iron, free from impurities and an excellent raw material for making steel.

Iron production had been important to medieval Sweden, though small deposits of bog ore rather than mineral ores were often used. By 1500, iron exports of 1,300 tons a year represented a substantial trade. Expansion had followed the introduction of the blast furnace in the fifteenth century and the separation of the smelting and refining processes which this involved; Swedish ironmasters took up many of the innovations originally introduced in the Low Countries, often by way of Dutch or Walloon intermediaries. Even in the heyday of copper production in the seventeenth century iron accounted for about half of all Sweden's exports. By 1720 iron made up 75 per cent of all exports, copper only 10 per cent. Between 1600 and 1720 iron output increased by five times and Sweden was producing perhaps as much as 35 per cent of Europe's total output of bar iron. For England, undergoing a crisis of production in the eighteenth century, imports of Swedish iron were of great significance, constituting as much as 40 per cent of English consumption in 1720 and accounting for 82 per cent of all imports of iron into England in that year. By about 1740, at the zenith of Sweden's importance, before Russian competition had seriously begun, Swedish iron production had grown to some 45,000 tons a year rising later to a fairly constant level of about 55,000 tons in the second half of the eighteenth century.

In Bergslagen the expansion of the iron industry had some of the characteristics of a pioneer movement of settlement into virgin land, for the operation of the blast furnaces required not only the building of the furnace near water-power and iron ore and the control over a supply of charcoal from nearby forests, but also the settlement of a forest population of woodcutters and charcoal burners and the acquisition or creation of arable farms to supply the grain needed by those dependent on the iron industry. As far as possible the units of iron-working were as self-sufficient as possible in both food supplies and raw materials, for the import of foodstuffs was expensive and difficult. In the period of expansion charcoal was frequently the medium of exchange by which forest workers and charcoal burners obtained food supplies from the truck shops set up by the iron-masters. The dependent and ancillary population on the new 'iron frontier' was usually far larger than the numbers actually engaged on iron production. In one area only 18 persons were concerned with producing iron as against 170 concerned in forestry, food production, charcoal burning, trading operations and so on.

In spite of its growth and prosperity in the seventeenth century and its importance in European trade, the iron industry suffered from restrictive policies from 1633 onwards. Forest resources in the neighbourhood of the mines and ore deposits were to be reserved for smelting only. Blast furnaces could therefore continue to operate within Bergslagen, but the forges in which the iron was refined were to be relegated to areas outside the zone of iron-mining itself. The policy was not wholly successful for vertical combinations of forges and furnaces persisted in the central area, but the spread of the forges to the periphery was started. To the north, new forges were constructed along the coast in Norrland and Värmland. To the west there was new expansion in the region between Bergslagen and Göteborg, the export route along which Bergslagen iron moved to the North Sea. A tradition of iron-working was here established on which later metal and engineering industries could be built. There was, similarly, a movement southwards of forges for refining from Bergslagen towards the Målar region, again establishing a basis on which modern industry has been built (most notably in the area of Eskilstuna).

In Bergslagen itself, ore was to hand and water power abundant. Charcoal supply represented a limiting factor on the expansion of output and also on the scale of each work unit. It may be that the restrictive policies of the seventeenth and eighteenth centuries were aimed at maintaining high prices in a market in which Sweden held a quasi-monopolistic position, but it is also abundantly clear that the restriction of charcoal supplies to the smelting industries in the neighbourhood of the Bergslagen ores was also aimed at making the most economic use of the limited charcoal supplies that were available within easy access of the iron ores. In the eighteenth century it took three to four tons of ore and six tons of charcoal to make one one ton of bar iron. In the late seventeenth century the average distance that charcoal was moved to the furnace was between three and ten miles.[12] For a given output of bar iron, it was therefore cheaper to move pig iron to available charcoal supplies outside the smelting area than to move iron ores or charcoal longer distances for smelting. Even in the absence of restriction, the expansion of iron output was severely limited by the economic limit of the field from which charcoal could be drawn.

It was also evident that the limited range from which charcoal could economically be moved to the blast furnace also tended to restrict the size of the blast furnace and the scale of operations at any one site. The Bergslagen industry consisted of a large number of small iron-works, numbering some 324 in 1695 and as many as 340 even in 1803, with an annual output rarely more than 200 tons. It was not until severe economies were made in the consumption of charcoal in the nineteenth century, and economies in transport by the building of the railways that the size of the unit was liberated from the limitations of local charcoal supply. Indeed, in 1950 only 0·65 to 0·70 tons of charcoal and 1·6 tons of ore were needed to make one ton of pig iron.[13]

The Swedish iron industry therefore provides a second example of the ways in which an expanding industry made use of a favourable combination of natural resources, and the scale of the industry and its rate of growth were closely geared to the nature and distribution of resources. So, too, was the quality of the product, and it was this above all, which assured Sweden of its external markets. Even in the absence of coal, the momentum established by the charcoal industry of the eighteenth century was never quite lost, and although it is unnecessary here to follow up the stages by which it survived the difficult years of the nineteenth century, it may be noted that steel and engineering industries built again upon these old foundations when electrical power made possible the greater emanicipation of steel industries from coal imports.

INDUSTRY IN FRANCE DURING THE *ANCIEN RÉGIME*

If statistics were available for the industrial output of the major European powers of the *ancien régime*, there is little doubt that

France, with its population of 18 to 20 million, would head the list. Its rate of growth would certainly have been lower than that of England by the second half of the eighteenth century, and England, Holland and the southern Netherlands would have probably outstripped France in terms of industrial output *per head*. The importance of the industrial revolution in England and the Low Countries at the very end of the period, and the concentration of historical research on the problems of its origins have tended to obscure the scale of French industry for the greater part of the *ancien régime*, but the classic age of the industrial revolution was one in which spectacular growth was still confined to a relatively limited range of industries, chiefly coal-mining, iron and textiles. These were industries in which it was quantity rather than quality that mattered, but France had led in trades in which it was quality and individuality that were important. One should therefore attempt to see the geography of industry in France in this period for its own sake rather than in terms of its relevance for the subsequent course of the industrial revolution. It may be useful then to consider first some of the more important general factors which affected the condition and distribution of industry in France, then to evaluate its general structure, and finally to analyse its geographical distribution.

It is often said that the expansion of the French economy and of its industry was repeatedly hampered by the almost continuous wars in which she was involved from the end of the Middle Ages to the Napoleonic wars. Periods of expansion during times of peace and stable administration alternated with stagnation or retrogression during periods of war and civil unrest. It may be easy to exaggerate the degree to which economic growth was disturbed, for Nef has pointed out that during the French wars of religion, for example, the areas directly affected by the armies were small and highly localised. Yet the wars of Louis XIV were costly in men and resources at the end of the seventeenth century and the emigration of many Huguenots, traditionally strong in industry and commerce and especially so in La Rochelle, Normandy and much of southern France, must have acted as a serious brake on industrial and commercial development after the revocation of the Edict of Nantes in 1685. The Seven Years' War was again a period of economic stagnation, followed by rapid recovery and renewed growth at an increasing rate to the end of the eighteenth century.

State intervention was the second general factor of importance in the French economy, and although it cannot be said that any major industrial area of France developed primarily through state intervention, it was important in many individual industries.[14] To stimulate domestic manufactures either for exporting or to substitute for imports was a cardinal principle of French mercantilistic policy from the sixteenth century. From the time of Francis I, great efforts had been made to imitate the luxury industries of Italy and thus to reduce imports of such 'fripperies'. In pottery, faience and goldsmiths' work, in tapestry and artistic crafts the crown began to replace the nobility in patronage of craftsmanship. Privileges and exemption from taxation were accorded to glass workers in an attempt to imitate and compete with fine Italian ware. The cultivation of the mulberry was encouraged by the state in order to nourish a domestic industry which would compete with that of Italy. The printing of fine books was encouraged by the crown. Inspectors and controllers of manufactures were instituted from 1572. The foundations were laid for the economic *étatism* of Colbert's age.[15]

It was indeed in the seventeenth century that the principle of state control of industry was most thoroughly developed. A few manufacturers were set up by the state, notably the art industries of Gobelins, the Savonnerie and the tapestry of Beauvais, and the military and naval workshops at Brest, Rochefort and Toulon. But the state was also responsible for the introduction of new industries and their subsequent protection and encouragement. Italian immigrants were attracted to establish some luxury industries such as the production of mirrors and fine lace; Swiss and Germans came to reorganise foundry work and mining; Dutch workers brought techniques for the production of fine cloth, shipbuilding and sugar-refining. The granting of privileges and monopolies was a further means of encouraging 'infant industries'. Interest-free loans were granted to the entrepreneurs of new industries and exemption from *taille* or from military duties for the workers. Traditional industries were also affected, for methods of production were often regulated in great detail in an attempt to raise quality or to standardise production or, occasionally, in the interests of efficiency. During the eighteenth century the number of inspectors of manufactures increased from 38 in 1715 to 64 in 1754 and their functions were extended from the supervision of cloth production to other industries. The mining, glass and paper industries were brought within the sphere of government control by way of the intendants. The medieval gilds had been gradually brought under the control of the state and became instruments through which government regulations were to be made effective. In order to secure better conformity with regulations and the protection of the urban craftsmen rural industry was officially forbidden until 1762, though official bans were largely ineffective in controlling the forces which were making for its spread.

It is difficult to gauge the effect of state intervention on the development of industry in France or on the geography of industrial development. Regulations designed to secure quality of product and to raise standards of production were much more of a hindrance than a help when they encouraged stagnation and prevented innovation. The spread of rural industry may have been hampered a little, but it was certainly not prevented. Many of the infant industries which had been nurtured by state protection grew into lusty maturity in the eighteenth century, and it has been claimed that in spite of many faults, the régime of industrial control and privileged manufacture paved the way for the extension of *la grande industrie* in the second half of the eighteenth century.[16]

A third characteristic of France during the *ancien régime* was the difficulty of internal communications. The sheer size of France and the distances between its major cities accorded them a degree of natural protection, but the other side of the coin was a tendency to regional isolation and the persistence of regional self-sufficiency. Scattered cloth industries producing for local markets and a wide distribution of iron industries producing poor-quality materials as well as the hesitancy of progress towards regional agricultural specialisation were associated with this fact. Internal communications had been notoriously bad in the seventeenth century, and although complaints were chiefly about the bad state of the roads linking Paris with the provinces, perhaps the major problem then as later lay in the poor quality of secondary and local roads. The post-roads of Tavernier's map of 1632 (see Fig. 10:1) give some idea of the roads of major importance before the advances of Colbert's régime towards the creation of a centralised administration of roads and bridges. Lyon, Paris and Orléans were the nodal points in the system, but wide areas of the Massif Central were not served, and no road penetrated towards Brittany further than to Caen in Normandy and Nantes. It was, however, not until the eighteenth century that large-scale road-building was begun. A school of civil engineering for roads and bridges was created in 1747; the budget was increased; and

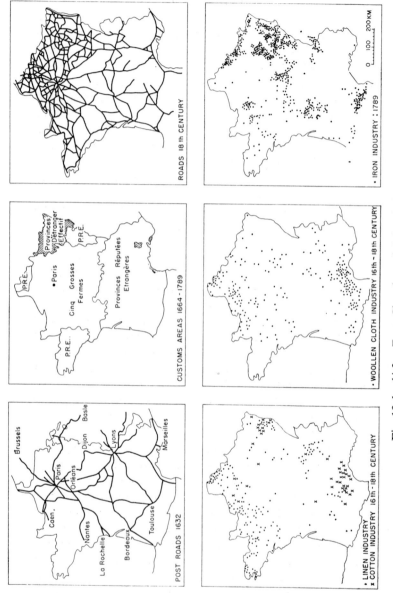

ROADS 18th CENTURY

CUSTOMS AREAS 1664-1789

P.R.E.

Provinces
à l'étranger
Effectif

P.R.E.

Paris

Cinq   Grosses   Fermes

Provinces   Réputées
Étrangères

P.R.E.

POST ROADS 1632

Brussels

Basle

Caen

Paris

Dijon

Orléans

Lyons

Nantes

La Rochelle

Bordeaux

Toulouse

Marseilles

• IRON INDUSTRY : 1789

0   100   200 KM

• WOOLLEN CLOTH INDUSTRY 16th-18th CENTURY

• LINEN INDUSTRY 16th-18th CENTURY
× COTTON INDUSTRY 16th-18th CENTURY

Fig. 10:1   (After East, Clough, and Atlas de France.)

the notorious forced labour of the *corvée* was used for the maintenance of highways. The military and strategic motives for road-building continued to be evident in the emphasis given to first class trunk roads and to communication with frontier zones, but government was also becoming conscious of internal transport as a public service which would strengthen economic unity. The results were seen and applauded by travellers like Arthur Young at the end of the century, when a network of major roads had been created which made the whole country fairly easily and quickly accessible from Paris, and which was particularly good in the north and east (see Fig. 10:1). By 1788 France possessed some 30,000 miles of good road and more were planned or under construction (a figure which may be compared with the railway mileage of France in 1937 of 26,500 miles). But the subsidiary roads remained very bad and effectively hindered the distribution of agricultural produce.

River navigation had always been the chief method (other than the coasting trade) of transporting bulk commodities. But there were many disadvantages: the rapidity of the Rhône current, the meanders of the Seine, the braided, shallow and shifting channels of the Loire, and the difficulties and delays engendered by weirs, fisheries and unfavourable winds. The navigation of the Seine, Loire, Dordogne and Garonne, the Rhône and the Saône had been improved to some extent in the régime of Colbert, and further work was undertaken in the eighteenth century on the Seine, Loire, Somme and other rivers of Nord as well on the Vilaine to Rennes. But the scale of the problem presented by the improvement of river navigation was much greater in France than in contemporary England, where most of the rivers were shorter, smaller, less braided and had less accentuated régimes. It was not until the nineteenth century that adequate techniques of civil engineering and capital for investment existed to permit large-scale improvements. Finally, the French had followed Italian and Flemish examples in the construction of canals, notably the Canal du Briare, begun in 1605 and completed in 1640 and linking the Seine and the Loire, and the famous Canal des Deux Mers in Languedoc, built between 1665 and 1681 to link Mediterranean and Atlantic and thus to provide a safe means of transport, but never much used because of the difficulty of feeding water to the summit area of the canal. But after a start in canal-building much earlier than that of England, little more was done until the second half of the eighteenth century and the Napoleonic régime.

Other obstacles to internal movement and to regional specialisation, whether of agriculture or industry, were of a different order, for they were the internal and provincial customs duties, tolls and prohibitions. A bewildering variety of tolls had survived from feudal times and even the administration of Colbert failed to secure freedom of internal trade. Three major divisions continued to exist in France up to the Revolution. The area known as the Five Great Farms (*Cinq Grosses Fermes*) consisted of the metropolitan region around Paris within which customs were unified by Colbert (see Fig. 10:1). This zone was surrounded by a tariff wall which varied in height at different provincial boundaries. Most of the remainder of France fell into the *Reputed Foreign* area, within which provinces levied their own duties, and finally, there were the *Effectively Foreign* areas, which were those most recently conquered by France (e.g. Alsace, Franche Comté) and which were virtually independent states from an economic point of view. Internal customs frequently prevented a logical growth of specialisation and these together with the uncertainties of bans and prohibitions made a chaos of the grain trade.

Compared with England over the same period, France continued to be characterised by a predominance of very small enterprises usually consisting of a master craftsman and a few apprentices or journeymen. In 1747, for example, there were 150 masters out of a total of 500 persons employed in the cloth industry of Poitiers. Even as late as 1851 there were 32,000 self-employed craftsmen working alone or with one employee, and only 7,000 employers with more than ten workmen. In France as a whole there were in the same year 124,000 employers in *la grande industrie* employing 1,306,000 workers, but there were also 1,548,000 small masters employing 2,800,000 workmen. To some extent, as Nef has pointed out, the need for capital investment and large-scale enterprise was sometimes less evident in the French equivalents of English industries. Thus salt production in England from salt deposits in Cheshire or elsewhere required coal supplies and investment in mining equipment. In France the equivalent industry used the evaporation of salt from natural brine by the sun on the south or west coasts, and this could be done efficiently by small enterprises with little capital. The same was true of wine production, to some extent the French counterpart of English beer-brewing, an industry which came to need heavier capital investment and which often used coal. Secondly, French industry was geared to a social structure much more strongly stratified than that of England. Among the nobility and the richer bourgeoisie demands were for high-quality luxury goods frequently custom-made or built to order and best produced by artisan industry. The mass demand of a rising middle class was much less important in France than in England. For example, the French continued to excel in the production of high-quality glass once the techniques had been learned from Italy in the sixteenth century, but it was in England that the greatest progress was made in the production of coarse glass for windows and cheap bottles. Finally, capital for investment was less readily available, for the French peasant farmer produced relatively few savings for investment and there were social barriers against investment by the nobility in industry.

The distributions of several important industries in eighteenth-century France are shown in Fig. 10:1. The production of woollen cloth was fairly widespread over the whole country except in Brittany, the south-west, the Massif Central and much of eastern France, but certain areas of concentration, particularly of finer cloths, may be singled out. In the north the industries of Valenciennes, Tournai, Lille, Picardy, St Omer and Amiens had formerly been associated with the spread of Flemish industry in the Middle Ages. Abbeville was the site chosen for the establishment of a fine woollen cloth industry by Van Robais, a Dutch merchant who migrated to France with some 50 Dutch workmen, and who was given privileges and subsidies to develop a cloth industry which would help to replace Dutch and English imports to France. By 1680 he had some 80 looms and was employing 1,700 workers. Cloth production in Normandy was also improved by a leaven of Dutch immigrants, particularly at Louviers, Fécamp and Elbeuf. Rouen, Caen and Evreux also became important centres of production.

The cloth industry of Languedoc had been of medieval importance particularly at Nîmes, where the wool from transhumant sheep was readily available, but the spread of industry to the Cévennes during the late seventeenth and eighteenth centuries provides an interesting example of the combination of state intervention, natural advantages and the importance of available markets.[17] Chiefly in order to supply an export commodity for the Levant trade through Marseilles, Colbert had instituted Royal manufactures at a number of places between Carcassonne and Clermont l'Hérault. As late as 1705 almost all of the woollen exports to the Levant were supplied from the Royal manufactures, organised on a large scale, often with as many as 500 to 800 workers. Private producers were given subsidies and by about 1715 equalled the production of the privileged Royal manufactures. In the rapid growth which followed the success of the light, cheap Languedoc cloth in the Levantine markets, it was the small-scale private producers who led. Output blossomed from some 7,000 cloths in 1710 to some 340,000 between 1730 and 1737. The manufacturing area was concentrated in a narrow zone from the valley of the Hérault in the north-east to the depression of the Naurouze and the valley of the Aude in the south-west, and on the southern slopes of the Garrigues, l'Espinouse and the Black Mountain. Water-power was available in much of the area but local wools had soon to be supplemented by imports, chiefly from Spain, but also from the Levant itself.

The linen industry and especially the production of coarse linens, had long been a speciality of Brittany, Normandy and Picardy. In the north, linen production was associated with the nearby Flemish industry; near Lyon with the lace for which the Auvergne had already acquired a strong reputation; and in Languedoc and Alsace it was linked with the growth of the cotton industry, and with the production of mixed goods of woollens and linens or cotton, the raw material mainly imported from the Levant through Marseilles. Finally the silk industry had been established in the Rhône valley from the fourteenth century and with the establishment of Italian immigrants and state help, the industry had emerged at and near Lyon as a large-scale industry for which imports from the Levant were needed to supplement the raw silk production of the Rhône valley itself. By 1700 the industry had spread towards St Chamond and St Etienne where it had become an important supplement to the inadequate agricultural incomes that could be got from poor land. Silk ribbons were the chief preoccupation of the marginal area towards St Etienne where a domestic small-scale industry existed in contrast to the large-scale organisation of Lyon.[18]

The iron industry, too, was widely distributed in many parts of France by 1789.[19] There were important centres of iron manufacture in Normandy and the Pyrenees but the margins of the Massif Central and the east carried about 70 per cent of the factories and were responsible for about 90 per cent of the output of pig iron. Total output was high for eighteenth-century Europe with an annual production of about 150,000 tons of pig iron, and 100,000 tons of wrought iron, but much of it was of poor quality and best-quality wrought iron had to be imported from Liège, Luxemburg, Sweden or Russia.[20] In France the balance of resources was very different from that of Sweden. Iron ores in France are widely scattered though many deposits are small and of poor quality. The Jurassic ores of eastern France are the most abundant, but the phosphorus content was too high to make good iron using the techniques that existed before the industrial revolution. The Silurian ores of western France on the margins of the Massif Central are widely scattered, often in very small quantities and greatly variable in quality and thickness of beds; it has been suggested that the limited deposits and their scattered nature here, in the Pyrenees and in the south of the Massif Central were factors contributory to a small-scale and widely scattered industry. The rich deposits of the Caen area were worked to make a better-quality iron and small outcrops of good ores in Jurassic rocks near St Etienne and in the Alps made good iron and steel. Tertiary ores in the Rhône valley were also worked and another source, not now used, was in the Neocomian beds of Champagne, an ore with a close English equivalent in the Weald Clay and Hastings Beds.

Iron ores in France, therefore, were fairly widespread; timber resources were much greater than those of contemporary England and there was a wide scatter of surviving woodland in areas of less attractive soils which had remained uncleared from medieval times, making supplies of charcoal obtainable on patches of poor soil or upland relief. Of the iron industry in the wooded scarps of Burgundy it was said in the eighteenth century that 'the multitude of forges and furnaces supports a branch of commerce all the more important since it is the only one which has succeeded in this part of Burgundy'. For some of the nobility, owning vast areas of poor woodland, the iron industry was seen as a means of exploiting land and timber which would otherwise have had very little value.

Water-power became a significant factor in the location of the French iron industry in the sixteenth century when the Walloon technique of separating blast furnace and refinery began to replace medieval bloomeries. In Sweden water-power was so readily available that it created few problems, but in France it was scarce enough to be a limiting factor in location, and it has been said that the proximity of water-power sometimes mattered more than the immediate presence of the raw material. Whereas Swedish river régimes are dominated by meltwaters and regulated by glacial lakes, seasonal low water during summer frequently made working impossible in France, as in Lorraine, Brittany and Normandy, unless regulating lakes were constructed. The Vosges, the Alpine margins and the eastern scarps of the Massif Central were much more favoured by steady régimes during the summer and a high stream density in upland areas, with a good fall of water over short distances.

The distributions of raw materials and of water-power were responsible for locating the iron industry in detail, but the over-riding factors in the wide scatter of the French iron industry were undoubtedly the poverty of internal transport and the internal taxes and prohibitions on the movement of raw materials or finished iron. Thus most provinces had to be self-sufficient in iron for most purposes, and only pure iron, used in nail-making, arms manufacture or the production of some kinds of ornamental work, was sufficiently scarce and costly to permit of long-distance trade and transport. The phosphoric iron of Brittany and Lorraine was largely consumed locally, but the purer irons of Champagne, Burgundy and St Etienne had wider circulation.

Each of the industries so far discussed had a fairly distinctive distribution pattern within France, but if the distributions of various industries are superimposed upon each other and the concentration of the silk industries around Lyon included, the outstanding feature is the wide dispersion of industry over almost the whole of the country. There were few areas without industry of some kind: the Alpine areas had some metal-working industries, woodworking and textiles and the Jura had varied domestic industries; but the high parts of the Massif Central, much of the Alpine area and the Landes were, of course, all areas of sparse and scattered population with relatively little activity of any kind. Southern Brittany and a broad zone of the centre-west from the Médoc peninsula to La Vendée had few textiles or iron industries but they were nevertheless regions of fishing and associated occupations, of salt and wine making. Finally a zone may be distinguished around Paris, extending to Poitou in the south-west and the Champagne in the east, in which there were relatively few industries to supplement earnings from agriculture, but this was a region of prosperous bourgeois grain farming for Paris and an area of early migration towards the higher wages offered in Paris itself. With these exceptions, then, industry was almost widespread throughout France. Much of it was still in the small towns, partly because of the power of urban gilds and state regulations, but rural industry was spreading widely long before it was permitted by the state in 1762. For in France, as in England, rural industry had advantages of cheap labour and freedom from regulation. In some areas water-power was an attraction to the countryside, but it is also noteworthy that rural industry was best developed in areas where landless labour sought supplementary wages in non-agricultural occupations or was found in impoverished regions of peasant farming where the family farm was too small, too divided, or too poor to provide adequate income and employment from agriculture or stock-rearing alone.

By the end of the eighteenth century large-scale industry, factory organisation and technological change had made strides in various parts of France and the foundations were being laid for an industrial revolution which was, however, very slow to come to fruition in the nineteenth century. In the cotton industry English technical innovation introduced by such men as Holker had been responsible for some factory industry, as at Rouen and Amiens, though by 1790 there were still only eight large spinning factories. In calico printing, chemicals and dyeing, the concentration of industry in factories proceeded as much from commercial organisation as from technological requirements, as at Mulhouse, the nucleus from which a rural cotton industry spread into the margins of the Vosges where abundant water-power was available. In the woollen cloth industry there was less emphasis on concentration and large-scale operation was in large measure an indirect product of government subsidies and privileges to those who introduced fine cloths. In the silk industry, the use of machinery and technical innovation was already well advanced, and it was partly organised in large-scale factories. In mining the exploitation of the Nord coalfield, discovered in the early eighteenth century, was largely in the hands of the Anzin Mining Company at first, a large-scale organisation, employing 4,000 workers in 1789. Similar large and highly capitalised enterprises existed at Carmaux and Alès, though much mining remained small-scale surface working by artisans, engaged on their own account with little capital. In the iron industry the society of Le Creusot had in 1782 shown the way to large-scale enterprise using coke furnaces in the English style. Wilkinson's iron foundry at Indret used only coal from 1777. But the iron industry remained a scattered and small-scale industry in most areas until the end of the century and it was not until 1826, for example, that coke blast and puddling furnaces were introduced into

St Etienne. In 1819, some 98 per cent of French iron was still produced by charcoal.

PATTERNS OF INDUSTRIAL DEVELOPMENT IN GERMANY

Compared with France, England or the Low Countries, German industry was relatively backward in 1800, though there was a sound substratum of skilled craftsmen and rural industrial workers widely distributed over most of the country. They were to provide a reservoir of great strength when the rapid industrialisation of Germany got under way in the nineteenth century. Even though large-scale industry was less well developed than in France, German industrial tradition was in mining, metallurgy and textiles—precisely the industries which benefited most from the transformations of the industrial revolution, for French industrial strength, reflecting to some extent its social structure, had been in luxury industries, fine woollens, silks, lace and *objets d'art*.

The losses and dislocations of the Thirty Years' War in Germany were much more severe than any that France experienced during the *ancien régime*, but when rapid revival got under way in the second half of the century, the restrictive and exclusive gild organisations of the towns were frequently challenged successfully, except in some parts of Prussia, by the growth of new rural industry. The organisation of the domestic or putting-out system was rather more hesitantly embarked upon than in England, but was stimulated by the high prices of raw materials, and, particularly in the textile industries, by the high expense of dyestuffs and alum. Yet the characteristic form of organisation remained the small independent craftsman working with a few journeymen or apprentices. Up to 1800 large-scale industry was largely restricted to concerns handling colonial resources (particularly sugar-refining in the major ports of Hamburg and Bremen), to some of the new industries of Berlin such as silk manufacturing, calico printing, iron foundries and luxury trades, and to the new iron industry of Silesia, established in the eighteenth century with a Prussian eye on the supply of armaments. Foreign innovation, particularly from France and by way of Huguenot immigrants after 1685 was important in the growth of many textile, clothing and luxury industries. The political fragmentation of Germany and the mercantilist policies of many small states were important in helping to develop or to preserve small-scale local industries by means of customs duties, tolls, privileges and monopolies.

In the Rhineland, metal and textile industries were already well established long before the industrial revolution made it possible to use the coal resources of the Ruhr on a substantial scale.[21] The major zone of metal industries before 1800 was the Sauerland massif to the south of the river Ruhr. Access to the navigable Rhine was relatively easy from the western part of the massif, but the region as a whole is one of poor soils developed on sandstones, slates and quartzites, and much of it was still wooded with the exception of a few pockets of more fertile soils developed on limestones. There was therefore an adequate supply of charcoal for iron industries, and for the smelting of lead, zinc, copper and silver. Iron ores of good quality existed in Siegerland, and though the ores of Sauerland were poorer in quality and quantity they were adequate for local iron industries. Water-power was also available from the valleys of the rivers Lahn, Sieg and Wupper and their tributaries. From the later Middle Ages, metal-working industries had become established in the territories of Berg and Mark, the provinces which shared the Siegerland and Sauerland massifs, and chiefly in the region between Solingen and Remscheid in the west and Iserlohn and Lüdenscheid in the east. This is now an area of steel and modern engineering industries partly based on a favourable position near the source of coal, power, and steel of the coalfield, but also on the skilled labour and industrial tradition which derives from the presence of metal-working industries developed long before the industrial revolution.

Three zones may be distinguished.[22] In the west the Solingen area had already acquired a reputation in the sixteenth century for the manufacture of edge tools, sickles, scythes and swords, and for its grinding and polishing mills, using the water-power of the Wupper valley. In the central zone, Breckerfelder had an important steel industry in the fifteenth century, and its merchants were to be found as far afield as England and Novgorod. In the eastern zone, Lüdenscheid was located well with respect to the Sauerland ores, and it had been the centre of medieval Osmund iron production using turf and bog ore as well as charcoal and ironstone in primitive furnaces and bloomeries. At Altena and Iserlohn, also in the eastern area, wire-drawing for the manufacture of nails and coats-of-mail was important. The central zone of Breckerfelder declined early, however, for its local surface ores were being worked out in the sixteenth century, and later its steelsmiths were reluctant to adopt the new water-worked trip hammers and slitting mills that were adopted successfully by the wire-drawing and nail-making industries further east. The finishing industries and manufacture of edge tools in Solingen and Remscheid persisted in the western province of Berg, which remained independent to 1800, but the eastern zone of Altena, Iserlohn and Lüdenscheid was in the province of Mark, early acquired by the Prussian state and therefore involved in mercantilist policies aimed at encouraging industry. Subsidies, state assistance in the siting and setting up of hammer works, drawbacks in charcoal, some freedom from taxation and the imposition of favourable customs duties, all favoured the establishment of new iron-works and finishing industries in the province of Mark during the eighteenth century. By the end of the century the eastern zone of Mark was one of rapid and widespread growth in a great variety of iron and steel products: small iron wares such as locks and nails, scythes and coarse iron goods such as firebacks, shovels, saws, hammers, anvils and cooking pots. The basis of skill and enterprise was laid for the later expansion of heavy engineering when the coal and steel of the Ruhr were developed.

The textile industries of the Rhineland may be seen as an area peripheral to the larger zone of textile manufacturing which extended from northern France through Belgium to the Netherlands. The production of woollen cloth was established at Düsseldorf, Krefeld and in the Palatinate, but the whole area was much better known for its flax and hemp production and for the weaving of linen cloth. Much of the bleaching and finishing of linens had been done in Haarlem and neighbouring Dutch towns in the seventeenth century, but Dutch and Belgian techniques were successfully absorbed and the finishing industry was later scattered in the towns on the left bank of the Rhine and in the provinces of Berg and Mark. Three areas were of particular importance by the end of the eighteenth century, all of them textile producers to this day.[23]

Krefeld was one of the towns which founded its wealth on linen and cloth production, but during the eighteenth century a thriving silk industry had also developed, using the labour of unemployed linen weavers. Innovation was very much the work of one family, for in 1790 90 per cent of Krefeld's silk was produced by one family enterprise employing 3,000 workers. At Aachen growth was restricted by ancient gild regulations, but protestant immigrants had established fine woollen cloth production, and between 1784 and 1806 the town was a pioneer in the introduction of machine spinning in

Germany. The numbers employed in textiles increased from about 3,000 to 16,000 during the period. Wuppertal was the third area of growth, chiefly at Elberfeld and Barmen in the Duchy of Berg. Linens made from locally grown flax and hemp had been the first preoccupation here too, but the emphasis had changed in the eighteenth century to cotton, with some silk. Elberfeld and Barmen became the commercial centres of a putting-out system which was extending in the surrounding countryside at the time when the iron and steel industries of Berg were contracting on to the two remaining centres of Solingen and Remscheid. In the early nineteenth century it was, indeed, the textile towns of the Rhineland that led in the growth of population. Krefeld, Elberfeld and Barmen each had about 50,000 and were much larger than the Ruhr coal towns or the metalworking towns of Berg and Mark. It was in the textile towns that the factory system made its first real impact in the Rhineland.

Saxony had already acquired many of the characteristics of an industrial region before 1800. Medieval wealth was based on a woollen industry of relatively local significance and on the much more important mining industry exploiting copper, silver and lead, but much of the impetus had been lost in the destruction and depression of the Thirty Years' War. When recovery began again in the second half of the seventeenth century new industrial growth was solidly based on an increasing rural population, but it was also given new direction by immigrants from the Netherlands and Huguenots from France who brought new techniques and some capital for the foundation of arms industries, silk, cotton, porcelain and faience industries, chiefly in Dresden, Leipzig, and Chemnitz (Karlmarxstadt).[24] The protectionist policy of the Saxon state assisted by providing subsidies and granting privileges for the foundation of new industries, and since Saxony was one of the larger and more prosperous German states the new industries had the advantage of a substantial domestic market as well as the prospect of sales in less industrially advanced Slav states to the east. Like the Rhineland, Saxony was endowed with suitable resources, reasonably good accessibility to external markets and an industrial tradition of skill going back to the Middle Ages. The mineralised rocks of the Erzgebirge, its wooded slopes and steep stream profiles still provided ores of iron, copper, and silver, timber for charcoal and constructional work, and water-power for the blast furnaces, stamping, grinding and slitting mills which were scattered over the area. In the lowlands to the north löss soils supported a dense rural population and provided food surpluses for the growing industrial population. Both the Elbe and the Saale provided easy access to the north-west and the area was crossed from east to west by the main routes linking Frankfurt and the Main valley with Dresden, Breslau and southern Poland.

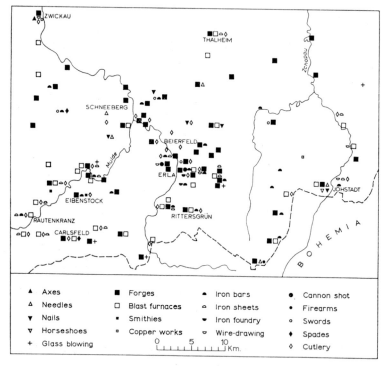

Fig. 10:2   Location of manufacturing in the Electorate of Saxony 1600–1800 (after Forberger).

The distribution of industry is shown in Figs. 10:2 and 10:3.[25] The major concentration was in the triangular area between Leipzig, Dresden and Plauen. The domestic woollen industry was very widely scattered, perhaps because excellent wools were locally available, and so too was the linen industry, also dependent on rural labour and locally grown materials. Cotton was best established in a more restricted zone about Zwickau, Chemnitz and Plauen, for it was from the towns that the raw materials were supplied. Cotton had been established from the sixteenth century by immigrants from the Netherlands, Switzerland and south Germany. It was mainly a small-scale domestic industry, though a few large firms had grown in Plauen and Chemnitz and machine-spinning had been introduced by the end of the century. Silk had been brought by Huguenot immigrants to Dresden and was established in Leipzig by 1674. Chemnitz

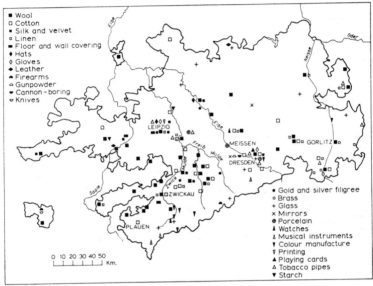

Fig. 10:3   Mining and metal industries in the western Erzgebirge to 1700
(after Forberger)

was spinning and weaving silk by 1745, and in the area as a whole the silk industry had remained almost entirely in the towns. Textile industries were the most important in Saxony but, in the eighteenth century as now, the area possessed a great variety of other industries: iron and metal manufactures, gold and silver, glass, arms, faience, porcelain, tobacco, musical instruments, printing and paper. The detailed locations of mills largely concerned with metal-working is shown for part of the western Erzgebirge in Fig. 10:2 and gives an impression of the intensity of activity in the upland areas.

Silesia may be taken as the third major region of German industry before the industrial revolution. Endowed with a range of resources broadly similar to those of the Rhineland, Silesia's development had been very closely linked to and strongly stimulated by the Prussian state, to which Silesia had been added in 1742. With its coal, copper, lead and zinc resources and with easy access to Berlin by way of the Oder, Silesia also had the great strategic advantage of being territorially contiguous with most of Prussia, unlike the Westphalian territories. In Silesia, the large landowners combined with government to invest capital in mining, iron and even textile industries in a manner which was impossible in the western zone, where small peasant proprietorship dominated and capital was difficult to accumulate or to mobilise. In mining and metal industries there had been very rapid growth during the eighteenth century, as there was also in the linen industry. Silesian linens had emerged from local importance in the sixteenth century as a result of the operations of foreign merchants who gained the support of feudal nobility in their efforts to organise a more efficient and finer-quality linen industry.[26] Opposition of the towns and the gilds to the rural spread of industry was powerless in the face of Junker support and the operations of foreign merchant-entrepreneurs. The contrasts in the social background to industrial development as between Silesia and the Rhineland or Saxony are of outstanding interest. In Silesia the predominance of landowning nobility and subservient peasantry indicated a pattern of development very different from that associated with the free peasantry and artisan tradition of the west; and whereas the Rhineland is an integral part of that greater area of indigenous industrial growth in the countries where the industrial revolution took place around the North Sea basin, Silesia had been a region of 'colonial penetration' by Dutch and German merchants. But industrial growth, though differently based, was nevertheless rapid. Silesian linen found markets in the Netherlands, England and the Spanish colonies in the seventeenth century and its linen merchants were wealthy and distinguished. Prosperity increased with the acquisition of the area by Prussia, for it received the concentrated attention of the Prussian state in its attempt not only to industrialise but also to germanise a predominantly slav-speaking area. The total population of Silesia increased from 1 million in 1741 to about 1,750,000 in 1791.

The Rhineland, Saxony and Silesia were by no means the only areas of industrial significance in Germany before 1800. Thuringia had iron and steel, armaments and toy industries; southern Germany retained its ancient interest in textile and metal industries and the occupational structure of its major regional centres shows a great variety of artisan industry.[27] Berlin, Hamburg and Bremen were major centres of urban growth.

Long before the industrial revolution had begun to make an impact on Germany, industrial concentrations were well developed in precisely those regions which were to benefit most from the introduction of coal-using techniques. At the margins of the Hercynian massifs in the northern Rhineland, Saxony and Silesia, the combination of ores, timber and water-power in upland regions had already favoured the growth of scattered textile and metal industries. In some of these areas the poverty of upland farming had been a stimulus to the adoption of part-time industrial occupations by a growing rural population. Access to markets by way of the Rhine, the Elbe system and the Oder were enduring advantages of the area. But it was fortunate for the subsequent development of German industry that industrial skills, capital and a dense rural population were already established on or near the coalfields.

Indeed, in Western Europe as a whole the pattern of developing industry before the age of steam and coke-iron coincides to a remarkable extent with the very areas in which coal was to be found. In southern Belgium and the West Midlands of England, the coalfield ores had already begun to play their part as location factors either because of the use of Coal Measure ores in smelting (as in England) or because coal was already being widely used, not in smelting or refining, but in the reworking of iron for metal manufactures, or in associated industries such as chemicals or glass. It would be interesting to have more detailed information on the use of coal in areas such as the Rhineland or St Etienne, but it would seem that in most areas other than southern Belgium and England, the use of coal was relatively unimportant, and the link between early industry and the occurrence of coal was no more than a tenuous relationship between areas of upland relief, poor soils, Palaeozoic rocks and associated coal, water-power and either timber for charcoal or pasture for sheep. In northern England, the Rhineland and Saxony, for example, the presence of coal was irrelevant in the early development of textiles, just as the proximity of iron and metal industries to the coal of the Ruhr seems to have had little importance before the nineteenth century. In some areas, indeed, coal was absent and industrial concentrations established before 1800 were able to survive using either water-power or imported coal until the development of electric power once again began to divorce industrial location from dependence on the coalfields in the twentieth century: examples are the Swedish iron industry; the textiles of the Swiss plateau; the varied industries of southern Germany and the textiles of the Vosges.

But by no means all of the developing industrial regions of Western Europe were oriented so clearly to environmental resources. Several were very clearly oriented to a dominant metropolitan centre: rural industries concerned with cotton and woollens near Barcelona, silk around Lyon or Milan, hosiery in the English Midlands were dominated from the major towns, most of them of ancient origin and long-standing commercial importance. But it was chiefly in England that a new generation of metropolitan centres, like Manchester and Birmingham, had already begun to emerge from an industrial environment.

REFERENCES

Abbreviation:
Ann. E.S.C. *Annales, Economies, Sociétés, Civilisations*, Paris.
1. K. BÜCHER, *Industrial Evolution* (1893), trans. S. M. Wickett, New York, 1907.
2. J. U. NEF, 'Industrial growth in France and England from 1540 to 1640', *Journ. of Political Economy*, vol. 44, 1936, pp. 289–317, 505–33, 643–66.
3. W. C. SCOVILLE, 'Huguenots in the French economy, 1650–1750', *Quart. Journ. Econ.*, vol. 67, 1953, pp. 423–44.
4. H. KELLENBENZ, 'Les industries rurales en occident de la fin du moyen âge au XVIIIe siècle', *Ann. E.S.C.*, vol. 18, 1963, pp. 833–83.
5. D. M. SMITH, 'The British hosiery industry in mid-nineteenth century', *Trans. Institute of British Geographers*, No. 32, 1963, pp. 125–42.
6. L. GUICCIARDINI, *Description de tout le pais bas*, Antwerp, 1567, p. 375.
7. J. LEJEUNE, *La Formation du Capitalisme moderne dans la Principauté de Liège au 16e siècle*, Paris, 1939.
8. L. DECHESNE, *Histoire économique et sociale de la Belgique*, Liège, 1932, pp. 306–9.
9. J. A. SPORCK, 'Le rôle de l'eau dans la localisation de l'industrie lainière dans la région vervetoise', *Bull. de la Soc. Belge d'Etudes Géogr.*, vol. 18, 1949, pp. 154–72.
10. E. HECKSCHER, *Economic History of Sweden*, Cambridge, Mass., 1954.
11. E. F. SÖDERLUND, The impact of the British industrial revolution on the Swedish iron industry, *Studies in the industrial revolution*, ed. L. S. Pressnell, London, 1960, pp. 52–65.
12. G. ARPI, 'Supply of charcoal to the Swedish iron industry, 1830–1950', *Geogr. Annaler*, vol. 35, 1953, pp. 11–27.

13. Ibid.
14. E. HECKSCHER, *Mercantilism*, 2 vols, London, 1935.
15. H. SEE, *Histoire économique de la France*, 2 vols, Paris, 1939–42, vol. 1, pp. 250 ff.
16. H. SEE, *La France économique et sociale au 18e siècle*, Paris, 1946, pp. 126–40.
17. P. MASSON, *Histoire du Commerce français dans le Levant au 18e siècle*, Paris, 1911.
18. M. PERRIN, *St Etienne et sa Région économique*, Tours, 1937.
19. N. J. G. POUNDS, 'Historical geography of the iron and steel industry of France', *Ann. Amer. Assoc. Geogr.*, vol. 47, 1957, pp. 3–14.
20. J. LEVAINVILLE, *L'industrie du fer en France*, Paris, 1922.
21. N. J. G. POUNDS, *The Ruhr*, London, 1952, pp. 27–56.
22. P. SCHÖLLER, 'Die Bedeutung einer alten Territorialgrenze für die heutige Verflochtenheit des Bergisch-Märkischen Indust riegebiets', *Petermanns Geogr. Mitterlungen*, vol. 97, 1953, pp. 187–92·
23. H. KISCH, 'Textile industries in the Rhineland and Silesia, a comparative study', *Journ. Econ. Hist.*, vol. 19, 1959, pp. 541–69.
24. F. G. DREYFUS, 'Economie et société en Allemagne au 18e siècle', *Rev. d'Histoire écon. et sociale*, vol. 38, 1960, pp. 477–93.
25. R. FORBERGER, *Die Manufaktur in Sachsen von Ende des 16 bis zum Anfang des 19 Jahrhunderts*, 2 vols, Berlin, 1958 and 1960.
26. Kisch, *Journ. Econ. Hist.*, vol. 19, 1959, pp. 541–69.
27. H. MAUERSBERG, *Wirtschaftliche und sozial Geschichte zentral europäischen Stadte in neuerer Zeit*, Göttingen, 1960.

POSTSCRIPT

In the years since this book was published, and even at the time it was being written, circumstances have changed in a variety of ways. It would be impossible to catalogue in any comprehensive way the nature and context of these changes, but three major categories may be mentioned. The first is that geographers have been finding new ways in which to look at their field of study, a fact which has in turn affected the way in which historical geographers look at the past. Within geography there has been something of an intellectual revolution, which was already under way in the mid-1960s, and to a greater or less extent this has also been true of the other disciplines in the social sciences with which the historical geographer is concerned. Secondly, no one could be unaware of the profound changes in the real world which have become apparent in the last fifteen to twenty years, and although the analysis of these changes forms no part of a book relating to Western Europe before 1800, it is important to recognise that contemporary changes interact with the general intellectual climate, and that as a result new themes of interest emerge which push the historian of an older world no less than the contemporary social scientist into new fields of inquiry or into new interpretations of old controversies. Similarly, burning issues of the 1950s, or even of the inter-war years, of which the embers were still glowing in 1960, are now cold and forgotten, the issues either resolved or, more frequently, abandoned. Thirdly, there have been new and important contributions of substance to the matters which are dealt with in the book. In part they arise simply from the continuous expansion of new knowledge about the past, and in part as a result of the changes in outlook mentioned above. A full-scale revision would incorporate the results of these researches, but unfortunately the exigencies of publishing make this impossible at the present time.

The first edition of this book was written at a time of rethinking about the tasks of historical geography. The preface comments briefly on the aims of historical geography as 'essentially a study in the changing landscape or as man's role in changing the face of the earth' and also as the reconstruction of past geographies, though with reservations which arise from the conceptual basis of geographical explanation which underlie this interpretation and which arise also from the pragmatic limitations which it sets. In fact, the emphasis was to be put on 'geographical change', a loose and imprecise term but one which was intended to stress the analysis of the processes operating to produce changes in spatial organisation. But it was also suggested 'that historical geography is now on the threshold of a new major task' (p. xv), which would be concerned more specifically with the exploration of geographical model-building with respect to an historical context.

It has often been said that the new emphasis accorded to spatial and ecological models and theories in the 1960s marked a fundamental intellectual shift in the geographers' approach to the real world. So far as historical geography is concerned, the argument may be briefly summarised along the following lines. In principle, there was to be a shift away from an empirical, inductive approach, regarded as traditional to much historical research as well as geography, by which information was collated, sifted and interpreted to yield insights about the real world of the past. Events, spatial patterns and their changes, or the relationships of man to his environment, were thought to be best understood in the light of 'conjunctural' situations which were to be seen as an aspect of complex functional relationships. In the traditional approach, spatial, sociological or political regularities underlying the observed patterns of behaviour were often assumed *a priori*, or emerged implicitly from the context of the study, but were often not very clearly specified or exposed explicitly. The emphasis tended in the main towards the interpretation of the complexity of forces involved in special and particular situations. The new approach was to enter the field of inquiry (represented by the real contemporary world or the record it contains of past conditions) with a formulated, explicit group of hypotheses to be tested against the evidence, and to be abandoned, reformulated, qualified or accepted in the light of the evidence acquired. Historical geography, like other branches of the subject, has moved some way towards this new paradigm. The record of the past is seen as a proving ground for the application, testing or elaboration of models relating to spatial processes. The specific aim is to tease out and examine closely the regularities of pattern or behaviour from the complexity of a conjunctural situation, rather than to interpret the uniqueness of a given historical context.

Perhaps the divergence between these two forms of approach is most apparent only at a highly abstract and even simplistic level. In economic history, for example, there has long been a difference of approach between economic historians whose concern it was to approach the past as a field in which to evolve, or to test, theories relating to some specific aspect of economic behaviour and those whose main concern was to bring a knowledge of economic principles to enlighten and inform their studies of the past, but these two categories overlap and are certainly not mutually exclusive. Historical geographers of former generations approached the vast and bewildering range of evidence from the past with preconceived ideas about what was relevant, and if their hypotheses were rarely explicity stated perhaps this was to a great extent because the hypotheses were highly generalised and assumed to be common ground among geographers. The differences lie in the precision and explicitness with which models should be formulated, and the fact that geographers are now possessed of a much greater range of middle order theories than was formerly the case. The benefits are reciprocal, for on the one hand a corpus of theory, concepts and techniques can generate new insights in our knowledge and interpretation of the past, and on the other hand the application of spatial models to past conditions can be expected to lead to a refinement, qualification or reformulation of the models themselves.

Quite apart from the culmination of this tend in geography as a whole over the past ten years or so, new areas of interest have emerged some of which may inform and stimulate the work of historical geographers. Behavioural studies have paid increasing attention to the ways in which the environment is perceived by the actors themselves rather than by the supposedly 'objective' external observer, and this is a point of view which clearly has much that is of relevance for ' istorical geographers, who have always been confronted to a greater or less extent with the problem of distinguishing between their own perceptions of what they interpret as objective truth about the real world of the past from the perception of those who have left records which bear witness about it. Hugh Prince's paper on 'Real, imagined and abstract worlds of the past' presents an interesting discussion and a challenge to the historical geographer in this field,though it is now many years ago that R. G. Collingwood advised historians to try to make the attempt to see events through the eyes of their participants. Concern with environmental problems of conservation, the destruction of resources and the revival of ecological approaches to man's relation to his environment have clear implications for the work of historical geographers who may be stimulated to pursue such themes in the past.

Interest in the conservation of man-made features of the landscape such as hedges, field patterns and even rural settlement patterns appear to have been a factor in reviving interest in the evolution and genesis of landscape as a study for its own sake. A. R. H. Baker and H. C. Prince, among others, have commented on the implications of these and other trends in the subject for the study of historical geography (see bibliography), and there is little need to elaborate further. But there is one other issue which is worthy of particular mention, and it arises to a considerable extent from the resurgence of interest in economic growth and regional development which stem from the real contemporary problems of the Third World. In historical terms, and with reference to Western Europe, this is certainly an area in which the interest of geographers in regional development, and the interest of economic and social historians in processes of growth and stagnation come together. Much of Part III of this book is concerned with problems of regional change, and this, too, is a direction in which there has been a considerable expansion of knowledge and information.

This book was written as a general introduction to the historical geography of preindustrial Western Europe, and perhaps it is right that such a book should be eclectic in its approach, reflecting current preoccupations of the subject. Some of the new themes, or the changes in emphasis in historical geography outlined above, have yet to make an impact on published work; others are duly represented in the bibliography below. A comprehensive review of the relevant trends is impossible in the space available, and what follows may perhaps be regarded as a brief commentary on some of the main topics.

Part I, on prehistory and the classical world, embodies several distinct aims. The sections on prehistory are concerned with the broader aspects of ecological adaptation of changing material cultures to changing physical and even social environments, but at the scale of Western Europe as a whole it also seemed important to pursue the processes ond orientations which were involved in the colonisation and settlement of Western Europe—an aspect of innovation and diffusion which is taken up again in the chapter on 'the peopling of Europe'. And in both this and earlier chapters, some considerable stress is laid on the evolution of racial and ethnic patterns. In part, this should be seen as a reaction against the intellectual passions which were raised in the 1940s by Aryan racial theories, now thankfully forgotten. In part, the emphasis on ethnicity was

intended to provide a background for the understanding of relationships between language and nationality, an issue of overwhelming
importance in the political geography of nineteenth- and early
twentieth-century Europe, but again, one which has receded in time.
Both these elements have been further pursued, and much has been
written on the geographical distribution of dialect and linguistic elements in particular regions. Archaeological work has tended to move
away from preoccupation with diffusion of cultures on a grand scale,
with all its doubts and uncertainties about chronology, provenance
and 'cultural influences'. The critique of Colin Renfrew of C14 and
tree-ring chronologies, for example, underlines the uncertainties
which are still involved, and Stuart Piggott has stressed the changes
in assumptions about cultural and material superiority which are
inherent in diffusionist ideas. The use of systems theory and spatial
models in archaeology has tended, however, to put an increasing
emphasis on ecological relationships and adjustments, and also to
replace earlier ideas of 'revolutions', notably the 'Neolithic revolution', by concepts of continuous adjustments and readjustments to
changing contexts of society and environment. A number of important books embody the results of these new approaches. Indeed,
European prehistory is one of the major fields in which new insights
have derived from the application of spatial and behavioural concepts, some of them derived from geographical writings.

The chapter on the classical world covers ground which has been
well worked from the late nineteenth century by geographers as well
as archaeologists and classicists, but Greek city states and ancient
Greek settlements have been the subject of detailed inquiry by
Doxiadis and his team, and the Greek colonial movement has been
reconsidered. The economy of the classical world, most relevant for
the understanding of its economic geography, has been the subject of
a massive study by A. H. M. Jones, and by M. I. Finley, but there has
also been further work on the Roman legacy in the rural and urban
landscapes of Western Europe.

The evolution of urban and rural settlement in Part II is much
concerned with the genesis of the cultural landscape, a theme which
has produced a substantial body of literature from historical geographers on agrarian structures, field systems, rural settlement patterns
and urban morphology. The initial tradition of the cultural landscape
in historical geography was primarily concerned with the evolution
of elements in the cultural landscape, but emphasis has moved from

comparatively simple genetic descriptions of landscape origins towards the use of landscape elements as evidence bearing directly on
the spatial arrangements adopted under specific social, economic and
demographic circumstances in rural and in urban society. Emphasis
has thus shifted from the interpretation of landscape features as an end
in itself towards the analysis of spatial organisation as a clue to, and
also as a product of, the times when they were created and the conditions under which they changed. Far from being a residual element
of an outmoded concept of geography, then, the analysis of agrarian
systems, field systems, rural settlement patterns and urban morphology may be seen in a different light as important keys to the understanding of spatial organisation, one of the most important current
concerns of geography as a whole.

The continuing interest of geographers in these themes has brought
forth a substantial body of literature, not only in Britain. It is evident,
for example, from a study of the work of historical geographers in
Britain, France, Germany and Scandinavia, that while interest in
historical geography in France has declined from the high level it
formerly attained, the study of genetic aspects of the rural landscape
has continued to engage the interest of geographers in Germany,
Scandinavia, and the Low Countries. An important symposium on
rural settlement and landscapes, held in Liège in 1969, represents a
landmark in this connection, hinting at the current work in progress
but also stressing the link, often previously neglected in the older
literature, between historical issues and current problems of planning
and rural consolidation in the modern world. Alan Mayhew's study
of Germany brings together a massive German corpus of publications on the theme of rural settlement, rural landscape, agrarian
structures and field systems. In common with much of the recently
published literature in German geographical periodicals, this is concerned as much with change through the late medieval and early
modern periods as with initial origins. Indeed, throughout Western
Europe there has been much more intensive study, for example, of the
contraction of settlement and the desertion of villages in the later
middle ages. Finally, one of the most welcome features has been the
increasing attention paid to local or regional studies of the evolution
of rural settlement and landscape in Spain, Portugal and Italy.

In urban studies there has been a similar transition towards the
historical study of urban morphology as an expression of the economic, social and political forces responsible for shaping the spatial

organisation of cities. Early street patterns, for example, have been minutely analysed, together with the details of urban properties. The explosion of urban planning in the modern world, the overwhelming predominance of the city in the advanced industrial world, and the resultant academic interest in urban planning and urban problems have also produced a spate of research in the historical dimension. Urban geography has become a major component in geographical courses compared with the minor role it held in the 1950s, with a much greater intellectual coherence stemming from the elaboration of sophisticated models relating to central place theory and internal urban differentiation, creating a stimulus and a challenge for historical geographers. Urban history has emerged as an acceptable subdiscipline of history, and interests in the city as a viable unit of historical study have thus converged from geography, architectural history, urban planning and sociology. The literature is now substantial, though much of it relates to individual cities, but there is still a shortage of comparative studies at any depth, and there is less than one might have hoped for in the application of central place theory, in its broadest aspects, to the pre-industrial period in Western Europe. J. C. Russell's work has focused on this problem for the medieval period, yet leaves much still to be done.

Demographic conditions are a fundamental key to understanding in historical geography and, of course, in economic and social history. The distribution of population at any given time is an essential foundation, for example, for the study of urban–rural relationships and the comparative study of urban life in terms of central place theory. It is not surprising, therefore, that much basic research continues to be done in the evaluation of records relating to population, taxation and assessments which have a bearing on the establishment of population density and distribution. N. J. G. Pounds is among those who have worked on past population distributions in continental Western Europe, but it is a topic which has engaged the attention of many others. In economic and social history, historical demography has come to occupy a much more central position in local and in general analysis, following the impetus given by Postan. The French and Scandinavian demographers have led in the application of demographic concepts to historical sources and have made possible a greater understanding of the mechanism of pre-industrial population growth, the significance of which was already apparent in the 1950s. Population change is central to the thesis of economic growth associated, for example, with the work of D. C. North and R. P. Thomas. But the more general analyses rest on the precise and detailed work of the schools of demographic historians who have taken up and extended the analysis of local parish records, pioneered by French historical demographers such as P. Goubert and Louis Henry, who have developed rigorous techniques of family reconstruction. Though largely concerned with the seventeenth and eighteenth centuries, the medieval period has not been neglected. Indeed, a thorough revision of this book would require a much more extensive treatment of population.

Part III, on the changing economic geography of Western Europe, touches on some of the demographic work published by the mid-1960s, but in general terms this part of the book is more closely related than earlier parts to the larger issues which have been the current preoccupation of economic historians. The general theme is concerned with the differential regional development of Western Europe in time and space, focusing attention on the areas of economic advance or decline, and attempting some analysis of the processes involved in regional change. Regional development is central to the work of geographers, involving as it must a dynamic approach to the regional themes which have so long been central to the subject, and supported by a massive, even bewildering, corpus of theory largely originating in recent concern with problems of economic and regional development in the Third World. Yet there has been relatively little interest by historical geographers in anything more than very local studies, and by far the greater bulk of interesting and stimulating work in this field has been done by economic historians, however lacking it may sometimes be in regional discrimination and a sense of place.

One of the most obvious features in the literature relating to pre-industrial Europe in the last ten years has been the very striking increase in the number of general studies in economic history. New views have been expressed on the early medieval trade of the Mediterranean, and there has been more intensive study of the Italian towns, banking, commerce and transport, the medieval fairs and their rôle in urban development, the towns and industries of the Low Countries.

Braudel's magisterial work on the Mediterranean in the sixteenth century has been translated into English; Venice, Ragusa and Ancona are among the cities for which important monographs have been published, and overseas expansion and its impact on European trade has been the theme of Ralph Davis's book on the rise of the Atlantic economies. New information has been forthcoming on the Baltic trade, and the Dutch economy of the seventeenth century has been intensively studied. These are the sections of the book which lie closest to the mainstream of economic history, focused as they are on trade and its relationship to the economic growth points of a developing Europe.

The chapter on agricultural and regional change revolves about a number of general concepts: the complex relationship between agriculture and population, involving both the Malthusian limits set to population growth by agricultural output and the issue of how far population growth was itself a stimulus to agricultural change. The former issue is one which can now be further pursued with the increasing number of detailed demographic studies. Both issues are a major theme in the work of North and Thomas, placing emphasis on the institutional change which made possible an escape from the vicious circle by higher productivity. Much more attention has been paid by economic historians to patterns of prices in time and space, and their relationship to internal changes within agriculture as well as in the balance between agricultural and industrial prices.

One of the major themes to be stressed in relation to regional change is not merely a general trend in the *ancien régime* towards a greater degree of agricultural specialisation, but also the regional expression of this tendency, articulated through the intensification of agriculture in areas of easy access to the urban centres of economic growth. These are areas of change in which, perhaps, one might discern the 'spread' effects of Gunnar Myrdal, in contrast to the remoter areas where agricultural specialisation might be interpreted in the light of 'backwash' effects. Case studies provide examples of this type of growth, though one might wish for closer study of remoter areas in which agricultural specialisation took on a more extensive form (in the context of von Thünen's ideas), and in which the gains from specialisation, concentrated in the hands of a dominant land-owning group, involved the impoverishment and displacement of a peasant population. The seventeenth and eighteenth centuries may be a period for which it would be rewarding to examine the applicability of those aspects of various regional development theories relating to the stagnation or impoverishment of peripheral satellite or backwash regions. In brief, it would be interesting to examine not only the agrarian changes happening within focal areas such as the Low Countries, south-east England, the Paris basin or north-eastern Spain, but also contemporary agrarian conditions in areas such as Ireland, the Scottish Highlands, the Auvergne, or southern Italy.

A regional approach, rather than a national approach, to agricultural change has much to commend it, certainly to historical geographers, and this would also seem to be true of industrial studies in the early modern period. Rural industry was inevitably closely linked with agrarian conditions, and very frequently with the range and quality of local resources of timber, water power, pastures or minerals. Urban, and particularly metropolitan industry were sometimes further removed from immediately regional contexts, but there would appear to be a real need for much more intensive study of the economic geography of industry in the eighteenth century, preferably in a form which would eschew, as far as possible, concentration on the overshadowing theme of the Industrial Revolution, and the question of the pre-conditions for it. Important work on what Mandels has called 'protoindustrialisation' has demonstrated the rich possibilities of detailed regional studies of process combining population change, migration and local industrialisation.

Perhaps one final postscript might usefully be added. Historical geography embraces, as it should, the interests of geography as a whole. Its distinctiveness as a subdiscipline lies in its preoccupation with the past, and its methodology is to some extent limited by the nature of the evidence of past conditions. Like any contemporary geography, it must attempt to resolve the problems which are set by the scale of spatial analysis, but it is also constantly involved with problems of temporal scale, and it may be that it is inherently difficult to maintain both in sharp focus except at very local scales of analysis. In this book the attempt is made to pursue a variety of themes with respect to a broad canvas of time and place. Some parts of the canvas are painted with a sharper focus and others, one might say, not at all. Yet the danger of distortion and misrepresentation in a general view are perhaps less serious than the prospect of historical geography as a collection of miniatures. Even Canaletto was forced to approximate and to generalise. There is still a need for works of synthesis in historical geography, both as a statement of the 'state of the art', and as a background for more detailed work.

BIBLIOGRAPHICAL NOTE

The following short bibliography of recent publications is not intended to be comprehensive, but lists important publications which have a bearing both on topics raised in various sections of the book and on the comments made in the postscript. Emphasis is placed on books and important articles relating to continental Western Europe, and the voluminous output relating specifically to the British Isles is excluded. Attention may also be drawn to the regular reviews of literature on the economic and social history of France, Germany, Scandinavia, the Low Countries and Italy, including many reviews and references of importance for the historical geographer which are published regularly in the *Economic History Review*, and to the summaries of selected publications appearing in Section D of *Geographical Abstracts*. The *Journal of Historical Geography*, which began publication in January 1975, carries reviews of important literature relevant to the historical geography of Europe.

Historical Geography in General

c. t. smith, 'Historical geography: current trends and prospects', *Frontiers in Geographical Teaching*, ed. R. J. Chorley and P. Haggett, London, 1965, pp. 118–43.

h. c. prince, 'Progress in historical geography', *Trends in Geography: an introductory survey*, ed. R. U. Cooke and J. H. Johnson, Oxford, 1969, pp. 110–22.

h. d. clout, *Themes in the Historical Geography of France*, London, 1977.

a. r. h. baker, r. a. butlin, a. d. m. phillips and h. c. prince, 'The future of the past', *Area*, vol. 4, 1969, pp. 46–51.

h. c. prince, 'Real, imagined and abstract worlds of the past', *Progress in Geography*, vol. 3, ed. C. Board *et al.*, London, 1971, pp. 4–86.

a. r. h. baker (ed.), *Progress in Historical Geography*, Newton Abbot, 1972. Includes articles by X. de Planhol on historical geography in France, H. Jäger on Germany, Austria and Switzerland, and by S. Helmfrid on Scandinavia.

Prehistory and the Classical World

a. goudie, 'Geography and prehistory, a survey of the literature with a select bibliography', *Jnl of Hist. Geog.*, vol. 2, no. 3, 1976, pp. 197–206.

d. collins, 'Culture traditions and the environment of early man', *Current Anthropology*, vol. 10, no. 4, 1969, pp. 267–316.

h. case, 'Neolithic explanations', *Antiquity*, vol. 42, 1969, pp. 176–86.

j. murray, *The First Agriculture: Osteological and Botanical Evidence, to 2000 B.C.*, Edinburgh, 1970.

594

P. VAN DOREN STERN, *Prehistoric Europe*, London, 1970.

S. STRUEVER, ed., *Prehistoric Agriculture*, Natural History Press, 1971, esp. Chapters 15 and 16 on agricultural dispersal and food production in Western Europe, By K. W. Butzer and H. T. Waterbolk.

C. RENFREW, *Before Civilization: the radio-carbon revolution and prehistoric Europe*, Cape, 1973.

D. D. A. SIMPSON, ed., *Economy and Settlement in Neolithic and Early Bronze Age Britain and Europe*, Leicester, 1971.

B. BENDER and P. PHILLIPS, 'The early farmers of France', *Antiquity*, vol. 46, 1972, pp. 97–105.

E. S. HIGGS, ed., *Papers in Economic Prehistory*, Cambridge, 1972.

E. S. HIGGS, *Palaeoeconomy*, Cambridge, 1975.

A. FLEMING, 'The genesis of pastoralism in European prehistory', *World Archaeology*, vol. 4, 1972, pp. 179–91.

S. PIGGOTT, *Ancient Europe from the Beginning of Agriculture to Classical Antiquity*, Edinburgh, 1965.

P. J. UCKO, R. TRINGHAM and G. W. DIMBLEBY, eds. *Man, Settlement and Urbanism*, London, 1972. Contains many contributions which concern prehistoric or classical Europe either directly or indirectly. There are papers on patterns of population growth in the prehistoric Aegean (Colin Renfrew), early Bronze Age settlements in the Cyclades, Minoan settlement in eastern Crete, and a study of town and country in ancient Greece (S. C. Humphreys); there is a paper on Roman urbanisation in Western Europe (M. W. C. Hassall), on central authority and patterns of rural settlement in classical Italy (J, B. Ward-Perkins), the beginnings of urban life in Europe (J. Alexander). and on the correlation of evidence on medieval urban communities (D. Sherdy), Papers of more general interest are concerned essentially with the evolution of settlement patterns, and with early rural–urban relationships.

D. COLLINS, R. WHITEHOUSE, M. HENIG and D. WHITEHOUSE, *Background to Archaeology: Britain in its European setting*, Cambridge, 1973.

P. PHILLIPS, *Early Farmers of West Mediterranean Europe*, London, 1975.

A. H. M. JONES, *The Later Roman Empire: a social, economic and administrative survey*, Oxford, 1964, 3 vols.

N. J. G. POUNDS, 'The urbanization of the classical world', *Ann. Ass. American Geographers*, 59 pp.

P. LEVÈQUE and P. CLAVAL, 'La signification géographique de la première colonisation grècque', *Revue de Géographie de Lyon*, vol. 45, pp. 179–200.

J. DEMANGEOT, 'Introduction à la géographie de la Méditerranée antique', *Acta Geographica*, Paris, vol. 3, no. 12, 1972, pp. 147–60.

C. A. DOXIADIS, 'Ancient Greek settlements', 1st, 2nd and 3rd annual reports, *Ekistics*, vols 325.

M. I. FINLEY, *The Ancient Economy*, London, 1973.

N. J. G. POUNDS, *An Historical Geography of Europe, 450 B.C.–1330 A.D.*, Cambridge, 1973.

Evolution of Urban and Rural Settlement
J. GEIPEL, *The Europeans: an ethnohistorical survey*, London, 1969.
R. PORTAL, *The Slavs*, London, 1969.
D. C. DOUGLAS, *The Norman Achievement*, London, 1969.
G. DUBY, *The Early Growth of the European Economy: warriors and peasants from the seventh to the twelfth century*, London, 1974.
A. M. LAMBERT, *The Making of the Dutch Landscape*, London, 1971.

There has been a continuing and very substantial output of articles and papers, particularly on the related themes of rural landscapes, agrarian structures, field systems and rural settlement, including a continuing interest in traditional rural house forms, especially in France and Germany. What follows is highly selected, and intended to be no more than representative.

Rural Settlement, Field Systems and Agrarian Structures
F. DUSSART, ed., *L'habitat et les paysages ruraux d'Europe* (Report of a symposium held in Liège in 1969) Liège, 1971.
J. BLUM, 'The European village as community: origins and functions', *Agricultural History*, vol. 45, no. 3, 1971, pp. 157–78.
X. DE PLANHOL, 'Les structures agraires de l'Europe du Nord-Ouest', *Revue de Géographie de l'Est*, vol. 6, 1966, pp. 109–14.
A. VERHULST, *Histoire du paysage rural en Flandre*, Brussels, 1966, 158 p.
'Colloque de Géographie sur la maison rurale, Poitou, 1967', *Norois*, vol. 16, no. 63, 1969, pp. 333–501.
H. D. CLOUT, 'The retreat of the wasteland of the Pays de Bray', *Trans. Inst. British Geographers*, vol. 47, 1969, pp. 171–89.
A. MAYHEW, *Rural Settlement and Farming in Germany*, London, 1973.
K. H. SCHRÖDER and G. SCHWARZ, 'Die ländlichen Siedlungsformen in Mitteleuropa', *Forschungen zur deutsche Landeskunde*, no. 175, 1969.
A. SIMMS, 'Deserted medieval villages and fields in Germany, a survey of the literature with a select bibliography', *Jnl Hist. Geog.*, vol. 2, no. 3, 1976, pp. 223–38.
W. R. MEAD, 'An atlas of settlement in sixteenth century Finland', *Jnl Hist. Geog.*, vol. 1, no. 1, 1975, pp. 17–20.
H. B. H. JENSEN, 'Origin, diffusion and distribution of medieval round churches in Scandinavia', *Pennsylvania Geographer*, vol. 8, no. 3, 1970, pp. 11–15.
R. M. NEWCOMB, *A Model of a Mystery: the medieval parish as a spatial system*, Aarhus, 1970.
F. CALVO, 'Formación del paisaje agrario de la huerta de Murcia', *Revista de Geografiia*, vol. 6, no. 1, 1972, pp. 5–33.
J. L. MARTIN GALINDO, 'Paisajes moriscos en Almería', *Estudios Geograficos*, vol. 36, 1975, pp. 673–96.

596

T. F. GLICK, *Irrigation and Society in Medieval Valencia*, Harvard, 1970.

H. DESPLANQUES, *Campagnes ombriennes*, Paris, 1969.

A. BLOK, 'South Italian Agro-towns', *Comparative Studies in Society and History*, vol. 11, 1969, pp. 121–35.

Urban

E. A. GUTKIND, *International History of City Development*, vol. 1, *Central Europe*, 1964; vol. 2, *Alpine and Scandinavian Countries*, 1965; vol. 3, *Southern Europe: Spain and Portugal*, 1967; vol. 4, *Southern Europe: Italy and Greece*, 1969; vol. 5, *Western Europe: France and Belgium*, 1971; vol. 6, *Western Europe: Netherlands and Great Britain*, 1971; vol. 7, *East Central Europe* (1), 1972; vol. 8, *East Central Europe* (2), 1972, New York.

G. SJOBERG, *The Pre-industrial City*, New York, 1960.

J. C. RUSSELL, *Medieval Regions and their Cities*, Indiana, 1972.

'Histoire et urbanisation', numéro spéciale *Annales, Économies, Sociétés, Civilisations*, vol. 25, no. 4, 1970, pp. 829–1208.

M. MITTERAUER, 'La continuité des foires et la naissance des villes', *Annales, Économies, Sociétés, Civilisations*, vol. 28, no. 3, 1973, pp. 711–34.

B. ROULEAU, *La Tracé des rues de Paris: formation, typologie, fonctions*, Paris, 1967.

E. JUILLARD, 'L'armature urbaine de la France pré-industrielle: pour une carte du réseau urbain et de l'organisation régional à la veille de l'établissement du réseau ferré', *Bull. de la Fac. des Lettres de Strasbourg*, vol. 48, 1970, pp. 299–307.

L. HOLZNER, 'The role of history and tradition in the urban geography of West Germany', *Ann. Ass. American Geographers*, vol. 60, no. 2, 1970, pp. 315–39.

W. KUHN, 'Die deutschen Stadtgründungen des 13 Jahrhundert in W. Pommern', *Zeitschrift für Ostforschung*, vol. 23, no. 1, 1974, pp. 1–58.

F. W. CARTER, *Dubrovnik: a classic city state*, London, 1972.

G. DE CARLO, *Urbino: the history of a city and plans for its development*, Cambridge, Mass., 1970.

D. RINGROSE, 'The impact of a new capital city: Madrid, Toledo and New Castile, 1560–1660', *Jnl Econ. Hist.*, vol. 33, no. 4, 1973, pp. 761–91.

G. A. LOPEZ, 'Valencia, Alicante y Denia: ciudades de origen romano', *Estudios Géograficos*, vol. 31, no. 121, 1970, pp. 651–60.

Historical Demography

Although there is no separate chapter on demography, the increase in academic interest in historical demography warrants the inclusion of a short list of references.

D. V. GLASS and D. E. C. EVERSLEY, eds, *Population in History*, London, 1965. Includes articles on pre-industrial demographic history of France, Scandinavia and Flanders, together with a more general survey of Italian demographic history.

D. V. GLASS and R. REVELLE, eds, *Population and Social Change*, London, 1972. Includes articles on demographic history of Spain in 18th and 19th centuries, pre-industrial Norway, 18th-century France and the Netherlands.

P. GOUBERT, *Beauvais et les Beauvaisis, de 1600 à 1730*, Paris, 2 vols.

P. GUILLAUME and J-P. POUSSOU, *Démographie historique*, Paris, 1970.

N. J. G. POUNDS and C. C. ROOME, 'Population density in fifteenth century France and the Low Countries', *Ann Ass. American Geographers*, vol. 61, pp. 116–30.

J. DUPAQUIER, 'Le peuplement du Bassin parisien en 1711: essai de cartographie historique', *Annales, Économies, Sociétés, Civilisations*, vol. 24, no. 4, pp. 976–98.

E. GAUTIER and L. HENRY, *La Population de Crulai, paroisse normande*, Paris, 1958.

The Changing Economic Geography of Western Europe
General Economic History and Historical Geography

C. M. CIPOLLA, ed., *The Fontana Economic History of Europe*, vol. 1, *The Middle Ages*; vol. 2, *Sixteenth and Seventeenth Centuries*; vol. 3, *The Industrial Revolution*, 1972–74.

N. J. G. POUNDS, *An Historical Geography of Europe, 450 B.C.–1330 A.D.*, Cambridge 1974.

M. M. POSTAN, *Essays on Medieval Agriculture and General Problems of the Medieval Economy*, Cambridge, 1973.

G. DUBY, *The Early Growth of the European Economy: warriors and peasants from the seventh to the twelfth centuries*, Ithaca, 1974.

A. FULLER and M. DOBB, *Economy and Society in Western Europe, 1300–1600*, London, 1971.

N. J. G. POUNDS, *An Economic History of Medieval Europe*, London, 1974.

H. A. MISKIMIN, *The Economy of Early Renaissance Europe, 1300–1460*, Cambridge, 1975.

M. MALOWIST, *Croissance et régression en Europe, 14–17ᵉ siècle*, Paris, 1972.

J. DE VRIES, *The Economy of Europe in an Age of Crisis: 1600–1750*, Cambridge, 1976.

W. W. ROSTOW, *How It All Began*, London, 1975.

R. DAVIS, *The Rise of the Atlantic Economies*, London, 1973.

D. C. NORTH and R. P. THOMAS, *The Rise of the Western World*, Cambridge, 1973.

P. EARLE, ed., *Essays in European Economic History, 1500–1800*, Oxford, 1973.

R. CAMERON, ed., *Essays in French Economic History*, Homewood, 1970.

C. WILSON, *The Dutch Republic and the Civilization of the Seventeenth Century*, London, 1968.

H. HAHN et al., 'Historische Wirtschaftskarte der Rheinlande um 1820', *Erdkunde*, vol. 24, no. 3, 1970, pp. 169–80.

598

Trade, Commerce and Transport

A. R. BRIDBURY, 'The Dark Ages', *Econ. Hist. Rev.*, vol. 22, no. 3, 1969, pp. 526–37.

R. S. LOPEZ, *The Commercial Revolution of the Middle Ages, 950–1350*, Cambridge, 1976.

A. O. CITARELLA, 'Patterns in medieval trade: the commerce of Amalfi before the Crusades', *Jnl Econ. Hist.*, vol. 28, 1968, pp. 531–55.

P. EARLE, 'The commercial development of Ancona, 1479–1551', *Econ. Hist. Rev.*, vol. 22, no. 1, 1969, pp. 28–44.

F. W. CARTER, 'The commerce of the Dubrovnik Republic, 1500–1700', *Econ. Hist. Rev.*, vol. 24, no. 3, 1971, pp. 370–94.

F. C. LANE, *Venice: a maritime republic*, Johns Hopkins Press, 1973.

R. T. RAPP, *Industry and Economic Decline in Seventeenth-Century Venice*, Harvard, 1976.

R. T. RAPP, 'The unmaking of the Mediterranean trade hegemony', *Jnl Econ. Hist.*, vol. 35, no. 3, 1975, pp. 499–525.

F. E. KOLLER, 'Geographical aspects of tenth and eleventh-century commercial growth in Bruges', *Jnl Geography*, vol. 3, no. 8, 1971, pp. 815–22.

F. E. KOLLER, 'Géographie de commerce médiéval flamande-italien', *Bull. de la Soc. de Géographie de Marseille*, vol. 80, no. 10, 1970, pp. 3–13.

M. BOGUCKA, 'Amsterdam and the Baltic in the first half of the seventeenth century', *Econ. Hist. Rev.*, vol. 26, no. 3, 1973, pp. 433–47.

P. DOLLINGER, *The German Hansa*, London, 1970.

A. C. LEIGHTON, *Transport and Communication in Early Medieval Europe, 500–1100*, New York, 1972.

G. ARBELLOT, 'La grande mutation des routes de France au milieu du 18e siècle', *Annales, Économies, Sociétés, Civilisations*, vol. 28, no. 3, 1973, pp. 765–91.

J. CERMAKAIAN, 'The Moselle river and canal from the Roman Empire to the EEC', *Toronto Research Publ.*, vol. 14, 1975, 162 p.

F. QUIROZ L., 'Fuentes para la geografía de la circulación en España: algunos libros sobre los caminos españoles en los siglos 18 y 19', *Estudios Geograficos*, vol. 32, no. 123, 1971, pp. 353–73.

D. RINGROSE, 'Transportation and economic stagnation in eighteenth-century Castile', *Jnl Econ. Hist.*, vol. 28, no. 1, 1968, pp. 51–79.

Agriculture

Numerous articles and papers on local and regional agricultural change are published in European geographical and historical journals, and there is also some overlap with the section devoted to the evolution of rural settlement and field systems. What follows is therefore a very brief selection.

J. GOODY, J. THIRSK and E. P. THOMPSON, *Family and Inheritance: rural society in Western Europe, 1200–1800*, Cambridge, 1976.

R. PEET, 'Influence of the British market on agriculture and related economic development in Europe before 1860', *Trans. Inst. British Geographers*, vol. 56, 1972, pp. 1–20.

599

B. SEXAUER, 'English and French agriculture in the late eighteenth century', *Agricultural History*, vol. 50, no. 3, 1976, pp. 491–505.

J. L. GOLDSMITH, 'Agricultural specialization and stagnation in early modern Auvergne', *Agricultural History*, vol. 47, no. 3, 1973, pp. 216–34.

K. SUTTON, 'La triste Sologne', *Norois*, vol. 16, no. 61, 1969, pp. 7–30.

J. DE VRIES, *The Dutch Rural Economy in the Golden Age, 1500–1700*, Yale, 1974.

W. ABEL, *Geschichte der deutschen Landwirtschaft von frühen Mittelalter bis zum 19 Jahrhundert*, Stuttgart, 1967.

F. LÜTGE, *Geschichte der deutschen Agrarverfassung vom frühen Mittelalter bis zum 19 Jahrhundert*, Stuttgart, 1967.

R. ZANGHERI, 'The historical relationships between agriculture and economic development in Italy', *Agricultural Change and Economic Development: the historical problems*, ed. E. L. Jones and S. J. Woolf, London, 1969, pp. 23–39.

G. A. LOPEZ, 'La introducción del maïs en Valencia y la sustitución de otros cereales', *Estudios Geograficos*, vol. 35, no. 135, 1974, pp. 147–56.

G. DUBY, *Rural economy and country life in the Medieval West*, translated C. Postan, London, 1968.

J. GARCIA, 'El cultivo del arroz y su expansión en el siglo 18 en . . . Valencia', *Estudios Geograficos*, vol. 32, no. 123, 1971, pp. 163–87.

Industry

Although many of the economic histories cited above contain studies of industrial development before the Industrial Revolution, and other books (not here cited) include summaries of industry immediately before it, there would appear to be relatively few studies of the geographical distribution of industry.

A. KLIMA, 'The role of domestic industry in Bohemia in the eighteenth century', *Econ. Hist. Rev.*, vol. 27, no. 1, 1974, pp. 48–56.

M. MAZZAOUI, 'The cotton industry of northern Italy in the later Middle Ages', *Jnl Econ. Hist.*, vol. 32, 1972.

H. VAN DER WEE, 'Structural changes and specialization in the industry of the southern Netherlands, 1100–1600', *Econ. Hist. Rev.*, vol. 28, no. 2, pp. 203–21.

H. FISCHER, 'Relikte der präindustrialische Wirtschaftslandschaft in nördliche lothringisch-luxemburgisch Industriegebiet', *Zeitschrift für Wirtschaftsgeographie*, vol. 16, no. 5, 1972, pp. 129–34.

P. IRADIEL, M., *Evolución de la industria textil castellana en los siglos 13–16*, Salamanca, 1974.

E. SCHREMMER, *Die Wirtschaft Bayerns vom höhen Mittelalter bis zum Beginn der Industrialisierung, Bergbau, Gewerbe, Handel*, Munich, 1970.

L'Industrie française au 18ᵉ siècle—l'industrie lainière, Économies et Sociétés, histoire quantitative de l'économie française, Paris, Cahiers de l'I.S.E.A., vol. 2, no. 8, 1968.

F. F. MENDELS, 'Social mobility and phases of industrialization', *Journal of Interdisciplinary History*, vol. 7, no. 2, 1976, pp. 193–216.

600

F. F. MENDELS, 'Industrialization and population pressure in eighteenth-century Flanders', *Jnl Econ. History*, vol. 32, 1972, pp. 241–61.

W. FISCHER, 'Rural industrialization and population change', *Comparative Studies in Society and History*, vol. 15, 1973, pp. 158–70.

INDEX

(Important references are italicised)

H.G.W.E.—20